DEVELOPING THE TEACHER WORKFORCE

DEVELOPING THE TEACHER WORKFORCE

103rd Yearbook of the
National Society for the Study of Education

PART I

Edited by
MARK A. SMYLIE AND DEBRA MIRETZKY

20 04

Distributed by THE UNIVERSITY OF CHICAGO PRESS • CHICAGO, ILLINOIS

#55855/63

National Society for the Study of Education

The National Society for the Study of Education was founded in 1901 as successor to the National Herbart Society. It publishes a two-volume Yearbook, each volume dealing with a separate topic of concern to educators. The Society's Yearbook series, now in its one hundred-third year, presents articles by scholars and practitioners noted for their significant work in critical areas of education.

The Society welcomes as members all individuals who wish to receive its publications. Current membership includes educators in the United States, Canada, and elsewhere throughout the world—professors, researchers, administrators, and graduate students in colleges and universities and teachers, administrators, supervisors, and curriculum specialists in elementary and secondary schools, as well as policymakers at all levels.

Members of the Society elect a Board of Directors. The Board's responsibilities include reviewing proposals for Yearbooks, authorizing the preparation of Yearbooks based on accepted proposals, and appointing an editor or editors to oversee the preparation of manuscripts.

Current dues (for 2004) are a modest $40 ($35 for retired members and for students in their first year of membership). Members whose dues are paid for the current calendar year receive the Society's Yearbook, are eligible for election to the Board of Directors, and are entitled to a 33 percent discount when purchasing past Yearbooks from the Society's distributor, the University of Chicago Press.

Each year the Society arranges for meetings to be held in conjunction with the annual conferences of one or more of the national educational organizations. All members are urged to attend these meetings, at which the current Yearbook is presented and critiqued. Members are encouraged to submit proposals for future Yearbooks.

Developing the Teacher Workforce is Part I of the 103rd Yearbook. Part II, published simultaneously, is titled *Towards Coherence Between Classroom Assessment and Accountability*.

For further information, write to the Secretary, NSSE, College of Education m/c 147, University of Illinois at Chicago, 1040 W. Harrison St., Chicago, Illinois 60607-7133 or see www.uic.edu/educ/nsse

ISSN: 0077-5762

Published 2004 by the
NATIONAL SOCIETY FOR THE STUDY OF EDUCATION
1040 W. Harrison St., Chicago, Illinois 60607-7133
© 2004 by the National Society for the Study of Education

First Printing
Printed in the United States of America

iv

Contributors to the Yearbook

Margaret Plecki, University of Washington, Seattle
Judi Randi, University of New Haven
Virginia Richardson, University of Michigan
Dirck Roosevelt, University of Michigan
Andrew W. Shouse, Michigan State University
Anthony G. Vandarakis, Chicago Public Schools
Ana María Villegas, Montclair State University
Suzanne M. Wilson, Michigan State University
Kenneth M. Zeichner, University of Wisconsin–Madison

Preface

During the past ten years, teacher quality and effectiveness has emerged as one of the nation's most important priorities for improving schools and student learning. Today, this issue joins accountability, standards, and choice as a primary focus and flash point for educational reform debate and policy development. Part I of the 103rd yearbook of the National Society for the Study of Education—this volume—focuses on improving teacher quality and effectiveness through teacher workforce development. Part II (Wilson, 2004) focuses on student assessment and its relationship to accountability. Standards-based reform was examined in a volume of the 100th yearbook (Fuhrman, 2001), and choice was the subject of several chapters of the 102nd yearbook's volume on educational governance (Boyd & Miretzky, 2003).

We chose to organize this volume around the idea of workforce development to allow contributors to explore and analyze problems of teacher development more comprehensively and systemically than generally occurs in current thinking, policy development, and practice. Thinking about teachers as a workforce creates opportunities to consider teacher development not simply as a problem of individual teacher growth and development or as a problem of developing the teaching profession at large. Although individual teacher development and development of the teaching profession are certainly important, what is often missing is attention to the development of collectivities of teachers, from school faculties to district staffs to district-wide and statewide supplies of potential teachers. A focus on workforce development draws our attention to such collectivities and to the fact that they are both diverse and dynamic and that, as a result, their development is more complex and demanding. This perspective would probably be self-evident to a school principal who must consider development of a faculty that consists of beginning teachers as well as seasoned veterans; teachers of various races, ethnicities, and cultures; and effective teachers who are at risk of leaving along with ineffective teachers who have every intention of staying. It would also be self-evident to a principal who has to manage the "churn" of a faculty that each year might lose several teachers to retirement, to other schools, or to other occupational pursuits. The problem is that this perspective is woefully underdeveloped in the education literature and in policy and practice.

This focus on workforce development also opens the door to thinking about teacher development not simply as a function of single, discrete practices but also as systems of strategies. It creates opportunities to think about how those strategies may interact at any given time and over the course of teachers' careers. It challenges us to think about teacher development not simply as a problem of, say, recruitment and initial preparation, but also as one of ongoing professional development, accountability, and retention. Likewise, a focus on workforce development draws our attention beyond a particular context or source to multiple contexts and sources in which and from which development might occur. It also draws our attention to the potential interactive influence of development efforts that emanate from multiple levels of the educational system—the school, the district, the state, and even the federal government.

These ideas are reflected in the selection of chapters and their organization in this book. The chapters are divided into three sections. The first section provides an overview of the broader issues underlying teacher workforce development. Richard Ingersoll opens the volume with an overview of four myths—restrictive entry barriers, teacher shortages, inadequate teacher preparation, and lack of control over teachers' work—that continue to surface in discussions about the quality of the teacher workforce. His chapter rejects these claims and their rationales and alternatively targets the semiprofessional status of teaching as the real source of teacher quality issues. In Chapter 2, Mark A. Smylie, Debra Miretzky, and Pamela Konkol argue that teacher development is fundamentally a problem and function of school organization. They provide a conceptual framework for a comprehensive, strategic, systems-oriented approach to workforce development that views teachers, individually and collectively, as the human resources of schools and school districts. In Chapter 3, Ana María Villegas and Tamara Lucas present a historical and contemporary analysis of diversity in the teacher workforce, describing the persistent demographics of White teachers teaching minority students. They argue that more aggressive systems of strategies, including more alternative routes to certification, are critical for attracting and retaining teachers of color, who they suggest bring particular skills and sensibilities to their work with students.

The second section of this volume contains chapters that examine specific teacher workforce development practices and strategies. In each chapter, the authors explore connections among the strategies they examine and others. In Chapter 4, Virginia Richardson and Dirck Roosevelt examine teacher preparation and certification and licensure.

They challenge policymakers to create strategies and practices that reflect the need for accountability at the local level but take contextual differences into account and that support teachers as "public intellectuals." In Chapter 5, Suzanne M. Wilson, Courtney Bell, Jodie Galosy, and Andrew W. Shouse situate recruitment, induction, and retention in the larger policy landscape, pointing out that both policy and practice decisions along the entire workforce continuum, as well as new teachers' conceptions of teaching, are profoundly shaped by our assumptions about the nature of teachers' work as labor, as professional work, or as vocation. In Chapter 6, Judi Randi and Kenneth M. Zeichner provide an overview of the status of professional development for practicing teachers and its continued reliance on a "one size fits all" approach. They describe emerging forms of collaborative teacher work that expand individual and collective teacher knowledge and encourage teachers to take responsibility for their own professional learning (and preparation programs to prepare them to do so). In Chapter 7, Edward Pajak and Angelique Arrington provide historical and contemporary perspectives on teacher accountability, via supervision and evaluation, noting that the criteria and the methods by which teachers have been assessed have changed little over the years. They point out, though, that today's expectations—and the ramifications for "failure" on the part of teachers—are higher than they have ever been, and they argue that this emphasis is unreasonable without more concrete support for teachers in the form of meaningful supervision, increased advocacy on the part of unions, and "opportunity-to-teach" standards that level the playing field. Carolyn Kelley and Kara Finnigan discuss compensation in Chapter 8, pointing out that little attention has been paid to the potential impact of compensation reform on the distribution of qualified teachers in general and to low-performing schools in particular. They see compensation as an effective strategy for recruitment but feel its potential can only be fully exploited when considered as part of a broader constellation of interventions. Finally, David Mayrowetz and Mark A. Smylie examine different approaches to the redesign of teachers' work as a means of workforce development in Chapter 9. They examine differences in the "logics" and the potential effectiveness of initiatives that seek to redesign the work of individual teachers or groups of teachers and that either redistribute existing work in schools or create opportunities for new types of work.

The third section of the book focuses on broader systems that influence, for better or for worse, teacher workforce development. In Chapter 10, M. Bruce King makes a case for leadership for teacher development and capacity building at the district level and encourages a district environment that combines a "top-down" responsibility to create and sustain a supportive context for system-wide learning while allowing for school-level flexibility to be innovative about teacher learning opportunities. In Chapter 11, Nina Bascia points out the irony of labeling union work on behalf of teachers as "self-interested" and nonprofessional. She applauds the growth of "reform unionism" but argues that traditional "bread and butter" issues like salary and working conditions—concerns that are unchallenged in other fields like medicine and law—are important and necessary components for recruiting and retaining quality teachers. In Chapter 12, Margaret Plecki and Hilary Loeb provide the final chapter of the volume with their examination of state and federal efforts to improve teacher quality. They find a disturbing policy emphasis on individual teacher development and on entrance into the profession, to the detriment of comprehensive and equitable policies that seek to address the full range of teachers' needs, and offer principles for more effective policy design and implementation.

The final section of the book contains commentaries on the subject of teacher workforce development. The inclusion of commentaries is new to an NSSE yearbook and, we believe, provides additional perspectives from a broad range of educational stakeholders. For this volume, a Chicago Public Schools classroom teacher, Anthony G. Vandarakis; the superintendent of the Boston Public Schools, Thomas W. Payzant; two of the deans of the College of Education at the George Washington University, Mary Hatwood Futrell and Janet Heddesheimer; the vice president of the Spencer Foundation, Paul Goren; and the president of the Chicago Teachers Union, Deborah Lynch, offer their own thoughts about how efforts to promote the development of teacher workforce might be enhanced at various levels.

Many of the ideas presented in this book are best considered to be "in progress." We hope that they will spur new ways to think about problems of teacher development and ways to address them. We also hope that they will suggest new questions and directions for future research and practice. We encourage readers who would like to offer their thoughts and discuss the contents of this book to visit the NSSE Web site at www.nsse–chicago.org

We acknowledge the following people for their help in reviewing drafts of chapters and providing helpful comments and suggestions: Patricia Anders of the University of Arizona, Mary Sue Baldwin of Samford University, Terry Cicchelli of Fordham University, Ben M. Harris of the University of Texas at Austin, James Horn of Monmouth

University, Sue Mutchler of the Texas Education Agency, Karl Rad-
nitzer of the University of Illinois at Champaign-Urbana, and Frances
Segan of the New York City Department of Education. We also thank
Jenni Fry for her help in shaping this volume throughout the editing
process. Finally, we would like to acknowledge Dr. Victoria Chou,
Dean of the College of Education at the University of Illinois at
Chicago, who was instrumental in establishing a home for NSSE at
UIC and who continues to provide invaluable support to the Society
in its endeavors.

Mark A. Smylie and Debra Miretzky

Editors

References

Boyd, W.L., & Miretzky, D. (Eds.). (2003). *American educational governance on trial:
Change and challenges. The 102nd yearbook of the National Society for the Study of Education*, Part I. Chicago: National Society for the Study of Education.

Fuhrman, S.H. (Ed.). (2001). *From the capital to the classroom: Standards-based reform in
the states. The one-hundredth yearbook of the National Society for the Study of Education*,
Part II. Chicago: National Society for the Study of Education.

Wilson, M. (Ed.). (2004). *Towards coherence between classroom assessment and accountability.
The 103rd yearbook of the National Society for the Study of Education*, Part II. Chicago:
National Society for the Study of Education.

Table of Contents

Part One
CHAPTER
Chapters

Part Two
Commentaries

Part One
CHAPTERS

CHAPTER 1

Four Myths About America's
Teacher Quality Problem

RICHARD M. INGERSOLL

Few educational issues have received more attention in recent times than the problem of ensuring that our nation's elementary and secondary classrooms are all staffed with quality teachers. Concern with the quality of teachers is neither unique nor surprising. Elementary and secondary schooling are mandatory in the United States, and children are legally placed into the custody of teachers for a significant portion of their lives. The quality of teachers and teaching are undoubtedly among the most important factors shaping the learning and growth of students. Moreover, the largest single component of the cost of education is teacher compensation. Especially since the publication of the seminal report *A Nation at Risk* (National Commission on Excellence in Education, 1983), a seemingly endless stream of studies, commissions, and national reports have targeted teacher quality as one of the central problems facing schools. Such critics have blamed the performance of teachers for numerous societal ills—the erosion of American economic competitiveness and productivity, the decline in student academic achievement, teenage pregnancy, juvenile delinquency and crime, the coarsening of our everyday discourse and culture, a decline in morals, gender and racial discrimination, and on and on.

As a result, in recent years reformers at the federal, state, and local levels have pushed a host of initiatives and programs seeking to upgrade the quality of teachers. These include a variety of teacher recruitment

Richard M. Ingersoll is Associate Professor of education and sociology at the University of Pennsylvania.

1

initiatives, increased teacher training and retraining requirements, improved teacher licensing examinations, performance standards, more
rigorous teacher evaluation, merit pay programs and, most recently,
state and national accountability mechanisms.

Although ensuring that our nation's classrooms are all staffed with
quality teachers is a perennially important issue in our schools, it is
also among the most misunderstood. This misunderstanding centers
on the supposed sources of the problem—the reasons behind the pur-
portedly low quality of teaching in American schools—and has under-
mined the success of reform efforts. Underlying much of the criticism
and reforms is a series of assumptions and claims as to the sources of
the problems plaguing the teaching occupation. In this chapter I will
focus on four of these.

The first is that the teaching occupation is plagued by unusually
restrictive and unnecessary entry barriers—teacher training and teacher
licensing requirements, in particular. In this view, as a result of these
rigid bureaucratic regulations large numbers of high-quality candidates
are discouraged from getting into the occupation.

The second is that severe teacher shortages are confronting our elementary and secondary schools, and our traditional teacher preparation
sources are simply not producing sufficient numbers of teachers to meet
the demand. Restrictive entry requirements may exacerbate this situation, but at the root of this school staffing crisis, according to this view,
are two converging macro demographic trends—increasing student enrollments and increasing teacher attrition due to a "graying" teaching
force. The resulting shortfalls of teachers, the argument continues, are
forcing many school systems to resort to lowering standards to fill
teaching openings, inevitably resulting in high levels of underqualified
teachers.

The third is that the teaching force is inadequately trained and prepared. Unlike the first view, this perspective argues that entry into the
occupation is not restrictive enough. In this view, the preservice preparation of teachers in college or university training programs and state
certification standards all too often lack adequate rigor, breadth, and
depth, especially in academic and substantive coursework, resulting in
high levels of underqualified teachers.

The fourth and final claim I will examine has to do with the control
and accountability of the teaching force once on the job. Schools, this
view claims, are far too loose, too disorganized, and lack appropriate control, especially regarding their primary activity—the work of teachers
with students. Teachers are not held accountable and simply do what

they want behind the closed doors of their classrooms. The predictable result, this view holds, is low-quality performance on the part of teachers.

These four claims are, of course, not the only explanations given for the problem of low-quality teachers and teaching, nor are these views universally believed. Indeed, each is the subject of much contention—and proponents of one may be opponents of another. But all are prominent views, all are part of the conventional wisdom as to what ails teaching, and all have had an impact on reform and policy.

The thesis of this chapter, however, is that each is largely incorrect. My theoretical perspective is drawn from the sociology of organizations, occupations, and work. My operating premise, drawn from this perspective, is that fully understanding issues of teacher quality requires examining the character of the teaching occupation and the social and organizational contexts in which teachers work. A close look at the best data available from this perspective, I argue, shows that each of these views involves a wrong diagnosis and a wrong prescription. In the following sections I review each of the above views and explain why I believe each provides an inaccurate explanation of the problems plaguing the teaching occupation. I then offer an alternative hypothesis to explain the problems undermining the quality of teachers and teaching.

Overly Restrictive Occupational Entry

Entry into many occupations and professions is regulated. That is, entry into many kinds of work typically requires a license, which is obtained only after completion of an officially sanctioned training program and passage of examinations. Indeed, it can be illegal to do many kinds of work, from plumbing or hairstyling to law or medicine, without a license. These credentials serve as screening or "gatekeeping" devices. Their official rationale is protection of the interests of the public by assuring that practitioners hold an agreed-upon level of knowledge and skill and by filtering out those who are unable to pass over these "bars" and "hurdles."

Rigorous entry requirements are one of the hallmarks of the traditional or established professions, such as law, medicine, university teaching, engineering, and science. Among those who study work and occupations, the underlying and most important quality distinguishing professions from other kinds of occupations is the degree of expertise and complexity involved in the work itself. In this view, professional work involves highly complex sets of skills, intellectual functioning,

4 FOUR MYTHS

and knowledge that is not easily acquired and not widely held. For this reason, professions are often referred to as the "knowledge-based" occupations. Accordingly, professions are usually more selective and characterized by higher training bars and narrower entry gates than nonprofessional occupations (Hall, 1968; Hodson & Sullivan, 1995). The importance of entry requirements is evidenced by the practice, especially common among those employed in the traditional professions, such as physicians, dentists, architects, and attorneys, of prominently displaying official documentation of their credentials in their offices.

Given the importance of credentials, especially in the traditional professions, the content and rigor of the licensing requirements for new teachers has been an important issue in school reform. (In teaching, licenses are usually referred to as teaching certificates.) But it has also been a source of contention. On one side are those who argue that entry into teaching should be more highly restricted, as in the traditional professions. From this viewpoint, upgrading the training and certification standards required of new teachers will upgrade the quality of teaching (see, e.g., National Commission on Teaching and America's Future, 1996, 1997), a perspective to which I will return.

On the other side are those who argue that entry into the teaching occupation is already plagued by unusually restrictive and unnecessarily rigid bureaucratic entry barriers (e.g., Ballou, 1996; Finn, Kanstoroom, & Petrilli, 1999; Hanushek & Rivkin, 2004). From this viewpoint, traditional teacher training and state certification requirements, in particular, are akin to monopolistic practices. These critics argue that there is no solid empirical research documenting the value of such entry requirements. These regulations, they charge, are motivated less by an interest in protecting the public and more by a desire to protect the interests of those in the occupation. As a result, this view holds, large numbers of high-quality candidates are discouraged from getting into the occupation. By doing away with these impediments, this argument concludes, schools could finally recruit the kinds and numbers of candidates they deem best, and this would solve the quality problems that plague teaching.

There are a number of different variants of the anti-restrictive-entry perspective. One of the more popular variants favors a training model analogous to that dominant in higher education. The preservice preparation of professors often includes little formal training in instructional methods. Similarly, from this perspective, having an academic degree in a particular subject is sufficient to be a qualified secondary school teacher in that subject. Content or subject knowledge—knowing *what* to teach—is considered of primary importance for a qualified teacher. Formal training in teaching and pedagogical methods—knowing *how* to teach—is considered less necessary (e.g., Finn, Kanstoroom, & Petrilli, 1999).

Another variant of the anti-restrictive-entry perspective is motivated by concern for the demographic diversity of the teaching force. From this viewpoint, teaching's entry requirements result in reduced numbers of minority candidates entering the occupation, either because the requirements are themselves racially or ethnically biased, or because they screen out otherwise worthwhile candidates who are unable to pass over particular hurdles because of an underprivileged background (see, e.g., Villegas & Lucas, this volume, chapter 3).

Proponents of the anti-restrictive entry perspective have pushed a range of initiatives, all of which involve a loosening of the traditional entry gates. Examples include alternative certification programs, whereby college graduates can postpone formal education training, obtain an emergency teaching certificate, and begin teaching immediately; and Peace Corps-like programs, such as Teach for America, which seek to lure the "best and brightest" into understaffed schools. It is important to note that proponents of these alternative routes into the occupation seek the same objective as those who propose to upgrade existing entry standards and programs—enhanced recruitment of higher quality candidates into teaching.

To be sure, there are at least two problems with existing teaching entry requirements. First, such requirements sometimes keep out quality candidates. Not everyone needs such qualifications to be a quality teacher. There are no doubt some individuals who are able to teach anything well, regardless of how few credentials they have. Moreover, especially in the absence of subsequent commensurate rewards, otherwise qualified candidates might be discouraged by the initial commitment and costs incurred by these entry hurdles. According to some, historically this has been the case in teaching. Attempts to upgrade the status of the occupation through more rigorous training and licensing standards or more selective entry gates appear to have often resulted in decreases in male entrants to teaching, who were eligible for, and more attracted to, occupations with better rewards (Strober & Tyack, 1980).

The second, and converse, problem with occupational entry barriers is that they sometimes do *not* keep out some who ought not be in a particular line of work. Entry selection criteria and mechanisms can be crude and sometimes fail. Moreover, the training itself can be flawed or of low quality. Having obtained credentials and completed exams does not, of course, guarantee that an individual is a quality teacher, nor even a qualified teacher. There are no doubt some individuals who are unable to teach anything well, regardless of how many hurdles they have passed and credentials they have obtained.

But these two problems exist in all occupations and professions. There are no doubt otherwise qualified individuals who cannot practice law because they did not complete a law school program and pass a state bar exam. Conversely, there are no doubt individuals who did complete law school and did pass a bar exam, but who ought not be practicing lawyers. Indeed, a major criticism of the traditional professions, like medicine and law, is that they have become monopolistic and have too little accountability to their clients. For example, critics of medicine hold that doctors do not adequately police their own ranks, and the public has few mechanisms to monitor or sanction incompetent doctors (Freidson, 1986). It is useful to place teaching's entry requirements, and the criticisms of them, in this context. The restrictiveness of occupational entry requirements is relative, and when evaluating the rules governing a particular occupation one must always pose the question, compared to what?

An Easy-In/Easy-Out Occupation

Compared with other developed nations, entry into the teaching occupation in the United States is not especially restrictive. Recent cross-national data indicate that the filters and requirements embedded in the process of becoming a teacher in the United States are less rigorous, less arduous, and less lengthy than those in a number of other countries, including Australia, England, Japan, Korea, the Netherlands, Hong Kong, and Singapore (Wang et al., 2003).

Moreover, the argument that entry into teaching is unusually restrictive stands in contrast to the perspective long held by organization theorists and among those who study work, organizations, and occupations in general. From a cross-occupational perspective, teaching has long been characterized as an easy-in /easy-out occupation. Compared with many other occupations and, in particular, compared with the traditional professions, teaching has a relatively low entry bar and a relatively wide entry gate (Etzioni, 1969; Ingersoll, 2000). There are some occupations, such as journalism, that do not require specialized training at either the undergraduate or graduate levels. However, many do require specialized training, often at an advanced level. Becoming a professor, lawyer, or dentist, for example, requires graduate-level training. This is also increasingly true for becoming an architect or engineer.

Other professions, such as accounting, do not require graduate-level training but do have relatively rigorous entry exams.

In his classic study of teaching, Lortie (1975) drew attention to a number of mechanisms that facilitate ease of entry into teaching. First, teacher training is relatively accessible. Beginning in the early part of the 20th century, the states created large numbers of low-cost, dispersed, and nonelitist teacher training institutions. Another aspect that facilitates entry is what Lortie calls "contingent schooling"—training programs geared to the needs of recipients and accessible to those already teaching. Persistors can increase their investment in occupational training, while others can choose to restrict their commitment to the minimum required. Teaching also has a relatively wide "decision range"—individuals can decide to become teachers at any number of points in their life span. Finally, most of those who desire to enter the teaching occupation are free to do so—individuals choose the occupation, not vice versa—a characteristic Lortie labeled the "subjective warrant." In contrast, the opposite prevails in many occupations and most traditional professions. Especially among the latter, occupational gatekeepers have a large say in choosing new members, and not all who desire to enter are allowed to do so.

In recent years, there has been a movement in a number of states to strengthen teacher certification standards. In the 1999-2000 school year, about 92% of public school teachers held a regular or full state-issued teaching certificate. Another 4% held only a temporary, emergency, or provisional certificate. About 4% of public school teachers held no teaching certificate of any type. Moreover, although not required in many states, a majority of private school teachers also are certified. In the 1999-2000 school year, about 59% of private school teachers held a regular or full teaching certificate. Another 4% held only a temporary, emergency, or provisional certificate. About 37% of private school teachers held no teaching certificate of any type (Ingersoll, 2004). By 2000, 74% of states required written tests of basic skills for those teachers entering the occupation, 58% had tests of content knowledge, and 48% had written tests for subject-specific pedagogy (*Education Week*, 2000). But the requirements to become an elementary- or secondary-level teacher are still neither uniform nor considered rigorous. While some states have implemented more rigorous certification criteria, others have passed legislation that waives requirements to meet certification criteria—an ambivalence reflecting the two opposing views described above.

Ironically, although teaching's entry training and licensing requirements are lower than those for many other occupations and lower in the United States than in some other nations, they appear to be subject to far more scrutiny than those in other occupations. There is an extensive body of empirical research, going back decades, devoted to evaluating the effects of teacher credentials on student performance (for reviews, see Allen, 2003; Murnane & Raizen, 1988). Accurately isolating and capturing the effects of teachers' qualifications on their students' achievement is difficult, and not surprisingly, the results from this literature are often contradictory. However, despite these problems, and contrary to the claims of the skeptics, many studies have indeed found teacher education and training, of one sort or another, to be significantly related to increases in student achievement (see, e.g., Greenwald, Hedges, & Laine, 1996; Raudenbush, Fotiu, & Cheong, 1999).

Such scrutiny of the value entry requirements add is useful from the perspective of the public interest. But this level of scrutiny also appears to be highly selective. In preliminary searches I have been unable to find analogous evaluative research—an effects literature—for a number of other occupations and professions. To be sure, there does appear to be interest in determining the best form of preparation of, for example, engineers and lawyers. But I have failed to find much debate over whether advanced training and education are necessary for these jobs. For example, there does not appear to be a "professor effects" literature that examines whether professors' qualifications have a positive effect on student achievement or on research quality (for a review, see e.g., Pascarella & Terenzini, 1991). Nevertheless almost all universities require a doctoral degree for academic positions.

My point is not to deny that existing training and entry requirements for teaching may be at times irrelevant, or that some worthy individuals have been denied entry into the occupation, or that financial obstacles and low-quality preparation programs exist, or that some entry requirements may be biased for or against particular groups. My point is simply that entry into the teaching occupation is relatively easy as compared to many other occupations, and as compared to the traditional professions.

The prescriptions offered by critics of teaching's entry requirements may be successful. Further loosening the entry gates to teaching may increase the flow of quality candidates, especially in the short term. But they may also do the opposite. If loosening the entry requirements involves further lowering an already low bar, this may make the occupation *less* attractive and reduce the flow of quality candidates, especially in the long term. Moreover, if new entry requirements neglect to provide particular kinds of practical training needed to function on the job, an additional burden would be placed on schools themselves to provide such training. In either event, regardless of the impact on the supply of new recruits, this kind of occupational deregulation and gate loosening, alone, will not solve the larger problem of ensuring a quality teacher in every classroom if it does not also address the issue of retention—the subject of the next section.

Severe Teacher Shortages

A second and related explanation for the problem of low-quality teaching in U.S. schools is teacher shortages. In this second view, the problem is that the supply of new teachers is insufficient to keep up with the demand. Restrictive entry requirements may exacerbate this condition, but the root of this gap, it is widely believed, is a dramatic increase in the demand for new teachers primarily resulting from two converging demographic trends—increasing student enrollments and increasing teacher retirements due to a "graying" teaching force. Shortfalls of teachers, this argument continues, have meant that many school systems have not been able to find qualified candidates to fill their openings, inevitably resulting in the hiring of underqualified teachers and ultimately lowering school performance. Teacher shortage crises are not new to the K-12 education system. In the early and mid-1980s, a series of highly publicized reports warned of an impending shortage crisis for the teaching occupation (see, e.g., Darling-Hammond, 1984; National Academy of Sciences, 1987; National Commission on Excellence in Education, 1983; for reviews of this issue, see Boe & Gilford, 1992). Indeed, teacher shortages have been seen as a cyclic threat for decades (Weaver, 1983).

The prevailing policy response to these school staffing problems has been to attempt to increase the supply of teachers through a wide range of recruitment initiatives. Some of these involve a loosening of entry requirements, some do not. There are career-change programs, such as the federally funded Troops to Teachers program, which aim to entice professionals to become teachers. Some school districts have recruited teacher candidates from other countries. Financial incentives such as signing bonuses, student loan forgiveness, housing assistance, and tuition reimbursement have all been used to aid recruitment (Hirsch, Koppich, & Knapp, 2001).

The best data for understanding these issues come from the nationally representative Schools and Staffing Survey (SASS), conducted by
the National Center for Education Statistics (NCES), the statistical
arm of the U.S. Department of Education. Begun in the late 1980s,
this is the largest and most comprehensive data source available on
teachers and school staffing. Indeed, it was originally created because
of a dearth of information on these very problems and issues. Over the
past few years I have undertaken a series of analyses of these data to
examine what is behind the teacher shortage. Below I will summarize
the results of this research. (The data and discussion below are drawn
from Ingersoll, 2001, 2003b). From these analyses, I have concluded
that the above efforts alone will not solve the problem schools have
staffing classrooms with qualified teachers.

The data show that the conventional wisdom on teacher shortages
is partly correct. Consistent with shortage predictions, demand for
teachers has increased over the past two decades. Since the mid-1980s
student enrollments have increased, teacher retirements have also
increased, most schools have had job openings for teachers, and the
size of the elementary and secondary teaching workforce has increased.
Most important, the data tell us that substantial numbers of schools
have experienced difficulties finding qualified candidates to fill their
teaching position openings.

After that the data and conventional wisdom begin to diverge.
National data on the supply of teachers trained, licensed, and certified
each year are difficult to obtain. One of the best sources is NCES's Integrated Postsecondary Educational Data System (IPEDS). This
source collects national data on the number of postsecondary degree
completions, by field and by year. These data suggest that, contrary to
the conventional wisdom, there are overall more than enough prospective teachers produced each year in the United States. But there are
also some important limitations to these data. An overall surplus of
newly trained teachers does not, of course, mean there are sufficient
numbers of graduates produced in each field. A large proportion of
education degree completions are in elementary education. The data
are unclear on whether a sufficient quantity of teachers is produced
each year in such fields as math, science, and special education.

On the other hand, the IPEDS data on degree completions under-
estimate the supply of newly qualified teachers because this database
does not include recipients of undergraduate degrees in areas other
than education who also completed the requirements for certification.
Moreover, newly qualified candidates, as counted in the IPEDS data,

are only one source of new hires in schools. Far more of those newly hired into schools each year are from what is often referred to as the "reserve pool." These include delayed entrants, those who completed teacher training in prior years but who have never taught, and reentrants, former teachers who return to teaching after a hiatus. The addition of these other types and sources of teachers lend support to the argument that there are more than enough teachers supplied each year.

However, the key question is not whether the overall national supply of teachers is adequate or inadequate but rather which schools have staffing problems and teacher supply and demand imbalances. Even in the same jurisdiction, the degree of staffing problems can vary greatly among different types of schools, and sites ostensibly drawing from the same teacher supply pool can have significantly different staffing scenarios. Some analysts have found, for example, that in the same metropolitan area in the same year, some schools have extensive waiting lists of qualified candidates for their teaching job openings, while other nearby schools have great difficulty filling their teaching job openings with qualified candidates (National Commission on Teaching and America's Future, 1997). This suggests that imbalances between demand and supply must be examined at the organizational level to be fully understood—an issue to which I will return.

There is also another problem with the conventional wisdom on shortages. The SASS data show that the demand for new teachers and subsequent staffing difficulties confronting schools are not primarily due to student enrollment and teacher retirement increases, as widely believed. Most of the demand for teachers and hiring is simply to replace teachers who have recently left their teaching jobs, and most of this teacher turnover has little to do with a "graying workforce."

The Revolving Door

The data tell us that large numbers of teachers leave their positions each year. I have found that, as an occupation, teaching has higher turnover rates than a number of higher-status professions (such as professors and scientific professionals), about the same as other traditionally female occupations (such as nurses), and less turnover than some lower-status, lower-skill occupations (such as clerical workers). But teaching is also a relatively large occupation. Teachers represent 4% of the entire civilian workforce. There are, for example, more than twice as many elementary and secondary teachers as there are registered nurses, and there are five times as many teachers as there are either lawyers or professors. The sheer size of the teaching force combined with its levels of annual turnover means that there are large numbers of teachers in some kind of job transition each year. For example, the data show that over the course of the 1999–2000 school year, well over a million teachers—almost one third of this large workforce—moved into, between, or out of schools. The image that these data suggest is one of a revolving door. The latter is a major, but unheralded, factor behind the difficulties many schools have in ensuring that their classrooms are staffed with qualified teachers.

Of course, not all teacher turnover is negative. Some degree of employee turnover is normal and beneficial in any workplace. Too little turnover of employees is tied to stagnancy in organizations; effective organizations usually both promote and benefit from a limited degree of turnover by eliminating low-caliber performers and bringing in new blood to facilitate innovation. But a revolving door is costly. In the corporate sector it has long been recognized that high employee turnover means substantial recruitment and training costs and is both the cause and effect of productivity problems (e.g., Bluedorn, 1982; Hom & Griffeth, 1995; Mobley 1982; Price, 1977, 1989). In contrast to the corporate sector, however, there has been very little attention paid to the impact of employee turnover in education. One notable exception is a recent attempt to quantify the costs of teacher turnover in Texas. This study concluded that teacher turnover costs the state hundreds of millions of dollars each year (Texas Center for Educational Research, 2000).

Some of the costs and consequences of employee turnover are more easily measured than others. One type of cost that is less easily quantified concerns the negative consequences of high turnover for organizational performance in work sites, like schools, requiring extensive interaction among participants. Much research has shown that the good school, like the good family, is characterized by a sense of belonging, continuity, and community (e.g., Coleman & Hoffer, 1987; Durkheim, 1925/1961; Grant, 1988; Kirst, 1989; Parsons, 1959; Waller, 1932). Continuity and coherence are especially important for long-term school improvement efforts. The capacity of schools to carry out successful reform often depends on the continuing presence of sufficient numbers of staff committed to the change (Fullan, 1991; Smylie & Wenzel, 2003). Thus, from an organizational perspective, teacher turnover is of concern not simply because it may be an indicator of sites of so-called shortages but because of its relationship to school cohesion and, in turn, school performance.

The data also show that turnover varies greatly among different kinds of teachers. Teaching is an occupation that loses large numbers

of its new members very early in their careers—long before their retirement years. A number of studies have found that after just five years,
between 40 and 50 percent of all beginning teachers have left teaching
altogether (Hafner & Owings, 1991; Huling-Austin, 1990; Murnane et
al., 1991). Other studies have also found that the "best and brightest"
among new teachers—those with higher test scores, such as on the
SAT and the National Teacher Exam—are the most likely to leave
(e.g., Henke, Chen, & Geis, 2000; Murnane et al.; Schlecty & Vance,
1981; Weaver, 1983). Moreover, the SASS data show that turnover also
varies greatly among different kinds of schools. High-poverty public
schools have far higher teacher turnover rates than do more affluent
schools. Urban public schools have more turnover than do suburban
and rural public schools.

These data raise two important questions: why is there so much
teacher turnover, and why are these rates so dramatically different between schools?

Contrary to conventional wisdom, the SASS data show that retirement accounts for only a small part—about one eighth—of the total
departures. Far more significant are personal reasons for leaving, such
as pregnancy, child rearing, health problems, and family moves. These
are a normal part of life and common to all workplaces. There are also
two other, equally significant reasons for teacher turnover—job dissatisfaction and the desire to pursue a better job inside or outside of the
education field. Together, these two reasons are the most prominent
source of turnover and account for almost half of all departures each
year. Of those who leave because of job dissatisfaction, most link their
departures to several key factors: low salaries, lack of support from
school administrators, lack of student motivation, student discipline
problems, and lack of teacher influence over school decision making.

What can we conclude from the data about the validity of the
teacher shortage diagnosis and its attendant prescriptions? The data
tell us that the root of the problem is not shortages, in the sense of too
few teachers being produced, but rather turnover—too many teachers
departing prior to retirement. Thus, the solution is not solely recruitment but also retention. In plain terms, recruiting thousands of new
candidates into teaching alone will not solve the teacher crisis if 40 to
50 percent of these new recruits leave the occupation in a few short
years, as the data tell us they do. The image that comes to mind is that
of a bucket rapidly losing water because there are holes in the bottom.
Pouring more water into the bucket will not be the answer if the holes
are not first patched.

Of course, nothing in the data suggests that plugging these holes will be easy. But the data do make clear that schools are not simply victims of inexorable societal demographic trends, and that there is a significant role for the organization of schools as workplaces and the treatment of teachers as employees in these workplaces. Improving the workplace conditions in our schools, as discussed above, would contribute to lower rates of teacher turnover, which in turn would slow down the revolving door, help ensure that every classroom is staffed with qualified teachers, and ultimately increase the performance of schools.

Too Many Underqualified Teachers

A third prominent explanation of low-quality teaching focuses on the qualifications, training, and licensing of prospective teachers. Rather than too many requirements, as in the earlier anti-restrictive entry perspective, this third view argues the opposite. In this view, a major source of the problem is inadequate and insufficient preservice training and certification standards. In response, reformers in many states have pushed tougher certification requirements and more rigorous coursework requirements for teaching candidates. However, like many similarly worthwhile reforms, these efforts alone will also not solve the problem because they do not address some key causes.

One of the least recognized of these causes is the problem of out-of-field teaching—teachers being assigned to teach subjects that do not match their training or education. This is a crucial issue because highly qualified teachers may actually become highly unqualified if they are assigned to teach subjects for which they have little training or education. There has been little recognition of this problem, however, largely because of an absence of accurate data—a situation remedied with the release of the SASS data in the early 1990s.

In analyses of these data, summarized below, I have found that out-of-field teaching is a chronic and widespread problem (the data and discussion below are drawn from Ingersoll, 1999, 2004). The data show, for example, that about one third of all secondary (grades 7-12) math classes are taught by teachers who have neither a major nor a minor in math or a related discipline such as physics, statistics, engineering, or math education. Almost one quarter of all secondary school English classes are taught by teachers who have neither a major nor minor in English or a related discipline such as literature, communications, speech, journalism, English education, or reading education. The situation is even worse within such broad fields as science and social studies.

Teachers in these departments are routinely required to teach any of a wide array of subjects outside of their discipline but still within the larger field. As a result, over half of all secondary school students enrolled in physical science classes (chemistry, physics, earth science, or space science) are taught by teachers who have neither a major nor a minor in any of these physical sciences. Moreover, more than half of all secondary school history students in this country are taught by teachers with neither a major nor a minor in history. The actual numbers of students affected are not trivial. For English, math, and history, several million secondary school students a year in each discipline are taught by teachers without a major or minor in the field.

Out-of-field teaching also varies greatly across teachers and schools. For instance, recently hired teachers are more often assigned to teach subjects out of their fields of training than are more experienced teachers. Low-income public schools have higher levels of out-of-field teaching than do schools in more affluent communities. Particularly notable, however, is the effect of school size; small schools have higher levels of out-of-field teaching. There are also differences within schools. Lower-achieving classes are more often taught by teachers without a major or minor in the field than are higher-achieving classes. Junior high classes are also more likely to be taught by out-of-field teachers than are senior high classes.

The data clearly indicate that out-of-field teaching is widespread. Some of it takes place in over half of all secondary schools in the United States in any given year—both rural and urban schools and both affluent and low-income schools. Each year over one fifth of the public teaching force for grades 7 to 12 does some out-of-field teaching. No matter how it is defined, the data show that levels of out-of-field teaching are alarming. I found, for example, that similarly high numbers of teachers do not have teaching certificates in their assigned fields. Indeed, when I upgraded the definition of a qualified teacher to include only those who held *both* a college major and a teaching certificate in the field, the amount of out-of-field teaching substantially increased. Moreover, out-of-field teaching does not appear to be going away; I found that levels of out-of-field teaching have changed little over the past decade.

The crucial question, and the source of great misunderstanding, is: why are so many teachers teaching subjects for which they have little background?

The Sources of Out-of-Field Teaching

Typically, policymakers, commentators, and researchers have assumed two related explanations for the continuing problem of out-of-field teaching. One involves the adequacy of teacher training; the other involves the adequacy of teacher supply. The first blames teacher preparation programs or state certification standards (e.g., American Council on Education, 1999; Committee for Economic Development, 1996; Darling-Hammond, 1999). One subset of this view argues that the problem can be remedied by requiring prospective teachers to complete a "real" undergraduate major in an academic discipline.

It certainly may be correct that some teacher preparation programs and teacher certification standards suffer from shortcomings, but these problems do not explain the practice of out-of-field teaching. The SASS data indicate that most teachers have completed basic college education and teacher training. Ninety-nine percent of public school teachers hold at least a bachelor's degree and almost half hold a master's degree or higher. Moreover, as mentioned earlier, in the 1999-2000 school year about 92% of public school teachers held a regular or full teaching certificate. Another 4% held only a temporary, emergency, or provisional certificate. About 4% of public school teachers held no teaching certificate of any type.

These data appear to conflict with conventional wisdom. In recent years, much attention has been focused on the plight of school districts, especially those serving low-income, urban communities that, according to popular belief, have been forced to hire significant numbers of uncertified teachers to fill their teaching vacancies. The national data suggest, however, that the number of teachers without a full certificate actually represents only a small proportion of the K-12 public teaching force.

My main point, however, is that the assumption that out-of-field teaching is due to teacher training deficits confounds and confuses two different sources of the problem of underqualified teaching; it mistakes teacher preservice education with teacher inservice assignment. The data show that those teaching out of field are typically fully qualified veterans with an average of 14 years of teaching experience who have been assigned to teach part of their day in fields that do not match their qualifications. At the secondary level, these misassignments typically involve one or two classes out of a normal daily schedule of five classes.

Why then is there so much misassignment? The second explanation of the problem of out-of-field teaching offers an answer—teacher shortages. This view holds that shortfalls in the number of available teachers have led many school systems to resort to assigning teachers to teach out of their fields (see, e.g., National Commission on Teaching and America's Future, 1996, 1997).

School staffing difficulties clearly are a factor in the degree of misassignment, but the data show that there are two problems with the shortage explanation for out-of-field teaching. First, it cannot explain the high levels of out-of-field teaching that the data indicate exist in fields that have long been known to have surpluses, such as English and social studies. Second, the data also indicate that about half of all misassigned teachers in any given year were employed in schools that reported no difficulties finding qualified candidates for their job openings that year.

The implications of these misdiagnoses for reform are important. The efforts by many states to recruit new teachers, to enhance their training, to enact more stringent certification standards, and to increase the use of testing for teaching candidates, although perhaps highly worthwhile, will not eliminate out-of-field teaching assignments and, thus, alone will not solve the problem of underqualified teaching in our nation's classrooms. In short, bringing in thousands of new candidates and mandating more rigorous coursework and certification requirements will help little if large numbers of such teachers continue to be assigned to teach subjects other than those for which they were educated or certified.

Human Resource Management

Rather than deficits in the qualifications and quantity of teachers, the data point in another direction. In a series of separate multivariate analyses designed to explore the sources of out-of-field teaching, I have found that the way schools are organized and teachers are managed accounts for as much of the problem of out-of-field teaching as do inadequacies in the supply of teachers. For example, I have found that, after controlling for school recruitment and hiring difficulties and for school demographic characteristics, factors such as the quality of principal leadership, average class sizes, the character of the oversight of school hiring practices provided by the larger district, and the strategies districts and schools use for teacher recruitment and hiring are all significantly related to the amount of out-of-field teaching in schools (Ingersoll, 2004).

The data tell us that decisions concerning the allocation of teaching assignments is usually the prerogative of school principals. These administrators are faced with resolving the tension between the many expectations and demands state and federal governments place on schools and the limited resources schools receive. School managers are charged with the often difficult task of providing a broad array of programs and courses with limited resources, limited time, a limited budget, and a limited teaching staff (Delany, 1991). Principals' staffing decisions are further constrained by numerous factors, such as teacher employment contracts, which, among other things, typically stipulate that full-time secondary school teaching staff must teach five classes per day. But, within those constraints, principals have an unusual degree of discretion in these decisions. There has been little regulation of how teachers are employed and utilized once on the job. Teacher employment regulations have been weak or rarely enforced, and, finally, most states have routinely allowed local school administrators to bypass even the limited requirements that do exist (*Education Week*, 2000; Robinson, 1985). In this context, principals may find that assigning teachers to teach out of their fields is often more convenient, less expensive, and less time consuming than the alternatives.

For example, rather than finding and hiring a new part-time science teacher to teach two sections of a newly state-mandated science curriculum, a principal may find it more convenient to assign a couple of English and social studies teachers to each cover a section in science. If a teacher suddenly leaves in the middle of a semester, a principal may find it faster and cheaper to hire a readily available, but not fully qualified, substitute teacher, rather than conduct a formal search for a new teacher. When faced with the choice between hiring a fully qualified candidate for an English position or hiring a lesser-qualified candidate who is also willing to coach a major varsity sport, a principal may find it more convenient to do the latter. When faced with a tough choice between hiring an unqualified candidate for a science teacher position or doubling the class size for one of the fully qualified science teachers in the school, a principal might opt for the former choice. If a full-time music teacher is under contract, but student enrollment is sufficient to fill only three music classes, the principal may find it both necessary and cost-effective in a given semester to assign the music teacher to teach two classes in English, in addition to the three classes in music, in order to employ the teacher for a regular full-time complement of five classes per semester. If a school has three full-time social studies teachers but needs to offer 17 social studies courses, or the equivalent of 3.4 full-time positions, and also has four full-time English teachers but needs to offer only 18 English courses, or the equivalent of 3.6 full-time positions, one solution would be to assign one of the English teachers to teach three English courses and two social studies courses.

All of these managerial choices to misassign teachers may save time and money for the school, and ultimately for the taxpayer, but they are not cost free. They are one of the largest sources of under-qualified teachers in schools.

A Lack of Workplace Control and Accountability

A fourth and final explanation often given for low-quality teaching focuses on the management of teachers and schools. This view holds that schools are highly disorganized and lack appropriate control, especially regarding their primary activity—the work of teachers with students. These critics argue that school systems are marked by low standards, a lack of coherence and control, poor management, and little effort to ensure accountability. The predictable result, they hold, is poor performance on the part of teachers and students. In short, this viewpoint finds schools to be the epitome of inefficient and ineffective bureaucracy (for reviews, see Conley, 1991; Tyler, 1988).

Over the past several decades this viewpoint has drawn a great deal of theoretical and empirical support from the interdisciplinary field of organization theory and from social scientists who study organizations, occupations, and work in general. To analysts in these fields schools are an interesting anomaly—an odd case. From this viewpoint, schools are unusual because, although they appear to be like other large complex organizations, such as banks, agencies, offices, and plants, they do not act like them. In particular, they do not seem to have the degree of control and coordination that such organizations are supposed to have. Schools have all the outward characteristics of other complex organizations, such as a formal hierarchy, a specialized division of labor, and a formal structure of rules and regulations, but, in actuality, according to these organizational analysts, schools exert very little control of their employees and work processes. Because of this seemingly contradictory behavior, organization theorists have adopted a colorful vocabulary to identify such settings. Educational organizations, they hold, are extreme examples of "loosely coupled systems" and "organized anarchies" (see, e.g., Cohen, March, & Olsen, 1972; Meyer & Scott, 1983; Weick, 1976). In this view, schools are oddly de-bureaucratized bureaucracies and, paradoxically, disorganized organizations—a situation that, they conclude, is often satisfying and of benefit to the staff involved but also a source of inefficient and ineffective organizational performance.

For many of those who subscribe to this view, the obvious antidote to the ills of the education system is to increase the centralized control of schools and to hold teachers more accountable. In short, their

objective has been to tighten the ship in one manner or another: increased teacher training and retraining requirements, standardized curricula and instructional programs, teacher licensing examinations, performance standards, more school and teacher evaluation, merit pay
programs, and state and national education goals, standards, and testing (see, e.g., Callahan, 1962; Elmore, 2000; Finn, Kanstoroom, & Petrilli, 1999).

But distinguishing the degree and character of accountability and
control in schools, as in any organization, depends on where and how
one looks. I found in an extensive project, summarized below, involving
analyses of international data, SASS data, and data from my own field
research in schools, that this "loosely coupled schools" perspective has
overlooked and underestimated some of the most important sources
and forms of organizational control and accountability in schools (the
data and discussion below are drawn from Ingersoll, 2003a).

In the first place, how one defines the job of teaching is important.
When it comes to assessing how centralized or decentralized schools
are and examining how much input and autonomy teachers do or
don't have, most researchers assume, reasonably enough, that classroom academic instruction is the primary goal and activity of schools
and teachers, and the most important place to look for evidence. Analysts typically focus on who chooses textbooks, who decides classroom
instructional techniques, and how much say teachers have over the
determination of the curriculum. Moreover, when it comes to evaluating the organization of schooling, most analysts look at the effects of
school characteristics on student academic achievement test scores.
This approach makes sense, but it also misses a very important point.

Schools are not simply formal organizational entities engineered
to deliver academic instruction, and schools do not simply teach children reading, writing, and arithmetic. Schools are also social institutions; they are akin to small societies whose purposes are in important
ways like those of another social institution—the family. Schools are
one of the major mechanisms for the socialization of children and
youth. This is so fundamental and so obvious it is, understandably
enough, easily forgotten and taken for granted. One of the central
contributions of sociology, in particular, to the study of schooling has
been to uncover and stress the importance of this fundamental social
role. Sociologists hold that this social role involves two highly charged
tasks, both of which profoundly shape the future lives of children. The
first involves the rearing and parenting of the young—in short, teaching children how to behave. The second involves the sorting of the

young according to their capacities and abilities, perhaps the most crucial part of which has become the determination of whether students are "college material" or not.

An empirical emphasis on the academic and instructional aspects of the job of teachers has meant a de-emphasis on these social dimensions of teaching in research on control in schools. However, to fully understand accountability and control in schools, it is necessary also to examine the control of these *social* aspects of the work of teachers in schools.

Second, assessments of organizational accountability and control are highly dependent on how one examines them. In school research, as in much organizational research, analysts often focus on the more direct, visible, and obvious mechanisms of control, accountability, and influence—such as rules and regulations, or "sticks and carrots." It is important to recognize, however, that control and accountability can be exerted in a wide array of ways in schools, as in other workplaces. Organizational analysts have shown that the most effective mechanisms by which employees are controlled are often embedded in the day-to-day organization of the work itself and, thus, can be taken for granted, invisible to insiders and outsiders alike (e.g., Braverman, 1974; Burawoy, 1979; Perrow, 1986).

Who Controls Teachers' Work?

Historically, in the United States, the control of elementary and secondary schooling developed in an unusual manner. In contrast to most European nations, public schooling in this country was originally begun on a highly democratized, localized basis. The resulting legacy is a current system of some 15,000 individual public school districts, governed by local school boards of citizens, each with legal responsibility for the administration and operation of publicly funded, universal, and mandatory elementary and secondary schooling. Local school districts in the United States are clearly no longer the autonomous bodies they once were. Nevertheless, the best international data available indicate that, despite these changes, schooling in the United States remains a relatively local affair in comparison with other nations.

Although the education system in the United States is relatively decentralized, schools themselves are not. Most public and private secondary schools are highly centralized internally. The SASS data show that although public and private school principals and public school governing boards often have substantial control over many key decisions in schools, teachers usually do not. As a result, teaching is an occupation beset by tension and imbalance between expectations and resources, responsibilities and powers. On one hand, the work of teaching—helping prepare, train, and rear the next generation of children—is both important and complex. But on the other hand, those who are entrusted with the training of this next generation are not entrusted with much control over many of the key decisions concerning their work. Perhaps not surprisingly, this is particularly true for those crucial and controversial activities that are most fundamentally social. The most highly controlled, most highly consequential, and most overlooked aspects of schools are the socializing and sorting of students that teachers do.

In my research I spent considerable time examining by what means and mechanisms, if any, administrators are able to exert control over the work of teachers and attempt to establish accountability in schools. I found that in schools, as in all bureaucratic organizations, there are large numbers of rules, policies, regulations, employee job descriptions, and standard operating procedures designed to direct and control the work of teachers. I also found that school administrators have numerous means, both formal and informal, by which they are able to supervise, discern, and evaluate whether teachers are complying with the rules and policies. In addition, I found that school administrators have numerous mechanisms, both formal and informal, to discipline or sanction those teachers who have not complied with the rules or have not performed adequately. A close look at schools reveals that administrators have a great deal of control over key resources and decisions crucial to the work of teachers, and these provide a range of direct and indirect levers—"sticks and carrots"—to exert accountability.

I also found that rules, regulations, supervision, and sanctions were not the only, nor perhaps the most effective, means of controlling the work of teachers. Teachers are also controlled in less visible and less direct ways. Schools are an odd mix of bureaucratic and non-bureaucratic characteristics. Some of these other genres of control are built into the formal structure of schools and the way the work of teachers is organized. Others are embedded in the workplace culture, the informal or social organization, of schools. Although these mechanisms are less direct and obvious than formal rules and regulations, they are no less real in their impact on what teachers actually do. Indeed, in some ways the pervasiveness of these other kinds of controls make it less necessary for school administrators to implement and require formal regulations and elaborate mechanisms of accountability. Higher-order decisions, over which teachers have little influence, set the parameters for lower-order decisions delegated to teachers in their classrooms. The use of relatively crude and direct levers is not necessary because, by definition, little of consequence is actually delegated to teachers.

The Teacher in the Middle

These less obvious controls are reflected in the role of teachers in schools. Teachers are akin to men or women in the middle. A useful analogy is that of supervisors or foremen caught between the contradictory demands and needs of their superordinates (school administrators) and their subordinates (students). Teachers are not the workers who do the work themselves, nor are teachers part of the management of schools. Teachers are in charge of, and responsible for, the workers—their students. Although teachers are delegated limited input into crucial decisions concerning the management of schools and their own work, teachers are delegated a great deal of responsibility for the implementation of these decisions. Like other middlemen and middlewomen, teachers usually work alone and may have much latitude in seeing that their students carry out the tasks assigned to them. This responsibility and latitude can easily be mistaken for autonomy, especially regarding tasks within classrooms. A close look at the organization of the teaching job shows, however, that although it involves the delegation of much responsibility, it involves little real power.

A little recognized but telling illustration of this mixed and in-between role is the widespread practice among teachers of spending their own money on classroom materials that they feel they need to do an adequate job with their students. Teachers often find, for a variety of reasons, that the school does not, or will not, provide the curriculum materials, stationery, and supplies they deem necessary. As the SASS data indicate, teachers have little access to, or control over, school discretionary funds. These monies must be requested through administrative channels, a sometimes frustrating and unsuccessful experience. A national survey of public school teachers conducted in 1990 by the Carnegie Foundation for the Advancement of Teaching found that teachers spent an average of about $250 of their own money per semester (or about $500 per year) for classroom materials and supplies they felt they needed to meet the needs of their students. Only 4% of the teaching force reported spending none of their own money for such supplies that year. Similarly, the 1996 Survey on the Status of the American Public School Teacher, conducted by the National Education Association, found that public school teachers spent, on average, about $408 of their own money that year for curriculum materials and classroom supplies. Only 6.3% reported spending none of their own money that year for such materials. Notably, this altruism was not merely a matter of youthful idealism; the data show that older teachers spent more of their own money than did younger teachers.

These data and indicators suggest a remarkable responsibility and accountability on the part of individuals in the face of a remarkable lack of responsibility or accountability on the part of the organizations that employ them. These nationally representative data suggest that in 1996, a workforce numbering about three million teachers donated a total of well over one billion dollars of educational materials to their schools. This kind of teacher subsidization of the school system received unprecedented recognition in federal legislation, proposed by the Bush administration in 2001, to provide tax deductions to teachers for their out-of-pocket expenditures for classroom materials.

Teacher financial subsidization of public schools is all the more notable because teaching is a relatively low-paying occupation. The SASS data indicate that the average starting salary for a public school teacher in the 1999-2000 school year was about $26,000, and the average highest possible salary was less than $50,000. The salaries of new college graduates who become teachers have long been consistently and considerably below those of new college graduates who choose most other occupations (Ingersoll, 2000). For instance, the average salary (one year after graduation) for 1993 college graduates who became teachers was almost 50% less than the average starting salary of their classmates who took computer science jobs. Moreover, this disparity remains throughout the career span. Comparing total yearly income, teachers earn less than those in many other occupations and far less than most traditional professionals. Data from a 1991 national survey show that the average annual earnings of teachers were one fifth the average annual earnings of physicians, one third that of lawyers, and just over half of the earnings of college and university professors (Ingersoll, 2000). Using these salary data, it is possible to make a crude calculation of an equivalent level of personal accountability for these other occupations. The lower $408 figure for out-of-pocket expenditures reported in the NEA survey represented about 1.5% of the average public school teacher salary that year. Thus, a rough equivalent of average out-of-pocket expenditures for the purchase of materials necessary to serve their clients would come to (in 1991 dollars): about $550 per year for professors; about $820 per year for lawyers; and about $1400 per year for doctors.

From the outside, this workplace ethos of individual responsibility and accountability may appear to involve a substantial degree of autonomy and discretion on the part of teachers. Although the structure of some schools may isolate and overextend them, teachers do appear to have a wide latitude of choice in how to respond to and cope with the manner in which their work is organized. From the loosely-coupled-schools perspective, this kind of autonomy held by teachers is considerable. However, from a workplace control perspective (e.g., Braverman, 1974; Burawoy, 1979; Simpson, 1985), such an interpretation misconstrues these phenomena. From this counter viewpoint, what may appear from the outside to be teacher autonomy and organizational decentralization is actually a form of centralized organizational control. The substitution of greater responsibility and greater latitude for a system of rigid rules and routinized procedures is not a form of decentralization and employee empowerment, but the opposite—an alternative and highly effective, yet highly invisible, form of centralized organizational control. Seen this way, the key distinction is between the delegation of *responsibility* and the delegation of *power*.

The critics of looseness in schools are correct—there is no question that the public has a right and, indeed, an obligation to be concerned with the performance of teachers. Schools, like all organizations designed to serve the collective needs of the public, need to be accountable to that public. However, the tighten-the-ship perspective and many of the reforms to come out of it commonly suffer from several problems. The first involves the accuracy of their diagnosis. The data show that there exists a high degree of centralization in schools and a lack of teacher control, rather than the opposite.

Second, accountability reforms are often unfair. For instance, proponents of top-down accountability reforms tend to overlook the unusual character of the teaching workforce. It is common among these policymakers and reformers to question and criticize the caliber and quality of teachers. A litany of such critics have told us again and again that teachers lack sufficient accountability, engagement, and commitment. But the data suggest that teachers have an unusual degree of public-service orientation and commitment compared with others. Unrecognized and unappreciated by these critics is the extent to which the teaching workforce is a source of human, social, and even financial capital in schools.

Third, for the above reasons accountability reforms often do not work. Top-down reforms draw attention to an important set of needs—accountability on the part of those doing the work. But these kinds of reforms sometimes overlook another, equally important set of needs—for autonomy and the good will of those doing the work. Too much organizational control may deny teachers the very control and flexibility they need to do the job effectively and may undermine their motivation. A high degree of organizational control may squander a valuable human resource—the unusual degree of commitment of those who enter the teaching occupation. Having little say in the terms, processes, and outcomes of their work may deny teachers the opportunity to feel that they are doing worthwhile work—the very reason many of them came into the occupation in the first place—and may end up contributing to the high rates of turnover among teachers. As a result, such reforms may not only fail to solve the problems they seek to address by offering a wrong prescription, but they may also end up making things worse. If top-down policies create an imbalance between power and responsibility, that is, if such policies hold teachers accountable for activities they do not control, they may decrease the very thing they seek to foster—improvements in teacher performance.

The Roots of the Teacher Quality Problem— An Alternative Hypothesis

In this section I offer an alternate hypothesis, drawn from the sociology of organizations, occupations, and work, to explain the problem of teacher quality and also the popularity of the four conventional explanations described above. From this perspective problems of teacher quality, low entry standards, chronic teacher turnover, teacher misassignment, and highly centralized workplaces are not new issues, and all can be traced to a common root—the stature and standing of the teaching occupation. Unlike in some European and Asian nations, in this country elementary and secondary school teaching has been largely treated as semiskilled work since the development of public school systems in the late 19th century (Etzioni, 1969; Lortie, 1975; Tyack, 1974). In his classic work, *The Sociology of Teaching* (1932), Willard Waller, for example, noted that, "The difficulties of the teacher . . . are greatly increased by the low social standing of the teaching profession and its general disrepute in the community at large. . . . Concerning the low social standing of teachers much has been written. The teacher in our culture has always been among the persons of little importance and his place has not changed for the better in the last few decades" (pp. 11, 58). Similarly, Mills (1951), in his classic study *White Collar*, classified schoolteachers as the "proletarians of the professions" (p. 129).

From this alternate perspective, the basis of occupational status lies in control over an important and scarce resource, such as knowledge of the causes of, and cures for, life threatening disease, as in the case of the medical profession (Abbott, 1988; Simpson, 1985). The demand for and importance of resources is tied to their scarcity or perceived scarcity. If the resource is something that is widely familiar or available, then the occupation will have difficulty claiming a monopoly of skill and jurisdiction and, thus, will have difficulty gaining the status associated with traditional professions (Wilensky, 1964).

Analysts of work and occupations have long classified teaching as a relatively complex form of work, characterized by uncertainty, intangibility, and ambiguity and requiring a high degree of initiative, thought, judgment, and skill to do well (e.g., Bidwell, 1965; Cohen, Raudenbush, & Ball, 2003; Lortie, 1975; Shulman, 1986). For example, in a comparative study of a number of occupations, Kohn and Schooler (1983) concluded that secondary teaching involved greater substantive complexity than the work of accountants, salespersons, machinists, managers, and officials in service industries and in the retail trade. What the work of elementary and secondary teachers lacks is not complexity but occupational legitimacy and prestige—leading sociologists to categorize teaching as a semi-profession (Etzioni, 1969; Lortie, 1969; Simpson, 1985). Although the work is relatively complex, the technical base of teaching does not appear to go beyond what the public thinks it knows. In other words, regardless of the reality, the public does not view teaching as equally skilled, sophisticated, intellectually difficult, or advanced work in comparison with the traditional professions.

Part of this public definition and perception may be traced to an unusual aspect of teaching—it is one of the few occupations whose clients have had extensive prior exposure to the work and its practitioners. In short, teaching is an occupation which many nonpractitioners believe they understand. Another factor closely tied to occupational status is gender—three fourths of the teaching force are women. The traditional professions, until recently, have been male dominated. In contrast, predominantly female occupations, such as teaching, have always been of lower prestige and status in the United States (Ingersoll, 2000).

Teaching as a Semi-Profession

From this occupational-status perspective, the semiprofessional stature of this feminized work is a large factor behind the first two of the four issues discussed in this chapter—entry requirements and shortages. Teaching is an occupation that has historically relied on recruitment, and not retention, to solve its staffing needs and problems. The emphasis was on ease of entry rather than raising admission standards or increasing teacher salaries. After the inception of the public school system in the late 19th century, teaching was socially defined and treated as a temporary line of work suitable for women, prior to their "real" career of child rearing (e.g., Lortie, 1975; Tyack 1974). For men, teaching was socially defined as a stepping stone to their "real" career in one of the male-dominated skilled blue-collar occupations or white-collar professions. Indeed, historically there was an ambivalence toward persistors in teaching, especially males, who had to account for why they continued to be "merely" teachers. To this day, low preservice training standards and requirements, relatively unselective entry criteria, and front-loaded salaries that pay newcomers relatively high salaries compared with veterans all tend to favor recruitment over retention. Moreover, low pay, isolated job conditions, little professional autonomy, and little sense of a career ladder all undermine longer-term commitment to teaching as a career and profession. Given these occupational characteristics, cyclic staffing problems, misdiagnosed as shortages, are to be expected.

The semiprofessional status of this feminized work also explains the irony, mentioned earlier, surrounding the relatively high scrutiny of teaching's relatively low entry requirements. Why is there such ongoing interest, compared with other occupations, in documenting and challenging whether teacher qualifications matter? Compared with other occupations, why is there social pressure to continually attempt to prove that teaching is a highly complex kind of work and that it takes both ability and advanced training to do well? In short, why is there a double standard?

From an occupational-status perspective, underlying the skepticism and double standard is the assumption that teaching is less complex and requires less ability and training than many other kinds of occupations and professions. Thus, for example, the assumption is that working with children and youth is less complex and requires less expertise than working with buildings (engineers), teeth (dentists), or financial accounts (accountants) or doing academic research (professors). In plain terms, the underlying assumption is that teaching is not especially difficult work to do well.

The semiprofessional status of teaching also explains the prevalence of out-of-field teaching—the third issue discussed in this chapter. The comparison with traditional professions is stark. Few would require cardiologists to deliver babies, real estate lawyers to defend criminal cases, chemical engineers to design bridges, or sociology professors to teach English. This also applies for the high-skill blue-collar occupations—for example, few would ask an electrician to solve a plumbing problem. The commonly held assumption is that such traditional male-dominated occupations and professions require a great deal of expertise and, thus, specialization is necessary. In short, for well-paid, well-respected professions and occupations, it is less acceptable to lower skill standards as a mechanism to increase the labor supply. In contrast, underlying out-of-field teaching appears to be the assumption that female-dominated, precollegiate school teaching requires far less skill, training, and expertise than many other occupations and professions and that specialization is less necessary and, thus, it is appropriate to use teachers like interchangeable blocks. Moreover, the tendency to misdiagnose these human resource management practices as deficits in teacher training or teacher supply further reflects the semiprofessional status of teaching.

Finally, the semiprofessional status of teaching also explains the fourth issue discussed in this chapter—the distribution of control in schools. One of the most important factors associated with the degree of professionalization and the status of an occupation is the degree of power and control practitioners hold over workplace decisions (Freidson, 1973, 1986; Kohn & Schooler, 1983; Mills, 1951; Perrow, 1986; Simpson, 1985). Professionalized employees usually have control and autonomy approaching that of senior management when it comes to organizational decisions surrounding their work. Academics, for example, often have equal or greater control than that of university administrators over the content of their teaching and research and over the hiring of new colleagues, and through the institution of peer review, over the evaluation and promotion of members and thus, over the ongoing content and character of the profession. Members of lower-status occupations usually have little say over their work. The SASS data show that in comparison with traditional professions, teachers have only limited authority over key workplace decisions, such as which courses they are assigned (or misassigned) to teach.

There is no question that some teachers are poorly trained, perform poorly, or are inadequate for the job in one way or another. Moreover, it is neither convincing nor valid to simply pass the blame for low-quality teaching and educational failure elsewhere—for instance, onto families. Teachers are important and do have an effect on students, and it is appropriate to scrutinize their training, qualifications, and performance. However, from an occupational-status perspective, solving the teacher quality problem will require addressing its underlying systemic roots. From this perspective, in order to improve the quality of teachers and teaching, it will be necessary to improve the quality of, and respect afforded, the teaching job and occupation. Moreover, piecemeal reform will not accomplish systemic change. Changes to entry standards, training, rewards, autonomy, and accountability must be enacted in concert to succeed. Increases in one must be accompanied by increases in the others. Simply raising preservice entry standards without also raising inservice rewards will not improve the quality of prospective entrants. Raising either entry standards or inservice rewards without also ensuring inservice accountability will not improve quality. Similarly, accountability and autonomy must be linked. Delegating power without commensurate responsibility is irresponsible and can even be dangerous and harmful. In other words, giving teachers more autonomy alone is not the answer. Likewise, accountability without commensurate power is unfair and can also be harmful. It does not make sense to hold somebody accountable for something they do not control, nor does it make sense to give someone control over something for which they are not held accountable. All of these individual changes are necessary, but none alone are sufficient to accomplish the larger systemic goal—ensuring quality teachers in every classroom.

REFERENCES

Abbott, A. (1988). *The system of professions: An essay on the division of expert labor.* Chicago: University of Chicago Press.

Allen, M. (2003). *Eight questions on teacher preparation: What does the research say?* Denver, CO: Education Commission of the States.

American Council on Education. (1999). *To touch the future: Transforming the way teachers are taught.* Washington, DC: Author.

Ballou, D. (1996). Do public schools hire the best applicants? *Quarterly Journal of Economics, 111*(1), 97-133.

Bidwell, C. (1965). The school as a formal organization. In J. March (Ed.), *Handbook of organizations* (pp. 973-1002). Chicago: Rand McNally.

Bluedorn, A.C. (1982). A unified model of turnover from organizations. *Human Relations, 35*, 135-153.

Boe, E., & Gilford, D. (1992). *Teacher supply, demand and quality.* Washington, DC: National Academy Press.

Braverman, H. (1974). *Labor and monopoly capitalism.* New York: Monthly Review Press.

Burawoy, M. (1979). *Manufacturing consent: Changes in the labor process under monopoly capitalism.* Chicago: University of Chicago Press.

Callahan, R. (1962). *Education and the cult of efficiency.* Chicago: University of Chicago Press.

Carnegie Foundation for the Advancement of Teaching. (1990). *The condition of teaching.* New York: Carnegie Foundation.

Cohen, D., Raudenbush, S., & Ball, D. (2003). Resources, instruction and research. *Educational Evaluation and Policy Analysis, 25*(2), 119-142.

Cohen, M., March, J., & Olsen, J. (1972). A garbage can theory of organizational decision making. *Administrative Science Quarterly, 17*, 1-25.

Coleman, J., & Hoffer, T. (1987). *Public and private schools: The impact of communities.* New York: Basic Books.

Committee for Economic Development. (1996). *American workers and economic change.* New York: Author.

Conley, S. (1991). Review of research on teacher participation in school decision making. In G. Grant (Ed.), *Review of Research in Education, 17*, 225-266. Washington, DC: American Educational Research Association.

Darling-Hammond, L. (1984). *Beyond the commission reports: The coming crisis in teaching.* Santa Monica, CA: Rand Corporation.

Darling-Hammond, L. (1999). *Teacher quality and student achievement: A review of state policy evidence.* Center for the Study of Teaching and Policy, University of Washington.

Delany, B. (1991). Allocation, choice and stratification within high schools: How the sorting machine copes. *American Journal of Education, 99*(2), 181-207.

Durkheim, E. (1925/1961). *Moral education: A study in the theory and application of the sociology of education,* E.K. Wilson and H. Schnurer (Trans.). New York: Free Press.

Education Week. (2000). Quality counts: A report on education in the 50 states. Washington, DC: Author.

Elmore, R. (2000). *Building a new structure for school leadership.* New York: Albert Shanker Institute.

Etzioni, A. (1969). (Ed.). *The semiprofessions and their organizations: Teachers, nurses and social workers.* New York: Free Press.

Finn, C., Kanstoroom, M., & Petrilli, M. (1999). *The quest for better teachers: Grading the states.* Washington, DC: Thomas B. Fordham Foundation.

Freidson, E. (1973). *The professions and their prospects.* Beverly Hills, CA: Sage.

Freidson, E. (1986). *Professional powers: A study in the institutionalization of formal knowledge.* Chicago: University of Chicago Press.

Fullan, M. (1991). *The new meaning of educational change.* New York: Teachers College Press.

Grant, G. (1988). *The world we created at Hamilton High*. Cambridge, MA: Harvard University Press.

Greenwald, R., Hedges, L., & Laine, R. (1996). The effect of school resources on student achievement. *Review of Educational Research, 66*, 361-396.

Hafner, A., & Owings, J. (1991). *Careers in teaching: Following members of the high school class of 1972 in and out of teaching* (NCES Report No. 91-470). Washington, DC: U.S. Department of Education, National Center for Education Statistics.

Hall, R. (1968). Professionalization and bureaucratization. *American Sociological Review, 33*, 92-104.

Hanushek, E., & Rivkin, S. (2004, forthcoming). How to improve the supply of high quality teachers. In D. Ravitch (Ed.), *Brookings papers on education policy*. Washington, DC: Brookings Institution.

Henke, R., Chen, X., & Geis, S. (2000). *Progress through the pipeline: 1992-93 College graduates and elementary/secondary school teaching as of 1997*. Washington, DC: National Center for Education Statistics.

Hirsch, E., Koppich, J., & Knapp, M. (2001). *Revisiting what states are doing to improve the quality of teaching: An update on patterns and trends*. Center for the Study of Teaching and Policy, University of Washington, Seattle.

Hodson, R., & Sullivan, T. (1995). Professions and professionals. In R. Hodson & T.A. Sullivan (Eds.), *The social organization of work* (pp. 287-314). Belmont, CA: Wadsworth.

Hom, P., & Griffeth, R. (1995). *Employee turnover*. Cincinnati: South-Western Publishing.

Huling-Austin, L. (1990). Teacher induction programs and internships. In W.R. Houston (Ed.), *Handbook of research on teacher education* (pp. 535-548). Reston, VA: Association of Teacher Educators.

Ingersoll, R. (1999). The problem of underqualified teachers in American secondary schools. *Educational Researcher, 28*, 26-37.

Ingersoll, R. (2000). The status of teaching as a profession. In J. Ballantine & J. Spade (Eds.), *Schools and society: A sociological perspective* (pp. 115-129). Belmont, CA: Wadsworth Press.

Ingersoll, R. (2001). Teacher turnover and teacher shortages: An organizational analysis. *American Educational Research Journal, 38*(3), 499-534.

Ingersoll, R. (2003a). *Who controls teachers' work? Power and accountability in America's schools*. Cambridge, MA: Harvard University Press.

Ingersoll, R. (2003b). *Is there really a teacher shortage?* Center for the Study of Teaching and Policy, University of Washington, Seattle. Available: http://ctpweb.org

Ingersoll, R. (2004). Why some schools have more underqualified teachers than others. In D. Ravitch (Ed.), *Brookings papers on education policy*. Washington, DC: Brookings Institution.

Kirst, M. (1989). Who should control the schools? In T.J. Sergiovanni & J. Moore (Eds.), *Schooling for tomorrow*. Boston: Allyn and Bacon.

Kohn, M., & Schooler, C. (1983). *Work and personality*. Norwood, New Jersey: Ablex.

Lortie, D. (1969). The balance of control and autonomy in elementary school teaching. In A. Etzioni (Ed.), *The semiprofessions and their organizations: Teachers, nurses and social workers* (pp. 1-53). New York: Free Press.

Lortie, D. (1975). *School teacher*. Chicago: University of Chicago Press.

Meyer, J., & Scott, W.R. (1983). *Organizational environments: Ritual and rationality*. Beverly Hills, CA: Sage.

Mills, C.W. (1951). *White collar*. New York: Oxford.

Mobley, W. (1982). *Employee turnover: Causes, consequences and control*. Reading, MA: Addison-Wesley.

Murnane, R., & Raizen, S. (1988). Indicators of teaching quality. In R. Murnane & S. Senta (Eds.), *Improving indicators of the quality of science and mathematics education in grades K-12* (pp. 90-118). Washington, DC: National Academy Press.

Murnane, R., Singer, J., Willett, J., Kemple, J., & Olsen, R. (Eds.). (1991). *Who will teach? Policies that matter.* Cambridge, MA: Harvard University Press.

National Academy of Sciences. (1987). *Toward understanding teacher supply and demand.* Washington, DC: National Academy Press.

National Commission on Excellence in Education. (1983). *A nation at risk: The imperative for educational reform.* Washington, DC: Government Printing Office.

National Commission on Teaching and America's Future. (1996). *What matters most: Teaching for America's future.* New York: NCTAF.

National Commission on Teaching and America's Future. (1997). *Doing what matters most: Investing in quality teaching.* New York: NCTAF.

National Education Association. 1972, 1982, 1987, 1992, 1996. *Status of the American public school teacher.* Washington, DC: National Education Association.

Parsons, T. (1959).The school class as a social system: Some of its functions in American society. *Harvard Educational Review, 29*, 297-318.

Pascarella, E., & Terenzini, P. (1991). *How college affects students: Findings and insights from twenty years of research.* San Francisco: Jossey-Bass.

Perrow, C. (1986). *Complex organizations: A critical essay.* New York: Random House.

Price, J. (1977). *The study of turnover.* Ames, IA: Iowa State University Press.

Price, J. (1989). The impact of turnover on the organization. *Work and Occupations, 16,* 461-473.

Raudenbush, S., Fotiu, R., & Cheong, Y. (1999). Synthesizing results from the trial state assessment. *Journal of Educational and Behavioral Statistics, 24*(4), 413-438.

Robinson, V. (1985). *Making do in the classroom: A report on the misassignment of teachers.* Washington, DC: Council for Basic Education and American Federation of Teachers.

Schlecty, P., & Vance, V. (1981). Do academically able teachers leave education? The North Carolina case. *Phi Delta Kappan, 63,* 105-112.

Shulman, L. (1986). Those who understand: Knowledge growth in teaching. *Educational Researcher, 15,* 4-14.

Simpson, R. (1985). Social control of occupations and work. *Annual Review of Sociology,* 415-436.

Smylie, M.A., & Wenzel, S.A. (2003). The Chicago Annenberg Challenge: Successes, failures, and lessons for the future (Final Technical Report of the Chicago Annenberg Research Project). Chicago: Consortium on Chicago School Research, University of Chicago.

Strober, M., & Tyack, D. (1980). Why do women teach and men manage? *Signs, 5,* 499-500.

Texas Center for Educational Research. (2000). *The cost of teacher turnover.* Austin, TX: Texas State Board for Educator Certification.

Tyack, D. (1974). *The one best system.* Cambridge, MA: Harvard University Press.

Tyler, W. (1988). *School organization.* New York: Croom Helm.

Waller, W. (1932). *The sociology of teaching.* New York: Wiley.

Wang, A., Coleman, A., Coley, R., & Phelps, R. (2003). *Preparing teachers around the world.* Princeton, NJ: Educational Testing Service.

Weaver, T. (1983). *America's teacher quality problem: Alternatives for reform.* New York: Praeger Publishers.

Weick, K. (1976). Educational organizations as loosely coupled systems. *Administrative Science Quarterly, 21,* 1-19.

Wilensky, H. (1964). The professionalization of everyone? *American Journal of Sociology, 70,* 137-158.

CHAPTER 2

Rethinking Teacher Workforce Development: A Strategic Human Resource Management Perspective

MARK A. SMYLIE, DEBRA MIRETZKY, AND PAMELA KONKOL

It might be said that the importance we attribute to teachers can be measured by the intensity of our ambivalence toward them. We are apt to blame teachers for many of the problems we see in our schools. At the same time, we look to teachers as a solution to these very problems. By this standard, today's teachers are held in the highest regard.

One does not have to look far to find charges that the failings of our schools can be attributed to teachers with "no skill in meeting classroom problems," to a tenure system that protects ineffective teachers, and to practices of selection and hiring that place the least qualified teachers in schools with the neediest children. Nor does one have to look far to find calls for improving teacher quality and effectiveness because of "[teachers'] immaturity entering the profession, the unevenness of their preparation, the lack of external stimulus connected with the practice of the profession, the complex nature of the work that must be entrusted to even the poorest teacher, the profound injury that results when the work is badly done, and the constant change in methods and curriculum." Such criticism has been commonplace across the decades. This particular critique, although it could have come from today's editorial pages, was published nearly a century ago in the National Society for the Study of Education's seventh yearbook, *The Relation of Superintendents and Principals to the Training and Improvement of Their Teachers* (Lowry, 1908, pp. 15 and 64).

This 103rd yearbook appears at a time when developing teacher quality and effectiveness is center stage. Increasingly, scholars are emphasizing the impact of both individual teachers and school faculties

Mark A. Smylie is a Professor and Chair of Policy Studies in the College of Education at the University of Illinois at Chicago. Debra Miretzky is Program Director of the National Society for the Study of Education and an Adjunct Instructor in education at UIC. Pamela Konkol is a Ph.D. student in Policy Studies in UIC's College of Education.

on student achievement (e.g., Darling-Hammond, 2000; Goldhaber & Anthony, 2004; Rice, 2003; Sanders & Horn, 1998; Wayne & Youngs, 2003). Developing teachers' "skill" and "will" is considered essential to the improvement of schools and classroom instruction and to the implementation of educational innovation (Newmann & Wehlage, 1995). As Fullan (2001) succinctly put it: "Educational change depends on what teachers do and think—it's as simple and complex as that" (p. 115). The goal of having a "highly qualified" teacher in every American classroom is embraced by such politically diverse organizations as the National Commission on Teaching and America's Future (1996) and the Thomas B. Fordham Foundation (1999). It is the cornerstone of the No Child Left Behind federal education legislation signed into law by President George W. Bush in 2002. Indeed, developing the quality and effectiveness of teachers has joined standards, testing, and accountability and market mechanisms as a primary policy instrument for educational reform (Murphy & Datnow, 2003).

What is problematic and in some dispute is how best to develop teacher quality and effectiveness (e.g., Darling-Hammond & Youngs, 2002; U.S. Department of Education, 2002). As the chapters in this volume demonstrate, creating and maintaining a high-quality teacher workforce is an extremely complex and challenging enterprise. It is often difficult to attract people to a profession that is demanding, poorly rewarded, and regularly castigated by the mass media. And it is difficult to attract people to teach in certain subject areas and in under-resourced or low-performing schools. Retention is becoming more and more of a problem, particularly among teachers in the early part of their careers and among those who teach in challenging settings. Teachers face increasing demands for improvement and accountability, often with inadequate resources and support. At the same time, they must work in schools and classrooms that may not be particularly conducive to their own development and performance. When schools try to develop their own faculties, they may be constrained by the policies and procedures of their districts or by collective bargaining agreements. Likewise, schools and districts may be constrained by policies and procedures at the state level.

Our contention is that schools and districts are much less effective than they could be in developing the quality and effectiveness of their teachers. We believe that one of the primary reasons for their lack of effectiveness is that they define and approach the problem incompletely. First, schools and districts fail to see that the task is more than developing the knowledge and skills of individual teachers or enhancing the teaching profession at large. It is both these things, but teacher development is also fundamentally a function of school organization. It is a problem of assembling, developing, and managing groups of teachers—faculties—in organizational context—schools—to work together to achieve organizational purposes—the education of children and youth. It is a task of workforce development and management. Second, schools and districts tend to think about teacher development in terms of a fairly limited range of discrete practices, often little more than recruitment, selection, and professional development. They fail to see how a broader range of practices, practices in which they already engage, can be used more strategically as an interrelated system that may be much more effective than individual practices or sets of disconnected practices. Third, schools and districts pay little attention to the variation and flexibility required to address the needs of teachers as a diverse and dynamic workforce and across the career span.

Drawing on recent concepts and theories of human resource management found in the literature on organization and management, we argue for the value of a comprehensive, strategic, systems approach to teacher development. This approach is gaining some purchase in the education literature, primarily in the form of critiques and calls for change in current policy and practice. We see this chapter as an opportunity to bridge the education literature and the literature on organization and management and to bring some potentially promising ideas to the problem of improving teacher quality and effectiveness (see Keep, 1993, for an earlier effort to bridge these literatures).

We begin with a brief review of conventional approaches to teacher workforce development and management, including current critiques of these efforts, their possible consequences, and an overview of the recent calls for more comprehensive, systemic approaches. This leads to a discussion of theoretical perspectives on strategic human resource management. After this discussion, we examine how these theoretical perspectives apply to the development and management of teachers through several examples of innovative practice at the school, district, and state levels. We conclude with a discussion of why using these perspectives to guide teacher development policy and practice may be difficult.

In this chapter, we intentionally focus on teacher development as a collective and organizational issue. In doing so, we do not wish to imply that a focus on the development of individual teachers or the development of the teaching profession is misplaced. It is not. In addition, by taking an organizational perspective, we do not mean to suggest that individual, organizational, and profession-level perspectives are mutually exclusive. Rather, they should be seen as "mutually constructive" (Horn, personal communication, April 25, 2004). Indeed, it is our hope that by emphasizing collective organizational issues, we will promote future thinking and practice that see teacher development as an interactive system of individual and collective, organizational growth.

Conventional Approaches to Teacher Workforce Development and Management

Developing and managing a workforce of teachers is quite complex. First, there is no such thing as a single teacher workforce. There are multiple, nested workforces that function at different levels of the educational system. School faculties are one level of teacher workforce that must be assembled, developed, and managed in a particular local context. We can think about all teachers who are employed by a school district as a workforce and all teachers who work in a state as another workforce. One can also imagine metropolitan, regional, and other workforces not necessarily defined by an organizational or governmental entity. Second, schools, districts, and states each have varying needs, interests, and authority to develop and manage teacher workforces at their particular levels. Each can develop and implement policies and practices to address those needs and interests within a particular range of influence. And efforts to shape the teacher workforce at the broadest levels are likely to affect efforts at the most local levels, not always productively (Darling-Hammond & Sykes, 2003; Kirp & Driver, 1995). Third, by definition, development and management imply some measure of coordination and control of individuals toward some collective, valued purpose. The balances between coordination and control and the individual autonomy and discretion needed to perform professional work in professional organizations—in this case, teaching in schools—is fraught with dilemmas and potential contradiction (Ogawa, Crowson, & Goldring, 1999; Weick & McDaniel, 1989). Moreover, there are many important issues to address concerning professional self-determinism and self-regulation as opposed to external bureaucratic control. We do not attempt to address these issues in this chapter, but what we have to say certainly implicates them.

We propose that it is most useful to think about the work of teacher workforce development and management first at the school level, where teachers—individually and collectively—are most likely to matter to student learning and development (Wang, Haertel, & Walberg, 1993), and then move outward to the district and state levels. As we have already noted, the development and management of a school faculty can be "bounded" by what districts and states do to develop and manage teacher workforces at their levels. Indeed, schools, districts, and states can be influenced by the dynamics of the broader workforces at, say, the regional level. The point is that, in our view, the district and state levels can be either supporting or impeding contexts for teacher development and management at the school level. (See Jennings, 2003, and Plecki and Loeb, this volume, Chapter 12, for additional treatment of state and federal policy contexts.)

So, what constitutes the work of teacher workforce development and management at the school, district, and state levels? Although it is impossible to capture the dimensions of this work completely, and although it is not to be assumed that all this work is performed or performed particularly well (a subject we will address shortly), we suggest that its scope looks something like that outlined in Table 1. This table lists the general tasks of teacher workforce development and management and gives examples of practices that might be performed at different levels of the educational system to accomplish those tasks (see Rebore, 2004; Wright & Snell, 1991). These tasks and examples are not meant to be exhaustive, and they certainly might vary by specific school, district, and state contexts.

In order to assemble, develop, and manage a faculty, a school must recruit and select new teachers. In recruitment and selection, a school must consider the characteristics and qualities of its current group of teachers, including their knowledge, skills, and values as well as their gender, race, ethnicity, and experience. It must also consider the needs of its students and the community and the characteristics and capabilities presented by potential hires. A school must induct new teachers into its philosophy, practices, and social-normative environment. It must assign teachers to grades and classes, and students to teachers. A school must manage teacher absenteeism and turnover from retirement and defection. It must try to retain effective teachers in danger of leaving and counsel out ineffective teachers who have every intention of staying. A school must supervise and evaluate its teachers and provide means for their ongoing professional development to address local learning needs and interests and to support the implementation of new policies and practices originating from external sources, including the district and the state. Although a school cannot reasonably alter the broad structure of teacher compensation and benefits, it can establish its own incentives, programs of recognition and reward, and sanctions. It can also create an environment that is conducive to

TABLE 1

Teacher Workforce Development: General Tasks and Examples of Practices
at the School, District, and State Levels

Task	Example of Practice		
	School	District	State
Develop general supply		Public promotion of opportunity and need	Credentialing and licensure; incentive programs
Promote quality of initial preparation	Support of school-based field experiences	Partnerships with local preparation programs	Accreditation of programs; promotion of innovative practices
Recruit, select, and hire	Informal networks; relationships with local preparation programs	Public promotion and incentive programs for minority teachers and teachers in high need areas; pipeline relationships with initial preparation programs; establishment of hiring criteria and procedures	
Allocate among schools and classrooms	Strategic placement to match teachers with student needs	Strategic placement to match teachers with school needs; monitor compliance with external mandates affecting teacher assignment (e.g., desegregation orders).	
Induct and socialize	School-based mentoring and informal practices	District-level orientation; programs of school-based mentoring and mentor support	
Provide opportunities for professional development	School-initiated programs and activities for local need; informal workplace learning	Programs for implementation of district programs and policies; identification and quality control of providers	Grants for district and school level professional development activity
Supervise and evaluate	Supplement district-level policies and procedures; deprivatization of practice in teacher professional learning community	General policies and procedures; professional practice standards and assessments; professional development for supervisors and evaluators	Standards and assessments; provisions for recertification and licensure
Retain and terminate	General professional and social support; counseling	General criteria and procedures for termination	
Motivate and promote performance	Supportive workplace conditions; administrative support; programs of recognition and reward; work redesign	Set compensation; work redesign initiatives and recognition and rewards programs; facilities management and standard operating procedures	
Manage labor relations	Manage building level personnel issues; initiate requests for contract waivers (e.g., to lengthen school day for joint planning and professional development)	Collective bargaining for contract, compensation, work rules, etc.	Legislate and regulate collective bargaining rights and processes

collaborative work, collective accountability, and motivated job performance. A school must do all these things (and perhaps more) with a group of teachers that is diverse in terms of age, experience, gender, race, and ethnicity and is dynamic in terms of turnover and mobility and individual and professional growth and need. And finally, a school must do all these things in a context of serving an ever-changing body of students and meeting external demands for improvement and higher levels of performance.

At the same time, the district in which the school is located must develop and manage its workforce. It must recruit new teachers to the district at large. Beyond the discretion it provides to schools to recruit and hire their own teachers, the district must manage the allocation of teachers across schools in the system and deal with problems of shortages and out-of-field teaching. The district also must promote racial, ethnic, and other forms of diversity. The district might provide opportunities for professional development, to meet general needs but also to support the implementation of district- or state-level initiatives or to facilitate compliance with state regulations or court orders. It might try to promote and regulate relationships between schools and external providers of professional development and other school improvement assistance. The district must set general teacher evaluation and supervision policies and procedures. Through collective bargaining, it must determine the structure and levels of teacher compensation and benefits, establish work rules, develop procedures for school-to-school transfers, and so forth. The district can guide teachers' work through the development of student learning standards, curricula, and instructional guides and materials. It can try to motivate teacher performance through work redesign and programs of recognition and reward. Finally, by its decisions in various areas, from facilities management to class-size policy to standard operating procedures, the district can create workplace conditions that can motivate, support, or impede teachers' work performance.

The state in which the district and school are located can promote the development and management of the teacher workforce at its level in a number of ways. States can develop the size and quality of the general supply of teachers through teacher credentialing and licensure (initial and renewal) and through accreditation of teacher preparation programs. States may also develop supply through various incentive programs to attract prospective teachers to preparation programs, into the workforce, and perhaps into high-need areas. States can create standards and accountability systems for evaluating teacher and student performance. Either administratively or legislatively, states can regulate teacher compensation and collective bargaining. Finally, states can support the entire enterprise of teacher workforce development and management through targeted and general funding.

Critiques of Conventional Approaches

How are schools, districts, and states likely to perform this work? In a word, poorly. Abundant literature, much of it cited throughout this yearbook, describes teacher workforce development and management as a hodge-podge of poorly planned, under-resourced, disconnected practices. For decades, these practices, which include initial teacher preparation, recruitment and selection, induction and socialization, ongoing professional development, supervision and evaluation, compensation and reward systems, and retention and termination, have been criticized as largely ineffective (see, e.g., Griffin, 1999; Henry, 1957; Lowry, 1908, Ryan, 1975).

Recently, a new critique has emerged. This one focuses less on individual practices of teacher development and management than on the "systems" of practices in which schools, districts, and states engage. This critique is no less damning, however, because these systems are judged to be anything but systemic. They are viewed as narrowly construed and built around a limited range of disconnected practices (Rebore, 2004). According to this critique, schools, districts, and states act on the assumption that different areas of teacher improvement serve discrete functions. Their efforts in these areas are therefore not likely to be coherently focused on broader educational objectives. Nor are these efforts likely to be well coordinated within or across school, district, or state levels of the educational system (Darling-Hammond, & Sykes, 2003; Rebore). As such, critics consider these efforts to be insufficient, inefficient, and ineffective (Darling-Hammond & Sykes; Hirsch, Koppich, & Knapp, 2001; Rebore).

This lack of relationship among the different areas of teacher workforce development and management can be reinforced by a number of factors. First, the orientation of most development and management practices is reactive instead of forward-looking and proactive (Keep, 1993; Rebore, 2004). The primary objective is typically solving immediate problems through a triage approach rather than accomplishing long-term goals. Schools and districts may be more concerned about filling vacant classroom positions, addressing teacher shortages in particular subject areas, or "retooling" teachers to meet new accountability demands than about pursuing long-term agendas of instructional reform. Second, different teacher development and management practices, be they at the school, district, state, or federal level, are often uniform and rigid, characteristics that reinforce their independence and constrain efforts to coordinate them. Moreover, this uniformity and rigidity limits variability and flexibility, which schools and districts require to satisfy changing demands and to meet the diverse and changing development needs of teachers throughout their careers.

These problems have deep roots that can be traced back to the early 1900s and the application of bureaucratic and scientific management models to education (Darling-Hammond, 1997). Through nearly a century of National Society for the Study of Education yearbooks (Bobbitt, 1913; Griffiths, 1964; Lowry, 1908; Spalding, 1946) and textbooks on educational administration (see Glass, 2004), one can see the influence of the view that educational administration consists of independent managerial tasks associated with "running a school" that fulfill discrete, specialized functions. According to this view, the improvement of teachers is a function of external coordination and control of individual work. The assumption was that an effective, uniform "technology" of schooling could be identified and then transferred into practice, primarily by selecting and training teachers to implement that technology and then holding them accountable through supervision and evaluation (see Tyack, 1974). The goal was efficient management and more effective performance of the current educational system (see Cuban, 1988). Despite the development of more humanistic and democratic views of schools and school administration during the 1940s and 1950s and the emergence in the 1960s and 1970s of more comprehensive theoretical perspectives of organizations and administration from the social and behavioral sciences, the view of school administration and administrative tasks established in the early 1900s has persisted (see McCarthy, 1999).

Moreover, the current critique of teacher workforce development and management practices is consistent with observations found in the literature on organization and management. In 1977, for example, Schein argued that the major problem with existing personnel development systems was that they were "fragmented, incomplete, and sometimes built on faulty assumptions about human or organizational growth" (p. 4). Fourteen years later, Wright and Snell (1991) characterized the practice of human resource management in organizations as being constructed around distinct specializations or subfunctions (e.g., hiring, training, performance appraisal, compensation). Typically, there were few connections between the different subfunctions and an organization's goals and strategy. When connections did exist, they usually were not strategic or mutually reinforcing. Wright and McMahan (1992) observed that the practice of human resource management had achieved little cross-functional integration. Different areas of human resource management had evolved from a technical, micro-level orientation—that is, from an effort to make the subfunctions operate more effectively but in relative isolation. Delery and Doty (1996) observed that a single, "universalistic," "best practice" approach dominates the field of human resource management and that human resource management traditionally has served a maintenance rather than a strategic development function.

The Consequences of Conventional Approaches

So what does it matter if the practice of teacher workforce development and management is typically limited in scope, fragmented, and lacking coherence? What does it matter if it lacks variability and flexibility and is disconnected from broader educational objectives? There is little evidence in the education literature to address these questions. The few studies that do exist focus less on the consequences of disconnectedness, for example, than on the actual or anticipated outcomes of more coherent and strategic systems of practices (e.g., D'Amico, Harwell, Stein, & van den Heuvel, 2001; Darling-Hammond et al., 2003; Elmore & Burney, 1997; Elmore, Peterson, & McCarthey, 1996; Hightower, 2002). We will discuss this literature later in the chapter.

Perhaps the best source of argument and evidence concerning the consequences of disconnected and fragmented workforce development and management practices is the literature on organization and management. In this literature, there is a small but growing body of research indicating that the methods an organization uses to develop and manage its human resources can have a substantial impact—both positive and negative—on organizational outcomes (Delery, 1998). This literature focuses specifically on the problems posed by discrete and disconnected practices that are general in nature, are not focused on the goals and tasks of the organization, and lack the variability and flexibility required to meet the different and changing needs of employees throughout their careers (see Arthur & Kram, 1989).

For instance, Wright and Snell (1991) argue that pursuing employee development through discrete, disconnected practices prevents an organization from seeing synergies or conflicts among those practices and thus increases the chances for inefficiency, inflexibility, and ineffectiveness within the organization. Such pursuits are also likely to generate practice-specific and potentially conflicting definitions of problems and to perpetuate the use of conventional (perhaps relatively ineffective) means for solving them, thus limiting the strategic alternatives available to the organization. Lepak and Snell (1999) contend that uniformity in employee development practices is also problematic. Uniformity assumes that there is a single, optimal architecture or strategy for developing and managing all employees. This assumption ignores the reality that employees in any organization are typically quite diverse, with different and dynamic development needs. In Lepak and Snell's estimation, a one-size-fits-all development practice, even in the guise of "best practice," is likely to be of limited effectiveness.

In one of the most comprehensive reviews of the theory and research on the consequences of employee development practices, Lado and Wilson (1994) reached the following conclusions: Organizations that invest in "non-firm specific" employee development practices do not perform as well as organizations that focus development practices on specific organizational needs and objectives. By this they mean that organizations that fail to systematically consider how new hires fit within the organization—how they will help the organization achieve its goals—do not perform as well as organizations that do consider this fit. Lado and Wilson also distinguish between employee development practices that focus on the performance of specific tasks and those that focus on broader organizational performance. They contend that the result of the former—"minimalist" practices that focus on operational efficiencies and short-term, person-to-job fit—is that organizations become "trapped by functional myopia" (p. 714). This effect may hinder the development of the broader, more important competencies that are necessary for the organization to be effective over time. Finally, Lepak and Snell found that overly bureaucratic, standardized, and inflexible employee development practices can impede individual and collective employee performance and engender a sense of "learned helplessness." Such an approach can foster dysfunction by compromising employee commitment to the organization and promoting unproductive or counterproductive behavior.

Calls for a More Comprehensive, Systemic Approach

In the late 1980s and early 1990s, several observers began to draw attention to the conflicts and inefficiencies that arise when different teacher development practices are disconnected, and they started to argue for greater coordination and coherence among these practices. For instance, McGreal (1989) and Wood and his colleagues (McQuarrie

& Wood, 1991; Wood & Lease, 1987) argued that the effectiveness of teacher evaluation, supervision, and professional development might be enhanced substantially if these practices were complementary and coordinated around a common instructional framework. Keep (1993) captured the issue more fully when he argued for a "genuine and coherent" system of teacher development. Without clear goals and strategic management in schools and school systems, he contended, individual teacher personnel initiatives would continue to be developed and implemented in isolation from one another. According to Keep, that approach has been both inefficient and ineffective. He reasoned, for example, that there is little value in developing a teacher compensation or reward system that fails to consider how teachers are evaluated. Moreover, neither compensation nor evaluation can reasonably be considered apart from the design of teachers' work or the opportunities available to teachers for ongoing professional development. Keep argued that teacher development issues should be viewed "as a whole," encompassing recruitment, selection, pay, evaluation, training and development, and the shape of work structures in order to create practices that work in mutually reinforcing ways (see also Thacker, 2000).

Similar arguments appeared in the National Commission on Teaching and America's Future's (NCTAF) benchmark report, *What Matters Most: Teaching for America's Future* (1996). This report outlined five broad recommendations that constitute a systemic, strategic program of related initiatives for improving the overall quality of teachers and teaching in the United States:

1. Develop standards for teacher and student knowledge, skills, and performance.
2. Reinvent teacher preparation and professional development as a career-long activity built around those standards.
3. Enhance the pathways to teaching and improve the ability of school systems to recruit, hire, and retain high-quality teachers, particularly in areas of high need.
4. Develop a career continuum for teachers that employs teacher assessment and compensation systems to reward knowledge and skill and to remove incompetent teachers.
5. Reform schools as workplaces to make them more conducive to teacher learning and development, high-quality teaching, and student learning.

More recently, NCTAF supplemented these recommendations by drawing attention to the problem of teacher retention (NCTAF, 2003). The

interrelated nature of these recommendations has been discussed by
Darling-Hammond (1997), who argued for a teacher development system consisting of "a coherent set of policies, linked to our educational
goals, that allow us to invest rationally and systemically in a career-
long continuum of powerful learning and productive teaching conditions for teachers" (p. 162). Darling-Hammond and Sykes (2003) have
called for policy changes and a greater government role in streamlining
and coordinating teacher development initiatives.

Arguments for more comprehensive, systemic approaches to teacher
development have also surfaced in a long-neglected area of educational
administration—human resource management. In a recent guidebook
for principals issued by the National Association of Elementary School
Principals, Clement (2000) argued that teacher recruitment and hiring
are only the first of several important aspects of school-level personnel
management. In addition, schools must provide administrative and
technical support for teachers. They must induct new teachers and offer
professional development opportunities across their careers. And,
schools must strive to promote effective working relationships among
the members of their faculties. These different aspects of personnel
management should be coordinated and mutually reinforcing.

The authors of three recent editions of educational administration
textbooks have made similar cases. In one, Smith (2001) argued that
effective human resource management 1) should be strategic and used
to promote school- and system-level goals; 2) should take into account
the needs of faculty across their careers; and 3) should be systemic in
that different elements of human resource management should be
carefully planned and coordinated. In a second text, Sergiovanni and
Starratt (2002) explored relationships among teacher supervision and
evaluation, professional development, and teacher leadership (as work
redesign). They concluded that all these practices should be viewed as
part of a single strategy for individual and collective teacher development and for school renewal. And in a third textbook, Rebore (2004)
argued that "the goals of the human resources function are to hire,
retain, develop, and motivate personnel in order to achieve the objectives of the school district, to assist individual members of the staff to
reach the highest possible levels of achievement, and to maximize the
career development of personnel" (p. 9). He identified eight areas of
human resource management in which schools and school systems
engage: 1) long- and short-range human resource planning keyed to
the goals of the school organization; 2) recruitment of personnel; 3)
selection and hiring; 4) placement and induction; 5) staff development

to help individual employees meet personal, professional, and organizational goals; 6) evaluation; 7) compensation; and 8) collective bargaining. According to Rebore, these are not discrete, isolated entities but, rather, integral aspects of the same strategic function.

A Strategic Human Resource Management Perspective

Such calls for more comprehensive approaches to teacher workforce development and management are similar to arguments for strategic systems of human resource management that have emerged in the literature on organization and management during the past 15 years. According to Wright and McMahan (1992), strategic human resource management refers to "the pattern of planned human resource deployments and activities intended to enable an organization to achieve its goals" (p. 298). Human resource management includes development of employee knowledge and skills but goes beyond this to encompass how human capacity is applied and managed in an organization. The arguments for these systems and their theoretical underpinnings are much more fully developed in the organization and management literature than in the education literature. They are indicative of a shift that is occurring in that field—from specialist, function-driven perspectives to more organizational and strategic perspectives (Brooks, 1994; Buller, 1988; Laabs, 1996; Ulrich, 1998).

Resource-Based Views of the Firm

The importance of employee development has long been recognized in the organization and management literature. Rosenblatt and Sheaffer (2001) observed that early organizational ecologists (e.g., Campbell, 1969; Stinchcombe, 1965) considered organizational effectiveness and survival to be contingent not only upon recruiting and retaining "the best and the fittest" employees but also upon developing and sustaining a complementary range of human capacities among employees—knowledge, skills, and commitments—that will best meet the organization's needs. In the early 1990s, emergent resource-based views of firms stressed that sustained organizational effectiveness is more than a function of how an organization positions itself in a competitive market. It is also, importantly, a function of strategic combinations, or "bundles," of resources possessed and employed by the organization, notably, its human resources (Wright, Dunford, & Snell, 2001). Nordhaug and Gronhaug (1994) observed that the different knowledge, skills, and values held by individuals within organizations form a "portfolio" of competencies that help organizations achieve their objectives. Wright and his colleagues (2001) referred to these collective competencies as "stocks of skills" and "strategically relevant" knowledge and behaviors (p. 706). Organizations will perform effectively, the logic goes, to the extent that they are able to strategically develop and blend the many competencies of their employees and coordinate and direct those competencies toward organizational purposes (Wright et al.; see also March & Simon, 1958).

Resource-based views of the firm emphasized the importance of employees and their development to organizational effectiveness. They also contributed to a new understanding of human resource management as a strategic organizational function (Wright & McMahan, 1992). Wright and Snell (1991) argued that organizations must perform two basic types of human resource management tasks: competence management and behavior management. Competence management refers to the acquisition, development, utilization, retention, and displacement of human capital—that is, of employees' knowledge, skills, and commitments. Behavior management refers to the coordination and control of that human capital so that it functions effectively within the organization. These functions can be performed through different types of human resource management practices such as personnel recruitment, selection, training, evaluation, and compensation. Wright and Snell contended that different aspects of competence and behavior management can be achieved with different combinations of such practices. Competence management might be achieved through recruitment, selection, and training. Behavior management might be achieved through evaluation and incentives provided through compensation. Moreover, the same practices might serve dual functions. For example, evaluation might develop employee competence through feedback on performance and at the same time manage employee behavior by communicating expectations for levels of performance. Compensation might attract new employees and thus promote competence within the organization at the same time that it motivates and controls particular employee behavior. Wright and Snell argued that specific human resource management practices are not in and of themselves important. What is important is the use of different practices in combination to develop and manage competence and behavior in ways that help an organization implement its strategies to meet its goals. Also important is coherence or congruence among these practices. In other words, it is "the pattern of planned human resource deployments and activities" in relation to an organization's work that enables the organization to achieve its goals (Wright & McMahan, p. 298). This link between human resource management and an organization's strategy is what distinguishes traditional perspectives on human resource management in organizations from more recent, strategic human resource management perspectives.

Concepts of Fit and Flexibility

Later, Wright and Snell (1998) reframed the basic ideas behind strategic human resource management in terms of the concepts of fit and flexibility (see Delery, 1998). "Fit" is generally referred to as the degree to which one organizational component is consistent or congruent with another. According to Wright and Snell, most theories of fit assume that when organizations achieve fit among components, they are more efficient and more effective relative to when a lack of fit, a misalignment, or a conflict exists. This is consistent with a general hypothesis of congruence in organizations which states that, all else being equal, the greater the total degree of congruence or fit between the various components of an organization, the more effective organizational behavior will be at multiple levels (Nadler & Tushman, 1977).

The concept of fit applies to strategic human resource management in two ways: vertically and horizontally. Vertical fit has several dimensions. First, it refers to the relationship between an organization's strategy and its objectives. It also refers to the relationship between an organization's strategy and objectives and the demands placed on the organization by its external environment. And importantly, it refers to the relationship between an organization's human resources and its strategy and objectives. In theory, an organization will encounter problems if it is unable to achieve fit among these elements, that is, if an organization's human resources are insufficient or incapable of enacting its strategy, making it difficult for the organization to achieve its objectives or meet external demands. Horizontal fit refers to the internal consistency or congruence among different human resource management activities. According to Delery (1998), the idea of horizontal fit shifts the focus from individual human resource management practices to the entire human resource management system. The assumption is that the effectiveness of any practice depends on the other practices in place. In a human resource management system with strong horizontal fit, the effect of that system on employee and organizational performance should be greater than the sum of the effects of each practice.

The problem, of course, is that fit is not something that can be achieved once and for all (Wright & Snell, 1998). Both vertical and horizontal fit are constantly challenged by the dynamic qualities of organizational environments and their demands and by the ever-changing nature of organizational workforces. An organization's workforce is in constant flux as employees flow in and out and as employees develop or fail to develop their knowledge and skills over time. Employee turnover and stagnation in human capacity can compromise an organization's ability to achieve its objectives. Organizational environments and the demands that they make on organizations change, often in unpredictable ways. New demands may challenge or render inadequate an organization's strategy. As an organization adapts its strategy to meet new demands, it may find that its human resources are inadequate.

These matters point to the importance of the concept of flexibility (Wright & Snell, 1998). "Flexibility" refers to an organization's ability to adapt to diverse and changing demands that may present themselves from sources within or outside the organization. Organizations that are able to modify their practices and develop their human resources in response to environmental or internal changes are likely to be more effective than those organizations that are not. Flexibility can be applied to human resource management in at least two ways. Because organizational environments are dynamic, organizations must be flexible in their strategies to meet new demands. As organizations find that they must adapt their strategies (and perhaps their objectives) to sustain the fit with external demands, they must also be flexible in their practices to develop and manage their human resources. And, because the human resources of an organization are themselves dynamic, the organization must be flexible in its practices to meet the changing needs of its employees and their varying ability to enact the organization's strategies effectively.

These ideas of fit and flexibility and of a systems perspective for human resource management are summarized well in an essay by Schein (1977) that anticipated much of this more recent thinking. Schein found that for an organization to have the capacity to perform effectively over a period of time, it must be able to recruit, manage, develop, dispose of, and replace human resources as warranted by the organizational tasks to be performed. He argued that human resource management in an organization operates best as a system of related components. Those components include processes for staffing the organization; monitoring the growth and development needs of employees; promoting employee growth and development to meet the needs of both the organization and the employees; confronting problems of decreasing employee effectiveness, obsolescence of skills, turnover, retirement, and other phenomena that reflect the need for employee growth or termination; and ensuring that people without requisite capacity move out of their jobs and are replaced by others with the appropriate capacity.

For Schein (1977), the most important component of a human resource management system is planning because "task requirements are likely to change as the complexity and turbulence of the organization's environment increase" (p. 5). According to his analysis, a key assumption underlying organizational performance is that the organization will face new demands and that the nature of work within the organization will need to change over time to meet those demands. These demands and changes must be continuously monitored in order to ensure that the right human resources are recruited or developed to do the organization's work. Schein reasoned that human resource management activities assume that some planning process has occurred, making it possible to assess whether or not those activities meet organizational needs, quite apart from whether they are promoting individual employee growth. He concluded that, because both individual and organizational needs change over time, the process of human resource management must be developmental. As external and internal (e.g., technological) demands require more diversity of knowledge and skills in the workforce, human resource management needs to be capable of dealing with a variety of employees, all at different stages of their careers.

Supporting Evidence

There is not a substantial amount of empirical research in the literature on organization and management that examines the effectiveness of strategic approaches to human resource management (Delery, 1998). Most research on human resource management in this literature focuses on individual practices rather than overall systems of practices (Huselid, 1995). Still, the few studies that do examine systems indicate that the approach has merit (Lado & Wilson, 1994).

For example, Delery and Doty's (1996) study of more than 1,000 banks found that the strategic combination of human resource management practices they used was more important to productivity than their specific individual practices. Buller's (1988) case studies of strategic planning and human resource management in eight companies showed that the integration of strategic planning and human resource functions in relation to a company's environment was critical to the company's success. These cases indicated that higher levels of integration may be necessary when a company's environment becomes more dynamic and demanding, pointing to the need for flexibility in a company's human resource management system. Huselid's (1995) study of more than 960 firms representing all major industries found that these firms' total investments in human resource management were associated with lower employee turnover and greater productivity. This study also found evidence that the internal fit between a firm's human resource management practices and its overall production strategy was somewhat positively associated with increases in firm performance. In light of other studies finding positive relationships and what he considered the compelling nature of the theoretical arguments, Huselid was cautiously optimistic about the efficacy of a strategic systemic approach to human resource management.

Application in Education: Evidence and Examples

As the chapters in this book indicate, there is an abundance of literature on the effectiveness (or lack thereof) of individual teacher development and management practices. However, there is little in the education literature that documents and analyzes how these practices might function together as a system or that examines the relationships among teacher workforce development and management practices across school, district, and state levels. The education literature also has yet to examine how concepts from the literature on organization and management such as fit and flexibility might apply in the context of school organization.

The few studies that do examine the function of multiple teacher human resource management practices tend to report positive outcomes. For instance, McLaughlin and Talbert (2003) found that school districts that were successful in their reform efforts employed integrated systems of teacher recruitment and professional development that were strategically tied to the districts' goals for improving teaching and learning. As we will describe in greater detail below, Elmore and his colleagues (1996) found in their case studies of restructuring elementary schools that those that adopted the most comprehensive and strategic systems of human resource management were most effective in promoting "deep" instructional improvement. So, too, did Louis and Miles (1990) find that the improvement of high schools in their study was supported by more comprehensive strategies for recruiting, developing, and transferring out teachers, pursuant to a particular vision for the school.

Several studies have been conducted of two school districts—District 2 in New York City and San Diego, California—widely known for their efforts to link systems of teacher human resource management practices with instructional improvement. The basic strategy for linking these practices with instructional improvement was developed by the District 2 superintendent and his staff. The superintendent transported this strategy, with some adaptation, to San Diego when he moved there. The components of the strategy include recruiting and hiring new teachers, providing intensive professional development using teacher networks and extensive external monitoring and consultation, establishing active teacher evaluation, moving ineffective teachers out of the district, preventing the transfer of ineffective teachers into the district, developing collaborative working relationships among teachers, redesigning teachers' work to provide new opportunities for leadership, and setting up a teacher incentive program—all focused on the implementation of the district's instructional framework and the achievement of its student learning standards.

Initial anecdotal evidence from District 2 indicated that this system of human resource management promoted changes in instruction in the direction of the framework (Elmore & Burney, 1997, 1998). Early evidence from San Diego suggested that this system had begun to alter the district's organization and the administration's orientation to teachers and instructional improvement (Hightower, 2002). This evidence also suggested that teaching practice across the district had begun to shift in the direction of the framework and that scores on standardized tests of student achievement had started to improve. Other evidence has suggested that these outcomes vary substantially by school and that additional flexibility may be needed to address differences in local school contexts and capacities for instructional reform (Darling-Hammond et al., 2003). As yet, there is no evidence available to indicate longer-term outcomes.

In addition to these few studies, there are several examples of schools, school districts, and states that have implemented more comprehensive, strategic approaches to teacher human resource management. These examples are largely descriptive. They illustrate how schools, school districts, and states can align their human resource management policies and practices with their respective organizational strategies for teaching and student learning. Unfortunately, most of these examples do not speak to the issue of strategic coordination of practices *across* levels (school, district, and state). And, not much evidence has been collected concerning whether the practices described in these examples have been effective in promoting school improvement or improving student learning. The reader is directed to other chapters in this book for examples of practices in other school districts and states.

School-Level Examples

Our school-level examples come from case studies of three elementary schools produced under the auspices of the Consortium for Policy Research in Education (CPRE) at the University of Pennsylvania. These case studies were conducted by Elmore, Peterson, and McCarthey (1996) between 1988 and 1991 and were designed to examine the relationship between efforts to restructure schools organizationally and instructional improvement. The case study schools are located in different geographic areas. One is in a poor, inner-city community. Another is located in a middle-class neighborhood of a larger city. The third is located in an outlying suburban area of a consolidated school system. The schools are relatively small, each serving between 250 and 475 students. At the time of the study, each school's student enrollment was racially and ethnically mixed and each had a critical mass of low-income students. One school was a relatively new alternative or "choice" school, founded about 15 years before the study. Another school was an "option" school under a city-wide school desegregation plan. Although the central focus of each study was on the relationship between organizational structure and teachers' work in classrooms, these cases also reveal different ways that the schools approached the issue of teacher development to promote their visions of effective teaching and learning.

Looking across the three cases, Elmore and his colleagues argued that each of the schools exemplified what the literature on school restructuring might call "enlightened practice." Each school had committed itself to a common vision of teaching practice, based on an intellectually ambitious conception of teaching and student learning. Each had established collegial decision making on a broad range of issues. Each had made recognizable changes in the structures by which students were assigned to teachers and by which teachers related to each other. Each provided frequent formal opportunities for teacher professional development. In each school, principals and teachers collaborated actively on issues of teaching and learning.

Elmore and his colleagues found that, even though the schools had "restructured" in these ways, and even though they had organized around a similar vision of ambitious teaching and learning, they varied considerably in the quality and consistency of instruction that occurred and in the depth of knowledge and understanding required of teachers to teach in intellectually ambitious ways. These differences were related to the manner in which the schools systemically and strategically developed and managed their teachers as faculties to promote the school's approach to teaching and learning.

The school that achieved the greatest depth and consistency of intellectually ambitious teaching and learning went further than the other schools in the strategic development of its faculty. The principal and teachers worked together to recruit and select only those teachers who were already committed to and relatively well prepared in the kind of teaching the school promoted. According to Elmore and his colleagues,

[These] teachers were expected to be practitioners of a certain kind of teaching when they entered the school. Some teachers were selected from the population of student teachers who regularly circulated through the school; some came to the school through professional networks; and in at least one case a teacher was "apprenticed" to another school for a year to learn how to teach art before being hired at [the case study school]. (p. 232)

This school put new teachers into an environment where discussion and observation—peer review—of teaching were "matter-of-fact" parts of everyday work. It set high expectations for teachers, creating and reinforcing a norm that every teacher should have a "consuming intellectual interest" that he or she should bring into the school. It formed internal and external networks of like-minded practitioners who were available to consult on problems of practice. The school took advantage of professional development workshops provided by the school district (although they were not viewed particularly highly by teachers at the school) and organized its own formal staff development activities. The school was also "crafty" at obtaining outside resources to help teachers learn and solve specific problems of practice.

In all, teacher development at this school was pursued through a coherent and systematic strategy of assembling a skilled, committed, like-minded faculty; socializing teachers into an environment defined by specific expectations for practice; linking teachers to internal and external sources of learning; and holding teachers accountable for their practice, primarily through peer interaction and professional expectations and norms of practice. The development of teachers was part and parcel of the "fabric of the organization" (Elmore et al., 1996, p. 233).

The other schools in the study failed to achieve such coherence and comprehensiveness in their approaches to teacher development.

District-Level Examples

Our first district-level example is District 34 in Glenview, Illinois, a suburban Chicago K-8 school system of approximately 3,200 students. Since the mid-1980s, District 34 has developed a system of multiple, coordinated strategies for the professionalization and development of its teachers (Smylie, 1993). The district began this work in 1984 by using a state grant to establish a teacher career development plan. This plan, called Project PEER (Promoting Excellence in Education through Recognition), was a work redesign initiative jointly developed by the district's central administration and the local teachers union. Project PEER established new teacher leadership roles at the school and district levels as well as commensurate compensation incentives. And, as a joint project of the administration and the union, it laid the foundation for a period of collaborative labor relations and "strategic bargaining," which produced the centerpiece of the district's reform efforts—its Constitution. This is an example of collaborative "professional unionism" aimed at teacher development and educational improvement (Bascia, this volume, Chapter 11; Kerchner & Caufman, 1993).

The Constitution replaced the conventional teacher contract and differed from it in significant ways. Rather than being negotiated by school board and union representatives, it was developed collaboratively by teams of teachers, school board members, union representatives, and school- and district-level administrators. It was ratified by nearly 80% of the system's teachers. The Constitution abandoned traditional work rules and replaced them with a preamble mission statement of service to students and the community and with statements of professional roles and responsibilities, expectations for teacher growth and development, and mutual accountability. In addition to these statements of principle, which were to guide the district and its professional employees, the Constitution established a structure of governance and decision making that placed teachers in key leadership roles at the school and district levels, in areas of responsibility that included curriculum and instruction, teacher professional development, personnel (including recruitment, hiring, evaluation, and retention), and finance. And, the Constitution outlined an enhanced salary structure for teachers, one tied less to academic degree attainment and years of experience than to work roles and responsibilities. The principles of professionalism and professional responsibility articulated in the Constitution, coupled with new curricular initiatives in literacy and in classroom technology, became strategic foci for the system's teacher development initiatives. These principles provided substantial latitude and flexibility for establishing teacher development programs and policies, conditions that would have been much less likely under a rigid set of work rules.

District 34 pursued an extensive agenda of teacher development activity aimed at enacting the principles of the Constitution and supporting its efforts to improve teaching and student learning. It established an aggressive program of professional development activity for teachers across the system. Project PEER and the Constitution provided new opportunities for teacher leadership and participation in school- and system-level governance. The district reasoned that not only would the teachers who assumed these new roles find opportunities for professional growth, they would also become sources of learning, development, and improvement for other teachers. The district also began aggressively recruiting and hiring teachers whose philosophies of teaching and professional orientations were consistent with its own.

In the early 1990s, District 34 designed and implemented a professional development school model with Chicago-area universities (Smylie, Attea, Brownlee-Conyers, & Miller, 1988). This model created an extended program of initial preparation and induction across university and district classrooms. Preservice teachers were hired by the district into multiyear internships to work alongside exemplary veteran teachers who, with university faculty, would have earlier taught them at the university and supervised them in initial practice settings. This model created a pipeline of new teachers into the district, provided a "grow your own" opportunity that was in line with system principles and objectives and, importantly, provided veteran teachers opportunities for leadership and professional development.

Our second district-level example is the Rochester City School District in New York. In 1987, in collaboration with the local teachers union, Rochester established its Career in Teaching Program (CIT). This program was considered to be a ground-breaking effort to restructure teaching, improve teachers' knowledge and skills, and improve student learning (Koppich, Asher, & Kerchner, 2002). The program established a new model of preparing, recruiting, and retaining teachers. It introduced shared decision making in all of the district's schools, it made a commitment to strengthen home-school relations, and it increased teacher salaries substantially. The CIT program was to be monitored by administrators, parents, and teachers and supported by the teachers union. The underlying logic of the program was that educational improvement would follow from the recognition and treatment of teachers as professionals (Murray & Grant, 1997).

The most significant piece of this program, and one more directly related to teacher human resource management, was the creation of a "career pathway" for educators. This plan included strategies for recruiting and hiring qualified teachers, supporting the induction of new teachers through mentoring, providing new opportunities for "highly accomplished" teachers to develop and share their knowledge and skills, establishing systems of peer review and assistance for teachers experiencing problems in their practice, and increasing the retention of effective teachers (Koppich et al., 2002). CIT contained provisions to develop schools to be more conducive to teaching and student learning. Based on the logic that professional support, effective teaching, and student learning are inextricably related, the Rochester program framed teacher development and the improvement of teaching as a career-long enterprise. It incorporated the sort of flexibility necessary to respond to teachers' professional needs at different stages of their careers. Although the primary focus of this program is on teachers within the system, CIT is noteworthy for involving parents and school- and system-level administrators as sources of development for teachers.

By and large, the Rochester plan seems to have had a significant impact on teacher retention. Koppich and her colleagues (2002) report that in 1998, 95% of the teachers who began their careers in Rochester ten years earlier and received mentoring were still teaching in the district. Because of significant changes in the school system, including changes in student demographics and the state testing program, it has been difficult to determine the effects of the CIT program on student achievement. However, one study of Rochester's teacher mentoring program found that improvement in student performance on some areas of state tests were attributable to the mentoring of beginning teachers (Murray & Grant, 1997).

State-Level Examples

Since the release of its 1996 report *What Matters Most*, NCTAF has been assisting states and districts to identify and develop policies and practices for the improvement of the quality of teaching. As part of this effort, NCTAF formed a state partnership network to strengthen the work of and connections among states across the country that are striving to improve teachers and teaching. Twenty-two states are members of this network: Alabama, Georgia, Hawaii, Idaho, Illinois, Indiana, Kansas, Kentucky, Louisiana, Maryland, Missouri, Montana, New

Mexico, North Carolina, Ohio, Oklahoma, Tennessee, Vermont, Virginia, Washington, West Virginia, and Wisconsin. Member states have been working in different ways, at different paces, and with varying degrees of success to design policy *systems* consistent with NCTAF recommendations.

Illinois is one of several NCTAF partner states to adopt an array of teacher workforce development initiatives (Pressley, 2002; see Plecki and Loeb, this volume, Chapter 12, for descriptions of initiatives in other NCTAF states). The conceptual foundation for these initiatives is outlined in the *Illinois Framework for Restructuring the Recruitment, Preparation, Licensure and Continuing Professional Development of Teachers*. This framework called for the development of professional teaching standards that would articulate what teachers are expected to know and be able to do. These standards would serve as the basis for the preparation, licensure, and continuing professional development of teachers. The framework called for 1) redesigning preservice teacher preparation programs around standards of practice; 2) developing new assessments for teacher licensure; 3) restructuring the state's licensure and certification system; 4) increasing the prevalence and quality of new teacher induction programs across the state; 5) improving the quality of ongoing teacher professional development; 6) promoting school-based learning communities for teachers; and 7) developing new incentives, alternative routes to certification, and processes for recruiting high-quality teachers and teachers in hard-to-staff subject areas and locations.

Since the adoption of this framework by the Illinois State Board of Education in 1996, the state has established an extensive array of professional teaching standards that articulate knowledge, skills, commitments, and practices that relate, at least conceptually, to the state's student learning standards. It has established new accreditation requirements based on those standards for the state's 96 teacher preparation programs. These professional teaching standards are also tied to a new, three-level certification system: an initial, five-year license for entry-level teachers; a subsequent, standard certificate, issued and renewed on the basis of ongoing professional development; and, finally, a master's certificate, linked to achievement of National Board certification. Teachers must earn the standard certificate to retain their eligibility to teach in the state after the initial license expires.

Illinois has sought to increase its recruitment of new teachers in general, and for high-need areas in particular, by establishing new grants and scholarship programs for teacher education students, encouraging the development of alternative routes to certification, and promoting new opportunities for teacher education coursework at the community college level. Illinois has also supported district-level beginning teacher mentoring and induction programs with new funding and has sought to promote ongoing teacher professional development by linking it to the standard teaching certificate. Finally, Illinois has sought to regulate the quality of teacher professional development by requiring that all professional development providers who offer "certification credits" be approved by the state.

Our second state example is Connecticut. Although not an NCTAF partner state, Connecticut has been engaged in systematic efforts to develop its teacher workforce for nearly 20 years (Wilson, Darling-Hammond, & Berry, 2001). It has sought to strategically integrate multiple programs and policies to enhance teacher quality from initial preparation throughout teachers' careers. As a case, Connecticut is notable for the breadth and coherence of its policies and programs, for developing strong relationships between state and local teacher development initiatives, and for the duration and apparent success of its efforts. It is also notable for its emphasis on inquiry and data-driven policy development, for flexibility in its programs and policies to meet the changing educational needs of the state, and for its ongoing bipartisan political commitment and support. Observers note that Connecticut has developed statewide surpluses of highly qualified teacher candidates, has improved the overall quality of teachers and teaching, and, as a result, has improved student achievement (Barron, 1999; Wilson et al.).

Connecticut's approach has been to develop a coherent system of policies aimed to enhance human capacity for providing high-quality education across all levels of the system, from local community stakeholders to state department of education staff, from classroom teachers to teacher educators. For teachers, these policies focus specifically on recruitment, initial preparation and support for ongoing professional development, and accountability for quality teachers and teaching and student learning. The state ties together professional teaching standards, student learning standards, teacher licensing and certification policy, a system of teacher assessment and professional development, school finance reform, and structures for teacher compensation.

As one of its earliest initiatives, Connecticut cultivated a supply of highly qualified teachers. To do so, it increased teacher salaries substantially. It provided teacher education scholarships to motivate candidates to prepare to teach in high-need content areas and locations. It also strengthened requirements for initial preparation programs to place greater emphasis on content knowledge and ability to work effectively with diverse groups of students and students with diverse learning needs. Connecticut provided induction support for new teachers through its Beginning Educator Support and Training (BEST) program. This program is grounded in a set of expectations for beginning teacher performance and development. Through mentoring experiences, classroom assessments, and professional development activity, the program seeks to develop beginning teachers' knowledge, skills, and practices, consistent with program expectations, and increase their capacity for ongoing learning and development. By training veteran teachers to serve as mentors, assessors, and professional development leaders, this program also seeks to promote the development of the teacher workforce more broadly.

In addition, Connecticut developed its Common Core of Teaching, a set of professional knowledge and skills that defines what it means to be an "accomplished" teacher. The Core emphasizes teachers' skills in diagnosing student learning needs and assessing student progress as the bases for making instructional decisions. The Core also serves as a foundation for the state's program of career-long teacher professional development activity.

Concluding Comments and Next Steps

In this chapter, we have argued for a comprehensive, systemic, strategic approach to teacher workforce development and management. Reviewing recent critiques and related research, we argued that conventional approaches that rely on a limited range of discrete practices—practices that may be poorly designed and implemented and are probably disconnected from the larger goals and strategies of the school organization—are likely to be inefficient and largely ineffective. We examined calls in the education literature for more comprehensive approaches to teacher workforce development and management. Turning to the literature on organization and management, we found that recent perspectives on strategic human resource management provide promising bases for new approaches to teacher workforce development and management. Finally, we showed what these more comprehensive strategic approaches might look like in action with examples of school-, district-, and state-level policies and practices.

Although there is an emerging, mostly descriptive body of research that points to the efficacy of a strategic human resource management approach, the argument for applying this approach to teacher workforce development and management is now largely theoretical and intuitive. As school districts and states develop and implement new policies and practices for teacher workforce development and management, there will be increasing opportunities for longitudinal, comparative study of these "natural experiments" to test the basic concepts of fit and flexibility in the context of educational organizations and to examine their relationship to the improvement of teaching and student learning. Attention to systems of practices, how they operate, and to what effect may bring additional focus and depth to the study of teacher development generally, an area of educational research that has been criticized for its lack of rigor and coherence (DeCourcy Hinds, 2002; see also American Educational Research Association, 1999; Burkhardt & Schoenfeld, 2003).

Even though more comprehensive, strategic systems of teacher workforce development and management appear promising, there are several related factors that might make the adoption of these systems difficult. First, as we alluded to at the beginning of the chapter, there are a number of tensions and dilemmas that are fundamental and enduring to school organization and to the professional work of teachers that make teacher workforce development and management extremely complicated (Ogawa, et al., 1999; Weick & McDaniel, 1989). These include tensions between individual teacher discretion and the achievement of school organizational objectives; between decentralization and centralization in governance and control across levels of the educational system; between self-determinism on the part of the teaching profession and administrative prerogative; and between leadership and management. A move toward more comprehensive, strategic systems of teacher workforce development and management would bring such tensions into sharper focus and may provoke political and philosophical conflict around them. Cochran-Smith and Fries (2001) warned that

unless underlying ideals, ideologies, and values are debated along with and in relation to "the evidence" about teacher quality, and unless we examine the discourse of teacher education policy reform, we will make little progress in understanding the politics . . . and the nuances and complexities of various reform agendas that are currently in competition with each other. (p. 13)

The prospect and difficulty of such a debate, one that should take place, may serve as a powerful deterrent to engaging these dilemmas anew and to making meaningful changes in policy and practice.

Second, as we have discussed throughout this chapter, there are structural and political impediments within school organizations that may make comprehensive, strategic systems approaches to teacher workforce development difficult to achieve (Wright & McMahan, 1992). As noted in the literature on organization and management and as suggested in the education literature, human resource management functions have traditionally been separated from strategic planning functions within organizations. In a school district, for example, it would not be uncommon to find a department that deals with human resource management to be only loosely connected, if connected at all, to departments or offices dealing with strategic planning and implementation, or with curricular and instructional improvement. One might also find that a department that deals with one aspect of human resource management, such as hiring, has little relationship with another department that deals with another aspect, such as teacher induction and professional development. Such structural disconnects would also likely be found within state education agencies and perhaps across state education agencies and other agencies at the state level that deal more generally with workforce and economic development issues. But the difficulty is not only that these departments, offices, and agencies may be structurally disconnected from one another. Over time, they may have developed strong political self-interests for influence and survival that "institutionalize" the structural fragmentation and impede coordination and collaboration. There is no reason to believe that the structural gaps between school, district, and state levels of the system would be any easier to bridge.

Finally, when moving toward new approaches to teacher workforce development and management, we are likely to confront long-standing, institutionalized patterns of thinking and belief about educational administration, teachers and the nature of their work, and how to improve teacher quality and effectiveness (see Meyer & Rowan, 1978; Sarason, 1990, 1996). We have already noted the historical mindset in the field of educational administration that views school administration as the performance of discrete managerial tasks and functions oriented toward efficiency and effectiveness of the current educational system, not necessarily its change. This mindset also tends to view teachers as semi-skilled labor and teaching as an identifiable set of practices that can be specified (and tested for effectiveness) and transmitted through training and evaluation (Darling-Hammond, 1997). This mindset, according to Callahan (1962) and McCarthy (1999), has guided the preparation of school administrators and has defined administrative practice for generations (see also Glass, 2004).

We are also likely to run into institutionalized perspectives on schools, teachers and teaching, and change in what are called the "assumptive worlds" of policymakers. These assumptive worlds are policymakers' "subjective understandings of the environment in which they operate" and are composed of "intermingled elements of belief, perception, evaluation, and intention as responses to the reality 'out there'" (Young, 1977, pp. 2, 3). According to Marshall, Mitchell, and Wirt (1989), values and policy choices become tangled in the assumptive worlds of a given environment. Policy actors "constrain their preferences to work within the assumptive worlds" of their policy environments (Marshall, Mitchell, & Wirt, 1985, p. 113). Once in this environment, policy actors "exist, talk, are inspired to act and to constrain their actions according to unstated mutual, reciprocal understandings shared with actors who occupy the same world" (Marshall, et al., p. 92). These worlds are extremely influential and difficult to change. They are "owned" and mutually reinforced by those who hold them. They become a basis for defining and pursuing individual and collective self-interest.

All of this suggests that institutionalized patterns of beliefs and assumptions are likely to inhibit our ability to see problems and issues of teacher workforce development and management with fresh eyes (Smylie, 1996). They may also constrain consideration of new, potentially promising approaches to address these problems. None of this means that more comprehensive, strategic systems approaches to teacher development are not worth pursuing. Good arguments and emerging evidence indicate that they are. Our point is that, however logical, however intuitively sensible, however justified by theory and research, movement from conventional practice to these more promising practices will require hard work over the long term. These approaches represent a substantial change from historical and deeply embedded patterns of thinking and practice around school organization. We believe that with persistent effort and thoughtful study, the hard work will be well worth it.

Authors' Note

We wish to acknowledge Carol Fendt for helping to identify and review the literature used in this chapter and Zehava Rosenblatt and David Mayrowetz for providing comments and suggestions on the structure of our argument.

REFERENCES

American Educational Research Association. (1999). Gorillas in our midst: Emerging themes on how to improve educational research. *On Capital Hill*, August/September. Retrieved January 14, 2004, from http://www.aera.net/gov/archive

Arthur, M.B., & Kram, K.E. (1989). Reciprocity at work: The separate, yet inseparable possibilities for individual and organizational development. In M.B. Arthur, D.T. Hall, and B.S. Lawrence (Eds.), *Handbook of career theory* (pp. 292-312). Cambridge, MA: Cambridge University Press.

Barron, J. (1999). *Exploring high and improving reading achievement in Connecticut.* Washington, DC: National Educational Goals Panel.

Bascia, N. (2004). Teacher unions and the teaching workforce. In this volume—M.A. Smylie & D. Miretzky (Eds.), *Developing the teacher workforce. The 103rd yearbook of the National Society for the Study of Education*, Part I (pp. 326-347). Chicago: National Society for the Study of Education.

Bobbitt, F. (1913). *The supervision of city schools. The twelfth yearbook of the National Society for the Study of Education*, Part I. Bloomington, IL: Public School Publishing Company.

Brooks, D.V. (1994). HR in the 90s: From tacticians to strategists. *HR Focus*, September, 12-13.

Buller, P.F. (1988). Successful partnerships: HR and strategic planning at eight top firms. *Organizational Dynamics, 17*, 27-42.

Burkhardt, H., & Schoenfeld, A.H. (2003). Improving educational research: Toward a more useful, more influential, and better-funded enterprise. *Educational Researcher, 32*(9), 3-14.

Callahan, R.E. (1962). *Education and the cult of efficiency.* Chicago: University of Chicago Press.

Campbell, D.T. (1969). Variations in selective retention in sociocultural evolution. *General Systems, 14*, 69-85.

Clement, M.C. (2000). *Essentials for principals: How to interview, hire, and retain high-quality new teachers.* Alexandria, VA: National Association of Elementary School Principals.

Cochran-Smith, M., & Fries, M.K. (2001). Sticks, stones, and ideology: The discourse of reform in teacher education. *Educational Researcher, 30*(8), 3-15.

Cuban, L. (1988). *The managerial imperative and the practice of leadership in schools.* Albany: State University of New York Press.

D'Amico, K., Harwell, M., Stein, J., & van den Heuvel, J. (2001, April). *Explaining the implementation and effectiveness of a districtwide instructional improvement effort.* Paper presented at the annual meeting of the American Educational Research Association, Seattle.

Darling-Hammond, L. (1997). School reform at the crossroads: Confronting the central issues of teaching. *Educational Policy, 11*, 151-166.

Darling-Hammond, L. (2000).Teacher quality and student achievement: A review of state policy evidence. *Education Policy Analysis Archives, 8*(1). Retrieved September 14, 2003, from http://epaa.asu.edu/epaa/v8n1/

Darling-Hammond, L., Hightower, A.M., Husbands, J.L., LaFors, J.R., Young, V.M., & Christopher, C. (2003). *Building instructional quality: "Inside-out" and "outside-in" perspectives on San Diego's school reform.* Seattle: University of Washington, Center for the Study of Teaching and Policy.

Darling-Hammond, L., & Sykes, G. (2003). Wanted: A national teacher supply policy for education: The right way to meet the "Highly Qualified Teacher" challenge? *Education Policy Analysis Archives, 11*(33). Retrieved September 21, 2003, from http://epaa.asu.edu/epaa/v11n33/

Darling-Hammond, L., & Youngs, P. (2002). Defining "highly qualified teachers": What does "scientifically-based research" actually tell us? *Educational Researcher, 31*(9), 13-25.

66   RETHINKING   TEACHER   WORKFORCE   DEVELOPMENT

DeCourcy Hinds, M. (2002). *Teaching as a clinical profession: A new challenge for education.* A Carnegie Challenge paper. New York: Carnegie Corporation of New York.

Delery, J.E. (1998). Issues of fit in strategic human resource management: Implications for research. *Human Resource Management Review, 8*, 289-309.

Delery, J.E., & Doty, D.H. (1996). Modes of theorizing in strategic human resource management: Tests of universalistic, contingency, and configurational performance predictions. *Academy of Management Journal, 39*, 802-835.

Elmore, R.F., & Burney, D. (1997). *Investing in teacher learning: Staff development and instructional improvement in Community School District #2, New York City.* New York: National Commission on Teaching and America's Future.

Elmore, R.F., & Burney, D. (1998). *Continuous improvement in Community District #2, New York City.* New York: National Commission on Teaching and America's Future.

Elmore, R.F., Peterson, P.L., & McCarthey, S.J. (1996). *Restructuring in the classroom: Teaching, learning, and school organization.* San Francisco: Jossey-Bass.

Fullan, M. (2001). *The new meaning of educational change* (3rd ed.). New York: Teachers College Press.

Glass, T.E. (2004). *The history of educational administration as viewed through its textbooks.* Lanham, MD: ScarecrowEducation.

Goldhaber, D., & Anthony, E. (2004). *Can teacher quality be effectively assessed?* Seattle: University of Washington, Evans School of Public Affairs and Urban Institute.

Goldring, E., & Greenfield, W. (2002). Understanding the evolving concept of leadership in education: Roles, expectations, and dilemmas. In J. Murphy (Ed.), *The educational leadership challenge: Redefining leadership for the 21st century. The one hundred-first yearbook of the National Society for the Study of Education,* Part I (pp. 1-19). Chicago: National Society for the Study of Education.

Griffin, G.A. (1999). *The education of teachers. The ninety-eighth yearbook of the National Society for the Study of Education,* Part I. Chicago: National Society for the Study of Education.

Griffiths, D. (Ed.). (1964). *Behavioral science and educational administration. The sixty-third yearbook of the National Society for the Study of Education,* Part II. Chicago: National Society for the Study of Education.

Henry, N.B. (1957). *In-service education for teachers, supervisors, and administrators. The fifty-sixth yearbook of the National Society for the Study of Education,* Part I. Chicago: National Society for the Study of Education.

Hightower, A.M. (2002). *San Diego's big boom: District bureaucracy support culture of learning.* Seattle: University of Washington, Center for the Study of Teaching and Policy.

Hirsch, E., Koppich, J.E., & Knapp, M.S. (2001, February). *Revisiting what states are doing to improve the quality of teaching: An update on patterns and trends.* Seattle: University of Washington, Center for the Study of Teaching and Policy.

Huselid, M.A. (1995). The impact of human resource management practices on turnover, productivity, and corporate financial performance. *Academy of Management Journal, 38*, 635-672.

Jennings, J. (2003). From the White House to the schoolhouse: Greater demands and new roles. In W.L. Boyd & D. Miretzky (Eds.), *American educational governance on trial: Change and challenges. The 102nd yearbook of the National Society for the Study of Education,* Part I (pp. 291-308). Chicago: National Society for the Study of Education.

Keep, E. (1993). The need for a revised management system for the teaching profession. *Education Economics, 1*(1), 53-59.

Kerchner, C.T., & Caufman, K.D. (1993). Building the airplane while it's rolling down the runway. In C.T. Kerchner & J. Koppich (Eds.), *A union of professionals: Labor relations and educational reform* (pp. 1-24). New York: Teachers College Press.

Kirp, D.L., & Driver, C.E. (1995). The aspirations of systemic reform meet the realities of localism. *Educational Administration Quarterly, 31*, 589-612.

Koppich, J., Asher, C., & Kerchner, C. (2002). *Developing careers, building a profession: The Rochester Career in Teaching Program.* New York: National Commission on Teaching and America's Future.

Laabs, J.J. (1996). Eyeing future HR concerns. *Personnel Journal,* January, 28-37.

Lado, A.A., & Wilson, M.C. (1994). Human resource systems and sustained competitive advantage: A competency-based perspective. *Academy of Management Review, 19,* 699-727.

Lepak, D.P., & Snell, S.A. (1999). The human resource architecture: Toward a theory of human capital allocation and development. *Academic of Management Review, 24,* 31-48.

Louis, K.S., & Miles, M.B. (1990). *Improving the urban high school: What works and why.* New York: Teachers College Press.

Lowry, C.D. (1908). *The relation of superintendents and principals to the training and professional improvement of their teachers. The seventh yearbook of the National Society for the Study of Education,* Part I. Bloomington, IL: Public School Publishing Company.

March, J.G., & Simon, H. (1958). *Organizations.* New York: Wiley.

Marshall, C., Mitchell, D., & Wirt, F. (1985). Assumptive worlds of education policy makers. *Peabody Journal of Education, 62*(4), 90-115.

Marshall, C., Mitchell, D., & Wirt, F. (1989). *Culture and education policy in the American states.* New York: Falmer.

McCarthy, M.M. (1999). The evolution of educational leadership preparation programs. In J. Murphy & K.S. Louis (Eds.), *Handbook of research on educational administration* (2nd ed., pp. 119-140). San Francisco: Jossey-Bass.

McGreal, T.L. (1989). Necessary ingredients for successful instructional improvement initiatives. *Journal of Staff Development, 10*(1), 35-41.

McLaughlin, M., & Talbert, J. (2003, September). *Reforming districts: How districts support school reform* (Document R-03-6). Seattle: University of Washington, Center for the Study of Teaching and Policy.

McQuarrie, F.O., Jr., & Wood, F.H. (1991). Supervision, staff development, and evaluation connections. *Theory into Practice, 30*(2), 91-96.

Meyer, J.W., & Rowan, B. (1978). The structure of educational organizations. In M.W. Meyer and Associates (Eds.), *Organizations and environments* (pp. 78-108). San Francisco: Jossey-Bass.

Murphy, J., & Datnow, A. (2003). The development of comprehensive school reform. In J. Murphy & A. Datnow (Eds.), *Leadership lessons from comprehensive school reform* (pp. 3-18). Thousand Oaks, CA: Corwin.

Murray, C., & Grant, G. (1997). Rochester's reforms. *Phi Delta Kappan, 79,* 148-155.

Nadler, D., & Tushman, M. (1977). A diagnostic model for organizational behavior. In J.R. Hackman, E.E. Lawler, & L.W. Porter (Eds.), *Perspectives on behavior in organizations* (pp. 83-100). New York: McGraw-Hill.

National Commission on Teaching and America's Future. (1996). *What matters most: Teaching for America's future.* New York: Author.

National Commission on Teaching and America's Future. (1997). *Doing what matters most: Investing in quality teaching.* New York: Author.

National Commission on Teaching and America's Future. (2003). *No dream denied: A pledge to America's children.* Washington, DC: Author.

Newmann, F.M., & Wehlage, G.G. (1995). *Successful school restructuring.* Madison: Center on the Organization and Restructuring of Schools, University of Wisconsin.

Nordhaug, O., & Gronhaug, K. (1994). Competencies as resources in firms. *The International Journal of Human Resource Management, 5,* 89-106.

Ogawa, R.T., Crowson, R.L., & Goldring, E.B. (1999). Enduring dilemmas of school organization. In J. Murphy & K.S. Louis (Eds.), *Handbook of research on educational administration* (2nd. ed., pp. 277-295). San Francisco: Jossey-Bass.

Plecki, M., & Loeb, H. (2004). Lessons for policy design and implementation: Examining state and federal efforts to improve teacher quality. In this volume—M.A.

Smylie & D. Miretzky (Eds.), *Developing the teacher workforce. The 103rd yearbook of the National Society for the Study of Education*, Part I. Chicago: National Society for the Study of Education.

Pressley, J. (2002, December). *Illinois policy inventory on teaching and learning*. Springfield, IL: Governors Council on Educatory Quality.

Rebore, R.W. (2004). *Human resources administration in education* (7th ed.). Boston: Allyn & Bacon.

Rice, J.K. (2003). *Teacher quality: Understanding the effectiveness of teacher attributes*. Washington, DC: Economic Policy Institute.

Rosenblatt, Z., & Sheaffer, Z. (2001). Brain drain in declining organizations: Toward a research agenda. *Journal of Organizational Behavior, 22*, 409-424.

Ryan, K. (Ed.). (1975). *Teacher education. The seventy-fourth yearbook of the National Society for the Study of Education*, Part II. Chicago: National Society for the Study of Education.

Sanders, W.L., & Horn, S.P. (1998). Research findings from the Tennessee Value-Added Assessment System (TVASS) database: Implications for educational evaluation and research. *Journal of Personnel Evaluation in Education, 12*, 247-256.

Sarason, S.B. (1990). *The predictable failure of educational reform*. San Francisco: Jossey-Bass.

Sarason, S. (1996). *Revisiting the culture of the school and the problem of change*. New York: Teachers College Press.

Schein, E.H. (1977). Increasing organizational effectiveness through better human resource planning and development. *Sloan Management Review, 19*, 1-20.

Sergiovanni, T.J., & Starratt, R.J. (2002). *Supervision: A redefinition* (7th ed.). Boston: McGraw Hill.

Smith, R.E. (2001). *Human resources administration: A school-based perspective* (2nd ed.). Larchmont, NY: Eye on Education.

Smylie, M.A. (1993). Glenview, Illinois: From contract to constitution. In C.T. Kerchner & J. Koppich (Eds.), *A union of professionals: Labor relations and educational reform* (pp. 98-115). New York: Teachers College Press.

Smylie, M.A. (1996). From bureaucratic control to building human capital: The importance of teacher learning in education reform. *Educational Researcher, 25*(9), 9-11.

Smylie, M.A., Attea, W.J., Brownlee-Conyers, J., & Miller, M. (1988, May). *The Glenview Public Schools-University of Illinois at Chicago Professional Development School Model*. Paper presented at the conference of the Midwest Regional Holmes Group, Chicago.

Spalding, W.B. (1946). Organizing the personnel of a democratic school system. In N.B. Henry (Ed.), *Changing conceptions in educational administration. The forty-fifth yearbook of the National Society for the Study of Education*, Part II (pp. 53-85). Chicago: National Society for the Study of Education.

Stinchcombe, A.L. (1965). Social structure and organizations. In J.G. March (Ed.), *Handbook of organizations* (pp. 142-193). Chicago: Rand McNally.

Thacker, R.A. (2000). Shifting the human resource management curriculum from the traditional to the strategic: Description of a process for curriculum revision. *International Journal of Leadership in Education, 3*, 399-409.

Thomas B. Fordham Foundation. (1999). The teachers we need and how to get more of them: A manifesto. In M. Kanstoroom & C. Finn (Eds.), *Better teachers, better schools* (pp. 1-18). Washington, DC: Author.

Tyack, D. (1974). *The one best system: A history of American urban education*. New York: Basic Books.

Ulrich, D. (1998). A new mandate for human resources. *Harvard Business Review, 76*, 124-134.

U.S. Department of Education. (2002). *Meeting the highly qualified teacher challenge: The Secretary's annual report on teacher quality*. Washington, DC: Office of Postsecondary Education, Office of Policy Planning and Innovation.

Wang, M.C., Haertel, G.D., & Walberg, H.J. (1993). Toward a knowledge base for school learning. *Review of Educational Research, 63*, 249-294.

Wayne, A.J., & Youngs, P. (2003). Teacher characteristics and student achievement gains: A review. *Review of Educational Research, 73*, 89-122.

Weick, K.E., & McDaniel, R.R., Jr. (1989). How professional organizations work: Implications for school organization and management. In T.J. Serviovanni & J.H. Moore (Eds.), *Schooling for tomorrow: Directing reforms to issues that count* (pp. 330-355). Boston: Allyn & Bacon.

Wilson, S.M., Darling-Hammond, L., & Berry, B. (2001). *A case of successful teaching policy: Connecticut's long-term efforts to improve teaching and learning.* Seattle: Center for the Study of Teaching and Policy, University of Washington.

Wood, F.H., & Lease, S.A. (1987). An integrated approach to staff development, supervision, and teacher evaluation. *Journal of Staff Development, 8*(1), 52-55.

Wright, P.M., Dunford, B.B., & Snell, S.A. (2001). Human resources and the resource-based view of the firm. *Journal of Management, 27*, 701-721.

Wright, P.M., & McMahan, G.C. (1992). Theoretical perspectives for strategic human resource management. *Journal of Management, 18*, 295-320.

Wright, P.M., & Snell, S.A. (1991). Toward an integrative view of strategic human resource management. *Human Resource Management Review, 1*, 203-225.

Wright, P.M., & Snell, S.A. (1998). Toward a unifying framework for exploring fit and flexibility in strategic human resource management. *Academy of Management Review, 23*, 756-772.

Young, K. (1977). Values in the policy process. *Policy and Politics, 5*(3), 1-22.

CHAPTER 3

Diversifying the Teacher Workforce: A Retrospective and Prospective Analysis

ANA MARÍA VILLEGAS AND TAMARA F. LUCAS

The topic of accountability has generated considerable attention in public discussions of education during the past ten years. Since the passage of the No Child Left Behind Act of 2001, however, the focus on accountability has become even more intense. No Child Left Behind requires that all students, not just some, make adequate progress toward meeting challenging academic standards, as determined by scores on standardized tests. This expectation, a significant departure from past practice, has profound implications for those concerned with teacher workforce issues.

As part of its mandate, No Child Left Behind calls for a "highly qualified" teacher in every classroom in the nation. Meeting this requirement is particularly challenging in the context of the shifting demographics of the student population. During the past 30 years, schools in the United States have become increasingly diverse. In 1972, students from racial/ethnic minority groups accounted for only 22% of total K-12 enrollments. By 2001, such students represented nearly 40% of all those served in elementary and secondary schools. A peek at the future shows that students from all minority groups combined will constitute the majority of the K-12 student population by 2035 (NCES, 2002e; U.S. Department of Commerce, 1996). Historically, schools have not succeeded in educating students of color[1] on a par with their White peers, as evidenced by numerous outcome measures, including scores on achievement tests (Lee, 2002) and high school completion rates (NCES, 2002a). Although this achievement gap is not new, the growing presence of racial and ethnic minorities in

Ana Maria Villegas is Professor of Curriculum and Teaching at Montclair State University. Tamara F. Lucas is Professor of Educational Foundations at Montclair State University. They recently co-authored *Educating Culturally Responsive Teachers: A Cohesive Approach*.

schools, in conjunction with current policies stemming from No Child Left Behind that hold schools and teachers accountable for student learning, demands a serious reassessment of the desired qualities of those we recruit into teaching, the strategies we use to recruit them, the structure and content of the preparation they receive, and the strategies we employ to retain them in the profession.

In this chapter, we argue that increasing the racial/ethnic diversity of the teacher workforce should be a key component of any system that aims to supply schools with well-prepared teachers for all students. We first explain why we think attention and resources should be devoted to increasing the diversity of the teacher workforce. We then provide a brief account of minority teacher and student representation in U.S. public schools since 1950, followed by a discussion of the reasons why the percentage of minorities in the teacher workforce declined significantly during the 1970s and 1980s. Because, to date, efforts to diversify the U.S. teaching force have focused largely on strategies for attracting more people of color into teaching, we devote an entire section to recruitment-related policy initiatives and program strategies. Following this, we highlight important issues beyond recruitment: the changes needed in the structures of colleges and universities—especially predominantly White institutions—to retain people of color through graduation, completion of teacher education programs, and attainment of teacher certification; the curricular changes needed in teacher education programs to adequately prepare candidates of color to teach a diverse student population well; the concerns raised by the concentration of teachers of color in urban schools; and the existing barriers to retaining teachers of color, especially those at the beginning of their teaching careers. We then review the current situation to gauge the extent of the progress made during the past decade toward diversifying the teacher workforce. Finally, we discuss the challenges ahead.

Why Increase Teacher Workforce Diversity?

There are two main arguments in support of increasing teacher workforce diversity. The most common argument is that, in a democratic society, minority teachers are needed as role models for all students, but especially for minority students. The second argument, discussed with less frequency, suggests that minority teachers are particularly suited to teaching minority students because they bring an inherent understanding of the cultural backgrounds and experiences of these learners to their work.

In a Democratic Society, Minority Teachers are Needed as Role Models for Students

School is a place where academic knowledge is constructed and transmitted, but it is also a setting where values are shaped, in ways most often subtle but always powerful. Having a disproportionately small number of people of color in the teacher workforce is contrary to the democratic values of equality and representation on which the United States was founded. Children of color see few people of their own backgrounds among the professional staff in schools, while White children see few people *un*like themselves in those roles. Either way, children are getting the message that the educational system is doing little to counteract the stratification that exists in the larger society. This message can alienate children of color from education as well as from the democratic process and can give White children the impression that existing inequalities are not problematic.

This argument in support of increasing the diversity of the teacher workforce first surfaced during the late 1960s and early 1970s as part of the move to achieve more racial balance among students in highly segregated districts across the United States. It resurfaced in the 1980s, when awareness of the influence of schooling on the formation of children's values led a number of scholars and several prominent professional organizations to consider the implications of exposing public school children to an overwhelmingly White teaching force (AACTE, 1987; Graham, 1987). Mercer and Mercer (1986), for example, argued that the racial/ethnic makeup of the teacher workforce communicates a strong message to children about the distribution of power in society. These scholars contended that the absence of minority teachers conveys to school children that White people are better suited to hold positions of authority in society. This implicit message contrasts markedly with the promise of equality espoused in the United States, a theme promoted within the formal school curriculum. Using this same line of reasoning, the Carnegie Forum on Education and the Economy (1986) also concluded that a democratic society should not condone exposing school children to few minorities in authority positions in schools. Although the literature skirts the issue of what might be considered the appropriate racial/ethnic makeup of the teacher workforce, parity is generally assumed—that is, a teaching force in which the proportion of minority teachers approximates the proportion of minority students enrolled in schools (Hidalgo & Huling-Austin, 1993).

Because most students of color live in poor communities and therefore tend to see relatively few successful professionals who are racially and ethnically like themselves, they are thought to derive special benefit from exposure to minority teachers (Adair, 1984; Riley, 1998). This exposure is assumed to boost the confidence of minority students and to enable them to grow up to become successful and contributing members of society, just like their racially and ethnically similar teachers (Stewart, Meier, & England, 1989; Zirkel, 2002). White students, too, are thought to benefit from exposure to a racially and ethnically diverse teaching force. For example, Waters (1989) contended that seeing minorities in professional roles challenges the myth of racial/ethnic inferiority that many White youngsters internalize about people of color.

Minority Teachers Are Particularly Suited to Teaching Minority Students

In addition to acting as role models, minority teachers can help minority students build cultural bridges to learning. The importance of establishing cultural links between home and school for students was supported by landmark studies in educational anthropology and cognitive science in the 1970s and 1980s that transformed our understanding of the learning process in cross-cultural settings (Cazden, John, & Hymes, 1972; Heath, 1983; Vygotsky, 1978). This research showed that learning, far from being a passive act of merely receiving new information, actually involves the active construction of ideas. It further showed that, whether inside or outside schools, learning takes place in a cultural context. In their attempts to make sense of new input, learners continuously strive to connect their prior knowledge and experiences—both individual and cultural—with the new information (Tharp & Gallimore, 1990; Tobin, 1998). Thus, children's prior knowledge and experiences are recognized as essential resources for learning. Effective teaching, by extension, has been redefined to mean helping learners build connections between what is familiar to them and the new content and skills to be learned.

These views of teaching and learning, and the growing recognition that culture plays a central role in the learning process, provide a solid theoretical grounding for the second main argument in support of increasing the racial/ethnic diversity of the teaching force (Villegas & Lucas, 2002). This argument has been most clearly articulated by Irvine (1988). Referring specifically to African Americans, Irvine explained that students from this group benefit from being taught by racially-like teachers, who are intimately familiar with the children's cultural backgrounds by virtue of their own life experiences. This cultural synchronicity, she argued, gives African American teachers a clear advantage over their White counterparts when assisting African American students in building the necessary bridges to learning. Such bridge-building strategies include selecting instructional materials that are of interest and relevance to the students, designing instructional activities that engage students in culturally appropriate ways, making use of pertinent examples and analogies drawn from the students' daily lives to introduce or clarify new concepts, managing the classroom in ways that take into consideration cultural differences in interaction styles, and using a variety of evaluation strategies to maximize students' opportunities to display what they actually know in ways that are familiar to them (Irvine & Armento, 2001).

A related argument in support of increasing the representation of minorities in teaching is that the personal insight minority teachers have into racial and ethnic inequalities in the United States allows them to establish special relationships with minority students (Foster, 1993). According to Foster, the trusting nature of these relationships enables minority teachers to challenge minority students to invest in learning, despite the many academic and social barriers these youngsters experience along the way. Because teachers of color are apt to have more credibility with students of color than would most White teachers, they are better positioned to help minority students understand the social and political consequences of choosing academic achievement or failure. Without this critical dialogue, many minority students would not engage in school learning.

Dilworth (1990) pointed out still another advantage of a diverse teacher workforce. She argues that minority teachers can use the inherent understanding of minority cultural backgrounds and experiences that they bring to the profession to help their White colleagues bridge the cultural gap separating them from a growing number of racial/ethnic minority students.

Consistent with these theoretical arguments that teachers of color can best facilitate learning for students of color, a few empirical studies have produced evidence that minority teachers have a positive impact on minority students. For example, Dee (2001) reanalyzed data from an experiment in Tennessee designed to test the effect of class size on the academic gains of students in kindergarten through third grade. Of the Black students in the original study, 45% were randomly assigned to Black teachers. Dee examined the effect of the Black teachers on the Black students' math and reading achievement test scores. He found that the students' scores significantly increased—by three to four percentage points during the first year of the experiment and by two to four percentage points each subsequent year. Class size proved to be a mediating factor in this investigation. That is, the race effect was significant in regular-size classes (defined as having 22 students), but was not in smaller classes. Correlation studies have also shown that students of color taught by a same-race/ethnicity teacher significantly increased their academic achievement in math and reading (Hanushek, 1992) and in a high school economics course (Evans, 1992).

Although Ehrenberg, Goldhaber, and Brewer (1995) reported that teacher race/ethnicity did not play an important part in students' academic gains, these researchers nevertheless found that minority students received higher subjective evaluations from minority teachers. Specifically, more minority teachers expected minority students to go to college, would recommend them for academic honors, reported that they related well to others, interacted with them outside of class, and believed they worked hard. Further research is needed to determine the impact of such evaluations on minority students, but the authors hypothesize that such evaluations reflect the degree to which teachers encourage students to strive for high levels of achievement. The literature also shows that minority students taught by a same-race/ethnicity teacher are better behaved in school (Meier & Stewart, 1991), have lower dropout rates (Ehrenberg & Brewer, 1993), and are less frequently absent from school (Farkas, Grobe, Sheehan, & Shuan, 1990). Although the results of these studies cannot be considered conclusive, they provide some empirical evidence to support policies and programs for diversifying the teacher workforce, much as earlier studies reporting similar positive findings for minority students taught by minority teachers (Arnez, 1978; Beady & Hansell, 1981; Crain & Mahard, 1978) had done during the school desegregation era of the late 1960s and early 1970s.

By highlighting the role that race/ethnicity plays in teaching and learning, we do not mean to imply that teachers must be of the same backgrounds as their students if the teachers are to be effective. Nor are we advocating assigning teachers to students based on these social characteristics. But we do find these arguments in support of increasing the diversity of the teacher workforce to be compelling. If teachers of color are essential role models for all students, especially students of color, in a democratic society, and if the life experiences of teachers of color infuse into the teacher workforce a critical source of cultural knowledge, then efforts to increase the diversity of the teacher workforce should be a key component in any system that aims to supply schools with well-prepared teachers for all students, particularly in light of the shifting demographics of the student population.

The Growing Disparity Between Minority Student and Minority Teacher Populations

Contradictory trends in the racial/ethnic makeup of student and teacher populations, first observed in the late 1960s as part of nationwide school desegregation efforts, was the phenomenon that ultimately brought national attention to the shortage of minority teachers in the late 1980s. Table 1 presents highlights of the troubling statistics. As shown, enrollments in public elementary and secondary schools became increasingly heterogeneous between 1971 and 1986, while the teacher workforce became more homogeneous. Despite a gain in diversity among the ranks of teachers from 1981 to 1986 (discussed below), the racial/ethnic disparity between students and educators more than doubled during this 15-year period.

TABLE 1

Percentage of Minority Teachers and Minority Students in
Public Elementary and Secondary Schools for Selected Years

Year	Teachers (%)	Students (%)	Difference (percentage points)
1971	11.7	22.2*	10.5
1976	9.2	23.8	14.6
1981	8.4	27.2	18.8
1986	9.4	30.9	21.5

Sources: NCES, 1997; U.S. Department of Education, 2001
*Data reported for 1972; no data were available for 1971.

Some scholars, educational leaders, and professional organizations issued warnings that this growing cultural mismatch between students and teachers was a matter with serious social and educational implications for the nation and its schools. They argued that without considerable intervention, the cultural divide already obvious in many classrooms would become even more severe in the 1990s, with the result that students—minority and White—would rarely be taught by minority teachers (Carnegie Forum on Education and the Economy, 1986; Graham, 1987; Irvine, 1988). In so doing, they helped define a critical workforce problem, the shortage of minority teachers.

Although the underrepresentation of minorities, as a group, in the teacher workforce became a well-established fact in the 1980s, differences in patterns of participation in the teaching profession evident between African Americans and members of other racial/ethnic minority groups merit attention. For African Americans, teaching had historically been a popular and respected profession (King, 1993; Stewart, Meier, & England, 1989). According to Foster (1995), half of all African American professionals employed in the United States in 1950 were teachers. This is not surprising because teaching was one of the few professions open to Black people during the long segregation era in the United States—the dual school system of the South needed Black educators to staff classrooms for Black students. Franklin (1990) reported that, prior to desegregation, African Americans held the teaching profession in high esteem and viewed Black teachers as community leaders.

Ironically, school desegregation markedly reduced the presence of African American teachers in elementary and secondary schools (Foster, 1995; Gordon, 2000; King, 1993). With the dismantling of the dual school system after the *Brown v. Board of Education* decision, approximately 38,000 African American teachers and school administrators who had staffed segregated Black schools had lost their jobs by 1970 though dismissal or nonrenewal of contracts (Ethridge, 1979). Among those placed in desegregated schools, many were assigned to teach subjects they were not certified to teach (Arnez, 1978). Others were assigned to lower-status positions that paid less than they had earned previously (Morris, 1967).

Between 1971 and 1986, the proportion of Black students enrolled in public schools grew by more than 12%. By contrast, the percentage of public school teachers who were Black fell from 8.1 to 6.9, a decrease of nearly 15% (NCES, 1997; U.S. Department of Education, 2001). Thus, the imbalance in the number of Black students and Black teachers became more pronounced over time. Although not advocating a return to segregation, African American scholars were quick to point out that the sharp decline in the participation of African Americans in teaching resulted in the loss of cultural linkages between home and school that had existed for African American students prior to desegregation (Arnez, 1978; King, 1993).

Compounding the sizeable loss of African Americans from the teacher workforce in the 1960s, the number of bachelor's degrees in education awarded to African Americans during the 1970s and 1980s declined significantly. (Although the same can be said for all racial/ethnic groups except Asians during these two decades, the decline experienced

78   DIVERSIFYING THE TEACHER WORKFORCE

by African Americans far surpassed that of any other group.) Data reported by Carter and Wilson (1992) show that in 1989 only 4,233 African Americans were awarded bachelor's degrees in education, down from 14,206 in 1976—a decline of more than 70% over 13 years. Such statistics prompted leaders of Historically Black Colleges and Universities—the major producers of African American teachers—to begin referring to the Black educator as an "endangered species" (Cole, 1986).

Hispanics, Asians, and Native Americans—unlike African Americans—had a history of limited representation in U.S. public education even before school desegregation became law in 1954. But, as the representation of Hispanic, Asian, and Native American students increased in elementary and secondary schools over the years, the degree of underrepresentation of teachers from these groups also grew (Holmes, 1990). Because there were relatively few non-African American minority teachers in the United States, *Education Statistics Digest* did not begin to report information about them by specific racial/ethnic category until 1991. Collectively, however, Hispanic, Asian, and Native American teachers constituted 3.6% of the K-12 teaching force in 1971. That figure dropped below 1% by 1981, before rebounding to 3.4% in 1986 (NCES, 1997). It should be noted that the concentrations of students from these minority groups in elementary and secondary public schools—which had been about half that of African American students throughout the 1970s—grew substantially in the 1980s (U.S. Department of Education, 2001). Thus, the cultural divide between teachers and their students actually widened during the 1980s for the fastest growing segment of the student population, despite a gain in the number of Hispanic, Asian, and Native American teachers in the second half of the decade.

Reasons for the Minority Teacher Shortage

A variety of reasons have been cited for the minority teacher shortage, in addition to the massive loss of African American teachers during the 1950s and 1960s discussed above. These can be broadly organized into four categories: (1) the small number of minorities eligible for postsecondary education and the high attrition rate among matriculants; (2) broader professional opportunities available to minorities as a result of the civil rights movement of the 1960s; (3) the widespread use of teacher testing in the 1970s and 1980s; and (4) the growing dissatisfaction with teaching as a profession.

Small number of minorities eligible for postsecondary education; high attrition rate for minority matriculants. After desegregation, minority students in elementary and secondary schools showed some improvements in various indicators of educational attainment, including scores on standardized tests of reading, writing, and mathematics (Berliner & Biddle, 1995). Such improvements were, no doubt, the result of policies and programs of the 1970s and 1980s intended to bring about a redistribution of educational opportunities. Despite this progress, the public education system continued to underserve minority students. Research confirms that students of color were taught by teachers who generally expected little of these children and who treated them in ways that stifled their learning (Irvine, 1990), were subjected to a non-inclusive curriculum that distanced them from learning (Banks, 1991), and were exposed to styles of interaction that clashed with the cultures of their homes and communities (Au & Kawakami, 1994). These and other disempowering practices help explain the underachievement of minority students during the 1970s and 1980s. It is not surprising, then, that proportionately many more minority students dropped out of school than did their White peers.

Among 18- to 24-year-olds, the dropout rate for White students was 12.3% in 1972, compared to a much higher rate of 21.3% for Black students and an even higher rate of 34.3% for Hispanic students (NCES, 2002b).[2] Although dropout rates were declining for White and Black students, similar discrepancies among the three groups persisted eight years later. In 1980, White students left high school at a rate of 11.4%, while Black and Hispanic students did so at rates of 19.1% and 35.2%, respectively. The pattern was repeated in 1988, when less than 10% of all White 18- to 24-year-olds dropped out, compared to 14.5% for Black students and 35.8% for Hispanic students (NCES, 2002b). In brief, disproportionately large numbers of Black and Hispanic students—but especially Hispanic students—left the education system before reaching the postsecondary level. This leak in the educational pipeline substantially limited the pool of potential minority candidates—for college in general, and for programs of teacher education more specifically—during the two decades in question.

An observable drop in the proportion of minority high school graduates attending college in the early 1980s contributed further to the diminishing ranks of potential minority teachers (Irvine, 1988; Stewart et al., 1989). For example, Zapata (1998) reports that 35.8% of Hispanics who had graduated from high school enrolled in college in 1976, but only 31% did so in 1983. The drop in college enrollments was even more marked for African Americans. According to Foster (1995), while half of all African American high school graduates attended college in 1977, only slightly more than one third enrolled in 1982. Dorman (1990) argued that this decline in minority college enrollments reflected cutbacks in federal financing of higher education, which redirected assistance from grants to loans in the early 1980s. Another explanation cited with frequency in the literature is the inadequate academic preparation and counseling that minority students received in high school, which left them ill-prepared to pursue a college degree.

Another factor that further constrained the pool of potential teachers of color during the 1980s was the high attrition rates observed among minority college students (Stewart et al., 1989). According to Vining Brown, Clewell, Ekstrom, Goertz, and Powers (1994), institutions of higher education, especially predominantly White colleges and universities, have historically had a poor minority retention record, particularly with first-generation college students from low-income backgrounds. Reasons cited for the low retention rates include the lack of attention given to cultural diversity on most college and university campuses, the lack of academic preparation for and understanding of college life on the part of many minorities, insufficient academic and social support for the college experience, and a resulting sense of alienation experienced by many minority students in predominantly White institutions (Dorman, 1990; Hood & Parker, 1991).

Broader professional opportunities available to minorities after the civil rights movement. One of the most frequently mentioned reasons for the loss of minority teachers in the 1970s and 1980s is the opening of new career opportunities for members of racial/ethnic minority groups resulting from the civil rights movement of the 1960s (Hawley, 1986). Prior to the passage of the Civil Rights Act of 1964, teaching was one of a few careers available to minorities. Afterward, there was a dramatic decline in the popularity of teaching among college students of color from the mid-1970s through the late 1980s. As shown in Table 2, minority undergraduates defected in large numbers from the field of education to business, engineering, and the health professions. Specifically, between 1976 and 1989, the number of bachelor's degrees awarded to minorities in the fields of business, engineering, and the health professions increased by 117%, 292.3%, and 57.6%, respectively, while bachelor's degrees in education awarded to minorities declined by 56.9%. This exodus was especially evident among Black students, who as a group received nearly 10,000 fewer education degrees in 1989 than in 1976. Of all minorities, Asians were the only group to show an increase in the number of undergraduate education degrees. But this increase can be attributed to the phenomenal growth of the group during the 1980s as a result of immigration. A close review of the table shows that the proportional increase in education degrees awarded to Asians pales in comparison with gains this group made in engineering, business, and the health professions.

TABLE 2

Number of Minority Bachelor's Degrees Conferred in Selected Fields, 1976 and 1989 and Percentage Change

	Education	Business	Engineering	Health Professions
Black				
1976	14,209	9,489	1,370	2,741
1989	4,233	15,088	3,237	3,973
% Change	−70.2	+59.0	+136.3	+44.9
Hispanic				
1976	2,831	2,467	841	901
1989	2,293	6,987	2,458	1,386
% Change	−19.0	+183.2	+192.3	+53.4
American Indian				
1976	742	426	150	166
1989	537	824	285	245
% Change	−27.6	+93.4	+90.0	+47.6
Asian American				
1976	776	1,829	951	847
1989	1,127	8,039	7,012	1,733
% Change	+45.2	+339.5	+622.1	+104.6
Totals				
1976	18,558	14,211	3,312	4,655
1989	8,190	30,938	12,992	7,337
Change (N)	10,368	16,727	9,680	2,682
Change (%)	-56.9	+117.7	+292.3	+57.6

Source: Carter and Wilson, 1992

Teacher education programs were also partly to blame for the defection of minority students to fields outside education. While other fields actively competed for academically prepared minority students by offering them scholarships and other incentives, teacher education programs—especially at predominately White institutions—generally put little effort into increasing their minority enrollments (Post & Woessner, 1987). According to Hood and Parker (1991), institutions of higher education made serious attempts to recruit students from minority communities only when they were funded specifically for this purpose, a rare occurrence in the 1980s, because they could not otherwise offer the incentives needed to attract minority students. A related barrier to recruiting minority students to predominately White institutions in general, and to teacher education programs at these institutions in particular, was the absence of procedures for identifying talented minority students who did not meet traditional admissions criteria (Hood & Parker, 1991).

Increased teacher testing. During the early 1980s, concern about the condition of public education in the United States generated widespread support for education reform. Within this context, teacher testing became an accountability measure, and its use grew steadily over the decade. In 1980, 15 states required prospective teachers to pass a standardized certification test as a condition for entry into the profession. By the end of the decade, 42 states had instituted this requirement (Villegas, 1997). Because the passing rates of minorities on these tests were lower than those of White candidates, the teacher competency test movement resulted in the exclusion of disproportionate numbers of people of color from teaching.

Various explanations for the poor showing of minorities on teacher tests appear in the literature of the 1980s. Critics of teacher tests charged that the content of these assessments unfairly discriminated against minorities (Hilliard, 1986). Teacher tests were criticized on other technical grounds as well, one of the more serious accusations being that there was little or no evidence that these tests accurately predicted how a person might perform as a teacher (Haney et al., 1987; Hilliard, 1986). Many observers also charged that the low minority pass rates on teacher competency tests were a reflection of the inadequate education students of color received in elementary and secondary and postsecondary educational institutions, as we discussed above.

Growing public dissatisfaction with the teaching profession. The intense criticism of teachers that followed the publication of *A Nation at Risk* in 1983 profoundly reduced the prestige of the teaching profession in this country. According to Darling-Hammond, Johnson, Pittman, and Ottinger (1987), this declining prestige severely dampened the interest in teaching among all racial/ethnic groups. This was especially so for minority groups, who by then had greater access to more prestigious and economically lucrative fields (Post & Woessner, 1987). The growing dissatisfaction with teaching not only kept many minorities from seeking a teaching career but also led some who had already overcome the obstacles and disincentives and become practicing teachers to consider leaving the profession (Dorman, 1990). A national poll conducted at the end of the 1980s showed that over 40% of minority teachers were likely to leave teaching before completing five years due to job dissatisfaction, compared to 25% of White teachers (Harris & Associates, 1988).

Because of these four issues, the ranks of minority teachers (especially African American teachers) were diminishing just as the student population was becoming significantly more racially/ethnically diverse. This rapidly growing demographic disparity between teachers and students prompted calls for the diversification of the teacher workforce through recruitment, resulting in a number of policy initiatives and program strategies.

Addressing the Shortage of Minority Teachers: A Focus on Recruitment

The professional literature frequently explains the shortage of minority teachers as being the result of a leaky pipeline. In this metaphor, the teacher education system is the pipeline, and when it is functioning properly, it facilitates students' movement from elementary school to middle school, from middle school to high school, from high school to college and teacher education programs, and from college to the teaching profession. The shortage of teachers of color is attributed to a significant loss of students of color as they make their way through the education pipeline. This loss—or leak—of human potential is said to occur most often at certain critical junctures, including graduation from high school, admission to college, admission to preservice teacher education programs, college graduation, and receipt of a teaching certificate. When the shortage of minority teachers is viewed in this manner, it becomes clear that nothing less than a comprehensive and coordinated initiative to expand the number of students of color in the pipeline and to stop the leak of human potential at the identified critical junctures will alter the demographic makeup of the teacher workforce in any significant way.

Policy Initiatives to Recruit Minority Teachers

At the end of the 1980s, a call to remedy the shortage of minorities in teaching set in motion a number of workforce initiatives designed to recruit more people of color into the profession. The Education Commission of the States (ECS) played a leading role in launching such initiatives. Building on the literature that examined reasons for the shortage of minority teachers, ECS (1990) argued that a systemic approach was needed to address this complex problem. Specifically, ECS called on school districts, institutions of higher education, and state education departments to adopt comprehensive and coordinated minority recruitment policies and programs aimed at improving elementary and secondary schools, particularly in high minority districts, by developing early teacher recruitment efforts targeting precollege minority students; expanding teacher recruitment pools to include both traditional and nontraditional minority candidates; creating more pathways to teaching; attracting more people of color into teacher education through incentives; and providing new recruits with a variety of supports to ensure that they will attain teaching certificates and find teaching positions.

By the end of the 1990s, 30 states were implementing minority teacher recruitment programs of some sort (Clewell, Darke, Davis-Googe, Forcier, & Manes, 2000). The state of Ohio, for example, established the goal of doubling the number of teachers from underrepresented groups by the year 2000 (Ohio State Legislative Office of Education Oversight, 1997). To attain this goal, the state focused its efforts on three different candidate pools—precollege students, college students, and career switchers. As part of this initiative, Ohio created a mentoring program for precollege students designed to cultivate their interest in teaching and to counsel them on curriculum choices that would provide the best preparation for college. The state also offered tuition remission to college students from underrepresented groups who enrolled in preservice teacher education programs. To attract career changers, including candidates of color, Ohio put in place an alternate licensing program. Other states have used a variety of strategies to promote the diversity of their teacher workforce, such as sponsoring annual conferences focused on minority recruitment, requiring school districts to submit a faculty diversification plan, reserving a given percentage of the funding available for teacher education scholarships specifically for candidates of color, and monitoring the racial/ethnic makeup of the teaching force in the state on a regular basis (ECS, 2000).

Private foundations also played a pivotal role in expanding the diversity of the teacher workforce during the 1990s. The two largest foundation-sponsored programs of this nature—the Ford Foundation Minority Teacher Education Program and the DeWitt Wallace-Reader's Digest Fund Pathways to Teaching Careers Program—were national in scope. The former included 50 sites in eight states and the latter involved 41 sites in 25 states. In addition to producing a large

number of minority teachers, these two programs served as demonstration sites for testing a variety of strategies for recruiting and preparing
people of color for teaching. In fact, the documented success of the
Pathways to Teaching Careers initiative (Clewell & Villegas, 1999,
2001; Dandy, 1998; Genzuk & Baca, 1998; Littleton, 1998; Villegas &
Clewell, 1998a, 1998b) prompted the Clinton administration to
include minority teacher recruitment programs as part of Title II of
the Higher Education Act of 1999, Teacher Quality Enhancement
Programs. Modeled after programs in the Pathways to Teaching
Careers initiative, these federally supported minority recruitment programs included two main features: 1) a strong partnership between one
or more preservice teacher education programs and one or more high-
need school districts; and 2) varied types of support to help participants
complete the program, obtain a teaching certificate, secure a teaching
position, and receive mentoring assistance to ensure retention.

*Programmatic Strategies for Expanding and Sealing the Teacher Workforce
Pipeline*

The prevalent program strategies used since the early 1990s to
expand the number of minorities in the teacher workforce include
early recruitment programs, articulation agreements between two-
and four-year colleges, career ladder programs for paraprofessionals,
and alternative routes to certification. Each of these strategies targets
individuals at a different point in the education pipeline and gives
them the support necessary for success, as we discuss below.

Early recruitment programs. One way of expanding the pool of
potential minority teachers is to identify likely candidates before their
senior year in high school—possibly as early as the middle grades—and
involve them in intervention programs designed to both foster the
young people's interest in teaching and enhance their preparation for
college. These early recruitment programs, which entail collaborative
efforts between institutions of higher education and neighboring school
districts, offer long-range plans for eliminating the minority teacher
shortage. Such programs use a variety of strategies to cultivate students'
interest in teaching, including Future Educators Clubs, introductory
teacher education courses that offer college credit to high school
juniors and seniors, mentor teachers and invited speakers who provide
students with information about the teaching profession and inspire
them to become part of it, summer programs that give students intensive teaching experiences as well as academic support, and work-study

programs in which minority students in the upper high school years tutor young children in community programs (Zapata, 1998).

To prepare the students for college, early recruitment programs (also known as teacher cadet programs when their goal is to recruit pre-college students into teacher education specifically) first administer a battery of tests to identify participants' academic needs and then provide tutorial assistance throughout the school year, usually after school or on Saturdays, to address problem areas. Summer enrichment programs, also designed to expand students' academic preparation, supplement the services offered during the school year.

Although teacher cadet programs have the potential to augment the pool of potential minority teachers, they are long-term efforts that take at least five to eight years to produce results. Equally important, although such programs have been shown to increase the number of minority college matriculants (Clewell et al., 2000), they do not necessarily guarantee that college recruits will actually seek admission into teacher education programs or that those who do and are admitted will continue in the field through graduation (Kirby & Hudson, 1993).

Articulation agreements between two- and four-year colleges. Community college students constitute another nontraditional pool from which teacher education programs at four-year colleges can recruit minority candidates (Hudson, Foster, Irvine, Holmes, & Villegas, 2002). Community colleges have traditionally enrolled more than half of all racial/ethnic minority students who are in higher education, but low proportions of them transfer into four-year colleges (Tinto, 1998). Teacher education programs that aim to increase their minority enrollments can greatly advance this goal by establishing partnerships with two-year colleges. To effectively tap the pool of minority students in community colleges, the four-year college must coordinate its programs with its partner two-year college (Anderson & Goertz, 1995). Typically, transfer programs require some curriculum development at the community college to ensure that the students will meet requirements for admission into teacher education at the four-year institution (Hudson et al., 2002; Terzian, 1991).

Anderson and Goertz (1995) found that several factors facilitate the success of two-year to four-year college transfer programs for future teachers. These include strong leadership and a solid commitment to preparing teachers at both institutions, careful selection of program participants at the two-year college to ensure that they will meet the admission requirements of the partner four-year institution in general and of its teacher education program in particular, and support services designed to meet participants' academic needs and facilitate their integration into the teacher education program at the four-year institution once the transfer occurs.

Career ladder programs for paraprofessionals. Paraprofessionals employed in local school districts are another untapped source of racial/ethnic minority candidates for teacher education (Clewell & Villegas, 2001; Dandy, 1998; Genzuk & Baca, 1998; Hidalgo & Huling-Austin, 1993; Littleton, 1998; Villegas & Clewell, 1998a; Yopp, Yopp, & Taylor, 1992). In urban schools in particular, many paraprofessionals are people of color who live in the same neighborhoods as their students and who are knowledgeable about the life circumstances of those children (Haselkorn & Fideler, 1996). Colleges and universities that have succeeded in attracting paraprofessionals into teacher education have developed programs to address the needs of this population, while building on their strengths. In these "career ladder" programs, paraprofessionals continue their salaried positions while taking courses each semester toward the completion of requirements for teaching certification and, in most cases, a bachelor's degree. In some programs, courses are taught on site at the partner schools or at community agencies to make them more accessible to the participants. A paraprofessional in this type of program will typically require three years or longer to graduate and attain certification. Therefore, career ladder programs for paraprofessionals are not an immediate solution to the shortage of minority teachers. Successful programs offer a variety of support services, including tuition assistance, to help participants stay with the program through graduation and certification (Clewell & Villegas; Villegas & Clewell). The success of such programs also hinges on their ability to restructure the student teaching experience so that paraprofessionals can fulfill their student teaching requirement without losing salary or benefits during this time (Villegas & Clewell).

School districts that employ paraprofessionals can play a central role in their recruitment into a career ladder program by publicizing the program and identifying promising candidates for participation. If districts view paraprofessionals as a strong population from which to draw future teachers, they are likely to provide tangible support for the program as well, such as giving participants release time to attend program-related activities and offering onsite classroom space for program courses (Clewell & Villegas, 2001).

Alternative routes to certification. Programs that offer an alternative route to teacher certification have been used to recruit people from minority groups who already hold bachelor's degrees in fields other than education—including midlife career changers and retirees. According to Newmann (1994), alternative route programs were originally adopted by states in the 1980s to address overall teacher shortages in inner city schools and rural areas as well as shortages of teachers for selected subjects, such as mathematics and science, and in particular fields, such as bilingual education and special education. To fill vacant positions in previous times of teacher shortages, school districts and states had issued emergency teaching certificates that allowed people without preparation in pedagogy to work as teachers for a period of time, usually up to three years. Alternative route programs were intended to replace this dubious practice. In such programs, those with academic preparation in the target subject matter undergo intense training in pedagogy and work as interns in classrooms before assuming the responsibilities of a teacher, and they receive mentoring and in-class support during their first year of teaching.

The chronic shortage of teachers in inner city schools that began in the 1980s and continues to the present has been attributed to many factors, chief among them the underfunding of urban education and the tight bureaucratic structures of urban schools, which result in poor working conditions that many teachers refuse to subject themselves to (Darling-Hammond, 1995). Another factor contributing to the shortage of teachers in urban schools is the apparent unwillingness of many traditional teacher education program graduates, the overwhelming majority of whom are White, to teach children in urban schools (Gordon, 1997). According to Stoddart (1993), part of the reason for this is that the majority of traditionally certified novice teachers experience difficulties relating to children who are racially, ethnically, and socially different from themselves. Instead, they prefer to teach students whose backgrounds are more similar to their own. In this context of growing teacher shortages in urban areas and increasing difficulties in attracting White teachers to urban schools, the idea of creating alternative route programs to recruit minorities into teaching, especially for difficult-to-staff schools in inner city districts, gained many advocates during the 1990s (Feistritzer, 1990).

Haberman (1991) argues that minorities with baccalaureate degrees and substantial professional experience are well suited for urban school teaching. As he explains, this population tends to be older and more mature, to possess a stronger sense of personal identity, and to have a deeper understanding of the life experiences of minority children than do White graduates of traditional teacher education programs. Such qualities, he argues, enable career switchers from racial/ethnic minority groups to work effectively in the challenging conditions of urban schools. It should not be surprising, then, that numbers of minorities have taken alternative routes into urban teaching (see Allen, 2003; Natriello & Zumwalt, 1993; Shen, 1997).

There is considerable controversy, however, surrounding alternative certification programs, whether or not they are specifically designed to recruit minorities into teaching. Although advocates see alternative certification as a solution to the severe teacher shortages in inner city schools and to the underrepresentation of minorities in the teacher workforce, opponents contend that these programs give participants inadequate opportunity during their preservice training to develop the skills needed to teach effectively, and that the supervision alternative-route teachers require upon entry into the profession rarely takes place (Neumann, 1994). Critics also charge that alternative certification programs raise serious equity questions because the overwhelming majority of those who enter teaching through this abbreviated pathway go on to teach minority children in inner city schools (Darling-Hammond, 1995).

Underlying the debate about the efficacy of alternative certification programs is a lack of clarity regarding what constitutes such a program. Zumwalt (1991) maintains that alternative route programs differ substantially in structure and, as such, ought to be evaluated based on the specific goals they were designed to meet. Similarly, Wilson, Floden, and Ferrini-Mundi (2001) argue that the wide variation in what counts as an alternative route makes it impossible to reach conclusions from the available research regarding the effectiveness of these programs. What is known, however, is that, compared to traditional teacher education programs, alternative-route programs attract higher percentages of minorities, and, overall, more participants who have experience living in urban settings, who are bilingual in English and another language, and who have high academic expectations for minority students (Zeichner & Schulte, 2001).

Since the early 1990s, educators and policymakers have responded to the need for teachers of color by calling for a comprehensive and coordinated approach to dealing with the problem. Because the problem was defined as a supply issue from the start—that is, as a shortage of teachers of color—the resulting state and federal policy initiatives and program strategies have focused on recruitment. Although attracting more people of color into teaching is a worthwhile and necessary goal, it is not enough to ensure the diversity of the teacher workforce. Issues related to the preparation of people of color for teaching and to their retention in the teacher workforce, which are slowly making their way into public discussions, must also be addressed.

Beyond Issues of Recruitment

During the past 10 years or so, preservice teacher education programs at predominately White institutions have increased their minority enrollments to some extent, as we discuss in the final section of this chapter. One of the rationales we have cited for promoting this increase is that the life experiences people of color bring to the profession can give them an advantage when teaching students of color. But this resource will have limited payoffs unless teacher education programs prepare their minority students to draw on it in their teaching. More to the point, it would be unfair to hold people of color accountable for becoming culturally responsive teachers without the benefit of professional growth experiences to support this. Similarly, it is unrealistic to expect that, without explicit preparation, future teachers of any racial/ethnic background will know how to orchestrate the types of interactions that can enable the teaching profession to benefit from the cultural expertise that people of color bring to it. Productive conversations about issues of race and ethnicity are difficult to get started, and even more difficult to sustain over time. If these conversations are to take place among teachers in schools, teachers-to-be must learn the value of such interactions and develop the skills required to talk across racial/ethnic lines. Unfortunately, preservice teacher education programs at predominately White institutions, in the main, are not preparing their students in this way (Villegas & Lucas, 2002).

The teacher education curriculum at predominately White institutions has changed somewhat to address issues of diversity, but those changes have been made largely in the service of the White preservice teacher population (Montecinos, 1995). It is not surprising, then, that empirical studies about multicultural teacher education conducted to date focus mostly on strategies for helping White preservice teachers to see student diversity as a positive situation rather than as a hurdle. This literature pays relatively little attention to strategies for using the unique strengths that people of color bring to teacher education—their knowledge about students of color—to shape pedagogy. Thus an important resource remains untapped, and thereby unacknowledged, in preservice programs, and candidates of color are left to figure out on their own how to use their insider's knowledge in the classroom. Lacking this pedagogical expertise, people of color become highly vulnerable to attrition once they assume teaching responsibilities, particularly in school districts with high minority enrollments.

A related issue surfaces in a number of studies published since 1998 that call into question the capacity of predominately White institutions to increase the number of degrees they grant to people of color (see Agee, 1998; Bennett, Cole, & Thompson, 2000; Burant, 1999; Cochran-Smith, 2000; Knight, 2002; Meacham, 2000; Rios & Montecinos, 1999; Sheets & Chew, 2002; Tellez, 1999). A prevalent theme in these works is that minority students in programs of preservice teacher education at predominantly White colleges can experience a profound sense of alienation. At the root of this isolation is what Sleeter (2001) called the "overwhelming presence of whiteness." Because they generally constitute a very small proportion of enrollments at these institutions, minorities come into contact with relatively few students who share their background experiences. They also see relatively few people who are racially/ethnically like themselves among the faculty, administration, and staff. Equally problematic, if not more so, they are exposed to a curriculum that ignores their strengths and needs, as we explained above. In this context of overwhelming whiteness, minorities tend to feel unsafe in classrooms, especially when discussing issues of race and multicultural education with their peers and faculty, many of whom lack sensitivity to these topics and show a lack of interest in them. According to this research, as the silencing process unfolds, minorities gradually detach themselves from the learning process and ultimately drop out of school. This phenomenon constitutes one of the leaks in the teacher education pipeline. These findings suggest that strategies for recruiting people of color into teacher education at predominately White institutions, no matter how useful they might be in increasing minority enrollments, are insufficient to increase the number of degrees these institutions will grant to people of color because of high minority attrition. Ultimately, the success of minority recruitment initiatives depends on the institutions' willingness to confront the cultural politics that excludes and silences minority students.

But the complexity of successfully staffing more classrooms with teachers of color goes beyond issues of recruitment and preparation. Referring to the teaching workforce in general, Ingersoll (1997; see also this volume, chapter 1) convincingly argues that issues of retention are at the root of current teacher shortages. According to him, teachers who are placed in schools with depressed salaries, high student discipline problems, and little faculty input into decision making tend to have high attrition rates. A large proportion of teachers of color are initially placed in hard-to-staff urban schools, many of which suffer exactly these problems; therefore an equally large proportion are at high risk of leaving the profession. But the challenges teachers face in urban schools go beyond those Ingersoll cites. Because the majority of the children who attend these schools live in poverty, they bring to school problems such as poor nutrition and uncertain living situations, which interfere with learning and make their teachers' jobs especially challenging. In addition, because most U.S. schools are still funded from local property taxes, urban schools have relatively few resources, and novice teachers are therefore less likely than their suburban counterparts to receive mentoring or ongoing, high-quality professional development. Further, because of seniority regulations, newer, less experienced teachers are often given the most challenging classroom assignments. Urban schools also tend to be highly bureaucratic, giving teachers little autonomy and few opportunities to make important decisions about their work life (Ingersoll, 1994). In recent years, and especially since the passage of No Child Left Behind, the intense pressure to raise their students' test scores has taken even more autonomy away from teachers, even in their own classrooms, and, for many teachers, it has also taken the joy out of teaching.

In sum, a number of issues other than recruitment need to be addressed if we are to increase the number of teachers of color. Predominantly White institutions need to find ways to incorporate the perspectives of students of color into their curricula and to cultivate vigilance so as not to silence such students and risk losing them to attrition. Teacher education programs need to give more attention to preparing teachers of color to effectively draw on the life experiences and insights they bring to teaching so as not to squander an important resource. All stakeholders—parents, teachers, teacher educators, policymakers—need to work to make the conditions of schools, especially urban schools, more supportive of teachers to increase the likelihood that they will remain in those schools beyond their first few years of teaching.

Accomplishments to Date and Challenges Ahead

Since the late 1980s, when the shortage of teachers of color first gained national attention, considerable progress has been made toward diversifying the teacher workforce. In this section, we first identify accomplishments to date by examining the current racial/ethnic makeup of the K-12 teaching force and reviewing important indicators of diversity along the educational pipeline that leads to teaching. We then reflect on the challenges that must be overcome in the years ahead to attain more diversity in the teacher workforce.

Accomplishments

Table 3 presents information about the racial/ethnic composition of the K-12 teaching force for 1987, 1993, and 1999, the last three years in which the Schools and Staffing Survey was administered. As shown, the overall percentage of minority teachers in elementary and secondary schools declined somewhat between 1987 and 1993 but then rebounded between 1993 and 1999, with a gain of three percentage points over those six years. The decline observed in 1993 resulted from a drop in the share of African American teachers. By 1999, the representation of African Americans increased but was still lower than the 8.3% observed six years earlier. The largest gain was made by Hispanics, who accounted for 5.6% of all teachers in 1999, up from 2.9% in 1987. Asians and Pacific Islanders, as a group, also showed an increase over the 12-year period, while the combined group of American Indians and Alaskan Natives posted a slight decline.

TABLE 3

Distribution (%) of Elementary and Secondary Public School Teachers, by Race/Ethnicity for Selected School Years

Race/Ethnicity	Year		
	1987	1993	1999
White	86.9	87.3	84.3
Racial/Ethnic Minority	13.1	12.7	15.7
Black, Non-Hispanic	8.3	6.8	7.6
Hispanic	2.9	4.1	5.6
Asian/Pacific Islander	0.9	1.1	1.6
American Indian/ Alaskan Native	1.0	0.9	0.9

Sources: NCES, 1997, 2002d

The gain in diversity evident among the ranks of teachers during the 1990s was not sufficient to keep pace with the phenomenal growth in the number of minority students in elementary and secondary schools, however. In 1999, for example, racial/ethnic minority students accounted for about 38% of total K-12 enrollments, while people of color constituted less than 16% of the teaching force. It seems reasonable to conclude that as the projected increases in minority enrollments materialize in the years ahead, considerably more resources than those currently available will be needed to bring more minorities into teaching just to keep the existing demographic disparity and the accompanying cultural gap between teachers and their students from widening any further.

Key indicators along the teacher education pipeline offer hope for a future increase in the diversity of the teaching force. Data from early in the pipeline show that between 1990 and 2000, high school completion rates increased by five percentage points for Hispanic 18- to 24-year-olds not enrolled in high school (going from 59.0% to 64.1%), while holding steady in the vicinity of 83% to 84% for African Americans. Black and Hispanic students still experienced considerably lower high school completion rates in 2000 (83.7% and 64.1%, respectively) than did their White counterparts (91.8%). Completion rates for Hispanic students lagged particularly far behind those of their Black and White peers, despite showing an 8.6% improvement between 1990 and 2000.

Further along the pipeline, minority enrollment in degree-granting institutions of higher education increased between 1996 and 2000, the years for which we were able to locate comparable data. Collectively, minorities totaled 4,071,796 in 2000, up from 3,637,400 four years earlier. Gains were most evident among Hispanics, whose enrollment rose from 1,166,100 to 1,370,604 (an 18% increase over four years) (NCES, 2002c).

Patterns of minority enrollment in schools, colleges, and departments of education during the 1990s are also encouraging (Table 4). And all minority groups—with the exception of Asian/Pacific Islanders—increased their share of bachelor's degrees in teaching between 1987 and 1998, as illustrated in Table 5. The gains African Americans and Hispanics have made are particularly noteworthy. At the master's level, however, only African Americans showed a relative increase in degrees attained among all minority groups.

These data, collected at critical junctures in the education pipeline, are consistent with the desired effects of the systemic approach to diversifying the teaching force that ECS proposed in the early 1990s. It is difficult to estimate the relative contribution that the new pathways to teaching described in this chapter have made to the overall gains in racial/ethnic diversity within the teacher workforce. It is doubtful, however, that the observed increases could have been possible without alternative certification programs, which have served as an important entry point to teaching for many people of color (Zeichner & Schulte, 2001).

TABLE 4

Distribution (%) of Total Enrollment in Schools, Colleges, and Departments
of Education, by Race/Ethnicity, 1989 and 1995

Race/Ethnicity	Year			
	1989		1995	
	n	%	*n*	%
White (non-Hispanic)	426,748	86.5	418,824	80.5
Black/African American	33,436	6.8	46,667	9.0
Hispanic	13,533	2.7	24,429	4.7
Asian/Pacific Islander	4,469	0.9	8,787	1.7
American Indian/ Alaska Native	2,282	0.5	3,593	0.7
Other	13,138	2.7	18,131	3.5

Sources: NCES, 1997, 2002d
Note: "Other" includes students who are international/nonresident or biracial.

TABLE 5

Distribution (%) of Bachelor's and Master's Degrees in Teaching,
by Race/Ethnicity, 1987 and 1998

Race/Ethnicity	Degree			
	Bachelor's		Masters	
	1987	1998	1987	1998
White (non-Hispanic)	89.5	83.0	88.0	80.0
Black/African American	4.9	7.0	7.0	8.0
Hispanic	2.5	6.0	3.0	3.0
Asian/Pacific Islander	2.6	2.0	1.5	1.0
American Indian/ Alaska Native	0.5	1.0	0.5	<1.0
Other	—	1.0	—	>7.0

Source: Patterson Research Institute, 2001
Note: "Other" includes those who reported being biracial.

Progress has also been made in research. As we have discussed in
this chapter, we now have some evidence, although inconclusive, that
students of color benefit academically from being taught by teachers
of color. We have a deeper understanding of strategies for recruiting
people of color into teaching. We have more knowledge about how
members of different minority groups view the teaching profession.

We have additional insight into the experiences of minority students in programs of preservice teacher education at predominantly White colleges and universities. We also have learned that recruitment efforts, although essential, will not result in a more diverse teaching workforce unless issues of preparation and retention receive greater attention.

Challenges Ahead

Continuation of the progress made since the 1990s toward diversifying the teacher workforce will depend, to a large extent, on how policymakers and educators handle a number of challenges that lie ahead, the most critical being the profound achievement gap that has existed over time, and persists today, between students of color and White students. Historically, students from racial/ethnic minority groups have not succeeded in schools at rates comparable to those of their White peers. Relative to White students, minority students have consistently attained lower scores on standardized tests of academic achievement (Lee, 2002). As a group, students of color have been overrepresented in special education programs, instructional groups designated as low achieving, and vocational curricular tracks (Oakes & Lipton, 1994). Minorities have also completed high school and enrolled in postsecondary education at much lower rates than White students (Chronicle of Higher Education, 1999). Although progress has been made on many of these fronts, the inadequate education that many minority students continue to receive in elementary and secondary schools, particularly in inner city districts, limits the number who are eligible to go on to higher education and leaves many of those who do enter college academically vulnerable. Unless this urgent problem is decisively addressed, adequate progress toward diversifying the teaching force is not likely to occur in the future.

Reducing the pressure of standardized testing is another challenge we must meet if we are to increase the number of teachers of color. As we discussed previously, states are placing ever greater emphasis on test scores in determining who can become a teacher, and high proportions of minorities achieve low scores on such tests. The reasons for these disproportionately low scores are varied, but they largely derive from the nature of the tests and the poor preparation of many students of color in public schools. To improve minority achievement on such tests, elementary and secondary schools must improve their record of educating minority students; equally important, interested educators must ensure that the skills, knowledge, and potential of minorities are accurately assessed. This may mean developing alternative assessments for entry into teacher education and advocating for changes in testing policies.

A narrow definition of teacher quality and the accompanying methods for identifying potentially successful teachers constitutes another challenge to increasing the diversity of the teacher workforce. In fact, we reveal what we value in teachers in the ways we assess applicants to teacher education programs. Potentially successful teachers are currently identified through a nearly exclusive focus on their performance on traditional academic indicators (e.g., test scores, grade point averages). Although such indicators provide important information about applicants' academic backgrounds, they tell us nothing about the special strengths that people of color bring to teacher education, including personal knowledge of racial/ethnic minority communities, firsthand experience of what it is like to be a minority group member, and the affirming views of diversity that these experiences tend to engender—factors that may significantly augment academic quality because of their potential role in the success of students of color. Unless we expand the definition of a good teacher to include such qualities, many people of color with the potential to become successful teachers will be excluded from teaching.

Admitting members of minority groups into teacher education programs is just the first step in producing more teachers of color. Predominately White institutions need to create more inclusive communities within teacher education programs and across the institutions so that students of color are integrated into the life of the university instead of feeling like outsiders. If they feel marginalized, they are less likely to remain through graduation and actually become teachers (Bennett, Cole, & Thompson, 2000; Dillard, 1994). Characteristics of an inclusive community include a commitment at all levels of the institution to increase the diversity of both student and faculty populations through recruitment and retention initiatives, ongoing efforts to raise the awareness and sensitivity of all members of the community to issues of diversity, and serious efforts to reflect and incorporate minority cultures across the institution (Villegas & Lucas, 2002).

Finally, if we are to succeed in increasing the number of minority teachers in U.S. schools, we need a better understanding of the issues raised in this chapter. We need ongoing, rigorous research that provides empirical evidence of the impact of minority teachers on minority students, successful ways to recruit more minorities into teaching, strategies for maximizing the cultural expertise of people of color in the teacher workforce, and the strategies used by minority teachers to build cultural bridges between home and school for minority students. We especially need more research on the particular nature of the challenges discussed above and on ways to address those challenges.

Conclusion

In this retrospective and prospective analysis of efforts to diversify the teaching profession, we have argued that the development of a diverse teacher workforce must begin early in the teacher education pipeline, long before the preservice preparation of teacher candidates, and it must continue through to the end of teachers' careers. Rather than merely searching for qualified minority candidates to recruit into teacher preparation, advocates and policymakers must give attention and resources to helping minorities qualify for postsecondary education in general and for teaching in particular. To date, most efforts have focused on strategies for expanding the pool of potential teachers of color and recruiting from that pool. Only recently have issues of teacher preparation, professional development, and retention in teaching begun to command serious attention among those concerned with increasing the diversity of the teaching force.

We have also argued that we cannot increase the number of minority teachers by concentrating on developing individuals; we need to address a number of factors that have an especially powerful impact on potential teachers of color as a group. These factors include the achievement gap in elementary and secondary schools, which results in lower rates of high school graduation and college enrollment for students of color than for White students; the alienation students of color can experience in predominantly White institutions of higher education, as well as the academic difficulties they may face if they attended inadequate K-12 schools, both of which can reduce college graduation rates; the challenges minority students face in making a strong showing on standardized tests, which can reduce the number who qualify to become teachers; and the placement of a disproportionately high number of new minority teachers in urban schools, which can lead to an equally disproportionate rate of early attrition due to poor working conditions and a lack of mentoring and professional development. If we successfully tackle these challenges, we predict that the pool of minority teachers will increase dramatically.

Although these challenges to increasing the diversity of the teaching force are formidable, current evidence and compelling arguments within the literature indicate that the teaching profession as a whole and, more importantly, the students in our schools stand to gain considerably from the infusion of expertise and knowledge of minority cultures that minority teachers bring to teaching. In addition to helping minority students make connections between home and school cultures that build bridges to learning, teachers with racial/ethnic backgrounds similar to the those of the students in a particular school or district can serve as a resource for teachers of other backgrounds— a resource that is currently wasted in most schools and school systems.

We conclude from the evidence and arguments presented in this chapter that the potential benefits minority teachers bring to the profession far outweigh the challenges to recruiting, supporting, preparing, and retaining them. This leads us to assert that increasing the racial/ethnic diversity of the teacher workforce should be a key component of any system that aims to supply well-prepared teachers for all students.

NOTES

1. We have chosen to use the terms *minority* and *people/students/teachers of color* interchangeably to refer to the large and varied group of people who differ from the White dominant group in terms of race or ethnicity.

2. Due to the small sample size, results for Asians and Native Americans were not reported separately by NCES.

REFERENCES

AACTE (American Association of Colleges for Teacher Education). (1987). *Minority teacher recruitment and retention: A public policy issue* (ERIC Document No. 298123). Washington, DC: Author.

Adair, A.V. (1984). Desegregation: The illusion of Black progress. Lanham, MD: University Press of America.

Agee, J. (1998). Confronting issues of race and power in the culture of schools. In M. Dilworth (Ed.), *Being responsive to cultural differences* (pp. 21-38). Thousand Oaks, CA: Corwin Press.

Allen, M.B. (April 2003). *Eight questions on teacher preparation: What does the research say?* Denver: ECS.

Anderson, B.T., & Goertz, M.E. (1995). Creating a path between two- and four-year colleges. In A.M. Villegas, et al. (Eds.), *Teaching for diversity: Models for expanding the supply of minority teachers* (pp. 48-71). Princeton, NJ: Educational Testing Service.

Arnez, N.L. (1978). Implementation of desegregation as a discriminatory process. *The Journal of Negro Education, 47*(1), 28-45.

Au, K.H., & Kawakami, A.J. (1994). Cultural congruence in instruction. In E.R. Hollins, J.E. King, & W.C. Hayman (Eds.), *Teaching diverse populations* (pp. 5-24). Albany, NY: SUNY Press.

Banks, J. (1991). A curriculum for empowerment, action, and change. In C.E. Sleeter (Ed.), *Empowerment through multicultural education* (pp. 125-141). Albany: SUNY Press.

Bennett, C., Cole, D., & Thompson, J.N. (2000). Preparing teachers of color at a predominantly white university: A case study of project TEAM. *Teaching and Teacher Education, 16*, 445-464.

Berliner, D.C., & Biddle, B.J. (1995). *The manufactured crisis: Myths, fraud, and the attack on America's public schools.* Reading, MA: Addison-Wesley.

Burant, T.J. (1999). Finding, using, and losing (?) voice: A preservice teacher's experiences in an urban educative practicum. *Journal of Teacher Education, 50*, 209-219.

Carnegie Forum on Education and the Economy, Task Force on Teaching as a Profession. (1986). *A nation prepared: Teachers for the 21st century.* Washington, DC: Carnegie Forum.

Carter, D.J., & Wilson, R. (1992). *Minorities in higher education: Tenth annual report.* Washington, DC: American Council on Education.

Cazden, C.B., John, V.P., & Hymes, D. (Eds.). (1972). *Functions of language in the classroom.* New York: Teachers College Press.

Clewell, B.C., Darke, K., Davis-Googe, T., Forcier, L., & Manes, S. (2000). *Literature review on teacher recruitment programs.* Washington, DC: The Urban Institute.

Clewell, B.C., & Villegas, A.M. (1999). Creating a nontraditional pipeline for urban teachers: The Pathways to Teaching Careers model. *Journal of Negro Education, 68*(3), 306-317.

Clewell, B.C., & Villegas, A.M. (2001). *Ahead of the class: Design lessons from the DeWitt Wallace-Reader's Digest Fund's Pathways to Teaching Careers Initiative.* Washington, DC: Urban Institute.

Cochran-Smith, M. (2000). Blind vision: Unlearning racism in teacher education. *Harvard Educational Review, 70*, 541-570.

Cole, B.P. (1986). The Black educator: An endangered species. *Journal of Negro Education, 55*(3), 326-334.

Dandy, E. (1998). Increasing the number of minority teachers: Tapping the paraprofessional pool. *Education and Urban Society, 31*(1), 89-103.

Darling-Hammond, L. (1995). Inequality and access to knowledge. In J. Banks (Ed.), *Handbook of multicultural education* (pp. 465-483). New York: Macmillan.

Darling-Hammond, L., Pitmann, K.J., & Ottinger, C. (1987). Career choices for minorities. Who will teach? Washington, DC: National Education Association and Council of Chief State School Officers.

Dee, T.S. (2001). *Teachers' race and student achievement in a randomized experiment.* Cambridge, MA: National Bureau of Economic Research.

Dillard, C. (1994). Beyond supply and demand: Critical pedagogy, ethnicity, and empowerment in recruiting teachers of color. *Journal of Teacher Education, 45*(1), 9-17.

Dilworth, M.E. (1990). *Reading between the lines: Teachers and their racial/ethnic cultures.* (Teacher Education Monograph No. 11). Washington, DC: ERIC Clearinghouse on Teacher Education and American Association of Colleges for Teacher Education.

Dorman, A. (1990). *Recruiting and retaining minority teachers: A national perspective* (North Central Regional Education Laboratory Policy Briefs No. 8). Oakbrook, IL: NCREL.

Education Commission of the States. (1990). *New strategies for producing minority teachers.* Denver, CO: Author.

Education Commission of the States. (2000). State notes. Teacher Recruitment/Retention. Information Clearinghouse. Denver, CO: Author.

Ehrenberg, R.G., & Brewer, D.J. (1993). Do school and teacher characteristics matter? Evidence from high school and beyond. *Economics and Education Review, 13*(1), 1-17.

Ehrenberg, R.G., Goldhaber, D.D., & Brewer, D.J. (1995). Do teachers' race, gender, and ethnicity matter? Evidence from the National Educational Longitudinal Study of 1988. *Industrial and Labor Relations Review, 48*(3), 547-561.

Ethridge, S.B. (1979). Impact of the 1954 *Brown vs. Topeka Board of Education* decision on black educators. *Negro Education Review, 30*(3-4), 217-232.

Evans, M.O. (1992). An estimate of race and gender role-model effects in teaching high school. *Journal of Economic Education, 25*(3), 209-17.

Farkas, G., Grobe, R.P., Sheehan, D., & Shuan, Y. (1990). Cultural resources and school success: Gender, ethnicity, and poverty groups within an urban school district. *American Sociological Review, 55*, 127-142.

Feistritzer, E. (1990). *Alternative teacher certification: A state-by-state analysis.* Washington, DC: Policy Studies Associates.

Foster, M. (1993). Educating for competence in community and culture: Exploring the views of exemplary African American teachers. *Urban Education, 27*(4), 370-394.

Foster, M. (1995). African American teachers and culturally relevant pedagogy. In J. Banks and C. Banks (Eds.), *Handbook on research on multicultural education* (pp. 570-581). New York: Macmillan.

Franklin, V.P. (1990). They rose and fell together: African-American educators and community leaderships, 1795-1954. *Journal of Education, 172*(3), 39-64.

Genzuk, M., & Baca, R. (1998). The paraeducator-to-teacher pipeline: A 5-year retrospective on an innovative teacher preparation program for Latinas(os). *Education and Urban Society, 31*(1), 73-88.

Gordon, J.A. (1997). Teachers of color speak to issues of respect and image. *The Urban Review, 29*(1), 41-66.

Gordon, J.A. (2000). *The color of teaching.* NY: Rutledge.

Graham, P.A. (1987). Black teachers: A drastically scarce resource. *Phi Delta Kappan, 68*(3), 598-605.

Haberman, M. (1991). Can cultural awareness be taught in teacher education programs? *Teaching Education, 4*(1), 25-31.

Haney, W., Madaus, C., & Krietzer, A. (1987). Charms talismanic: Testing teachers for improvement of American education. In E. Rothkopf (Ed.), *Review of Research in Education, 14*, 169-238. Washington, DC: American Educational Research Association.

Hanusheck, E. (1992). The trade-off between child quality and quantity. *Journal of Political Economy, 100*(3), 84-118.

102   DIVERSIFYING THE TEACHER WORKFORCE

Harris & Associates. (1988). *The Metropolitan Life survey. The American teacher 1988: Strengthening the relationship between teachers and students.* New York: Metropolitan Life Insurance Co. (ERIC Document Reproduction Service No. ED305357)

Haselkorn, D., & Fideler, E. (1996). *Breaking the class ceiling: Paraeducator pathways to teaching.* Belmont, MA: Recruiting New Teachers.

Hawley, W.D. (1986). Toward a comprehensive strategy for addressing the teacher shortage. *Phi Delta Kappan, 67,* 712-718.

Heath, S.B. (1983). *Ways with words: Language, life, and work in communities and classrooms.* London: Cambridge.

Hidalgo, F., & Huling-Austin, L. (1993). Alternate teacher candidates: A rich source for Latino teachers in the future. In R.E. Castro & Y.R. Ingle (Eds.), *Reshaping teacher education in the Southwest—A forum: A response to the needs of Latino students and teachers* (pp. 13-34). Claremont, CA: TRC.

Hilliard, A.G. (1986). From hurdles to standards of quality in teacher testing. *Journal of Negro Education, 55*(3), 304-315.

Holmes, B. (1990). *New strategies are needed to produce minority teachers* [Guest commentary] (North Central Regional Educational Laboratory Policy Briefs No. 8). Oakbrook, IL: NCREL.

Hood, S., & Parker, L. (1991). Minority students informing the faculty: Implications for racial diversity and the future of teacher education. *Journal of Teacher Education, 45*(3), 164-171.

Hudson, M., Foster, E., Irvine, J.J., Holmes, B., & Villegas, A.M. (2002). Tapping potential: Community college students and America's teacher recruitment challenge. Belmont, MA: Recruiting New Teachers.

Ingersoll, R.M. (1994). Organizational control in secondary schools. *Harvard Educational Review, 64*(2), 150-172.

Ingersoll, R.M. (1997) Teacher turnover and teacher quality: The recurring myth of teacher shortages, *Teachers College Record, 91*(1), 41-44.

Irvine, J.J. (1988). An analysis of the problem of the disappearing Black educator. *Elementary School Journal, 88*(5), 503-514.

Irvine, J.J. (1990). *Black students and school failure.* New York: Greenwood Press.

Irvine, J.J., & Armento, B.J. (2001). Culturally responsive teaching: Lesson planning for elementary and middle grades. NY: McGraw-Hill.

King, S.H. (1993). The limited presence of African-American teachers. *Review of Educational Research, 63*(2), 115-149.

Kirby, S.N., & Hudson, L. (1993). Black teachers in Indiana: A potential shortage? *Educational Evaluation and Policy Analysis, 15*(2), 181-194.

Knight, M.G. (2002). The intersections of race, class, and gender in the teacher preparation of an African American social justice educator. *Equity & Excellence in Education, 35*(3), 212-224.

Lee, (2002). Racial and ethnic achievement gap trends: Reversing the progress toward equity? *Educational Researcher, 31*(1), 3-12.

Littleton, D.M. (1998). Preparing professionals as teachers for the urban classroom: A university/school collaborative model. *Action in Teacher Education, 19*(4), 149-58.

Meacham, S. (2000). Black self-love, language, and the teacher education dilemma: The cultural denial and cultural limbo of African American preservice teachers. *Urban Education, 34*(5), 571-596.

Meier, K.J., & Stewart, J. (1991). *The politics of Hispanic education: Un paso pa'lante y dos pa'tras.* Albany, NY: SUNY.

Mercer, W.A., & Mercer, M.M. (1986). Standardized testing: Its impact on Blacks in Florida's educational system. *Urban Educator, 8*(1), 105-113.

Montecinos, C. (1995). Teachers of color and multiculturalism. *Equity & Excellence in Education, 27*(3), 34-42.

Morris, E.W. (1987). Facts and factors of faculty desegregation in Kentucky, 1955-1965. *The Journal of Negro Education, 36*(1), 75-77.

Natriello, G., & Zumwalt, K. (1993). New freedom for urban schools? The contribution of the provisional teacher program in New Jersey. *Education and Urban Society*, *26*, 49-62.

NCES (National Center for Education Statistics). (1997). Selected characteristics of public school teachers: Spring 1961 to spring 1996. In *Digest of Education Statistics*, *1997*. Retrieved June 2003 from http://nces.ed.gov/programs/digest/

NCES (National Center for Education Statistics). (2002a). Elementary and secondary education. Dropout rates in the US: 2000. High school completion rates by race/ethnicity. In *Digest of Education Statistics, 2001*. Retrieved July 2003 from http://nces.ed.gov/programs/digest/

NCES (National Center for Education Statistics). (2002b). Elementary and secondary education. Percent of high school dropouts (status dropouts) among persons 16 to 24 years old, by sex and race/ethnicity: April 1960 to October 2000. In *Digest of Education Statistics, 2001*. Retrieved June 2003 from http://nces.ed.gov/programs/digest/

NCES (National Center for Education Statistics). (2002c). Postsecondary education. Total fall enrollment in degree-granting institutions, by type and control of institution and race/ethnicity of student: 1976 to 1999. In *Digest of Education Statistics, 2001*. Retrieved June 2003 from http://nces.ed.gov/programs/digest/

NCES (National Center for Education Statistics). (2002d). *Estimates of numbers and percent of public school teachers: 1999-2000*, derived from the Schools and Staffing Survey. Analysis conducted upon request, November 13, 2002.

NCES (National Center for Education Statistics). (2002e). Elementary and secondary education. Racial/ethnic distribution of public school students. In *Digest of Education Statistics, 2002*. Retrieved June 2003 from http://nces.ed.gov/programs/digest/

Newmann, R.A. (1994). Reconsidering emergency teaching certifications and alternative certification programs as responses to teacher shortages. *Urban Education*, *29*(1), 49-62.

Oakes, J., & Lipton, M. (1994). Tracking and ability grouping: A structural barrier to access and achievement. In J. Goodlad & P. Keating (Eds.), *Access to knowledge: The continuing agenda for our nation's schools* (pp. 187-204). New York: College Board.

Ohio State Legislative Office of Education Oversight. (1997). *Availability of minority teachers*. Columbus, OH: Author. (ERIC Document Reproduction Service No. ED 409 292)

Post, L.M., & Woessner, H. (1987). Developing a recruitment and retention support system for minority students in teacher education. *Journal of Negro Education*, *56*(2), 203-211.

Riley, R.W. (1998). Our teachers should be excellent, and they should look like America. *Education and Urban Society*, *31*(1), 18-29.

Rios, F., & Montecinos, C. (1999). Advocating social justice and cultural affirmation: Ethnically diverse preservice teachers' perspectives on multicultural education. *Equity & Excellence in Education*, *32*(3), 66-76.

Sheets, R.H., & Chew, L. (2002). Absent from the research, present in our classrooms: Preparing culturally responsive Chinese American teachers. *Journal of Teacher Education*, *53*(2), 127-141.

Shen, J. (1997). Has the alternative certification policy materialized its promise? A comparison of traditionally and alternatively certified teachers in public schools. *Educational Evaluation and Policy Analysis*, *19*, 276-283.

Sleeter, C. (2001). Preparing teachers for culturally diverse schools: Research and the overwhelming presence of whiteness. *Journal of Teacher Education*, *52*(2), 94-106.

Stewart, J., Meier, K., & England, R. (1989). In quest of role models: Change in black teacher representation in urban school districts, 1968-1986. *Journal of Negro Education*, *58*, 140-152.

Stoddart, T. (1993). Who is prepared to teach in urban schools? *Education and Urban Society*, *26*(1), 29-48.

Tellez, K. (1999). Mexican American preservice teachers and the intransigency of the elementary school curriculum. *Teaching and Teacher Education, 15,* 555-570.

Terzian, A.L. (1991). A model in community college transfer programs. *New Directions for Community Colleges, 19*(2), 87-92.

Tharp, R.G., & Gallimore, R. (1990). *Rousing minds to life: Teaching, learning, and schooling in social contexts.* NY: Cambridge University Press.

Tinto, V. (1998). Colleges and communities: Taking research on student persistence seriously. *Review of Higher Education, 21*(2), 167-178.

Tobin, K. (1998). Sociocultural perspective on the teaching and learning of science. In M. Larochelle, N. Bednarz, & J. Garrison (Eds.), *Constructivism and education* (pp. 195-212). NY: Cambridge University Press.

U.S. Department of Commerce. (1996). *Current population reports: Population projections of the United States by age, sex, race, and Hispanic origin: 1995-2050.* Washington, DC: Author.

U.S. Department of Education. (2001). *Bureau of the Census, October Current Population Surveys, 1972-2000.* Table 3-1 Percentage distribution of public school students enrolled in grades K-12 who were minorities: October 1972-2000. Retrieved July 2003 from http://nces.ed.gov/programs/coe/2002/section1/tables/t03_1.asp

Villegas, A.M. (1997). Increasing the diversity of the U.S. teaching force. In B. Biddle, T. Good, and I. Goodson (Eds.), *The international handbook of teachers and teaching* (pp. 297-336). The Netherlands: Kluwer Academic Publishers.

Villegas, A.M., & Clewell, B.C. (1998a). Increasing teacher diversity by tapping the paraprofessional pool. *Theory Into Practice, 37*(2), 121-130.

Villegas, A.M., & Clewell, B.C. (1998b). Increasing the number of teachers of color for urban schools. *Education and Urban Society, 31*(1), 42-61.

Villegas, A.M., & Lucas, T. (2002). *Educating culturally responsive teachers: A coherent approach.* Albany: SUNY.

Vining Brown, S., Clewell, B.C., Ekstrom, R.B., Goertz, M.E., & Powers, D.E. (1994). *Research agenda for the Graduate Record Examinations Board minority graduate education project: An update.* Princeton, NJ: Educational Testing Service.

Vygotsky, L.S. (1978). *Mind in society.* Cambridge, MA: Harvard University Press.

Waters, M.M. (1989). An agenda for educating Black teachers. *The Educational Forum, 53*(3), 267-279.

Wilson, S.M., Floden, R.E., & Ferrini-Mundy, J. (2001, February). Teacher preparation research: Current knowledge, gaps, and recommendations. Seattle, Center for the Study of Teaching and Policy, University of Washington.

Yopp, R.H., Yopp, H.K., & Taylor, H.P. (1992). Profiles and viewpoints of minority candidates in a teacher diversity project. *Teacher Education Quarterly, 19*(3), 29-48.

Zapata, J. (1998). Early identification and recruitment of Hispanic teacher candidates. *Journal of Teacher Education, 39,* 19-23.

Zeichner, K.M., & Schulte, A.K. (2001). What we know and don't know from peer-reviewed research about alternative teacher certification programs. *Journal of Teacher Education, 52*(4), 266-282.

Zirkel, S. (2002). Is there a place for me? Role models and academic identity among white students and students of color. *Teachers College Record, 104*(2), 357-376.

Zumwalt, K. (1991). Alternate routes to teaching: Three alternative approaches. *Journal of Teacher Education, 42*(2), 83-92.

CHAPTER 4

Teacher Preparation and the Improvement of Teacher Education

VIRGINIA RICHARDSON AND DIRCK ROOSEVELT

> There are, in their ultimate analysis, but three primary problems in education. The first is that of how properly to finance a school system. The second is how to secure a trained teaching force for it. The third is how to supervise it to produce leaders for its management and improvement. The financial one always underlies the other two.
>
> —Ellwood Cubberley, 5th Yearbook of the
> National Society for the Scientific Study of Education, 1906

The improvement of teaching and teacher education has recently become the central focus of national policies and legislation such as the No Child Left Behind Act of 2001 (NCLB, 2002). Concerns about improving the quality of the teacher workforce are offered as justification for, indeed an imperative for, a stronger federal presence in the regulatory processes of licensing, certification, and accreditation of teachers and teacher education institutions. Competing views and proposals about the ways in which the quality of teaching should be enhanced often focus both on the design and operation of the regulatory processes that screen individuals entering the profession and on the curriculum and characteristics of preservice teacher preparation programs. The states, meanwhile, struggle to assert their role and protect their prerogatives in the face of increasing federal pressure, sometimes in uneasy conjunction with professional organizations' parallel struggles. There is, then, a fight for control over the preparation of teachers and their entrance into the teaching profession, and, in fact, over the definition of quality teaching. In these conflicts, the educative aims of quality teaching—whether for K-12 youngsters or for those who would teach them—are often forgotten.

Virginia Richardson is Professor of Educational Studies at the University of Michigan and is currently a Visiting Scholar at the Carnegie Foundation for the Improvement of Teaching in Palo Alto, California. Dirck Roosevelt is the Director of Teacher Education and Assistant Professor at the University of Michigan.

Many of the solutions being pressed for and experimented with today focus on the teacher as being instrumental in a child's education and the key figure in (or target of) educational reform.[1] Although this may seem the obvious place to center attention, past reforms have often ignored the teacher. Previous solutions have focused on curriculum standards and content, input factors such as funding, and commercial instructional programs and materials sold as being easy to implement with short in-service programs.

However, this shift in focus to teaching and teachers has historical antecedents and might almost be characterized as a stage in a familiar cycle. Although some reform efforts of the 1960s, for example, sought "teacher proof" curricula,[2] the conviction that the teacher is the critical factor in schooling and that teachers' qualities and capacities must be directly engaged, appraised, and promoted can be found at the opening of the last century, in the deliberations of scholars concerned with understanding and improving public education, as our chapter epigraph suggests. The contributors to the 5th NSSE Yearbook (Holmes, 1906), for example, found the teacher to be categorically "the most important single factor in determining the efficiency of our educational system" (p. 8). It seemed to these scholars uncontroversially obvious that the consequentiality of teaching and the "educational rights of children" together make prospective teachers' academic and professional education, ethical standards, and attitudes toward democracy and its institutions of critical importance. Furthermore, teachers were subject to standards set and regulated by the state as conditions of entry, and properly so, according to the contributors (p. 8). Perhaps, then, we should approach our present task, and the current enthusiastic embrace of teaching as the most promising area for the improvement of schooling, with some modesty.

Today, most commentators, whether from the policy arena, within the profession, within the academy, or among the lay public, agree that, although curricula, standards, instructional programs, and funding are critical elements in the reform of education, the teacher is the one who must orchestrate all of these factors in a classroom, which is located within a school and a community that provide both unique and generic opportunities and challenges. Yet, a focus on teaching should not be allowed to lead to excessive and singular blame of teachers and teacher education for the failure of the educational system to educate to a desirable standard all students in the system. All critical elements, including the local context in which the schools reside and operate, must also be considered when addressing the quality of the teaching workforce specifically, and school reform generally.

The ideas we explore in this chapter ultimately revolve around improving the quality of the teacher workforce through the pursuit of two related goals: 1) teachers who are hired by school districts will have as beginning professionals the acquired knowledge, habits of mind, and skills necessary to meet the needs of the students within the particular contexts of the schools in which they teach; and 2) teachers will have dispositions and ways of thinking that will allow them to continue to develop their understandings and skills such that they continually improve their practice.

We discuss two types of approaches to meeting these goals: one regulatory, through licensing, certification, and accreditation; and the other educative, through preservice teacher preparation in its various forms. Regulatory approaches are examined as important elements of the policy context and in relation to screening individuals seeking entry into the teaching profession and improving preparation programs. When considering preservice preparation, we focus on the nature of teacher education programs and on what we might know or understand about the processes of learning to teach that might be of use to those engaged in teacher preparation, responsible for educational policy, or both.

However, in order to understand and make judgments concerning the nature of the various proposals and regulations designed to improve the quality of *teachers*, it is important to examine the work of *teaching*. Thus, in the next section we focus on fundamental considerations of the nature of good and effective teaching. We then place this discussion within the policy context of teaching and teacher education and describe how that context has changed over the last number of years. We follow this with descriptions of the various forms of regulatory activities and types of preservice teacher education and an account of recent research on certification and the effects of teacher preparation.

Finally, we present our conclusions, but with a caveat: Although we focus on preservice teacher preparation and teacher licensing and accreditation programs in this chapter, we do not assume that enhancing these alone will necessarily lead to an overall improvement of the teacher workforce, particularly in difficult-to-staff schools and school districts such as those in urban areas, unless other reform elements are also put in place. To rely solely on the improvements suggested in this chapter, we would have to count on the graduates of excellent teacher education programs to make the following decisions: 1) to teach, 2) to teach in a challenging district and school, and 3) to remain in teaching for more than three years. This would require a very different approach to preparation, recruitment, support, retention, and professional development than is currently in place. Our conclusions thus bring the teacher preparation focus of this chapter together with other elements that may lead to the improvement of the teacher workforce and make its deployment more equitable across urban, suburban, and rural districts.

The Work of Teaching

Characterizations of teaching abound. On the one hand, the meaning of *teaching* is often taken to be self-evident; on the other, it is represented as an "uncertain" craft (Floden & Buchmann, 1993; Jackson, 1986; McDonald, 1992), a "moral" endeavor (Hansen, 2001; Tom, 1984), a "process of human improvement" (Cohen, 1988), and increasingly today, a procedure of applied "science" (NCLB, 2002; U.S. Department of Education, 2002; and others). The existence and persistence of these multiple characterizations is itself noteworthy. We suggest that no one-dimensional account of what teaching "is" can suffice in the context of public schooling in America in the early 21st century. Thus, our account is both deeply structured and normative.

Teaching is at once:

- a purposeful, *ends-driven activity*;[3]
- a materially, historically, culturally, and politically situated *relationship*; and
- a complex, potent social *signifier* (an image of considerable symbolic value, a screen on which are projected multiple meanings, hopes, and fears).

It is a normative practice: ways of doing and thinking, shaped by beliefs and habits, entailing traditions of lore and skill, linked by the common intent of influencing the immediate and long-term dispositions, capacities, and conduct of the young, constrained by the need to manage the complex social dynamic of young people's involuntary presence in the classroom. Replete with attributes of a craft, it is nonetheless, like other human arts and "helping professions," value-saturated. It results in no product[4] and is irreducible to technique. It is a profession concerned with contested and elusive ends, bound up with the question of what kind of adults we want children to become, which has long been understood as equivalent to asking what kind of society we wish to live in, a question that is properly a matter of contention and debate (Hampshire, 2000). In this, teaching is unlike, for example, medicine, which is concerned with relatively stable ends (health, or the mitigation of disease) and is therefore susceptible, to a large extent, to progressively improved means. Teaching is more like a practice of philosophy[5] (addressed to ultimate questions and, as a discipline, not cumulative) than one of science (progressive, cumulative, organized around hypotheses that are, although unavailable to certainty, at least capable of falsification).

Teaching's status *as* a profession, meanwhile, remains debated. It is often valorized as an act of service and as a public trust—a tenuous notion today, when the social solidarity that would underwrite it is so little evident. On the contrary, community outrage when a teacher in Kansas sanctions high school students for cheating (Bellamy, 2002) and recurrent observations that families of color, in a school system still largely staffed by White teachers and administrators, feel that their children are positioned as "other" and withhold affirmation of school practices (G. McHaney-Trice, personal communication, May 16, 2003), for example, suggest that teaching's legitimacy is widely in question.

Given this general framework and these deeply structured dimensions of teaching, we do not offer a value-free discussion of teaching, which, even were it possible, would not take us far (Fenstermacher & Richardson, in press). Instead, we bring forward a number of distinctive, normative characteristics of teaching—features of the kind of work we find it to be—of special relevance for those charged with educating prospective teachers or formulating policy intended to shape teacher education.

Teaching is highly context-specific work. The classroom is shaped by what students and teachers bring with them, including both prior knowledge and the heterogeneous influences of cultures and of society. The classroom is a social setting in which students, each with distinctive experiences, interact with each other and with the teacher. It is axiomatic that each is equipped with desire, will, disposition, proclivities, skills, and shortcomings insofar as formal learning is concerned. All of these contextual factors strongly affect what it means to teach particular material to particular students in a particular time and place. And, of course, particular pedagogical purposes and disciplinary frameworks additionally, perhaps decisively, as Ball and others argue (e.g., Ball & Bass, 2000), constitute distinct contexts for teaching. Most of these variables are moving targets, as it were, though they do not move synchronously. In coming together in the classroom, they create a condition of simultaneity of meaning, perception, and action (Doyle, 1992; Lampert, 1985, 2001). Competing goods and multiple consequences, many of them invisible (Jackson, 1986), attend every pedagogical decision.

Contexts then are material, temporal, psychological, social, and, certainly, cultural. What a teacher *means*—certainly, how he or she is *understood*—is in part a function of the conceptions of authority, the roles of "teacher" and "student," and other manifestations and constructions of age and race and gender, that obtain in the students' worlds outside of school, inflected but not determined by those of the dominant culture (see, e.g., Ballenger, 1999; Delpit, 1988; Gee, 1989). A teacher cannot issue instructions, directions, or sanctions independent of this web of meaning, though he or she can make many choices about a stance toward it—assuming he or she has some understanding of it.

Teaching is relational work. Lampert (2001) persuasively defines teaching as "working in relationships." Her elegant model elucidates the density and interconnectedness of the relationships between student and student, student and teacher, and student and content. Here, we simply stipulate the ineluctably social dimension of teaching. Accounts of teaching from Socrates to Paley (e.g., 1990), along with scholarly treatments of Britzman (1991), Hollingsworth, Dybdahl, & Minarik (1993), Lampert, and others, demonstrate that the dynamics of power, attraction, and resistance; the nuances of giving and withholding recognition, voice, and assent; the poles of cooperation and autonomy; and the impossibility of complete privacy are not simply circumstances amid which some other activity (e.g., "imparting knowledge," "inquiry," etc.) takes place. They are material with which and from which knowledge and understanding, as well as confusion and error, are constructed.

As a manifestation of human relationship, classroom teaching has certain distinguishing features. The fact that students, until they are somewhere between 15 and 17 years old (depending on state regulations) in the United States and in many other countries, are involuntary parties to the relationship is certainly a key one, with special importance for what it means to teach and to learn to teach. That teaching is almost always understood to involve the teacher's elicitation and subsequent appraisal of student performances may be seen as a recurring manifestation of the willed/coerced, dominant/subordinate quality of the teacher-student(s) relationship. The teacher, moreover, is involved in a continuous public performance, although, as has often been remarked, that "public" is typically not an audience of peers.

Teaching is work premised on the teacher's possession of knowledge that is itself, as a central objective of the work, to be made available to students. Thus teaching necessarily enacts assumptions about the *nature* of knowledge and the nature of persons qua learners; these in turn entail assumptions about what it is to be human and to be young. Many arguments and assumptions are made about the contribution of subject matter learning to the purposes of schooling—that there are straightforward instrumental values, that it enables participation in humanity's "conversation" with itself (Oakeshott, 1990), that it is a site for the student's expansion of experience and realization of his or her own powers (Dewey, 1902/1956, 1938/1963), that it is a catalyst for the development of democratic culture (Roosevelt, 1998), that it is a medium of entry into the "discourse of power" (Delpit, 1988, 1992), that is a refuge of a certain form of equality in an inequitable system (Ball, 1995), that it serves as an occasion for learning the use of cultural tools (Egan, 1999), that it is intrinsically a source of delight, and more.

Bracketing these important questions, there is no doubt that the knowledge of some more or less specifiable "stuff" deemed valuable for learners is a precondition for teaching. There is in our time a now deep and broad investigation into the *kind* of subject matter knowledge necessary for teaching and what it means to know a subject in order to be able to teach it (Schwab, 1978; Shulman, 1986, 1987; and, more recently, with a review of much of the intervening work, Leinhardt, 2001). Shulman's construct of pedagogical content knowledge has given conceptual and, to an increasing extent, practical, purchase on challenges of pedagogy in teacher education that had previously been obscured. This is not to say that it has simplified them.

The design of instruction betrays a perspective (or several, as coherence cannot be assumed) on the nature of knowledge and the nature of learning at every turn. A view of knowledge as discrete, inert, more or less convertible with information, warranted by authorities far removed from the messiness of teaching and learning, although easy to caricature, remains discernible in many practices of teaching, curriculum, and assessment and useful as an analytic foil. Such a view positions the learner as a relatively passive consumer or recipient. Conversely, "constructivist" views of knowledge (see Phillips, 2000; Richardson, 2003) and "situative" perspectives on learning (see, e.g., Putnam & Borko, 2000) frame knowledge as a human product dependent on social norms and agreements, and position learning as an active, contextualized, participatory process.

These varying perspectives also entail a range of views on expertise and authority, the role of inquiry, and the proper quality of relationships between children and adults and children and each other (Hawkins, 1967/1974; Lampert, 2001; Roosevelt, 2003; Wenger, 1998). These are matters of both symbolic and concrete import.

Teaching is work that has moral significance (Fenstermacher, 1990b; Hansen, 2001; Noddings, 1992; Sockett, 1993; Tom, 1984). This fact flows directly from the relational essence of teaching, the question of how humans ought to treat one another, residing as it does at the heart of morality and ethics. The coerced presence of students in schools sharpens the moral implicature of teaching, which is perhaps expressed most obviously in the daily regime of "disciplinary" and "management" practices. But the fundamental moral proposition that we treat human persons as ends in themselves, not as means (Kant, 1785/1959) is a live issue at the deepest levels of schooling: for example, in the logic (touched on above) that finds a conception of knowledge to entail a conception of learning and of learners, which in turn entails a conception of persons as, for example, relatively passive objects of instruction or as active subjects capable of some self-determination. Indeed, whenever the quality of students' lived experience is subordinated to larger purposes—even such unassailable ones as the establishment of a good society—the challenge that we treat others as ends in themselves presses itself uncomfortably upon the teaching as it is both understood and enacted.[6]

In summary, and for all of these reasons, *teaching is work that entails judgment, and is agentive.* The simultaneity of thought and action in the classroom and the moral nature of the relational decisions compel a particular form of judgment that relies, in part, on the acquisition of practical knowledge gained from experience. It is called, variously, "thinking on one's feet," *phronesis* in the Aristotelian typology, "knowing with" (Broudy, 1977), "tact" (Van Manen, 1991), and "reflection-in-action" (Schön, 1988). Several of these concepts are informed by Dewey's (1933/1989) ideas about reflective thinking. Further, teaching is work that is performed by purposeful, deliberative actors attempting to engage the efforts and capacities of other actors, themselves possessed of desires, needs, and intentions. Agency, therefore, is an essential criterion of this work.

The implications of this picture for the professional preparation of teachers are considerable. Educating people of any age and aspiration to take full responsibility for the consequences of their purposeful and habitual actions in other people's lives may be said to be an unmet challenge—though it may also be said to lie at the heart of the democratic assumption and its expression in universal public schooling. Educating people, including prospective teachers just barely adults themselves, to see themselves as others see them (e.g., through multiple lenses of culture and value) and to consider how the meanings of their actions (e.g., instruction) are informed by those perceptions, is a challenge. So, too, is educating these same people to be wise managers of the human relationships in which they themselves are necessarily participant. And the ability to make knowledge accessible requires not only its possession in the first place, but its flexible possession: an understanding that its value for education is measured by its enrichment of students' and ultimately citizens' individual and communal lives and the teacherly ability to simultaneously command an overview of the subject at hand and appreciate the particular, context-bound understandings and needs of specific learners in order to identify potential links between the two (Ball, 1993; Dewey, 1902/1956).

These are complex challenges to which varied rational approaches can and have been taken, none of which can be said to be conclusively superior in all respects, for all contexts. Still, there are clearly *better* approaches that can be described and analyzed (as in, e.g., the AACTE/NCTAF-sponsored work of Darling-Hammond, 2000) and ways of conceptualizing the task that make it more manageable, by acknowledging, not reducing, its complexity (as in the work of Feiman-Nemser, 2001). However, the agentive work described above implies a certain degree of instructional autonomy and trust in teachers' judgments and decisions that is generally not present today. So there are problems nested within problems: The work in question is extraordinarily complex as well as contested as to its basic conceptualization and as to its loci of authority. There are multiple uncertainties about how best to prepare people to do this work, and it is quite probably ultimately to be performed in settings not hospitable to this complexity, conflict, and uncertainty. Or, in Labaree's (1998) words: "We ask teacher education programs to provide ordinary college students with the imponderable so they can teach the irrepressible in a manner that pleases the irreconcilable, and all without knowing clearly either the purposes or the consequences of their actions."

The policy context described in the next section reflects tensions between conceptions of teaching, for teacher education appears as a very different enterprise and problem depending on how teaching is seen. The situated, judgment-intensive, morally, socially, and culturally literate, agentive work described above will not be learned in the same fashion as the relatively straightforward technical activity, performed according to standards set by often-distant others, that teaching is sometimes understood to be. And a conception that suggests that teaching is a natural, spontaneous human capacity that is present to an effective degree in some identifiable subset of the population requires hardly any formal preparation at all. Choices about investment of resources in selection, preparation, retention, systems of evaluation, and research all may be seen to reflect, tacitly or otherwise, such differences in conception. Analysis that surfaces, and lends or withdraws warrant from, particular conceptions of teaching may also, it is hoped, inform such choices.

The Policy Context: The Shift to Nationalization

Since *A Nation at Risk* (National Commission on Excellence in Education, 1983), the policy world has sought to locate blame for what is viewed as the unsatisfactory academic performance of our K-12 students on various elements of the educational system and then to develop often one-variable procedures for fixing the problems. For a number of years, the focus was on teachers and schools, more recently on standards and assessments. Although these are of continuing concern in policy and practice, there has recently been a pronounced shift to teacher preparation.

As with the turning of attention to teaching and teachers, this shift toward their preparation has ample historical precedent. Early 20th-century promoter of a "science" of education Ellwood Cubberley and his fellow *Yearbook* editors and authors (Holmes, 1906) are again instructive. Cubberley and his colleagues blamed provincialism, immaturity of the field, excessive reliance on examinations, and inadequacies of preparation for the existence of a "great mass of poorly educated and poorly trained teachers who . . . work on low standards, work for small wages, and too often serve to discredit the name and work of a teacher" (Cubberley, 1906, p. 77). He called for a substantial, intellectually ambitious, and practically grounded professional education for teachers—*and* adequate funding—as the means of improvement. Committed to higher standards, he was wary of centralization (p. 48).

Today's shift in the culprit-focus from teaching to teacher preparation has led to some quite significant, often competing policy recommendations and decisions, some of which echo the arguments of a hundred years ago. Currently, two very different approaches to the improvement of teaching dominate policy debates on the topic. Although both work toward nationalization of elements of regulatory procedures, they are very different in their conceptions of teaching and teacher education (see also Cochran-Smith & Fries, 2001, for a discussion of these differences).

One perspective, which we call "natural teaching," is evident in recent federal government policies and pronouncements that attempt to reduce (or eliminate) traditional preservice preparation that takes place in schools and colleges of education and replace it with truncated "alternative" preparation that emphasizes subject matter knowledge.[7] The view of teaching inherent in this position was advocated by Stephens (1967) and described and critiqued by Murray (1996a). It suggests that teachers simply require subject matter knowledge in combination with a set of natural human tendencies such as "the tendency to talk about what one knows" (Murray, p. 4). Hiring teachers would involve assessing their subject matter understanding and their innate natural teaching tendencies. Thus, formal preparation in pedagogy is a nonissue, and gatekeeping logically bears the brunt of "quality control." And, as will be described below, there is a strong push to nationalize this gatekeeping function.

The second approach, which we label "professionalization," attempts to professionalize the quality of traditional preservice preparation through higher standards in and standardization of what are thought to be improved, evidence-based processes and accountability procedures. Teaching is seen as a highly complex profession that requires extensive preparation in a number of forms of knowledge and skills, including disciplinary (subject matter) knowledge, understanding of student learning, pedagogy, pedagogical content knowledge, social and moral foundations of education, and pedagogy for special populations of students. Coupled with this belief is a sense that the best (or perhaps only) way to improve teacher education is by standardization of what are thought to be effective teacher education processes through the setting of high standards and the administration of required assessments.

There are also those who find themselves advocating neither approach. These people believe that teaching is complex, and they approve strongly of quality preservice preparation of teachers. However, they fear the effects of national mandates such as standards and high-stakes testing. There is a deep concern among these practitioners and scholars that locating the process of standards setting and assessment development and implementation at the federal level will have a devastating effect on practitioners' sense of agency at the local level. As pointed out by Fenstermacher (2002):

There is a cost to democracies when decisions of consequence to all are appropriated at progressively higher political levels. The usual consequence is that those at the periphery feel disqualified from the debate and its resolution, thus experiencing a sense of powerlessness and concomitant disaffection. (p. 21)

Furthermore, our previous analysis of the work of teaching suggests that excessive or ill-considered constraint of practitioners' sense of agency inherently poses a threat to professional capacity and to the quality of teaching itself. For some of the people who feel these concerns, the improvement of preservice teacher education may be handled through extensive, deep, and context-relevant program assessments that focus, in part, on preservice students and what they take with them from the program.[8]

The perceived need to increase the quality of the teacher workforce strongly influences discussions of possible changes to the content, locus of responsibility, or both, for the regulatory processes designed to screen individuals seeking entry into the profession and to monitor teacher preparation programs. Traditionally, these processes have been the function of the individual states. However, the dissimilarity of regulatory procedures and criteria among the various states is thought to have led to great variance in the quality of teachers entering the profession, and there is concern that some school districts—notably, urban districts—are particularly hurt by this variance. That is, a higher proportion of entering teachers in urban areas are either not certified at all or are teaching "out of area" (i.e., in a subject other than the one in which they have been prepared) (Darling-Hammond, Berry, & Thoreson, 2001). In fact, it appears that some entering teachers in urban areas such as Houston are neither certified nor hold a bachelor's degree (Raymond, Fletcher, & Luque, 2002). Thus, the federal government and various professional associations are working toward standardizing, at the national level, the procedures for licensing teachers and accrediting teacher education programs. Although many of the assessments are, at this point, considered voluntary—that is, a particular state or school may or may not choose to use a particular examination process—there is considerable pressure from national policy leaders for states to adopt more standard approaches for licensing teachers and accrediting programs. For example, the board of the American Association of Colleges for Teacher Education (AACTE) has recently called for a common national assessment for all new teachers, regardless of the nature of their preservice teacher preparation (or lack thereof) (AACTE, 2003a).

A significant component of policy attention at present is thus focused on the state regulations for providing teacher education program approval, the national teacher education accreditation programs, and the licensing/certification of teachers. The next section will address these issues.

Regulation: Accreditation, Licensing, Certification

The regulatory procedures of licensing and certification undertaken at the state level function both to screen beginning teachers and to shape teacher preparation programs. Although the second function is often understated, there is no doubt that licensing and certification requirements can and do strongly affect teacher education curricula. Accreditation, however, is a process designed to directly affect the teacher education programs' structures and curricula by setting high expectations for and assessing teacher preparation institutions. Over the last several years, these regulatory functions have become more complexly linked than in the past, in part because of the increased emphasis on the use of standards and assessments in accreditation and competency testing in the licensing procedure.

Program Approval and Accreditation

Program approval and accreditation are two somewhat different processes, but the terms are often used synonymously. We pair them in this chapter because the two processes are coming ever closer together. Program approval is a mandatory state-level process. As part of its responsibility for teacher licensure, a given state uses a set of standards and criteria to examine each teacher education program and determine whether it should be approved. Until recently, candidates graduating from approved programs automatically received state licensing. More recently, however, in most states, students attending an approved institution also have to pass tests of basic skills, content, and/or pedagogy in order to receive a license. Again, until quite recently, this process was designed to license new teachers at a minimum level of expertise.

Accreditation, in contrast, is a voluntary national process run by the profession and designed to provide the public with assurance about the quality of teacher education preparation programs and institutions as well as to provide guidance to institutions for improving their programs. All teacher education institutions undergo state-level program approval processes, but all do not undertake accreditation review. In 1996, for example, somewhat fewer than half of the teacher education institutions in the United States were nationally accredited, although the accredited institutions prepared approximately two thirds of the new teachers (NCTAF, 1996).

Recently, however, there has been a substantial effort on the part of the oldest national accreditation agency, the National Council on Accreditation of Teacher Education (NCATE), to engage states in adopting NCATE processes for program approval. At present, 48 states have agreed to partner with NCATE in various ways and to use elements of the NCATE processes in their approaches. And several states now require institutions to undergo a national accreditation process, which may be altered somewhat to permit state standards to be examined.[9] As of recently, however, only four states required that all of their teacher education programs be professionally accredited (Darling-Hammond, 2001).

There are now two national accreditation organizations in the United States through which individual institutions may apply for accreditation. NCATE is the oldest council and has undergone several major revisions of its standards. For example, until very recently, NCATE standards focused on teacher education program elements and processes, but a 1987 reform led to the inclusion of standards in relation to the "knowledge base" for teaching.

A relatively new national organization, the Teacher Education Accreditation Council (TEAC), provides an alternative to NCATE. By adapting the concept of audit teams used in other parts of the world for the assessment of programs in higher education, TEAC aims to encourage colleges of education to define a quality program for themselves, within their own context and within a set of general standards specified by TEAC, and to conduct a self-assessment with respect to program effects on students' knowledge, skills, habits of mind, and moral virtues. The colleges are also expected to make a case for the validity of the evidence provided in the self-assessment. Those who advocate a TEAC approach to accreditation suggest that the opportunity for a program to develop and specify its own set of desired outcomes and assessments not only is of educative value within the program but also helps the assessment process account for contextual issues.[10]

NCATE has also increasingly focused some of its standards on performance outcomes; a very recent decision, however, has given priority to the standard related to knowledge of the curriculum content that the candidate will eventually teach. This is another indication of the degree to which the national government is attempting to standardize regulatory processes, standards, and assessments within the "natural teacher" model. To achieve legitimacy in the eyes of state governments, educational accreditation agencies must be recognized by the federal accreditation oversight panel of the U.S. Department of Education. Recently, that panel informed NCATE that in order to retain its recognition, NCATE must use exam pass rates as the primary factor in accreditation decisions. Thus, the NCATE board decided that, as a requirement of accreditation, 80% of the institution's teacher candidates must pass the content examinations used in their state's licensure decisions. Although NCATE stresses that other standards are important, the passing rate on the content examinations will undoubtedly be viewed as a priority standard (AACTE, 2003b). At present, NCATE is working with the Educational Testing Service to promote the PRAXIS examination for future teachers as a national model, if not a standard requirement, for NCATE-accredited schools.

Teacher Licensing and Certification

Although the terms *licensing* and *certification* are often used interchangeably in teaching, they are not in other professions (Roth, 1996). Licensing, as applied to teaching and other professions, describes a state's decision to permit an individual to practice his or her profession in that state. Certification, in other professions, is the recognition of high levels of competence. In teaching, however, there were until recently no certification procedures available for such recognition. Although advanced certification is now available with the National Board for Professional Teaching Standards,[11] the distinction between licensing and certification is not usually employed. We therefore use the terms interchangeably in this chapter to refer to the state's responsibility for screening candidates into the profession.

An individual who is interested in teaching can obtain a license to teach in a number of different ways, with both inter- and intrastate variations. Each of the following routes is typically accompanied by a requirement that the candidate pass one or a set of specified examinations, depending upon the particular state in which one is interested in teaching. Basic skills tests (sometimes required for program entry) are increasingly the norm (required in at least 40 states as of 2003), but subject matter tests are almost as common (34 in 2003, an increase of about 33% since 1990) (*Education Week*, 2003; see also NCES, 2003). Tests of pedagogical knowledge are less common (23 in 2003), performance assessments (a loosely defined category including assessment by portfolio) still less so (14 in 2003) (NCES, 2003).

1. Approved Program Certification: An individual attends an institution that runs a teacher education program that has received program approval from the state. The institution recommends the graduate to the state; the state issues the certification as a matter of course.
2. Emergency Certification: In times of teacher shortage, an individual may be granted short-term certification, directly by the state or by school districts in cooperation with the state.
3. Alternative Certification: Similar to an approved programs approach; institutions offering alternative certification programs (described in the next section) apply to the state for certification on behalf of their graduates.

It is also sometimes possible for an individual to apply directly to a state board of education for certification, typically by submitting a portfolio and other evidence of qualifications.

Alternative Routes to Certification

In the mid 1980s, so-called alternative certification programs were developed, in part, to deal with teacher shortages in a way that was considered to be better than emergency certification. It was thought that these programs would draw from a population of talented and educated college graduates who wished to switch careers or head directly into teaching without an extended preparation program.

Fenstermacher (1990a) offered four additional reasons for the development of these programs that suggest bids for control over the certification process and other political goals: 1) to "break the lock that teacher education institutions appear to have on entry into the teaching profession"; 2) to "provide political capital for politicians and policymakers who want to be identified with the school reform movement"; 3) to "offer a means for other actors, such as foundations and corporations, to become players in the formation of teaching policy"; and 4) to "increase the range of choices or alternatives available for career entry, consistent with the emerging, more pervasive political ideology favoring choice and deregulation" (p. 160). These reasons are still relevant today as the national policy apparatus ever more strongly encourages alternative routes to certification. Another rationale for alternative certification programs that has developed in recent years is that these programs would improve the quality of the teaching force, particularly in urban areas, by attracting an increasing number of African Americans, Latinos, and other persons of color into the profession.[12]

Alternative certification programs vary considerably. They range from very little pre-preparation, with an emphasis on in-the-field mentoring (e.g., Troops to Teachers, organized by the Department of Deense) and a radical reduction in pedagogical coursework, to 12-month, full-time, intensive programs, often located within colleges or universities. The latter programs, though dubbed "alternative," may and often do include clinical experiences and pedagogical coursework comparable in nature and quantity to that provided in "traditional" programs. Several states have developed alternative certification procedures beyond emergency programs, and the number of alternative certification programs is increasing. However, as pointed out by Humphrey et al. (2000), the percentage of teachers who are licensed through alternative certification programs (not counting emergency certification) is relatively low.

The push toward nationalizing teacher assessment and eliminating teacher education institutions from the licensing process has led to a new national alternative certification program. The American Board of Certification of Teacher Excellence offers a series of assessments to determine whether experienced professionals and military personnel who are interested in becoming teachers are qualified to do so. No evidence of formal professional preparation is required. The program has received the approval of and funds from the U.S. Department of Education and, effectively, the Secretary's imprimatur (U.S. Department of Education, 2003) and one state has now recognized this new certification process.[13]

The licensing of teachers is no longer accomplished solely through the approval or accreditation of teacher education institutions within a given state. Licensing also involves testing prospective teachers on content and pedagogical knowledge and sometimes their application of this knowledge. These new assessment procedures are discussed in the next section.

Assessment for Licensing

Current national concern about the quality of teachers has led to an increase in the use of competence testing in the licensing process. As mentioned, in 2003, 40 states required candidates to pass basic-skills tests in order to enter an accredited teacher education program or upon completion of the program. An increasing number of states are also developing tests for subject matter knowledge, and many have paper-and-pencil tests for pedagogical knowledge (*Education Week*, 2003). More recently, performance testing has been added to the battery of tests in a number of states.

Two big players in assessment for teacher licensing are Education Testing Service (ETS) and Interstate New Teacher Assessment and Support Consortium (INTASC). ETS has developed the PRAXIS series of assessments, which covers three assessment categories: academic skills, subject matter knowledge, and classroom performance. The classroom performance assessments require classroom observation as well as documentation prepared by the candidate and semi-structured interviews. This means that states using this assessment must provide all candidates with a temporary license so that their performances in the classroom can be evaluated.[14]

INTASC is a consortium of 30 states that developed a set of model standards for what every beginning teacher should know and be able to do. The INTASC licensing system includes a subject matter examination, a test of teaching knowledge, and an assessment of classroom performance through videotapes, sample lessons and assessments, and student work. A major difference between the PRAXIS and INTASC efforts is that ETS is a testing agency, whereas INTASC is not. States pay ETS to administer and assess ETS products; states wishing to use INTASC products pay INTASC a fee to do so and then administer and score the tests themselves.

Research on Certification

As all aspects of teacher education enter the political arena, the demand for the use of teaching practices and approaches to teacher preparation and licensure that have been validated through rigorous evaluation have grown quite loud.[15] The current calls for research that will provide evidence distinguishing more and less successful practices focus attention on the conflict between the two approaches to improvement of the teacher workforce that we have described—the natural teacher approach (no need for pedagogical preparation beyond subject matter), and the professionalization approach (requiring subject matter as well as strong pedagogical preparation in classes and in the field). That is, the question of whether traditional teacher education in colleges and universities produces better teachers than alternative certification programs that entail reduced numbers of pedagogy courses is a major concern among advocates for both approaches, but for different reasons. A second concern focuses on the certification process itself: Are state certification processes complex and antiquated, and are they therefore keeping out of the profession people who would, in fact, be quality teachers? The question of whether teachers who are licensed to teach through standard state procedures actually become better teachers than those who are not has also been of strong interest to advocates for both approaches.

However, the politicization and conceptual complexity of the issues appear to render these general questions quite meaningless when research is conducted, or when research findings are interpreted for policy purposes. For example, the Department of Education has been making a case for the reduction of pedagogical course requirements in certification processes and for rendering student teaching and attendance at schools of education optional (U.S. Department of Education, 2002). The department cites a report by Walsh (2001) that bases recommendations for reforming present certification programs on "solid research." Darling-Hammond and Youngs (2002), however, make a compelling case for the absence or misuse of research in the Walsh report.

At the same time, the various pieces of research used to suggest or deny that certification does, in fact, make a difference in the quality of teaching suffer deeply from conceptual and political problems (see recent reviews of the literature in Bracey & Molnar, 2003; Darling-Hammond, 2001; Humphrey et al. 2000; Wilson, Floden, & Ferrini-Mundy, 2001). Certification processes and requirements are remarkably different from state to state; therefore, examining certified versus noncertified teachers across states may be quite misleading. The term *certified teacher* in one state or study may include emergency certified teachers, or it may not. An *uncertified teacher* may be one who has been certified in one state but has recently moved to another that does not recognize that certification, or the so-called uncertified teacher may be one whose credential simply has not yet been processed by the state. The term *alternative certification* may include emergency certified teachers but usually doesn't.

Often, the term *certified teacher* is used to mean only teachers who have graduated from teacher education programs in institutions of higher education, as it was in the Laczko-Kerr and Berliner (2002) study that examined the differences in student learning between classrooms with certified teachers and those with uncertified teachers. Thus, for some analysts, certification is good because certified teachers attended a teacher education institution; for others, present-day certification regulations are bad for the same reason and also because it is thought that these regulations keep potentially excellent teachers out of the profession. Some studies compare the quality of certified teachers (and therefore teachers who have attended higher education teacher education programs) with alternatively certified teachers, even though most alternative certification programs are sponsored by institutions of higher education. Because of the lack of conceptual clarity as well as the often political motivation in the use of research to support a particular policy, a single study finding may be used to argue for teacher education programs and against them.[16] Therefore, any research that uses the term *certification* and relates the process to any indicators of quality teaching must be examined very carefully to determine both how the term is being conceptualized and the motivation for conducting the research.

Preservice Teacher Preparation

Earlier in the chapter, we suggested a number of characteristics of the work of teaching: It is context-specific, relational, morally significant, and agentive. At the same time, it is premised on the teacher's possession of knowledge and understanding of a content area and entails different forms of judgment, including the ability to think quickly on one's feet. The question of how a teacher education program can effectively prepare its students for this work is under heavy scrutiny today. As mentioned, there are those who feel that the most important—and perhaps only—element of a teacher's preparation relates to subject matter knowledge. Others feel that pedagogical preparation is even more important now than in the past, given both the current goals of educational equity and the daily requirements of higher order thinking. We find ourselves in the second group, and the next section explains why. Following this, we discuss the research on preservice teacher education and the effects of that research.

Why Require Preservice Teacher Preparation?

The question to be addressed in this section is whether preservice preparation beyond preparation in subject matter knowledge and a B.A. or B.S. should be a requirement for entering the teaching profession. This is not a question that would have been asked 10 or 15 years ago, but it is now a strong factor in national policy debates. Some pronouncements out of Washington even suggest that student teaching contributes little to the preparation of teachers.[17]

There are powerful reasons to advocate preservice teacher preparation as a necessity for fostering well-grounded beginning teachers who will continue to develop good and successful practices by reflecting on and inquiring into their experiences. All professions require preservice preparation because it is thought that there are foundational understandings, ways of thinking, and skills that should be learned prior to, and will be of help in, the first years of practice and that will provide the basis for further learning.

Our view of the nature of the work of teaching, as explicated in the characteristics that are outlined earlier in the chapter, suggests the need for (and the difficulty of) providing teacher education students with the appropriate knowledge, habits of mind, and skills they will need when they join the profession. An alternative to such preparation is a reliance on formula teaching that is not effective for very long, in part because the variation among students in any classroom requires that teachers use multiple and sometimes inventive approaches to ensure that all students learn. If teachers have little formal knowledge of education systems, student learning, action alternatives, and how these may or may not work together, they will not be able to generate immediate solutions for meeting the needs of all students.[18] Teacher preparation should introduce the dispositions and ways of thinking that allow the continued development of skills and of understandings and beliefs about teaching, learning, and subject matter. These qualities help beginning teachers become expert teachers who are both competent and centered in their work. In fact, studies that have examined the preconceived understandings and beliefs about teaching and learning that preservice teachers bring with them into their programs suggest that teachers without strong preparation programs that help students question and alter their beliefs will have a remarkably difficult time in the classroom and may not stay there very long (Darling-Hammond & Sykes, 2003).

Perhaps one way of becoming convinced of the importance of preservice teacher preparation is to spend time with committed and exemplary teacher educators. We are fortunate to be surrounded by such people and even more fortunate that they have written about their work. We also know of many, many exemplary teacher educators around the country and the world who engage in the scholarship of teaching and write for others about their work. For example, the teacher educators who are involved in subject matter methods courses bring together subject matter knowledge with pedagogical considerations. Their teaching combines a deep respect for and a focus on subject matter with a commitment to providing their students ways of thinking about and experiences in teaching and learning. Many use technology extensively in their courses, including videocases of teaching and learning. These cases help bring together formal and practical knowledge, which leads to a better sense of the subject matter and offers ways of involving students in the constructs and practice of the subject matter. The curricula in these classrooms engage preservice students in deeply intellectual and practical material that helps them understand the complex thinking and understanding that is required in classrooms today.[19]

Our experiences with excellent teacher educators who are committed to the improvement of teaching though the development of thoughtful, knowledgeable, skilled, and committed beginning teachers leads us to worry about elementary teachers who have not had such experiences prior to teaching. We also worry about their students.

Obviously, we are disposed in favor of preservice teacher preparation as a necessity beyond subject matter preparation, but we are also aware that some preservice programs are not particularly effective in preparing their students to become competent beginning teachers nor in providing them with the grounding to become experts over time. One way of improving teacher education is through the inquiry process. The next section focuses on research on and assessment of teacher education programs and processes.

Research on and Assessments of Teacher Preparation

Recently there have been a number of articles and reports that decry the dearth of viable research linking teacher preparation program structures and content to outcomes such as the knowledge, skills, and dispositions of the graduating teachers or the achievements of their students (Humphrey et al., 2000; Wilson, Floden, & Ferrini-Mundy, 2001, 2002). Humphrey et al., for example, stated that

In general, research directions for improving teacher preparation in the 1990s have focused on questions, issues, and methods that yield little guidance for the design of evaluations that are concerned with outcomes and accountability (p. 20). . . . The evaluative frame of mind has not yet penetrated teacher education programs (p. 30).

This seems quite remarkable given that there are a number of journals devoted specifically to teaching and teacher education (e.g., *Journal of Teacher Education* and *Teaching and Teacher Education*) and handbooks of research on teacher education such as Houston (1990), Murray (1996b), and Sikula (1996). Given the research that does exist, why is there not more rigorous research that focuses on outcomes?

One consideration in this inquiry revolves around the purposes of research on teacher education. For those who call for rigorous evaluative research requiring large-scale samples, the purpose appears to relate primarily to policy formation. For example, Wilson et al.'s (2001) research review was conducted in response to a request from the U.S. Department of Education to consider "five questions posed by policymakers, educators, and the public" (p. 4). Two of those questions concerned subject matter study and education coursework—pointing to the current policy tension regarding the nature of quality teaching. Whether or not the research or its review will immediately change the minds of those in a position to formulate policies related to teacher education—and there are those such as Cohen and Garrett (1975) who would suggest that research doesn't do that—it is felt that a solid argument in favor of or opposed to a particular policy issue cannot be made without the backing of rigorous research.

Wilson et al. (2002) define rigorous work within six categories of research: four quantitative, one qualitative, and one that can be either. The descriptions of rigor are in terms of traditional quantitative criteria. For example: "For experimental and quasi-experimental studies, they must have used random assignment to groups or some form of matching for entering characteristics" (p. 38). Such forms of research and criteria suggest large-scale and expensive research designs, usually well beyond the finances, sample size, and contexts of an individual teacher education program or teacher educator.

However, as pointed out by Florio-Ruane (2002) and others in alternative representations and in responses to the Wilson et al. (2002) article, there is more than one purpose for research on teacher education. In particular, some research helps those engaged in or interested in teacher education to understand its processes, structures, participants, contexts, and effects and how these aspects interact. The purpose of much of the research that leads to this understanding is to improve the many processes that make up a teacher education program. Although a considerable amount of this work is small scale, local (Florio-Ruane), and interpretive and is often self-study (conducted by teacher educators around their own programs), there is also a body of descriptive research that provides data on the nature of the teacher education system (e.g., Howey, Arends, Galluzzo, Yarger, & Zimpher, 1995; Howey & Zimpher, 1989). Much of this work was not cited in Wilson et al. or Humphrey et al. (2000), perhaps because of what might be considered a lack of emphasis on outcomes, lack of rigor, or a belief that it would be of little interest to policymakers. Nonetheless, this work can provide useful information and ways of thinking for the improvement of teacher education. This is particularly the case when articles that focus on the same processes and outcomes are brought together in a synthesis.

One such synthesis related to an outcome of teacher education focuses on preservice teacher beliefs and belief change. In some educational theories, belief change (in the philosophical sense of belief) is presented as the most important goal of teaching. For Green (1971),

Teaching has to do, in part at least, with the formation of beliefs, and that means that it has to do not simply with *what* we shall believe, but with *how* we shall believe it. Teaching is an activity which has to do, among other things, with the modification and formation of belief systems. (p. 48)

Fenstermacher (1979) extended this view to teacher education. He argued that one goal of teacher education is to help teachers and future teachers transform their tacit or unexamined beliefs about teaching, learning, and the curriculum into objectively reasonable or evidentiary beliefs.

A large number of small-scale, often qualitative studies exist that examine preservice teachers' beliefs and belief changes as they move through their programs. Syntheses of these studies suggest that preservice students' entering beliefs are often highly idealistic, loosely formulated, deeply seated, and traditional (Richardson, in press; Wideen, Mayer-Smith, & Moon, 1998). The results of efforts to instigate belief change in preservice teacher education, however, have been somewhat discouraging in that students hold on to their entering beliefs, acquired during years of experience as students (Bolin, 1990; Korthagen, 1988; Zeichner, Tabacknick, & Densmore, 1987).

Several of the studies did, however, report at least some belief change after one class or at the completion of the academic element of the program (Wideen, Mayer-Smith, & Moon, 1998). Elements that seem to make a difference in affecting beliefs in these classes include various attempts at bringing propositional and practical knowledge together through, for example, an accompanying practicum (field experience) that is well coordinated with the class (Featherstone, 2003); the use of cases, particularly videocases that bring K-12 classrooms visually into the university classroom (Lampert & Ball, 1999; Richardson & Kile, 1999); and the conceptual coordination of the program across classes (Feiman-Nemser, McDiarmid, Melnick, & Parker, 1989). Without these or similar program elements, it is doubtful that belief change will occur in the academic elements of teacher education programs.

Findings such as these are difficult to translate into policies that are set at a considerable distance from the practice of teacher education, although we might hope that such studies would help policymakers to understand the complex nature of the teacher education process and the problems inherent in designing policies that focus on one or two "magic bullets." At the same time, this research is critical to those who are actively engaged in the teacher education process and in structuring programs designed to foster well-grounded beginning teachers.

This analysis indicates that a variety of effects studies around teacher education are called for. Large-scale policy studies within relatively stringent criteria for rigor are helpful in considerations of policies that are formulated at the state and national levels and in providing evidence for arguments put forth within policy contexts. At the same time, small-scale studies that do not match the criteria used by those who are interested in teacher education research for policy purposes are nonetheless very important for teacher educators as they work to improve their programs. Such studies lead to or elaborate on theories that are useful in considering alternative preparation programs.

Putting It All Together:
Elements Required for Teacher Workforce Improvement

Early in this chapter, we distinguished between educative and regulatory approaches to the improvement of the quality of teaching. Regulatory approaches, in turn, can be subdivided into those aimed more or less directly at controlling the entry of *individuals* into the profession and those aimed at governing and guiding professional preparation *programs*. We suggested that neither the educative nor the regulatory route will necessarily or in isolation improve the quality of teaching in urban and other school districts, particularly those serving predominantly poor students and students of color. There are great shortages of qualified teachers in these districts, particularly in certain specializations such as mathematics and special education. However, as Darling-Hammond and Sykes (2003) point out, there is not an *overall* shortage of qualified teachers; rather, not enough qualified teachers are choosing to teach in these school districts, and those who do apply and are hired[20] often stay only a short time. Thus, strategies for solving these workforce problems must go beyond improving the preparation of individuals who may or may not eventually enter the teaching profession. Nor is gatekeeping an obvious solution. Inviting qualified people through the gates is certainly in order; however, persuading people to remain once they have entered is equally, or, indeed, more necessary.

Darling-Hammond and Sykes (2003) suggest that there should be national initiatives that focus on encouraging a more equitable distribution of the supply of qualified teachers across school districts through the provision of incentives to both prospective teachers and teacher preparation programs and partnerships, among other means. They urge that these initiatives should *not* include lowering teacher standards—for example, by allowing states to designate uncertified teachers as "highly qualified" as long as they have appropriate subject matter preparation and are enrolled in an alternative certification program.[21]

But although the equitable distribution and retention of qualified teachers are critical for improving the quality of the teacher workforce, teacher preparation can and should be improved. We think that such improvement is vastly more likely to occur if the quality of discussion about systematic, designed, and deliberate efforts to educate beginning teachers itself continues to improve and is accompanied by systematic inquiry. As over a century of scholarship and practice demonstrates, these are not simple or tractable matters. Clarity around effects research—that is, greater consistency and transparency of terms and categories (e.g., what is meant by "certified" or "alternative program")— would certainly help. We also need to observe a conceptual distinction between large-scale, necessarily crude effects research, and practice- and context-sensitive research aimed at understanding what learning to teach entails and how it occurs (and/or misfires).

It is also evident, we believe, that coherent and productive discussion of these issues properly rests in and returns to a consideration of the nature of teaching and learning and conceptions of *quality* teaching and learning. These are not matters that can be deeply investigated, far less addressed through policy and programs, absent discussion of purpose and beliefs. Finally, it seems clear that learning to teach, and the development of teaching as a profession on terms suitable to the nature of the craft and to its role in a system of mass compulsory public education, requires a conception of life-long learning and consideration of the school as a learning environment for teachers as well as students. In this we come back to our contention that neither regulation nor preparation alone can solve the teaching problems of our most hard pressed, under-resourced, schools. Various elements, then, must be considered if a satisfactory policy for improvement of the teaching workforce is to be designed.

Recruitment

The recruitment process in large urban areas should focus on two significant populations: the districts' own K-12 students and teacher education students whose values related to social improvement make teaching in urban areas of intellectual and moral interest to them. Although school administrators, teachers, and staff should be involved in the recruitment of the first population, students would perhaps view these efforts as more legitimate if community activists were also participants in the recruitment process. Integrating the practical wisdom of community activists into the process of recruiting students should start in middle school. As civil rights activist and educator Myles Horton suggested, "those who have the problem have the solution" (1990).

For the recruitment of individuals from the second population, we should learn from the current Teach for America program[22] and from Teacher Corps and other programs of the 1960s. Many idealistic college students attracted to these programs, now as in the 1960s, view teaching as a compelling activity and a venue for social improvement. Our own experience also suggests that there is a segment of the college-going population for whom the intellectual challenges of teaching, in combination with the social commitment aspects and the powerful human-relations component of teaching, are, if properly presented, a potential draw. For example, in a survey of preservice teachers, Watt & Richardson (2003) found that intrinsic factors related to personal interest in teaching as well as a perception of ability to teach were stronger motivators for entering the teaching profession than were extrinsic factors. Attention should be given to these and other similar findings during the recruitment process.

Thus, we should seek to tap into the persistent interest in social improvement among children of relative privilege and into the energy, commitment, and local knowledge of children of communities that historically have been and presently are underserved and misserved, too much of the time, by schools. These strategies, it is worth pointing out, imply an acceptance, if not an embrace, of the value dimension of teaching.

Professional Education Over the Worklife of the Teacher

Feiman-Nemser (2001) and others have suggested the importance of thinking about professional education in teaching as a continuum that spans the worklife of the teacher, from preservice through induction and finally into continued professional development.[23] Viewing professional education in this way contributes not only to the improvement of teaching, but, perhaps just as importantly in urban areas, to teacher retention. For example, research on California's Beginning Teacher Support and Assessment system suggests that teacher attrition in districts where this mentoring and assessment program is operating has dropped to less than 10% (Wood, 1999). Feiman-Nemser (2001) delineates the forms of knowledge that teachers should be focusing on in the three stages. These are summarized below with suggestions for processes that should be considered in implementing the attendant programs.

Preservice teacher education. As their central tasks during preservice teacher education—both traditional and alternative—students should 1) examine their own beliefs critically in relation to visions of good teaching; 2) develop subject matter knowledge for teaching; 3) develop an understanding of learners, learning, and issues of diversity; 4) develop a beginning repertoire of teaching strategies; and 5) develop the tools and dispositions to study teaching, including their own (Feiman-Nemser, 2001). Summaries of the literature suggest that programs for preparing students for urban settings should explicitly and deliberately address the characteristics of such settings and the teaching of students of color and should include professional development for teachers and administrators in the school in which students are interning (see Anders, Hoffman, & Duffy, 2001; Dilworth & Brown, 2001; Ladson-Billings, 2000; Richardson & Anders, in press). Of considerable importance in these programs is the nature of the attempts at conceptual coherence, both within the academic elements of the program itself and between the academic elements and the field experiences (Grossman, 2000). This suggests that the field experience should be extensive, focused, and well structured; and cooperating teachers, who exert great influence on the student teachers, should be well prepared for their role, as should the receiving school (Wilson et al. 2001; see also Darling-Hammond, 2000).

Induction years. Feiman-Nemser (2001) suggests that beginning teachers and programs designed to support them should focus on 1) learning the context—the students, the curriculum, and the school itself; 2) learning how to design a responsive instructional program; 3) learning how to create a classroom learning community; 4) enacting a beginning repertoire; and 5) developing a professional identity.

Mentoring programs should provide both psychological and instruction-related support, should be reasonably long-term, and should be developmentally appropriate for the beginning teacher. Hare and Heap (2001) also suggest that one-on-one mentoring and mandatory participation for all new teachers are important features of successful programs. According to the National Center for Research on Teacher Learning (NCRTL, 2000), mentoring within successful induction programs 1) is connected to a vision of teaching that is understood by all involved; 2) is informed by an understanding of how one learns to teach; 3) defines the mentoring role as a professional practice, not just a new and additional role for experienced teachers; and 4) is affected by the professional culture of the school and broader policies and values.

Professional development. Feiman-Nemser (2001) suggests that professional development beyond the induction years should help teachers to 1) extend and deepen subject matter knowledge for teaching; 2) extend and refine repertoires in curriculum, instruction, and assessment; 3) strengthen skills and dispositions to study and improve their own teaching; and 4) expand responsibilities and develop leadership skills, including mentoring of preservice and induction years teachers.

There are many summaries of professional development research that suggest characteristics of staff development programs that lead to change in teachers' beliefs and practices, and a few studies suggesting that these characteristics in turn lead to changes in student learning (Garet, Porter, Desimone, Birman, & Yoon, 2001; Hawley & Valli, 1999). These summaries also suggest that professional development should be long-term with follow-up and should involve buy-in from the participants as well as agreement on vision and goals. Further, an inquiry approach to professional development is thought to provide the possibility for deep changes in beliefs and practices.

However, urban areas present particular difficulties for implementing professional development programs that lead to successful change. Research on professional development programs described as successful—that is, programs in which teachers change beliefs and practice and their students appear to achieve more—are often based on small, very labor-intensive projects, with the researchers themselves working extensively with the teachers in a given school. It is difficult to determine how to turn this knowledge into efforts that involve many schools and teachers. Fishman, Marx, Best, and Tal (2003) have provided considerable insight into the problems and promise of planning and implementing a large-scale professional development program that maintains the characteristics of successful smaller-scale programs. Their program makes extensive use of technology, and they are developing teacher leaders to take on the role of facilitators and coaches.

What is important is that the teachers in the school system develop an intrinsic improvement orientation in which they continue to question their actions and add to their knowledge and understandings about their subject matter, their students, and the consequences of their actions. It is essential that the school district support teachers through programs that respect individual differences, autonomy, and expertise.

Retention

Resolving the problems of retention involves several steps. One is further inquiry: A fuller, more nuanced understanding of the issues is necessary. However, we know enough to wisely invest some intellectual and fiscal resources right now. As the work of Ingersoll (2001) and Darling-Hammond and Sykes (2003) show, shortages of teachers and disproportionate reliance on inexperienced teachers are situated, not global, problems that are associated first and foremost with poverty and race. Migration, not just simple attrition, for example, is a pronounced problem in under-resourced, administratively sclerotic, urban areas (thus, as we know, further penalizing poor and minority families). In few situations, though, would sustained, coherent, learning-and learner-focused professional development, along the lines just suggested, be superfluous; in the most hard-pressed districts, it is essential. The development of systematic and coherent programs that both provide mentorship to beginning teachers and support experienced teachers in their continued learning is perhaps the step with the greatest probability of implementation and success at this time. Consistent with Ingersoll's (e.g., 2001) findings, a third and more complex step toward the resolution of retention problems is to change the culture of schools, making them places where teachers' judgments, deliberations, and inquiries are at the heart of an environment conducive to "professional citizenship" (Roosevelt, 2003; see also McLaughlin & Talbert, 2001; Meier, 2002).

In any event, although increases in teacher salaries are in order, as New York City's recent experience demonstrates (see also Kelley & Finnigan, chapter 8, this volume), as are other material incentives (for example, all schools should be physically decent and humane settings), it is clear that retention requires considerably more. It requires, for teachers, a sense that the school districts care about their struggles, rejoice in their successes, and are willing to support their efforts at improvement through programs that are based on a deep understanding of how teachers learn over their work life.

Conclusions

This chapter points to two trends concerning teacher education that appear to be in some conflict in the development of workforce policy, but which could and should work together in the improvement of the education of teachers and students. The first relates to major gains in the development of a better understanding of the nature of teaching and learning to teach, particularly around approaches to teaching and learning that honor independent, complex, and educationally and morally sound thinking and action. The second is an increased interest in and concern about teaching and teacher education within the policy contexts of government as well as the profit and nonprofit sectors of the economy.

On one hand, the concept of teaching that frames this chapter leads to a sense of the need for individual autonomy and context-specific educational decision making. It suggests that teachers and teacher educators should be treated as professionals and experts, and that they should be allowed the dignity and autonomy to make educative decisions within their classrooms, schools, and programs. The improvement of teaching and teacher education within this conception of teaching requires support for in-depth involvement of the professionals in assessing their goals, beliefs, and classroom actions and support for improvement through individual and group reflection and experimentation. This conception of teaching, however, may lead to a sense of highly individualistic goals, curricula, methods, and outcomes that will make it particularly difficult for students to move from one grade to another, or from one school to another school. Although it is possible to think in terms of collective autonomy (Little, 1992; Pendlebury, 1990), this conception presents a challenge for policymakers as they contemplate local, state, and national policies that would support such improvement programs.

On the other hand, the increased politicization of teaching and teacher education is leading to attempts at overall improvement of teaching through the institution of national and state standards and assessments. A potential, indeed, predictable, outcome of such policies is the standardization of teaching practices that are noneducative (such as teaching to the test), inappropriate for a particular context, or both. The national and nationalization efforts cannot take into account the complexity and context-specific nature of teaching and teacher education and will undoubtedly lead to unintended negative consequences.

The question, then, is how to set workforce development policies and practices that operate somewhere between the extremes of individual autonomy, derived in part from research based on individual teacher learning, and national standards for practice, which by necessity reduce the importance of context. This process requires an understanding that accountability must accompany autonomy and that students need some stability in goals, approaches, and curriculum structure as they move from grade to grade, school to school, and perhaps even state to state.

What we suggest is a middle-level approach to workforce development policies—that is, one that provides for accountability at the local level but also allows for strong context differences. Most importantly, these policies should be framed with the goal of providing conditions of professional dignity and appropriate autonomy for the individual teachers who make up the workforce. The conception of teaching should neither be one of technical work nor one of an enlightened but amateur approach to a natural task. Instead, what is called for is a "public intellectual" conception that is more appropriate to the work of teaching and that allows for the understanding of the teaching act as one that creates an empowering and enlightened classroom for our children.

AUTHORS' NOTE

We thank Karen Corvino, Gary Fenstermacher, and Donald Kollisch for their contributions.

NOTES

1. For example, the National Commission on Teaching and America's Future (NCTAF, 1996) states: "what teachers know and can do is the most important influence on what students learn" (p. iv).

2. For example, Jerome Bruner's *The Process of Education* (1960/1977) gave a compelling and influential account of reform via curriculum. (The 1977 edition includes a brief apologia for having given insufficient consideration to the role of the teacher.)

3. By which we do not mean to take a utilitarian stance: as folk wisdom rightly says, in human affairs, ends cannot escape their means.

4. Unless test scores have (as a veteran teacher recently said to one of us) become its products. We take it as given that it is not acceptable to refer to human beings themselves as "products."

5. A Deweyan conception (Dewey, 1916/1966), not to mention a Socratic one, at odds with more scientist views now prevailing (as, for example, Reid Lyon's: see AACTE, 2002, p. 7).

6. Thanks to Helen Featherstone (personal communication) for helping clarify this.

7. In a speech that introduced the report *Meeting the Highly Qualified Teachers Challenge* (U.S. Department of Education, 2002), Secretary of Education Rodney Paige stated: "We now have concrete evidence that smart teachers with solid content knowledge have the greatest effect on student achievement" (Keller & Galley, 2002, p. 25). The report itself suggests that certification be redesigned to focus on teachers' verbal ability and content knowledge, and to reduce the emphasis on pedagogy.

8. See, for example, the Teacher Education Accreditation Council's (TEAC, www.teac.org) approach to accreditation (Murray, 1999) and the Delta Project, funded

by the Carnegie Commission for the Improvement of Teaching (http://www.carnegie foundation.org/TeacherEd/index.htm).

9. See, for example, the literature on the three forms of state partnerships with NCATE, available at http://www.ncate.org/partners/3types.htm

10. See the TEAC procedures for accreditation in Murray (1999); also available at http://teac.org/literature/wingspread.pdf

11. See http://www.nbpts.org/ for a description of the board.

12. See Humphrey et al. (2000) and Wilson, Floden, & Ferrini-Mundy (2001), who suggest that some alternative programs are, indeed, attracting prospective teachers of color at a somewhat greater rate than "traditional" programs are.

13. See http://www.abcte.org/passport.html. At the time of the first draft of this chapter, two states were involved. However, one of these states—Pennsylvania—has reversed course, requiring that candidates who have passed the ABCTE nonetheless enroll in a state-approved program for the specific purpose of having a supervised student teaching or internship experience (Keller, 2004, p. 10).

14. For information about PRAXIS, see http://ets.org/praxis/

15. Note that practitioners in other fields may find educators' calls for "evidence-based" approaches somewhat naive at times. Nuland (2002), a clinical professor of surgery at Yale, for example, disparages "claims that the new so-called 'evidence-based' medicine, in which decisions are said to emerge from a review of all pertinent studies . . . can somehow convert diagnosis and therapeutics into an exact science" (p. 11). He continues by saying that medicine "is not a science at all. It (is) . . . an art that uses science as well as it can" (p. 11). In the *British Medical Journal*, Smith (1991) estimated that "only about 15% of medical interventions are supported by solid scientific evidence" (p. 798); see also Millenson (1997).

16. The Goldhaber and Brewer (2000) article, for example, is used by the U.S. Department of Education (2002) to argue that subject matter degrees have a greater effect on student achievement than certification in subject matter. Darling-Hammond & Youngs (2002), however, suggest that this same study "found strong influences of teacher certification on student achievement in high school mathematics and science, above and beyond the effects of teachers' subject matter degrees" (p. 16).

17. In the *Secretary's Annual Report on Teacher Quality* of 2002, for example, readers are advised that "unpaid student teaching" is a "hurdle" that does not lead to "improved quality . . . according to the best available current research" (U.S. Department of Education, 2002, p. 40). The *Second Annual Report* is both more positive and more cautious. The assertion that "training in pedagogy (and) the amount of time spent practice teaching . . . have yet to be linked to increases in student achievement" (U.S. Department of Education, 2003, p. 2) is followed by the "caveat" that "neither last year's report nor the present report contend that attributes like training in pedagogy or time spent in the field practice teaching are not valuable. All the reports suggest is that the evidence linking these attributes to increases in student achievement is weak, and certainly not as strong as the evidence linking general cognitive ability, experience and content knowledge to teacher effectiveness" (p. 3).

18. Jere Brophy (1976) once suggested that we should work toward a Merck Manual in teaching that every teacher could have on his or her desk. The Merck Manual in medicine provides information on diagnosing medical conditions that takes into account a number of variables for each diagnosis. But there is no longer a sense that this would be possible in teaching.

19. Examples of such work are found in Bain (2001), Davis (2002), Feiman-Nemser & Featherstone (1992), Lampert & Ball (1999), and others. There is also wonderful work at many other institutions here and abroad. See Loughran, Hamilton, LaBoskey & Russell (in press) for thorough descriptions and explications of the self-study movement.

20. A recent study of urban school district hiring practices found that many highly qualified teachers do apply for positions in urban schools, but these school districts wait too long to hire new teachers. Thus, the applicants accept positions elsewhere (Levin & Quinn, 2003).

21. We found this notion in several Department of Education Requests for Proposals. Darling-Hammond and Sykes (2003) refer to the following: 34 C.F.R. pt. 200, Fed. Reg., vol. 67, no. 231, p. 71,712 (Dec. 2, 2002).

22. See http://www.teachforamerica.org/certification.html

23. Again, there is precedent for taking this long view: The editors of the 5th NSSE Yearbook suggested that a good system for selecting qualified teachers might also be expected to aid in "keeping them alive professionally" once they are appointed (Holmes, 1906, p. 10).

REFERENCES

AACTE (American Association of Colleges for Teacher Education). (2002, December). Report calls for rigorous evidence, randomized trials in education. *AACTE Briefs, 23*(17), 1, 7.

AACTE (American Association of Colleges for Teacher Education). (2003a, March). AACTE accountability statement. Retrieved December 17, 2003, from http://aacte.org/Membership_Governance/accountabilitystmt.htm

AACTE (American Association of Colleges for Teacher Education). (2003b, May). President's comments. *AACTE Briefs, 24*(6), 2, 3.

Anders, P., Hoffman, J., & Duffy, G. (2000). Teaching teachers to teach reading: Paradigm shifts, persistent problems, and challenges. In M. Kamil, P. Mosenthal, P.D. Pearson, & R. Barr (Eds.), *Handbook of reading research* (Vol. 3, pp. 719-742). Mahwah, NJ: Erlbaum.

Bain, R.B. (2001). *Characterizing and developing subject matter and pedagogical reasoning in history methods class.* Paper presented at the annual meeting of the American Educational Research Association, Seattle, WA.

Ball, D.L. (1993). With an eye on the mathematical horizon: Dilemmas of teaching elementary school mathematics. *Elementary School Journal, 93*(4), 373-397.

Ball, D.L. (1995). Transforming pedagogy—Classrooms as mathematical communities: A response to Lensmire and Pryor. *Harvard Educational Review, 65*(4), 670-677.

Ball, D.L., & Bass, H. (2000). Interweaving content and pedagogy in teaching and learning to teach: Knowing and using mathematics. In *Multiple perspectives on the teaching and learning of mathematics* (pp. 83-104). Westport, CT: Ablex.

Ballenger, C. (1999). *Teaching other people's children: Literacy and learning in a bilingual classroom.* New York: Teachers College Press.

Bellamy, C. (2002). Teacher resigns in plagiarism case. *Associated Press Online.* Retrieved November 19, 2003, from LexisNexis database.

Bolin, F. (1990). Helping student teachers think about teaching: Another look at Lou. *Journal of Teacher Education, 41*(1), 10-19.

Bracey, G.W., & Molnar, A. (2003). *Recruiting, preparing and retaining high quality teachers: An empirical synthesis.* Tempe, AZ: Educational Policy Studies Laboratory, College of Education, Arizona State University. Retrieved December 15, 2003, from http://edpolicylab.org

Britzman, D. (1991). *Practice makes practice: A critical study of learning to teach.* Albany: SUNY Press.

Brophy, J. (1976). Reflections on research in elementary schools. *Journal of Teacher Education, 27*, 31-34.

Broudy, H.S. (1977). Types of knowledge and purposes of education. In R.C. Anderson, R.J. Spiro, & W.E. Montague (Eds.), *Schooling and the acquisition of knowledge* (pp. 1-17). Hillsdale, NJ: Erlbaum.

Bruner, J. (1960/1977). *The process of education.* Cambridge, MA: Harvard University Press.

Cochran-Smith, M., & Fries, M.K. (2001). Sticks, stones, and ideology: The discourse of reform in teacher education. *Educational Researcher, 30*(8), 3-15.

Cohen, D.K. (1988). *Teaching practice: Plus ça change* (Issue Paper 88-3). East Lansing: Michigan State University, National Center for Research on Teacher Education.

Cohen, D.K., & Garrett, M. (1975). Reforming educational policy with applied social research. *Harvard Educational Review, 45*(1), 17-43.

Cubberley, E.P. (1906). The certification of teachers: A consideration of present conditions with suggestions to future improvement. In M.J. Holmes (Ed.), *The 5th yearbook of the National Society for the Scientific Study of Education*, Part II (pp. 47-88). Bloomington, IL: Public School Publishing Company.

Darling-Hammond, L. (Ed.). (2000). *Studies of excellence in teacher education.* New York: American Association of Colleges for Teacher Education.

Darling-Hammond, L. (2001). Standard setting in teaching: Changes in licensing, certification, and assessment. In *Handbook of research on teaching* (4th ed., pp. 751-776). Washington, DC: American Educational Research Association.

Darling-Hammond, L., Berry, B., & Thoreson, A. (2001). Does teacher certification matter? Evaluating the evidence. *Education Evaluation and Policy Analysis, 23*(1), 57-77.

Darling-Hammond, L., & Sykes, G. (2003, September 17). Wanted: A national teacher supply policy for education: The right way to meet the "highly qualified teacher" challenge. *Education Policy Analysis Archives, 11*(33). Retrieved September 16, 2003, from http://epaa.asu.edu.epaa/v11n33

Darling-Hammond, L., & Youngs, P. (2002). Defining "highly qualified teachers": What does "scientifically-based research" actually tell us? *Educational Researcher, 31*(9), 13-25.

Davis, B. (2002). Scaffolding prospective elementary teachers in critiquing and refining instructional materials for science. In P. Pell, R. Stevens, & T. Satwicz (Eds.), *Proceedings of the fifth international conference of the Learning Sciences (ICLS)*. Seattle, WA: Lawrence Erlbaum.

Delpit, L.D. (1988). The silenced dialogue: Power and pedagogy in educating other people's children. *Harvard Educational Review, 58*(3), 280-298.

Delpit, L.D. (1992). Acquisition of literate discourse: Bowing before the master? *Theory Into Practice, 31*(4), 296-302.

Dewey, J. (1902/1956). *The child and the curriculum.* Chicago: University of Chicago Press.

Dewey, J. (1916/1966). *Democracy and education.* New York: Macmillan.

Dewey, J. (1933/1989). How we think. In J.A. Boydston (Ed.), *The later works, 1925-1953* (Vol. 8, pp. 105-352). Carbondale: Southern Illinois University Press.

Dewey, J. (1938/1963). *Experience and education.* New York: Collier/Macmillan.

Dilworth, M., & Brown, C. (2001). Consider the difference: Teaching and learning in culturally rich schools. In V. Richardson (Ed.), *Handbook of research on teaching* (4th ed., pp. 643-667). Washington: American Educational Research Association.

Doyle, W. (1992). Curriculum and pedagogy. In P. Jackson (Ed.), *Handbook of research on curriculum* (pp. 486-516). New York: Macmillan.

Education Week. (2003). Quality counts 2003: The teacher gap. *Education Week on the Web, 22*(17), 90. Retrieved February 15, 2004, from http://www.edweek.org/sreports/qc03/reports/quality-t1.cfm

Egan, K. (1999). Education's three old ideas, and a better idea. *Journal of Curriculum Studies, 31*(3), 257-267.

Featherstone, H. (2003, April). *Preparing teachers of elementary math: Evangelism or education?* Paper presented at the annual meeting of the American Educational Research Association, Chicago.

Feiman-Nemser, S. (2001). Preparation to practice: Designing a continuum to strengthen and sustain teaching. *Teachers College Record, 103*(6), 1013-1055.

Feiman-Nemser, S., & Featherstone, H. (Eds.). (1992). *Exploring teaching: Reinventing an introductory course.* New York: Teachers College Press.

Feiman-Nemser, S., McDiarmid, G.W., Melnick, S.L., & Parker, M. (1989). *Changing beginning teachers' conceptions: A description of an introductory teacher education course* (Research Rep. No. 89-1). East Lansing: Michigan State University, National Center for Research on Teacher Education.

Fenstermacher, G. (1979). A philosophical consideration of recent research on teacher effectiveness. In L.S. Shulman (Ed.), *Review of research in education* (Vol. 6, pp. 157-185). Itasca, IL: Peacock.

Fenstermacher, G. (1990a). The place of alternative certification in the education of teachers. *Peabody Journal of Education, 67*(3), 155-182.

Fenstermacher, G. (1990b). Some moral considerations on teaching as a profession. In J.L. Goodlad, R. Soder, & K.A. Sirotnik (Eds.), *The moral dimensions of teaching* (pp. 130-151). San Francisco: Jossey-Bass.

Fenstermacher, G. (2002). Reconsidering the teacher education reform debate: A commentary on Cochran-Smith and Fries. *Educational Researcher, 31*(6), 20-22.

Fenstermacher, G., & Richardson, V. (in press). Determinations of quality in teaching. *Teachers College Record*.

Fishman, B., Marx, R., Best, S., & Tal, R. (2003). Linking teacher and student learning to improve professional development in systemic reform. *Teaching and Teacher Education, 19*, 643-658.

Floden, R., & Buchmann, M. (1993). Between routines and anarchy: Preparing teachers for uncertainty. In *Detachment and concern: Conversations in the philosophy of teaching and teacher education* (pp. 211-221). New York: Teachers College Press.

Florio-Ruane, S. (2002). More light: An argument for complexity in studies of teaching and teacher education. *Journal of Teacher Education 53*(3), 205-215.

Garet, M., Porter, A., Desimone, L., Birman, B., & Yoon, K. (2001). What makes professional development effective? Results from a national sample of teachers. *American Educational Research Journal, 38*(4), 915-945.

Gee, J.P. (1989). (Tech. Rep. No. 2). Newton, MA: Literacy Institute, Educational Development Center.

Goldhaber, D.D., & Brewer, D.J. (2000). Does teacher certification matter? High school teacher certification status and student achievement. *Educational Evaluation and Policy Analysis, 22*(2), 129-146.

Grossman, P. (2000). Thoughts on evaluation of partnerships grants program. [Memo to United States Department of Education.] Washington, DC: U.S. Department of Education.

Green, T. (1971). *The activities of teaching*. New York: McGraw Hill.

Hansen, D.T. (2001). Teaching as a moral activity. In V. Richardson (Ed.), *Handbook of research on teaching* (4th ed., pp. 826-857). Washington, DC: American Educational Research Association.

Hampshire, S. (2000). *Justice is conflict*. Princeton, NJ: Princeton University Press.

Hare, D., & Heap, J.L. (2001). *Effective teacher recruitment and retention strategies in the Midwest: Who is making use of them?* Chicago: North Central Regional Educational Laboratory.

Hawkins, D. (1967/1974). I, thou, and it. In *The informed vision: Essays on learning and human nature* (pp. 48-62). New York: Agathon.

Hawley, W., & Valli, L. (1999). The essentials of effective professional development. In L. Darling-Hammond & G. Sykes (Eds.) *Teaching as the learning profession: Handbook of policy and practice* (pp. 127-150). San Francisco: Jossey-Bass.

Hollingsworth, S., Dybdahl, M., & Minarik, L.T. (1993). By chart and chance and passion: The importance of relational knowing in learning to teach. *Curriculum Inquiry, 23*(1), 5-35.

Holmes, M.J. (Ed.). (1906). *The fifth yearbook of the National Society for the Scientific Study of Education*. Bloomington, IL: Public School Publishing Company.

Horton, M. (with Kohl, J., & Kohl, H.). (1990). *The long haul*. New York: Doubleday.

Houston, R. (Ed.). (1990). *Handbook of research on teacher education*. New York: Macmillan.

Howey, K., Arends, R., Galluzzo, G., Yarger, S., & Zimpher, N. (1995). *RATE VIII: Teaching teachers—relationships with the world of practice*. Washington, DC: American Association of Colleges for Teacher Education.

Howey, K., & Zimpher, N. (1989). *Profiles of preservice teacher education: Inquiry of the nature of programs*. Albany, NY: SUNY Press.

Humphrey, D., Adelman, N., Esch, C., Riehl, L., Shields, P., & Tiffany, J. (2000). *Preparing and supporting new teachers: A literature review*. Menlo Park, CA: SRI International.

Ingersoll, R.M. (2001). Teacher turnover and teacher shortages: An organizational analysis. *American Educational Research Journal, 38*(3), 499-534.

Jackson, P.W. (1986). *The practice of teaching*. New York: Teachers College Press.

Kant, I. (1959). *Foundations of the metaphysics of morals* (L.W. Beck, Trans.). Indianapolis: Library of Liberal Arts (Bobbs-Merrill). (Original work published 1785.)

Keller, B. (2004). Alternative teacher licensing exam has setback in Pa. *Education Week*, 23(20), 10.

Keller, B., & Galley, M. (2002, June 19). Paige uses report as a rallying cry to fix teacher education. *Education Week*, p. 25.

Korthagen, F.A.J. (1988). The influence of learning orientations on the development of reflective teaching. In J. Calderhead (Ed.), *Teachers' professional learning* (pp. 35-50). Philadelphia: Falmer.

Labaree, D. (1998). *The peculiar problems of preparing teachers: Old hurdles to the new professionalism*. Paper presented at the Professional Actions and Cultures of Teaching, Hong Kong.

Laczko-Kerr, I., & Berliner, D.C. (2002). The effectiveness of "Teach For America" and other under-certified teachers on student academic achievement: A case of harmful public policy. *Educational Policy Analysis Archives*. Retrieved October 11, 2003, from http://epaa.asu.edu/epaa/v10n37.html

Ladson-Billings, G. (2000). Fighting for our lives: Preparing teachers to teach African-American students. *Journal of Teacher Education*, 51(3), 206-214.

Lampert, M. (1985). How do teachers manage to teach? *Harvard Educational Review*, 55(2), 178-194.

Lampert, M. (2001). *Teaching problems and the problems of teaching*. New Haven: Yale University Press.

Lampert, M., & Ball, D. (1999). *Investigating teaching: New pedagogies and new technologies for teacher education*. New York: Teachers College Press.

Leinhardt, G. (2001). Instructional explanations: A commonplace for teaching and location for contrast. In V. Richardson (Ed.), *Handbook of research on teaching* (pp. 333-357). Washington, DC: American Educational Research Association.

Levin, J., & Quinn, M. (2003). *Missed opportunities: How we keep high-quality teachers out of urban classrooms*. New York: New Teacher Project.

Little, J. (1992). The black box of professional community. In A. Lieberman (Ed.), *The changing contexts of teaching. The Ninety-first yearbook of the National Society for the Study of Education*, Part I (pp. 157-178). Chicago: National Society for the Study of Education.

Loughran, J.L., Hamilton, M.L., LaBoskey, V.K., & Russell, T.L. (Eds.). (in press). International handbook of self-study of teaching and teacher education practices. The Netherlands: Kluwer Academic Publishers.

McDonald, J.P. (1992). *Teaching: Making sense of an uncertain craft*. New York: Teachers College Press.

McLaughlin, M., & Talbert, J. (2001). *Professional communities and the work of high school teaching*. Chicago: University of Chicago Press.

Meier, D. (2002). *In schools we trust: Creating communities of learning in an era of testing and standardization*. Boston: Beacon.

Millenson, M.L. (1997). Demanding medical excellence: Doctors and accountability in the information age. Chicago: University of Chicago Press.

Murray, F. (1996a). Beyond natural teaching: The case for professional education. In F. Murray (Ed.), *The teacher educators' handbook: Building a knowledge base for the preparation of teachers* (pp. 3-13). San Francisco: Jossey-Bass.

Murray, F. (Ed.) (1996b). *The teacher educators' handbook: Building a knowledge base for the preparation of teachers*. San Francisco: Jossey-Bass.

Murray, F. (1999) *Accreditation reform and the preparation of teachers for a new century*. Paper presented at the Wingspread Conference: New Teachers for a New Century, Racine, Wisconsin.

National Commission on Excellence in Education. (1983). *A nation at risk: The imperative for educational reform*. Washington, DC: U.S. Department of Education.

NCES (National Center for Education Statistics). (2003, May). Statistics in brief. Washington DC: U.S. Department of Education Institute of Education Sciences.

(NCLB) No Child Left Behind Act of 2001, Pub. L. No. 107-110 (H.R.1), 115 Stat. 1425 (2002).

NCRTL (National Center for Research on Teaching Learning). (2000). Available at http://ncrtl.msu.edu/
NCTAF (National Commission on Teaching and America's Future). (1996). *What matters most: Teaching for America's future.* New York: Author.
Noddings, N. (1992). *The challenge to care in schools: An alternative approach to education.* New York: Teachers College Press.
Nuland, S.B. (2002). Whoops! [Review of the book *Complications: A surgeon's notes on an imperfect science.*] *New York Review, 49*(12), 10-13.
Oakeshott, M. (1990). A place of learning. In T. Fuller (Ed.), *The voice of liberal learning: Michael Oakeshott on education* (pp. 17-42). New Haven: Yale University Press.
Paley, V. (1990). *The boy who would be a helicopter.* Cambridge: Harvard University Press.
Pendelbury, S. (1990). Community, liberty and the practice of teaching. *Studies in Philosophy and Education, 10,* 263-279.
Phillips, D. (Ed.). (2000). *Constructivism in education. The Ninety-ninth yearbook of the National Society for the Study of Education,* Part I. Chicago: National Society for the Study of Education.
Putnam, R.T., & Borko, H. (2000). What do new views of knowledge and thinking have to say about research on teacher learning? *Educational Researcher, 29*(1), 4-15.
Raymond, M., Fletcher, S., & Luque, J. (2002). *Teach for America: An evaluation of teacher differences and student outcomes in Houston, Texas.* Palo Alto, CA: Hoover Institute, Stanford University, Center for Research on Education Outcomes.
Richardson, V. (in press). Preservice teachers' beliefs. In J. Raths & A. McAnench (Eds.), *Advances in teacher education* (Vol. 6). Greenwich, CT: Information Age Publishers.
Richardson, V. (2003). Constructivist pedagogy. *Teachers College Record, 105*(9), 1623-1640.
Richardson, V., & Anders, P. (in press). Professional preparation and development of teachers in literacy instruction for urban settings. In *Literacy in urban settings.* Newark, DE: International Reading Association.
Richardson, V., & Kile, R.S. (1999). The use of videocases in teacher education. In M. Lundberg, B. Levin, & H. Harrington (Eds.), *Who learns from cases and how? The research base for teaching with cases* (pp. 121-136). New Jersey: Erlbaum.
Roth, R.A. (1996). Standards for certification, licensing, and accreditation. In J. Sikula (Ed.) *Handbook of research on teacher education* (2nd ed., pp. 242-278). New York: Macmillan.
Roosevelt, D. (1998). "Unsuspected literatures": Public school classrooms as laboratories for the creation of democratic culture. *Theory into Practice, 37*(4), 271-279.
Roosevelt, D. (2003, April). *"What gives you the right?": Searching for intrinsic authority to teach as a task for beginning teachers.* Paper presented at the annual meeting of the American Educational Research Association, Chicago.
Schön, D.A. (1988). *Educating the reflective practitioner.* San Francisco: Jossey-Bass.
Schwab, J.J. (1978). Education and the structure of the disciplines. In I. Westbury & N.J. Wilkof (Eds.), *Science, curriculum, and liberal education* (pp. 229-272). Chicago: University of Chicago Press.
Shulman, L. (1986). Those who understand: Knowledge growth in teaching. *Educational Researcher, 15*(2), 4-14.
Shulman, L. (1987). Knowledge and teaching: Foundations of the new reform. *Harvard Educational Review, 57*(1), 1-22.
Sikula, J. (Ed.). (1996). *Handbook of research on teacher education* (2nd ed.). New York: Macmillan.
Smith, R. (1991). Where is the wisdom? The poverty of medical evidence. *British Medical Journal, 303,* 798-9.
Sockett, H. (1993). *The moral base for teacher professionalism.* New York: Teachers College.
Stephens, J.M. (1967). *The process of schooling: A psychological examination.* Austin, TX: Holt, Rinehart & Winston.

Tom, A.R. (1984). *Teaching as a moral craft*. New York: Longman.

U.S. Department of Education. (2002). *Meeting the highly qualified teachers challenge: The Secretary's annual report on teacher quality*. Washington, DC: U.S. Department of Education, Office of Postsecondary Education, Office of Policy, Planning, and Innovation.

U.S. Department of Education. (2003). *Meeting the highly qualified teachers challenge: The Secretary's second annual report on teacher quality*. Washington, DC: U.S. Department of Education, Office of Postsecondary Education, Office of Policy, Planning and Innovation.

Van Manen, M. (1991). *The tact of teaching: The meaning of pedagogical thoughtfulness*. Albany, NY: SUNY Press.

Walsh, K. (2001). *Teacher certification revisited: Stumbling for quality*. Baltimore: Abell Foundation. Retrieved December 22, 2003, from http://www.abell.org

Watt, H.M.G., & Richardson, P.W. (2003, April). *Motivational factors leading to teaching as a career choice: Development and validation of the FIT-Choice scale*. Paper presented at the annual meeting of the American Educational Research Association, Chicago.

Wenger, E. (1998). *Communities of practice: Learning, meaning, and identity*. Cambridge: Cambridge University Press.

Wideen, M., Mayer-Smith, J., & Moon, B. (1998). A critical analysis of the research on learning to teach: Making the case for an ecological perspective on inquiry. *Review of Educational Research, 68*(2), 130-178.

Wilson, S., Floden, R.E., & Ferrini-Mundy, J. (2001). *Teacher preparation research: Current knowledge, gaps, and recommendations* (Research report prepared for the U.S. Department of Education). Seattle, WA: University of Washington, Center for the Study of Teaching and Policy. Retrieved December 18, 2003, from http://www.ctpweb.org

Wilson, S., Floden, R.E., & Ferrini-Mundy, J. (2002). Teacher preparation research: An insider's view from the outside. *Journal of Teacher Education 53*(3), 205-215.

Wood, C. (1999). How can new teachers become the best? In M. Scherer (Ed.) *A better beginning: Supporting and mentoring new teachers* (pp. 120-123). Alexandria, VA: Association for Supervision and Curriculum Development.

Zeichner, K., Tabacknick, R., & Densmore, K. (1987). Individual, institutional, and cultural influences on the development of teachers' craft knowledge. In J. Calderhead (Ed.), *Exploring teachers' thinking* (pp. 21-59). London: Cassell.

CHAPTER 5

"Them That's Got Shall Get": Understanding Teacher Recruitment, Induction, and Retention

SUZANNE M. WILSON, COURTNEY BELL, JODIE A. GALOSY, AND ANDREW W. SHOUSE

In this age of heightened concern about teacher quality, calls for new policies and practices concerning recruitment, induction, and retention are familiar to many. Policymakers legislate new mandates intended to recruit more teachers, and school districts hire consultants who can help them develop marketing strategies, glossy brochures, and recruitment teams. District-sponsored induction programs open new offices and collect data on how their efforts are affecting retention rates in the schools. Experienced teachers learn to become mentors, supporting new teachers so that their entry into the profession is smooth.

In many—if not most—cases, these new policies and programs are inserted into the already functioning educational bureaucracy. The problems with this approach—the gradual accretion of offices and programs that make the educational system alternately unwieldy and fractionalized—have been noted by many scholars (e.g., Cohen & Spillane, 1993; Cusick, 1992; Smith & O'Day, 1991). Numerous coalitions form and reform, pressing for their self-interests. Teachers confront multiple, sometimes conflicting messages about what and how they are to teach. The current enthusiasm for policies to recruit, support, and retain new teachers runs the risk of adding more clash and clang to an already cacophonous policy environment. What would it mean to reimagine policies concerning teachers' early careers in ways that did not treat them as "add-ons" but rather as part of a larger system of policies and practices? This is our charge in this chapter.

Suzanne M. Wilson is a Professor in the Department of Teacher Education at Michigan State University. Courtney Bell, Jodie A. Galosy, and Andrew W. Shouse are doctoral candidates in the Department of Teacher Education at Michigan State University.

To inform our inquiry, we looked at recent developments in teacher recruitment, induction, and retention policies and practices in the United States and abroad, at both the state and district levels. We also looked to other fields. All professions struggle with the transition from student to practitioner. Understanding how to help the student of medicine become a doctor or the student of law become an attorney, for example, is a perennial problem faced by those professions. As Turow (1977) writes,

In baseball it's the rookie year. In the navy it is boot camp. In many walks of life there is a similar time in trial and initiation, a period when newcomers are forced to be the victims of their own ineptness and when they must somehow master the basic skills of the profession in order to survive. For someone who wants to be a lawyer, that proving time is the first year of law school. (p. 9)

In our quest to understand more about this transition—and the policies and pedagogies used to enable it—we examined literature on the clergy, medicine, law, the armed forces, and public service (e.g., Bosk, 1979; Breyer, 2000; Carroll, Wheeler, Aleshire, & Marler, 1997; Gawande, 2002; Turow, 1977).

We begin our chapter by briefly describing the factors that have historically influenced entry into teaching. We structure the rest of the chapter around the troika of policies concerning teacher recruitment, induction, and retention, describing current understandings of these phenomena, as well as new developments in both policy and practice. We conclude by exploring the question, "What kind of work are new teachers being recruited and inducted into?" Wrestling with this question is essential to understanding the potential power and pitfalls of those policies.

The Factors That Shape Entry into Teaching

The results of teacher surveys by the National Education Association (NEA, 2003) over the past 30 years replay five themes that Lortie (1975) identified as attracting people to teaching: an interest in interacting with (young) people; making a difference in society; finding ways to remain affiliated with school or subject matters; reaping material benefits, including money, prestige, and employment security; and an attraction to teaching's time demands (the length of school day, say, or summer breaks).[1] For instance, in the most recent NEA (2003) analysis, almost three fourths (73%) of the 2001-2002 survey respondents selected "a desire to work with young people" as one of the three main reasons they originally decided to become teachers. The next most frequent response was the "value or significance of education in society" (44%), and an "interest in a subject matter field" (36%) was the third. These items were similarly ranked as the three main reasons teachers continued to teach.

The other two themes Lortie identified appear to play an important role in current teachers' career decisions as well. Although financial rewards were not one of the main attractors to teaching (2.4%) or a primary reason for remaining in teaching (5.5%), "low salary" was the most frequently cited reason for leaving the profession. Another material benefit—job security—seemed to matter to teachers much more than financial rewards, especially over time. Less than one fifth (16.7%) of teachers chose job security as a major reason for becoming a teacher, but more than one fourth (27.3%) selected job security as a main reason they were currently teaching. Finally, a "long summer vacation" was selected by one fifth of the teachers surveyed as a main reason for entering teaching and by about one fourth as a reason for staying.

Several other survey responses indicated differences between what might attract teachers to teaching and what keeps them there. The influence of significant others, especially respondents' former teachers (32%) or family members (19.5%), was a major reason for entering the profession. About one fifth (19%) also indicated that they entered teaching because they had "never considered anything else." However, the influence of others and long-held career aspirations appeared much less important (all below 10%) as reasons to remain in teaching. Another response—"too much invested to leave now"—was chosen by almost one third of teachers (30.2%) as a key reason they were currently teaching.

Although it might be easy to assume that what teachers have "invested" is financial—for instance, steps on a salary scale or the time it takes to earn a credential—teachers also refer to very different kinds of investments. NEA survey results and in-depth interviews (Johnson & Birkeland, 2003) continue to document the centrality of intrinsic, rather than extrinsic, rewards as motivating factors for teaching careers. For instance, when Nieto (2003), working closely with a small group of urban high school teachers, raised the question, "What keeps teachers going—in spite of everything?" the answers included commitments to social justice, a love of children, and a belief in the promise of public education as a private and public good. As one teacher put it, "I have spent my work life committed to a just cause: the education of Boston high school students" (p. 18). Another reflected on the matchless value of her relationships with students:

So, despite everything in our way, why do some of us end up staying? Is it because our lives continue to be changed forever, for the better, by our students? What would my life be without Sonie, without Jeramie? It is an addictive thing, teaching. (p. 18)

The sentiments of these present-day teachers are very similar to those Lortie quoted in his earlier work. Yet, although the factors shaping entry into and commitment to the profession show little change over the last few decades and continue to resonate with teachers of today, school districts find themselves scrambling to recruit, support, and retain good teachers. We begin by considering the evolution of the "problem" of recruitment.

Recruitment: Responding to a Distribution Problem

School districts across the country this year received a windfall of applicants. The weakened economy is drawing people to the relative stability of teaching from such battered fields as technology and business management. Other factors include more aggressive recruitment campaigns, pay hikes, and the steep rise of alternative credential programs, which make it easier and faster for people with college degrees to become teachers. (Hayasaki, 2003)

Americans have been worried about who will teach their children since the mid-18th century. In fact, Sedlak (1989) argues that in the history of the American teacher workforce, shortages are the norm. After 1970, however, the problem was reconceptualized as shortages related to a worrisome "brain drain" rather than the previously articulated more general shortages. Specifically, well-qualified, talented people who formerly filled the teaching ranks (especially women and people of color) began taking advantage of new labor market options. The "best and the brightest" found other, more attractive employment opportunities (Schlechty & Vance, 1983; Sedlak, 1989; Sedlak & Schlossman, 1986).

At the turn of the 21st century, the problem has been reconceptualized again, for a number of recent studies indicate that the United States does not currently have a teacher shortage. Instead, the problem is one of distribution (Darling-Hammond & Sykes, 2003; Ingersoll, 2001; Murphy, DeArmond, & Guin, 2003; NASBE, 1998). On the basis of numbers alone, there are enough certified teachers to staff U.S. public schools (NASBE, 1998). Yet, studies of out-of-field teachers (teachers without a degree and/or certification in the subjects they teach) reveal that the highest proportion of out-of-field teaching occurs in "pockets"—in particular school districts and teaching fields.

Large urban districts serving high numbers of students who are poor, minority, and English language learners (NCES, 1999) tend to have more out-of-field teachers than their suburban counterparts (Ingersoll, 2001; Urban Teacher Collaborative, 2000). These are the same schools required by No Child Left Behind legislation to hire highly qualified teachers for any programs funded through Title I and to ensure that all of their teachers are highly qualified by the end of the 2005-2006 school year. The challenges these urban districts face in attracting qualified teachers are so great that many of them have been labeled "hard-to-staff" and targeted for recruitment assistance (Education Commission of the States, 1999).

Teacher qualification studies document the sharp contrasts in the distribution of certified teachers within states. For instance, Lankford, Loeb, and Wyckoff (2002) found several key distribution patterns of qualified teachers across New York State: teachers are systematically sorted across schools and districts such that some schools employ substantially more qualified teachers than others do; differences in the qualifications of teachers in New York State occur primarily between schools within districts and between districts within regions, not across regions—with the exception of New York City, which, on average, employs substantial numbers of teachers who do not meet standards for "highly qualified" teachers; and non-White, poor, and low-performing students, particularly those in urban areas, attend schools with less qualified teachers (p. 54).[2]

Distribution patterns like these echo the sentiments of the song "God Bless the Child": "Them that's got shall get, them that's not shall lose." In other words, teacher recruitment is a very different (and more formidable) task for an administrator in a large urban district like Chicago than for an administrator in one of the smaller, wealthier suburbs to its north (UPI, 2001). Stretching the extremes, in Chicago (or another urban center) it might appear to be a case of choosing the lesser of two evils ("Is an electrical engineer with no teaching experience a better choice to teach middle school physical science than a second-year certified middle school biology teacher?"), whereas in a northern Illinois suburb (or many other suburbs nationwide) it may feel more like selecting the most desirable alternative ("Is a 'traditional,' experienced, certified physics teacher a better choice to teach middle school physical science than an inexperienced, certified physical science teacher who claims to be 'inquiry oriented'?").

The unequal distribution patterns in schools and districts are further exacerbated by shortages in particular fields. National shortages in mathematics, science (especially physical science), and special education teachers and emergent English language specialists (Hirsch, 2001; NCTAF, 2002) create a "buyer's market" for these positions. Again, wealthy suburban districts have the edge over large urban districts that are not well positioned to offer financial or other incentives (small class sizes, compliant students, or "involved" parents) to attract teachers (NASBE, 1998).

A study by the Philadelphia Education Fund (PEF, 2002) illustrates the problem for large urban districts. Pennsylvania produces a surplus of teachers, and many districts in Pennsylvania do not have teacher shortages. Yet, employment of emergency-certified teachers is on the rise and is especially high in certain subject areas such as special education, science, and mathematics. As Philadelphia well knows, hard-to-staff positions in hard-to-staff schools equals ongoing and troublesome teacher shortages.

In order to enlarge the pool of qualified teacher applicants for hard-to-staff schools, recruitment strategies are being leveraged from both the supply side—through university teacher education and alternative certification programs designed to prepare teachers for hard-to-staff schools—and the demand side—through state, district, and local school recruitment efforts. We explore each.

Strategies on the Supply Side

Supply-side goals concerning the teaching force include increasing the percentage of minority teachers, developing urban teacher preparation programs, attracting graduates with prestigious university credentials, and fostering better subject matter preparation for prospective teachers. One traditional strategy used to recruit new teachers entails increasing salaries to attract teachers, especially those who can earn more in other occupations within their field, as in mathematics and science. An American Federation of Teachers (AFT, 2001) analysis found the average salary offered to college graduates in other occupations was almost $13,000 more than the average starting salary of teachers. Milanowski (2002) reports that about a 45% increase in average starting salaries for teaching would significantly increase the number of mathematics, science, and technology undergraduates willing to consider teaching as a career.

Another increasingly popular recruitment strategy involves alternative certification. The underlying logic of these programs is that many fine and qualified teaching candidates are out there, deterred only by the rigidly structured, time consuming, or irrelevant curricula of traditional teacher preparation programs. Many alternative certification programs, or other alternative routes into teaching, find ways to increase the supply of potential teachers by making the route simpler, more obstacle free. Included here are "grow your own" programs (often known as "pipeline" programs) as well as tuition reimbursement and scholarships especially for minority teacher recruitment programs. In some of these programs, prospective teachers are recruited as high school students and supported in their pursuit of undergraduate degrees and teaching credentials (Clewell, Darke, Davis-Googe, Forcier, & Manes, 2000; Hirsch, 2001).

Alternative certification and "grow your own" programs are often pursued in the name of diversifying the workforce—increasing the number of male teachers and teachers from racial minority groups. Recent surveys estimate that about 85% of K-12 teachers are White and approximately 70% are female. In contrast, only about 60% of all U.S. public school students are White; about 50% are female (National Center for Education Statistics, 2002). The overrepresentation of White women in teaching has been attributed to an entangled set of social, cultural, and political factors, including expectations that women assume "primary caregiving and homemaking responsibilities" (Bierema, 2001, p. 56). The occupational structure of teaching allows women to move more easily in and out of the workforce as well as match schedules with their children who attend school.

Minority teacher recruitment programs have received more focused attention during the last two decades, especially in response to studies that reveal a growing "disparity between teacher and student populations with regard to race and ethnicity" (Yasin & Albert, 1999, p. 6). Reasons for these disparities include demographics (a region, state, or school district contains few minorities locally available for its teacher pool); burn out and frustration (due to poor working conditions, discipline problems, spreading school violence, or a lack of support from colleagues); inadequate schooling that leaves some minority students ill-prepared and unmotivated for higher education; standardized tests that often have cutoff scores that exclude minority students from higher education, teacher training, and teacher certification programs; licensure tests that disproportionately screen out minorities; salaries that are lower than those for other professionals, which lowers the prestige and social value of a career in teaching for many potential minority teachers; and more career opportunities outside of teaching (NEA, 2001).

Minority recruitment strategies attempt to address many of these concerns with a variety of initiatives, many of which have been privately funded (NEA, 2001; Yasin & Albert, 1999). These efforts include precollegiate programs (e.g., future teacher clubs, mentoring, teaching internships), as well as collegiate support for minority students interested in teaching (e.g., financial assistance, mentoring, placement services). Some of the most promising minority recruitment programs appear to be those that target students in two-year colleges and paraprofessionals as well as those developed locally to encourage students of color to become teachers and return to teach in their community's schools.

Meeting the Demand

Recent teacher recruitment analyses (Education Week, 2003; Hare & Heap, 2001; Hirsch, 2001; PEF, 2002) report that states, districts, and local schools are using a variety of strategies to increase teacher supply in underserved schools and content areas, including temporary licensure, aggressive recruiting practices, streamlined hiring practices, financial incentives, and improved working conditions. A survey of Midwest school district superintendents (Hare & Heap), for instance, found temporary licensure to be a common practice to fill vacant positions, especially in large districts and high-poverty districts. As the report indicates, a teacher with a temporary license should not be assumed to be underqualified for the position. For example, teacher credentialing is not necessarily reciprocal across states, so temporary licenses are initially issued to highly qualified teachers who are new to a state until they are able to meet that state's requirements. To reduce the need for issuing temporary licenses to qualified teachers, some states have revised their policies to allow reciprocal certification across states.

Districts also mount recruiting campaigns. A study by *Education Week* (2003) reports that districts with hard-to-staff schools are trying to increase the number of applicants through campaigns that include hiring public relations specialists, sponsoring job fairs, creating appealing Web sites, and forming partnerships with teacher preparation and alternative certification programs. For example, Montgomery Township, one of the fastest growing townships in New Jersey, sponsors job fairs, participates in college recruiting programs, and aggressively advertises for teachers (Sargent, 2003). Some large urban districts have even started recruiting mathematics and science teachers from Europe. During a panel discussion in Washington on the urban teacher shortage, the Chicago public school district human resources director reported that his district "has been certified as having a shortage of math and science teachers, which has allowed the Immigration and Naturalization Service to issue visas to fill those needs" (UPI, 2001).

The costs—marketing, public relations, and recruiting—are considerable. In 2000-2001, Houston spent $100,000 on radio, television, billboards, and newspaper advertising to attract new teachers. Louisville spent $120,000 on classified ads to recruit fully credentialed teachers in 2000-2001. These expenses are miniscule when compared to those faced by large urban districts: Chicago spent $5.1 million in 1999-2000 to recruit and hire new teachers, whereas New York spent $8 million for an advertising campaign to hire 10,000 new teachers in 2001-2002 (Price, 2002). Costs, of course, are not simply financial. Many school districts have developed elaborate systems of recruitment and selection, including interview and performance assessments. Montgomery Township, for example, uses a three-interview process: The first, brief interview is conducted by the school principal and screens out all but the most promising candidates. In the second interview, the candidate teaches a demonstration lesson observed by the principal and other teachers in the school, who then question the candidate about instructional practice, discipline, and alternative methods for teaching the same class in the future. Candidates who have a successful second interview proceed to a third interview with the principal and school superintendent (Sargent, 2003).

A third set of strategies involves developing incentives, including flexibility in compensation (differential pay), bonuses, tuition assistance for retraining and certification, loan forgiveness, housing incentives, and tax credits. Price (2002) reports that, although additional longitudinal data are needed before the effectiveness of financial incentive programs can be more fully assessed, "preliminary participation rates indicate that financial incentives are attracting teachers' attention and are drawing teachers to schools they might not have considered otherwise" (p. 32).

Price (2002) offers some "lessons learned" about financial incentive strategies:

- The incentive has to be large enough to matter and must be targeted to generate the desirable result, or the impact will be diminished (e.g., if the desired result is to increase qualified teachers in high-poverty schools, the incentive should apply only to those schools);
- Imposing a repayment penalty for failing to uphold the terms of agreement will increase the likelihood of retention, as will spreading out the bonus payments over several years (with the biggest payoff awarded last);

- The incentive should be structured so that teachers are not penalized when school performance improves, and it should be renewable;
- More incentives should be designed to attract experienced teachers, rather than new recruits, to high-poverty, low-performing schools;
- Districts cannot do it alone, and substantial reallocation of current resources as well as new money will be necessary for financial incentive strategies to be effective.

Financial incentives targeted at alleviating teacher distribution problems are similar to those used to attract applicants to federally funded occupations perceived to be "high intensity" or "less desirable," such as air traffic control and the military. The Federal Aviation Administration, for example, provides salary (as well as other incentives) for air traffic controllers willing to staff high-activity, high-stress airports, like Chicago O'Hare (FAA, 1997). Similarly, the U.S. Diplomatic Corps and the U.S. military offer "hazard pay" for staff willing to assume positions in places that may be remote or less friendly to U.S. citizens (United Nations, 2002; United States Government, 2001). Recently, Darling-Hammond and Sykes (2003) have argued for a new federally organized and supported teacher supply program modeled on similar efforts in medicine that have been used to ease physician shortages in both high-need communities and medical specialties.

But, as Darling-Hammond and Sykes (2003) note, increasing supply does not guarantee employment. A newly released study by the New Teacher Project (Levin & Quinn, 2003) of four urban districts' hiring practices has both good and bad news about the success of teacher-recruitment strategies. The researchers found that by implementing "high-impact recruitment strategies," all four districts received at least five to seven times the number of applications as available teaching positions. However, the researchers also discovered that "despite having hundreds of applicants in high-need areas (mathematics, science, special education, and education for English Language Learners) and many more applicants than vacancies to fill, each district was left scrambling at the 11th hour to fill its openings" (p. 5).

Why? The researchers discovered that the districts could not make contract offers until mid-to-late summer. Consequently, "anywhere from 31 percent to 60 percent of applicants withdrew from the hiring process, often to accept jobs with districts that made offers earlier." Of those who withdrew, "50 percent to 70 percent cited the late hiring

timeline as a major reason they took other jobs" (p. 5). Even more disturbing from a teacher quality standpoint, the applicants who withdrew were stronger candidates (using indicators like grade point average, educational coursework, and degree) than those who remained in
the district pool—some of whom the district eventually hired. The
irony is palpable: the very teachers the district worked so hard to
recruit were literally at the door and still could not find their way in.
Other researchers have noted this "late fill" problem as well (Murphy,
DeArmond, & Guin, 2003).

According to Levin and Quinn (2003), three policies typical of
most urban districts and outside of the control of human resources
departments were primarily responsible for late hiring practices: late
vacancy notification policies for resigning and retiring teachers;
teacher union transfer policies that give currently employed teachers
"first pick" of job openings; and late state budget timelines. The
authors conclude with recommendations for revising policies that
constrain what an otherwise hefty investment in recruitment might
actually accomplish—high-quality teachers for all children.

In South Carolina, some districts contend that the school funding
policies in that state place poor rural districts at a disadvantage for
attracting teachers, forcing them to hire high numbers of uncertified
teachers. Eight of the poorest districts are suing the state for lack of
money to hire "first string" teachers (AP, 2003). A state administrator
testified during court proceedings: "Students in [poor] districts need the
best teachers in South Carolina. Instead they are getting a larger number of new, inexperienced teachers because of money." The administrator indicated that the majority of new hires in these districts held a
bachelor's degree in a subject area but had no teacher training. "They
show up at the school, they're handed the keys to that room, and they're
told to teach," she said, "All we know is they have a degree in business,
and they were a shoe salesman." The court decision in the ten-year old
lawsuit, which finally went to trial in late summer 2003, is still pending.

Although recruitment efforts and hiring policy changes might
seem the most promising routes for attracting teachers to school settings and teaching fields experiencing teacher shortages, Ingersoll
(2001) points out that efforts to get teachers in the door are only as
good as the efforts to keep them there. His detailed analyses of data
from the Schools and Staffing Survey suggest that the unequal distribution of teacher shortages is not a problem of recruitment but rather
one of retention—a phenomenon he aptly refers to as the "revolving
door" of teaching.

Ingersoll (2001) contends that this "revolving door" operates at an accelerated rate in some locations and teaching fields. In other words, you may be able to get teachers into hard-to-staff locations or teaching fields, but they will leave quickly. Urban teachers leave as soon as they find jobs in the suburbs; science and mathematics specialists find their way back to careers outside of education. Johnson and Birkeland (2003) found that, above all else, teachers' decisions to stay depended on whether they believed they could be successful with their students. Working conditions such as "collegial interactions, opportunities for growth, appropriate assignments, adequate resources, and schoolwide structures supporting student learning" were the most important factors which influenced that decision (p. 259).

Findings from Philadelphia (PEF, 2002) resonate with these claims. Philadelphia, like many other large, urban systems, experiences problems with teacher staffing in high-poverty schools. A comparison between high- and low-poverty schools in Philadelphia shows higher teacher turnover and a higher percentage of noncertified teachers in high-poverty schools. High turnover leads to high percentages of new teachers in schools, especially in the highest poverty schools. In six of the highest poverty middle schools, for example, 46% of teachers had taught at the school for two years or less.

This finding is particularly troubling in light of research that points to teacher experience as one of the most consistently verifiable factors in student achievement (Darling-Hammond & Sykes, 2003; Goldhaber & Brewer, 1997; Greenwald, Hedges, & Laine, 1996; Hanushek, Kain, & Rivkin, 1998; Kain & Singleton, 1996; see also Wilson & Floden, 2002, for a synthesis). We cannot be satisfied to simply find new teachers—we also have to keep them. We now turn our attention to induction programs created to do just that.

Induction

Historically, new teachers were left to their own devices, to "sink or swim." Recall Ralph, the new schoolmaster in Eggleston's (1871/1984) *The Hoosier Schoolmaster*, who arrives at "Flat Crick" School excited and ready to teach. One of the school's trustees, "old Jack Means," assesses his chances:

"WANT to be a school-master, do you? You? Well, what would you do in Flat Crick deestrick, I'd like to know? Why, the boys have driv off the last two, and licked the one afore them like blazes. You might teach a summer school, when nothin' but children come. But I 'low it takes a right smart man to be schoolmaster in Flat Crick in the winter. They'd pitch you out of doors, sonny, neck and heels, afore Christmas."

The young man, who had walked ten miles to get to the school in this district, and who had been mentally reviewing his learning at every step he took, trembling lest the committee should find that he did not know enough, was not a little taken aback at this greeting from "old Jack Means," who was the first trustee that he lighted on. The impression made by these ominous remarks was emphasized by the glances which he received from Jack Means' two sons. The older one eyed him from the top of his brawny shoulders with that amiable look which a big dog turns on a little one before shaking him. Ralph Hartsook had never thought of being measured by the standard of muscle. This notion of beating education into young savages in spite of themselves dashed his ardor. (p. 2)

We've come a long way from those "survival of the fittest" days. And today's educators understand that recruitment is not a "one-shot deal." That is, a school district might successfully recruit new teachers, but the investment (both in terms of time and financial resources) is considerable. Making good on that investment means finding ways to support the ongoing development of new teachers once they arrive in their classrooms and schools.

Programs for beginning teachers—variously termed "induction," "new teacher orientation," or "novice teacher institutes"—may be administered by university-based teacher education programs, school district staff development offices, local schools, or others outside of the formal educational system. Indeed, induction does not "belong" to any one organizational entity. Nor does induction happen only within the context of formal programs. School-level staff development efforts, informal teacher exchanges, classroom experiences, a school's curriculum—all of these and still other factors contribute to the formal and informal, intentional and unintentional, induction of new teachers.

Induction, which occurs at the crossroads of preparation and practice, interests diverse stakeholders for quite different reasons. At the extremes, supporters of induction include both members of the educational establishment and its staunchest critics. To critics, induction is a welcome substitute for university-based teacher preparation. They contend that formal programs of teacher preparation are little more than barriers to entry for smart applicants who would otherwise enter teaching (Ballou & Podgursky, 1998). Although these criticisms often originate from outside of the public K-12 system, the underlying sentiments are not foreign to insiders. In fact, teacher education graduates often attribute their own knowledge and skill in the classroom to their knowledge of the subject (especially at the secondary level) or to their practical experience. Historically, they have attributed little value to their formal teacher preparation (Lanier & Little, 1986; Lortie, 1975).

Supporters, including many (but not all) teacher educators and educational researchers, point out that, at best, a novice teacher is but a well-launched beginner. They see induction as a place along a continuum of professional education that begins in preparation and carries a teacher through his or her career (Feiman-Nemser, 2001; Feiman-Nemser, Schwille, Carver, & Yusko, 1999). From this perspective, induction is a bridge between preparation and practice that builds on teacher preparation and extends through the early phase of professional teaching (Tickle, 2000).

Given this broad support, induction programs are proliferating internationally and nationally, at both state and local levels. One recent study described induction practices within 11 nations (Moskowitz & Stephens, 1997; see also Britton, Paine, Pimm, & Raizen, 2003, for another international study of induction). Domestic surveys document that 22 states currently fund induction programs at some level and that 11 other states require, but do not fund, induction (Fideler & Haselkorn, 1999; NCTAF, 2003).

Purposes

The purposes of these programs vary. First, there is the issue of new teachers acquiring knowledge of their new schools and communities. Teacher preparation programs prepare new teachers for schools across their home states and, in many cases, across the country. Thus, teacher preparation programs cannot prepare new teachers with knowledge of the particular needs and character of the school district where they will eventually be employed. This has increasingly become the case as entrepreneurial urban school districts recruit new teachers from across the country and, in some cases, the world. Orientation sessions (often held near the beginning of the year) provide new teachers with much local knowledge, be it bureaucratic paperwork and routines, union rules, community expectations, or the diverse needs of the local student population.

Another purpose of induction programs is associated with the perennial problem in learning to teach: bridging the gap between theory and practice, or the university and the schools. Some argue that teacher preparation programs simply are not in touch with the realities of schools or are not practical enough. And indeed, there is much room for improvement in teacher preparation. But some challenges associated with learning to teach are unavoidable, for learning how to put ideas into practice requires practice. This is a problem all professions face. Gawande's (2002) description of learning to become a surgeon is a poignant reminder of how hard—and unavoidable—this process is. "Mine were not experienced hands," he notes (p. 12). "In surgery, as in anything else, skill and confidence are learned through experience—haltingly and humiliatingly" (p. 18). Teacher induction is no different, although it is often less dramatic than learning to make an incision in a living person. And many induction programs are designed to help new teachers make this difficult transition—with the support of more experienced colleagues—from novice to proficient practitioner, from someone who might "know" what to do but cannot yet enact that vision to someone who has skill and can make responsible, appropriate judgments on the spot.

A third purpose of induction programs is retention. Many urban school districts that suffer from high attrition have designed induction programs with the express purpose of keeping teachers rather than lose them to their more affluent neighbors. This attention to district or school retention is related to but separate from retention in the profession, an issue that is of concern to all schools. As we have already noted, the literature on teacher quality suggests that experience matters. Retention, then, becomes critical if teachers are to have the time they need in order to develop into highly qualified practitioners.

Multiple Actors: Who Staffs Induction?

In addition to having multiple purposes, induction programs also involve multiple actors. Staff members typically include central office personnel who have some responsibility for professional development, principals, and mentor teachers or coaches. There is considerable variation in how mentors are selected, whether they participate in professional development designed to help them enact the role of mentor or coach, whether they are full-time teachers or have been released from all or part of their teaching, and how they are matched with new teachers. There is also considerable variation in how much opportunity principals have had to learn how to support new teachers, as well as in the common procedures mentors and principals use for providing feedback and support.

Recently, additional actors have entered the induction game. The new Carnegie Corporation of New York initiative, Teachers for a New Era, explicitly requires that the participating teacher education programs create induction supports for their graduates.[3] In 1998, in response to an increasing enrollment of new teachers in its Teacher Institute (TI), the Exploratorium—a hands-on museum in San Francisco—created a two-year Teacher Induction Program (TIP) to support novice middle and high school science teachers in the San Francisco Bay area with funding from the National Science Foundation.[4] During the academic year, TIP offers participants support-group meetings, content and pedagogy work-shops (called Saturday workshops), and classroom coaching and mentor-ing assistance. Mentors and coaches are selected from TI/TIP staff and TI alumni.

During the summer between participants' first and second years in the program, TIP participants join TI participants in a four-week sum-mer institute. During the institute, participants attend discipline- and grade level–specific workshops, work with their mentors to develop a science curriculum unit, and share demonstration lessons. Because the institute takes place at the Exploratorium, workshop leaders use the museum's exhibits to demonstrate and explain phenomena, providing time for teachers to build similar classroom-size models in the Explor-atorium workshop. The Exploratorium also houses an extensive library of curriculum materials.

In addition to supporting novices, TIP provides support for the experienced teachers who work with the novices as mentors or coaches. TIP mentors participate in a four-week leadership institute that takes place during the summer and overlaps for three weeks with the new teachers' summer institute. During the weeks of overlap, mentors have 90 minutes each day to work with new teachers in developing curricu-lum materials (Shouse, Galosy, & Wilson, 2003).

This program is just one example of a growing number of programs that are developing outside of the educational establishment. The New England Aquarium also offers a program designed to provide ongoing learning opportunities for new teachers. The National Science Founda-tion has awarded grants to numerous partnerships to create similar pro-grams. In addition, there are consultants and organizations like Harry Wong (Breaux & Wong, 2003; Wong & Wong, 2001), Charlotte Daniel-son (1996), Susan Villani (2001), and the Educational Testing Service (makers of the PRAXIS III classroom performance assessments) that offer materials and support for the creation of induction programs. Indeed, when facing mandates to provide induction to their new teach-ers, districts often seek out these existing materials and make use of them as best they can.

Who Is the "New" Teacher?

We should also note that there is variation in the teachers who are being served by the induction programs. Programs begin and end at different times, and so there is variation in how "new" the new teachers are: Some participants are experienced teachers who have recently moved to a new school district; others are experienced teachers who have recently changed assignments (moving to a new grade level or subject area, for example). Some participants are newly certified first-year teachers, others have been teaching for two, perhaps three years. Some programs require certification as a prerequisite, whereas others open their doors to anyone who has teaching responsibilities, including those who are teaching with partial certificates or emergency credentials, or are participants in alternative certification processes.

The Content and Pedagogy of Induction

Finally, there is considerable variation in what teachers are expected in learn in induction (the content), as well as in expectations of how new teachers learn (the pedagogy). In one recent study of induction programs in Michigan (Wilson, Bell, Galosy, Harris, & Shouse, 2002), we found that induction programs across the state of Michigan included information on special education requirements and student aggression, assessment strategies and survival skills, cooperative learning and trust building, laws and legislation, CPR, how to be a good mentee, working with diverse learners and classroom management, preparing for state and local standardized tests, back-to-school night and standards, instructional strategies and how to work with parents, legal issues, and writing across the curriculum. They were also offered content-specific professional development (how to teach writing or reading, mathematics or social studies) and were given a range of resources such as books by Harry Wong and Charlotte Danielson.

In addition to this wide array of topics, the pedagogy of induction—the opportunities to learn that new teachers are offered—also varies. The mainstay of most induction programs is some form of mentoring or coaching, although (as we noted earlier) what it means to coach or mentor a new teacher varies considerably across programs. Other structures are used as well. Orientation sessions, workshops, summer institutes, lesson study groups, and book groups are just a few of the pedagogical alternatives that are used to support new teacher learning.

In sum, there is considerable activity brewing in the name of induction in the United States, and new teachers interact with a variety of stakeholders in a variety of settings and learn a variety of things. Despite this increased interest in and commitment to teacher induction programs, we know little about the impact of these various programs, or about which program features are tied to improved teaching practice or increased student learning. Some research is beginning to emerge. For example, Smith and Ingersoll (2003) found that beginning teachers who were provided with mentors from the same content area and who participated in collective induction activities (such as co-planning) were less likely to move to other schools and less likely to leave teaching after their first year. Other forms of assistance—for instance, having a reduced teaching load—did not appear to have the same effects. Schwille and Feiman-Nemser (2001) found that mentors—or "advisors," as they are called in the Santa Cruz New Teacher Project—helped new teachers learn to create effective environments for student learning; to engage and support the learning of all students; to understand and organize the subject matter for the purposes of teaching; to plan and design instruction; and to grow as a professional. Much more research is needed to shed light on questions around which supports have the most impact in the induction phase of a teacher's career. Currently, one major proxy used for assessing an induction program's success is teacher retention, and it is to policies concerning retention that we now turn.

Retention: The Problem of the "Revolving Door"

The common perception, widely reported in the press, is that we just don't have enough teachers, especially good ones, to go around. But as often happens, the conventional wisdom turns out to be too conventional and too little wisdom. Our inability to support high-quality teaching in many of our schools is driven not by too few teachers coming in, but by too many going out, that is, by a staggering teacher turnover and attrition rate. (NCTAF, 2002, p. 3)

Finally, there is the issue of retention: If teacher quality depends, to some extent, on experience, then schools need to keep their teachers well after the early years of their career. This is no small feat, for less than 50% of the teaching supply in any given year can be made up of returning teachers (Boe, 1997). The teaching force churns.[5] As John Merrow explained: "The pool keeps losing water because no one is paying attention to the leak. That is, we're diagnosing the problem as recruitment, when it's really retention. Simply put, we train teachers poorly and then treat them badly—so they leave in droves" (as quoted in Claycomb, 2000, p. 18).[6]

Teachers leave their teaching assignments for many reasons: They retire, they take new jobs in education that do not involve teaching, they leave to raise children, or they leave to take jobs outside of education. Popular wisdom suggests that urban and high-poverty schools have higher rates of teacher turnover, and that teacher retirements account for much of the loss of the teaching force. But recent research suggests otherwise. Ingersoll (2001), for example, found that small private schools have higher rates of teacher turnover than suburban or urban schools. After controlling for characteristics of both teachers and schools, Ingersoll (2001) found that four factors—low salaries, student discipline problems, limited administrative support, and limited input into school decision making—all contributed to higher rates of turnover. Although many teachers retire, research suggests that the combined number of new entrants into teaching and reentrants far exceeds the retirement rate (NCTAF, 2002). Other research suggests that many teachers become "voluntary movers": they opt to search out new jobs where the work environment fosters both satisfaction and teaching success (Johnson & Birkeland, 2003; Kardos, Johnson, Peske, Kauffman, & Liu, 2001). This finding, too, is not new, for Becker (1952) found a similar pattern of "lateral moves" for Chicago public school teachers who were in search of less stressful, more comfortable school settings in which to teach.

Induction programs are seen as part of the solution to this problem. But other factors need to be addressed if one is to conceptualize retention systemically. Other critical factors include salaries (e.g., Brewer, 1996; Hanushek, Kain, & Rivkin, 1998; Murnane & Olsen, 1989; Murnane, Singer, & Willett, 1989; see also Kelley & Finnigan, this volume, chapter 8), working conditions (Corcoran, Walker, & White, 1988; Firestone, 1994; Ingersoll, 2001, 2003; Loeb, Darling-Hammond, & Luczak, forthcoming), and teacher preparation (NCTAF, 2002).

To counteract these forces, schools and school districts have experimented with new policies. Some programs focus on the pipeline problem—how to get teachers interested in and committed to working in a district's schools. The St. Paul Schools, Minneapolis, and the University of St. Thomas, for example, have worked together to create a 13-month, highly competitive program to prepare urban teachers from underrepresented groups. Upon graduation from the program, the teachers teach in the city's elementary schools. Over twice as many applicants are turned away as accepted (Claycomb & Hawley, 2000). Some policies focus on hiring practices: In 1998, New York

City gave its schools their budgets in April so that the schools would know how many teachers they would need to hire and could afford to hire in the spring. This allowed the district to make job offers early enough to compete with other districts.

Other strategies have involved changing the assignments of new teachers. Renard (2003), for example, suggests that schools ought not require new teachers to team teach, assign new teachers outside extra-curricular responsibilities like coaching or editing the yearbook, or assign new teachers to the most difficult classes in the school. Other recommendations include giving new teachers fewer preparations, arranging for mentors and new teachers to have the same planning period, and keeping new teachers in the same grade levels or courses for the first two years of their assignments.

Many incentives for retention, however, remain compensatory: signing bonuses, low-interest home mortgages, and extra years of service toward retirement. These compensatory practices, however, do not touch the core problem: changing the nature of the work and workplace. As Claycomb (2000) notes, this would require

such things as rebuilding crumbling buildings, raising teachers' salaries, and reconfiguring management structures to allow teachers to share in decision-making. Ultimately, it may mean investing in whole-school and community renewal efforts that reinvigorate families, curb violence, beautify neighborhoods, and build a sense of community. (p. 20)

Consider an example of how one school changed other policies to increase teacher retention and satisfaction. The Timber Lane Elementary School in Virginia fought this revolving door syndrome by changing to a year-round calendar. This allows teachers more flexibility in their work schedules, as well as reducing stress with more frequent, albeit shorter, breaks. The year-round schedule also allows for more professional planning time; teachers can receive stipends for meeting during their intersessions to reflect on their teaching and plan for the coming term (Haser & Nasser, 2003). By changing the ways in which teachers experienced their normal workday, Timber Lane built an environment more conducive to teaching and learning to teach.

Conceptualized as a reform that would affect the work of all teachers, this shift in working conditions also has direct implications for the support and retention of new teachers. It is a point that Willard Waller (1932/1967) brought home poignantly in his classic, *The Sociology of Teaching*: "Their daily work will write upon them; what will it write?"

(p. 380). In the final section of this paper we turn to this question by considering the multiple conceptions of "teaching" that these policies concerning recruitment, induction, and retention embody and promote.

What Work Are Teachers Being Inducted Into?
How Policies Shape and Are Shaped by Conceptions of Teaching

Faced with the need to attract, support, and keep good teachers, the educational system is doing what it always does when faced with a new challenge: busily trying to develop policies and practices to increase the recruitment of good teachers, smooth their entry into the profession during the early stages of their careers, and ensure their retention. Some of these policies are developed independent of one another. In other cases, school districts or states conceptualize recruitment, induction, and retention as a package of policies that must be aligned.

But what does it mean to "align" such policies? And how broadly ought we cast our net across the relevant policies? To answer these questions, we must first consider, What is the nature of the work that teachers are being recruited and inducted into?

Educators and the American public answer this question in many different ways. Some argue that teachers are civil servants; others, that teachers are professionals. Some argue that teaching is moral work; others, that it is technical. Teaching is alternately seen as an art or a science. Although some might say that these discussions are the stuff that academic conversations are made of, we argue that presumptions about what teaching is—as work—are inextricably woven into our decisions about what policies and practices will best attract, support, and keep new teachers. Offering a higher salary as an incentive is qualitatively different than changing the conditions of one's workplace or teaching assignment. Both can act as incentives, and both can send implicit messages about how the work of teaching is valued and understood. Let us briefly consider a few alternative conceptualizations of teaching before reflecting on the implications for policies that support teacher quality: teaching as professional work, teaching as labor, and teaching as vocation.

Teaching as Professional Work

Much has been written about teaching as professional work. Scholars have alternately argued that teaching is professional or quasi-professional work that requires specialized knowledge not available to the ordinary citizen on the street (e.g., Lortie, 1969; Shulman, 1983, 1986,

1987; Sykes, 1983). In the larger discourse on professionalism, there are several different approaches to defining what one actually means by "profession." One dominant paradigm has conceptualized professions as "organized bodies of experts who applied esoteric knowledge to particular cases. They had elaborate systems of instruction and training, together with entry by examination and other formal prerequisites. They normally possessed and enforced a code of ethics or behavior" (Abbott, 1988, p. 4).

Within this paradigm, the commonplaces of professional work include a knowledge base, specialized training, entry and certification by examination, a code of ethics, and a community obligation to police practice within its ranks. Professions, such as medicine and law, also exhibit other features, including professional associations with regular meetings and journals that publish new knowledge.[7]

Professions also have particular ways of recruiting and inducting new members. Consider medicine. New doctors are not expected to know everything they need to or have all of the requisite skills upon graduation from medical school. And so they participate in residencies. The profession exercises social control through rounds—work, chart, attending, grand—and through mortality and morbidity conferences. These structures serve both to monitor the quality of care offered to patients and as learning communities in which less-experienced physicians gradually enter the profession and take on more and more responsibility (Bosk, 1979).

A recent and prominent example of the conception of teaching as professional work can be seen in the development and evolution of the National Board for Professional Teaching Standards (NBPTS). The NBPTS has created standards for the knowledge base of teachers (across different content domains and developmental stages of students) and a certification process by which candidates for NBPTS certification are judged by other teachers. The National Commission on Teaching and America's Future (NCTAF) offers another example. NCTAF argues for the creation of professional standards boards in every state; rigorous accreditation for all schools of education (and the closure of all inadequate schools of education); licensing teachers based on demonstrated performance (including tests of subject matter knowledge, teaching knowledge, and teaching skill); and the use of NBPTS standards for judging accomplished teaching (NCTAF, 1996).

Recruitment, induction, and retention policies within a framework of "teacher as professional" would focus on controlling access to students, assessing and enhancing a novice teacher's knowledge and skill, and increasing autonomy. Novice teachers, for instance, might participate in sheltered experiences with students, perhaps even in apprenticeships with their more experienced and knowledgeable colleagues. At our own university, all teaching candidates must participate in an internship year after they receive an undergraduate degree. During that year, they gradually take on the responsibilities of full-time teaching, as well as participate in seminars designed to support their capacities to critically reflect on and learn from experience. Induction into a profession might include mechanisms like this, designed to extend one's professional knowledge and skill. Induction might also include rigorous and challenging assessments of competence such as portfolios or performance assessments like those used in the state of Connecticut (Wilson, Darling-Hammond, & Berry, 2001; Youngs, 2002). Similarly, the assessments and standards developed by the Interstate New Teacher Assessment and Support Consortium, including tests of teacher content knowledge and portfolios, presume that teaching is professional work and that induction ought to include policies that assess new teachers' professional capacities.[8]

Teaching as Labor

Another, very different way to think of teaching is as "labor" or "civil service." In fact, in many countries, teachers are civil servants. Because education is a local enterprise in the United States, and participation of all—parents, local community members, industry officials— is accepted and expected, teachers are seen by some as civil servants, employees of the local school board—labor, if you will (Lipsky, 1980).

Mitchell and Kerchner (1983) argue that laboring work is not distinguished by being a "low-level" occupation, "but rather by the rationalized and preplanned character of tasks and direct inspection of how those tasks are performed" (p. 217):

Loyalty and insubordination are the most important concepts in evaluating laboring work. It is very important for laborers to give allegiance to the organization for which they work and to respond energetically and promptly to directions given by superiors. (p. 217)

Policies that support the recruitment, induction, or retention of civil servants might be quite different from those formulated within a teacher-as-professional framework. And, indeed, when state school boards of education have considered whether teachers ought to sit for NBPTS certification, debates have included discussions of whether or not teachers are professionals and therefore have the right to exercise control within their ranks, or are civil servants and are thus controlled by their superiors. This is not surprising, because the public remains skeptical as to whether teaching requires specialized knowledge (Johnson & Birkeland, 2003). Incentives like signing bonuses, loan forgiveness, housing incentives, and tax credits might reinforce a conception of teaching as labor. Programs that deemphasize the need for professional knowledge—for instance, alternative routes that do not prepare new teachers with the knowledge and skills necessary to succeed—might send explicit or implicit messages to new teachers that the work they will do does not require specialized knowledge but rather "energetic and prompt" response to mandates from above.

Teaching as Vocation

A third conception of teaching is as a vocation. Vocation, Buechner claims, is "the place where your deep gladness and the world's deep hunger meet" (cited in Palmer, 1998, p. 30). Some people become teachers for reasons less related to labor or professionalism and more related to "life work" (Hall, 1993). The women in Casey's (1993) *I Answer With My Life*—Catholic nuns in social justice ministry, Jewish women in inner-city schools, and black women working for the promotion of racial minorities—all reflect such commitment. Others have focused on teaching as moral, ethical work (e.g., Green, 1971; Hansen, 1995; Noddings, 1988; Tom, 1984). As Bryk (1988) has argued, "good teaching is also an intensely personal activity." This "personalism" that Bryk describes "vitalizes the concept of the teacher as an agent of personal transformation and not just a subject matter specialist. . . . It is a teacher's sense of agape that can unite the academic and moral aims of education and engage students in an education of intellect and will" (pp. 278-279).

Perhaps the most prominent contemporary voice for this "teaching as vocation" perspective is Parker Palmer. Palmer's focus is on both recognizing and integrating the intellectual, emotional, and spiritual. He explains that he uses the heart in the "ancient sense," as the place where intellect, emotions, and spirit join together. He argues that the heart of teachers is critical to good teaching and that "good teaching cannot be reduced to technique . . . [it] comes from the identity and integrity of the teacher" (p. 10).

For Palmer, the heart, not simply the mind, is the source of good teaching. He argues that we must nurture both the minds and hearts of teachers in order to have excellent teaching. If book sales and speaking engagements are any indication, Palmer's perspective has resonated with thousands of teachers, in both K-12 schools and higher education. Perhaps unsurprisingly, similar concerns exist in other professions, including medicine, where there is a need to educate doctors for both moral and technical work (Bosk, 1979), and the clergy, where formation—human, spiritual, intellectual, and pastoral—is a critical aspect of both a new minister's preparation and what the minister does for parishioners. Recruitment, in this context, takes on a very different meaning. Breyer (2000) describes her yearlong process of "discernment," during which her denomination assessed and tested her "call to ministry." The process begins with an orientation:

Each applicant brings an entourage and carries copious documentation. We have psychological assessments, medical and financial records, a stack of required reading, commentary forms for the Parish Committees on Ministry to fill out, and a schedule for interviews with both bishops in Washington. Our rectors and parish committee representatives are in tow, a group with whom we will continue to discuss our callings regularly over the next four months. Finally, a lay mentor—a person who, though not a member of the clergy, is very active in his or her church as well as in some community ministry—is assigned to each aspirant. (p. 5)

The implications for policies are quite different if one conceptualizes teaching as vocation. For these teachers, the work of teaching is that of connecting, of interacting with students through subject matter and ideas, through personal passions, through what Schwab (1978) named the teacher's and student's Eros. Recruiting teachers, from this perspective, might bear a resemblance to the discernment process for the clergy. Teachers might need to undergo psychological assessments and collect attestations from local sponsors, as well as attest to their commitment and calling.

The rewards of the work within this view are one's sense of personal connection with students as people and learners. The very ability to enter a classroom and teach, interact, listen, and learn is a reward. Retention within such a model would require helping teachers find ways to connect with their students, feel personally renewed, be valued as human beings, and work in conditions that allow them to act out their beliefs about personal connection.

Teaching, of course, is not simply any one of these things—it is part labor, part profession, part vocation. Teachers are recruited and inducted into all of these versions of teaching. They need to know about the district's paperwork and they need to know how to relate to children.

They want higher salaries and they need to have professional knowledge. The tensions inherent in understanding that teaching is a moral enterprise that requires professional expertise and exists within a public bureaucracy resonate with tensions experienced by other workers, including professionals like doctors and lawyers. Ingersoll (2003) describes the tension as such:

On the one side is a rationalistic viewpoint that stresses the importance of workplace coordination, predictability, and accountability for the success of collective enterprises. On the other side is the humanistic viewpoint that stresses the need for workplace democracy, worker autonomy, and employee well-being for organizational success. These counterarguments are central to a larger discussion among social scientists of the character of middle-class employment as a whole—is it proletarianized or professionalized? Are essential white-collar occupations like teaching more akin to professional vocations, based on expertise, training, and skill, or are they closer to factory-like jobs, which underutilize human resources and alienate employees? And what should they be? (p. 15)

Our aim here is not to claim that one paradigm deserves pride of place. Rather, we want to reiterate Mitchell and Kerchner's (1983) argument: underlying assumptions about the nature of teaching—that is, the kind of work that new teachers are recruited to and inducted into—fundamentally shape our understanding of both policy and practice. We decide how to recruit, induct, and retain teachers based on our assumptions about the nature of the work. Reflexively, through our recruitment, induction, and retention practices, we shape how new teachers conceptualize and enact the work of teaching. The current mix of policies and practices—ranging from signing bonuses to restructured school years, from school loan forgiveness to performance assessments for new hires, from induction as training for the district's standardized test to induction as seminars devoted to learning more about electricity—are an eclectic mix. This variability can be understood in part as rooted in different conceptions of the work of teaching. As Mitchell and Kerchner argue, this mix is to be expected, but "care must be taken to ensure that policies do not become mutually contradictory and self-destructive" (p. 237). This is easier said than done.

Conclusion: Situating Recruitment, Induction, and Retention in the Larger Policy Landscape

We end by taking Mitchell and Kerner's argument one step further. Teacher quality policies exist in a system of other policies—policies about school finance, labor relations, curriculum, student accountability, and the like. Even though these policies appear unrelated to teacher quality policies, they too send messages about the nature of the work. For example, when a school district mandates a "teacher-proof" curriculum"—that is, a curriculum that teachers are required to work with as a script—it sends an explicit message about the nature of teaching: it is labor, not professional work. A professional would need to critically evaluate and adapt the materials; laborers need to demonstrate loyalty by doing what they are told. As Ingersoll (2003) and others have pointed out, policies like this de-skill teaching:

Teacher-proof curricula reserve the conceptual portion of the complex craft of teaching—for a small number of highly trained, highly skilled, highly paid outside experts. Reducing the need for skill, knowledge, and training for the majority of inside employees, the teachers, reduces their value and the level at which they should be paid. Moreover, by reducing the need for skill, knowledge, and training, these mechanisms ease the replacement of teachers and can thus reduce the threat of teacher turnover and strikes. (p. 158)

Policies that mandate particular curricula or pedagogies can directly or indirectly shape how policies and practices of recruitment, induction, and retention are interpreted, received, and implemented. Policies concerning student accountability, labor relations, and the like can have a similar effect. If, for example, a teacher is inducted into a professional view of teaching through association with scientists and science teachers at the Exploratorium in summer institutes and then is hired in a school where she is directed to teach a particular curriculum in a specific way, there is the possibility that these mixed messages of who she is as a teacher—professional or civil servant—will, as Mitchell and Kerchner (1983) suggest, be self-destructive. Conversely, if a district strictly mandates a curriculum, that mandate might attract teachers who are passive and willing to be imprisoned in what Weber (cited in Krause, 1996, p. 2) called the "iron cage of bureaucratization." The same policy might very well discourage new teachers in alternative routes who come from prestigious undergraduate institutions (like those attracted to teaching through programs like Teach for America) and want to proactively create and teach intellectually rigorous curricula.

Consider Distar and Direct Instruction (DI) (Adams & Engelmann, 1996), two curricula that include scripted lesson plans. For some teachers, such clear structure and direction is reassuring; others find it off-putting. Or consider the New York City public schools, where recently adopted "teacher quality" policies are meant to emphasize professional expertise and to "inspire effective educators to teach in [New York] City's schools" (New York City Department of Education, 2003). At the same time, curriculum mandates handed to teachers in the fall of 2003, like those regulating mathematics and reading instruction in the "famously fractious and diffusely organized" New York City schools (Traub, 2003), had a "totalitarian" feel for some teachers and parents. Policies dictated that "every single literacy and math class must hew to the same topics and utilize the same teaching methods . . . each literacy and math class [must also] be the exact same length and be given at the same time in every school in the city" (Stern, 2003, p. 2). As New York City schoolteachers received memos that included strict specifications (subject to "disciplinary action") for seating arrangements and checklists of what must be visible in every classroom (Williams, 2003), conformity and compliance moved center stage as markers of a "good" teacher. This vision directly contradicts that of the teacher as a professional who is autonomous and trusted to make wise decisions about the curriculum and instruction.

Of particular importance is an understanding of how state and federal mandates are playing an increasingly dominant role, and the consequences of that encroachment. Historically, the state has always been antagonistic toward what Krause (1996) calls "guilds"—associations (including professions) and "institutions created by groups of workers around their work, their skill or craft" (p. 3). Guilds exercise power through association by controlling both the workplace and the market. The state sees this guild power as "the enemy and limitation of production as a plot against the consumer" (p. 6). In the case of teacher quality policies, conceptions of teaching as profession or vocation resonate with the notion of guilds, or associations. In the current political climate, marked as it is with a procapitalist, free-market ideology, such associations are seen as the "enemy" of the state. Krause argues that

Guild power . . . is declining as state power and capitalist power encroach upon it. Where state and capitalist power have won out, they and not the profession control the aspects of professional life that we call "the workplace" and "the market" and determine to a large extent how much associational group power the profession has left vis-à-vis the state and capitalism. (p. 22)

Ingersoll's (2003) analysis and Johnson and Birkeland's (2003) descriptions clearly demonstrate how little control teachers have over their workplace, the schools. As the "state," in the form of both state policies and federal legislation like No Child Left Behind, increasingly encroaches on the market and workplace, teachers are pressed more and more into civil service and labor orientations toward teaching in their daily work. Teacher recruitment, induction, or retention policies that either presume a different orientation toward teaching (teaching as vocation or profession, for instance) or ignore the other messages new teachers receive about the nature of their work run the risk of being thwarted from the start. As Carroll and his colleagues (Carroll, Wheeler, Aleshire, & Marler, 1997) noted in their study of theology schools: "Powerful educational cultures, often unacknowledged, play a very big part in the formation of students' characters and capacities" (p. 279). This is no less true of teachers. In fact, those cultures come into sharp focus (and sometimes conflict) for teachers in schools. Recent scholarship suggests that critical leverage points in recruitment, induction, and retention are the nature and structure of the workplace. Whatever version of teaching teachers is being bought into, if we are to change the status quo we must improve workplace features such as salaries, class sizes, pupil loads, teacher input into decision making, opportunities for intellectual engagement, the appropriateness of teaching assignments, basic support, and the accessibility of school-level leadership (Darling-Hammond & Sykes, 2003; Ingersoll; Johnson & Birkeland).

The larger educational and political context of the steady advance of the state into the direct governance of a broad array of issues concerning teaching, learning, and the schools promises to have significant implications for how any recruitment, induction, and retention policies are implemented and received. We close by returning to Waller (1932/1967):

These recruits who face teaching as a life work are ready to learn to teach, and they are ready, though they know it not, to be formed by teaching. When teaching has formed them, what shape will it give them? Their daily work will write upon them; what will it write? (p. 380)

As policymakers and practitioners, we need to consider the messages about teaching that are both embodied in and created by the policies we use to recruit, support, and retain good teachers. Individual policies may presume teachers to be, alternatively, laborers, professionals, or people with a calling. Furthermore, because these policies are woven into a complex web of other policies concerning curriculum and assessment, teacher quality, school finance, and workplace conditions, we must also strive to understand how the messages sent by this eclectic mix of policies resonate with or contradict one another. As Waller notes, policies shape and are shaped by teachers. As such, they will "write" important lessons on the hearts and minds of the next generation of teachers. It behooves us all to understand what those lessons are.

AUTHORS' NOTE

Work on this chapter was supported by the Educational Policy Center at Michigan State University, as well as two National Science Foundation grants. The first grant funds an evaluation of the New Teacher Induction program at the Exploratorium (a collaboration between Wilson, Galosy, and Shouse at MSU); the second supports a study of mathematics and science teacher induction in the United States (a collaboration between Edward Britton, Tania Madfes, and Frances Montell at WestEd and Lynn Paine, Brian Delany, Steve Ryan, and Suzanne Wilson at MSU).

NOTES

1. Lortie analyzed data collected from 94 intensive teacher interviews in the Boston metropolitan area and several surveys conducted by the National Education Association during the mid-1960s to early 1970s.

2. Lankford and his colleagues went beyond out-of-field teaching in their study, employing multiple measures of teacher quality in addition to certification (e.g., experience, degree, etc.). However, because their measures were highly correlated, we use their work as an "out-of field" study from which teacher shortages can be inferred.

3. See http://www.carnegie.org/sub/program/teachers.html

4. See http://www.exploratorium.edu/ti/programs/index.html#new

5. We note, however, that Harris and Adams (2003) found that the turnover rates for teaching do not differ dramatically from similar fields, including nursing, social work, and accounting.

6. Of course, retention is not an unequivocal good. A program's capacity to weed out underprepared or less-than-highly qualified teachers is also important. Thus, retention needs to be understood as the retention of good teachers.

7. Scholars interested in the sociology of the professions have taken multiple perspectives on the domain. Some approach the study of professions by considering the workplace; others, by considering the "traits" of the profession (as we do here) (e.g., Krause, 1996; Larsen, 1977). Another paradigm focuses instead on jurisdiction—that is, how groups of professionals compete for control over certain domains and how they establish relationships with other groups, including other groups of professionals. For example, although the mentally ill were originally the jurisdiction of the law, gradually the medical profession—specifically the arm that emerged as psychiatry—claimed that jurisdiction and redefined the problem as one not of maintaining order but of treating disease (Abbott, 1988). Although we do not delve into these issues here, questions of jurisdictional competition are particularly helpful in considering arguments over what constitutes preparation for teachers, and whether and who (schools of education, K-12 schools, or the state) should certify teachers' competence.

8. See http://www.ccsso.org/projects/Interstate_New_Teacher_Assessment_and_Support_Consortium/

REFERENCES

Abbott, A. (1988). *The system of professions: An essay on the division of expert labor.* Chicago: University of Chicago Press.

Adams, G.L., & Engelmann, S. (1996). *Research on Direct Instruction: 25 years beyond Distar.* Seattle: Educational Achievement Systems.

AFT (American Federation of Teachers). (2001). *Survey and analysis of teacher salary trends 2001.* Retrieved January 6, 2003, from http://www.aft.org/research/survey01/index.html

AP (Associated Press). (2003, September 23). *Expert says poor districts are being forced to hire inexperienced teachers.* Associated Press Newswire.

Ballou, D., & Podgursky, M. (1998). The case against teacher certification. *Public Interest, 132,* 17-29.

Becker, H.S. (1952). The career of the Chicago public schoolteacher. *American Journal of Sociology, 57,* 470-477.

Bierema, L.L. (2001). Women, work, and learning. In T. Fenwick (Ed.), *Sociocultural perspectives on learning through work* (Vol. 92, pp. 53-72). San Francisco: Jossey-Bass.

Boe, E.E. (1997). Whither didst thou go? Retention reassignment, migration, and attrition of special and general education teachers from a national perspective. *The Journal of Special Education, 30,* 371-389.

Bosk, C.L. (1979). *Forgive and remember: Managing medical failure.* Chicago: University of Chicago Press.

Breaux, A.L., & Wong, H.K. (2003). *New teacher induction: How to train, support, and retain new teachers.* Mountain View, CA: Harry Wong Publications.

Brewer, D. (1996). Career paths and quit decisions: Evidence from teaching. *Journal of Labor Economics, 14,* 313-339.

Breyer, C. (2000). *The close: A young woman's first year at seminary.* New York: Basic Books.

Britton, E., Paine, L., Pimm, D., & Raizen, S. (2003). *Comprehensive teacher induction: Systems for early career learning.* Dordrecht, the Netherlands: Kluwer Academic Publishers.

Bryk, A. (1988). Musings on the moral life of schools. *American Journal of Education, 96,* 256-290.

Carroll, J.W., Wheeler, B.G., Aleshire, D.O., & Marler, P.L. (1997). *Being there: Culture and formation in two theological schools.* New York: Oxford University Press.

Casey, K. (1993). *I answer with my life: Life histories of women teachers working for social change.* New York: Routledge.

Claycomb, C. (2000). High-quality urban school teachers: What they need to enter and to remain in hard-to-staff schools. *State Education Standard,* Winter, 17-20.

Claycomb, C., & Hawley, W.D. (2000). *Recruiting and retaining effective teachers for urban schools: Developing a strategic plan for action.* Washington, DC: National Partnership for Excellence and Accountability in Teaching.

Clewell, B., Darke, K., Davis-Googe, T., Forcier, L., & Manes, S. (2000). *Literature review on teacher recruitment programs.* Washington, DC: U.S. Department of Education Planning and Evaluation Service.

Cohen, D.K., & Spillane, J. (1993). Policy and practice: The relations between governance and instruction. In S. Fuhrman (Ed.), *Designing coherent education policy* (pp. 35-95). San Francisco: Jossey-Bass.

Corcoran, R., Walker, L.J., & White, J.L. (1988). *Working in urban schools.* Washington, DC: The Institute for Educational Leadership.

Cusick, P.A. (1992). *The educational system: Its nature and logic.* New York: McGraw-Hill.

Danielson, C. (1996). *Enhancing professional practice: A framework for teaching.* Alexandria, VA: Association for Supervision and Curriculum Development.

Darling-Hammond, L., & Sykes, G. (2003). Wanted: A national teacher supply policy for education: The right way to meet the "Highly Qualified Teacher" challenge.

Education Policy Analysis Archives, 11(33). Retrieved September 16, 2003, from http://epaa.asu.edu/epaa/v11n33

Education Commission of the States. (1999). *Teacher recruitment, preparation and retention for hard-to-staff schools.* Retrieved October 23, 2003, from http://www.ecs.org

Education Week. (2003). *If I can't learn from you: Ensuring a highly qualified teacher for every classroom.* Retrieved February 1, 2003, from http://www.edweek.org/sreports/QC03/

Eggleston, E. (1871/1984). *The Hoosier school-master.* Bloomington: Indiana University Press.

FAA (Federal Aviation Administration). (1997). *ARP hard-to-staff facilities/positions.* Retrieved January 26, 2003, from http://www1.faa.gov/ahr/policy/prib/pribs/ARP/Prib009e.cfm

Feiman-Nemser, S. (2001). From preparation to practice: Designing a continuum to strengthen and sustain teaching. *Teachers College Record, 103,* 1013-1055.

Feiman-Nemser, S., Schwille, S., Carver, C., & Yusko, B. (1999). *A conceptual review of literature on new teacher induction.* Washington, DC: National Partnership for Excellence and Accountability in Teaching.

Firestone, W.A. (1994). Incentives for teachers: Mixing the intrinsic with the financial. In B.A. Jones & K.M. Borman (Eds.), *Investing in U.S. schools: Directions for educational policy* (pp. 53–67). Norwood, NJ: Ablex Publishing.

Fideler, E.F., & Haselkorn, D. (1999). *Learning the ropes: Urban teacher induction programs and practices in the United States.* Belmont, MA: Recruiting New Teachers.

Gawande, A. (2002). *Complications: A surgeon's notes on an imperfect science.* New York: Picador.

Goldhaber, D.D., & Brewer, D.J. (1997). Why don't schools and teachers seem to matter? Assessing the impact of unobservables on educational productivity. *Journal of Human Resources, 32,* 505-523.

Green, T. (1971). *The activities of teaching.* New York: McGraw-Hill.

Greenwald, R., Hedges, L., & Laine, R.D. (1996). The effect of school resources on student achievement. *Review of Educational Research, 66,* 361-396.

Hall, D. (1993). *Life work.* Boston: Beacon Press.

Hansen, D.T. (1995). *The call to teach.* New York: Teachers College Press.

Hanushek, E.A., Kain, J.F., & Rivkin, S.G. (1998). *Teachers, schools, and academic achievement* (Working Paper No. 6691). Cambridge, MA: National Bureau of Economic Research.

Hare, D., & Heap, J.L. (2001). *Effective teacher recruitment and retention strategies in the Midwest: Who is making use of them?* Paper prepared for the North Central Regional Laboratory. Retrieved January 15, 2003, from http://www.ncrel.org/policy/pubs/html/strategy/

Harris, D., & Adams, S.J. (2003). *Turning over the turnover debate: A comparison of teachers with other professionals.* Unpublished manuscript.

Harris, P. (2002). *Survey of California teachers.* Rochester, NY: Peter Harris Research Group.

Haser, S.G., & Nasser, I. (2003). Teacher job satisfaction in a year-round school. *Educational Leadership, 60*(8), 65-67.

Hayasaki, E. (2003, February 10). Teacher shortage abates. *Los Angeles Times,* p. A1.

Hirsch, E. (2001). *Teacher recruitment: Staffing classrooms with quality teachers.* Denver, CO: State Higher Education Executive Officers.

Ingersoll, R.M. (2001). *Teacher turnover, teacher shortages, and the organization of schools.* Seattle: University of Washington, Center for the Study of Teaching Policy.

Ingersoll, R.M. (2003). *Who controls teachers' work? Power and accountability in America's schools.* Cambridge, MA: Harvard University Press.

Johnson, S.M., & Birkeland, S.E. (2003). Pursuing "a sense of success": New teachers explain their career decisions. *American Educational Research Journal, 40,* 518-618.

Kain, J., & Singleton, K. (1996). Equality of educational opportunity revisited. *New England Economic Review* (May/June), 87-114.

Kardos, S.M., Johnson, S.M., Peske, H.G., Kauffman, D., & Liu, E. (2001). Counting on colleagues: New teachers encounter the professional cultures of their schools. *Educational Administration Quarterly, 37*, 250-290.

Kelley, C., & Finnigan, K. (2004). Teacher compensation and teacher workforce development. In this volume—M.A. Smylie & D. Miretzky (Eds.), Developing the teacher workforce. *The 103rd yearbook of the National Society for the Study of Education*, Part I (pp. 253-273). Chicago: National Society for the Study of Education.

Krause, E.A. (1996). *Death of the guilds: Professions, states, and the advance of capitalism, 1930 to the present*. New Haven, CT: Yale University Press.

Lanier, J.E., & Little, J.W. (1986). Research on teacher education. In M.C. Wittrock (Ed.), *Handbook of research on teaching* (3rd ed., pp. 527-569). New York: Macmillan.

Lankford, H., Loeb, S., & Wyckoff, J. (2002). Teacher sorting and the plight of urban schools: A descriptive analysis. *Educational Evaluation and Policy Analysis, 24*, 37-62.

Larsen, M.S. (1977). *The rise of professionalism*. Berkeley: University of California Press.

Levin, J., & Quinn, M. (2003). *Missed opportunities: How we keep high-quality teachers out of urban classrooms*. New York: New Teacher Project.

Lipsky, M. (1980). *Street-level bureaucracy: Dilemmas of the individual in public services*. New York: Russell Sage Foundation.

Loeb, S., Darling-Hammond, D., & Luczak, J. (forthcoming). *Teacher turnover: The role of working conditions and salaries in recruiting and retaining teachers*. Stanford, CA: Stanford University School of Education.

Lortie, D. (1969). The balance of control and autonomy in elementary school teaching. In E. Amitai (Ed.), *The semi-professions and their organization* (pp. 1-53). New York: Free Press.

Lortie, D. (1975). *Schoolteacher: A sociological study*. Chicago: University of Chicago Press.

Milanowski, A. (2002). *An exploration of the pay levels needed to attract mathematics, science and technology majors to a career in K-12 teaching*. Retrieved January 1, 2003, from http://www.wcer.wisc.edu

Mitchell, D.E., & Kerchner, C.T. (1983). Labor relations and teacher policy. In L.S. Shulman & G. Sykes (Eds.), *Handbook of teaching and policy* (pp. 214-237). New York: Longman.

Moskowitz, J., & Stephens, M. (1997). *From students of teaching to teachers of students: Teacher induction around the Pacific Rim*. Washington, DC: Asia Pacific Economic Cooperation.

Murnane, R.J., & Olsen, R.J. (1989). Will there be enough teachers? *American Economic Review, 79*, 242-246.

Murnane, R.J., Singer, J.D., & Willett, J.B. (1989). The influences of salaries and opportunity costs on teachers' career choices: Evidence from North Carolina. *Harvard Educational Review, 59*, 325-346.

Murphy, P., DeArmond, M., & Guin, K. (2003). A national crisis or localized problems? Getting perspective on the scope and scale of the teacher shortage. *Education Policy Analysis Archives, 11*(23). Retrieved August 5, 2003, from http://eppa.asu.edu/epaa/v11n23/

NASBE (National Association of State Boards of Education). (1998). *The numbers game: Ensuring quantity and quality in the teaching workforce*. Alexandria, VA: Author.

NCES (National Center for Education Statistics). (1999). *Digest of Education Statistics*. Washington, DC: Author.

NCES (National Center for Education Statistics). (2002). *Digest of Education Statistics*. Washington, DC: Author.

NCTAF (National Commission on Teaching and America's Future). (1996). *Doing what matters most: Investing in quality teaching*. New York: Author.

NCTAF (National Commission on Teaching and America's Future). (2002). *Unraveling the "teacher shortage" problem: Teacher retention is the key*. A symposium of the National Commission on Teaching and America's Future and NCTAF State Partners, August 20-22, 2002, Washington, DC.

NCTAF (National Commission on Teaching and America's Future). (2003). *No dream denied: A pledge to America's children*. New York: Author.

NEA (National Education Association). (2001). *National directory of successful strategies for the recruitment and retention of minority teachers*. Washington, DC: Author.

NEA (National Education Association). (2003). *Status of the American public school teacher 2000-2001* (Research report). Washington, DC: Author.

New York City Department of Education. (2003). School Chancellor Joel L. Levin announces two new programs to recruit teachers for New York City Public Schools. Retrieved November 17, 2003 from http://www.nycenet.edu/press/02-03/n61_03.htm

Nieto, S.M. (2003). What keeps teachers going? *Educational Leadership, 60*(8), 14-18.

Noddings, N. (1988). An ethic of caring and its arrangements for instructional arrangements. *American Journal of Education, 96*(2), 215-230.

Palmer, P.J. (1998). *The courage to teach: Exploring the inner landscape of a teacher's life*. San Francisco: Jossey-Bass.

PEF (Philadelphia Education Fund). (2002). *Teacher staffing in the school district of Philadelphia: A report to the community*. Philadelphia: Author.

Price, C.D. (2002). *Higher pay in hard-to-staff schools: The case for financial incentives*. Retrieved December 5, 2002, from http://www.aasa.org/issues_and_insights/issues_dept/higher_pay.pdf

Renard, L. (2003). Setting new teachers up for failure . . . or success. *Educational Leadership, 60*(8), 62-64.

Sargent, B. (2003). Finding good teachers—and keeping them. *Educational Leadership, 60*(8), 44-47.

Schlechty, P.C., & Vance, V. (1983). Recruitment, selection and retention: The shape of the teaching force. *Elementary School Journal, 83*, 469-487.

Schwab, J.J. (1978). Eros and education: A discussion of one aspect of discussion. In I. Westbury and N.J. Wilkof (Eds.), *Science, curriculum, and liberal education: Selected essays* (pp. 105-132). Chicago: University of Chicago Press.

Schwille, S.A., & Feiman-Nemser, S. (2001, April). *The impact of induction on new teachers' practice: Observations of novices and their mentors*. Paper presented at the annual meeting of the American Educational Research Association, Seattle, WA.

Sedlak, M.W. (1989). Let us go and buy a schoolmaster. In D. Warren (Ed.), *American teachers: Histories of a profession at work* (pp. 257-290). New York: Macmillan.

Sedlak, M., & Schlossman, S. (1986). *Who will teach? Historical perspectives on the changing appeal of teaching as a profession*. Washington, DC: RAND.

Shouse, A.W., Galosy, J.A., & Wilson, S.M. (2003). *The Exploratorium's Teacher Induction Program: Annual evaluation report*. Unpublished document, Michigan State University College of Education.

Shulman, L.S. (1983). Autonomy and obligation: The remote control of teaching. In L.S. Shulman & G. Sykes (Eds.), *Handbook of teaching and policy* (pp. 484-504). New York: Longman.

Shulman, L.S. (1986). Those who understand: Knowledge growth in teaching. *Educational Researcher, 15*(2), 4-14.

Shulman, L.S. (1987). Knowledge and teaching: Foundations of the new reform. *Harvard Educational Review, 57*, 1-22.

Smith, M.S., & O'Day, J. (1991). *Putting the pieces together: Systemic school reform*. (Consortium for Policy Research in Education Policy Brief No. RB-06). Philadelphia: University of Pennsylvania Graduate School of Education.

Smith, T.M., & Ingersoll, R.M. (2003, April). *Reducing teacher turnover: What are the components of effective induction.* Presentation at the annual meeting of the American Educational Research Association, Chicago, IL.

Stern, S. (2003, September 2). One enemy is inside the tent. *New York Post.*

Sykes, G. (1983). Public policy and the problem of teacher quality: The need for screens and magnets. In L.S. Shulman & G. Sykes (Eds.), *Handbook of teaching and policy* (pp. 97-125). New York: Longman.

Tickle, L. (2000). *Teacher induction: The way ahead.* Buckingham, UK: Open University Press.

Tom, A. (1984). *Teaching as moral craft.* New York: Longman.

Traub, J. (2003, August 3). New York's new approach. *New York Times*, 4A, 20.

Turow, S. (1977). *One L.* New York: G.P. Putnam's Sons.

United Nations. (2002). *What is hazard pay?* Retrieved January 27, 2003, from http://www.un.org/Depts/OHRM/salaries_allowances/allowances/hazard.htm

UPI (United Press International). (2001, August 15). Is the teacher shortage real? *United Press International.*

United States Government. (2001). *Pay for duty involving physical hardship or hazard.* Retrieved January 27, 2003, from http://frwebgate.access.gpo.gov

Urban Teacher Collaborative. (2000). *The urban teacher challenge: Teacher demand and supply in the Great City Schools.* Retrieved on October 23, 2003, from http://www.rnt.org

Villani, S. (2001). *Mentoring programs for new teachers: Models of induction and support.* Thousand Oaks, CA: Corwin Press.

Waller, W. (1932/1967). *The sociology of teaching.* New York: John Wiley & Sons.

Williams, J. (2003, October 10). Teachers getting out of their rockers to rally. *New York Daily News.*

Wilson, S.M., Bell, C.A., Galosy, J.A., Harris, D., & Shouse, A. (2002). *Keeping teachers teaching.* A proposal to the Education Policy Center at Michigan State University. Unpublished document, Michigan State University College of Education.

Wilson, S.M., Darling-Hammond, L.D., & Berry, B. (2001). Steady work: The story of Connecticut's reform. *American Educator, 25*(3), 34-39, 48.

Wilson, S.M., & Floden, R.F. (2002). *Creating effective teachers: Concise answers for hard questions.* Washington, DC: ERIC Clearinghouse on Teaching and Teacher Education.

Wong, H.K., & Wong, R.T. (2001). *The first days of school: How to be an effective teacher.* Mountain View, CA: Harry Wong Publications.

Yasin, S., & Albert, B. (1999). *Minority teacher recruitment and retention: A national imperative.* Washington, DC: American Association of Colleges for Teacher Education.

Youngs, P. (2002, November). *State and district policy related to mentoring and new teacher induction in Connecticut.* Paper prepared for the National Commission on Teaching and America's Future (NCTAF). New York: NCTAF.

CHAPTER 6

New Visions of Teacher Professional Development

JUDI RANDI AND KENNETH M. ZEICHNER

Recent scholarship has focused attention on teaching as "the learning profession" (Darling-Hammond & Sykes, 1999). In other professions, individuals are typically responsible for their own learning and individuals' learning is thought to enhance the collective, the profession as a whole. In education, however, the structure of school has typically situated teacher learning within the context of the organization, rather than the entire teaching profession, as the collective. Teacher professional learning has historically been viewed as a means for organizational development or school improvement (Elmore, 2002; Fullan & Steigelbauer, 1990; McLaughlin & Marsh, 1978).

School reform has often been the ultimate goal of staff development. The content of staff development at any given time has been largely determined by concurrent reform efforts (Fullan, 2000; Little, 2002). The current emphasis on accountability for student performance on national and state tests is but one example in a long history of externally driven staff development agendas (Borko, Elliott, & Uchiyama, 2002; Sykes, 1996; Youngs, 2001). Accountable for student achievement, some schools select particular curriculum interventions and research-based practices they deem most likely to improve instruction and increase student achievement and then design staff development programs around the content of those interventions (Le Fevre & Richardson, 2002; McLaughlin & Marsh, 1978; Smagorinsky, Lakly, & Johnson, 2002). Pressed to demonstrate immediate results, schools may pay more attention to "what works" in the short term than to research findings about how best to design and sustain teacher professional learning opportunities for the continuing growth of both teachers and students.

In a recent review of the literature, Wilson and Berne (1999) examined professional development projects that attended to content

Judi Randi is an Assistant Professor of Education at the University of New Haven. Kenneth M. Zeichner is Hoefs-Bascom Professor of Teacher Education and Associate Dean at the University of Wisconsin-Madison.

and pedagogy, to both "*what* teachers learn and *how* teachers are taught" (p. 176). In this chapter, we argue that schools may be attending more often to the *what* than the *how* of staff development. Although the literature has focused attention on *how* best to design staff development, the learning opportunities actually offered to teachers have typically been driven by others' visions of *what* teachers need to learn. The danger in this approach is not so much that someone else is deciding what teachers ought to know but that any decision to focus narrowly on some content to the exclusion of other content may limit teachers' access to knowledge, no matter where they teach. Although some may argue that it takes no specialized knowledge to teach, the Holmes Group (1986) has reminded us that certain knowledge is the "hallmark of competent professionals." Teachers' professional knowledge includes a

broad and deep understanding of children, the subjects they teach, the nature of learning and schooling, and the world around them. [Teachers] exemplify the critical thinking they strive to develop in students, combining tough-minded instruction with a penchant for inquiry. (Holmes Group, 1986, p. 28-29)

Since the Holmes Group report, several research programs have focused on the nature of teachers' knowledge and how teachers acquire their knowledge (Borko & Putnam, 1995; see also Wilson & Berne, 1999). One difficulty in defining the professional knowledge base for teaching may be the scope and complexity of teachers' knowledge—it is a knowledge base that continues to expand as teachers share their knowledge with researchers and others. A substantial body of research on teaching and learning does exist (e.g., Richardson, 2001), and efforts have been made to make this research more widely accessible to teachers (see, e.g., Ornstein, 1995). Thus, the knowledge base potentially available to teachers includes both the existing research canon as well as teachers' own knowledge construction, through such efforts as teacher research or inquiry on practice. Therefore, as teachers seek and construct knowledge, their own knowledge base grows. And, as they share their knowledge among colleagues, both within and across schools, their shared "professional knowledge base" grows as well.

Thompson and Zeuli (1999) argue that professional development is "learning by widening circles of teachers, so that it is not only these teachers' knowledge but also the whole profession that develops" (p. 367). In their view, circles of professionals can be widened as teachers share their knowledge with colleagues. This idea that teacher knowledge is connected to the development of the profession raises the question of whether or not some staff development practices may have slowed the development of teaching as a profession, by constraining, rather than affording, opportunities to take responsibility for their own learning. Staff development practices have typically attempted to solve problems for teachers by defining what teachers need to know in particular situations or by giving them certain materials they can use to improve student learning outcomes. Some might argue that teachers have neither the resources nor the inclination to take responsibility for their own learning, much less school improvement. Modern psychological theory explains why this may be so.

Describing how people acquire personal characteristics that lead to success in school and in the workplace, Corno explains that "qualities of deliberating, planning, and coping . . . emerge from the *flow of information* exchanged" (emphasis added) in educational situations over time, and thus "education enhances an individual's overall functioning" (Corno, in press, p. 39). This is how education develops "aptitude," defined as "being equipped to work in a particular situation" (Corno, p. 38; see also Snow, 1992). In schools where teachers both work and learn, the "flow of information" exchanged with colleagues may provide teachers opportunities to understand why certain students behave as they do, have difficulty in certain academic situations, and so forth. Teachers' particular experiences in problem solving, over time, may lead to the development of more generalized problem-solving skills that "equip" teachers to learn in the context of their work. On the other hand, for example, if the learning environment does not include opportunities for problem solving, or if the information exchanged suggests to teachers that they are not successful problem solvers, then it is unlikely that teachers will acquire these more generalized problem-solving skills that they can then apply to new problems as they arise in the context of practice. Without opportunities to take responsibility for their own learning, and without the need to seek knowledge beyond their own schools and classrooms, teachers may not have sufficient opportunities in the "flow of information" to develop the aptitude, as individuals and as a profession, for the kinds of learning, thinking, planning, coping, and problem solving that professional work demands.

There has been considerable debate in the literature about whether or not teaching is a profession or even a quasi profession (Ingersoll, this volume, chapter 1; Lortie, 1975; for a discussion of alternative conceptions of teaching, see Wilson, this volume, chapter 5). Recognizing this debate, we make a distinction between an organizational, performance-oriented workforce and a professional, learning-oriented workforce. In an organizational workforce, workers' goals are typically focused on accomplishing specific tasks that contribute to the productivity of the organization (Vancouver, 2000). Meeting a sales goal, staying within a budget, or raising student achievement scores are examples of performance-oriented goals. In performance-oriented environments, learning opportunities are provided for *work's* sake. For example, salespersons who need to make a weekly sales quota may be offered learning opportunities focused on strategies for closing a sale, contacting new clients, and so forth. In contrast, in learning-oriented environments, work is accomplished for *learning's* sake. For example, in classroom learning environments, students' tasks (i.e., their work), such as solving mathematical problems or writing an essay, are viewed as learning experiences. In learning environments, work produces learning (see also Randi, in press[a]). Similarly, teaching has been characterized as the *learning* profession (Darling-Hammond & Sykes, 1999). Some argue that the work of teaching cannot be accomplished without learning; teaching requires learning within the context of practice—teachers' work (Ball & Cohen, 1999). This conception of teaching suggests that *learning* is central to teachers' work and that teachers' work may best be accomplished for learning's sake. Thus, in a learning profession, individuals' goals are focused not on learning to work more efficiently but rather on working to learn more effectually.

Consistent with the conception of teaching as a learning profession, our vision of a professional teacher workforce is one in which teachers do take responsibility for their own learning—their work. Teachers' work involves drawing on the shared professional knowledge base—knowledge that is shared by all teachers—to solve the problems of teaching and learning in particular situations. Teachers' work enriches the organization and the profession because teachers refresh the "flow of information" (Corno, in press) by bringing in knowledge that they construct in the course of their work as well as knowledge they may acquire through their other knowledge-seeking activities.

But this type of work is different from what has been asked of teachers in the past, in the organizational workforce. Supporting teachers' transition from workers to learners may require learning opportunities of a different type—work opportunities offered for learning's sake rather than learning opportunities provided for work's sake. To trace the evolution of teachers as learners, we examine past and current staff development practices in light of our new vision of *profession* development, in which teachers' knowledge-seeking goals are valued and supported and their work affords them opportunities to achieve their goals. We seek to understand the differences between staff development opportunities typically offered to "schools of teachers" and learning opportunities that situate teaching in a broader professional context. First, we describe these different orientations toward teacher professional development and illustrate them with examples of past and current practices. Next, we examine the theories of learning and teacher knowledge that may explain these differences. Finally, we review promising new practices such as teacher research in which teachers work together within and across schools to contribute to the professional knowledge base and the improvement of the teaching profession. We conclude that, when teacher learning is situated in a broader, overarching context, teachers' knowledge serves individual student needs and school improvement goals as well as the profession as a whole.

Understanding Past Practices

The history of staff development practices chronicles the evolving nature of the teacher workforce and its slow, "forward and backward" progress in its quest for professional status. Staff development practices have been closely aligned with the debate about whether or not teaching should be considered a profession. This ambivalence is reflected in the language used to describe teacher learning. For example, "staff development" implies that teachers are staff members and that "training" or "developing" the membership improves the organization. On the surface, "teacher professional development" acknowledges teachers as professionals, yet still implies a deficit model of staff development in which teachers need to be "developed." The term *inservice* is commonly used to distinguish learning opportunities for practicing teachers from *preservice* teacher preparation programs. One justification for this distinction may be the prevailing theory that novices learn differently than experts do (Eraut, 1994). Novices tend to focus on concept formation and seek rules, whereas experts ground their learning in practice (Daley, 1999). The two distinct terms, however, separate teacher learning into "before" and "after" categories, implying a separation between theory and practice.

In the third NSSE Yearbook, *The Relation of Theory to Practice in the Education of Teachers*, John Dewey (1904) forewarned educators about assigning the teaching of theory exclusively to teacher preparation programs and the development of practice exclusively to mentors of classroom teachers. Dewey thought preparation programs should elicit examples of theory from teacher candidates' prior knowledge and experience.

Similarly, Dewey expected practicing teachers to take an intellectual stance toward teaching and evaluate teaching practices in light of educational theory. But even as early as 1904, the school organization and "the eagerness of those in authority to secure immediate practical results at any cost" challenged teachers' intellectual independence (Dewey, 1904, p. 16).

In education, as in other disciplines, apprentice and experienced professionals share a common body of knowledge. In other disciplines, however, the language used to describe learning across career stages emphasizes a shared, professional knowledge base. In the medical field, for example, medical students learn in "medical education" programs and practicing (and retired) physicians update their knowledge by participating in "continuing medical education," often attending seminars at medical schools (Manning & DeBakey, 2002). Nurses and other medical workers, on the other hand, participate in "staff development" to update their knowledge (Alspach, 1995). In contrast to the language adopted in other fields, the language used to describe teacher learning not only mirrors ambivalence about teaching as a profession but also reflects the thinking that theory and practice are somehow separate.

Subsequent to the 1904 Yearbook, no fewer than nine NSSE volumes have focused on the study of teacher education. The titles of these NSSE Yearbooks reflect the field's contradictory stances toward teacher learning. Some describe teachers as professionals (e.g., *The Professional Preparation of High School Teachers*, 1919; *Education for the Professions*, 1962). Others describe teachers as staff members to be trained or developed (e.g., *The Education and Training of Secondary Teachers*, 1905; *Staff Development*, 1983). One reflects both views in its title (e.g., *The Relationship of Superintendents and Principals to the Training and Professional Improvement of Their Teachers*, 1908).

The titles also reflect the distinction between inservice and preservice teacher education, typically linking inservice education to the school organizational structure (*The Relationship of Superintendents and Principals to the Training and Professional Improvement of Their Teachers*, 1908; *In-service Education of Teachers, Supervisors, and Administrators*, 1957). Preservice programs are described in volumes focusing on teacher education, typically situated in the university (*Teacher Education*, 1975; *The Education of Teachers*, 1999). The 1999 NSSE Yearbook (*The Education of Teachers*), however, described a trend toward providing preservice teachers with more field experiences and developing university-school partnerships that make it increasingly difficult to assign the responsibility for teacher preparation exclusively to the university (Griffin, 1999). True to its title, however, the 1999 Yearbook focused almost exclusively on preservice teacher education, leaving inservice teacher education for another volume.

In the 1957 NSSE Yearbook, Stephen Corey, dean of Teachers College at Columbia University and director of the Horace Mann-Lincoln Institute for School Experimentation, discussed some of the changes that had taken place in the way "inservice teacher education" (ISTE) had been thought of since the inception of formal teacher education, in the form of the teacher institute and the normal school, in the United States in the mid-nineteenth century. These included a shift in thinking about the purpose of ISTE, from correcting teachers' deficiencies to promoting teacher improvement, with an emphasis on groups of teachers cooperating to solve common school problems. Even with this shift in thinking, however, Corey acknowledged that "much of what goes on for in-service education is uninspiring and ineffective" (1957, p. 1). The workshop was viewed as the dominant form of ISTE at that time, although other forms, such as cooperative action research and teacher study groups, had begun to be used more widely.

The conception of ISTE advocated in the 1957 Yearbook attempted to move away from a deficit model of administrators telling teachers what they should do to a more teacher-initiated form of learning and problem solving that

provides maximum opportunity for individuals and particularly groups to a) identify the particular problems on which they want to work, b) get together to work on these problems in ways that seem most productive to the group, c) have access to a variety of resources, d) try out in reality situations those modifications in practice that give a priori promise, and e) appraise and generalize from the experience. (pp. 8-9)

The emphasis in this type of teacher professional development is on solving school problems and on the continuous improvement of teachers and other staff, rather than on "fixing" the problems of individual teachers. Teachers were viewed as playing an important role in the enactment of this activity rather than serving as passive receptacles to the directives of others. The emphasis on group processes that is evident in this literature is similar in a way to the focus on "communities of practice" in the current teacher professional development literature (Gallucci, 2003).

Focusing on teacher research, the 1994 NSSE Yearbook (*Teacher Research and Educational Reform*) offered an integrated perspective on teacher professional development by viewing teacher learning through the lenses of theory and practice, educational reform, and the professional nature of teaching. Importantly, this volume acknowledged teacher research as a form of teacher learning in both preservice and inservice education (see, e.g., Cochran-Smith, 1994; Richardson, 1994a). Equally important, teacher research has the potential not only to contribute to teachers' individual knowledge, but also to enhance the professional knowledge base as well as the immediate settings in which teachers work (Zeichner, 1994).

Those who promote the professionalization of teaching, however, have noted contradictions between the school organizational structure and teacher professionalism (e.g., Darling-Hammond & McLaughlin, 1995; Zeichner, 1991). As workers, teachers may have been given more opportunities to learn for work's sake than they were afforded opportunities to work for learning's sake. Researchers have noted the tensions between teacher learning and the development of "staff" to improve the organization (see also Miretzky, Smylie, & Konkol, this volume, chapter 2). Staff development practices have reflected these tensions, and efforts to resolve them may explain the "forward and backward" progress of the teaching profession.

What Practicing Teachers Learn: Lessons from the Past

As Dewey (1904) predicted, during the last three decades practicing teachers' development experiences have coincided with waves of school reforms. Veteran educators report that development programs have introduced them to repeated cycles of "new" instructional strategies that mirror ever-changing reform agendas (see, e.g., Hong, 1996). Reform has often been the catalyst for teacher learning (see, e.g., Hong). Although the literature began to call for teachers' more active involvement in their own learning, traditional teacher development programs continue to afford teachers few opportunities to take the initiative for both seeking and generating knowledge.

Staff Development. In the 1970s and 1980s, teacher development focused primarily on teachers as staff members who could be trained to implement particular practices. Since the 1970s, staff development has been recognized as a critical factor in facilitating school change (McLaughlin & Marsh, 1978). Early research on teaching in the process-product paradigm generated a legacy of general pedagogical techniques that promised to improve student achievement (McLaughlin, 1991). Consequently, during the 1970s and 1980s, the content of staff development focused almost exclusively on the dissemination of the products of educational research (Little, 1989). Because the purpose of this type of staff development was to equip teachers with the technical skills needed to faithfully implement specific teaching behaviors that had been found to improve student achievement, the "theory, demonstration, and practice" model dominated staff development practices throughout much of the 1980s (Joyce & Showers, 1980, 1988). Consistent with the view of teacher as technician, much of the staff development during this time focused on the acquisition of pedagogical skills.

Professional Development. Gradually, the focus shifted away from passive "skills training" to more active forms of staff development, more accurately described as professional development. In 1993, Little called attention to the inadequacy of staff development that focuses on skills training. In an influential essay on professional development in a climate of educational reform, Little also warned about the folly of professional development that focuses on implementation of specific reforms. Little identified five streams of reforms that posed new and complex challenges: 1) subject matter standards, curriculum, and pedagogy; 2) equity issues among diverse student populations; 3) the nature and uses of assessment; 4) social organization of schools; and, 5) the professionalization of teaching. These reforms demanded a different form of teacher professional development—one that developed in teachers the capacity to study, investigate, and invent new teaching practices. Little invited teachers to participate in a more active role, not only as consumers but also as critics and producers of research (Little, 1993).

A growing interest in the teacher as reflective practitioner (Schön, 1983) provided the rationale for a new vision for staff development in the 1990s (Lieberman & Miller, 1991). In this vision, teachers are active learners in charge of their own professional growth, rather than passive recipients of others' ideas. Researchers began to envision schools as professional communities that supported teachers' efforts to transform their own practice (Lieberman, 1990; McLauglin & Talbert, 1993).

Thus, attention began to focus, at least theoretically, on the role of the teacher in changing school culture (Fullan & Steigelbauer, 1990). Consistent with cognitive theories of learning, staff development now aimed to change teachers' thinking, including their beliefs about the innovations they were encouraged to implement (Richardson, 1994b). Some changes in the approach to teacher professional learning gradually made their way into some schools, but, despite decades of research intended to improve the quality of teacher professional development, much of what teachers actually experience remains the same as it has always been—a variety of short-term specific activities designed to introduce teachers to new curricular practices or a smorgasbord of content-specific off-site courses (Elmore, 2002; Sparks, 2002).

Understanding the Present: Repeating History

Despite calls for assigning teachers more active roles in their own professional learning, contemporary reform agendas still seek ways to define what constitutes teacher professional learning. For example, standards-based reforms have been viewed as a driving force for professional development as teachers are challenged to ensure that diverse student populations meet rigorously uniform standards. Moreover, the prescriptions of the 1970s and 1980s have resurfaced, this time in the form of curriculum programs intended to "help" teachers bring all students up to standards (e.g., with scripted curriculum materials). We argue that some of these practices may limit teachers' access to knowledge, especially when they focus teachers' learning experiences on single instructional programs rather than giving teachers access to theoretical principles of teaching and learning that can be applied to different situations.

Assessment-Driven Reforms as Motivation for Learning

One pressing concern of contemporary educators is accountability to national and state standards, typically measured by external testing programs. Preparing students for these tests has been the focus of staff development programs in many school districts (Borko, Elliott, & Uchiyama, 2002; Goertz & Duffy, 2001; Koretz, Barron, Mitchell, & Stecher, 1996; Youngs, 2000).

Considerable research has investigated staff development focused on state reforms in Kentucky, one of the first states to implement standards-based reforms driven by assessment (Borko, Elliott, & Uchiyama, 2002; McDiarmid & Kelly, 1997; Stecher, Barron, Kaganoff, & Goodwin, 1998; Stecher & Barron, 2001; Youngs, 2001). In one survey conducted in 1996-97, Kentucky teachers reported that they had changed their instructional practices as a result of professional development they received in portfolio development and scoring (Stecher et al.). In related research, Stecher and Barron conducted a statewide survey of teaching practices at grade levels in which state-mandated tests were given in particular subject areas. They found substantial differences in practice between tested and nontested grades. In this survey, teachers reported that they had received more professional development for the subjects that were assessed in their grade.

Qualitative research provides a more in-depth view of what Kentucky's test-based staff development looks like in practice. Borko and her colleagues (2002) conducted case studies of professional development in four Kentucky schools and described offerings focused on portfolio development, analysis of student work, curriculum alignment with state frameworks, and graphic organizers developed by resource teachers to assist students in constructing answers to open-response items on state assessments. In one school, teachers observed demonstration lessons on such "assessed" topics as persuasive and narrative writing, on-demand writing, and answering open-ended response questions.

Staff development intended to facilitate assessment-driven reform tends to focus teachers' efforts on what will enable students to perform well on the test, rather than what will enable them to achieve an intellectual understanding of the content (Sheldon & Biddle, 1998). Thus, the motivation for both teacher and student learning derives from the pressure to perform well on specific tasks rather than the pursuit of broader learning goals. Teachers' own learning is focused on mastering particular instructional practices rather than gaining access to the broader professional knowledge base.

Scripted Curricula as Motivation for Learning

Another practice that has resurfaced amid reform agendas advocating high standards for all students is the use of scripted curricula. Initially designed to ensure fidelity to treatment in intervention studies, scripts are also being used to "teacher proof" curricula and to ensure uniform implementation of innovative practices adopted by school districts (see, e.g., Randi & Corno, 1997, for a review of implementation research). Implementation of prescribed curricula has long provided the content for staff development (McLaughlin & Marsh, 1978), and learning the script remains the focus of many district-wide staff development initiatives.

Arguing that low-performing students need the consistency that a uniform curriculum provides, some urban school districts have adopted highly structured, scripted curricula as a means for improving low-performing schools. In New York City, for example, teachers in low-performing schools have been required to use a single, highly scripted reading program (Goodnough, 2003a). This uniform approach for failing schools has been criticized for creating a class system that allows middle-class students access to more innovative teaching while students in high-poverty schools are bound by a mandated curriculum and schedule (Goodnough, 2003a). Equally important, teachers in these schools, who are often novices, experience staff development that focuses on the implementation of specific curricular programs rather than professional development that contributes to their growth as teachers. Some argue that such "rule-based" staff development is more appropriate for novices (Daley, 1999). Other research has found that even novice teachers are constrained by scripts (Smagorinsky, Lakly, & Johnson, 2002). In either view, teachers' growth as professionals may be limited without sufficient opportunities for learning grounded in practice.

Unfortunately, in many urban districts, the adoption of a common curriculum typically requires that experienced teachers as well as novices teach in uniform ways. Moreover, such curriculum programs typically come and go with each new administration (Goodnough, 2003b). Consequently, even when highly scripted programs are exchanged for less-regimented ones, teachers—both novice and experienced—still participate in the same kind of "teacher training" that focuses on learning to implement the new curriculum rather than learning about the broader concepts underlying the program's research base or attaining the subject matter knowledge necessary to teach the content in more than a superficial way.

In low-performing urban schools, teachers also are likely to come and go (Ingersoll, 2001). In other districts, however, beginning teachers receive support, such as mentoring, rather than prescriptions. Some research has found that beginning teachers supported by mentors were more likely to remain in teaching through the first seven to eight years than those in neighboring districts who received no mentor support (Strong & St. John, 2001). Moreover, about one quarter of the teachers in the study reported that mentoring was a factor in their decision to stay in teaching. Although learning to implement curriculum materials may be a place to start for novice teachers, it seems likely that mentors can play an important role in helping them thoughtfully interpret and adapt the curriculum for the different students they teach rather than mindlessly follow one script for all.

Some teachers report that some curriculum-based professional development helps them change their classroom practices, especially if they are given opportunities to work through the curriculum as their students will do. Researchers used data from a 1994 survey of California elementary teachers to examine the influence of assessment, curriculum, and professional development on teacher practice and student achievement (Cohen & Hill, 2000). These researchers found that student achievement was higher in schools where teachers were given an opportunity to learn to teach specific math content than in schools where teachers participated in professional development based on general pedagogy. Moreover, teachers reported that professional development grounded in the student curriculum made a difference in their classroom practices. On the other hand, teachers who participated in issue-specific workshops, such as cooperative learning or "Family Math," less often described changes in their teaching practices.

The curriculum-centered professional development these teachers described included learning to implement "replacement units," curriculum modules on specific topics in mathematics developed to make the existing curriculum consistent with the California Curriculum Framework. This framework intended to reform the teaching of mathematics so that instruction placed an emphasis on mathematical reasoning and explanation rather than skills and facts. Teachers could use the units to replace existing units in their mathematics textbook. In their professional development activities, teachers were given an opportunity to learn not only the new curriculum modules but also the mathematics content their students would study.

Because this research was based on teachers' reported practices and did not include classroom observations, it is difficult to determine whether or not these teachers actually changed their classroom practices and, if so, in what way. For example, were these teachers able to adapt activities in the replacement units to meet individual student needs or design other activities to provide additional support or challenges for their students? Perhaps more important, did these teachers implement instructional practices consistent with the reform movement's principles when they taught other units from their mathematics textbooks? Cohen and Hill (2000), noted that the teachers reported that, rather than abandoning their past instructional practices entirely, they incorporated the newly learned elements into them, which suggests that these teachers used the curriculum materials in flexible ways.

One important question for further research is whether or not these teachers were able to use the reform-oriented curriculum units as models for designing and delivering instruction on other topics in their mathematics curriculum in ways that promote students' conceptual understanding. Put another way, it is important to understand whether or not providing teachers with such models, together with access to a common body of knowledge—which, in this case, included the underlying principles of the discipline of mathematics—helps them to transfer their knowledge to new teaching situations. If not, even reform-oriented curriculum modules risk producing the same types of superficial and short-term changes in teaching practice described in the long history of implementation research (see, e.g., Randi & Corno, 1997).

Content as Design

There is some evidence that the selection of the content to be learned drives the design of staff development. This is another example of paying more attention to *what* teachers need to know than to *how* best to design professional development. When the staff development topic focuses on the implementation of a specific instructional program rather than broader teaching concepts, the workshop model of training persists, despite efforts to design teacher development programs that facilitate rather than direct learning.

Researchers who conducted a descriptive study of staff development in five early reading intervention programs found that the content of the staff development determined, in part, its structure, even when the staff development was specifically designed to be facilitative (Le Fevre & Richardson, 2002). The staff development facilitators viewed their role differently depending on the program they were promoting. The facilitators employed to promote *Success for All* (Slavin et al., 1994), a highly scripted reading intervention, and *Reading Recovery* (Clay, 1991), a structured, individualized reading intervention, sought to ensure that teachers would follow the structures of the programs. At the other end of the continuum, the staff development facilitator for the implementation of the State Standards Project encouraged teachers' active participation. In this project involving four school districts, teachers developed ways to apply the state standards to their own classroom instruction. In the middle of the continuum were two staff development programs designed to assist teachers in adapting externally developed curriculum materials to their own school settings. Thus, the content of the staff development ranged from learning to implement or adapt externally developed programs to developing local standards and practices consistent with state standards.

In short, the nature of the content itself invited more or less active teacher participation. Although participation levels varied, the content of each intervention, scripted or not, was uniform across the district, and all teachers participated in the same staff development related to the curriculum initiative. Moreover, although the facilitator of the State Standards Project invited teacher input, she had to balance her desire to give teachers choice and autonomy with the need to maintain consistency across teachers. Such consistency has been thought to build organizational capacity by developing a critical core of teachers prepared to implement common practices and, ultimately, to disseminate those new practices throughout the organization (Elmore, 2002). But, in this case at least, it seems that the uniform content constrained teachers' knowledge construction, even though they seemed to be taking a more active role in their learning.

The State of Practice: One Size Fits All

Although focused staff development activities designed to introduce or sustain the implementation of a common curriculum may build organizational capacity and unite teachers around the shared visions of the organization, they provide teachers little choice about their own professional learning and little autonomy in instructional decisions. Put another way, limiting teachers' choices about their own learning limits their access to knowledge and may leave them with an insufficient knowledge base to apply to different teaching situations. Individualized staff development has been criticized for being fragmented (Elmore, 2002; Newmann, King, & Youngs, 2000). Unfortunately, however, capacity-building staff development that seeks to develop a critical core of teachers devoted to a narrow range of particular instructional practices also has its disadvantages. Such staff development may carry with it the implicit message not only that one size fits all but also that a little knowledge is enough, for teachers and for students.

Some might argue that it is the organization's responsibility to provide staff development focused on particular school improvement efforts, not to support individual teachers' quests for knowledge. After all, teachers are free to seek professional learning opportunities on their own time. But how many teachers are willing to support their own professional learning? The *National Center for Education Statistics* (Choy & Ross, 1998) surveyed teachers in 1993-94 and found that almost 90% participated in district-sponsored inservice programs, compared to 50% who participated in activities sponsored by professional associations and only 25% who took college or university courses. Thus, most teachers participate in what the districts provide and fewer teachers seek opportunities outside the district. This may be because of a lack of initiative on the part of teachers, or lack of district support, including funding and approval. More research is needed to determine the reasons why so few teachers take responsibility for their own learning and what resources teachers need to encourage and support their independence as learners.

A more recent *National Center for Education Statistics* study (U.S. Department of Education, 2001) surveyed a representative sample of 5,253 public school teachers in 50 states and the District of Columbia and found that not much had changed on the district staff development menu. Teachers most frequently reported participating in professional development related to state or district curriculum and performance standards. Most of the professional development these teachers reported was of a short duration; they reported that they typically spent one day or less on specific activities. Based on this recent survey, much of what teachers experience is still short-term activity linked to state or district priorities. These statistics suggest that school districts exercise considerable control in teachers' access to knowledge—what districts offer is what most teachers learn.

Funding Staff Development

Historically, spending for professional development has not been a priority in the nation's school districts. The National Commission on Teaching and America's Future (Darling-Hammond, 1997) called for an investment in teacher professional development, citing the nation's low expenditures on teacher professional development compared to those of other countries and compared to U.S. corporate expenditures for employee development. A recent study analyzed professional development expenditures by U.S. school districts using data from the Census Bureau (Killeen, Monk, & Plecki, 2002). Researchers found that from 1992 to 1998 districts devoted approximately 3% of their total yearly expenditures to professional development, reflecting a flat trend in new investments in teacher development. This alarming trend continues despite considerable evidence that policies and institutional practices that improve teacher quality also make a difference in student learning (Darling-Hammond, 2000).

Some research suggests that what makes a difference in the quality of professional development is not so much what the district spends as how the district chooses to spend the funding it has. Researchers evaluated professional development in districts that received funding from the Eisenhower Professional Development Program, the federal government's substantial investment focused on developing the knowledge and skills of classroom teachers (Garet, Porter, Desimone, Birman, & Yoon, 2001). Districts may use Eisenhower funds to support a wide range of professional development activities, including workshops and conferences, study groups, and networks. Researchers surveyed a national sample of 1,027 mathematics and science teachers participating in professional development funded by the Eisenhower program and asked them to report the degree to which participation in particular activities enhanced their knowledge and skills.

The researchers drew from prior research and best-practice models to identify six features of high-quality professional development. Activities were categorized by three structural features: form (traditional or reform); duration (contact hours and time span); and participation (collective participation from one department or school or individual activities). Reform activities included study groups, teacher networks, mentoring relationships, and individual research projects. Traditional activities included workshops, courses, and conferences. In addition, activities were also categorized by three core features: the degree of content focus (i.e., focus on subject matter content and how students learn that subject matter); the opportunities for active learning; and coherence or alignment with state, district, and individual professional development goals. The structural and core features were interrelated. For example, reform activities were more likely to be of longer duration and include collective participation, but traditional activities that were of longer duration and offered collective participation opportunities produced similar outcomes (as measured by teachers' reports of the impact of the activity on their practice).

Results indicated that only 23% of the teachers surveyed participated in reform types of professional development. Moreover, most teachers reported participating in activities that did not have collective participation or a major emphasis on content, that were of short duration, and that had limited coherence and a small number of active learning opportunities (see also Desimone, Porter, Garet, Yoon, & Birman, 2002). This research found much variation in professional development and teaching practices within schools, suggesting that, even within schools, not all teachers have equal access to high-quality professional development. We view this as a "knowledge property" issue. Shouldn't every teacher have access to high-quality professional development?

The researchers cautioned that cost is a major impediment to implementing extensive high-quality professional development and that, even with external funding, schools often must choose between serving large numbers of teachers with short-term, superficial learning activities or fewer teachers with more in-depth, sustained professional development activities. Some districts, however, may have more capacity than others when it comes to providing teachers with access to high-quality professional development. Some research has investigated how districts' management strategies relate to the quality of professional development they provide teachers (Desimone, Porter, Birman, Garet, & Yoon, 2002). Drawing from the Eisenhower national sample, researchers interviewed a sample of district professional development coordinators about district-sponsored professional development activities. Certain strategies, such as aligning district activities to national standards, continuous improvement efforts, and teacher involvement in planning were associated with high-quality professional development. This research suggests that, in addition to funding, certain other strategies need to be implemented to provide high-quality professional development.

Not all districts spend professional development funds wisely. One study, for example, conducted a cross-case analysis of professional development spending in seven elementary schools in a large urban district. Schools within the district varied widely in their levels of professional development funding, depending on school performance, availability of discretionary funds, and staff preferences (Fermanich, 2002). Other research found that even when districts allocate considerable funds for professional development, most of the investments are spent on district-controlled activities, typically in ineffective ways and for unclear purposes (Corcoran, 1995). But is it not reasonable to expect that those who invest in staff development also control its content? Schools, after all, are organizations that expect returns on their investments. The Education Commission of the States (1999) compared schools to private sector corporations and recommended that schools align training strategies with organizational goals. But is this not what schools are doing when they choose staff development programs expressly designed to raise student achievement on standardized, high-stakes tests? Like private sector corporations, schools are increasingly evaluated in terms of results and performance, so they may be pressed to invest in short-term staff development to achieve the organization's immediate goals or to serve large numbers of teachers rather than to support in-depth teacher learning sustained over time that could potentially contribute to the profession as a whole.

Present Practices Summarized

Given limited resources and the pressure to achieve immediate results, performance-oriented schools may find it increasingly challenging to provide high-quality professional development. As school districts provide fewer personally relevant, meaningful professional development opportunities, teachers' access to high-quality professional development may depend on their own initiative—on their willingness to seek out learning opportunities beyond their school districts as well as their aptitude for learning within their classrooms, from their own teaching.

There is evidence that some teachers may leave schools that do not give them opportunities to learn. Johnson and Birkeland (2003) followed the career paths of 50 new teachers in Massachusetts for four years. Eight of these teachers, termed *voluntary movers*, left their original schools to seek better working conditions, including more supportive learning environments with such things as opportunities to learn and grow together with their colleagues, reasonable assignments, and accessible, respectful leaders who talked with teachers about instruction. All but one of these voluntary movers had entered teaching after pursuing other careers, that included law and engineering.

Other research has found similar patterns. Researchers conducted a longitudinal study that surveyed 392 teachers entering the New Jersey teaching force in 1987 through traditional and alternative teacher preparation programs (Natriello & Zumwalt, 1992). Of these teachers, 13 from the traditional programs and 12 from the alternative programs participated in interviews that followed their career paths. Of the 12 alternatively prepared teachers, 4 left their original schools voluntarily and accepted employment in other schools within the first six years of their teaching career. Two of these teachers were "second career" teachers and two entered alternative programs immediately after receiving their undergraduate degrees. Teachers' reasons for leaving schools included unsupportive working environments, difficult teaching assignments, and salary, as well as leaving in order to "do other things." These "other things" included graduate coursework and teaching in a private school. Interestingly, no teachers in the traditionally prepared group left their original school districts voluntarily, although some left their original schools and accepted teaching positions elsewhere because of circumstances such as lay-offs or family situations requiring a move out of the state (see also Randi, in press). Further research is needed to investigate these patterns in teacher turnover.

The National Commission on Teaching and America's Future suggests that teacher attrition is as much an issue of quality as of quantity. A school may benefit when ineffective teachers leave (NCTAF, 2003). But the reverse is also true; neither the school nor the profession benefits from an exodus of effective teachers. Further research might investigate possible links between learning opportunities offered teachers and teacher turnover, considering not only how many teachers leave but which teachers leave, and for what reasons.

Visions of the Future

In striking contrast to the workshop-style development teachers typically experience, the current staff development literature presents a futuristic fantasy in which teachers are given the time and support for collaborating with colleagues, analyzing student work, and reflecting on their practice. The National Staff Development Council (NSDC) and other advocates of teacher professional learning have argued that high-quality professional development ought to be recognized, fully funded, and institutionalized at the school and district levels. But few schools have the capacity to support such visions.

The NSDC envisions teacher teams that collectively assume the responsibility for student achievement, supported by high-quality staff development that

- focuses on deepening teachers' content knowledge and pedagogical skills;
- includes opportunities for practice, research, and reflection;
- is embedded in educators' work and takes place during the school day;
- is sustained over time; and
- is founded on a sense of collegiality and collaboration among teachers and between teachers and principals in solving important problems related to teaching and learning (Sparks, 2002, p. I-4).

Unfortunately, schools can more easily offer workshops addressing content and pedagogy to large numbers of teachers than they can change schools into learning communities where all teachers are given the time, resources, and organizational structure to support collective problem solving. Restructuring the school day to make common time for reflection, collaboration, and problem solving has more often been a vision than an accomplishment.

In contrast to the NSDC's vision, a report from the National Foundation for the Improvement of Education (NFIE) has encouraged teachers to "take change of their own learning" (Renyi, 1996). Viewing teacher professional development as critical for student success, this report includes lessons for both teachers and schools. Like the NSDC, the NFIE urges schools to reallocate time and funding for teacher professional learning. But, recognizing that schools may not provide these resources, the NFIE views teachers as professionals who are ultimately responsible for their own learning. For example, the NFIE report encourages teachers to form partnerships with parents, seek resources for learning among community members, and join teacher networks focused on subject matter expertise.

Lieberman (1996) proposed an expanded view of teacher professional learning that addressed the needs of both the individual and the collective. She envisioned a continuum of teacher professional learning opportunities, including learning that takes place both in school and out of school. In addition to the formal learning experiences typically provided by organizations, Lieberman described informal in-school teacher learning opportunities as well as out-of-school learning experiences, such as teacher networks. Notably, these less formal types of teacher learning require less support from the organization. Although some in-school experiences require some degree of support from the school organization, such as peer coaching, teacher leadership opportunities, and school site management teams, other professional learning experiences described in Lieberman's continuum, both in school and out of school, can be accessed by teachers with little or no support from the school. For example, teachers can reflect on their practice through journal writing, conduct teacher research in their own classrooms, and engage in online discussions with colleagues.

This vision of professional development represents a fundamentally different notion of staff development—one that, paradoxically, might be easier to facilitate than the workshop model or formal professional development programs that require substantial time, resources, and restructuring. Rather than provide workshops on specific skills, schools might profitably offer teachers opportunities to engage in new teaching practices, reflect on the processes of learning, and work with their colleagues to pose and solve problems, thus capitalizing on learning opportunities that already exist embedded in the daily routines of school. Similarly, out-of-school experiences afford learning opportunities for teachers, such as teacher-to-teacher networks and partnerships with youth-based organizations. Such professional learning experiences in school as well as opportunities beyond school may be more accessible to teachers than capacity-building practices, which are often envisioned but seldom implemented.

Digging Deeper: Best Practices Examined

Contemporary staff development literature suggests that teachers learn little from traditional inservice workshops and that they should engage in more experiential professional learning. But what teachers actually learn in more contemporary forms of staff development has not often been investigated. Wilson and Berne (1999) conducted a review of the literature, selecting exemplary projects that focused on both content and pedagogy. These researchers examined projects that focused on one of three categories: subject matter, student learning, or teaching practices. Wilson and Berne then identified three themes that connected all of the projects. First, all involved learning communities that attempted to redefine teaching practices. Second, in contrast to traditional staff development delivered in workshops, these projects enabled teachers to be active learners, discovering and activating new knowledge about teaching and learning. Much in the manner of scientists, teachers in these projects inquired into the subject matter they taught, into the nature of student learning, and into their own teaching practice. Third, in all of the projects, building collegiality was critical to engendering the professional discourse in the learning community. One salient finding was that the development of community might differ depending on the context of the community (e.g., in school or outside school). This finding may indicate the importance of teacher participation in a range of both in-school and out-of-school learning experiences, as described in Lieberman's (1996) continuum. The nature of the professional discourse understandably depends on the nature of the community. Out-of-school networks, for example, may focus on general concerns about subject matter, student learning, or teaching, whereas in-school networks may focus more closely on particular students or school contexts.

High-Quality Professional Development: A Consensus?

During the past decade, the staff development literature has converged around several important features that characterize effective staff development. For example, there is agreement that teacher professional learning should focus on instruction and student learning outcomes (Abdal-Haqq, 1995; Corcoran, 1995; Darling-Hammond & McLaughlin, 1995; Elmore, 2002; Renyi, 1996), be sustained and continuous rather than short term (Elmore; Garet et al., 2001; Lieberman, 1996), and provide teachers with opportunities for reflection on practice (Abdal-Haqq; Elmore; Lieberman; Sparks, 2002; Wilson & Berne, 1999). Hawley and Valli (1999) have described the convergence around these characteristics as an "unprecedented consensus" among researchers and professional developers.

One problem with identifying characteristics of "effective" staff development is that there is little research directly linking the effect of different types of professional development to student learning. Such research would require carefully designed experiments comparing a number of different forms of professional learning while holding other variables constant. As Guskey (2003) explains, research on effective professional development is complicated by the varied contexts and goals of the different programs. In reviewing the literature, Guskey found that programs identified as being "effective" vary widely depending on the criteria used to determine effectiveness. Also, programs that appear to be similar may produce widely different results, depending on context. Guskey argues, for example, that less-qualified teachers may show significant improvement after participating in staff development programs, whereas more-qualified teachers participating in similar programs may show little improvement.

Consistent with Guskey's report, our review of the literature found little consensus on several important aspects of professional development. For example, who should design and choose professional learning experiences? Some argue that teachers should take control of their own learning (Renyi, 1996), others argue that schools and teachers should work together to design staff development (Sparks, 2002), and still others argue that professional development should be designed and organized by schools to improve capacity (Elmore, 2002). Similarly, there is disagreement on whether or not staff development should be voluntary, as is often the case when teachers choose to participate in off-site teacher networks (Lieberman & Wood, 2001) or mandated, as is typical in reform-oriented staff development (Borko, Elliott, & Uchiyama, 2002; Youngs, 2000).

Another issue focuses on the location of staff development. A growing movement casts professional development as integral to school operations and situates professional development in school contexts (Hawley & Valli, 1999). The staff development literature includes both examples of "job-embedded" staff development, deeply rooted in school contexts (Elmore, 2002; Youngs, 2000), as well as examples of off-site professional development networks, such as university-school partnerships, teacher networks, and teacher center projects (Lieberman, 1996). There seems to be no clear consensus that job-embedded staff development is more or less effective than off-site learning experiences. When opportunities for both in-school and off-site professional learning experiences are offered to teachers, teachers' learning is enriched by variety and choice, and the organization is enriched by teachers' learning as well (Lieberman).

In Lieberman's (1996) continuum, individuals and organizations are viewed as mutually supportive. Yet, in practice and in the literature, tensions still exist; researchers and practitioners debate the role of the individual in the collective. Those interested in large-scale school reform view individuals as assisting or hindering change efforts. Individual teachers have few choices about their own learning when staff development focuses on large-scale reforms intended to institutionalize particular innovative practices (Elmore, 2002; Fullan, 2000). Elmore, for example, argues that the knowledge gap for effective staff development is not so much in how to design staff development as it is in how to institutionalize the "ideal prescriptions" in schools (p. 11).

Others view the organization as supporting individual change. Drawing on research in a number of different areas, including learning in general, teacher learning, and organizational change, Loucks-Horsely and Matsumoto (1999) described contexts supporting teacher learning, such as organizations that facilitate learner-centered and knowledge-centered environments. Optimal learning environments provide teachers with feedback and opportunities to learn together in a community. New formats for professional development have been created, including curriculum development; immersion in a subject area, such as doing hands-on science work; and collaborations with experts and mentors, both inside and outside school contexts. Drawing on the organizational change literature, the researchers emphasize the important conditions that promote teaching learning, such as leadership and consistency of focus over time. This research suggests that learner-friendly organizations facilitate rather than prescribe individuals' learning opportunities as well as allow for both in-school and out-of-school learning, thus widening teachers' access to knowledge.

Teacher Learning in Context

One promising line of research focuses on teacher professional learning within school contexts. Little (2003) describes a spontaneous form of learning arising from teachers' individual classrooms and developing through out-of-classroom interactions with colleagues in the teachers' own schools or subject area departments. Through case studies, Little investigated the collegial interactions among teachers of mathematics and English in two high schools. Little's research focused on teacher groups with a clear collective identity and a professional task orientation. For example, these groups identified themselves by name (e.g., Algebra Group, Academic Literacy Group) and focused their interactions on improvement-oriented professional work. Participation was voluntary, and the groups were organized around topics of common interest. The Academic Literacy Group included five teachers who agreed to develop a new ninth grade course on reading comprehension. Meeting informally during the school day or after school, teachers in these groups discussed problems of practice, which, although particular to their own classrooms, demonstrated common themes in the teachers' collective classroom experiences. At one meeting, teachers in the Academic Literacy Group analyzed actual samples of student work, discussed the feedback they had provided to their students, and examined the teaching practices that had led to the desired student performance. In the Algebra Group, teachers focused on collectively solving a problem of practice brought to the discussion table by a novice teacher—how to teach a range of students with differing motivations and abilities.

What is particularly striking about these teacher groups is that they operated informally within the existing school structure, suggesting that teachers might have access to this form of teacher professional development with or without organizational supports. In schools, there are countless opportunities for teachers to organize informally around social or personal interests, such as sports or hobbies. But in these two cases, teachers had organized themselves in a local community of practice centered on teaching and learning. In fact, each group differed in the resources or artifacts that afforded learning opportunities. For example, in the Algebra Group, teachers examined students' thinking and learning difficulties in mathematics. In the Academic Literacy Group, teachers examined their own classroom teaching practices, such as the tasks they assigned their students. The language used was specific to each group, characterized by vernacular rather than formal terms (for example, teachers used terms such as "warm-ups" or "guess and check" to describe instructional practices). Despite the different learning opportunities, informal structure, and localized discourse, these teacher groups were engaged in ongoing professional learning: teacher interactions in each group focused on student learning, were sustained over time, and afforded opportunity for reflection on practice.

In these cases, teachers' own learning and engagement in professional activities apparently contributed to the improvement of practice in these particular schools. It seems only logical to assume that students and schools also benefit from teachers' knowledge. The teachers' persistent use of vernacular language, however, may be viewed as evidence that teacher learning is not situated in the broader context of the profession as the collective. The use of the vernacular may indicate that the professional knowledge base is not available to these teachers, that they have not yet accessed it, or that they have labeled their own discoveries much as researchers and theorists label constructs. In any case, these local communities of practice might be viewed as fledgling professional communities that reflect the evolving nature of teaching as a profession—working for learning's sake.

Understanding Differences Through Learning Theory

When examined through the lens of learning theory, staff development practices reveal subtle differences related to beliefs about the knowledge base deemed necessary for teaching and to fundamental beliefs about how people learn. These differences may explain, in part, the lack of consensus about the characteristics of effective staff development. To understand these differences, we next explore theories of teacher knowledge, learning in general, and adult learning.

Teacher Knowledge

Substantial research exists on teacher knowledge and expertise (see, e.g., Borko & Putnam, 1995; Shulman, 1987). Elmore (2002) categorized teacher knowledge into three domains: knowledge of subject matter, general pedagogical·knowledge, and pedagogical content knowledge. In this view, the knowledge and skills that constitute teacher expertise are forms of declarative and procedural knowledge that can be imparted to teachers in traditional staff development and teacher preparation programs.

Others believe that knowing "what and how" is not sufficient for teaching. Teaching requires knowing when and how to apply particular instructional strategies within the context of particular and dynamic classroom situations. Translating research into practice in this way requires a different kind of knowledge, termed *craft knowledge* or *practitioner knowledge*. Distinguishing practitioner knowledge from research knowledge, Hiebert, Gallimore, and Stigler (2002) have identified three features of practitioner knowledge that make it especially useful and valuable for teachers: First, practitioner knowledge is deeply rooted in classroom practice, and its creation is motivated by particular problems of practice. Second, practitioner knowledge differs from research-generated knowledge in its specificity. Critics of practitioner knowledge might argue that it is so specific that it is not useful to other teachers in different situations. Knowledge from research, on the other hand, is generalized and thus applicable to a wide variety of situations. Yet, given the difficulties in translating generalized knowledge into practice, some might argue that research-generated knowledge is not as useful to teachers as practitioner knowledge. In fact, there is value in both research-generated and practitioner knowledge, and one lesson learned from this debate might be the recognition of a different role for staff development—one in which researchers work with teachers to facilitate the generation of practitioner knowledge (see also Richardson, 1994c; Randi & Corno, 2000). The third feature of practitioner knowledge that Hiebert, Gallimore, and Stigler identified also distinguishes it from research-generated knowledge. Practitioner knowledge draws on and connects aspects of knowledge to solve problems of practice. Hiebert, Gallimore, and Stigler called for making practitioner knowledge public so that it might be examined in wider contexts.

Others have noted similar distinctions. Cochran-Smith & Lytle (1999) distinguished three different conceptions of teacher learning. The first, knowledge-*for*-practice, consists of formal knowledge of pedagogy and subject matter, and this conception is based on the assumption that teachers' knowledge is acquired from experts outside the classroom. The second, knowledge-*in*-teaching, consists of craft knowledge generated by teachers as they reflect on their practice. Professional development and teacher education that facilitate the acquisition of knowledge typically use teaching cases and videos of practice as learning resources while a facilitator guides inquiry and reflection on practice. The third type, knowledge-*of*-practice, consists of knowledge generated by systematic inquiry into one's practice, often in collaboration with researchers. Professional development schools and teacher networks supporting teacher research are examples of the contexts for such inquiry. One distinguishing feature of this third type of teacher knowledge is that it is typically linked to larger reform efforts and positions the teacher as change agent.

These fundamentally different conceptions of teacher learning promote dramatically different types of professional development. The first focuses on the passive acquisition of externally generated knowledge, and the others on the generation of knowledge by teachers, whether individually, collectively, or in collaboration with researchers. Both externally generated and teacher-constructed knowledge are important. Knowledge about teaching and learning can be acquired, but learning how to apply that knowledge to the problems of practice requires work for learning's sake. Thus, the generation of new knowledge derives from the work of teaching.

Social Cognitive Learning

The idea that teachers learn by discussing problems of practice with colleagues is a fairly common theme in contemporary teacher professional development literature (Abdal-Haaq, 1995; Elmore, 2002;

Sparks, 2002). Drawing on social cognitive learning theory, researchers propose that these communities of practice form around the common ideas, norms, values, and tools of the discipline practiced by community members (Lave & Wenger, 1991). There is a growing body of literature on social cognitive learning theory, which provides insights into how individuals learn in informal, out-of-school contexts. In contrast to formal, in-school learning, informal learning tends to emphasize broad goals rather than specific learning outcomes, is typically voluntary, and is supportive of individual differences (Schauble, Beane, Coates, Martin, & Sterling, 1996). Participation in informal learning opportunities typically results in a product or performance rather than the acquisition of specific knowledge and skills. Learners are motivated by participation in a community where knowledge is shared and created by its members. Put simply, in this theory, individuals matter.

Studies of apprentices learning trades have contributed to our understanding of how learning occurs in natural settings where opportunities for learning are afforded by participation in work practices rather than structured by master tradesmen in the form of directions for accomplishing specific tasks (Lave & Wenger, 1991). In these situations, individuals are apprenticed into a community of practice through their direct involvement or participation in the work valued by the community and through their interactions with mentors and others in the community. In these communities, learners avail themselves of the resources, tools, and learning opportunities afforded them by participation in the community of practice.

As members of communities of practice, experienced teachers, for example, apprentice novice teachers into the teacher workforce, and they themselves continue to learn from practice. In communities of practicing teachers, the artifacts of teaching—lesson plans, student work samples, and instructional tasks—are likely to afford learning opportunities, both individually and collectively. Individual teachers draw on such resources for improving their own practice and come together to share what they have learned with others, engaging in discourse around the common problems of practice (Little, 2003). Rather than depend on organizational structures that potentially both support and limit their learning, teacher communities work around the constraints of practice, finding time to engage in meaningful discourse that often generates new knowledge.

In contrast, in more structured learning situations, teachers, staff developers, facilitators, and others provide resources and, by implication, limit learning (Lave & Wenger, 1991). Thus, although teachers may be given opportunities to reflect collectively on their practice, their experiences, when structured by the institution and organized around specific learning outcomes, may more closely reflect older learning theories underlying traditional instructional practices, such as teacher-directed (or organization-directed) instruction, than more contemporary learning theory.

Most important, social cognitive theory has taught us that individuals contribute in unique ways to the collective, and in so doing, they change the nature of the collective. Individual expertise is valued and differences are welcomed and celebrated (Lave & Wenger, 1991). As applied to teacher professional development, social cognitive theory encourages teacher autonomy and participation in activities uniquely attuned to their needs. There is little tolerance for prescription; without the introduction of new ideas, the shared knowledge base would remain fixed. Our vision of *profession* development is consistent with social cognitive theory. As individuals learn and share their expertise with colleagues, both within schools and across schools, the knowledge base of the profession, the collective, changes.

Adult Learning

Research on adult learning converges with social cognitive learning theory and suggests that adults—teachers—learn best outside formal educational settings. In pioneering research on adult learning, Brookfield (1986) studied adults learning in such varied out-of-school contexts as work settings, single-parent groups, and citizens' action committees. Brookfield reported observing several common features not unlike those observed in studies of communities of practice. For example, participants engaged voluntarily in a purposeful exploration of knowledge, skills, and experiences in a group setting, bringing their own individual prior knowledge to bear on solving problems of common interest. Based on this research, Brookfield proposed six characteristics of effective practice for facilitating adult learning: 1) participation in learning is voluntary; 2) there is respect among the participants; 3) facilitation is collaborative, and leadership and facilitation roles are shared among participants; 4) praxis is at the heart of facilitation, and learning revolves around reflection on and interpretation of one's own work; 5) facilitation aims to foster critical reflection and renewal of practice; and 6) the aim of facilitation is the nurturing of self-directed, empowered adults (pp. 9-11).

Other research also focuses on how adults learn in work settings. Drawing on social cognitive theory, Billett (2002) proposed a theory of workplace pedagogy. In Billet's theory, workers are afforded opportunities to learn through participation in work activities, direct guidance (e.g., mentoring by coworkers), and indirect guidance (e.g., observing others in the workplace). The workplace constrains learning when workers are restricted to performing routine tasks and when they are not given direct guidance. Workplace pedagogy uses existing resources (i.e., coworkers and workplace artifacts) to develop workers' expertise. As Billett points out, workplace pedagogy may be especially important in organizations unwilling or unable to provide funding for the continuing education of their employees.

Other scholarship on adult learning focuses on the implications for learning in the context of professional practice. Daley (2002) discussed these implications in a review of the research on continuing professional education in law, nursing, and social work. Daley argued that professionals are more likely to align themselves with the principles of the broader professional community than with the organization that employs them. That is, in the professions, the larger community, and *not* the specific organization, defines the roles and responsibilities of its members. Lawyers, for example, regardless of the particular firm in which they practice, view the practice of law consistently. Moreover, informal collegial networks may contribute as much to lawyers' learning as formal continuing professional education programs. Daley argued that these social interactions increase lawyers' allegiance to the profession and have an impact on what they learn and how they use information in their practice.

Taken together, this body of research raises questions about formal and informal learning experiences in school contexts. Do capacity-building staff development programs promote teachers' allegiance to the school rather than to the profession? Do schools, rather than the profession, define teachers' roles and responsibilities when they select and invest in particular staff development initiatives? Can workplace pedagogy which, paradoxically, may be less dependent on formal organizational support than other forms of staff development, promote teacher professionalism? How can schools be encouraged to afford more opportunities for teacher learning, such as assigning teachers' varied teaching assignments and mentoring responsibilities? Studying educational reforms in England and Wales, Hargreaves (1994) suggested that providers of continuing professional education must be responsive to professionals' definitions of their needs. Calling for a synthesis of professional and institutional development, Hargreaves not only recognized that individuals contribute to organizational capacity, he also emphasized the important role organizations serve in the development of individuals. This idea is supported by research in organizational psychology that found that when organizations support individuals' personal goals, individuals are more likely to invest effort in their work, and that motivation for job performance derives from an optimized psychological climate in the workplace (Brown & Leigh, 1996).

Promising Practices:
Toward a New Theory of Teacher Professional Education

Taking into account teachers' practical knowledge, social cognitive theory, and adult learning theory, as well as what we have learned from a history of staff development practices, a new theory of teacher professional learning has begun to emerge, one that pays as much attention to the design of staff development as to its content. In this theory, the content arises naturally from the experiences of the participants, who come together voluntarily around problems of practice that are of common interest. Learning resources are the artifacts of teaching that participants bring to the discussion. The discourse typically centers on problems of practice that have surfaced in individual classrooms. Together, teachers pool their expertise to solve these problems and, in turn, generate new knowledge about the particular teaching and learning situation. The voluntary nature of and the respect for teachers' knowledge in this form of teacher professional learning are consistent with adult learning theory and may serve as intrinsic motivators that are typically absent in staff development that affords teachers few choices about their own learning. Most important, this form of teacher professional learning contributes to the development of both the individuals and the profession and generates new knowledge from the sharing of expertise among members of teacher learning communities.

Several teacher professional development practices are consistent with this emerging theory of teacher professional learning. These include teacher networks, teacher study groups, teacher-university collaborations, and teacher research. In all these forms of professional development, teachers take the initiative for their own learning, and their learning is grounded in their own practice. Thus, future teachers may need to develop an aptitude for learning from practice as self-regulated learners responsible for their own learning (Randi, in press).

Teacher Networks

Although teacher networks are not new and have been associated with school reform, they are consistent with the emerging theory of teacher professional learning. Researchers have for some time viewed teacher networks as vehicles for educational change (Parker, 1977). Writing about teacher networks and school reform, Lieberman and McLaughlin (1992) differentiated networks from the teacher centers of the 1970s. Unlike the generic teacher centers, teacher networks select a clear focus of activity, establish an identity, and develop a learning community around common interests. Networks may be regional but typically expand nationally. Some networks, such as the Urban Mathematics Collaboratives and the National Writing Project, focus on particular subject matter. Other networks, such as the Foxfire Teacher Outreach Network, grow around common interests in particular teaching philosophies. A hallmark of teacher networking is teacher involvement in a professional community in which teachers shape their own learning (Lieberman & McLaughlin, 1992).

Lieberman and Grolnick (1996) conducted a study of sixteen teacher networks. The researchers interviewed network leaders and collected newsletters and print materials. They found common themes across the networks, including a facilitative leadership approach, collaborative learning, challenging agendas, "movement-like" rather than organizational structures, and a respect for both context-specific and generalized knowledge. These networks were described as a "new look for professional development." Networks, although still examined as vehicles for reform, were now viewed as a new form of teacher professional development that characterized staff development less as a tool for organizational development and more as a grassroots teacher movement focusing on the development of individual teachers.

As one example of a teacher network, the National Writing Project was the focus of a study by Lieberman and Wood (2001). The primary focus of this study was on the teacher network as a professional development opportunity rather than a vehicle for school reforms. The study focused on the work of individual teachers as they shared their own teaching practices, both teaching others and receiving feedback from like-minded colleagues teaching in schools across the nation. Although not specifically intended as a reform movement, the National Writing Project has contributed to the development of a pool of teachers capable of sharing their expertise with colleagues, both in their own schools and across schools. An important distinction between teacher networks and more traditional forms of professional development is the centrality of teacher knowledge and teaching practice in the teacher network learning community. Perhaps more important than what teachers learn about teaching literacy is what they learn about how to learn in a community of practice. The former may address the immediate needs of students and schools; the later prepares teachers to solve future problems as they arise in the context of practice.

Teacher Research

A second promising form of teacher professional learning is teacher research (Freedman, 2001; Richardson, 1994a). Since the 1980s, there has been a tremendous growth in the United States in teachers doing research on their own practices. There is much variety in the ways in which teacher research has been conceptualized, organized, and supported across the nation. Although some teachers have conducted research as individuals (e.g., Gallas, 1998), much of this work has taken place in the context of teacher research communities, either in small collaborative groups (e.g., Freedman, Simons, Kalnin, Casareno, & the M-Class Team, 1999) or in school faculty groups involving most of a school's staff (e.g., Calhoun, 1994). This teacher research has been sponsored by teachers themselves, as well as school districts, teacher unions, colleges and universities, regional educational laboratories, educational foundations, state and federal governments, and school-university partnerships (Zeichner & Noffke, 2001).

Some of the teachers doing research have followed a classic action research spiral of "plan, act, observe, and reflect" or some variation thereof (Elliott, 1991), but much of this inquiry in the United States has taken on a more narrative form, with multiple questions under investigation at once or with the immediate aim being a closer look at one's practice rather than a change in practice (Fishman, 2000). Although there have been many testimonials as to the value of teacher research as a professional development activity for teachers, there has been relatively little systematic research documenting its impact on teachers, their pupils, and schools.

Zeichner (2003) reviewed the research that has been conducted in the United States on the impact of teacher research and concluded that there are several features that appear to be important to the power of teacher research as a transformational professional development activity for teachers. When teacher research is conducted within the context of a teacher research community, these features include voluntary participation by teachers, a culture of inquiry that respects the voices of teachers and the knowledge that they bring to the research experience, a balance between honoring teachers' voices and expertise and asking them to critique what they know (i.e., a balance between safety and support and intellectual challenge), and teachers' ownership of their research focus and methodology. Zeichner also found it important that the research be conducted over a substantial period of time (at least a year) and that rituals and routines be established within the groups to build community and to provide structure to the discourse about teachers' research projects.

Although the focus in much of the teacher research in the United States has been on improving teaching within one's individual classroom, some of these inquiries have focused on improving schools and influencing educational policymaking (e.g., Meyers & Rust, 2003). One way in which the tension between school and school district improvement priorities and teachers' own definitions of their individual professional development needs has been handled is for a school or school district to organize teacher research groups around areas of institutional priority but to then give teachers ownership and control over their individual inquiries within these priority areas (Zeichner, 2003). Openness to teachers' ownership and control of their research studies will not be attractive to those who would like to move teachers' practices in particular, predetermined directions (e.g., in relation to standards), but it seems to be essential to teacher research that makes a difference for teachers and their pupils.

When schools invest in building teachers' capacity to conduct research under the kind of conditions outlined above, teachers often become more confident about their ability to promote student learning and more proactive about dealing with difficult situations that arise in their teaching. They also frequently acquire habits and skills of inquiry that they continue to use beyond their research experience, and they become more focused on the needs and thinking of their pupils. Finally, there have been links established between these conditions and improvements in pupil attitudes, behavior, and learning. For example, in a study of the teacher research program in the Madison, Wisconsin, school district, Zeichner and Klehr (1999) reported evidence of improvements in student learning associated with teachers' participation in year-long, district-sponsored research groups. As teachers conducted research, they implemented a variety of new practices with their students, including new grouping and scheduling patterns, multicultural literature, student journals, writing workshops, service learning projects, and so on. Many of these teachers' research reports documented improvements in students' attitudes, learning, and behavior that were associated with these interventions.

The evidence for these changes is provided by focused teacher observations, careful documentation of classroom activities, analyses

of student work samples, and teacher-designed assessments of particular learning activities. Some of the evidence documented learning
improvements for specific students over a period of time, and other
evidence documented learning improvements for different students
with a particular curriculum (e.g., how well kindergarten students
learned to write from one year to the next given changes in the
teacher's approach to teaching writing).

Teacher Study Groups

Another promising form of teacher professional learning is the
study group. Typically, study groups are school-based groups organized
by teachers, and the group's agenda arises from topics of interest to the
participants (Loucks-Horsley, Love, Stiles, Mundry, & Hewson, 2003).
Study groups may focus on teaching particular subject matter, implementing particular strategies, or reading and discussing research.
Because study groups require a substantial commitment from teachers
and support from administrators (e.g., released or common planning
time or resources), this form of professional development may be difficult to institutionalize in schools (Loucks-Horsley et al., 2003).

Lesson study, a type of teacher study group originating in Japan,
has been recognized as a powerful form of teacher professional development (Lewis, 2002). In lesson study groups, teachers first set a learning goal for their students and then collaboratively plan instructional
strategies that lead students to achieve that goal. The product of this
collaborative planning is an actual lesson plan. Fernandez (2002) conducted an empirical study of two groups of teachers participating in
lesson study in the United States. Japanese teachers recruited as mentors facilitated one group; Fernandez and her research team introduced
the other group to lesson study. Data included videotaped meetings
and lessons, participant interviews, field notes, and the actual lesson
plans. The results of the study revealed challenges in the adoption of
lesson study as a staff development activity in the United States. The
success of lesson study as a learning experience depends on the participants' stance toward inquiry. That is, Japanese teachers view lesson
study as a form of inquiry, turn their goals into researchable questions,
collect evidence as they implement the lessons, and interpret the results
in such a way as to generate a principle of practice or a question for
further study. American teachers struggled with examining their own
practice in this way, and their learning was limited to incidental knowledge gained from observing their colleagues teaching lessons. Fernandez suggested that lesson study and other forms of self-generated

inquiry may be especially difficult for U.S. teachers because they have had little experience in designing their own learning, having most often participated in the delivery model of staff development.

The challenges in implementing lesson study might also arise in implementing teacher research and other forms of teacher-driven professional development. It makes sense, then, for practitioners to seek more collaboration with researchers and university-based teacher educators. Such collaborations accentuate the continuing nature of teacher education across a teaching career and reconnect the inservice experience to the context of the university. It is important, however, that in these interactions, university researchers work with teachers in genuinely collaborative ways and do not seek to subvert teachers' intellectual responsibility for grappling with the complexities involved in studying one's teaching practice (Zeichner, 1995).

School-University Collaborations

Because of the challenges that may arise in facilitating teacher-driven professional development, the university-school partnership has been viewed as a promising concept for supporting teacher learning. Miller and O'Shea (1996) defined *partnership* as a set of reciprocal relationships. Describing one school-university partnership, the Southern Maine Partnership, the researchers found that members influenced each other through conversation, interactions, and common work, creating an egalitarian structure. Selected as a "promising practice" by the U.S. Department of Education (1998), the Southern Maine Partnership was initially established as a formal organization, with eight school districts contributing annual dues to participate in monthly discussions of research of interest to practitioners. The Southern Maine Partnership is one example of partnership, but university-school collaborations include a range of partnership structures—professional development schools, research programs such as Cognitively Guided Instruction, and individual teacher-researcher collaborations, to name a few.

First proposed by the Holmes Group (1986), professional development schools have been viewed as extensions of teacher education programs. The Holmes Group envisioned them as a kind of teaching laboratory in which novice teachers could hone their skills under the guidance of experienced teachers. Importantly, the Holmes Group vision also provided for different learning opportunities for teachers at different stages of their careers. Lieberman and Miller (1992) viewed professional development schools as opportunities for experienced teachers to engage in continuous inquiry into practice. Like teacher networks, professional development schools provide opportunities for teachers to collaborate with colleagues and focus their study on their teaching practices. For example, in professional development schools, teachers are typically introduced to innovative practices and encouraged to try out the new practices with support from colleagues who observe lessons and provide feedback. Unlike networks, professional development schools have a narrower constituency (i.e., a single school or district partnering with a particular university). Often, professional development schools are connected with colleges of education, providing both preservice and inservice teachers guidance in learning from practice, as professionals learn. Without such guidance, novice teachers may be left to acquire only a tacit knowledge of how professionals learn the context of their practice.

Another form of university-school partnership arises from research programs. In these programs, researchers disseminate their findings to practitioners through professional development and ongoing support for implementing practices consistent with research and contemporary learning theory. Unlike traditional staff development, in which teachers are expected to implement a particular innovation in prescribed ways, these programs focus on helping teachers understand the particular underlying theory so that they can adapt their instruction accordingly. One prominent example is Cognitively Guided Instruction, a program that helps teachers understand how children think mathematically (Carpenter, Fennema, & Franke, 1996). Based on the assumption that children construct knowledge of mathematics, the program encourages teachers to analyze children's mathematical thinking. Rather than delivering knowledge to teachers, researchers help teachers use analysis of children's thinking to guide their own instructional practices. A similar program in reading encourages teachers to analyze students' metacognitive reading strategies, developing metacognitive teachers as well as metacognitive readers (Duffy, 1993).

In other subject areas, similar university-teacher collaborations have provided "thoughtful" professional development. For example, Grossman, Wineburg, & Woolworth (2001) brought together 22 English and social studies teachers for the purpose of engaging them in discussions to deepen their knowledge of subject matter. As in Cognitively Guided Instruction, the researchers guided teachers to analyze thinking in the subject matter—this time, their own. For example, teachers themselves, in the manner of historians, analyzed primary sources and delved into research on historical thinking. As in networks, teachers formed a community of learners, shared ideas with each other, and brought primary sources and their "historical thinking" from the project back to their classrooms.

Individual teacher-university partnerships have also provided a range of opportunities for teacher professional development. In a broad sense, individual teachers pursuing graduate coursework might be considered a teacher-university partnership. But universities often provide other professional development opportunities to individual teachers as well. For example, teacher education programs may invite experienced teachers to teach preservice courses or deliver presentations and demonstration lessons for beginning teachers. Such experiences provide leadership and professional development opportunities for these teachers. As another example, individual teachers may be invited to collaborate with researchers to develop innovative curricula based on theory (see, e.g., Randi & Corno, 2000, for a description of teacher innovations in self-regulated learning).

In short, collaborative partnerships are increasingly viewed as legitimate professional development experiences. Summarizing the research on change and teacher professional development, researchers have described partnerships as meeting contemporary standards for effective professional development and leading to changes in instructional practices (Loucks-Horsley et al., 2003). That is, partnerships provide professional development driven by a well-defined and research-based image of effective classroom learning and teaching and provide opportunities for teachers to collaborate in learning new instructional approaches that they will ultimately use with their students. Loucks-Horsley and her colleagues extend the concept of university-school partnership to include partnerships with scientists and mathematicians in business and industry as well as in universities.

In these partnerships, the focus is on an intellectual understanding of content, whether the content is the subject matter (e.g., history or mathematics) or educational theory (e.g., research-based curriculum projects). Thus, this form of professional development serves to link theory and practice in ways that matter to classroom teachers. The theory teachers learn through this practice-oriented collaborative work has direct application to their work with students.

One Size Does Not Fit All

Common themes run through these promising practices. Teacher networks, teacher research, teacher study groups, and university-school collaborations each involve teachers in inquiry into their own practice. Knowledge is not delivered by external presenters; the agenda is teacher-driven. Consistent with contemporary social cognitive learning theory, learning occurs in a community of practice in which participants share their expertise and engage in discourse while drawing on the artifacts of teaching (e.g., student work samples, lesson plans). Some caution is warranted, however. These forms of teacher professional learning, in and of themselves, do not ensure success. Thompson and Zeuli (1999) note, for example, that some teacher study groups deteriorate into emotional support groups. We suggest that the more attention teachers give to accessing, sharing, and contributing to the professional knowledge base, the less likely their activities and dialogue will drift to other topics. We argue that teacher ownership is important in professional development, including teacher ownership of the professional knowledge base.

Subtle distinctions differentiate these promising practices, suggesting that all may coexist as teacher professional development options. In fact, they may serve as alternatives for meeting the varying needs of teachers at different points in their careers. Some teachers, for example, may prefer to broaden their perspective by collaborating with colleagues across the nation—an opportunity that networks typically offer. Teachers whose teaching philosophies may be inconsistent with mainstream practices in their schools, those who seek to bring innovative practices to their schools and classrooms, and those who prefer to participate in teacher professional development during summers and weekends might be attracted to teacher network opportunities. Other teachers sufficiently fortunate to work in schools with a core of like-minded colleagues and supportive organizational structures might benefit from initiating teacher study groups. For others interested in teacher research, mentoring, or leadership opportunities, professional development schools and university-school partnerships might offer supportive learning environments.

To illustrate and distinguish teacher *profession* development from other forms of professional development, we offer two hypothetical scenarios.

Scenario A. Improving student writing has been identified as a district priority. The decision to focus on writing was based on an analysis of student achievement on the writing portion of the state test. Results showed a gradual decline in students' test scores during the previous three years. The district has invested considerable time and funding in realigning the district writing curriculum to state standards. A teacher's guide has been developed by a committee of teachers to assist the teachers in implementing the new writing curriculum. All teachers must attend weekly workshops with staff developers and members of the curriculum committee to learn about the curriculum. Because the district's priority is now "writing across the curriculum" and professional development funding is limited, teachers' requests to attend out-of-district professional development activities in areas other than writing are typically denied. Teachers are required to submit a teaching portfolio each year as part of the district's teacher evaluation plan. The portfolio must include samples of student writing that document student progress at benchmark points in the writing curriculum.

Scenario B. Improving student writing has been identified as a district priority. The decision to focus on writing was based on an analysis of student achievement on the writing portion of the state test. Results showed a gradual decline in students' test scores during the previous three years. The principal shared these results at a faculty meeting, and teachers cited examples of student writing that were consistent with the test results. The faculty decided that student performance in writing was a problem that needed to be addressed. Weekly faculty meetings were set aside to work on this problem. Some teachers formed a study group and shared articles they had read. Some teachers conducted inquiry on their own teaching and shared their work with other teacher researchers. Other teachers joined lesson study groups and collaboratively planned writing lessons and assessed student work. Some teachers joined the National Writing Project; other teachers attended conferences on writing and writing-related topics, including writing for publication. One teacher who had started a writing lab invited a new teacher to work with her in the lab. Another teacher, who was writing an article with her graduate school instructor, shared her work with colleagues and asked them for feedback on her own writing. Once a month, the faculty meeting was devoted to a whole-group sharing session. Although writing was the immediate focus of teachers' attention, requests to attend conferences unrelated to writing were approved. Because of limited funds, teachers understood that they might not receive financial support for the activity. Nonetheless, teachers were encouraged to seek such learning opportunities and to bring back information, which might be critical for solving, anticipating, and preventing future problems.

Which approach to staff development, Scenario A or Scenario B, is more likely to improve student achievement? Currently, there is no clear consensus in the literature, nor is there sufficient empirical research to allow an evidence-based judgment about the advantage of one above the other. There is a critical need for empirical research that contributes answers to this question. The question speaks not to the *what* but to the *how* of professional development practices.

In the interim, there are other questions to ask: Which approach to staff development, Scenario A or Scenario B, is more likely to facilitate teachers' access to knowledge—knowledge that they might draw on to solve problems of practice now and in the future? In these scenarios, which teachers demonstrate more knowledge-seeking capacity? Which teachers take responsibility for their own learning and their students' learning? Which teachers would we choose to staff our schools?

Learning from History: Promised Practices

Profession development is a slow, steep process that depends on knowledge-seeking teachers to take up the challenge to access, share, and contribute to the professional knowledge base. These knowledge-seeking teachers can take up this challenge outside the contexts of their school organizations, as in teacher networks or in study groups sponsored by national organizations, or they can take up this challenge in schools, either in their own classrooms or in collaborative learning cultures. Profession development is not about learning to work more efficiently. As learning professionals, teachers are working to learn more effectually so that they may bring their knowledge to bear on the particular problems of practice.

Schools, including schools of education, can facilitate profession development by widening teachers' access to the professional knowledge base and by providing learning opportunities that prepare teachers for contributing to it themselves. One way to do this is for university teacher education programs to develop in individuals the aptitude to learn from teaching. For example, teacher education might develop teachers' understanding of the theoretical principles underlying practice and prepare teachers to engage in inquiry on practice. Colleges of education might also collaborate more closely with schools in the continuing education of teachers, just as schools collaborate with teacher preparation programs in the preservice education of teachers.

Schools might also support profession development, not by offering a smorgasbord of staff development activities or prescribing particular "remedies" to improve teachers, but by encouraging teachers to participate in activities that require them to tap into the professional knowledge base and work together to apply their knowledge to solve problems of practice. Ironically, the trend toward decreasing funding for staff development may afford teachers opportunities to take charge of their own learning. In a community of practice, constraints and affordances are often what the participants make of them. Some might view lack of funding as a constraint, while others might see it as an opportunity for innovation. Schools, for example, may find it more sensible to afford teachers resources for learning in the artifacts of teaching than in purchased programs; the resources for solving the complex problems of schools may derive from the teachers themselves.

No matter what form the future of professional development takes, given the history of failed attempts to "develop" teachers in traditional workshops, and the increasingly fewer resources available for teacher professional development, it seems clear that the quality of teacher professional learning may rest on teachers' willingness to seek out opportunities for their own learning. Certainly the responsibility for learning falls on teachers themselves, as some might argue it should in a profession. If the quality of teacher professional learning and, by extrapolation, of the profession depends on teachers themselves, then it seems to make perfect sense for organizations (both schools and teacher preparation programs) to support teachers in their continuing education efforts. In the end, the quality of education that will be available in our public schools will depend on the quality of professional learning opportunities available to teachers.

REFERENCES

Abdal-Haqq, I. (1995). *Making time for teacher professional development.* Washington, DC: ERIC Clearinghouse on Teaching and Teacher Education (ERIC Digest 95-4).

Alspach, J.G. (1995). *The educational process in nursing staff development.* St. Louis: Mosby.

Ball, D., & Cohen, D. (1999). Developing practice, developing practitioners: Toward a practice-based theory of professional education. In L. Darling-Hammond & G. Sykes (Eds.), *Teaching as the learning profession: Handbook of policy and practice* (pp. 1-32). San Francisco: Jossey-Bass.

Billett, S. (2002). Toward a workplace pedagogy: Guidance, participation, and engagement. *Adult Education Quarterly, 53*(1), 27-43.

Borko, H., Elliott, R., & Uchiyama, K. (2002). Professional development: A key to Kentucky's educational reform effort. *Teaching and Teacher Education, 18*, 969-987.

Borko, H., & Putnam, R. (1995). Expanding a teacher's knowledge base: A cognitive psychological perspective on professional development. In T. Guskey & M. Huberman (Eds.), *Professional development in education: New paradigms and practices* (pp. 35-65). New York: Teachers College Press.

Brookfield, S. (1986). *Understanding and facilitating adult learning: A comprehensive analysis of principles and effective practices.* San Francisco: Jossey-Bass.

Brown, S., & Leigh, T. (1996). A new look at psychological climate and its relationship to job involvement, effort, and performance. *Journal of Applied Psychology, 81*, 358-368.

Calhoun, E. (1994). *How to use action research in a self-renewing school.* Alexandria, VA: Association for Supervision and Curriculum Development.

Carpenter, T., Fennema, E., & Franke, M.L. (1996). Cognitively guided instruction: A knowledge base for reform in primary mathematics instruction. *Elementary School Journal, 97*(1), 3-20.

Choy, S.P., & Ross, M. (1998). *Toward better teaching: Professional development in 1993-94* (NCES No.98-230). Washington, DC: National Center for Educational Statistics.

Clay, M. (1991). *Becoming literate: The construction of inner control.* Auckland, New Zealand: Heinemann.

Cochran-Smith, M. (1994). The power of teacher research in teacher education. In S. Hollingsworth & H. Sockett (Eds.), *Teacher research and educational reform. The Ninety-third yearbook of the National Society for the Study of Education*, Part I (pp. 142-165). Chicago: National Society for the Study of Education.

Cochran-Smith, M., & Lytle, S. (1999). Relationships of knowledge and practice: Teacher learning in communities. In A. Iran-Nejad & P.D. Pearson (Eds.), *Review of Research in Education* (Vol. 24, pp. 249-306).

Cohen, D.K., & Hill, H.C. (2000). Instructional policy and classroom performance: The mathematics reform in California. *Teachers College Record, 102*, 294-343.

Corcoran, T.B. (June 1995). *Helping teachers teach well: Transforming professional development.* CPRE Policy Briefs. Philadelphia: University of Pennsylvania.

Corey, S. (1957). Introduction. In N.B. Henry (Ed.), *Inservice teacher education for teachers, supervisors and administrators. The Fifty-sixth yearbook of the National Society for the Study of Education*, Part I (pp. pp.1-10). Chicago: National Society for the Study of Education.

Corno, L. (in press). Work habits and work styles: Volition in education. (Introduction to the special issue). *Teachers College Record.*

Daley, B.J. (1999). Novice to expert: An exploration of how professionals learn. *Adult Education Quarterly, 49*(4), 133-148.

Daley, B.J. (2002). Context: Implications for learning in professional practice. *New Directions for Adult and Continuing Education, 96*, 79-88.

Darling-Hammond, L. (1997). *Doing what matters most: Investing in quality teaching.* New York: National Commission on Teaching and America's Future.

Darling-Hammond, L. (2000, January). Teacher quality and student achievement: A review of state policy evidence. *Education Policy Analysis Archives, 8*(1). Retrieved December 1, 2003, from http://epaa.asu.edu/epaa/v8n1

Darling-Hammond, L., & McLaughlin, M.W. (1995). Policies that support professional development in an era of reform. *Phi Delta Kappan, 76*(8), 597-604.

Darling-Hammond, L., & Sykes, G. (Eds.). (1999). *Teaching as the learning profession.* San Francisco: Jossey-Bass.

Desimone, L.M., Porter, A., Birman, B., Garet, M.S., & Yoon, K. (2002). How do district management and implementation strategies relate to the quality of professional development that districts provide to teachers? *Teachers College Record, 104*(7), 1265-1312.

Desimone, L.M., Porter, A., Garet, M.S., Yoon, K., & Birman, B. (2002). Effects of professional development on teachers' instruction: Results from a three-year longitudinal study. *Educational Evaluation and Policy Analysis, 24*(2), 81-112.

Dewey, J. (1904). The relation of theory to practice in education. In F.M. McMurry (Ed.), *The relation of theory to practice in the education of teachers. The third yearbook of the National Society for the Study of Education,* Part I (pp. 9-30). Bloomington, IL: Public School Publishing Company.

Duffy, G.G. (1993). Rethinking strategy instruction: Four teachers' development and their low achievers' understandings. *Elementary School Journal, 93*(3), 231-247.

Education Commission of the States. (1999). *Teacher preparation and professional development: A view from the corporate sector* (Policy Brief: Teacher Education).

Elliott, J. (1991) *Action research for educational change.* Philadelphia: Open University Press.

Elmore, R.F. (2002). *Bridging the gap between standards and achievement.* Washington, DC: Albert Shanker Institute.

Eraut, M. (1994). *Developing professional knowledge and competence.* Washington, DC: Falmer Press.

Fermanich, M.L. (2002). School spending for professional development: A cross-case analysis of seven schools in one urban district. *Elementary School Journal, 103*(1), 27-50.

Fernandez, C. (2002). Learning from Japanese approaches to professional development: The case of lesson study. *Journal of Teacher Education, 53*(5), 393-405.

Fishman, S. (2000). Charter conceptions of teacher research. In S. Fishman & L. McCarthy, *Unplayed tapes: A personal history of collaborative teacher research* (pp. 13-32). New York: Teachers College Press.

Freedman, S. (2001). Teacher research and professional development: Purposeful planning or serendipity? In A. Lieberman & L. Miller (Eds.), *Teachers caught in the action: Professional development that matters* (pp. 188-208). New York: Teachers College Press.

Freedman, S., Simons, E., Kalnin, J., Casareno, A., & the M-Class team. (1999). *Inside city schools: Investigating literacy in multicultural classrooms.* New York: Teachers College Press.

Fullan, M. (2000). The return of large-scale reform. *Journal of Educational Change, 1,* 1-25.

Fullan, M., & Steigelbauer, S. (1990). *The new meaning of educational change.* New York: Teachers College Press.

Gallas, K. (1998). *Sometimes I can be anything: Power, gender, and identity in a primary grade classroom.* New York: Teachers College Press.

Gallucci, C. (2003) *Theorizing about responses to reform: The role of communities of practice in teacher learning.* Seattle: Center for the Study of Teaching and Policy.

Garet, M., Porter, A., Desimone, L., Birman, B., & Yoon, K.S. (2001). What makes professional development effective? Results from a national sample of teachers. *American Educational Research Journal, 38*(4), 915-946.

Goertz, M.E., & Duffy, M. (2001). Assessment and accountability systems in the 50 states: 1999-2000 (Research Rep. No. RR-046). Philadelphia: University of Pennsylvania, Consortium for Policy Research in Education.

Goodnough, A. (2003a, January 19). A strict curriculum, but only for failing schools, mostly in poor areas of New York. *New York Times*.

Goodnough, A. (2003b, January 22). City is converting reading and math to uniform course. *New York Times*.

Griffin, G. (1999). Changes in teacher education: Looking to the future. In G. Griffin (Ed.), *The education of teachers. The Ninety-eighth yearbook of the National Society for the Study of Education* (pp. 1-17). Chicago: National Society for the Study of Education.

Grossman, P., Wineburg, S., & Woolworth, S. (2001). Toward a theory of teacher community. *Teachers College Record, 103*(6), 942-1012.

Guskey, T.R. (2003). What makes professional development effective? *Phi Delta Kappan, 84*(10), 748-756.

Hargreaves, D. (1994). The new professionalism: The synthesis of professional and institutional development. *Teaching and Teacher Education, 10*(4), 423-438.

Hawley, W.D., & Valli, L. (1999). The essentials of effective professional development. In L. Darling-Hammond & G. Sykes (Eds.), *Teaching as the learning profession*. San Francisco: Jossey-Bass.

Hiebert, J., Gallimore, R., & Stigler, J.W. (2002). A knowledge base for the teaching profession: What would it look like and how can we get one? *Educational Researcher, 31*(5), 3-15.

Holmes Group. (1986). *Tomorrow's teachers: A report of the Holmes Group*. East Lansing, MI: The Holmes Group.

Hong, L.K. (1996). *Surviving school reform: A year in the life of one school*. New York: Teachers College Press.

Ingersoll, R.M. (2001). *Teacher turnover, teacher shortages, and the organization of schools*. Seattle, WA: University of Washington, Center for the Study of Teaching Policy.

Ingersoll, R.M. (2004). Four myths about America's teacher quality problem. In this volume—M.A. Smylie & D. Miretzky (Eds.), *Developing the teacher workforce. The 103rd yearbook of the National Society for the Study of Education*, Part I (pp. 1-33). Chicago: National Society for the Study of Education.

Johnson, S.M., & Birkeland, S.E. (2003). The schools that teachers choose. *Educational Leadership, 60(8)*, 20-24.

Joyce, B., & Showers, B. (1980). Improving inservice training: The messages of research. *Educational Leadership, 37*, 379-385.

Joyce, B., & Showers, B. (1988). *Student achievement through staff development*. New York: Longman.

Killeen, K.M., Monk, D.H., & Plecki, M.L. (2002). School district spending on professional development: Insights available from national data (1992-1998). *Journal of Education Finance, 28*(1), 25-50.

Koretz, D.M., Barron, S.I., Mitchell, K., & Stecher, B. (1996). *The perceived effects of the Kentucky Instructional Results Information System (KIRIS)*. MR-792-PCT/FF. Santa Monica, CA: RAND.

Lave, J., & Wenger, E. (1991). *Situated learning: Legitimate peripheral participation*. New York: Cambridge University Press.

Le Fevre, D., & Richardson, V. (2002). Staff development in early reading intervention programs: The facilitator. *Teaching and Teacher Education, 18*(4), 483-500.

Lewis, C. (2002). Everywhere I looked: Levers and pendulums. *Journal of Staff Development, 23*(3), 59-65.

Lieberman, A. (Ed.). (1990). *Schools as collaborative cultures: Creating the future now*. New York: Falmer Press.

Lieberman, A. (1996). Practices that support teacher development. In M.W. McLaughlin & I. Oberman (Eds.), *Teacher learning: New policies, new practices* (pp. 185-201). NY: Teachers College Press.

Lieberman, A., & Grolnick, M. (1996). Networks and reform in American education. *Teachers College Record, 98*(1), 7-45.

Lieberman, A., & McLaughlin, M.W. (1992). Networks for educational change: Powerful and problematic. *Phi Delta Kappan, 73*(9), 673-677.

Lieberman, A., & Miller, L. (1991). Revisiting the social realities of teaching. In A. Lieberman & L. Miller (Eds.), *Staff development for education in the '90s* (pp. 92-112). New York: Teachers College Press.

Lieberman, A., & Miller, L. (1992). The professional development of teachers. In M. Alkin (Ed.), *Encyclopedia of educational research* (6th ed., vol. 3, pp. 1045-1053). New York: Macmillan.

Lieberman, A., & Wood, D. (2001). When teachers write: Of networks and learning. In A. Lieberman (Ed.), *Teachers caught in the action: Professional development that matters* (pp. 175-187). New York: Teachers College Press.

Lieberman, A., & Wood, D.R. (2002). The National Writing Project. *Educational Leadership, 59*(6), 40-43.

Little, J.W. (1989). District policy choices and teachers' professional development opportunities. *American Educational Research Journal, 11*(2), 165-179.

Little, J.W. (1993). Teachers' professional development in a climate of educational reform. *Educational Evaluation and Policy Analysis, 15*(2), 129-151.

Little, J.W. (2002). Locating learning in teachers' communities of practice: Opening up problems of analysis in records of everyday work. *Teaching and Teacher Education, 18*(8), 917-946.

Little, J.W. (2003). Inside teacher community: Representations of classroom practice. *Teachers College Record, 105*, 913-945.

Lortie, D. (1975). *Schoolteacher: A sociological study.* Chicago: University of Chicago Press.

Loucks-Horsley, S., Love, N., Stiles, K., Mundry, S., & Hewson, P. (2003). *Designing professional development for teachers of mathematics and science.* Thousand Oaks, CA: Corwin Press.

Loucks-Horsley, S., & Matsumoto, C. (1999). Research on professional development for teachers of mathematics and science: The state of the scene. *School Science and Mathematics, 99*(5), 258-271.

Manning, P.R., & DeBakey, L. (2002). Continuing medical education: The paradigm is changing. *Journal of Continuing Education in the Health Professions, 21*(1), 46-54.

McDiarmid, G.W., & Kelly, P.P. (1997). *Teachers planning professional development in a reform context: The case of Kentucky.* Paper presented at the annual meeting of the American Educational Research Association, Chicago.

McLaughlin, M.W. (1991). Enabling professional development: What have we learned? In A. Lieberman & L. Miller (Eds.), *Staff development for education in the '90s* (p. 61-82). New York: Teachers College Press.

McLaughlin, M.W., & Marsh, D. (1978). Staff development and school change. *Teachers College Record, 80*(1), 69-94.

McLaughlin, M.W., & Talbert, J.E. (1993). *Contexts that matter for teaching and learning.* Stanford: Center for Research on the Context of Secondary Teaching.

Meyers, E., & Rust, F. (2003). (Eds.) *Taking action with teacher research.* Portsmouth, NH: Heinemann.

Miller, L., & O'Shea, C. (1996). School-university partnership: Getting broader, getting deeper. In M.W. McLaughlin & I. Oberman (Eds.), *Teacher learning: New policies, new practices* (pp. 161-184). New York: Teachers College Press.

Miretzky, D., Smylie, M.A., & Konkol, P. (2004). Thinking differently about teacher workforce development. In this volume—M.A. Smylie & D. Miretzky (Eds.), *Developing the teacher workforce. The 103rd yearbook of the National Society for the Study of Education*, Part I (pp. 34-69). Chicago: National Society for the Study of Education.

National Commission on Teaching and America's Future. (2003). *No dream denied: A pledge to America's children.* Washington, DC: National Commission on Teaching and America's Future.

Natriello, G., & Zumwalt, K. (1992). Challenges to an alternative route for teacher education. In A. Lieberman (Ed.), *The changing contexts of teaching. The Ninety-first yearbook of the National Society for the Study of Education* (pp. 59-78). Chicago: National Society for the Study of Education.

Newmann, F.M., King, M.B., & Youngs, P. (2000). Professional development that addresses school capacity: Lessons from urban elementary schools. *American Journal of Education, 108*(4): 259-299.

Ornstein, A.C. (1995). *Teaching: Theory into practice.* Boston: Allyn and Bacon.

Parker, A. (1977). *Networks for innovation and problem solving and their use for improving education: A comparative overview.* Washington, DC: School Capacity for Problem Solving Group, National Institute of Education.

Randi, J. (in press[a]). Teachers as self-regulated learners. *Teachers College Record.*

Randi, J. (in press[b]). Final choices: Surveying career options. In K. Zumwalt & G. Natriello (Eds.), *The New Jersey Teacher Education Study* [tentative]. New York: Teachers College Press.

Randi, J., & Corno, L. (1997).Teachers as innovators. In B.J. Biddle, T. Good, & I. Goodson (Eds.), *International handbook of teachers and teaching* (pp. 1163-1221). Dordrecht, The Netherlands: Kluwer.

Randi, J., & Corno, L. (2000). Teacher innovations in self-regulated learning. In P. Pintrich, M. Boekaerts, & M. Zeidner (Eds.), *Handbook of self-regulation* (pp. 651-685). San Diego: Academic Press.

Renyi, J. (1996). *Teachers taking charge of their own learning: Transforming professional development for student success.* Washington, DC: National Foundation for the Improvement of Education.

Richardson, V. (1994a). Teacher inquiry as professional staff development. In S. Hollingsworth & H. Sockett (Eds.), *Teacher research and educational reform. The Ninety-third yearbook of the National Society for the Study of Education,* Part I (pp. 186-203). Chicago: National Society for the Study of Education.

Richardson, V. (1994b). *Teacher change and the staff development process: A case in reading instruction* (135-159). New York: Teachers College Press.

Richardson, V. (1994c). Conducting research on practice. *Educational Research, 23*(5), 5-10.

Richardson, V. (Ed.). (2001). *Handbook of research on teaching* (4th ed.). Washington, DC: American Educational Research Association.

Schauble, L., Beane, D.A., Coates, G.D., Martin, L.M., & Sterling, P. (1996). Outside classroom walls: Learning in informal environments. In L. Schauble & R. Glaser (Eds.), *Innovations in learning: New environments for education* (pp. 5-24). Mahwah, NJ: Erlbaum.

Schön, D.A. (1983). *The reflective practitioner: How professionals think in action.* New York: Basic Books.

Sheldon, K., & Biddle, B. (1998). Standards, accountability, and school reform: Perils and pitfalls. *Teachers College Record, 100*(1), 164-180.

Shulman, L.S. (1987). Knowledge and teaching: Foundations of the new reform. *Harvard Educational Review, 57,* 1-22.

Slavin, R.E., Madden, N.A., Dolan, L., Wasik, B.A., Ross, S.M., & Smith, L.J. (1994). Whenever and wherever we choose: The replication of "Success for All." *Phi Delta Kappan, 75*(8), 639-647.

Smagorinsky, P., Lakly, A., & Johnson, T. (2002). Acquiescence, accommodation, and resistance in learning to teach within a prescribed curriculum. *English Education, 34*(3), 187-213.

Snow, R.E. (1992). Aptitude theory: Yesterday, today, and tomorrow. *Educational Psychologist, 27,* 5-32.

Sparks, D. (2002). *Designing powerful professional development for teachers and principals.* National Staff Development Council. Retrieved March 1, 2003, from http://www.nsdc.org/library/leaders/sparksbook.cfm

Stecher, B., & Barron, S. (2001). Unintended consequences of test-based accountability when testing in "milepost" grades. *Educational Assessment, 7,* 259-281.

Stecher, B., Barron, S., Kaganoff, T., & Goodwin, J. (1998). *The effects of standards-based assessment on classroom practices: Results of the 1996-97 RAND survey of Kentucky teachers of mathematics and writing* (No. CSE Tech Report No. 482). Los Angeles: UCLA Center for Research on Evaluation, Standards, and Student Testing.

Strong, M., & St. John, L. (2001). *A study of teacher retention: The effects of mentoring on beginning teachers.* (Research Working Paper No. 3). Santa Cruz, CA: University of California.

Sykes, G. (1996). Reform of and as professional development. *Phi Delta Kappan, 77*(7), 468-476.

Thompson, C., & Zeuli, J.S. (1999). The frame and the tapestry: Standards-based reform and professional development. In L. Darling-Hammond & G. Sykes (Eds.), *Teaching as the learning profession* (pp. 341-375). San Francisco: Jossey-Bass

U.S. Department of Education. (1998). *Promising practices: New ways to improve teacher quality.* Retrieved December 1, 2003, from http://www.ed.gov/pubs/PromPractice

U.S. Department of Education, National Center for Education Statistics. (2001). *Teacher preparation and professional development: 2000.* Washington, DC: Office of Educational Research and Development.

Vancouver, J.B. (2000). Self-regulation in organizational settings: A tale of two paradigms. In P. Pintrich, M. Boekaerts, & M. Zeidner (Eds.), *Handbook of self-regulation* (pp. 303- 342). San Diego: Academic Press.

Wilson, S. (2004). "Them that's got shall get": Understanding teacher recruitment, induction, and retention. In this volume—M.A. Smylie & D. Miretzky, *Developing the teacher workforce. The 103rd yearbook of the National Society for the Study of Education,* Part I (pp. 145-179). Chicago: National Society for the Study of Education.

Wilson, S.M., & Berne, J. (1999). Teacher learning and acquisition of professional knowledge: An examination on contemporary professional development. In D.P.A. Iran-Nejad (Ed.), *Review of Research in Education* (Vol. 24, pp. 173-209).

Youngs, P. (2000, April). *Connections between district policy related to professional development and school capacity in urban elementary schools.* Paper presented at the annual meeting of the American Educational Research Association, New Orleans.

Youngs, P. (2001). District and state policy influences on professional development and school capacity. *Educational Policy, 15*(2), 278-301.

Zeichner, K. (1991). Contradictions and tensions in the professionalization of teaching and the democratization of schools. *Teachers College Record, 92*(3), 363-560.

Zeichner, K. (1994). Personal renewal and social construction through teacher research. In S. Hollingsworth & H. Sockett (Eds.), *Teacher research and educational reform. The Ninety-third yearbook of the National Society for the Study of Education,* Part I (pp. 66-85). Chicago: National Society for the Study of Education.

Zeichner, K. (1995) Beyond the divide of teacher research and academic research. *Teachers and Teaching, 1*(2), 153-172.

Zeichner, K. (2003) Teacher research as professional development for P-12 educators in the U.S. *Educational Action Research, 11*(2), 301-325.

Zeichner, K., & Klehr, M. (1999). *The nature and impact of action research in one urban school district.* Paper presented at the annual meeting of the American Educational Research Association, Montreal.

Zeichner, K., & Noffke, S. (2001). Practitioner research. In V. Richardson (Ed.), *Handbook of research on teaching* (4th ed., pp. 298-332). Washington, DC: American Educational Research Association.

CHAPTER 7

Empowering a Profession: Rethinking the Roles of Administrative Evaluation and Instructional Supervision in Improving Teacher Quality

EDWARD PAJAK AND ANGELIQUE ARRINGTON

In the complex environment of 21st-century public education, a consensus has emerged among policymakers, researchers, and educational practitioners that the single most important factor contributing to student learning is the quality of teaching. Despite this unanimity in principle, the practical matter of guaranteeing high-quality instruction for every student in every classroom poses a serious challenge with no simple solution in sight. Embedded in conversations about teacher preparation, induction, and professional development are dilemmas about how to properly support teachers and develop their capacities and skills while holding them accountable so that the best will stay and the worst are persuaded to leave.

Calls for evidence of a more effective teacher workforce from policymakers, federal agencies, state departments of education, and local school districts have resulted in a trend of increasingly stringent accountability measures. Some fairly recent formulations—for example, the "report card" requirements for teacher preparation programs included in the 1998 reauthorization of the Higher Education Act of 1965 and the "highly qualified teacher" provision of the No Child Left Behind Act of 2001—emphasize punitive consequences for weak results. In the case of the Higher Education Act, teacher preparation programs that are judged to be "low performing" lose their accreditation. Similarly, No

Edward Pajak is a Professor currently serving as Interim Director of the Graduate Division of Education at Johns Hopkins University. Recent publications include "Loosely coupled organizations, misrecognition, and social reproduction" in the *International Journal of Leadership in Education* and *Honoring Diverse Teaching Styles: A Guide for Supervisors*. Angelique Arrington is an Assistant Professor in the Department of Teacher Preparation at Johns Hopkins University.

Child Left Behind encourages the dismissal of teachers who do not meet certification requirements. Laws such as these have received strong bipartisan support in Congress and in state legislatures and appear to be endorsed by the media and a broad segment of the general public.

In another trend spurred by the same calls for quality teaching, some experts and organizations are seeking to "professionalize" teaching through innovations that would empower teachers to police their own ranks, provide peer assistance for inexperienced and less-successful teachers, and reward teachers who display excellence or take on greater responsibilities for schoolwide success. The National Board for Professional Teaching Standards, for example, recognizes excellence in teaching and offers opportunities for teachers who distinguish themselves to share their expertise with less-accomplished colleagues. The National Commission on Teaching and America's Future (NCTAF) has issued recommendations for the selection and training of teachers that propose a career-long perspective with multiple sources of support and encouragement (NCTAF, 1996, 2003). Similar initiatives by the National Education Association (NEA) and the American Federation of Teachers (AFT) sponsor programs that support mentoring of new teachers and career paths for veteran teachers to become teacher leaders (Green, 2001). Advocates of professionalizing teaching maintain that providing support and rewarding excellence will result in significant improvement in teaching quality nationwide.

The contrasting trends evident in today's pursuit of quality teaching are by no means new. Earlier versions of many current proposals have been debated and some have even been implemented in the past, though never on a national scale. Their parallel presence in today's reform movement may be viewed as the most recent manifestation of a historical tension between competing bureaucratic and professional impulses, forces that have influenced determinations of teacher quality in public education since the early 20th century (Glanz, 1998).

Traditionally, the attempt to ensure quality teaching has been addressed through two distinct, yet closely related, organizational processes—administrative evaluation and instructional supervision. These processes typically overlap because they share common historical roots, are sometimes performed by a single person (often the principal), and ultimately work toward the same purpose of ensuring quality teaching. But the underlying assumptions, sources of influence, and practices associated with administrative evaluation and instructional supervision are quite different, generally reflecting the bureaucratic–professional dichotomy noted above. Administrators address managerial issues such as scheduling, facilities, finance, and hiring and firing personnel; supervisors deal mainly with matters relating to instruction, curriculum, and the professional development of teachers.

At the risk of oversimplifying, the primary difference between administrative evaluation and instructional supervision is this: After hiring the most qualified teachers that can be found, a school administrator monitors teacher performance in order to make informed decisions about whom to retain and whom to dismiss. Consistent with "summative" assessment (Scriven, 1967), a school administrator makes an eventual determination about whether a teacher's performance is satisfactory enough to justify continued employment. An instructional supervisor also favors hiring the best teachers available but monitors teacher performance for different reasons—to provide feedback to teachers about how they are doing and to determine the kinds of professional support that teachers need to guarantee that as many as possible succeed. Such "formative" assessment (Scriven, 1967) assumes that the potential for competence exists and is used to inform decisions about how teaching can be improved.

In this chapter, we first look at the history of administrative evaluation and instructional supervision within education. Then we review the current context of teacher accountability and the present uses of administrative evaluation and instructional supervision in efforts to improve teacher quality. Finally, to restore a balance between administrative evaluation and instructional supervision that will better ensure teacher quality, we recommend empowering the teaching profession by 1) actively including teachers' unions as partners in systemic efforts to ensure teacher quality; 2) more fully embracing and expanding a graduate-level medical model of preparation to develop a generation of teachers who are highly qualified in both academic knowledge and pedagogical skill; and 3) adopting national "opportunity to teach" standards to uniformly improve teaching conditions in all schools so that highly qualified teachers remain in the profession.

Administrative Evaluation and the Legacy of Rating Scales

The national preoccupation with achieving quality in teaching can be traced back almost one hundred years. The influence of Frederick Taylor's *Principles of Scientific Management* (1911) on the nascent practice of school administration has been well documented. Based on time–motion studies of workers at Bethlehem steel plants in the United States, Taylor's industrial logic advised managers of factories to identify and enforce a single most efficient way of accomplishing a task, to separate the planning of work from its execution, and to link pay directly to performance. History suggests that instead of improving efficiency and precision, the application of Taylor's principles to schools more often resulted in bureaucratic rigidity, the pursuit of trivial outcomes, and a loss of meaningful purpose (Callahan, 1962; Flinders, 1998; Tyack, 1974).

Among the most influential advocates of applying Taylor's ideas to education was Franklin Bobbitt, a professor of educational administration at the University of Chicago, who believed that classrooms and schools would be more efficient if they operated more like factories (Bobbitt, 1913). This view became exceedingly popular in education just prior to World War I and resulted in the publication of many books and journal articles devoted to the subject of applying quantitative measures to practically every aspect of schooling, including the development and proliferation of rating scales intended to measure teacher efficiency (e.g., Bobbitt; Boyce, 1915; Whipple, 1916).

An illustrative example published in an early NSSE Yearbook (1915) proposed that a teacher could be rated along a scale ranging from "very poor" to "excellent" on 45 different items. Some of these items, such as "grasp of subject matter," "sense of justice," "skill in stimulating thought," and "attention to individual needs," remain recognizable today as arguably related to effective teaching. Other items on the scale, however, describe personal traits over which teachers have little control, that are irrelevant to instructional effectiveness, or that require a capricious judgment. The observer was encouraged, for instance, to rate the teacher on items that refer to the teacher's "general appearance," "health," and "voice" (Boyce, 1915, p. 42).

Rating scales continue to be widely used in summative evaluation of teachers across the United States, mainly because they take little time to complete and they provide documentation that a contractual obligation (i.e., classroom observation) has been fulfilled. These expediencies derive from the fact that the observer simply sits in judgment of the teacher's performance and is not required to make a serious effort to understand or even think about the uniqueness of the particular classroom context, why something may or may not be happening, or what steps ought to be taken to improve learning.

The primary advantage that a rating scale offers teachers is that, unlike a laundry list of arbitrary criticisms that could change from day to day, a scale limits the number of criteria against which teaching can be assessed. The teacher can then make a deliberate effort to exhibit

EMPOWERING A PROFESSION

the behaviors required to comply with whatever passes as "satisfactory" teaching.

A modern-day classroom performance assessment tool, the Framework for Teaching, now widely used for evaluating teachers, became
popular several years ago. Twenty-two "components of professional
practice" make up the framework. The components are said to be
based on research conducted at Educational Testing Service, tied to
the PRAXIS III criteria by which most states license qualified teachers, and informed by National Board for Professional Teaching Standards documents and other contemporary sources (Danielson, 1996).

Table 1 shows that at least 15 of these "components" (slightly more
than two thirds) are virtually identical to items from the rating scale published in that early 20th-century NSSE Yearbook. The newer framework
clusters 22 components into four "domains"; the older "Efficiency Record"
grouped 45 "qualities" into five categories, one of which, labeled "results,"
focused on student learning and development. Further, where the modern
framework prescribes rating teachers according to four levels of performance—"unsatisfactory," "basic," "proficient," and "distinguished"—the
earlier instrument provides five categories for making such distinctions—
"very poor," "poor," "medium," "good," and "excellent." Although it may
be unfair to suggest that no progress has been made in our ability to assess
teacher performance in the 81 years between 1915 and 1996, the obvious
similarities between these two instruments raise questions about whether
administrative evaluation has really come very far at all.

TABLE 1
Selected Criteria for Evaluating Teachers: 1915 versus 1996

NSSE (1915)	Danielson (1996)
Interest in lives of pupils	Knowledge of students
Adaptability and resourcefulness	Flexibility and responsiveness
Interest in the life of the school	Contributing to the school and district
Neatness of room	Organizing physical space
Discipline (governing skill)	Managing student behavior
Grasp of subject matter	Knowledge of content and pedagogy
Definiteness and clearness of aim	Selecting instructional goals
Stimulation of community	Establishing a culture for learning
Organizing of subject matter	Designing coherent instruction
Professional interest and growth	Growing and developing professionally
Skill in questioning	Using questioning and discussion techniques
Care of routine	Managing classroom procedures
Skill in motivating work	Engaging students in learning
Accuracy	Maintaining accurate records
Use of English	Communicating clearly and accurately

Yet not only the components of rating scales but also the very idea behind their use should be called into question. Promoted as eliminating the subjective judgment of a classroom observer, rating scales instead simply mask observers' inherent idiosyncrasies and create an impression of impartial accuracy by limiting the range of the observations and the vocabulary of the observers' responses. When rating scales are used to evaluate teachers, validity and reliability are problematic because the context of teaching is ignored. "Even when [evaluators receive extensive training], some drift over time in their understanding of the defining attributes [inevitably occurs]" (Iwanicki, 1998, p. 164).

Perhaps the most serious limitation of rating scales, however, is that in failing to consider the uniqueness of particular situations, they continue to enforce, in the tradition of Frederick Taylor, a "one best way" of teaching. A standardized instrument may ensure that every teacher is measured against the same criteria, which ostensibly guarantees some level of equitable treatment, but it makes little sense that the same instrument used to evaluate teaching at the kindergarten level should be applied with equal vigor and confidence for determining the worthiness of high school instruction (Killian & Post, 1998). It is also highly questionable whether the same scheme for evaluating the quality of teaching in mathematics is appropriate for assessing teachers' efforts in history, literature, or science, because the pedagogical knowledge and skills needed for teaching different content areas vary considerably (Shulman, 1987a). Although "well-defined standards and criteria" can be useful for determining whether a candidate is fit for initial licensure, more complex understandings of teaching quality are necessary when the purpose is to guide a teacher's development (Iwanicki, 1998, p. 163).

Instructional Supervision and Democratic Professionalism

As public education became institutionalized, especially after World War I, instructional supervision developed an identity separate from administrative evaluation, one that emphasized democratic professionalism over bureaucratic control (Glanz, 1998) as the proper path for improving the quality of teaching and learning. One early author described instructional supervision as being closely related to "the democratic motive of American education" (Elliott, 1914, p. 2). He distinguished "supervisory efficiency," which relied upon "*decentralized, cooperative, expert* supervision" (emphasis in the original) from "administrative efficiency," which demanded "centralization of administrative power" (p. 78). The misapplication of administrative control to the work of teachers and the accomplishments of students was denounced as stifling to creativity and individuality (Elliott).

Authors of early supervision texts throughout the 1920s emphasized the importance of democracy as a guiding principle of American education (Ayer & Barr, 1928; Burton, 1927; Hosic, 1920; Stone, 1929). One popular textbook, *The Supervision of Instruction*, noted that Frederick Taylor's principles of industrial management had "never been especially popular" and appeared "to have had little influence" (Barr & Burton, 1926, p. 75). According to Callahan and Button (1964), the reason the industrial management movement had little influence on instructional supervision in education is because "the problems of supervision and teaching method were not readily amenable to investigation in the management frame of reference nor with the techniques available" (p. 90).

Indeed, John Dewey's (1929) writings, which combined democratic principles with scientific thinking, exerted a much stronger force on the evolution of supervision in education than is generally recognized (Glanz, 1992). Dewey's conception of collegial, scientific problem solving differed greatly from industrial management theory in that it advocated reflective inquiry as a guide to practice instead of generating prescriptive rules through pseudoscientific machinations. Beginning in the 1930s and throughout the next several decades, democratically inspired, consciously reasoned, cooperative problem solving became the hallmark of supervision in education (e.g., Association for Supervision and Curriculum Development, 1960; Barr, Burton, & Brueckner, 1938; Department of Supervisors and Directors of Instruction, 1934; Department of Supervisors and Directors of Instruction, 1943; Franseth, 1955).

During the 1950s and 1960s, however, several factors contributed to instructional supervision becoming less democratic and less distinct from administrative evaluation in its orientation, particularly at the district level. A greater federal role in public education and a burgeoning of educational innovations (e.g., "new" math, open space schools, etc.) resulted in the notion that supervisors should become "change agents" who make their positions clear and share their objectives with school faculties and staff only *after* identifying problems, establishing priorities, and deciding to whom, where, and how an intervention would be introduced (e.g., Cunningham, 1963).

The adoption of collective bargaining in many states also effectively usurped supervisors' traditional methods (e.g., cooperative planning and problem solving), redefined decisions affecting instruction and curriculum as conditions of employment, and left supervisors in an untenable no-man's-land between the interests of management and labor (Kinsella, Klopf, Shafer, & Young, 1969). Finally, rapid growth in the size and complexity of schools and districts required supervisors to devote more time and attention to programmatic goals and long-range planning (Alfonso, Firth, & Neville, 1975; Ogletree, 1972).

At about the time that district-level supervision began drifting away from the ethos of democratic professionalism, Morris Cogan (1973) developed the idea of clinical supervision at Harvard University. Cogan coordinated a Master of Arts in Teaching program in the late 1950s that prepared liberal arts graduates for teaching careers. An internship lasting an entire year was central to the program, but both students and university faculty recognized that it was not providing a satisfactory induction experience. Cogan developed the concept and techniques of clinical supervision—essentially, a pre-observation conference between the teacher and supervisor, a classroom observation, and a post-observation conference—in response to the need for meaningful feedback that would improve the success of beginning teachers.

Along with his colleagues (Goldhammer, 1969; Mosher & Purpel, 1972), Cogan (1973) believed that data gathered during observations should be used strictly as formative feedback to improve teaching and learning and never for summative assessment. The Harvard group proposed the very powerful idea that every lesson plan ought to be considered a hypothesis that is framed during the pre-observation conference and then tested by the teacher in the laboratory of the classroom. Verbal and nonverbal behaviors occurring during a lesson and recorded by the supervisor in verbatim notes provided data for determining whether the "hypothesis" was supported by available evidence.

Cogan's name for this method for observation and feedback, *clinical supervision*, along with the method's emphasis on practical, democratic problem solving by professional colleagues, implied a close affinity with medicine, psychology, and social services and represented an important departure from industrial management imagery (Garman, 1986). Over the last several decades, clinical supervision has evolved into a variety of approaches (technical, didactic, artistic, humanistic, developmental, reflective) that can accommodate and support a wide array of teaching styles (Pajak, 2000, 2003). When a teacher's preferred style is recognized as the proper starting point for planning professional growth, clinical supervisors can then provide teachers with appropriately differentiated learning environments. The implication is that supervisors should strive to work with teachers in ways that are consistent with how teachers are expected to work with students—by responding to diversity in ways that enhance the likelihood of success (Pajak, 2003).

The Current Context of Teacher Accountability

Currently, both administrative evaluation and instructional supervision are bogged down in legal procedures and negotiated policies that blur important distinctions between them. Competing duties of school leaders prevent the investment of the time and effort necessary to make classroom observation, data collection, analysis, and conferencing effective, so teachers do not receive immediate feedback grounded in the context of students' learning needs. Also, because data gathered for formative purposes can potentially be used as evidence in legal proceedings, trust and openness between professionals is seriously compromised. The recent shift to test scores as the sole measure of school success ignores gross inequities in the availability of material and human resources that already exist and diverts time, effort, and attention away from capacity building, particularly in schools that need it most.

Since the 1960s, increasing wariness of litigation has resulted in legal definitions and procedures dominating almost every aspect of public education (Hendrie, 2003). State statutes, rules, regulations, and courts rarely distinguish between formative and summative teacher assessment (Hazi, 1998). As a result, interactions between educators that involve assessment are narrowly prescribed and generally defensive, and thus neither administrative nor supervisory functions in schools are particularly effective (Areglado, 1998).

Experienced teachers in public schools are usually protected from dismissal because of tenure, a property right to employment that is normally prescribed by state law after a teacher demonstrates satisfactory performance over several years. Once tenure is acquired, teachers can be dismissed from their jobs for a limited number of reasons. Maryland state law, for example, allows school boards to dismiss teachers for five specific reasons: "incompetency, misconduct in office, willful neglect of duty, insubordination, and immorality" (Fischer, Schimmel, & Stellman, 2003, p. 31). Nontenured teachers are similarly protected from dismissal without legal cause during the contract year, though school boards in most states may decide not to renew their employment at the end of that period without having to provide justification.

In most states, specific procedures must be followed before a tenured teacher can be dismissed. These typically include making a statement of formal charges and holding a hearing with legal representation, subpoenaed witnesses, testimony given under oath, recorded proceedings, a written decision, and right to appeal (Fischer, Schimmel, & Stellman, 2003). Also, the courts and many states require school districts to provide assistance and a reasonably adequate period of time to allow a teacher to remediate the deficiencies noted in the charges (Fischer, Schimmel, & Stellman). Significantly, several instances are on record of tenured teachers being dismissed because their students consistently scored low on standardized tests (Hazi, 1998).

Classroom observation and data collection, the central aspects of instructional supervision, have become important sources of evidence in cases where teacher incompetence or neglect of duties is alleged. Tenured teachers usually cannot be dismissed because of a single incident of incompetence, especially if ratings of their performance in the past have been satisfactory. Rather, a pattern of events over time must be established through documentation that may include student grades, lesson plans, instructional materials and tests, records of observations and conferences, lesson transcripts, and even cursory notes. All of these are subject to subpoena as evidence in hearings (Hazi, 1998).

Despite increased attention to accountability in recent decades, according to a recently published estimate, fewer than 1% of teachers nationwide "receive anything other than the highest marks on the summary evaluation report." But teachers and school administrators readily admit in private, according to this same source, "that 15 to 20 percent of permanent teachers are functioning at a less than satisfactory level" (McGrath, 2000, p. 2).

Teachers are sometimes awarded tenure without having demonstrated competence because of factors that prevent school administrators from evaluating teachers effectively (Painter, 2000). Many principals avoid both formative and summative assessments of teacher performance because conducting regular classroom observations, recording and analyzing data, and providing support to new or struggling teachers (tasks for which principals are often not adequately trained) takes a great deal of time and effort. Evaluating an entire faculty, which can easily range from 100 to 150 teachers in a typical high school, competes with other duties that may seem more urgent in the immediate press of daily events, including paperwork, attending meetings, dealing with student misbehavior, and conferencing with parents. Teacher dismissal becomes even more time consuming and expensive in states with strong teacher unions, where administrative actions are routinely challenged as violations of collective bargaining agreements. Avoiding and delaying serious evaluation of teachers because of these reasons too often results in serious problems of teacher performance that might have been corrected before tenure was awarded (Painter, 2000).

When administrative and supervisory functions are both assigned to the same person, as is often the case with a school principal, trust and open communication can be compromised. Teachers may be reluctant to admit deficiencies or even disclose minor concerns to someone who will eventually decide whether they are awarded a contract or granted tenure. Indeed, principals themselves experience difficulty and stress from trying to balance these conflicting duties (Areglado, 1998; McLaughlin, 1984). Many experts (e.g., Joyce & Showers, 1988) advise, therefore, that the supervisory function should be assigned to someone other than the principal, such as an individual or group charged exclusively with making formative assessments and providing necessary professional support.

Partly because traditional administrative evaluation has failed to improve teacher quality, policymakers now emphasize assessment at school and state levels on the assumption that classrooms are directly connected to these larger units and are also influenced by social and political forces (Boyd & Kerchner, 1987; Fuhrman, 1993; NCTAF, 1996). No Child Left Behind, for example, seeks to guarantee teacher quality through accountability processes that focus on uniform performance standards and on student learning outcomes as measured by standardized tests at multiple organizational levels.

Complicating any discussion of teacher quality in relation to system-wide accountability, however, are the extreme differences among school districts in the socioeconomic levels of students' families and the per capita funding of classrooms. The disparities are greater in some states than in others and, as Jonathan Kozol (1991) demonstrated in *Savage Inequalities*, more affluent districts commonly spend two to three times more money per classroom than schools in less affluent areas. Teachers in poorer districts, usually in urban or rural areas, must accomplish similar academic goals with fewer resources and less professional support. Problems created by such inequities result in many of the best teachers in poorer schools becoming frustrated and leaving for better funded settings within the first few years of their employment (Haycock, 2000). This often leaves the classrooms populated by children of color and poverty with teachers who are less experienced and less qualified. In essence, the students who need the most help academically often receive it from teachers who are the least prepared to provide it (Haycock, 2003; NCTAF, 2003).

These harsh realities draw attention to important dilemmas that recent calls for greater accountability as manifested in No Child Left Behind too easily overlook or brush aside.

First, the testing, reporting, and other requirements of No Child Left Behind will consume tremendous amounts of time, effort, and other resources (Hoff, 2000), yet schools are likely to become even more understaffed and underfunded in coming years, especially in already economically depressed urban and rural areas, given the financial deficits facing state and local governments (Neill, 2003). If greater accountability is sought without adequate resources forthcoming, then time and funds will have to be reallocated. Teachers already protest that overzealous testing requirements imposed by states and districts severely curtail the time and resources available for instruction (Goldberg, 2004; Pedulla, 2003). Mandates for accountability are also likely to compete for time and funding that could be spent building teacher and school capacity (Elmore, 2003).

Second, if standards for student achievement are set much higher than current norms, many teachers are unlikely to attain those standards without additional support. At a time when highly qualified teachers are said to be in short supply, it makes little sense to terminate the employment of those who do not quite measure up, especially those who work in challenging school environments where teacher success and retention are most difficult. On the other hand, if norms are set at current levels of performance, or readjusted downward as many states are already doing with student tests to avoid parental backlash, the utility of imposing a cumbersome and expensive assessment apparatus becomes highly dubious.

Third, if greater attention to accountability discloses clear differences in performance among teachers and schools, a highly probable outcome, the inevitable next question is, "What will be done?" Some advocates of system-wide accountability measures favor redirecting resources to those teachers and schools that are highly successful, as a kind of pay for performance (Teaching Commission, 2004). An alternative that seems less popular with policymakers is to muster adequate support for less successful teachers and schools, those in greatest need of help, to ensure that all students have access to effective instruction (Odden, 2001).

Finally, and most important, assessment data are not valid indicators of teacher quality when those who are being assessed do not have both adequate resources and sufficient control to do their jobs well (Ingersoll, 2004; Neill, 2003). In the current environment of policy mandates, ballooning deficits, and budget cuts, these prerequisites are less likely than ever to be met.

We are not suggesting that teacher accountability is unnecessary or undesirable. Parents and the public in general certainly have a right to insist that teachers measure up to high standards of quality. Nor are we implying that proposals for greater accountability are inherently flawed. But we are proposing that current perspectives and reform efforts are woefully incomplete, are overly dependent on administrative evaluation, and have essentially forsaken the democratic, professional, and formative legacy of instructional supervision.

Three Policy Recommendations to Better Ensure Teacher Quality

If current reform efforts are incomplete and inappropriate, what is needed to truly ensure teacher quality in the United States? We believe that a restored balance between administrative evaluation and instructional supervision will create a solid foundation for effective professional practice and system-wide improvement of teacher quality. To achieve this balance, we recommend empowering the teaching profession by 1) actively including teachers' unions as full-fledged partners in efforts to ensure teacher quality; 2) more fully embracing a graduate-level medical model of teacher preparation to develop a generation of teachers who are highly qualified in both academic knowledge and pedagogical skill; and 3) adopting national "opportunity-to-teach" standards to uniformly improve the working conditions of teachers in all schools, so that highly qualified teachers will remain in the profession. These recommendations are both necessary and appropriate for the extraordinary levels of responsibility and accountability that the teaching profession now faces.

A New Role for Teachers' Unions

As noted earlier, teacher evaluation and dismissal of incompetent teachers is a time consuming and expensive process, especially in states with strong teacher unions, where administrative actions are routinely challenged as violations of collective bargaining agreements. This partly explains why school administrators avoid giving serious attention to teacher evaluation (Painter, 2000). Unlike other professional associations, such as the American Medical Association and the American Bar Association, teachers' unions have been comparatively uninvolved with ensuring the effectiveness of the teaching profession as a whole, viewing their primary purpose as protecting the contractual rights of individual teachers. Recently, however, teachers' unions have begun to expand their mission by providing professional support and development opportunities for members and exercising greater responsibility for accountability within their ranks.

In 1997, newly elected National Education Association president Bob Chase announced a commitment to "new unionism," which meant putting teacher quality and student achievement at the center of the union's mission. The next year, the American Federation of Teachers adopted a policy resolution titled, "The Union Role in Assuring Teacher Quality." A task force appointed to make specific recommendations called upon universities, professional associations, unions, government agencies, and foundations to work together toward this new vision. In particular, K-12 union locals were charged with assuming "greater responsibility for the clinical experience by working with the district and the higher education institutions to identify and train excellent teachers to serve as cooperating teachers" (AFT K-16 Teacher Education Task Force, 2000, p. 11).

Following these developments at the national level, the Montgomery County (Maryland) Education Association (MCEA), the third largest NEA local in the United States, achieved an unusual level of positive engagement with its school district. Collaboration between MCEA and the Montgomery County Public School (MCPS) system, which borders Washington, D.C. and employs more than 11,000 teachers in 193 schools, has been exceptional in focusing on the goals of improving student learning and professional development opportunities for teachers (Montgomery County Public Schools, 2001).

One of their collaborative projects is the Professional Growth System (PGS), intended "to create a professional learning community in each school focused on improving achievement of all students" (MCEA-MCPS, 2002, p. 2). The PGS, phased in between 2000 and 2003, includes a full-time staff development teacher in every school, teacher-initiated professional development plans, a multiyear professional growth and evaluation cycle differentiated according to teacher experience, clear performance standards for teaching within a rigorous evaluation system, and a Peer Assistance and Review (PAR) program (MCEA-MCPS, 2002).

The PAR program, initiated, designed, implemented, and evaluated by MCEA in collaboration with the district's administration, empowers some teachers in Montgomery County with a voice in deciding which teachers keep their jobs and which do not. These 45 consulting teachers are assigned full-time for three years to simultaneously provide support and evaluate the performance of all new teachers and veteran teachers who have been identified by their principals as needing improvement. The consulting teacher–client ratio is 16 to 1. In the first year of implementation, 253 teachers underwent peer review. Of these, only two teachers had their contracts terminated involuntarily, but 29 resigned before a PAR panel composed of six teachers and six administrators could pass judgment on them. Another 30 were awarded a contract provisionally for an additional year, during which time they were required to improve their skills (Archer, 2001).

Thus, sharing responsibility for the assessment of teacher performance with the union clearly improved the effectiveness of both administrative evaluation and instructional supervision in Montgomery County. The 24% of teachers whose performance was determined to be lacking, for example, is a much higher proportion than the 1% "unsatisfactory" ratings given nationally and is consistent with the estimated 15% to 20% of teachers who are performing at a less than satisfactory level nationally (McGrath, 2000). Although the employment of half the teachers whose performance was judged inadequate in Montgomery County was terminated, the half that remained received additional support over an entire year to demonstrate improvement.

MCEA has also formed a partnership with Johns Hopkins University to create the Center for Teacher Leadership, which opened in July 2003. Cochaired by a faculty member from Hopkins and a former president of the MCEA, the center is supported with resources contributed by both organizations and with grants from the National Educational Association and the Foundation for the Improvement of Education. The primary purpose of the center is to support, encourage, and train teacher leaders.

In its first year of operation, the center is focusing its efforts on development work, publicity, and building infrastructure, including the formation of a national advisory board to be chaired by Maryland's state school superintendent. The center has also launched six initiatives aimed at promoting a vision for teacher unions that places the quality of teaching and student learning at the top of the agenda:

- A National Board of Professional Teaching Standards network of teachers meets monthly and functions as a think tank to explore, systematize, and model ways to improve schools, attract the best teachers to the most challenging schools, and support colleagues who apply for National Board Certification.
- Hopkins's faculty, in consultation with teachers who serve on Councils for Teaching and Learning and as consulting teachers in

the Peer Assistance and Review program, are planning a master's program and noncredit courses aimed at developing knowledge and skills related to teacher leadership and peer collaboration.

- Several "teacher development schools," possibly corresponding to existing Professional Development School sites in Montgomery County, are being designated. Affiliated with the center, these schools will promote instructional leadership among teachers within a "career lattice" framework that allows teachers to exert schoolwide influence without necessarily leaving the classroom.
- Existing MCEA/MCPS initiatives, such as an ongoing joint intervention that empowers teachers in a low-performing elementary school, will be independently documented and evaluated, along with new goals and projects associated with the center.
- Workshops, summer institutes, and a virtual community will be provided for emerging teacher union leaders from outside the local region to promote the "new union" concept of placing the quality of teaching and learning at the center of the union's work.
- Professional development and support services will be provided, as requested by the school district, to supplement existing collaborative efforts intended to improve student learning.

As Bascia (this volume, chapter 11) suggests, teachers' unions can be credible partners, rather than adversaries, in the effort to improve teacher quality. Although they are uniquely suited to the task of identifying, reporting, and responding to the work-related needs of the teaching profession, as Bascia notes, teacher unions face serious difficulties in shaping educational policy despite the nascent spirit of new unionism. We believe that these unions can play an integral part in restoring the balance between administrative evaluation and instructional supervision through partnerships like the Professional Growth System and the Center for Teacher Leadership, which unite the interests and expertise of higher education, teachers, school administrators, and the state department of education in the common purpose of improving both teacher quality and student learning.

A Medical Model of Teacher Preparation and Clinical Support

In contrast to the industrial imagery associated with administrative evaluation, the developers of clinical supervision (Cogan, 1973; Goldhammer, 1969; Mosher & Purpel, 1972) deliberately drew upon the medical profession for an analogy to frame their empirical approach to teacher development and instructional improvement (Garman, 1986).

Later, during the 1980s, the Holmes Group (1986) recommended that teacher preparation should be housed in professional schools of education, as is the case for medicine and law, and also proposed the establishment of Professional Development Schools (PDS) as a way for teacher preparation to emulate that of physicians. Universities in at least 38 states and hundreds of K-12 schools (AACTE, 2003) responded by forming partnerships to bring the PDS concept to life:

Like teaching hospitals in medicine, these schools aim to provide sites for state-of-the-art practice that are also organized to support the training of new professionals, extend the professional development of veteran teachers, and sponsor collaborative research and inquiry. (Darling-Hammond, 2000b, p. 169)

In a collaboration between Johns Hopkins University and PDS sites in Baltimore, clinical supervision has been combined with the PDS concept in an environment that supports the preparation, induction, and professional development of novice and experienced K-12 teachers. Teacher interns engage in problem-based learning combined with didactic instruction in new content, develop strategies for problem solving, and participate in guided reflection. They are given opportunities to make connections between theory and practice by applying new knowledge in their classrooms and by summarizing lessons learned through an interactive process of self-study.

All this is accomplished through an eight-step clinical approach for transferring theoretical knowledge to classroom practice, one derived from the approach used in teaching hospitals and aptly named the "Operating Theatre." All interns begin their Operating Theatre cycle by reading articles or a book on a "focus topic" that is related to instruction or classroom management. University faculty then demonstrate how the focus topic is applied in a campus-based seminar or workshop setting called "Clinic I: Discussion & Modeling."

During Clinic I, teacher interns use an observation guide aligned with the topic being studied while observing a "round" of expert classroom teachers who apply the focus topic in their classroom with real students. Facilitators and interns then "unpack" what has been learned in debriefing during the second week of the cycle.

Teacher interns next observe a second round of teachers, this time using another focused observation guide to deepen their understanding. Only after this phase do the interns practice the focus topic with their own students. This practice session is videotaped; afterward, the teacher interns view and reflect on their lesson with veteran teachers. In the last phase of the cycle, the teacher interns analyze and critique the second set of observations as well as their own growth with the facilitators and teachers in a final debriefing.

As might be expected, this type of intensive engagement and support of teacher interns requires considerable investments of time and other resources. But the Operating Theatre approach is used at most of the Johns Hopkins PDS sites and informs induction practices throughout the Department of Teacher Preparation.

Examining the preparation of medical practitioners can indeed offer insights that may improve the preparation of teachers (Shulman, 1987b; 1998). Extending this reasoning to the policy level, Darling-Hammond and Sykes (2003) recently called upon the federal government to initiate an incentive-based teacher supply model, which would parallel programs that have long existed to support the training of physicians in underrepresented areas of specialization and to encourage their distribution to high need urban and rural communities. Their vision includes, among other recommendations, "new forms of professional development schools that emulate the teaching hospitals used to develop state-of-the-art medical practices" (p. 37).

We believe that the Operating Theatre approach is a promising innovation. If teacher preparation and instructional supervision fully embrace a medical analogy rather than the early 20th-century industrial analogy, classrooms can become laboratories for the discovery of solutions to problems of instruction in local contexts, and schools can become learning communities that promote professional development for teachers at every stage of their careers.

Opportunity-to-Teach Standards

In her response to the high-stakes testing debate, Darling-Hammond (2000a) reminds us that earlier national policies aimed at reforming education, dating back to the compensatory efforts of the late 1960s, never adequately addressed issues of substandard educational resources for poor and minority students. She predicts that top-down reforms that call for identifying and designating certain schools and teachers as underachieving, such as the No Child Left Behind Act of 2001, will similarly fail because no allowance is made for vast disparities that schools face in the availability of financial resources, physical facilities, qualified and capable teachers, challenging curricula, and effective instruction.

Darling-Hammond (2000a) proposes that the legislative adoption of "opportunity-to-learn" standards (NCEST, 1992; O'Day & Smith, 1993) would guarantee equitable inputs for schools before expectations for equivalent student achievement are imposed. If the United States is serious about ensuring that all students have access to high-quality teaching, we suggest that a set of "opportunity-to-teach" standards is also necessary, both to provide an optimal environment for teaching and learning and to stem the loss of talented but demoralized teachers who each year simply give up in frustration (Ingersoll, 2001).

Opportunity-to-teach standards have the potential to refocus school administration on the task of ensuring that adequate conditions for successful professional practice exist in every classroom. Such standards are also needed to reorient instructional supervision to the central task of ensuring that all teachers receive support, especially early in their careers, within an organization that makes successful practice possible and encourages professional growth. Finally, opportunity-to-teach standards are necessary to provide teachers with a level of power commensurate with the extraordinary levels of responsibility and accountability they are being asked to accept. At the very least, such standards ought to guarantee the following to teachers at every school:

- A reasonable number of daily lesson preparations, limited exclusively to the grade level and content area for which a teacher is certified, with a class size that makes individualized instruction possible;
- Electronic access to accurate student data, and administrative paperwork kept to an absolute minimum;
- Daily scheduled time to plan, assess, reflect upon, and refine instruction, and weekly scheduled time to develop new techniques, update subject matter knowledge, and engage in other forms of professional renewal;
- Intensive mentoring during the first three years of teaching, with opportunities thereafter to experiment with innovative strategies and styles of teaching in a safe, nonthreatening environment;
- An administrative evaluation process based on portfolios that include sample lesson plans, instructional materials, teacher-made tests, input from colleagues, and multiple forms of data collected during classroom observations;
- An effective and efficient school administration dedicated to securing adequate equipment, supplies, and facilities;
- Decision-making power commensurate with responsibility, perhaps even including the right to refuse to teach students who are violent or chronically disruptive.

Advocates of system-wide changes for the improvement of student achievement tout rigorous outcome standards and high-stakes testing as panaceas that will bring coherence to chaotic organizations. In doing so, they ignore or downplay the effects of vast inequities in resources, governance, and professional support available at different schools. Unless and until some consistent expectations for the work environment are established, equivalent student outcomes will never be achieved and schools that most need to attract and retain highly qualified teachers will continue to struggle unsuccessfully.

The solution to the problem of ensuring an adequate supply of highly qualified teachers has as much to do with retaining the teachers we already have as it does with finding new teachers to replace those who are lost each year to attrition (Ingersoll, 2001; NCTAF, 2003). Adopting the opportunity-to-teach standards proposed here directly addresses two of the major reasons that teachers leave their current teaching assignments, namely, poor working conditions and lack of professional support (Darling-Hammond, 2003). Addressing these factors promises not only to improve teacher retention generally, but can also help keep teachers in schools that serve impoverished populations where turnover is most acute (Johnson & Birkeland, 2003).

Ensuring High Quality in the Teaching Workforce

Bascia (this volume, chapter 11) observes that most current proposals for the improvement of teacher quality stress centralized control, a strengthened administrative structure, and standards and policies that demand teacher compliance. Teachers are expected to simply obey and conform to these remotely controlled, one-best-way prescriptions. Lack of compliance from teachers, let alone resistance, is portrayed by both the media and policy researchers as evidence of the sorry state of the teaching profession. Such a view, she notes, denies the possibility that teachers' noncompliance may be the result of informed judgments for best practice and ignores the limiting effect that poor working conditions can have on the quality of that practice. The situation Bascia describes sounds remarkably similar to what existed at the beginning of the 20th century, with administrative evaluation squaring off against democratically inspired instructional supervision. Worse, we are very likely to make the same mistakes, by using principles and tools that are almost identical to what has already been tried and proven ineffective.

If improving and ensuring the quality of teaching is truly the purpose behind state and national policy initiatives, more drastic changes are needed in the educational system to achieve this goal. A better balance between the bureaucratic (administrative evaluation) and the professional (instructional supervision; high-quality preparation, induction, and professional development; adequate working environments) must be restored for accountability to be an accurate measure of teacher quality, and the only way to bring that about is to move radically beyond existing structures. Involving experienced teachers in both processes is the key, but such participation cannot simply involve delegation of administrative responsibility to a few individuals. If the intention is to make accountability a more useful and effective tool, then teachers' involvement should be collective and exercised through professional associations, as is the case for the American Medical Association and the American Bar Association.

Teachers' unions, in the interest of their members and of public education generally, should be integrated at all levels of effort that support high quality in the teacher workforce. A major contribution from teachers' unions would be to reach consensus about what constitutes high standards of professional practice and then proceed to actively enforce those standards among rank and file members through local agreements like those in Montgomery County. To have it otherwise is to continue to subordinate teachers and their profession to the efficiencies of the organization and the winds of politics. As advocates for teachers, teachers' unions should endorse the "opportunity to teach" standards recommended earlier, or similar minimal conditions for practice, and then work with others who favor improvement of schools to have them codified into local, state, and national laws, statutes, and policies.

Two independent sources of power—bureaucratic and professional—are needed in schools, and should complement and balance each other in the service of students. As for hospital administration, the primary purpose of school administration should be to ensure that conditions for professional practice (e.g., resources, facilities, equipment, supplies, and support staff) are present so that the highest level of service from teachers is rendered. The community of teachers, acting through their professional associations, can then assume instructional supervision responsibilities by monitoring, improving, and enforcing high standards of teaching through routine classroom visits. If university partners and professional development schools are included in this formula, responsibility for ensuring the success of new and experienced teachers can be shared and teaching may begin to approach the level of control over entry into its ranks and working conditions that the medical profession attained at the beginning of the 20th century.

Partnerships that include universities, school districts, state depart-ments of education, and teachers' unions have the potential to restore the balance between administrative evaluation and instructional super-vision to arrive at a professionally justifiable integration of these processes for purposes of licensure and the awarding of tenure. To avoid the accusations of monopolistic practice that are sometimes lodged at the traditional professions (Ingersoll, 2003), state agencies might grant renewable licenses to teachers that would be valid for a specified length of time (e.g., seven or ten years) based on a process of peer review. Ideally, the bureaucratic and professional aspects of teach-ing should intersect, with accountability becoming a context in which teachers work naturally with little need for external control.

References

AACTE (American Association of Colleges of Teacher Education). (2003). *Frequently asked questions*. Retrieved March 1, 2004, from http://www.aacte.org/Frequent_Questions/professional_dev_schools.htm

AFT K-16 Teacher Education Task Force. (2000). *Building a profession: Strengthening teacher preparation and induction*. Washington, DC: American Federation of Teachers.

Alfonso, R.J., Firth, G.R., & Neville, R.F. (1975). *Instructional supervision: A behavior system*. Boston: Allyn & Bacon.

Areglado, R.J. (1998). Supervision in elementary schools. In G.R. Firth & E.F. Pajak (Eds.), *Handbook of research on school supervision* (pp. 591-600). New York: Macmillan.

Archer, J. (2001). New roles tap expertise of teachers. *Education Week, 20*(38), 1, 16-19.

Association for Supervision and Curriculum Development. (1960). *Leadership for improving instruction* (1960 Yearbook). Washington, DC: Author.

Ayer, F.C., & Barr, A.S. (1928). *The organization of supervision: An analysis of the organization and administration of supervision in city school systems*. New York: Appleton.

Barr, A.S., & Burton, W.H. (1926). *The supervision of instruction*. New York: D. Appleton.

Barr, A.S., Burton, W.H., & Brueckner, L.J. (1938). *Supervision: Principles and practices in the improvement of instruction*. New York: Appleton-Century.

Bascia, N. (2004). Teacher unions and the teaching workforce: Mismatch or vital contribution? In this volume—M.A. Smylie & D. Miretzky (Eds.), *Developing the teacher workforce. The 103rd yearbook of the National Society for the Study of Education*, Part I (pp. 326-347). Chicago: National Society for the Study of Education.

Bobbitt, F. (1913). *The supervision of city schools. The twelfth yearbook of the National Society for the Study of Education*, Part 1. Bloomington, IL: Public School Publishing Company.

Boyce, A.C. (1915). *Methods for measuring teachers' efficiency. The fourteenth yearbook of the National Society for the Study of Education*, Part II. Bloomington, IL: Public School Publishing Company.

Boyd, W.L., & Kerchner, C.T. (1987). *The politics of excellence and choice in education* (1987 yearbook of the Politics of Education Association). New York: Falmer.

Burton, W.H. (1927). *Supervision and the improvement of teaching*. New York: Appleton-Century.

Callahan, R.E. (1962). *Education and the cult of efficiency*. Chicago: University of Chicago Press.

Callahan, R.E., & Button, H.W. (1964). Historical change of the role of the man in the organization, 1865-1950. In D.E. Griffiths (Ed.) *Behavioral science and educational administration. The sixty-third yearbook of the National Society for the Study of Education*, Part II (pp. 73-94). Chicago: National Society for the Study of Education.

Cogan, M.L. (1973). *Clinical supervision*. Boston: Houghton Mifflin.

Cunningham, L.L. (1963). Effecting change through leadership. *Educational Leadership, 21*(2), 75-79.

Danielson, C. (1996). *Enhancing professional practice: A framework for teaching*. Alexandria, VA: Association for Supervision and Curriculum Development.

Darling-Hammond, L. (2000a). New standards and old inequalities: School reform and the education of African American students. *Journal of Negro Education, 69*(4), 263-287.

Darling-Hammond, L. (2000b). Teacher quality and student achievement: A review of state policy evidence. *Education Policy Analysis Archives, 8*(1). Retrieved January 14, 2004, from http://epaa.asu.edu/epaa/v8n1/

Darling-Hammond, L. (2003). Keeping good teachers: Why it matters, what leaders can do. *Educational Leadership, 60*(8), 6-13.

Darling-Hammond, L., & Sykes, G. (2003, September 17). Wanted: A national teacher supply policy for education: The right way to meet the "highly qualified teacher" challenge. *Education Policy Analysis Archives, 11*(33). Retrieved September 29, 2003, from http://epaa.asu.edu/epaa/v11n33/

Dewey, J. (1929). *The sources of a science of education.* New York: Horace Liveright.
Department of Supervisors and Directors of Instruction. (1934). *Scientific method in supervisory programs.* Seventh Yearbook of the Department of Supervisors and Directors of Instruction. New York: Teachers College, Columbia University.
Department of Supervisors and Directors of Instruction. (1943). *Leadership at work.* Washington, DC: Author.
Elliott, E.C. (1914). *City school supervision.* New York: World Book.
Elmore, R.F. (2003). A plea for strong practice. *Educational Leadership, 61*(3), 6-10.
Fischer, L., Schimmel, D., & Stellman, L.R. (2003). *Teachers and the law* (6th ed.). Boston, MA: Allyn & Bacon.
Flinders, D.J. (1998). Industrial dimensions of supervision. In G.R. Firth and E.F. Pajak (Eds.) *Handbook of research on school supervision* (pp. 1123-1138). New York: Macmillan.
Franseth, J. (1955). *Supervision in rural schools* (Bulletin 1955 No. 11). Washington, DC: U.S. Department of Health Education and Welfare, Office of Education.
Fuhrman, S.H. (1993). *Designing coherent education policy.* San Francisco: Jossey-Bass.
Garman, N. (1986). Clinical supervision: Quackery or remedy for professional development, *Journal of Curriculum and Supervision, 1*(2), 148-157.
Glanz, J. (1992). Curriculum development and supervision: Antecedents for collaboration and future possibilities. *Journal of Curriculum and Supervision, 7*(3), 226-244.
Glanz, J. (1998). Histories, antecedents, and legacies of school supervision. In G.R. Firth & E.F. Pajak (Eds.), *Handbook of research on school supervision* (pp. 39-79). New York, Macmillan.
Goldberg, M.F. (2004). The test mess. *Phi Delta Kappan, 85*(5), 361-366.
Goldhammer, R. (1969). *Clinical supervision: Special methods for the supervision of teachers.* New York: Holt, Rinehart, & Winston.
Green, R.L. (2001). New paradigms in school relationships: Collaborating to enhance student achievement. *Education, 121*(4), p. 737.
Haycock, K. (2000). No more settling for less. *Thinking K-16, 4*(1), 3-12.
Haycock, K. (2003). Toward a fair distribution of teacher talent. *Educational Leadership, 60*(4), 11-15.
Hazi, H.M. (1998). Policy and legal considerations in supervision. In G.R. Firth & E.F. Pajak (Eds.), *Handbook of research on school supervision* (pp. 968-986). New York: Macmillan.
Hendrie, C. (2003, November 12). Group says "lawsuit culture" hampers schools. *Education Week, 23*(11), 5.
Hoff, D.J. (2004). Debate grows on true costs of school law. *Education Week, 23*(21), 1, 22.
Holmes Group. (1986). *Tomorrow's teachers: A report of the Holmes Group.* East Lansing, MI: Holmes Group.
Hosic, J.F. (1920). The democratization of supervision. *School and Society, 11*, 331-336.
Ingersoll, R. (2001). Teacher turnover and teacher shortages: An organizational analysis. *American Educational Research Journal, 38*(3), 499-534.
Ingersoll, R. (2003). *Who controls teachers' work?: Power and accountability in America's schools.* Cambridge, MA: Harvard University Press.
Ingersoll, R. (2004). Four myths about America's teacher quality problem. In this volume—M.A. Smylie & D. Miretzky (Eds.), *Developing the teacher workforce. The 103rd yearbook of the National Society for the Study of Education,* Part I (pp.1-33). Chicago: National Society for the Study of Education.
Johnson, S.M., & Moore, S.E. (2003). The schools that teachers choose. *Educational Leadership, 60*(8), 20-24.
Joyce, B., & Showers, B. (1988). *Student achievement through staff development.* New York: Longman.
Killian, J.E., & Post, D.M. (1998). Scientific dimensions of supervision. In G.R. Firth & E.F. Pajak (Eds.), *Handbook of research on school supervision* (pp. 1032-1054). New York: Macmillan.

Kinsella, B.W., Klopf, G.J., Shafer, H.T., & Young, W.T. (1969). *The supervisor's role in negotiation*. Washington, DC: Association for Supervision and Curriculum Development.

Kozol, J. (1991). *Savage inequalities*. New York: Crown.

McGrath, M.J. (2000). The human dynamics of personnel evaluation. *School Administrator, 57*(9), 1-8.

McLaughlin, M.W. (1984). Teacher evaluation and school improvement. *Teachers College Record, 86*(1), 193-207.

MCEA-MCPS Labor Management Collaboration Project (2002). *Status report: TURN-Broad Foundation initiative*. Rockville, MD: Montgomery County Public Schools and Montgomery County Education Association.

Montgomery County Public Schools. (2001). *Workforce excellence in the Montgomery County Public Schools*. Rockville, MD: Montgomery County Public Schools.

Mosher, R.L., & Purpel, D.E. (1972). *Supervision: The reluctant profession*. New York: Houghton Mifflin.

NCEST (National Council on Education Standards and Testing). (1992). *Raising standards for American education*. Washington, DC: U.S. Government Printing Office.

NCTAF (National Commission on Teaching and America's Future). (1996). *What matters most: Teaching for America's future*. New York: Author.

NCTAF (National Commission on Teaching and America's Future). (2003). *No dream denied: A pledge to America's children*. Washington, DC: Author.

Neill, M. (2003). Leaving children behind: How No Child Left Behind will fail our children. *Phi Delta Kappan, 85*(3), 225-228.

O'Day, J.A., & Smith, M.S. (1993). Systemic reform and educational opportunity. In S.H. Fuhrman (Ed.), *Designing coherent education policy: Improving the system* (pp. 250-312). San Francisco: Jossey-Bass.

Odden, A. (2001). The new school finance. *Phi Delta Kappan, 83*(1), 85-91.

Ogletree, J.R. (1972). Changing supervision in a changing era. *Educational Leadership, 29*(6), 507-510.

Painter, S. (2000). Easing dismissals and non-renewals. *School Administrator, 57*(9), 40-43.

Pajak, E. (2000). *Approaches to clinical supervision* (2nd ed.). Norwood, MA: Christopher-Gordon.

Pajak, E. (2003). *Honoring diverse teaching styles: A guide for supervisors*. Alexandria, VA: Association for Supervision and Curriculum Development.

Pedulla, J.J. (2003). State-mandated testing: What do teachers think? *Educational Leadership, 61*(3), 42-46.

Scriven, M. (1967). The methodology of evaluation. In R.W. Tyler (Ed.), *Perspectives in curriculum evaluation* (pp. 39-83). Chicago, IL: Rand McNally.

Shulman, L.S. (1987a). Knowledge and teaching: Foundations of the new reform. *Harvard Educational Review, 57*, 1-22.

Shulman, L.S. (1987b). The wisdom of practice: Managing complexity in medicine and teaching. In D.C. Berliner & B.V. Rosenshine (Eds.), *Talks to teachers: A Festshrift for N. L. Gage* (pp. 369-386). New York: Random House.

Shulman, L.S. (1998). Theory, practice, and the education of professionals. *The Elementary School Journal, 98*(5), 511-526.

Stone, C.R. (1929). *Supervision of the elementary school*. Boston: Houghton Mifflin.

Taylor, F.W. (1911). *Principles of scientific management*. New York: Harper & Row.

Teaching Commission. (2004). Teaching at risk: A call to action. Retrieved February 23, 2004, from http://www.theteachingcommission.org/

Tyack, D.B. (1974). *The one best system: A history of American urban education*. Cambridge, MA: Harvard University Press.

Whipple, G.M. (Ed.). (1916) *Standards and tests or the measurement of the efficiency of schools and school systems. The fifteenth yearbook of the National Society for the Study of Education*, Part I. Bloomington, IL: Public School Publishing Company.

CHAPTER 8

Teacher Compensation and Teacher Workforce Development

CAROLYN KELLEY AND KARA FINNIGAN

The federal No Child Left Behind Act of 2001 highlights the importance of teacher quality by calling for a "highly qualified" teacher in every classroom by the end of the 2005-06 school year (for more details, see U.S. Department of Education, 2002). Teacher quality has been found to be an important predictor of student success in school (Rice, 2003; Rockoff, 2003; Sanders & Horn, 1996; Wright, Horn, & Sanders, 1997), yet nearly half of the nation's middle and high school teachers fail to meet the definition of "highly qualified" (U.S. Department of Education, 2003a).[1] Calls for high-quality teachers emerge periodically, but prior to No Child Left Behind, the federal government had never mandated a system-level change of this magnitude.

Through No Child Left Behind, states receive funds that can be used to address "challenges to teacher quality, whether they concern teacher preparation and qualifications of new teachers, recruitment and hiring, induction, professional development, teacher retention, or the need for more capable principals and assistant principals to serve as effective school leaders" (U.S. Department of Education, 2003b, p. 7). These factors provide examples of some of the barriers that policymakers have identified as impeding the improvement of both the quality of the teaching force and the distribution of high-quality teachers.

In this chapter, we focus on the role that one policy area—teacher compensation—can play in inhibiting or advancing teacher quality through its impact on attracting, retaining, and developing a high-quality teaching force. Because compensation reform is at a nascent stage of development, we rely on a variety of information sources for our review, including empirical research studies examining the role that

Carolyn Kelley is Chair and Associate Professor in the Department of Educational Leadership and Policy Analysis at the University of Wisconsin-Madison. Kara S. Finnigan is Assistant Professor of Educational Leadership at the Warner Graduate School of Education and Human Development, University of Rochester.

compensation plays in influencing teacher behaviors, theoretical studies, and case studies of innovative uses of compensation to affect
teacher behavior. In some cases, the empirical research is based on
small sample sizes, reflecting the difficulty of obtaining good data
sources for the study of compensation systems and the lack of good
examples to study. Although the chapter focuses solely on compensation, we find significant evidence to suggest that changes in compensation must be part of a larger, systemic reform strategy to strengthen the
teacher workforce that focuses on modifying or enhancing a variety of
components of teachers' work.

In our examination of compensation for teacher workforce development, we also focus on the unique situation high-poverty, low-performing urban schools face because of the particular challenges to
attracting and retaining high-quality teachers in these schools. The
demographics of the student population in public schools have shifted
dramatically over the past few decades, following the patterns of the
larger U.S. population. Both minority and low-income populations
have grown but are not equally distributed—urban areas have larger
proportions of both types of student. In fact, although minority students make up approximately 39% of the total population of students
in U.S. public schools, they represent 62% of students in large or mid-
size cities, 35% in urban fringe areas, and 20% in small town or rural
areas (Hoffman, 2002). Cities are also more likely than rural, small
town, or urban fringe areas to have children living in poverty (NCES,
2003). Students and teachers in the highest poverty schools face other,
related challenges, including high rates of absenteeism and low rates of
parent involvement (NCES, 2003).

Furthermore, high-poverty schools are more likely than other
schools to be staffed by unqualified or underqualified teachers. The
1993-94 Schools and Staffing Survey data showed that students in low-
income and high-minority schools were far less likely than other students to have highly qualified teachers, as measured by educational
attainment, percentage of staff certified in their field, years of teaching
experience, prior education related to subject matter, and teachers'
self-assessments of their ability to teach in their assigned field (Jerald,
2002; NCES, 1997). Policies aimed at reducing inequities in the distribution of education dollars across schools and districts within states
have failed to alleviate inequitable distributions of highly qualified
teachers. The concentration of poor and minority students makes
teacher quality particularly a problem facing *urban* educational settings
(Lankford, Loeb, & Wyckoff, 2002).

Public schools are also facing new and higher-stakes accountability policies at the state and federal levels. The idea of accountability in education is not new, but recent policies represent a shift toward primarily holding schools accountable for *outcomes* rather than *inputs* (Fuhrman, 1999). These policies typically have two types of consequences: 1) public reporting and 2) rewards or sanctions. Those that incorporate rewards or sanctions are considered the more high-stakes approaches (O'Reilly, 1996). Urban schools are particularly vulnerable to being sanctioned under these accountability policies, as they tend to have more minority and low-income students, are larger in size, have higher rates of teacher absenteeism and student behavior problems, and have fewer resources for teachers (NCES, 1996).

In the next section, we describe teacher compensation in the United States as a background for an examination of the role that compensation plays and could play in teacher workforce development.

Teacher Pay

The average teacher salary in the United States in 2002 was $44,367 (not taking into account pay for additional job responsibilities), with significant variation across states. California paid the highest average salary, at $54,348, whereas the lowest average was $31,383, in South Dakota (American Federation of Teachers, 2003). Significant regional differences also exist within states.

Currently, nearly all public school teachers are paid according to the single salary schedule, in which pay is based on years of experience and the accumulation of educational credits and degrees. The single salary schedule has the advantage of being objective, predictable, and relatively easy to administer, even in large urban systems. By decoupling pay from evaluation, the single salary schedule succeeded in reducing the subjectivity of merit pay systems, in which administrators provided pay increases for teacher "merit," often based on limited objective evidence of teacher performance. With the single salary schedule, teachers rely less on administrator approval, and over time the culture of the education system has begun to shift to a more egalitarian work environment, giving teachers greater autonomy in the classroom (Odden & Kelley, 2002).

In many districts, the single salary schedule has become increasingly elaborated, such that teachers need to commit many years to teaching and obtain a Ph.D. in order to achieve the highest levels on the salary scale. One clear disadvantage of the single salary schedule is that it provides no recognition for knowledge, skill, or effort; the most

gifted teacher is paid according to the same years-on-the-job and edu-
cation-level scale as the least gifted teacher. In addition, many districts
set a maximum limit on the number of years of experience they will
recognize when teachers transfer from other districts, so a teacher
with 20 years of experience, for example, may only receive credit for 5
years of experience if he or she moves to a different school district.
Thus, teachers have a strong incentive to move early in their careers
and to move into districts with higher levels of compensation and better working conditions. Gifted experienced teachers who would face
significant financial loss if they were to move to another school district
may choose to move to other schools within the district that have better working conditions or to leave the teaching ranks in favor of promotion to administrative positions (although in many districts, principals are paid less on an hourly basis than experienced teachers in the
same district) (Odden & Kelley, 2002).

In the last few decades, there have been some attempts to alter the
single salary schedule. In 1983, *A Nation at Risk* recommended that
teacher salaries be "professionally competitive, market-sensitive, and
performance-based" (National Commission on Excellence in Education, 1983, p. 30). Districts and states responded to the report with a
flurry of activity, establishing merit pay, career ladder, and other incentive pay programs for teachers, most of which were short-lived.

Merit pay programs are typically defined as providing rewards to
individual teachers for outstanding performance. Several studies have
sought to understand why merit pay programs are rarely institutionalized (Educational Research Service, 1978; Hatry, Greiner, & Ashford,
1994; Jacobson, 1987; Johnson, 1986; Murnane & Cohen, 1986).
Nearly all have reached the same conclusions:

1. By identifying a small percentage of the best and brightest teachers, merit pay runs counter to efforts to create cultures of collegiality, cooperation, and trust that characterize effective schools
   (Bryk & Schneider, 2002; Rosenholtz, 1989).
2. Excellence is rarely defined clearly.
3. The procedures for identifying excellence are typically flawed in
   fundamental ways.
4. Districts and states rarely provide consistent funding for these
   programs, significantly reducing their motivational value.

Career ladder programs attempt to reform compensation by providing strong teachers with an opportunity to advance to new roles and

responsibilities in the profession yet remain connected to the classroom. Most career ladder programs engage teachers outside the classroom for some portion of their day, during which they spend time on other tasks such as curriculum development and teacher training. Cornett (1994) found that in Arizona, among students taught by teachers in the career ladder program, achievement increased, dropout rates declined, and graduation rates increased. Despite these successes, career ladder programs tend to be short-lived, and most of the programs established in the 1980s were phased out by the mid-1990s (Hatry, Greiner, & Ashford, 1994). One explanation for the lack of long-term commitment to career ladder programs is that the programs tend to be costly. As teachers move up the career ladder, their duties are shifted toward mentoring and other administrative support. This increases the overall cost of instruction as additional teachers are needed to replace the instructional time no longer provided by the promoted teachers.

Beginning in the 1990s, a number of states and districts began to pay bonus awards to groups of teachers within a school, or to entire school staffs, for the achievement of specific educational goals.[2] These school-based performance award programs arose as part of the movement toward greater accountability in public education. With the passage of No Child Left Behind, compensation and accountability have become further intertwined. The act requires that schools either meet state standards or face sanctions and provides funding to states for professional development, recruitment, tenure reform, and performance pay (U.S. Department of Education, 2002).

Also in the 1990s, a number of states and districts instituted incremental pay increases or bonuses for National Board Certified teachers in an effort to compensate teachers for advanced knowledge and skills. The pay increases or bonuses typically ranged from $2,500 to $10,000 per year for the 10-year life of the certificate (Kelley & Gardner, 2002; Kelley & Kimball, 2001). State-to-state comparisons of the number of National Board Certified teachers show that states with pay incentives for National Board Certification have much larger numbers of Board Certified teachers than states without these incentives, suggesting that the incentives were successful (Kelley & Kimball).

Beyond providing pay increases for the development and demonstration of specific teaching competencies, knowledge and skills–based pay systems have been designed to completely replace the single salary schedule. A theoretical advantage to this type of system is that it can provide formative as well as summative feedback to teachers, thereby helping to shape their ongoing professional growth and development

(Danielson & McGreal, 2000). In this type of system, teachers advance through the salary schedule as they demonstrate successive levels of mastery of teacher knowledge and skills (Odden & Kelley, 2002). This differs from traditional merit pay systems in that 1) it is standards based; 2) every teacher has an opportunity to achieve mastery; and 3) the system is designed to support teacher growth and development. The goal is to align pay with teacher professional development to provide consistent feedback, support, and growth opportunities for teachers to develop their teaching skills. Although such systems have been conceptualized and piloted in Cincinnati (Ohio) and in the state of Iowa, and this type of system is currently in place in the Vaughn New Century Charter School in Los Angeles, knowledge and skills–based pay systems are rare.[3]

Teacher Compensation as a Tool for Attracting, Retaining, and Developing High-Quality Teachers

In this section, we consider teacher compensation in light of the research on teacher attraction, teacher retention and mobility, and the professional growth and development of the teaching workforce.

Attraction

A large body of literature suggests that teacher supply is enhanced when salaries for teachers are made more competitive relative to pay in other professions (Brewer, 1996; Lankford et al., 2002; Manski, 1987; Murnane, Singer, & Willett, 1989). Calls to raise teacher salaries are premised on the idea that higher pay will attract a larger pool of teacher candidates, thereby increasing the pool of more capable teachers. But the supply of teachers depends not only on teacher pay levels but also on the pay levels of other jobs that potential teachers are qualified to pursue. For example, the average beginning teacher salary in the United States in 2002 was $30,719 (with significant regional variation). Even accounting for the shorter work year for teachers, this compares unfavorably to average beginning salaries in engineering ($49,702), math/statistics ($46,744), computer science ($46,495), accounting ($41,162), economics/finance ($41,102), and business administration ($40,242) (American Federation of Teachers, 2003). Several studies have found that teachers in particular fields, such as science and math, have particularly high rates of attrition (Hanushek, Kain, & Rivkin, 1999; Kirby & Grissmer, 1993; Murnane, 1987). Thus, some teacher shortages, such as in science, could be explained by the competitive labor market for individuals with these skill sets (Mila-nowski, 2003).

Although there is little doubt that pay level influences career deci-sions, the relationship between compensation and occupational choice is complex and involves consideration of a number of factors related to the match between the career and individual interests, personality, and values. Thus, even a small increase in beginning pay for teachers might attract an additional set of candidates from the employment pool, specifically those whose personalities and career interests are most closely aligned with the characteristics of a career in teaching (Mila-nowski, 2003). Furthermore, not only beginning teacher salaries but also the earnings potential for teachers across the entire span of the teaching career may influence teacher employment decisions. Teaching, a highly unionized profession, is characterized by elaborate pay struc-tures that reward seniority and education. Recent increases in pay have been largely invested in increasing pay for senior teachers, rather than boosting starting pay (Ballou & Podgursky, 1997).

Increased compensation for teachers could boost the quality of the candidate pool if the higher pay results in more highly qualified indi-viduals seeking teaching careers. Some researchers speculate that, with increased compensation, the quality of teachers hired could increase even if the group of individuals seeking teaching careers remained at the current distribution of talent. This is because the increased pay could lower the attrition rate for existing teachers, thereby enabling administrators to be more selective in filling the resulting smaller num-ber of vacancies (Ballou & Podgursky, 1997; Murnane et al., 1989).

Because teachers face very different career path choices depending on their field of study, general increases in pay are considered some-what inefficient mechanisms for raising the quality of the teacher can-didate pool. In other words, raising teacher pay generally raises pay the same amount for teachers in every field of study, even though history and science teachers (for example) face very different salary trade-offs when comparing their earning power in teaching to other types of positions that they may be qualified to pursue. Furthermore, an overall increase in pay raises compensation levels for teachers regardless of the quality of their contribution. This has led some researchers to theorize that increasing teacher pay will have more impact on teacher quality if pay increases are provided as rewards for high-quality teacher perfor-mance (Ballou & Podgursky, 1997).

Even so, pay incentives may be inadequate to attract teachers to the highest need schools. In a study of compensation and teacher quality in the State of New York, Loeb (2000) found that the largest variation in pay occurred across, rather than within, regional labor markets in the state. Further, an examination of teacher qualifications suggested that teacher sorting occurred primarily *within* districts. That is, the more highly qualified teachers self-sorted away from the high-need schools within their districts.

Policies intended to address these problems include the provision of signing bonuses or housing allowances to lure teachers to less-desirable areas or to higher cost urban and suburban districts. Scant research exists on these recruitment strategies, but one study of Massachusetts is worth noting. In 1998, Massachusetts began a program awarding $20,000 signing bonuses over a four-year period. Teachers were attracted to the program, but retention became a problem: after three years, 47% of the teachers recruited under this program had left their positions (Archer, 2002). Liu, Johnson, and Peske (2003) studied 13 of the 59 individuals who received these bonuses during the first year of implementation and found that the bonuses were too weak an inducement to *retain* teachers. These researchers found that many teachers had left because of inadequate working conditions, including a lack of support at their schools. The following paragraphs describe the literature on teacher retention in more detail.

Retention and Mobility

The teaching profession is characterized by relatively high rates of teacher turnover, with as much as half of that turnover representing movement between schools and districts. Using data from the Schools and Staffing Survey, Ingersoll (2001) found that 14% of teachers left their schools in 1993-94. Turnover is higher for new teachers. A 1997 NCES study found that 9% of public school teachers left teaching before they had completed their first year in the classroom. In addition, 25% to 30% of teachers leave within their first five years, with low-performing schools losing teachers at even higher rates (Certo & Fox, 2002; NCREL, 2001).

Teacher mobility appears to have a detrimental effect on urban schools. A study in New York State found that New York City experienced a higher-than-average rate of teacher transfer to other school districts. This higher transfer rate had an adverse effect on teacher quality in New York City schools because teachers who transferred out of the district were found to have higher qualifications on average than those who stayed in the same school or transferred within their own districts (Lankford et al., 2002; Murnane et al., 1989):

Those transferring [from New York City] to another district have failed the
certification exams half as often as those remaining in the same school. They
are twice as likely to have attended a most or highly competitive college, and
about half as likely to have attended the least competitive college. (Lankford
et al., 2002, p. 50)

Pay clearly influences teachers' decisions to transfer to another
school or leave the profession altogether (Certo & Fox, 2002; Hanushek, Kain, & Rivkin, 2001; Ingersoll, 2001; Shen, 2001). A study of
teachers in seven Virginia districts found that salary was the top reason
that teachers reported for leaving the profession (Certo & Fox). Other
factors identified included a lack of administrative support, student discipline problems, lack of student motivation, lack of influence over
decision making, and lack of planning time (Certo & Fox; Ingersoll).
The characteristics of the work environment, such as the races and
achievement levels of students, have also been identified as important
predictors of teacher decisions to move to other schools or districts
(Hanushek et al.; Shen). Thus, teacher pay is a contributing factor to
teachers' decisions to stay or leave, but the context of teacher work is
also critically important.

Professional Growth and Development of the Teacher Workforce

Teacher compensation can also be in the form of incentives and
rewards for teacher performance and for the growth and development
of teachers throughout their careers. The single salary schedule, which
is currently the dominant structure of teacher compensation, has been
criticized because advancement on the schedule is not associated with
teacher performance or knowledge and skill development. Although
research suggests that experience is related to teacher quality in the
first few years of teaching, in subsequent years there is no statistically
significant relationship between years of experience and teacher performance (Murnane & Phillips, 1981). Furthermore, although some
studies have found that having a degree in the subject taught has a
small positive effect on teacher performance at the high school level, in
general, educational credits and degrees are also a weak indicator of
teacher quality (Lankford et al., 2002).

Therefore, here we consider the potential role that compensation
might play in shaping the professional growth and development of the
teaching force. We consider two new types of pay—school-based
performance pay and knowledge and skills–based pay—as alternative
approaches to compensating teachers that could be used to shape teacher
workforce development.

Pay for Performance. School-based performance award policies attempt to motivate changes in individual teacher behavior that will lead to improved school-level performance. In most cases, these policies provide individual bonuses to all teachers when a school meets a particular standard or growth target. The underlying theory of these policies is that school performance will improve when the level, focus, and quality of teacher effort is improved.

Past research has found that performance for some students does appear to improve when school-based performance award programs are in place. For example, the performance of Hispanic and White students (see Ladd, 1999), as well as elementary students (see Poggio, 2000), improved under these programs. Schools that improve under such plans are characterized by high teacher expectancy (Kelley, Heneman, & Milanowski, 2000). That is, student performance improves in schools where teachers have a strong belief in their own abilities and in their collective ability to achieve the accountability goals set for them. Teacher expectancy, in turn, is affected by certain organizational conditions such as a belief among the teachers that the reward program is fair, opportunities for teachers to receive and understand student performance feedback, no conflicts with other school goals, and strong and committed principal leadership and support (Kelley & Finnigan, 2003).

Although some benefits of school-based performance award programs have been identified, concerns remain about the implementation of these policies. First, without systematic realignment and investment in teacher knowledge and skills and improvements in organizational performance, performance pay plans can work only to the extent that teachers already have the capacity to change their practices to improve student performance. Thus, empirical studies on group-based performance pay systems have shown that, typically, short-term gains in student performance reflect stepped-up efforts to align instructional content with state standards and to prepare students for the test by familiarizing them with its approach and emphasizing its importance. Longer-term gains reflect improvements in teacher capacity produced by intensive and focused professional development; opportunities for increased problem solving among teachers; more sophisticated efforts at curriculum alignment and refinement, both within and across grade levels; and systematic evaluation of student performance data with feedback into curriculum and program design (Kannapel, Coe, Aagaard, Moore, & Reeves, 2000; Kelley, 1998; Kelley & Protsik, 1997; Stecher & Barron, 1999).

Second, whether the program motivates changes in teacher behavior is only one measure of its effectiveness. An equally important question is whether the accountability incentives produce *desirable* behaviors. Some researchers and practitioners have expressed concern that school-based performance award programs may overly narrow the curriculum; divert it from important instructional goals that are not assessed; and negatively influence educator behaviors, including encouraging administrator and teacher flight from low-performing schools (Kannapel et al., 2000; King & Mathers, 1997; Ladd & Walsh, 2002; McNeil, 2000; Poggio, 2000; Stecher & Barron, 1999). However, it is also the case that accountability systems with a school-based performance award component have focused teacher efforts in some desirable ways, providing focus and attention to data to inform instructional decisions, promoting collaboration among teachers, enhancing and focusing professional development for teachers, and promoting improvements in student achievement (Kelley et al., 2002).

The research shows that the measure of student performance chosen and the overall incentive design shape behavioral outcomes. The research suggests that pay can clearly provide an incentive that motivates changes in teacher and administrator behaviors. However, we note that it is relatively easy to get the incentives "wrong," and much more difficult to get them "right."

Pay for Knowledge and Skills. Pay for the development and demonstration of teacher knowledge and skills, such as National Board Certification, is another form of compensation for teachers designed to enhance the quality of the teaching workforce. Because teachers with National Board Certification are overrepresented in states with incentive policies, pay appears to motivate teachers to undergo this process. Teachers participating in the process say that Board Certification is a powerful professional development activity (Belden, 2002; Buday, 2001; Kelley & Gardner, 2002; Kelley & Kimball, 2001; NBPTS, 2002); therefore, pay for National Board Certification could be viewed as pay for knowledge and skill development as teachers hone their skills in preparation for, and during their participation in, the certification process. An issue of concern in state-level pay incentives for National Board Certification is that, due to the unequal distribution of qualified teachers, there may be few teachers in the lowest performing schools who even qualify to apply for Board Certification. Furthermore, research has shown that minority candidates are less likely than others to achieve National Board Certification (Bond, 1998). Some states have tried to use Board Certification as a mechanism for identifying excellent teachers and encouraging them to move to low-performing schools (Belden). Additional research is needed to understand the impact of these targeted policies.

Another use of knowledge and skills–based pay has been to replace the single salary schedule with an elaborated set of rewards for the demonstration of teacher knowledge and skills. The only known example of this approach is the Vaughn New Century Charter School. Vaughn is a PK-6 school with a history of low performance located in an extremely impoverished neighborhood of South Central Los Angeles. It became a charter school in 1993 and adopted an alternative pay plan in 1997-98 (Kellor, 2003a). Although this is a unique case in that the school is led by a particularly strong and charismatic principal, it provides one of the few examples of a fully implemented knowledge and skills–based pay program. Vaughn adopted its pay strategy to improve recruitment to a highly challenged school in a very tight teacher employment market (California).

The principal has used the pay plan to reward teachers for the development and demonstration of knowledge and skills. Evaluation data suggest that the school has become more competitive in attracting new teachers and has retained them by providing opportunities to achieve much higher initial salaries and salary advancement that outpaces other schools in the Los Angeles Unified School District. In 2002-03, Vaughn paid $33,150 as a base salary, with an additional $2,000 for a California Teaching Credential, $2,000 for a master's degree, and up to $4,500 for knowledge and skills in English as a Second Language, Mathematics, Special Education Inclusion, Classroom Management, or Lesson Planning. The additional pay may be particularly attractive to teachers in the Los Angeles market, where the cost of living is prohibitively expensive for many new teachers. A validation study of the program showed that teacher evaluation ratings were significantly related to student performance gains in reading, but not in math (Gallagher, 2002).

Although this type of compensation system can focus attention on the goals and expectations for teachers, knowledge and skills–based pay systems are difficult to implement. A key challenge is developing the institutional capacity required to assess teacher knowledge and skills accurately across all skill levels, with sufficient reliability and defensibility to assign pay based on the judgments of evaluators (Gallagher, 2002). In this case, capacity includes having highly skilled evaluators who can assess teaching practice accurately from the lowest to the highest skill levels and investing the resources needed to collect sufficient teaching evidence (typically through multiple observations and review of curricular materials and lesson plans) to make an informed and accurate assessment of teaching practice. Principals are the primary evaluators in most schools but they may lack the knowledge, skills, and time necessary to effectively implement such a pay system. Furthermore, when the stakes on evaluation are high, the process can quickly become politicized, to the detriment of the formative goals of the evaluation system (Halverson, Kelley, & Kimball, 2003).

Thus, the limited research on knowledge and skills–based pay suggests that compensation can provide incentives for knowledge and skill development and can contribute to focusing and motivating teachers to work toward specific goals, but more research is needed to determine how well these systems work in practice. Furthermore, pay plays an important role in attracting and retaining teachers, but it will be most effective when disparities in school resources and working conditions are also addressed.

Teacher Compensation and Low-Performing Schools

Compensation has the potential to be an important policy lever for improving teacher quality by enhancing the ability of schools and districts to attract, retain, and encourage the development of the teacher workforce. However, measures of the success of these incentives should consider whether they have achieved the equitable distribution of high-quality teachers across districts and states to ensure that even the highest poverty, lowest performing schools benefit from these policies.

Attracting and Retaining Teachers in Low-Performing Schools

Attracting and retaining high-quality teachers in low-performing schools is a critical issue given the No Child Left Behind requirement that schools either meet standards or face sanctions. Currently, most districts use the same pay scale for all teachers within the district, regardless of school assignment. Policies that increase teacher pay district-wide would not provide an incentive for teachers within a district to select the highest need schools. Instead, district or state policies would have to provide additional funds to teachers in the lowest performing schools.

Furthermore, teacher retention is a critical problem for urban schools serving low-income and minority populations. Turnover is much higher in teaching than in other professions (Ingersoll, 2001), and low-performing schools frequently lose their best teachers to higher paying school districts with higher performing student populations, typically those with fewer minority students (Lankford et al., 2002). The evidence suggests that teachers who stay in teaching migrate from lower to higher paying districts, and from lower to higher performing schools, particularly in high-stakes accountability environments (Hanushek et al., 2001; Ladd, 2001; Lankford et al.). Lankford, Loeb, and Wyckoff found that highly qualified teachers were likely to move to schools with higher wages and better working conditions, including schools with significantly lower proportions of poor and non-White students, smaller class sizes, and salaries that were between 12% and 22% higher than their original districts. Teachers who leave indicate that pay is the most important factor for their leaving, followed by a number of other issues related to working conditions, including the challenges characteristic of teaching at-risk populations of students in low-performing schools (Certo & Fox, 2002; Ingersoll).

Similar results were found in a study of teacher transfer and exit in Wisconsin public schools. In a quantitative analysis of teacher transfer behaviors in Milwaukee and surrounding districts, Imazeki (2000) found that high-need districts had higher teacher transfer rates. The regression models suggested that increasing the wages of teachers in high-need districts relative to other districts could reduce both exit and transfer attrition, but a 25% to 33% salary differential would be needed to equalize transfer rates for Milwaukee teachers (for example) with those for teachers in surrounding districts.

Juxtaposed with consideration of the structure of compensation, it is not surprising that the best and brightest teachers choose to leave low-performing urban schools for higher pay and less-challenging working conditions in the suburbs. Urban settings are often more expensive than suburban settings, and the structure of teacher pay is such that it takes years to work one's way up the pay scale. As gifted and talented individuals see their friends in other professions moving ahead, they face a 30-year climb to the top of the pay scale, complete with the promise of evenings and weekends committed to additional graduate study to get ahead.

Because some districts limit the number of years of experience that transferring employees can claim on the pay scale (see, e.g., Ballou, 2000), the imperative to move early is reinforced, and teachers are encouraged to select a district they know they can live with for a long time. There is plenty of research to show that teachers are sensitive to pay levels in their decisions to transfer (Ingersoll, 2001; Lankford et al., 2002) and that higher pay would encourage them to stay in the more challenging learning environments (Imazeki, 2000). But the size of the pay increase required to entice teachers to stay would likely be prohibitive if it were applied according to the current lock-step pay scale.

Compensation Strategies Focused on Low-Performing Schools

The challenge for urban districts is to develop attractive, competitive, and cutting-edge compensation strategies that enable them to retain an advantage over their suburban competitors. The desire to attract qualified teachers is high, and the resources available to many suburban districts enable them to quickly match and better alternative pay strategies currently offered by urban districts in an attempt to attract and retain a high-quality teaching force.

State-level efforts to reduce district practices of limiting the number of years of experience credited to transferring teachers and to encourage district experimentation with pay approaches that reward the development and demonstration of teacher knowledge and skills can also enhance teacher willingness to commit some portion of their careers to working in challenging school settings. These efforts need to be combined with purposive strategies to reward teachers for their experiences in challenging educational settings, including creating expectations that excellent leaders will commit at least a portion of their careers to working in these settings and will be rewarded for this service with both pay and career advancement.

Increasing entry-level pay could serve as an additional factor in attracting highly qualified teachers to low-performing schools. Even the most dedicated teacher needs to be able to pay the rent, and in many areas, teacher pay is wholly insufficient to provide even a minimum standard of living. Increased pay for beginning teachers could provide an important incentive to attract qualified (certified) teachers to challenged school environments. Opportunities for increased pay combined with other rewards for strong performance may provide an important incentive to attract *and* retain more highly qualified teachers to challenged schools. These incentives are likely to be more effective than signing bonuses, which provide the initial attraction but do little to encourage teacher retention (see, e.g., Archer, 2003).

It is important to retain a systemic approach to the issue of teacher quality and consider the range of factors that contribute to an unequal distribution of teacher quality within schools and across schools and districts. Most teachers identify compensation *and* working conditions as key factors in their decisions to leave their current schools. Policymakers and administrators must consider a variety of approaches to compensate for the additional challenges facing educators in schools with very low-income and highly at-risk populations of students. Along with restructured pay systems, such compensation could include reduced class sizes, reduced teaching loads, more opportunities for mentoring and professional growth and development, increased teaching resources, opportunities to serve under strong and effective school leaders, more opportunities for long-term career advancement, and cultures that encourage service rotations across the district rather than unidirectional migration out of the lowest performing schools. These other non-monetary types of compensation may be as important as competitive salaries and other monetary rewards for attracting teachers to challenged schools, as evidenced by recent strikes over health insurance in four districts (Keller, 2003).

Although knowledge and skills–based pay systems provide a unique opportunity to reward teacher growth and development, the success of these types of systems depends in part on the abilities of the principals (or others who serve as evaluators) to provide meaningful, accurate, developmental feedback to teachers. They also require a significant time investment in order to observe and review evidence for the evaluation. Thus, such systems can be somewhat costly to administer. Very low-performing schools may be the ones least likely to have the capacity to effectively implement them. These schools are likely to need significant investment in evaluator training, teacher professional development, and staffing to implement the evaluation piece of a knowledge and skills–based pay system effectively.

Finally, accountability policies may increase the inequality among schools, as strong teachers seek opportunities in districts that are more likely to be rewarded and less likely to be identified as poor performing. The evidence cited from New York City and Milwaukee suggests that this is true, as it is the more highly qualified teachers who move out of the urban district to seek higher pay and better working conditions. Policymakers must find ways to hold schools accountable without discouraging the most effective teachers. Careful research is needed on the impact of accountability pressure on teacher supply, retention, and mobility to inform policy decisions about the kinds of incentive structures that will improve the performance of these schools without chasing away the very best teachers.

Conclusion

Teacher compensation policies provide powerful incentives and have a significant role to play in attracting and retaining high-quality teachers and developing the teacher workforce. However, the limited research in this area also suggests that a systemic approach involving districts and states that invests in positive changes to organizational cultures and capacities, combined with changes in teacher compensation, has the potential to attract more highly qualified teachers to low-performing schools and to enhance the quality of the teaching force more generally. As the language of No Child Left Behind suggests, no single intervention is likely to significantly enhance the quality and distribution of the teaching force. Instead, attention should be paid to a constellation of factors contributing to persistent school failure, including but not limited to the distribution of resources, leadership, social capital, culture and climate, management, and parent and community support.

In this chapter, we have tried to raise a number of important issues related to the role of compensation reforms in developing the teaching workforce because the research in this area, to date, has paid little attention to either the impact of these reforms on altering the distribution of teacher qualifications across schools and districts or the effect of these policies on low-performing schools. Further attention is needed to understand current disparities and to identify ways that compensation can be used as part of a broader strategy to address them.

NOTES

1. No Child Left Behind defines "highly qualified" as those who hold a bachelor's degree from a four-year college, have state certification, and demonstrate competence in the subject they teach.

2. Early innovators in school-based performance awards include Douglas County, Colorado; Dallas, Texas; Boston, Massachusetts; Charlotte-Mecklenburg, North Carolina; Kentucky; Texas; and Florida. Other examples include programs in Denver, Colorado; Atlanta, Georgia; California; Maryland (which paid awards to schools for discretionary school spending); and Ontario, Canada. These programs vary widely in context, design, and implementation, but all represent a movement to link pay in the form of school-wide bonuses to student performance outcomes.

3. In addition, the state of Idaho is exploring the development of a statewide knowledge and skills–based salary schedule; Minnesota has just announced a proposal to create a pilot program to award excellent teachers up to $100,000 in bonuses for working in one of the state's five most difficult schools; in 2004, Florida will begin piloting programs for a 2004-05 requirement that all school districts in that state implement a career ladder program for classroom teachers that includes four salary levels: associate, professional, lead, and mentor teacher (Kellor, 2003b).

REFERENCES

American Federation of Teachers. (2003). Survey and analysis of teacher salary trends 2002. Washington, DC: Author. Retrieved August 12, 2003, from http://www.aft.org/research/survey02/SalarySurvey02.pdf

Archer, J. (2002, December 4). Mass. bonus program to favor ed. schools. *Education Week on the Web*. Retrieved October 9, 2003, from http://www.edweek.com/ew/ewstory.cfm?slug=14bonus.h22

Ballou, D. (2000). *Teacher contracts in Massachusetts*. Boston, MA: Pioneer Institute for Public Policy Research.

Ballou, D., & Podgursky, M. (1997). *Teacher pay and teacher quality*. Kalamazoo, MI: W.E. Upjohn Institute for Employment Research.

Bond, L. (1998). Disparate impact and teacher certification. *Journal of Personnel Evaluation in Education, 12*(2), 211-220.

Brewer, D.J. (1996). Career paths and quit decisions: Evidence from teaching. *Journal of Labor Economics, 14*(2), 313-339.

Bryk, A.S., & Schneider, B.L. (2002). *Trust in schools: A core resource for improvement*. New York, NY: Russell Sage Foundation.

Certo, J.L., & Fox, J.E. (2002). Retaining quality teachers. *The High School Journal, 86* (Oct/Nov), 57-75.

Cornett, L.M. (1994, April). Ups and downs of incentive programs. *Southern Regional Education Board Career Ladder Clearinghouse*. Atlanta, GA: Southern Regional Educational Board.

Danielson, C., & McGreal, T. (2000). *Teacher evaluation to enhance professional practice*. Alexandria, VA: Association for Supervision and Curriculum Development.

Educational Research Service. (1978). *Methods of scheduling salaries for teachers*. Arlington, VA: Educational Research Service.

Fuhrman, S. (1999). *The new accountability*. Philadelphia: Consortium for Policy Research in Education.

Gallagher, H.A. (2002, April). *The relationship between measures of teacher quality and student achievement: The case of Vaughn Elementary*. Paper presented at the annual meeting of the American Educational Research Association, New Orleans, LA.

Halverson, R., Kelley, C., & Kimball, S. (2003, April). *Implementing teacher evaluation systems: How principals make sense of complex artifacts to shape local instructional practice*. Paper presented at the annual meeting of the American Educational Research Association, Chicago, IL.

Hanushek, E.A., Kain, J.F., & Rivkin, S.G. (2001). Why public schools lose teachers. Cambridge, MA: National Bureau of Economic Research.

Hatry, H.P., Greiner, J.M., & Ashford, B.G. (1994). *Issues and case studies in teacher incentive plans* (2nd ed.). Washington, DC: Urban Institute Press.

Hoffman, L. (2002). Overview of public elementary and secondary schools and districts: School year 2000-2001 (NCES 2002-356). Washington, DC: U.S. Department of Education, National Center for Education Statistics.

Ingersoll, R.M. (2001). *Teacher turnover, teacher shortages, and the organization of schools* (Document No. R-01-1). Center for the Study of Teacher Policy, University of Washington.

Imazeki, J.Y. (2000). *School finance reform and the market for teachers*. Unpublished doctoral dissertation, Department of Economics, University of Wisconsin-Madison.

Jacobson, S.L. (1987). Merit pay and teaching as a career. In K. Alexander and D.H. Monk (Eds.), *Attracting and compensating America's teachers. Eighth annual yearbook of the American Educational Finance Association*, (pp. 161-177). Cambridge, MA: Ballinger.

Jerald, C.D. (2002). *All talk, no action: Putting an end to out-of-field teaching*. Washington, DC: Education Trust.

Johnson, S.M. (1986). Incentives for teachers: What motivates, what matters? *Educational Administration Quarterly, 22*(3), 54-79.

Kannapel, P.J., Coe, P., Aagaard, L., Moore, B.D., & Reeves, C.A. (2000). Teacher responses to rewards and sanctions: Effects of and reactions to Kentucky's high stakes accountability program. In B.L. Whitford and K. Jones (Eds.), *Accountability, assessment and teacher commitment: Lessons from Kentucky's reform efforts* (pp. 127-146). New York: SUNY Press.

Keller, B. (2003, October 15). Health costs obstructing contract settlements. *Education Week on the Web.* Retrieved October 22, 2003, from http://www.edweek.org/ew/ewstory.cfm?slug=07health.h23

Kelley, C. (1998). The Kentucky school-based performance award program: School-level effects. *Educational Policy, 12*(3), 305-324.

Kelley, C., & Finnigan, K. (2003). The effects of organizational context on teacher expectancy. *Educational Administration Quarterly 39*(5), 603-634.

Kelley, C., & Gardner, D. (2002, April). *Good return on the investment? Teacher perceptions of the value of incentives and rewards for National Board Certification.* Paper presented at the annual meeting of the American Educational Research Association, New Orleans, LA.

Kelley, C., Heneman, H.G., III, & Milanowski, A. (2002). Teacher motivation and school-based performance awards. *Educational Administration Quarterly, 38*(3), 372-401.

Kelley, C., & Kimball, S. (2001, September). Financial incentives for National Board Certification. *Educational Policy, 15*(4), 547-574.

Kelley, C., & Protsik, J. (1997). Risk and reward: Perspectives on the implementation of Kentucky's school-based performance award program. *Educational Administration Quarterly, 33*(4), 474-505.

Kellor, E.M. (2003a). Catching up with the Vaughn Express: Four years of performance pay and standards-based teacher evaluation. CPRE UW Working Paper Series TC-03-02, University of Wisconsin-Madison. Retrieved October 28, 2003, from http://www.wcer.wisc.edu/cpre/papers/pdf/Vaughn2003.pdf

Kellor, E.M. (2003b). State and local initiatives. *October 2003 CPRE-UW e-newsletter.* Retrieved October 20, 2003, from http://www.wcer.wisc.edu/cpre/tcomp

King, R.A., & Mathers, J.K. (1997). Improving schools through performance-based accountability and financial rewards. *Journal of Education Finance, 23*, 147-176.

Kirby, S.N., & Grissmer, D. (1993). *Teacher attrition: Theory, evidence, and suggested policy options.* Santa Monica, CA: Rand.

Ladd, H.F. (1999). The Dallas school accountability and incentive program: An evaluation of its impact on student outcomes. *Economics of Education Review, 18*(1), 1-16.

Ladd, H.F. (2001). School-based educational accountability systems: The promise and the pitfalls. *National Tax Journal, 54*(2), 385-400.

Ladd, H.F., & Walsh, R.P. (2002). Implementing value-added measures of school effectiveness: Getting the incentive right. *Economics of Education Review, 21*(1), 1-17.

Lankford, H., Loeb, S., & Wyckoff, J. (2002). Teacher sorting and the plight of urban schools: A descriptive analysis. *Educational Evaluation and Policy Analysis, 24*(1), 37-62.

Liu, E., Johnson, S.M., & Peske, H.G. (2003, April). *New teachers and the Massachusetts signing bonus: The limits of inducements.* Paper presented at the annual meeting of the American Educational Research Association, Chicago, IL.

Loeb, S. (2000, November 8). *How teachers' choices affect what a dollar can buy: Wages and quality in K-12 schooling.* Proceedings from the Symposium on the Teaching Workforce, Albany, New York: Education Finance Research Consortium.

Manski, C.F. (1987). Academic ability, earnings, and the decision to become a teacher: Evidence from the National Longitudinal Study of the High School Class of 1972. In D.A. Wise (Ed.), *Public sector payrolls* (pp. 291-312). Chicago: University of Chicago Press.

272   TEACHER   COMPENSATION

McNeil, L.M. (2000). *Contradictions of school reform: Educational costs of standardized testing.* New York: Routledge.
Milanowski, A. (2003, December 27). An exploration of the pay levels needed to attract students with mathematics, science and technology skills to a career in K-12 teaching, *Educational Policy Analysis Archives, 11*(50). Retrieved November 13, 2003 from http://epaa.asu.edu/epaa/v11n50/
Murnane, R.J. (1987). Understanding teacher attrition. *Harvard Educational Review, 57,* 177-182.
Murnane, R.J., & Cohen, D.K. (1986). Merit pay and the evaluation problem: Why most merit pay plans fail and a few survive. *Harvard Educational Review, 56,* 1-17.
Murnane, R.J., & Phillips, B.R. (1981). Learning by doing, vintage, and selection: Three pieces of the puzzle relating teaching experience and teaching performance. *Economics of Education Review, 1*(4), 453-465.
Murnane, R.J., Singer, J.D., & Willett, J.B. (1989). The influences of salaries and "opportunity costs" on teachers' career choices: Evidence from North Carolina. *Harvard Educational Review, 59*(3), 325-346.
National Commission on Excellence in Education. (1983). *A nation at risk: The imperative for education reform.* Washington, DC: U.S. Department of Education.
NCES (National Commission on Education Statistics). (1996). *Urban schools, the challenge of location and poverty.* Washington, DC: U.S. Department of Education, Office of Education Research and Improvement.
NCES (National Commission on Education Statistics). (1997). *America's teachers: Profile of a profession, 1993-94.* Washington, DC: U.S. Department of Education, Office of Educational Research and Improvement.
NCES (National Center for Education Statistics). (2003). *Conditions of education.* Washington, DC: U.S. Department of Education, Institute of Education Sciences.
NCREL (North Central Regional Educational Laboratory). (2001, June). *Policy Issues.* Naperville, IL: Author. Retrieved December 9, 2003, from http://www.ncrel.org/policy/pubs/html/pivol8/june2001.htm
Odden, A., & Kelley, C. (2002). *Paying teachers for what they know and do: New and smarter compensation strategies to improve schools* (2nd ed.). Thousand Oaks, CA: Corwin Press.
O'Reilly, F. (1996). *Educational accountability: Current practices and theories in use.* Philadelphia: Consortium for Policy Research in Education.
Poggio, J.P. (2000). Statewide performance assessment and school accountability. In R.S. Pankratz & J.M. Petrosko (Eds.), *All children can learn: Lessons from the Kentucky reform experience* (pp. 75-97). San Francisco: Jossey-Bass.
Rice, J.K. (2003). *Teacher quality: Understanding the effectiveness of teacher attributes.* Washington, DC: Economic Policy Institute.
Rockoff, J.E. (2003). The impact of individual teachers on student achievement: Evidence from panel data. Cambridge, MA: Harvard University Kennedy School of Government. Retrieved December 9, 2003, from http://econwpa.wustl.edu/eps/pe/papers/0304/0304002.pdf
Sanders, W.L., & Horn, S.P. (1994). The Tennessee value-added assessment system (TVAAS): Mixed model methodology in educational assessment. *Journal of Personnel Evaluation in Education, 8,* 299-311.
Shen, J. (2001). Teacher retention and attrition in public schools: Evidence from SASS91. *Journal of Educational Research, 91*(2), 81-88.
Stecher, B.M., & Barron, S. (1999, April). *Test-based accountability: The perverse consequences of milepost testing.* Paper presented at the annual meeting of the American Educational Research Association, Montreal, Canada.
U. S. Department of Education. (2002). *No Child Left Behind: A Desktop Reference.* Retrieved December 10, 2003, from http://www.ed.gov/admins/lead/account/nclbreference/index.html

U.S. Department of Education. (2003a). *Meeting the highly qualified teachers challenge: The secretary's second annual report on teacher quality.* Washington, DC: U.S. Department of Education, Office of Postsecondary Education.

U.S. Department of Education. (2003b). Improving teacher quality: Non-regulatory guidance. Revised Draft, September 12, 2003. Washington, DC: Academic Improvement and Teacher Quality Programs, Office of Elementary and Secondary Education, Author. Retrieved October 16, 2003, from http://www.ed.gov/policy/elsec/guid/edpicks.jhtml?src=fp

Wright, P.S., Horn, S.P., & Sanders, W.L. (1997). Teacher and classroom context effects on student achievement: Implications for teacher evaluation. *Journal of Personnel Evaluation in Education, 11*, 57-67.

CHAPTER 9

Work Redesign that Works for Teachers

DAVID MAYROWETZ AND MARK A. SMYLIE

Over the past two decades, scholars and practitioners in a variety of industries have considered work redesign among a constellation of strategies to promote employee recruitment and retention, development, motivation, and performance. In the second wave of responses to the alarming rhetoric of *A Nation at Risk* (i.e., between the mid-1980s and the mid-1990s; NCEE, 1983), many of the nation's school systems followed the business world's lead. At the state and school district levels, the resulting proliferation of teacher work redesign initiatives included countless varieties of career ladder plans; mentor, master, and lead teacher programs; and participative decision making and school-based management.

Although educational policymakers in the middle to late 1990s shifted their attention to standards (NCTM, 1989, 1991), systemic reform (Clune, 2001; Smith & O'Day, 1991), assessments (Popham, 1987; Shepard, 1989), and accountability (Goertz, 2001), teacher work redesign remains in schools in both familiar and unfamiliar forms. We see the development of new teacher leader roles, particularly around the tasks of curricular and instructional improvement. We continue to witness an emphasis on teacher participation in school decision making. And we note the emergence of new responsibilities for teachers associated with efforts to promote teacher research, distribute school leadership, and build communities of practice. These last efforts are not typically thought of as work redesign, but in this chapter we will demonstrate how they are, and how they represent new, potentially effective approaches to the promotion of teacher development and school improvement.

Unlike much of the literature on work redesign, our analysis is not confined to the level of the individual employee—the teacher. Instead,

David Mayrowetz is an Assistant Professor in Policy Studies in the College of Education at the University of Illinois at Chicago. Mark A. Smylie is a Professor and Chair of Policy Studies in the College of Education at UIC.

we focus on workforce-level issues, on the prospects that work re-design might serve as a mechanism for recruiting and retaining good teachers, as a means of developing teachers' knowledge and skills, and as a motivational tool for improving teacher performance. We propose that work redesign can function as a means for the development not only of the teacher whose work is being changed but also of other teachers as individuals or in work groups and even of entire faculties.

In this chapter, we explore the promise of work redesign for teacher workforce development by examining both the theory of redesign and the research on its effectiveness. After categorizing work redesign along two dimensions—whose work is changed (the individual or the collec-tive) and in what way (reassigned or redefined)—we conclude that ini-tiatives that redefine jobs rather than simply reassigning tasks and that focus on collective rather than individual work should be most effec-tive, especially for promoting teacher performance.

Evolving Concepts of Work Redesign

Work redesign is a vague and often ambiguous concept. In general, it refers to "the alteration of specific jobs (or interdependent systems of jobs) with the intent of increasing both the quality of employees' work experience and their on-the-job productivity" (Hackman, 1977, p. 98). It is "the deliberate, purposeful planning of the job, including any or all of its structural or social aspects" (Umstot, Bell, & Mitchell, as cited in Hart, 1990, p. 33). It is a term used generically to include a broad range of strategies such as job rotation, job enlargement, and job enrichment (Strauss, 1974).

Historical Highlights

Theorists and organizational leaders have puzzled for more than a century about the relationship between the design of work and em-ployee efficiency and effectiveness (Kelly, 1982; Parker & Hall, 1998). In the early 1900s, leading intellectuals and industrialists promoted a revolution in the way work should be accomplished. They argued that, in the interests of efficiency and effectiveness, organizations should break the complex work that most employees do into smaller parts. Each employee would then become an expert in achieving a few of those simpler tasks, and so the end product (or service) would be com-pleted in an extraordinarily efficient manner. But this work design led to unintended consequences such as worker boredom and alienation because of what was later termed a "de-skilling" process (Littler, 1978).

The adoption of these "scientific management" philosophies by schools has been well documented (Callahan, 1962; Tyack, 1974). Early 20th century administrators re-formed schools from the one-room schoolhouse to mimic the paragon of efficient organizational models, the factory. Most significantly, they tracked and graded class-rooms. School administrators, who were largely male, de-skilled and wrested power from the mostly female teacher workforce as they strove for legitimacy and respectability among the larger public (Blount, 1999; Tyack, 1974).

In the 1950s and 1960s, organizational theorists began to look more closely at the relationships between individuals and organiza-tions. They suggested new hypotheses for the person-job relationship, namely, that redesigning, "re-complicating," enlarging, or enriching jobs might be necessary to promote greater worker performance and efficiency. By the late 1960s and early 1970s, a number of companies had implemented work redesign initiatives based on the premise that providing employees with richer job experiences could make the work-place more humane and enhance job performance. However, reports on the failure of such "job enrichment" programs to make widespread changes in settings like the General Foods plant in Topeka, Kansas (Walton, 1975), as well as organized labor's general distrust of the motives and methods of the organizational scientists behind these re-forms (Gomberg, 1973), intimated an end to work redesign. In defense of these initiatives, Hackman (1975) argued that better, more theoreti-cally grounded work redesign initiatives could improve workplace con-ditions, productivity, and efficiency, but only if they were implemented with the proper seriousness, prior study, and preparation of the target employees and those who work with them.

In 1980, Hackman and Oldham followed this defense with their seminal book, *Work Redesign*. This book and the job characteristics the-ory it introduced seemed to give work redesign a "second wind." *Work Redesign* remains perhaps the most authoritative and influential treat-ment of the subject today. Hackman and Oldham's analysis proceeded from a premise that the person-job relationship should be the center-piece of workplace reform. Although there are always several ways that employers try to shape employees (professional development, training, etc.), supervisors ought to shift attention to something they have more control over, namely, the design of work. This strategy contrasts with others such as altering employee titles, increasing pay or rewards, or re-structuring the company's organizational chart. Instead, by changing the nature of the actual work that front-line employees do, those workers will become motivated and the company's bottom line will benefit. We will explicate this theory and the associated Job Characteristics Model (JCM) later in the chapter.

Over the years, researchers have divided work redesign initiatives into two basic categories—job enlargement and job enrichment. Although there is some ambiguity in the meaning of these categories and in the classification of specific redesign efforts as they are implemented in practice (Rosenblatt, 2001), job enlargement is usually defined as a "horizontal integration of skills" (Rosenblatt, p. 348). The employee with an enlarged job takes on tasks of equal complexity and responsibility that are commonly reserved for other employees at the same level in the organization (Campion & McClelland, 1993). In contrast, job enrichment is the "vertical integration of skills" (Rosenblatt, p. 348)—that is, a combination of current work with tasks that imply the leadership skills performed by and responsibilities held by one's supervisor (Campion & McClelland; Rosenblatt).

Unfortunately, these ways of thinking about work redesign are not particularly helpful, especially in terms of job characteristics theory, because they tend to confound changes in task with changes in role and status. Although researchers and practitioners must consider power when formulating and implementing work redesign, letting the role and status elements creep into the definitions keeps the theory from being sufficiently parsimonious. Hackman and Oldham (1980) originally conceived work redesign as focusing "squarely on the actual work that people perform in organizations" (p. 66), not on contextual considerations like politics, although such organizational variables can be moderators in the JCM, as we will explain.

Furthermore, the enrichment/enlargement distinction precludes ways of thinking about redesign that do not have to do with simply reallocating existing work. Work can also be redesigned in ways that completely redefine the nature of one's job and create new types of assignments not previously performed by anyone in the organization. If organizations are to grow, mature, and improve, it is difficult to imagine that the sum of the organization's work can remain static. New work and new roles have to be created to achieve new goals.

Similarly, we think it is likely that educators allow considerations of role or status to overwhelm their conceptions of work redesign. For them, redesign is probably synonymous with the creation of a lead teacher position or the implementation of a career ladder program. Sometimes, but not always, a redesign is accompanied by changes in title, status, and/or pay. Although some teachers might welcome work redesign as a chance for career advancement, others might view the prospect with fear, anticipating additional responsibilities without sufficient compensation (financial or otherwise).

Our examination of work redesign proceeds from a somewhat different starting point. Instead of thinking about work redesign from the perspective of employee role, be it the role the employee occupies or the role in which the employee's new work is usually performed, we think about work redesign along two different dimensions. On one dimension, a redesigned job can contain either routine or new elements. That is, an employee can be reassigned extant tasks previously performed by somebody else in the organization but new to that employee, or the whole job can be redefined and entirely new tasks created. For the employee who is reassigned existing tasks, the basic nature of the work remains unchanged. For the employee who is assigned new tasks, the nature of the job is modified so much that the indigenous characteristics and understanding of what the job entails has been altered. On a second dimension, work redesign can apply to one person or a group (collective). To look at work redesign along these dimensions opens up new possibilities for analyzing its potential effectiveness and explaining its outcomes.

Work Redesign and Teacher Workforce Development

Now that we have established a definition of work redesign that connects to the basics of the Job Characteristics Model, we will explore the potential for different work redesign reforms to develop the teacher workforce. By teacher workforce development, we mean four things: recruiting more quality teachers, retaining them in the schools, motivating them to excel, and otherwise promoting their capacity to perform (i.e., teach). In the following sections, we discuss the four models of work redesign that can be derived from the two dimensions of work redesign outlined earlier: individual task reassignment, collective task reassignment, individual task redefinition, and collective task redefinition. For each model, we report a) its applications; b) the theory and/or policy logic behind how it might enhance teacher workforce development; c) empirical evidence of its effectiveness for the four aspects of teacher workforce development; and d) a discussion of its strengths and weaknesses. We conclude with implications for policymakers, educators, and researchers.

In Table 1, we present school reforms categorized by the two critical dimensions of work redesign as we see it: whose work is changed and in what way. To be sure, some school reforms might fit into multiple cells within this table because common understandings of work redesign and, more importantly, the manner in which they have been implemented in schools are not based on our two-dimensional definition. For example, the creation of teacher teams within a school is a collective redesign, but depending on the tasks performed, the effort could be construed as either a reassignment or redefinition. The same could be said for the genesis of a career ladder program, although the rungs on that ladder usually contain tasks that are routinely part of the organizational mission and therefore constitute a task reassignment (and specifically, job enlargement; Smylie, 1997). For purposes of this chapter, we will address each of these reforms in terms of only one of the four models.

TABLE 1
School Reform Initiatives, by Work Redesign Dimension

Method	Focus	
	Individual	Collective
Task reassignment	Mentor teacher Lead teacher Instructional coordinator	Participative decision making Teacher teams
Task redefinition	Teacher-researcher	Collective teacher research Communities of practice Distributive leadership

Work Redesign Model 1: Individual Task Reassignment

As we have already mentioned, most scholars and practitioners understand and recognize forms of work redesign in schools that require individual teachers to accept responsibilities and tasks usually reserved for others. We refer to these work redesign initiatives as *individual task reassignments*. Normally, reforms such as mentor and master/lead teachers fall into this category. Teachers who climb career ladders are also generally engaged in individual task reassignment (Smylie, 1997).

Theories of Individual Task Reassignment

There are two theories of how individual task reassignment could develop the teacher workforce. The first is really a theory of action or policy logic (Argyris & Schön, 1974), not a formal theory. The policymakers (not educators) who created teacher career ladders believed that such programs would attract the best and brightest to the field of education (Brandt, 1987; Malen, 1986). The underlying policy logic is fairly straightforward: if opportunities for advancement and financial rewards are present (and relatively comparable to other professions), then confident and talented young people will choose education as a career and select a district with a career ladder as a place of employment.

However, the idea that school systems can change work to retain teachers, motivate them to excel, and promote better performance is consistent with a second, formal theory, Hackman and Oldham's (1980) job characteristic theory. According to this theory, having new tasks incorporated into an employee's daily work changes the "core job characteristics" of that work. Hackman and Oldham postulated five ways to change jobs that would lead to positive outcomes:

1. Increase the variety of skills necessary to perform a job (skill variety)
2. Give employees the ability to work on a whole task (task identity)
3. Ensure that the task is significant to other people (task significance)
4. Give workers independence and discretion (autonomy)
5. Provide direct and clear information about performance (feedback)

This Job Characteristics Model holds that altering work in this manner will provide employees with more experienced meaningfulness, more experienced responsibility, and greater knowledge of the fruits of their labors—three psychological states that, according to Hackman and Oldham, motivate employees and increase their job satisfaction. These scholars believed that, eventually, "the quality of performance should improve as a direct function of the increased motivating potential of the work" (Hackman & Oldham, 1980, p. 92).

In a lead teacher position, for example, educators will certainly experience higher skill variety, and probably greater task identity and task significance, than they would in a normal teacher position. Also, with a higher position on a career ladder, a teacher may have more autonomy in his or her work. Notably, the school reforms associated with individual task reassignment do not necessarily increase feedback, the fifth job characteristic in the JCM. This point is significant because authors of a meta-analysis of research on work redesign programs in a variety of industries found that feedback on performance was the most important job characteristic. It affected all three psychological states mediating the desired outcomes of increased motivation, satisfaction, and performance (Fried & Ferris, 1987). Therefore, what seems to be the most powerful core job characteristic in work redesign theory frequently could be absent in the most prevalent individual task reassignments in schools.

Several scholars have challenged and refined the job characteristics theory over the years. Although empirical research in the management literature confirms the basic premises of the JCM, several holes remain. First and foremost, the model is more predictive of changes in motivation than changes in job performance (Fried & Ferris, 1987). In study after study, the impact of work redesign on performance is very low or insignificant (Fried & Ferris; Johns, Xie, & Fang, 1992). What accounts for this major shortcoming in the JCM? Clearly, Hackman and Oldham's reliance on an increase in motivation to spark higher performance is insufficient. Recently, scholars have begun to explore how other mechanisms such as learning and enhanced self-efficacy could be used to translate the aforementioned psychological states into increased performance (Axtell & Parker, 2003; Parker, 1998).

Also, it is likely that Hackman and Oldham underestimated the importance of moderators on the ability of work redesign to enhance the other two outcomes in the JCM, motivation and job satisfaction. These moderators fall into three categories: individual worker characteristics such as experience, expertise, and burning desire for personal accomplishment (known as "growth need"); workplace characteristics; and the degree to which pay is perceived as relating to performance (i.e., instrumentality). Researchers have downplayed the significance of these moderators (Johns et al., 1992), but our analysis of the empirical studies in schools demonstrates the strength of the first two.

Empirical Evidence of the Effectiveness of Individual Task Reassignment in Schools

For almost every aspect of teacher workforce development, the evidence supporting the effectiveness of individual task reassignment in schools is extraordinarily mixed.

Recruitment. Of all the individual work redesign initiatives, the career ladder is most obviously concerned with recruiting and retaining teachers. But studies suggest that the ability of career ladder programs to recruit teachers is uncertain. In survey studies, Arizona teachers believed that the career ladders in their districts would attract effective teachers (Packard & Bierlein, 1986). Teachers in Tennessee, however, came to the opposite conclusion (Reddick & Peach, 1986). In Utah, new teachers with "promise" did select school districts with career ladders for initial employment (Hart & Murphy, 1990).

Retention. Although theory would predict that changing job characteristics—perhaps by attaining a higher rung on the career ladder—would make employees happier and increase their desire to stay in the organization, it is difficult to summarize its impact in schools based on previous research. According to Rosenblatt (2001), Israeli teachers who have jobs with high skill variety and who utilize these skills report a lower tendency to quit than other teachers. But two studies of American career ladder districts, where skill flexibility and utilization should be high, provided no firm answers on the issue of retention. One pair of authors (Taylor & Madsen, 1989) found that effective teachers remained in districts that had a career ladder program for the first few years after its initiation. Another research team (Ebmeier & Hart, 1992) working in the same state found no statistical differences in intention to quit between participants and nonparticipants in the career ladder program they studied.

Our view of the empirical evidence is that the moderating variables in the JCM (i.e., personal and workplace characteristics) are crucial to the success of individual task reassignment in schools. We know that the introduction of work redesign initiatives like career ladders can be fraught with political infighting and can lead to changes in the school climate, sometimes for the better and sometimes for the worse (Smylie, 1997). Because work redesigns like career ladders, lead and master teacher programs, and even well-designed mentoring programs challenge the prevalent norms of teaching (e.g., privacy, nonjudgment, egalitarianism, and equity), the degree to which these norms exist in an individual school or district before the introduction of individual task reassignment might determine their effect (Hart, 1990).

Furthermore, the individual characteristics of teachers also seem to moderate the impact reforms have on retention. For example, many young teachers in the career ladder districts in Utah (many of whom may have been attracted by the ladders in the first place) reported being more likely to leave the profession than other teachers did (Murphy, Hart, & Walters, 1989). Unlike the mid-career teachers who were relatively more optimistic about the possible outcomes of career ladders (Ebmeier & Hart, 1992), these beginners were wary of making a long-term commitment to teaching (Hart, 1994).

Motivation. The empirical research is slightly more optimistic about the ability of lead teacher, mentor teacher, and career ladder programs to motivate teachers. Perhaps these findings should not be surprising given that the job characteristics theory is geared toward increasing motivation on the premise that it will precipitate growth in the other outcomes.

In a review of literature, Smylie (1997) concluded that becoming a lead teacher can be rewarding and can help the lead teachers develop new skills. Simultaneously, though, becoming a lead teacher is often stressful. Educators report being underprepared for the new tasks and overcommitted during the day. They also feel tension if they are charged with supervising their peers, thereby challenging the traditional teacher norms of privacy and egalitarianism.

Similarly, teachers who become formal mentors have both positive and negative reactions to that form of work redesign. They believe that their new positions broaden their outlook on the organization. The relationships they build with protégés can provide professional satisfaction (Hart, 1985). Most studies show an overall positive affective result from mentoring (Smylie, 1997). Those findings are consistent with other research that shows that performing nonteaching duties in school increases skill flexibility and skill utilization and, in turn, better work attitudes for teachers (Rosenblatt, 2001). At the same time, though, mentoring newer teachers can lead to stress and overload (Bird & Little, 1983; Evertson, Wade, & Smithey, 1993).

Capacity Development and Performance. As we have mentioned, individual work reassignment generally does not improve work employee performance of central duties. Lead teacher programs have "few benefits at the classroom level" (Smylie, 1997, p. 548) and do not seem to have an impact on other teachers in the school (Smylie, 1993). In short, the benefits of these initiatives rarely spread beyond the individual who becomes a master teacher (Smylie, 1994). But when teachers are engaged in jobs that require skill flexibility, their principals will rate their job performance higher than other teachers' job performance (Rosenblatt & Inbal, 1999).

We know of no studies that demonstrate whether being a mentor increases the learning or achievement of the mentor's students (Smylie, 1997), although in many cases, protégés feel that their mentors provide them with the moral support and instructional leadership they crave (Feiman-Nemser & Parker, 1994). With regard to career ladders, again, the evidence is equivocal. Some studies revealed that students in career ladder districts scored high on achievement tests; in others, researchers found no statistically significant difference in test scores between districts with and without career ladders.

Strengths and Weaknesses of Individual Task Reassignment

Individual task reassignment has a track record in schools. Studies suggest that its strength is motivating the teachers who have their work redesigned, as long as the redesign occurs under proper conditions. The individual characteristics of the teacher and the workplace context (e.g., amount of support from a supervisor) appear to be crucial variables in determining the degree to which these reassignments will lead to workforce development. We suspect that the conflicting reports on its effectiveness indicate differences in these moderators.

In general, individual task reassignment is best suited to enhancing teacher motivation and job satisfaction, and only for the teacher whose job is redesigned. The exception to this rule is that mentor teacher programs can support more junior members of the faculty. However, all types of individual task reassignment have minimal impact on the core technology of teachers, teaching, and learning (Smylie, 1994). Therefore, individual task reassignment has limited power to improve performance and enhance student achievement.

Work Redesign Model 2—Collective Task Reassignment

A second way of redesigning work in schools is through *collective task reassignment*. In this model, teachers are placed into a group to perform tasks that they normally do not do, or at least do not do together. Most forms of teaming would fall into this category, as would the participative decision making reforms prevalent in the early 1990s. Hackman and Oldham (1980) also suggested ways in which work should be redesigned for groups. In schools, however, the evidence of the efficacy of collective task reassignment is just as uncertain as it is for individual task reassignment.

Theory of Collective Task Reassignment

Collective task reassignment, like individual task reassignment, is based on job characteristics theory and, conceivably, can enhance teacher workforce development. Reaching back further into the intellectual ancestry of job characteristics theory, we find that collective task reassignment is supported by sociotechnical systems theory, originally formulated by British thinkers in the 1960s and 1970s (Cherns, 1976;

Davis & Trist, 1974). The basic thrust of sociotechnical systems theory is that both the technical and social aspects of work must be "jointly optimized" in the service of organizational goals. Many (perhaps too many) theorists suggest the same tool for achieving this objective— autonomous or semiautonomous work groups. These special groups of workers are given access to and control over the resources they need to do their work (Parker & Hall, 1998). Over time, the group should become a team, working together, developing the knowledge, skills, and commitments necessary for effective production (Hackman, 1998).

In *Work Redesign*, Hackman and Oldham (1980) borrow from sociotechnical theory and also proffer their own ideas about how to enhance the effectiveness of what they call "self-managing work groups" (p. 164). As in their job characteristics model for individual work redesign, they suggest that by organizing certain elements of a group's work, employers can create intermediate conditions that set the stage for successful work group outcomes. They argue that by focusing on the nature of the task, the composition of the group, and the internal norms regarding work process, organizations can create circumstances under which groups can work effectively. The intermediate conditions are necessary effort, knowledge, and performance strategies to get the job done. Hackman and Oldham define groups as effective when they "meet or exceed organizational standards for quality and quantity" (p. 168), when workers are more satisfied than frustrated, and when the group survives over time.

We highlight the fact that although the intermediate conditions in this model are not psychological, as they are in the JCM, they do deal with some of the personal characteristics and group dynamics that are analogous to the moderators in the JCM. The Hackman and Oldham theory of collective redesign does not, however, consider the group within its ecological context. As we have noted, context is an important moderator in the individual work redesign theory. But, when devising their collective redesign theory, Hackman and Oldham were concerned only with how to create a healthy and productive dynamic inside a newly formed work group. An equally important but frequently overlooked factor is that administrators must manage the boundaries between a group and the rest of the organization, even when that group is autonomous, semiautonomous, or self-managing (see Sundstrom, De Meuse, & Futrell, 1990, for a discussion of the importance of viewing work groups in their ecological contexts).

But when Hackman (1975) bemoaned the fact that the necessary employees in the General Foods plant example we cited earlier were not properly trained to work with those who had redesigned jobs, he essentially flagged the importance of boundary management. In 1998, Hackman revisited this point when he concluded that both internal and external team leadership are necessary for a work group to achieve its potential. Without strategic vision and strong coordination of work groups from external administrators, organizations with multiple groups risk serious fragmentation.

Empirical Evidence of the Effectiveness of Collective Task Reassignment in Schools

Because collective task reassignment efforts like participative decision making (PDM) and teacher teaming are not geared toward recruiting teachers to the profession or to schools, it is not surprising that no researchers have measured their impact on recruitment. However, there is quite a bit of evidence about the effects that such efforts have on job satisfaction (which could be associated with retaining teachers), motivating teachers to perform, and capacity development and performance.

As was the case for individual task reassignment, the picture of how these reforms work in schools is remarkably fuzzy because of seemingly contradictory reports. In many instances, principals and teachers expect collective task reassignments such as PDM to improve school conditions and enhance their work professionally (Smylie, 1997). In practice, the efficacy of teacher teams and participative decision-making bodies depends on several factors consistent with the moderating variables of the JCM. For collective task reassignment, these factors include the initiation and political context of the reform, and internal and external organizational support.

Retention. When schools introduce participative decision making or teacher teams, the implications for teacher retention appears mixed. Although we know of no studies that attempt to connect taking part in these reforms in schools with intentions to quit, we do know how it affects job satisfaction. Participation in decision making, especially for issues related to teaching and learning, generally keeps teachers satisfied, but too much or too little participation could decrease job satisfaction (Conway, 1976). Too little participation on issues that teachers care about, or "decision deprivation," has been associated with work alienation (Benson & Malone, 1987). Moreover, the launch of a new PDM initiative might lead to increased commitment but also could result in role ambiguity and conflict as teachers wrestle with their work responsibilities inside and outside the classroom. For example, teachers studied by Hannaway (1993) were both more enthusiastic and more frustrated when working within the participative decision-making model. As a result, these teachers reported lower levels of job satisfaction and might have been more willing to quit their jobs.

Motivation. PDM and teaming can lead to both positive and negative affective outcomes for teachers. Much like other forms of work redesign, the positive consequences arise because of the excitement and growth potential of being in a new situation. Specifically, studies reveal that PDM can enhance self-efficacy (Lee, Dedrick, & Smith, 1991), morale (Chapman & Boyd, 1986), and organizational responsibility (Smylie, 1997). The negative consequences from PDM are role ambiguity and the stresses of working with others in a field (teaching) that values autonomy and self-reliance. For example, when some teachers are on decision-making committees for the entire school, there can be tension over whether the teachers on the committee truly represent the voices of others (Weiss, Cambone, & Wyeth, 1992). It is crucial that someone (e.g., an administrator or teacher) manage the boundary between the decision-making group and others in the organization.

Teacher teams are similarly inconsistent in their ability to promote positive emotions and motivated employees. In a comparative study of two middle schools (grades 7-9), teachers in the teamed school were more satisfied with their professional growth and with their jobs than teachers in the non-teamed school (Pounder, 1999). However, in the teamed school, two grade-level teams had pronounced difficulty in maintaining positive interpersonal dynamics. In one grade, some teachers were blamed for shirking responsibilities. In another, the team split into two because of ideological and personal differences (Crow & Pounder, 2000). Although these studies involve only a small number of teachers and teacher teams, the findings represent the wide spectrum of affective outcomes one can expect from collective task reassignment.

Capacity development and performance. When teachers participate in decision making at the school or grade level, they must communicate, collaborate, and exchange information. These actions provide opportunities for professional growth and commitment to the profession. Smylie (1997) reports that in most survey and case study research, teachers recount positive instructional changes and school improvement when they participate in decision making. However, a number of case studies demonstrate that PDM does not translate into actual changes at the classroom level, let alone improved student performance (Conway,

1984; Conway & Calzi, 1996). Furthermore, half of the research investigating the relationship between PDM and student learning reports no impact; half shows a positive correlation (Smylie, 1997).

Teacher teams also create opportunities for professional growth for those involved in them. Many teachers on the grade-level teams studied by Crow and Pounder (2000) believed that they gained from the experience. But the impact of teams rarely reaches the school organization or the students (Smylie, Conley, & Marks, 2002). In high schools, departments have been shown to hinder communication, collaboration, and curricular coherence (Herriott & Firestone, 1984). Interdisciplinary teams in middle schools can shift focus away from school-wide goals and onto the stresses, tensions, and issues associated with work groups (Kruse & Louis, 1997). And, in three of the four groups studied by Crow and Pounder, the new configuration of teachers primarily resulted in a willingness to share the responsibility for student interventions. Only one team turned a collective critical focus back onto the pedagogy of its members. Those energetic, aggressive, and sometimes impolitic teachers created interdisciplinary teaching units. Notably, compared to its sister school in Utah, students in the teamed school were more satisfied with teachers, fellow students, and discipline (Pounder, 1999).

Importance of Context

In the studies of PDM and teacher teams, the moderating variables in the JCM (e.g., individual characteristics and organizational context) were consistently shown to be of paramount importance. Specifically, these ideas were operationalized in schools as leadership from those at the head of the organizational hierarchy, organizational stability, and trust among colleagues (Conway & Calzi, 1996; Crow & Pounder, 2000; Smylie, 1997).

For example, if a principal uses PDM as a tool to advance his or her own agenda, then the effort could lead to teacher frustration and resentment (Firestone, 1977). But, if a principal engages his or her faculty openly, then teachers could gradually increase their influence in the school's decision-making processes. Administrators will generally trust faculty with decisions dealing with issues of teaching and learning, and over time, teachers' voices will spill into spheres of administrative decisions. Eventually, the principal's influence will expand too, into spheres of teaching and learning (Smylie, 1993; Tannenbaum, 1962). Lawler (1988) predicts that this form of work redesign will flatten the organizational hierarchy as both groups share their traditional spheres of work. Similarly, teacher teams need the proper organizational context. They seem to work best when there is strong internal leadership and when team members are familiar with the school setting and have previous experience working in groups (Smylie, Conley, & Marks, 2002).

Strengths and Weaknesses of Collective Task Reassignment

On the whole, we are faced with a set of mixed reviews for collective task reassignment similar to those we see for individual task reassignment. There are circumstances when collective task reassignment can lead to job satisfaction (and probably retention), motivation, and even enhanced capacity and performance. However, there is no consistency with these reforms because organizational context is a determining factor for their success. Another weakness to this model of redesign is that there is no evidence that it can attract teachers to the profession.

Work Redesign Model 3—Individual Task Redefinition

Until now we have investigated the common forms of work redesign that we characterize as task reassignment (i.e., an individual or group acquiring tasks previously performed by others in the organization). Embedded in these conceptions of work redesign are assumptions of an organizational hierarchy and a clear distinction between the roles and functions of middle line administration and the operating core of teachers that must be overcome. Additionally, there is no explicit recognition that organizations operate in open systems or that they might need to perform new work in order to achieve goals or even survive. By introducing the concept of task redefinition, we aim to show how meaningful work redesign can occur without a change in role or status, simply by the acquisition of new work. The same core ideas from the JCM are manifest in school reforms where teachers engage in new work and thereby redefine the very nature of their jobs. For example, teacher-researchers collect and analyze data on their classroom practice. A supervisor might also have performed this task, but probably in a different way and with different objectives in mind. When the teacher engages in classroom research, that action can redefine what the expectations are for what a "real" teacher does.

Theories of Individual Task Redefinition

As Henson (1996) recounts, the idea of employing teachers to conduct research has been around for a century. But in the past fifteen years, we have witnessed a proliferation of teacher research efforts, or more aptly, a teacher research movement. For *teacher research*, we borrow our meaning from Cochran-Smith and Lytle (1999), who define it as "systematic, intentional, and self-critical inquiry about one's work in . . . classrooms, schools" (p. 22).

In a recent review, Zeichner and Noffke (2001) enumerate the multiple reasons teachers have for engaging in research. On the most immediate and personal level, teacher research can improve individual practice. By engaging in research, teachers can reflect on what they do in the classroom, how students interact with one another, the environment of the class, what constitutes appropriate behavior or the right answer, and any number of issues specific to the context of that particular classroom. Additionally, teacher researchers can turn a critical eye on themselves, uncovering inconsistencies between espoused beliefs and practices and illuminating their tacit assumptions on a whole range of topics.

At the macro level, teacher research challenges the dominant patterns of knowledge construction in the field and in the academy. Some teacher-researchers also center race, gender, or socioeconomic class in their inquiry, seeking to highlight and rectify oppressive schooling practices. Indeed, there is a consistent theme in this research: the power residing in institutions that preserve the status quo (e.g., cultural definitions of teaching and learning, epistemological claims about knowledge construction, or systemic inequities in society and schools) needs to be contested if a more just and democratic society is to evolve (Cochran-Smith & Lytle, 1999).

Finally, teachers engage in research to promote school improvement and professional growth, thereby enhancing both craft knowledge and the status of the profession. Seen in this light, teacher research is consistent with job characteristics theory, although few (if any) educational researchers recognize this. Teacher-researchers experience the five elements of redesigned work as conceived by Hackman and Oldham (1980). Specifically, teachers who engage in research must employ different skills than they usually do. They have control over a meaningful endeavor from start to finish, all with the intent of providing feedback on practice. According to the JCM, by engaging in teacher research, a form of work that rates high in the five key job characteristics, teachers should be motivated to remain at their jobs and improve their performance.

Empirical Evidence of the Effectiveness of Individual Task Redefinition in Schools

Because the large majority of teacher-researchers approach the enterprise from either a personal or a political perspective, they do not collect data that provide specific evidence regarding the efficacy of teacher research for workforce development as we define it. We suspect that teacher research would not necessarily attract people to the profession, but it might lead to better retention rates. Once a person engages in a research project, it is logical that he or she would want to complete it and make changes in teaching or schooling practices in response to the findings. Additionally, although we surmise that teachers who conduct research are already motivated individuals, we also suspect that the process of doing research will maintain their passion for teaching and the constant improvement of practice.

We see in teacher research the promise of building capacity for school and student performance. Teacher research requires data collection and analysis, and it implies reflection on those results. Conventional wisdom suggests that teacher research would facilitate a learning process for individual teachers. That learning process, which is missing from a lot of the work redesign we categorize as task reassignment, could bridge the distance between the psychological states achieved by the redesigned work (i.e., experienced meaningfulness, experienced responsibilities, and knowledge of actual results) and the increased effectiveness Hackman and Oldham promised more than 20 years ago.

Strengths and Weaknesses of Individual Task Redefinition

In sum, we see substantial potential in teacher research for developing the teacher workforce but no significant evidence, as of now. The structured reflection implied by teacher research should trigger individual learning about teaching as well as the motivation mechanism hypothesized by the JCM. Therefore, we think it is likely that this form of individual task redefinition will have more powerful effects on capacity development and performance than a standard task reassignment.

Additionally, the whole endeavor of teacher research poses a challenge to traditional schooling practices (e.g., the strict organizational hierarchy) that have been impediments to teacher workforce development. However, a lot of teacher research is individual, especially when it is classroom based. Without explicit structures for sharing information with other teachers in a school or district, we fear that the effects of teacher research will be minimal.

Work Redesign Model 4—Collective Task Redefinition

Collective teacher research, the establishment of communities of practice, and attempts to distribute leadership in schools all fall into our final category of work redesign, *collective task redefinition*. These initiatives, like teacher research, are usually not recognized as work redesign, and researchers who study these reforms usually do not collect data that respond to the four aspects of teacher workforce development that we have noted. But these work redefinition reforms share prominent elements with the JCM.

Theories of Collective Task Redefinition

Currently, there are three models of distributive leadership discussed by educational researchers (Smylie, Conley, & Marks, 2002). One view is that school leadership does not exist in roles but in functions (Heller & Firestone, 1995; Mayrowetz & Weinstein, 1999). These crucial functions are 1) providing and selling a vision; 2) providing encouragement and recognition; 3) obtaining resources; 4) adapting standard operating procedures; 5) monitoring the innovation; and 6) handling disturbances (Heller & Firestone, 1995). Whoever performs these leadership functions, whether that person works at the top, the bottom, or even outside the organizational hierarchy of a school, is a leader. Furthermore, redundant performance of these six actions will increase the chances of successful school innovation.

A second model of distributive leadership holds that leadership should be construed as an organizational quality (Ogawa & Bossert, 1995). Drawing on institutional theory, these scholars argue that leadership exists in the social web of relationships within the school. Teachers and administrators maintain areas of expertise in the decoupled organization, and by sharing their knowledge, individuals or groups of individuals are able to exert influence, or leadership, across the school.

Most recently, Spillane, Halverson, and Diamond (2000, 2001) proposed their "distributed leadership" model. They approach leadership as a human activity conducted in a social and situational context. Borrowing concepts from the cognitive sciences, these scholars maintain that leadership (like learning) is distributed or "stretched over" the context in which it is performed. Because context enables and constrains individual agency, it is part of the exercise of leadership. In other words, leadership cannot be viewed separately from the school or the relationships among individuals within the school. One could argue that this conception of leadership accounts especially well for the moderating variables from the JCM by simply absorbing context into the leadership theory.

Prestine and Nelson (2003) note the overlapping conceptual terrain between this third model (i.e., distributed leadership) and the notion of communities of practice (Lave & Wenger, 1991). A community of practice is a "joint enterprise" in which a group of individuals are "mutually engaged" for technical and social purposes. Over time, the community develops a "shared repertoire of communal resources" that members draw on as they continually renegotiate their structures, relationships, norms, and goals (Wenger, 1998). Wenger distinguishes a community of practice from a team (and, by implication, from sociotechnical theory) by arguing that the former is bound together by "shared knowledge and interest" rather than by the need to complete a project or meet a deadline.

With this focus on employee interest rather than task, there are some obvious differences between job characteristics theory and the community of practice. However, if schools were to legitimize existing communities of practice with missions of school improvement and student achievement or "seed and nurture" new ones, we argue that work redesign would quickly follow. Teachers in the community of practice would have their jobs redefined because they would be expected to become members of that community (peripherally or centrally) and to engage in a range of tasks necessary to membership maintenance.

Empirical Evidence of the Effectiveness of Collective Task Redefinition

Collective task redefinition is incredibly difficult to achieve in schools, and there have been few empirical studies of how these theoretical constructs operate within the school context. As with most of the other models of work redesign, there is no evidence as to whether collective task redefinition can aid in the recruitment of teachers. However, studies suggest that in schools with well-developed organizational leadership, there may be higher teacher retention rates.

Retention. Distributive leadership is not necessarily an innovation that must be adopted by a school, because it describes the way in which influence operates in schools. In other words, each school already has some amount of distributive leadership.

As previously mentioned, researchers have found that leadership functions are frequently performed by individuals in multiple roles (e.g., administrators, teachers, parents, paraprofessionals, community activists) to reform schooling practices (Heller & Firestone, 1995; Mayrowetz & Weinstein, 1999). In an interview study of Chicago elementary school teachers, Spillane, Hallet, and Diamond (2003) found that administrators, teachers, and curriculum specialists all had influence over instructional practice. However, teachers had the most diverse array of influence mechanisms and were most frequently cited as bearers of expert power. Also using surveys, Pounder, Ogawa, and Adams (1995) found that organizational leadership varied among the 57 schools they studied.

But Pounder and colleagues also found that higher degrees of total organizational leadership were ultimately correlated with lower faculty and staff turnover, as measured in a three-year window. Thus, there is some evidence that collective task redefinition, which in many ways mirrors distributive leadership, could lead to teacher retention.

Motivation. There is no specific evidence on how collective task redefinition would motivate teachers. Communities of practice assume shared interests and therefore some degree of motivation already. With regard to one type of community of practice, a teacher network, Pennell and Firestone (1996) found that the California teachers who volunteered to join their network had much more motivation and enthusiasm than did Vermont teachers who were forced to participate. Those who try to create communities of practice must consider how teachers perceive the effort (Stein & Spillane, 2003). In work redesign terms, they must consider how the JCM moderating variables of organizational context, individual experience, and instrumentality will operate in the minds of teachers. These considerations are especially important for an emergent community of practice that will exist, by necessity, alongside the traditional structures, hierarchy, and policies omnipresent in today's schools. In an environment of multiple and overlapping formal and informal structures, educators must be somewhat comfortable in their work if they are expected to stay motivated.

Capacity development and performance. The greatest promise of collective work redefinition lies in the area where other work redesigns fall short—capacity development and performance. If multiple educators redefine their roles in the school, we can envision the creation of a community of practice where leadership flows throughout the organization. In these schools with higher degrees of organizational leadership, reforms are more likely to take root (Mayrowetz & Weinstein, 1999), teachers perceive that their schools are more effective (Pounder et al., 1995), and student achievement as measured by the Stanford Achievement Test increases (Pounder et al.).

Collective teacher research is one initiative that schools can undertake to achieve these ends. For example, Tikunoff, Ward, and Griffin

(1979) studied a collaborative model of action research in which teachers, a researcher, and a staff developer identified problems within a school and implemented a staff development program to address some of those issues. They reported significant schoolwide reform in teacher practice. Similarly, Cycle of Inquiry programs in the Annenberg-funded Bay Area School Reform Collaborative (BASRC) resulted in some remarkable schoolwide innovations (Center for Research on the Context of Teaching, 2000; Copland, 2001). In many of the 86 schools involved in the BASRC, teachers engaged in action research to identify organizational goals and worked to achieve them. They created new leadership structures for themselves, such as rotating or joint principalships. They also were able to address instructional issues. These teachers evaluated student work together, created new curricula, and piloted new pedagogical techniques.

There have been a few studies of how communities of practice work in school contexts. Murphy and Prestine (2001) found that simply collecting teachers and administrators and having them meet does not create a community of practice. Instead, these communities, often a subset of teachers within a school, typically work together to maintain a vision of instructional change, offer emotional and technical support, and buffer potentially discordant external messages (McLaughlin & Mitra, 2001). Clearly, these groups can promote not only the structural changes associated with traditional work redesigns (i.e., task reassignments) but also promote cultural and social change in the school and reassessment of the meaning of being a teacher. That being said, they can also protect the status quo, especially if there is no serious, in-depth dialogue about the nature of teaching and learning (Coburn, 2001). Indeed, Little (2003) recently reported how teacher communities can both enable and constrain learning.

Although the empirical evidence supporting the efficacy of collective task redefinition for teacher workforce development is not yet present, we believe that, of the four models we have presented, it holds the greatest potential. The creation of new, nonroutine work rather than the reassignment of existing tasks may enhance the motivational potential of work redesign and should initiate other mechanisms (i.e., learning, enhanced self-efficacy) that would lead to improved performance. Learning, in particular, may be the mechanism that creates more consistent outcomes for the employee in a redesigned job with the improved attitude and disposition toward work to perform better. But again, if an initiative like teacher research remains limited to an individual teacher, the likelihood that benefits will accrue to the organization as a whole is minimal. Communication and the establishment of social connections within the school are required by the collective nature of these efforts and will put teachers in contact with each other. Given the proper conditions, redesigning work for groups may evoke new sources of motivation, influence, and learning for the benefit of the collective as well as the individual. Without sufficient empirical evidence, however, we do not know the strength of the impact the moderating variables of individual experience, organizational context, and instrumentality will have on collective task redefinition.

Summary and Conclusion

Despite extensive implementation and research, the impact of individual task reassignment in schools is unclear. There are equivocal results about the ability of individual task reassignment to retain, recruit, and motivate teachers, usually explainable by individual or contextual differences (e.g., the way the reform is introduced, the experience or skill level of the teachers). More troubling, however, is that the positive outcomes of these reforms rarely expand beyond the teacher whose job has been redesigned and usually do not include enhanced classroom performance. Researchers have come to similar conclusions when studying groups of teachers undertaking reassignment initiatives together (e.g., participative decision making or grade-level teaming). These efforts can easily fail as a result of contextual differences such as poor boundary management or a lack of internal or external leadership. Also, when the reforms do increase motivation, those positive emotions rarely translate into improved classroom performance.

But in a redefinition form of work redesign like teacher research or distributive leadership, we see greater promise because of the likelihood that a teacher will be reflecting on practice and learning. Learning may be the mechanism that creates more consistent outcomes for the employee in a redesigned job and results in an improved attitude and the disposition to perform better. But again, if an initiative like teacher research remains limited to an individual teacher, the likelihood that benefits will accrue to the organization as a whole is minimal. We conclude, therefore, that collective task redefinition provides the greatest hope for teacher workforce development, especially for improved performance. Not only does it imply learning; its collective nature could enable increased capacity and performance throughout a school.

Although our best analysis of the theory and the limited empirical evidence suggests that collective work redefinition does hold promise for developing the teacher workforce, the research on the effects of the redefinition forms of work redesign needs to be much stronger before we can recommend them without reservation. We suspect that there are several scholars investigating teacher research, communities of practice, and distributive leadership in schools at the time of this publication. We suggest that these researchers consider Hackman and Oldham's (1980) job characteristic theory as a framework for analysis. We urge them to measure the outcomes that represent a full picture of teacher workforce development, namely, recruitment, retention, motivation, and capacity development and performance. Concurrently, we need to know how teachers' individual experience, the organizational context, and the degree to which teachers perceive pay as related to performance moderate these workforce development outcomes.

We note that Fullan (2001) argues that researchers would do well to study the conditions that lead to successful school reform as much as the reforms themselves. The moderating variables in the job characteristics model appear to influence the success of work redesign in schools substantially. Perhaps it is time to pay attention to these contextual variables when developing the teacher workforce at individual sites.

For policymakers and educators, our analysis suggests a strategy for teacher workforce development that relies on more than increasing motivation and will. Although these elements are important, the mixed results from what we call task reassignment suggest that attempts to redesign work need to utilize another strategy for reforms to impact teaching and learning in the classroom. For this reason, we suggest that administrators experiment with redesign reforms that redefine the nature of teachers' work, especially in groups. Although such efforts may take a great deal of commitment and learning, we suspect that it is exactly those elements which will keep good teachers in schools and keep them motivated to excel, and that should lead to increased student outcomes. Policymakers must support these experiments with money and with patience, two commodities that we know are in short supply. Unless these reforms are designed and implemented within proper conditions—that is, with internal and external leadership and in a political context that is not perceived as manipulative or punitive—then work redesign has little chance of working for teachers.

298   WORK REDESIGN THAT WORKS FOR TEACHERS

REFERENCES

Argyris, C., & Schön, D.A. (1974). *Theory in practice: Increasing professional effectiveness.* San Francisco: Jossey-Bass.

Axtell, C.M., & Parker, S.K. (2003). Promoting role breadth self-efficacy through involvement, work redesign and training. *Human Relations, 56*(1), 113-131.

Benson, N., & Malone, P. (1987). Teachers' beliefs about shared decision making and work alienation. *Education, 107,* 244-251.

Bird, T., & Little, J.W. (1983, April). *Finding and founding of peer coaching: An interim report of the application of research on faculty relations to the implementation of two school improvement experiments.* Paper presented at the annual meeting of the American Educational Research Association, Montreal.

Blount, J.M. (1999). Manliness and the gendered construction of school administration in the USA. *International Journal of Leadership in Education, 2*(2), 55-68.

Brandt, R.M. (1987, April). *An ethnography of career ladder planning and implementation.* Paper presented at the annual meeting of the American Educational Research Association, Washington, DC.

Braver, M.W., & Helmstadter, G.C. (1989). *Executive summary: Impact of career ladders on student achievement.* Report presented to the Joint Legislative Committee on Career Ladders, Phoenix, AZ.

Callahan, R.E. (1962). *Education and the cult of the efficiency.* Chicago: University of Chicago Press.

Campion, M.A., & McClelland, C.L. (1993). Follow-up and extension of the interdisciplinary costs and benefits of enlarged jobs. *Journal of Applied Psychology, 78*(3), 339-351.

Center for Research on the Context of Teaching. (2000, May). *Assessing results: Bay Area School Reform Collaborative—Year 4.* Stanford, CA: Center for Research on the Context of Teaching, Stanford University.

Chapman, J., & Boyd, W.L. (1986). Decentralization, devolution, and the school principal. Australian lessons on statewide educational reform. *Educational Administration Quarterly, 22*(4), 28-58.

Cherns, A. (1964). The principles of socio-technical design. *Human Relations, 29,* 783-792.

Clune, W.H. (2001). Toward a theory of standards-based reform: The case of nine NSF statewide systemic initiatives. In S. Fuhrman (Ed.), *From the capital to the classroom: Standards-based reform in the states. The one-hundredth yearbook of the National Society for the Study of Education,* Part II (pp. 13-38). Chicago: National Society for the Study of Education.

Coburn, C.E. (2001). Collective sensemaking about reading: How teachers mediate reading policy in their professional communities. *Educational Evaluation and Policy Analysis, 32*(2), 145-170.

Cochran-Smith, M., & Lytle, S.L. (1999). The teacher research movement: A decade later. *Educational Researcher, 28*(7), 15-25.

Conway, J.A. (1976). Test of linearity between teachers' participation in decision making and their perceptions of their schools as organizations. *Administrative Science Quarterly, 21*(1), 130-139.

Conway, J.A. (1984). The myth, mystery, and mastery of participative decision making in education. *Educational Administration Quarterly, 20*(3), 11-40.

Conway, J.A., & Calzi, F. (1996). The dark side of shared decision making. *Educational Leadership, 53*(4), 45-49.

Copland, M.A. (2001, April). *Shared school leadership: Moving from role to function in an inquiry-based model of school reform.* Paper presented at the annual meeting of the American Educational Research Association, Seattle, WA.

Crow, G.M., & Pounder, D.G. (2000). Interdisciplinary teacher teams: Context, design, and process. *Educational Administration Quarterly, 36*(2), 216-254.

Davis, L.E., & Trist, E.L. (1974). Improving the quality of work life: Sociotechnical case studies. In J. O'Toole (Ed.), *Work and the quality of life* (pp. 246-284). Cambridge, MA: MIT Press.

Dickson, L. (1990, April). *Student achievement and career ladder status.* Paper presented at the annual meeting of the American Educational Research Association, Boston.

Ebmeier, H., & Hart, A.W. (1992). The effects of a career ladder program on school organizational processes. *Educational Evaluation and Policy Analysis, 14*(3), 261-281.

Evertson, C.M., Wade, M.W., & Smithey, M.W. (1993, April). *Learning to mentor: Redefining knowledge, roles, and self.* Paper presented at the annual meeting of the American Educational Research Association, Atlanta, GA.

Feiman-Nemser, S., & Parker, M.B. (1994). *Mentor teachers: Local guides or educational companion?* East Lansing: Michigan State University, National Center for Research on Teacher Learning.

Firestone, W.A. (1977). Participation and influence in the planning of educational change. *The Journal of Applied Behavioral Science, 13*, 167-183.

Fried, Y., & Ferris, G.R. (1987). The validity of the job characteristics model: A review and meta-analysis. *Personnel Psychology, 40*, 287-322.

Fullan, M. (2001). *The new meaning of educational change* (3rd ed.). New York: Teachers College Press.

Goertz, M. (2001). Standards based accountability: Horse trade or horse whip? In S. Fuhrman (Ed.), *From the capital to the classroom: Standards-based reform in the states. The one-hundredth yearbook of the National Society for the Study of Education,* Part II (pp. 39-59). Chicago: National Society for the Study of Education.

Gomberg, W. (1973, June). Job satisfaction: Sorting out the nonsense. *American Federationist, 80,* 14-20.

Hackman, J.R. (1975). On the coming demise of job enrichment. In E.L. Cass and F.G. Zimmer (Eds.), *Man and work in society* (pp. 97-115). New York: Nostrand, Reinhold.

Hackman, J.R. (1977). Work redesign. In J.R. Hackman & J.L. Suttle (Eds.), *Improving life at work: Behavioral science approaches to organizational change* (pp. 98-162). Santa Monica, CA: Goodyear.

Hackman, J.R. (1998). Why teams don't work. In R.S. Tinsdale et al. (Eds.), *Theory and research on small groups* (pp. 245-267). New York: Plenum.

Hackman, J.R., & Oldham, G.R. (1980). *Work redesign.* Reading, MA: Addison-Wesley.

Hannaway, J. (1993). Decentralization in two school districts: Challenging the standard paradigm. In J. Hannaway & M. Carnoy (Eds.), *Decentralization and school improvement* (pp. 135-162). San Francisco: Jossey-Bass.

Hart, A.W. (1985, April). *Formal teacher supervision by teachers in a career ladder.* Paper presented at the annual meeting of the American Educational Research Association, Chicago.

Hart, A.W. (1990). Impacts of the school social unit on teacher authority during work redesign. *American Educational Research Journal, 27*(3), 503-532.

Hart, A.W. (1994). Work feature values of today's and tomorrow's teachers: Work redesign as an incentive and school improvement policy. *Educational Evaluation and Policy Analysis, 16*(4), 458-473.

Heller, M.F., & Firestone, W.A. (1995). Who's in charge here? Sources of leadership for change in eight schools. *Elementary School Journal, 96*(1), 65-86.

Henson, K.T. (1996). Teachers as researchers. In J. Sikula, T.J. Buttery, & E. Guyton (Eds.). *Handbook of research on teacher education* (pp. 53-64). New York: Macmillan.

Herriott, R.E., & Firestone, W.A. (1984). Two images of schools as organizations: A refinement and elaboration. *Educational Administration Quarterly, 20*(4), 41-57.

Johns, G., Xie, J.L., & Fang, Y. (1992). Mediating and moderating effects in job design. *Journal of Management, 18*(4), 657-676.

Kelly, J.E. (1982). *Scientific management, job redesign, and work performance.* New York: Academic Press.

Kruse, S.D., & Louis, K.S. (1997). Teacher teaming in middle schools: Dilemmas for the school-wide community. *Educational Administration Quarterly, 33*(3), 261-289.

Lave, J., & Wenger, E. (1991). *Situated learning: Legitimate peripheral participation*. New York: Cambridge University Press.

Lawler, E.E. (1988). Substitutes for hierarchy. *Organizational Dynamics, 17*(1), 5-15.

Lee, V.E., Dedrick, R.F., & Smith, J.B. (1991). The effect of the social organization of schools on teachers' efficacy and satisfaction. *Sociology of Education, 64*(3), 190-208.

Little, J.W. (2003). Inside teacher community: Representations of classroom practice. *Teachers College Record, 105*(6), 913-945.

Littler, C.R. (1978). Understanding Taylorism. *British Journal of Sociology, 29*(2), 185-202.

Malen, B. (1986, April). *Career ladder policymaking in Utah: State perspective*. Paper presented at the annual meeting of the American Educational Research Association, San Francisco.

Mayrowetz, D., & Weinstein, C.S. (1999). Sources of leadership for inclusive education: Creating schools for all children. *Educational Administration Quarterly, 35*(3), 423-449.

McLaughlin, M.W., & Mitra, D. (2001). Theory-based change and change-based theory: Going deeper, going broader. *Journal of Educational Change, 2*, 301-323.

Murphy, M., & Prestine, N.A. (2001, October). *A slow, painless death: A study of an urban high school's five-year effort to create professional learning communities*. Paper presented at the Fall Conference of the University Council for Educational Administration, Cincinnati, OH.

Murphy, M.J., Hart, A.W., & Walters, L.C. (1989, April). *Satisfaction and intent to leave of new teachers in target populations under redesigned work*. Paper presented at the annual meeting of the American Educational Research Association, San Francisco.

NCEE (National Commission on Excellence in Education). (1983). *A nation at risk: The imperative for educational reform*. Washington, DC: Author. Retrieved February 22, 2004, from http://www.ed.gov/pubs/NatAtRisk/risk.html

NCTM (National Council of Teachers of Mathematics). (1989). *Curriculum and evaluation standards for school mathematics*. Reston, VA: Author.

NCTM (National Council of Teachers of Mathematics). (1991). *Professional standards for teaching mathematics*. Reston, VA: Author.

Ogawa, R.T., & Bossert, S.T. (1995). Leadership as an organizational quality. *Educational Administration Quarterly, 31*(2), 224-243.

Packard, R.D., & Bierlein, L. (1986). *Arizona career ladder research and evaluation project: Research and development for effective educational change and reform*. Flagstaff, AZ: Northern Arizona University.

Parker, S.K. (1998). Enhancing role breadth self-efficacy: The roles of job enrichment and other organizational interventions. *Journal of Applied Psychology, 83*(6), 835-852.

Parker, S., & Hall, T. (1998). *Job and work redesign: Organizing work to promote well-being and effectiveness*. Thousand Oaks, CA: Sage.

Pennell, J.R., & Firestone, W.A. (1996). Changing classroom practices through teacher networks: Matching program features with teacher characteristics and circumstances. *Teachers College Record, 98*(1), 46-76.

Popham, J. (1987). The merits of measurement driven instruction, *Phi Delta Kappan, 68*(9), 679-82.

Pounder, D.G. (1999). Teacher teams: Exploring job characteristics and work-related outcomes of work group enhancement. *Educational Administration Quarterly, 35*(3), 317-348.

Pounder, D.G., Ogawa, R.T., & Adams, E.A. (1995). Leadership as an organization-wide phenomena: Its impact on school performance. *Educational Administration Quarterly, 31*(4), 564-588.

Prestine, N.A., & Nelson, B.S. (2003, April). *How can educational leaders support and promote teaching and learning? New conceptions of learning and leading in schools*. Paper presented at the Annual Meeting of the American Educational Research Association, Chicago.

Reddick, T.L., & Peach, L.E. (1986, November). *Career ladder level II and level III teachers' perceptions of the effectiveness of the Tennessee career ladder program*. Paper presented at the annual meeting of the Mid-South Educational Research Association, Memphis, TN.

Rosenblatt, Z. (2001). Teachers' multiple roles and skill flexibility: Effects on work attitudes. *Educational Administration Quarterly, 37*(5), 684-708.

Rosenblatt, Z., & Inbal, B. (1999). Skill flexibility among school teachers: Operationalization and organizational implications. *Journal of Educational Administration, 37*(4), 345-366.

Shepard, L. (1989). Why we need better assessments. *Educational Leadership, 46*(7), 4-9.

Smith, M., & O'Day, J. (1991). Systemic school reform. In S. Fuhrman & B. Malen (Eds.), *The politics of curriculum and testing* (pp. 233-67). Bristol, PA: Falmer Press.

Smylie, M.A. (1993). When teachers are school district decision makers. In T.A. Astuto (Ed.), *When teachers lead* (pp. 57-72). University Park, PA: University Council for Educational Administration.

Smylie, M.A. (1994). Redesigning teachers' work: Connections to the classroom. In L. Darling-Hammond (Ed.), *Review of Research in Education: Vol. 20* (pp. 129-177). Washington, DC: American Educational Research Association.

Smylie, M.A. (1997). Research on teacher leadership: Assessing the state of the art. In B.J. Biddle et al. (Eds.), *International handbook of teachers and teaching* (pp. 521-592). Dordrecht, The Netherlands: Kluwer Academic.

Smylie, M.A., Conley, S., & Marks, H.M. (2002). Exploring new approaches to teacher leadership for school improvement. In J. Murphy (Ed.), *The educational leadership challenge: Redefining leadership for the 21st century. The one-hundred first yearbook of the National Society for the Study of Education*, Part I (pp. 162-188). Chicago: National Society for the Study of Education.

Spillane, J.P., Halverson, R., & Diamond, J.B. (2000). *Towards a theory of leadership practice: A distributed perspective*. Evanston, IL: Northwestern University, Institute for Policy Research.

Spillane, J.P., Halverson, R., & Diamond, J.B. (2001). Investigating school leadership practice: A distributed perspective. *Educational Researcher, 30*(3), 23-28.

Spillane, J.P., Hallet, T., & Diamond, J.B. (2003). Forms of capital and the construction of leadership: Instructional leadership in elementary schools. *Sociology of Education, 76*(1), 1-17.

Stein, M.K., & Spillane, J.P. (2003, April). *Research on teaching and research on educational administration: Building a bridge*. Paper presented at the annual meeting of the American Educational Research Association, Chicago.

Strauss, G. (1974). Job satisfaction, motivation and job redesign. In G. Strauss, R.E. Miles, C.C. Snow, & A.S. Tannenbaum (Eds.), *Organizational behavior: Research and issues* (pp. 19-49). Madison, WI: Industrial Relations Research Association.

Sundstrom, E., De Meuse, K.P., & Futrell, D. (1990). Work teams: Applications and effectiveness. *American Psychologist, 45*(2), 120-133.

Tannenbaum, A.S. (1962). Control in organizations: Individual adjustment and organizational performance. *Administrative Science Quarterly, 7*(3), 236-257.

Taylor, B., & Madsen, J. (1989, March). *Career ladder process in Missouri: A report on how districts are realizing the goals of the program*. Paper presented at the annual meeting of the American Educational Research Association, San Francisco.

Tikunoff, W.J., Ward, B., & Griffin, G.A. (1979). *Interactive research and development on teaching study: Final report*. Far West Laboratory for Educational Research and Development.

Tyack, D.B. (1974). *The one best system: A history of American urban education*. Cambridge, MA: Harvard University Press.

Walton, R.E. (1975). The diffusion of new work structures: Explaining why success didn't take. *Organizational Dynamics, 3*(3), 3-22.

Weiss, C.H., Cambone, J., & Wyeth, A. (1992). Trouble in paradise: Teacher conflicts in shared decision making. *Educational Administration Quarterly, 28*(3), 350-367.

Wenger, E. (1998). Communities of practice. Learning as a social system. *Systems Thinker*. Retrieved December 30, 2003, from http://www.co-i-l.com/coil/knowledge-garden/cop/lss.shtml

Zeichner, K.M., & Noffke, S.E. (2001). Practitioner research. In V. Richardson (Ed.), *Handbook of research on teaching* (pp. 298-330). Washington, DC: American Educational Research Association.

CHAPTER 10

School- and District-Level Leadership for Teacher Workforce Development: Enhancing Teacher Learning and Capacity

M. BRUCE KING

More than 90 years ago, in the Seventh NSSE Yearbook, Charles Lowry (1908), then the Chicago district superintendent of schools, outlined five avenues for the improvement of teachers: 1) supervision, 2) work undertaken voluntarily by teachers, 3) work required of teachers, 4) work stimulated by rewards or advancement in position, and 5) miscellaneous efforts. Fast-forward to the mid-1990s, when Goertz, Floden, and O'Day (1996) captured an emerging consensus for improvement when they argued for five different avenues for building capacity for systemic reform: 1) articulate a vision for reform; 2) provide instructional guidance to help realize the vision; 3) restructure governance and other organizational structures to facilitate learning; 4) provide necessary resources; and 5) establish evaluation and accountability measures that help provide incentives and address barriers. These recommendations suggest that teacher workforce development is best addressed through a coherent system of strategies across many levels and activities (e.g., initial preparation and induction, recruitment and selection, evaluation and compensation). Thus, leadership for teacher development and capacity building, the central theme of this chapter, becomes critical.

In the conventional form of U.S. school and district organization, educational leaders manage a bureaucracy and the workforce within it, and the practice of leadership is largely hierarchical and gendered. Leadership responsibilities are associated with specific, official positions within the hierarchy and tend to focus on administrative matters rather than instructional ones (e.g., Elmore, 2000; Smylie & Hart, 1999). As with most attempts at educational innovation and reform, changes in

M. Bruce King is a Research Scientist at the Wisconsin Center for Education Research at the University of Wisconsin, Madison.

leadership practice have tinkered around the edges of the core technologies of schooling, teaching and learning, rather than addressing them head on. The result: "Direct involvement in instruction is among the least frequent activities performed by administrators of any kind at any level, and those who engage in instructional leadership activities on a consistent basis are a relatively small proportion of the total administrative force" (Elmore, 2000, p. 7). Not much has changed since Cuban (1988) showed how the job of education leaders has historically encompassed three main roles—the managerial, the political, and the instructional—and how the first two have clearly dominated the third.

If successful school reform rests largely on the capabilities of individual teachers and groups of teachers to deliver high-quality instruction (Little, 1999), then a key component of teacher workforce development is teacher learning. One of the prominent ways in which educational leaders shape school conditions and teaching practices is through their beliefs and actions regarding teacher learning. Of course, leaders must still attend to myriad important matters, such as selection, assignment, and retention of teachers; utilization of financial and other material resources; and cultivation of school-level leadership and school-family-community relations. But the shift to a greater emphasis on the instructional role of leaders should be paramount. In this chapter, I will address school- and district-level leadership for teacher workforce development through improving teacher learning and capacity.

What conditions promote effective teacher learning? Research (see Darling-Hammond & McLaughlin, 1996; Desimone, Porter, Birman, Garet, & Yoon, 2002; Elmore, 2002; Hargreaves, 1995; Little, 1993; Lytle & Cochran-Smith, 1994; Newmann, King, & Youngs, 2000; Renyi, 1996; Richardson, 1994) suggests at least the following four conditions. First, teacher learning is most likely to occur when teachers focus on instruction and student outcomes in the specific contexts in which they teach. Because traditional inservice activities and other forms of professional development often present material that teachers see as irrelevant to student learning in their specific school settings, teachers often do not learn and apply what these experiences offer.

Second, teacher learning is most likely to occur if teachers have sustained opportunities to study, to experiment with, and to receive helpful feedback on specific innovations. Yet, most professional development entails brief workshops, conferences, or courses that make no provision for long-term follow-up and feedback.

Third, teacher learning is most likely to occur when teachers have opportunities to collaborate with professional peers, both within and outside of their schools, and have access to the expertise of external researchers and program developers. Peer collaboration offers a powerful vehicle for ongoing teacher learning and is an important supplement to materials and advice from other authorities. In contrast, traditional approaches rely almost exclusively on outside experts and materials, without integrating these resources into strong systems of peer collaboration.

Fourth, teacher learning is most likely to occur when teachers have influence over the substance and process of their learning activities. If teachers have some control over the course of their professional development, it increases their opportunity to connect it to specific conditions in their schools and provides opportunities for them to exercise professional discretion. Empowerment facilitates a sense of personal ownership or "buy-in," which promotes internalization of learning. Traditionally, however, school, district, or state authorities often dictate staff development experiences without significant input from teachers.

Teacher learning would clearly be enhanced if formal and informal professional development opportunities met these conditions, but whether this would necessarily advance student achievement across a substantial portion of schools depends on the acceptance of at least one additional idea—that an approach to teacher learning that focuses only on the learning of *individual* teachers is insufficient. Success in boosting student achievement depends on the teacher's ability to implement knowledge and skills within a particular school. But each school contains a unique mix of many teachers' competencies and attitudes, a unique mix of many students' competencies and attitudes, and a unique set of social, cultural, and political conditions, all of which influence what teachers do with students. Individual teacher learning is, of course, the foundation for improved classroom practice, but teachers must learn to exercise their individual knowledge, skills, and dispositions to advance the *collective* work of the school under a unique set of conditions. To the extent that teacher development efforts focus only on individual learning while neglecting to help whole school faculties to integrate their learning for the advancement of all students in that school, substantial and equitable achievement gains cannot be expected. Thus, school and district leadership to promote teacher development needs to attend to not only how individual teachers learn but also how groups of teachers, particularly the staff of a school, learn and develop together.

Teachers' Individual and Collective Capacities

Individual teacher competence is necessary for effective classroom practice. Teachers must be able to integrate knowledge of students, subject matter, pedagogy, and teaching context in planning units and lessons, carrying out instruction, assessing student work, and reflecting on practice. At the same time, to promote achievement among all students from one year to the next, teachers must employ their individual knowledge, skills, and dispositions—their individual capacity— in ways that advance the shared work of their schools. The power of an entire faculty to strengthen student performance throughout their school can be summarized as teachers' collective capacity.

All teaching staff must be professionally competent in curriculum, pedagogy, assessment, and classroom management, and they must maintain high expectations for student learning. The influence of teachers' individual capacity on student achievement is well recognized in the literature on teacher education, licensure, and professional development (e.g., Cohen & Hill, 2000; Darling-Hammond, 1998). But individual teacher competence must be exercised in organized, coherent ways that foster teachers' collective capacity. Collective capacity emphasizes the educative importance of social resources in the school, or school-wide *professional community*. Definitions of professional community vary in the literature. In recent work on professional development in low-achieving, high-poverty elementary schools (King, 2002; King & Newmann, 2000; Newmann et al., 2000; Youngs & King, 2002), my colleagues and I defined professional community as having these dimensions: 1) shared goals for student learning; 2) meaningful collaboration among faculty members; 3) in-depth inquiry into assumptions, evidence, and alternative solutions to problems; and 4) opportunities for teachers to exert influence over their work. Studies have shown higher levels of professional community to be associated with higher student achievement (Lee & Smith, 1996; Louis, Kruse, & Associates, 1995; Louis & Marks, 1998). Despite this evidence, one must also take into account the possibility that strong teacher communities can be less effective if teachers collaborate to reinforce practices that don't work, or if they promote shared values to the extent that minority viewpoints are unwelcome or that disagreement and diversity are perceived as a threat (e.g., Fullan, 2001; King, 2002; McLaughlin & Talbert, 2001).

Fostering collective capacities of teachers through professional community relates to the recent work on schools as learning organizations.

Schools as learning organizations help teachers interrogate, integrate, and apply knowledge and values in the process of continual improvement (Argyris & Schön, 1996; Crowther, Kaagan, Ferguson, & Hann, 2002; Leithwood & Louis, 1999; Louis & Marks, 1999). This focus on learning organizations assumes, as Goodlad (1983) argued twenty years ago, that the individual school should become the key unit for educational improvement. The idea of schools as learning organizations addresses one of the major barriers to successful reform and teacher development. That barrier is the normative environment, which "is a direct result of an institutional structure that is deliberately and calculatedly incompetent at influencing its core functions" (Elmore, 2000, p. 7) and which often reflects a dysfunctional level of respect for the autonomy of individual teachers. One consequence of this kind of environment is a reliance on teacher volunteerism to improve practice, which inhibits school-wide efforts. Another result is teacher isolation. One of the critical problems in teacher learning is teachers' inability and reluctance to work accountably together across grades, classrooms, and subject matter at a school to ensure that students meet high standards for learning (McDonald, 2001). Schools with strong professional communities overcome these problems and as such are learning organizations.

School Leadership That Enhances Teacher Capacity

Effective school-level leadership plays a critical role in fostering teachers' individual and collective capacities. The importance of principal leadership has long been recognized in the literature (see, e.g., Hallinger & Heck, 1998), and principals clearly have the authority to affect school conditions and teacher learning opportunities in positive or negative ways and to varying degrees, depending on the quality of their leadership. Principals can enhance teachers' knowledge, skills, and dispositions by connecting teachers to external expertise, by creating internal structures for collaboration, and by establishing trusting relations with school staff. School leaders can promote collaboration and reflective inquiry by allocating time for teachers to meet on a consistent basis (Bryk, Lee, & Holland, 1993; Johnson, 1990). Shared commitment is strengthened when principals work with teachers to establish shared goals for student learning (Hallinger & Heck, 1996; Leithwood, 1994), to align such goals with school-wide professional development (Conley & Goldman, 1994; Goldring & Rallis, 1993), and to buffer their schools from conflicting external influences (Louis, Kruse, & Marks, 1996).

Studies have revealed substantial differences in the nature of principal leadership between schools with strong professional communities and those with weak professional communities (Louis et al., 1996; Useem, Christman, Gold, & Simon, 1997). These differences involve how school leaders enact their roles and the relationships they establish, as opposed to how their roles are formally defined. When principals foster social trust with staff members, teacher capacity is likely to be strengthened. Research indicates that trust develops between principals and teachers when school leaders' beliefs and actions are consistent with school goals, when principals support teachers' work on a consistent basis, and when principals manage conflict among staff members proactively and effectively (Bryk et al., 1993; Bryk & Schneider, 2002; Smylie & Hart, 1999). Sharing responsibility with teachers is also conducive to building trust (Goldring & Rallis, 1993; Louis et al.). When principals encourage teachers to have influence over decisions related to curriculum, hiring, and professional development, they can increase trust among teachers and enhance collective responsibility for student learning (Spillane, Halverson, & Diamond, 2001).

It is clear that school leadership does not and should not reside solely in the principalship. It should be distributed throughout the organization (Elmore, 2000; Gamoran et al., 2003; Spillane et al., 2001), and principals can play a key role in cultivating leadership among teachers. Thus, leadership becomes an organizational property (Ogawa & Bossert, 2000; Smylie & Hart, 1999) and a key component of a school's organizational strength (Newmann et al., 2000).

School leadership can advance comprehensive approaches to teacher learning that promote the development of both individual and collective capacities. A comprehensive approach must exhibit high levels of *program coherence*, which can be defined as the extent to which programs, policies, and activities at a school are coordinated, directed at clear learning goals, and sustained over time. Program coherence can be thought of as a measure of organizational integration. Schools frequently adopt innovations unconnected to a central focus and pursue innovations for short periods of time. Leadership is often seduced by a continuing series of "hot" reforms in pursuit of a quick fix. But such patterns of unconnected, short-term innovations are unlikely to improve instructional quality or enhance teacher development (Newmann et al., 2000; Newmann, Smith, Allensworth, & Bryk, 2001). Student and staff learning can be weakened by organizational fragmentation when schools implement programs that are unrelated to each other, that address only limited numbers of students and staff, or that end after short periods of time. A lack of coherence at the school level can weaken commitment to shared goals for student learning and teachers' collective capacity. Although there has not been much empirical research on the effects of program coherence on student achievement, Newmann et al. (2001) recently found a strong relationship between instructional program coherence and student achievement in Chicago elementary schools. Though I have focused here on the school level, it is important to note that leadership can also connect student learning, teacher professional learning, and system-wide learning with one another and with learning goals to promote coherence (Knapp, Copland, & Talbert, 2003) I will discuss this issue later in the chapter. The more that the broader array of strategies for teacher workforce development—state education policies, preservice preparation, selection and assignment to schools, induction and socialization, supervision and evaluation, working conditions, allocation and use of resources, and professional learning opportunities—are consistent, coordinated, focused, and sustained, the more one would expect to see improvements in teaching and learning (Ladwig & King, 2003; Newmann, 1993).

Some of the important aspects of principal leadership played out in different ways at two elementary schools that participated in a study of professional development that my colleagues and I recently conducted (King & Newmann, 2000; Newmann et al., 2000; Youngs & King, 2002). Principals expanded the individual and collective capacities of teachers even though their schools pursued very different approaches to reform. The first, Lewis Elementary School, implemented a highly structured, externally developed program; the second, Renfrew Elementary School, implemented a program developed by the staff.

Lewis Elementary School

The Lewis Elementary student body is 78% Latino, 15% White, and 7% African American, and 93% of the students receive free or reduced-price lunches. At Lewis, reform centered on implementing Success for All (SFA; Slavin, Madden, Dolan, & Wasik, 1996) reading in grades K-5 and SFA math in grades 3-5. The common curriculum and instructional strategies that teachers used formed a solid base for shared commitment to clear learning goals. Staff members consistently articulated that the school's main goal was to improve student performance in reading and math through SFA.

Lewis's principal, at the helm for more than 10 years, was committed to whole-school development through SFA, and he structured sustained time for professional development related to SFA. Under his leadership, the school created eight half days of professional development each year by adding five instructional minutes per day to the required daily schedule. He promoted shared goals and teacher commitment to SFA by involving teachers in the initial selection of this particular reform program, holding frequent grade-level and whole-faculty meetings related to SFA, and insisting that the school stay the course with the program. He structured daily common planning time for grade-level teams and regular meetings of teams and individual teachers with the school-based SFA reading and math facilitators, and he himself met monthly with team leaders. By arranging training and "implementation checks" by SFA and working closely with the school-based facilitators, he ensured that teachers at Lewis participated collaboratively in school-wide reform activities. Further, he provided substitutes and allocated funds for teachers to attend local and national SFA conferences. Although there was minimal staff turnover, the principal looked for new teachers who were prepared to teach SFA; in this regard, he was able to hire teachers who had interned at the school and to involve them immediately in further SFA training. These SFA-related professional development activities continually addressed specific teaching strategies in reading, writing, and mathematics.

Renfrew Elementary School

At Renfrew Elementary, the student body is 44% Latino, 38% White, 14% African American, and 4% Asian, and 54% of the students receive free or reduced-price lunches. In contrast to Lewis, the staff at Renfrew developed their own program for improvement; thus, reform was more organic and school based. Each year, the staff developed or reaffirmed two "essential questions," which focused reform efforts and enhanced shared commitment and teacher influence. During our study, one of their essential questions concerned the pattern of unequal achievement across different student groups. In addition, the staff focused on literacy instruction and achievement for multiple years and worked in grade-level teams to develop outcomes and assessments for reading comprehension and writing.

The principal, at the school for 10 years, structured numerous forums for collaborative work among teachers. These included grade-level teams, whole-staff institutes prior to the start of the school year and at midyear, and biweekly inquiry groups. In the meetings we observed, teachers consistently voiced ideas, proposals, concerns, feedback, and criticisms, with direct encouragement for this kind of dialogue from the principal. In facilitating whole-staff institutes, she

designed activities for the staff that included examining achievement data disaggregated by race/ethnicity and social class, discussing instructional strategies and other teacher behaviors that might help students from different backgrounds, and reviewing results from a staff survey to identify areas needing attention. Teachers were always involved in co-planning these activities as well as helping to facilitate them during the institutes. To make formal policy and plans for professional development, the principal consulted with the lead teachers from the grade-level teams, and no major change was made without wide support throughout the faculty. These actions reflect a shared, or distributive, style of leadership that fostered empowerment and collective capacity.

Under the principal's guidance, staff scrutinized conditions of schooling relevant to equity and social justice. Although it was extremely challenging for teachers to examine issues of racism and prejudice in their own attitudes and practice, it helped generate and reinforce commitment to shared learning goals. Inquiry both involved and contributed to collaboration in that teachers' beliefs and their students' achievement levels were subject to collective scrutiny in a supportive environment. For a school principal to facilitate and participate in these kinds of professional discussions, without the cloud of administrative evaluation derailing the effort, is extremely rare in schools. Renfrew's inquiry was successful, according to the district's superintendent, because the school had a principal who passionately believed that teachers needed to be actively engaged in examining their own and their peers' practices.

These brief vignettes of two urban elementary schools illustrate productive principal leadership that strengthened individual and collective teacher capacity. Principals kept professional development activities focused on the school's vision for reform and on issues of teaching and learning. They structured, and expected, collaborative work, reflection, and responsibility among the staff.

Similarly, at the high school level, McLaughlin and Talbert (2001) found that leadership made a significant contribution to whether professional communities developed in ways that positively affected student learning outcomes. In their study, the theme of principals taking on a role other than the traditional one of manager was again apparent. They showed that principals rated low on leadership by their teachers were seen as "managers who provide little support or direction for teaching and learning." Principals rated high by their teachers were "actively involved in the sorts of activities that nurture and sustain strong teacher community" (p. 110). School reform and the teacher development that it requires are unlikely to become sustained without this type of leadership and support for organizational learning. As Fullan (2001) explained, "Organizations transform when they can establish mechanisms for learning in the dailiness of organizational life. . . . Leaders in a culture of change create these conditions for daily learning" (pp. 130-131).

District Leadership That Enhances Teacher Capacity

School districts have often been thought of as "forgotten players" (Tyack, 2002), but district-level leadership can profoundly shape teacher learning and capacity. Schools and districts, once part of the "loosely coupled" system, are becoming more tightly connected. Standards, high-stakes assessments, and accountability require it. Although these three tools for improved school performance are now common across districts and states in this country, they are still subject to considerable research and debate as to their effectiveness.

Recent systemic approaches to school improvement tend to reflect a centralized strategy. That is, educational policies rely on mandatory curriculum frameworks or standards, high-stakes student testing, and aligned teacher professional development. Considerable problems have been identified with excessively centralized approaches, such as limited teacher buy-in (Clune, 1993; Smylie, 1996). Yet a reliance on site-based approaches can leave many schools behind because they do not have the capacity to generate or sustain significant improvements. Concerns for more equitable student achievement demand some central oversight. School districts can provide important external guidance for enhancing the quality of teaching and learning on a large scale. But districts must combine centralized strategies with more decentralized ones, including those related to teacher learning, in order to effectively build local school capacity (Bryk, Sebring, Kerbow, Rollow, & Easton, 1998).

Historically, however, educational policy has proceeded from the logic that "problems of schooling are due in large part to lack of direction, excessive discretion, and low accountability within the educational system. This theory claims that these conditions can best be corrected through external regulation and bureaucratic control" (Smylie, 1996, p. 9). Consistent with this logic, districts typically take a centralized approach to teacher learning, providing a menu of professional development sessions from which teachers must choose or mandating professional development in a specified program or topic for most or all staff members of a school or schools.

But it is unlikely that successful reform can be built to any significant degree through this approach alone. "One does not change the 'face' of schools through the central office" (Freire, quoted in Weiner, 2003, p. 92). Teacher development opportunities that are not well linked to student learning in teachers' specific school settings tend to diminish individual and collective development of knowledge, skills, and dispositions. Also, highly specific prescriptive professional development opportunities that are mandated by external authorities can deny school staff members both the commitment and authority they need to work collaboratively to achieve a clear purpose for student learning. In a study my colleagues and I made of urban elementary schools (Newmann et al., 2000), districts with excessively centralized approaches tended to exacerbate the problem of school program coherence. For three schools, district-sponsored professional development was aimed toward meeting dozens of mandatory standards for curriculum and assessment, in different subjects at different grade levels, and failed to help faculties generate common missions for their schools. Although standard setting by districts may not always threaten program coherence, the standards in each of these contexts were made up of lengthy lists of discrete skills and items of knowledge that lacked thematic coherence. At one school, the district required teachers to participate in math workshops that had no connection at all to what the school was trying to do in their own reform efforts in math.

But some districts have taken alternative approaches to professional learning that seem to hold more promise for effective teacher development and school reform. In the remainder of this section, I will summarize what recent research has revealed about the role of districts in enhancing teacher learning. Two critical dimensions of this research are school-level professional development and districts as a whole evolving into learning organizations.

Successful district approaches to professional learning entail a shift to more decentralized and participatory management practices, where professional development is school based. The role of the district may include such strategies as making structural accommodations for peer observations and consultation both within and across schools, providing release time for teacher inquiry groups, and hiring consultants to work with staff in a sustained way that is focused on areas identified by the school as its main targets for school improvement. This shift in district role does not preclude centralized policies or regulations. Indeed, given that educational reforms generally fail to influence persisting patterns of teaching and that concerns for equity require fundamental changes in many schools, school districts must address the issue of building school capacity on a large scale. Standard setting and account-ability systems, targeting particular subject areas, requiring school improvement plans, and the like all may be used to guide, rather than control, teacher learning and school reform. High-quality professional development can be provided both from the central office and from the local school (Smylie, Allensworth, Greenberg, Harris, & Luppescu, 2001). The nature of the balance between centralized and decentral-ized initiatives in school systems, and how systems and schools negoti-ate this balance, remain critical issues for further research.

In districts where professional development is largely school based, different schools may embrace different programs for teacher learning. Professional development in some schools may center on implement-ing comprehensive programs of curriculum, instruction, and assess-ment developed by external agencies, such as the Success for All pro-grams in reading and mathematics. In other schools, professional development may aim more toward organic forms of school improve-ment, such as the creation of school-based assessments and perfor-mance outcomes. The critical issue is not whether the program of pro-fessional development is prescriptive or organic for the school, for teachers' knowledge and skills and professional community can be addressed by either approach (Newmann et al., 2000). Teachers at dif-ferent schools vary in their existing levels of capacity and, thus, warrant different strategies (Slavin, 1997). District leadership can either estab-lish a compelling vision for teaching and learning to guide professional development or support teachers and schools in developing their own visions (Gamoran et al., 2003). Districts can leverage effective profes-sional development at the school level while maintaining quality con-trol over external partners and providers (Smylie et al., 2001).

School districts can play a critical role in establishing the context for productive professional development (e.g., Desimone et al., 2002; Elmore, 1997; Knapp et al., 2003; Spillane, 1996; Spillane & Jennings, 1997; Spillane & Thompson, 1997), and a growing body of research documents significant success in some districts' approaches to profes-sional development. For example, Community School District 2 in New York City employed an innovative strategy that featured school-based consultants, peer observations, and a professional development laboratory that enabled teachers to visit accomplished colleagues in their classrooms for extended periods of time. In addition, District 2 focused for several years on improving instruction and student perfor-mance in reading and writing and, more recently, in mathematics. This content focus applied to all district elementary schools. Thus, the district's approach stressed school-site decision making for selecting the teachers who would receive training and support, the consultants who would be employed over a specific period, and the professional networks that would foster teacher collaboration. But the approach also gave district staff a major share of the responsibility for deciding which instructional areas would receive priority attention, for maintaining focus on those areas, for forming and maintaining relationships with consultants who delivered training and support to schools in the priority areas, and for keeping school-site decisions focused on district-wide policies (Elmore). The district's strategy targeted school-level improvement through professional development, placing a great deal of weight on principals and their ability to create strong, unified learning communities within their schools, as well as offering different schools different kinds of attention from the district administration (Stein & D'Amico, 1998). It remains to be seen whether or not this kind of approach can be successfully sustained.

A recent study of professional development that my colleagues and I undertook (King, Newmann, & Youngs, 1999; Youngs, 2000) showed that some districts have facilitated school-based professional development that seems to have promise for building capacity. One district's approach to professional development explicitly emphasized enhancing individual school capacity. The district's model of professional development was evolving into one based on specific requests and identified needs from individual schools, as opposed to the traditional model of centrally mandating the same inservice activities for all. To this end, the district formed a Leadership Center for Systemic Change. All schools participated by sending a team to critically address issues of school improvement in collaboration with other teams and district personnel.

Schools in three other districts received sustained support from central office staff that was well coordinated with their mission and focus. In one, the district's coordinator for curriculum, instruction, and assessment was a trained Accelerated Schools coach, and she provided ongoing assistance to the school that adopted that reform model. In a second school, a district-based "resource teacher" worked in the school one day each week. She visited classrooms regularly, responded to requests for assistance, and facilitated the development of the school improvement plan. Throughout one semester, she worked closely with a team of teachers, helping them to align social studies and science curricula with state tests. At the third school, the district offered a graduate course in "emergent literacy" to the whole staff. The school had targeted literacy in its five-year plan for school improvement, and, through this course, teachers increased their knowledge of instructional strategies and reinforced their shared focus.

Renfrew Elementary School's district established policies and programs that specifically addressed teacher inquiry, a key aspect of teacher professional community. The district enabled teacher inquiry groups at each school through district funding and grants from the state and from independent reform projects. While supporting teacher inquiry groups at individual schools, this district adopted a system-wide approach to the development of performance standards and assessments in math and literacy. Thus, district leadership directly confronted the tension between sponsoring and supporting school-based professional development on one hand and implementing district-level initiatives on the other. To the extent that this system-wide focus represents a major shift in program substance and professional development, however, it could subvert capacity by conflicting with coherence and shared learning goals at a school like Renfrew that had developed its own approach to reform.

Particular school district strategies are associated with high-quality professional development. Analysis by Desimone et al. (2002) showed that alignment with standards and assessments, coordination and co-funding of programs, continual improvement efforts, and teacher involvement in district-level planning are important ways districts can support professional development. The researchers noted problems in defining and measuring alignment, but one must also question the extent to which alignment with standards and assessments exacerbates program *incoherence* if what they align with is an overstuffed curriculum or a high-stakes test that reflects a superficial and fragmented vision of learning (see McNeil, 2000).

These recent studies indicate, however, that some districts have implemented innovative strategies and approaches to professional development that have potential for improving teachers' individual and collective capacities. They also show that, in adopting new approaches, districts do not abandon systemic policies or regulations. Policies and other approaches to school and teacher development can have elements of both centralization and decentralization. Despite the potential of new approaches to professional development to enhance teacher capacity, however, they can generate significant tension as districts attempt to strike the most productive combination of decentralized and centralized initiatives, school-based and system-wide reform. The critical challenge for districts is to promote both school reform and system coherence (Bryk et al., 1998). Thus, one of the critical issues is how districts can establish parameters for professional development without turning them into bureaucratic controls that diminish capacity.

One recently completed study offers important insights into how district leadership can make a difference for teacher learning and capacity. The Learning First Alliance's study (Togneri & Anderson, 2003) of five school districts that varied in size, demographics, region, and urbanicity found a similar set of strategies to improve instruction. One of the study's major contributions is that it strongly points to the need for a district to be a professional learning community and not (only) a bureaucracy (see also McLaughlin & Talbert, 2002). Of importance here are the common actions leaders in these districts took to build the political will for reform. They publicly acknowledged that student achievement was unacceptably low; accepted responsibility for the problem of low achievement; clearly communicated the expectation that all stakeholders needed to be part of the solution; and committed themselves to supporting innovations over the long term.

These districts also established a system-wide approach to improving instruction. Common components across the different districts' approaches included "a vision focused on student learning and instructional improvement" (Togneri, 2003, p. 4). The existence of the vision was not unique; most districts have them. But what was unique was the fact that these districts actually used their visions to guide instructional improvement. The visions were active and vibrant, and superintendents made it clear that the visions were driving their programmatic decisions.

Importantly, leadership was distributed across stakeholders. Leadership before instructional reforms were instituted was diffuse, and there was no coordinated training of leaders. "There was limited support for principals to become instructional leaders [and] teacher leaders existed but were not used in a coordinated, explicit manner" (Togneri, 2003, p. 7). After reform was initiated, or as part of the reform strategy itself, districts "created networks of instructional leaders that provided significant support to teachers. Districts expected principals to be instructional leaders and provided significant support. Districts formed networks of teacher leaders who provided instructional assistance to teachers, principals, and central office administrators" (p. 7).

These examples make clear that districts undertaking successful reforms have redefined leadership roles. This was one of the key findings of the Learning First Alliance study. Leadership was focused on instructional change, as opposed to managerial, administrative, or political roles. Leadership was expanded and shared, and different stakeholder groups took on elements of reform that they were well suited to lead. For example, school boards set policies that supported changes in instruction, and central offices took charge of creating systems to improve principal leadership and system-wide support for new teachers.

As Togneri and Anderson (2003) have noted, the creation of the infrastructure for district-wide instructional reform might suggest an excessively top-down approach. But this was not the case in the districts they studied. The reform efforts were not a simplistic dichotomy of centralization versus decentralization. Principals and teachers led and implemented reforms at their school, but these efforts were not isolated from district efforts. Districts showed varying degrees of centralization, but the schools in each of them had considerable flexibility to pursue productive change. Leaders purposefully sought a balance between district-level support and school-level flexibility to innovate. "[District] leaders expressed the understanding that, because challenges varied from school to school, school leaders would need flexibility to address challenges specific to their environments" (Togneri & Anderson, p. 22). As noted above, this involves attending to administrative matters—hiring teachers, determining the use of funds, and structuring schedules—as well as providing leadership for teacher learning. Similarly, Massell and Goertz (2002) documented how professional development was approached differently in large urban and smaller districts, depending on fiscal and human resources. There is no single recipe, but the focus should be on building the individual and collective capacities of teachers in their schools.

This last finding from the Learning First Alliance study echoes Fullan's (2001) claim that different leadership strategies are needed for different circumstances. He argues,

The need for external intervention is inversely proportionate to how well the school is progressing. In the case of persistent failure, dramatic, assertive leadership and external intervention appear to be necessary. In the long run, however, effectiveness depends on developing internal commitment in which ideas and intrinsic motivation of the vast majority of organizational members become activated. Along the way, authoritative ideas, democratic empowerment, affiliative bonds, and coaching will all be needed. (p. 46)

This is a potent reminder to those reformers who put incredible faith in less hierarchical power relations and leadership structures, and reel from the idea of top-down, authoritarian mandates. As I noted earlier, significant problems have been identified with excessively centralized approaches. But if concerns for schooling's role in reproducing social inequalities (e.g., the persisting problem of inequitable student achievement across racial and economic groups) are taken seriously, there must be honest assessments of what particular schools and teachers do and do not do, and how some merit top-down navigation and central control over change.

Conclusions

The focus on school- and district-level leadership for teacher capacity suggests a fairly radical rethinking of educational leadership from its traditional grounding in administrative and managerial functions. Productive school reform and both individual and collective teacher development that improves the learning of all students require, among other things, "skillful school and district leaders who guide continuous instructional improvement" (Elmore, 2002, p. 38). This rethinking of leadership, though, does not provide a recipe or checklist for quick fixes, for there really aren't any (Fullan, 2001). There are, however, some principles for leadership that we can summarize here, as well as draw out some implications from them.

Elmore (2000) sets down five principles for leadership for large-scale reform:

- The purpose of leadership is the improvement of instructional practice and performance, regardless of role.
- Instructional improvement requires continuous learning.
- Learning requires modeling.
- The roles and activities of leadership flow from the expertise required for learning and improvement, not from the formal dictates of the institution.
- The exercise of authority requires reciprocity of accountability and capacity. (pp. 20-21)

School and district leadership exercised in ways that are consistent with these principles is likely to productively promote teacher development and capacity. But implicit in these principles is one more important consideration—the relational quality of leadership. Relationships are crucial to leadership (Fullan, 2001). We can see the centrality and importance of relationships in Elmore's (2000) discussion of school leadership: "The job of administrative leaders is primarily about enhancing the skills and knowledge of people in the organization, creating a common culture of expectations around the use of those skills and knowledge, holding various pieces of the organization together in a productive relationship with each other, and holding individuals accountable for their contributions to the collective result" (p. 15).

Leadership is about relationships, and thus, *social interaction* as the building block of leadership is critical (Bryk & Schneider, 2002; Ogawa & Bossert, 2000). From this perspective, leadership is not unidirectional and it is not located in formal roles. Thus, leadership should focus on reciprocity and enhancing leadership in others—the mutual obligations and value of sharing knowledge among organizational members (Fullan, 2001). A strong professional community, with a shared purpose for student learning, collaboration, inquiry, and empowerment, seems to require a distribution of both leadership and knowledge.

Individual leaders take responsibility to share what they know, to be proactive listeners, to appreciate dissent, and to privilege respectful and caring treatment of others—a far cry from the distant and controlling leader of the past (see Bruner, 2002, for an analysis of traditional and nontraditional conceptions of the superintendency). Leaders remove barriers to sharing, create mechanisms for sharing, and reward those who share. Inclusivity, as opposed to hierarchically imposed exclusivity, becomes valued. Individual *and* organizational development are thereby enhanced. Because commitment cannot be generated from the top, "it must be nurtured up close in the dailiness of organizational behavior, and for that to happen there must be many leaders" (Fullan, 2001, p. 133). As I have stressed throughout this chapter, it is more a question of building strong collectivities of educators in organizations than of developing great individual leaders.

A plan for teacher development through the enhancement of individual and collective capacities cannot be fashioned independently of the school community members. A school community must genuinely make its model or approach to reform and improvement its own and policy should assist schools in this endeavor. The implication here is that different schools need different kinds of support for teacher development and building teacher capacity, but state and district policies still tend to reflect a one-size-fits-all approach, which can diminish commitment and overall capacity. Policies need to be flexible enough to fit particular school contexts and needs. Leadership then takes center stage, at the school and district levels, in ways that further the work of the members of each school.

Previously, I discussed the persistent problem of educational inequality and its implications for the extent of centralization in district efforts to improve teachers and schools. This equity concern encourages one further notion in rethinking leadership. If teachers' capacity focuses their individual and collective power to enhance achievement for all students, leadership must purposefully support these efforts to confront inequities. In a stratified society, with economic and cultural resources unequally distributed across racial/ethnic and socioeconomic groups, educational leaders can work to minimize the impact of power and privilege and the school's role in reproducing these inequalities. We are now familiar with many high-performing teachers and schools of excellence and equity; the challenge for leadership for widespread reform is still ahead.

322   SCHOOL- AND DISTRICT-LEVEL LEADERSHIP

REFERENCES

Argyris, C., & Schön, D. (1996). *Organizational learning II.* Reading, MA: Addison-Wesley.

Bruner, C.C. (2002). A proposition for the reconception of the superintendency: Reconsidering traditional and nontraditional discourse. *Educational Administration Quarterly, 38*(3), 402-431.

Bryk, A.S., Lee, V.E., & Holland, P.B. (1993). *Catholic schools and the common good.* Cambridge, MA: Harvard University Press.

Bryk, A.S., & Schneider, B. (2002). *Trust in schools: A core resource for improvement.* New York: Russell Sage Foundation.

Bryk, A.S., Sebring, P.B., Kerbow, D., Rollow, S., & Easton, J. (1998). *Charting Chicago school reform.* Boulder, CO: Westview Press.

Clune, W.H. (1993). The best path to systemic education policy: Standard/centralized or differentiated/decentralized? *Educational Evaluation and Policy Analysis, 15*(3), 233-254.

Cohen, D.K., & Hill, H.C. (2000). Instructional policy and classroom performance: The mathematics reform in California. *Teachers College Record, 102*(2), 294-343.

Conley, D.T., & Goldman, P. (1994). Ten propositions for facilitative leadership. In J. Murphy & K.S. Louis (Eds.), *Reshaping the principalship: Insights from transformational reform efforts* (pp. 265-281). Thousand Oaks, CA: Corwin Press.

Crowther, F., Kaagan, S.S., Ferguson, M., & Hann, L. (2002). *Developing teacher leaders: How teacher leadership enhances school success.* Thousand Oaks, CA: Corwin Press.

Cuban, L. (1988). *The managerial imperative and the practice of leadership in schools.* Albany: SUNY Press.

Darling-Hammond, L. (1998). Teachers and teaching: Testing policy hypotheses from a national commission report. *Educational Researcher, 27*(1), 5-15.

Darling-Hammond, L., & McLaughlin, M.W. (1996). Policies that support professional development in an era of reform. In M.W. McLaughlin & I. Oberman (Eds.), *Teacher learning: New policies, new practices* (pp. 202-218). New York: Teachers College Press.

Desimone, L., Porter, A.C., Birman, B.F., Garet, M.S., & Yoon, K.S. (2002). How do district management and implementation strategies relate to the quality of the professional development that districts provide to teachers? *Teachers College Record, 104*(7), 1265-1312.

Elmore, R.F. (with Burney, D.). (1997). *Investing in teacher learning: Staff development and instructional improvement in Community School District #2, New York City.* New York: National Commission on Teaching and America's Future.

Elmore, R.F. (2000). *Building a new structure for school leadership.* Washington, DC: Albert Shanker Institute.

Elmore, R.F. (2002). Bridging the gap between standards and achievement: The imperative for professional development in education. Washington, DC: Albert Shanker Institute.

Fullan, M. (2001). *Leading in a culture of change.* San Francisco: Jossey-Bass.

Gamoran, A., Anderson, C.W., Quiroz, P.A., Secada, W.G., Williams, T., & Ashmann, S. (2003). *Transforming teaching in math and science: How schools and districts can support change.* New York: Teachers College Press.

Goertz, M.E., Floden, R.E., & O'Day, J. (1996). *Systemic reform.* Washington, DC: Office of Educational Research and Improvement.

Goldring, E.B., & Rallis, S.F. (1993). *Principals of dynamic schools: Taking charge of change.* Newbury Park, CA: Corwin Press.

Goodlad, J.L. (1983). The school as workplace. In G.A. Griffin (Ed.). *Staff development. The Eighty-second yearbook of the National Society for the Study of Education,* Part II (pp. 36-61). Chicago: National Society for the Study of Education.

Hallinger, P., & Heck, R.H. (1996). Reassessing the principal's role in school effectiveness: A review of empirical research, 1980-1995. *Educational Administration Quarterly, 32*(1), 5-44.

Hallinger, P., & Heck, R.H. (1998). Exploring the principal's contribution to school effectiveness: 1980-1995. *School Effectiveness and School Improvement, 9*(2), 157-191.

Hargreaves, A. (1995). Development and desire: A postmodern perspective. In T.R. Guskey & M. Huberman (Eds.), *Professional development in education: New paradigms & practices* (pp. 9-34). New York: Teachers College Press.

Johnson, S.M. (1990). *Teachers at work: Achieving success in our schools.* New York: Basic Books.

King, M.B. (2002). Professional development to promote school wide inquiry. *Teaching and Teacher Education, 18,* 243-257, 2002.

King, M.B., & Newmann, F.M. (2000). Will teacher learning advance school goals? *Phi Delta Kappan, 81*(8), 576-580.

King, M.B., Newmann, F.M., & Youngs, P. (1999). *District initiatives to build school capacity: The role of professional development.* Madison, WI: Wisconsin Center for Education Research, University of Wisconsin-Madison.

Knapp, M.S., Copland, M.A., & Talbert, J.E. (2003). *Leading for learning: Reflective tools for school and district leaders.* Seattle, WA: Center for the Study of Teaching and Policy, University of Washington.

Ladwig, J.G., & King, M.B. (2003). *Education systems and school organizational capacity: A cross-national analysis.* Paper presented at the annual meeting of the American Educational Research Association, Chicago.

Lee, V.E., & Smith, J.B. (1996). Collective responsibility for learning and its effects on gains in achievement for early secondary students. *American Journal of Education, 104*(1), 103-147.

Leithwood, K. (1994). Leadership for school restructuring. *Educational Administration Quarterly, 30*(4), 498-518.

Leithwood, K.A., & Louis, K.S. (Eds.). (1999). *Organizational learning and school improvement: Linkages and strategies.* Lisse, Netherlands: Swets and Zeitlinger.

Little, J.W. (1993). Teachers' professional development in a climate of educational reform. *Educational Evaluation and Policy Analysis, 15*(2), 129-151.

Little, J.W. (1999). Organizing schools for teacher learning. In L. Darling-Hammond & G. Sykes (Eds.). *Teaching as a learning profession: Handbook of policy and practice* (pp. 376-411). San Francisco: Jossey-Bass.

Louis, K.S., Kruse, S.D., & Associates. (1995). *Professionalism and community: Perspectives on reforming urban schools.* Thousand Oaks, CA: Corwin Press.

Louis, K.S., Kruse, S.D., & Marks, H.M. (1996). School-wide professional community: Teachers' work, intellectual quality, and commitment. In F.M. Newmann & Associates, *Authentic achievement: Restructuring schools for intellectual quality* (pp.179-203). San Francisco: Jossey-Bass.

Louis, K.S., & Marks, H.M. (1998). Does professional community affect the classroom? Teachers' work and student experiences in restructuring schools. *American Journal of Education, 106*(4), 532-575.

Louis, K.S., & Marks, H.M. (1999). Teacher empowerment and the capacity for organizational learning. *Educational Administration Quarterly, 3*(5), 707-750.

Lowry, C. (Ed.). (1908). *The relation of superintendents and principals to the training and professional improvement of their teachers. The seventh yearbook of the National Society for the Scientific Study of Education* (pp. 11-66). Bloomington, IL: Public School Publishing Company.

Lytle, S.J., & Cochran-Smith, M. (1994). Inquiry, knowledge, and practice. In S. Hollingsworth & H. Sockett (Eds.), *Teacher research and educational reform. The Ninety-third yearbook of the National Society of Education,* Part I (pp. 22-51). Chicago: National Society for the Study of Education.

Massell, D., & Goertz, M.E. (2002). District strategies for building instructional capacity. In A. Hightower, M.S. Knapp, J.A. Marsh, & M.W. McLaughlin (Eds.), *School districts and instructional renewal* (pp. 43-60). New York: Teachers College Press.

McDonald, J.P. (2001). Students' work and teachers' learning. In A. Lieberman & L. Miller (Eds.). *Teachers caught in the action: Professional development that matters* (pp. 209-235). New York: Teachers College Press.

McLaughlin, M.W., & Talbert, J.E. (2001). *Professional communities and the work of high school teaching.* Chicago: University of Chicago Press.

McLaughlin, M.W., & Talbert, J.E. (2002). Reforming districts. In A. Hightower, M.S. Knapp, J.A. Marsh, & M.W. McLaughlin (Eds.). *School districts and instructional renewal* (pp. 173-192). New York: Teachers College Press.

McNeil, L. (2000). *Contradictions of school reform: Educational costs of standardized testing.* New York: Routledge.

Newmann, F.M. (1993). Beyond common sense in educational restructuring: The issues of content and linkage. *Educational Researcher, 22*(2), 4-13, 22.

Newmann, F.M., King, M.B., & Youngs, P. (2000). Professional development that addresses school capacity: Lessons from urban elementary schools. *American Journal of Education, 108*(4), 259-299.

Newmann, F.M., Smith, B., Allensworth, E., & Bryk, A.S. (2001). Instructional program coherence: What it is and why it should guide school improvement policy. *Educational Evaluation and Policy Analysis, 23*(4), 297-321.

Ogawa, R.T., & Bossert, S.T. (2000). Leadership as an organizational quality. In *The Jossey-Bass reader on educational leadership* (pp. 38-58). San Francisco: Jossey-Bass.

Renyi, J. (1996). *Teachers take charge of their learning: Transforming professional development for student success.* Washington, DC: National Foundation for the Improvement of Education.

Richardson, V. (Ed.). (1994). *Teacher change and the staff development process: A case in reading instruction.* New York: Teachers College Press.

Slavin, R.E. (1997). *Sand, bricks, and seeds: School change strategies and readiness for reform.* Baltimore: Center for Research on the Education of Students Placed at Risk, Johns Hopkins University.

Slavin, R.E., Madden, N.A., Dolan, L.J., & Wasik, B.A. (1996). *Every child, every school: Success for all.* Newbury Park, CA: Corwin.

Smylie, M.A. (1996). From bureaucratic control to building human capital: The importance of teacher learning in educational reform. *Educational Researcher, 25*(9), 9-11.

Smylie, M.A., Allensworth, E., Greenberg, R.C., Harris, R., & Luppescu, S. (2001). *Teacher professional development in Chicago: Supporting effective practice.* Chicago: Consortium on Chicago School Research.

Smylie, M.A., & Hart, A.W. (1999). School leadership for teacher learning and change: A human and social capital development perspective. In J. Murphy & K.S. Louis (Eds.). *Handbook of research on educational administration* (2nd ed., pp. 421-441). San Francisco: Jossey-Bass.

Spillane, J.P. (1996). School districts matter: Local educational authorities and state instructional policy. *Educational Policy, 10*(1), 63-87.

Spillane, J.P., Halverson, R., & Diamond, J.B. (2001). Distributed leadership: Toward a theory of school leadership practice. *Educational Researcher, 30*(3), 23-28.

Spillane, J.P., & Jennings, N.E. (1997). Aligned instructional policy and ambitious pedagogy: Exploring instructional reform from the classroom perspective. *Teachers College Record, 98*(3), 449-481.

Spillane, J.P., & Thompson, C.L. (1997). Reconstructing conceptions of local capacity: The local education agency's capacity for ambitious educational reform. *Educational Evaluation and Policy Analysis, 19*(2), 185-203.

Stein, M.K., & D'Amico, L. (1998). *Content-driven instructional reform in Community School District #2.* Pittsburgh, PA: Learning Research and Development Center, University of Pittsburgh.

KING325

Togneri, W. (2003). *Beyond islands of excellence: What districts can do to improve instruction and achievement in all schools—A leadership brief.* Washington, DC: Learning First Alliance.

Togneri, W., & Anderson, S.E. (2003). Beyond islands of excellence: What districts can do to improve instruction and achievement in all schools. Washington, DC: Learning First Alliance.

Tyack, D. (2002). Forgotten players: How local school districts shaped American education. In A. Hightower, M.S. Knapp, J.A. Marsh, & M.W. McLaughlin (Eds.). *School districts and instructional renewal* (pp. 9-24). New York: Teachers College Press.

Useem, E.L., Christman, J.B., Gold, E., & Simon, E. (1997). Reforming alone: Barriers to organizational learning in urban school change initiatives. *Journal of Education for Students Placed at Risk, 2,* 55-78.

Weiner, E.J. (2003). Secretary Paulo Freire and the democratization of power: Toward a theory of transformative leadership. *Educational Philosophy and Theory, 35*(1), 89-106.

Youngs, P. (2000). *Connections between district policy related to professional development and school capacity in urban elementary schools.* Madison, WI: Wisconsin Center for Education Research, University of Wisconsin-Madison.

Youngs, P., & King, M.B. (2002). Principal leadership for professional development to build school capacity. *Educational Administration Quarterly, 38*(5), 643-670.

CHAPTER 11

Teacher Unions and the Teaching Workforce: Mismatch or Vital Contribution?

NINA BASCIA

While the focus on improving teaching and learning affords an opportunity for the state to exercise proactive leadership, realistically speaking, there are limits to what can be accomplished through the vehicle of state policy action. Establishing and sustaining quality teaching is equally dependent on the capacity of organizations and networks at regional, district and school levels to productively engage in improvement efforts that are realized in the classroom. (Shields & Knapp, 1997)

When educational policy analysts and policymakers speak in terms of the "teacher workforce," they are articulating concerns about the daunting challenge of ensuring an adequate number of teachers to address the educational needs of the vast number of children and youth in public school systems. Such concerns have been raised with the most urgency in times, like these, of population growth through significant immigration or increases in the native birth rate, and in times of significant teacher turnover, when a generational cohort of educators retires or when large numbers of teachers, dissatisfied with a teaching career, leave before retirement. The "teacher workforce" evokes military and industrial images, huge numbers of workers who must be trained, deployed, and managed. Efficiency becomes the paramount virtue, and centralized, hierarchical controls seem the obvious strategy. Systemic reform—that is, the coordination of recruitment, preparation, and retention efforts across levels of government and across institutions within the greater educational infrastructure—seems the logical solution.

Held up against these images, teacher unions appear at best anomalous and at worst counterproductive: unless aligned in both purpose

Nina Bascia is Chair of the Department of Theory & Policy Studies at the Ontario Institute for Studies in Education of the University of Toronto (OISE/UT). She is the author of *Unions in Teachers' Professional Lives* and co-editor of *The Contexts of Teaching in Secondary Schools, Making a Difference about Difference, The Sharp Edge of Educational Change*, and *The International Handbook on Educational Policy*.

and function with other organizations in order to ensure compliance and quality control in relation to centralized authority, what useful role could they perform? Indeed, assessments of teacher unions' impact on the educational infrastructure most often reflect this viewpoint, either implicitly or explicitly. Unions themselves have been struggling to articulate a convincing answer to this question as the educational reform context has changed and their desire to improve their effectiveness as educational players has increased. What is the useful contribution of organizations whose primary function is to advocate for teachers and who sit partly inside and partly outside of the formal educational authority structure?

This chapter draws attention to two of the major and unique contributions teacher unions have made to the quality of the teacher workforce over the past several decades. It draws from more than a decade of research on U.S. and Canadian teacher unions' roles in both the backwaters and the frontiers of educational reform (Bascia, 1994, 1997, 1998a, 1998b, 1998c, 2000, 2001, 2003, in press; Bascia, Stiegelbauer, Jacka, Watson, & Fullan, 1997; Lieberman & Bascia, 1991). Some of this research (e.g., Bascia et al.; Lieberman & Bascia) was commissioned on behalf of union organizations concerned about their ability to improve the quality of educational practice. Other studies (e.g., Bascia, 1994, 2000, 2003) were part of larger research projects that explored the relative impact of a variety of influences on teaching quality.

Specifically, this chapter describes unions' efforts with respect to attracting and retaining teachers (otherwise known as teacher compensation and the conditions of teaching) and to improving the quality of teachers' professional preparation and ongoing learning. By recasting these relatively familiar but undervalued union priorities (compensation and working conditions) and by illuminating their often overlooked work (with respect to teachers' professional learning), the chapter challenges educational policy research that suggests unions ought to either profoundly change, have their impact reduced, or disappear entirely. Unions are in a unique position to enhance the quality of the teacher workforce in meaningful and potentially measurable ways, and we ignore their real and potential contributions at our peril. No other organization or entity can identify, report, and respond to the work-related needs of the teaching profession the way unions can. No other entity can combine the strengths of playing both insider and outsider roles within the larger educational infrastructure—working across levels and in many locations and, while lacking in formal authority, able to critique, challenge, and seek alternative solutions to educational problems.

The section that follows provides a historical overview of teacher unions' presence and activities with respect to educational policy and practice, noting both the enduring challenges these organizations face and the unique roles they perform. Two sections take up in detail the motives, opportunities, and impact of unions with respect to teacher attraction and retention and teachers' preparation and professional learning. A fourth section identifies the conditions necessary to ensure that unions can make these contributions. The final section returns to the notion of the workforce metaphor, revealing some of its pitfalls and suggesting a reconceptualization of the terms by which teacher quality is ensured.

A Whirlwind History of Teacher Unions

The evolution of teachers' organizations, not surprisingly, has occurred in ways that parallel the evolution of the larger educational infrastructure. The establishment of large urban educational systems occurred about a century ago; the emergence of these infrastructures created a new bureaucratic order organized hierarchically and governed by administrative "experts" who asserted their authority to tell teachers, for the first time, what and how to teach (Darling-Hammond, 1997; Tyack & Hansot, 1982). One enduring result of the educational systems' blueprint has been that this power structure has been hardwired in, so to speak: not only has the dominant status of administrators been maintained, but the involvement of teachers in educational policymaking has remained much more tenuous (Carlson, 1992). At the same time, this educational authority structure has frequently been challenged by teachers as well as parents and others (Larson, 1977; Murphy, 1990; Smaller, 1991; Urban, 1982).

Within the educational establishment, the most common standard to which teacher unions have been held, since their inception, is the degree to which their priorities are congruent with prevailing policy directions and administrative preferences. Teachers' organizations first became the focus of policy research with the passage of legislation enabling collective bargaining in the 1960s and 1970s, when decision makers had to contend with a newly organized and stronger union presence. The literature that emerged during this period first raised concerns about the potential challenges unions might pose to state/province-, district-, and school-level administrative discretion (Johnson,

1983, 1984; Kerchner & Mitchell, 1986; Lawton, Bedard, MacLellan, & Li, 1999).

To a great extent, teacher unions' effectiveness is shaped by formal educational policy system parameters. Educational labor law took a big step forward when teachers' organizations' formal representative role was recognized for the first time, but this recognition was provisional, a "great compromise" that set serious limits on their roles. U.S. states and Canadian provinces, which have constitutional jurisdiction over educational policy, determine whether collective bargaining is permitted and by what terms it will be carried out. In the main, teacher unions can negotiate on their members' behalf with respect to compensation, other benefits, and working conditions, but formal decision making about substantive issues is the purview of legislators and administrators (Carlson, 1992). In schools, at the district level, and with respect to the educational policymaking processes of the state/province, the substantive involvement of union members (teachers), staff, and elected officials in decision making is subject to the willingness of administrators and elected officials to involve them or consider their input. While labor laws can be modified and the productivity of working relationships between union staff and decision makers certainly varies, the basic terms of union involvement restrict them from participating as equal or even consistently effective partners in educational decision making (Bascia, 1998b; Carlson; Larson, 1977).

In recent years, the trend in the U.S. and Canada has been toward increased centralized control (through state/provincial legislation) of significant domains of what had formerly been negotiated locally, including teacher salary, class size, and other working conditions. Further, several Canadian provinces have systematically reduced unions' authority by revising labor law, weakening membership requirements, and establishing new bodies called "colleges of teachers," touted as "teachers' real professional organizations," which set and regulate teaching qualifications, standards of conduct, and the terms for teachers' initial and continuing certification. Provincial establishment of such entities tends, both in real and symbolic terms, to displace some of the limited authority Canadian teacher unions have had. All of these trends further marginalize teacher unions' efforts to work in the larger educational system on their members' behalf.

The media and policy researchers alike tend to criticize teacher unions by maintaining the perspective that compliance should be the standard by which these organizations' actions are judged. But teacher

330 TEACHER UNIONS AND THE TEACHING WORKFORCE

unions are not a common topic of research. When they do attract the attention of policy analysts, teacher unions have often been viewed as focused on inappropriate goals, such as increasing teacher salary even in tight fiscal contexts, and with promoting ineffective solutions rather than promoting quality teaching and learning. Most educational policy research has viewed unions as not quite legitimate decision makers, at best benign or irrelevant, but frequently obstructive, rarely visionary, and tending to promote mediocrity. For example, in their influential work on systemic reform, Marshall Smith and Jennifer O'Day wrote, "If the union emphasis in contract negotiations is only on increases in salaries and benefits ... it will be very difficult for [a] district to ... develop a creative and productive instructional environment" (1990, p. 256). Such comments tend to be speculative, based on what "everybody knows" about teacher unions rather than grounded in solid evidence, since there is not much empirical research on unions' roles relative to educational quality, and much of the reform research has ignored unions or attempted to make do with scant evidence. Policy documents that have noted unions' productive reform efforts (e.g., National Commission on Teaching and America's Future, 1996) have been encouraged by a handful of individual cases of innovation rather than being able to report on more widespread trends.

Unions and Teacher Quality

While prevailing opinion assumes teacher unions are uncommitted to educational improvement, a closer reading of the research on these organizations suggests a somewhat different picture, that of organizations concerned about educational quality as it is manifested in and through teachers' work. This concern may be evident even when the directions unions choose appear to contradict prevailing policy preferences. While there has been much of a speculative nature written about the negative impact of union presence on educational practice, most actual empirical research has revealed a more nuanced picture, with union officials attempting to establish productive working relationships with district and school administrators and to compensate for the limitations of the educational bureaucracy (Kerchner & Mitchell, 1986; Johnson, 1983, 1984, 1987). Starting in the second half of the 1980s, Charles Kerchner and colleagues Douglas Mitchell and later Julia Koppich first articulated the work of, and then supported unions in adopting a stance of, "joint stewardship" for educational reform (Kerchner & Mitchell, 1988; Kerchner & Koppich, 1993). Joint stewardship trades adversarial for cooperative practices and works with district decision makers to support local school reform (Bascia, 1994; also Lieberman & Bascia, 1991; Rosow & Zager, 1989). Empirical studies that followed describe changes in local governance to involve union leaders as well as members in substantive decision making and various reforms in support of increased teacher quality, such as school- and district-level support, innovation in initial teacher education, recruitment, and retention, and a wide range of professional development strategies (Bascia, 1998a; Bascia et al., 1997; Johnson, 1988; Murray & Grant, 1998; Martin Macke, 1998).

Kerchner and Mitchell's assertion, in the late 1980s, that teacher unions were entering a new phase of their evolution, beyond organizing, contract maintenance, and adversarial relationships to cooperation and reform-mindedness, may have been a bit overconfident; evaluation research has also revealed the fragility of these new arrangements and the enduring, intractable nature of some major union concerns. But there is some evidence to support Kerchner and Mitchell's claims that these organizations are evolving (or are at least different from the ways most of the literature has portrayed them). In some cases, unions are less likely to assert their own interests at the "expense" of students and more likely to view quality teaching and learning as mutually supportive. Within these organizations are individuals who have read the research critical of teacher unions and are concerned about their organizations' capacities to respond effectively to a changing reform climate. As an organizational type, teacher unions are becoming more interested in and more able to initiate and support educational innovation.

Though it is not well documented (but see McClure, 1991; Ogawa, 1994; Rauth, 1990), there have been a range of recent efforts to "scale up" union reform—to expand the quality and quantity of unions' support for educational improvement. Staff in the offices of national teachers' organizations in both the U.S. and Canada have been supporting reform since at least the mid-1980s. Various networks of union organizations (sometimes supported by foundation funding) have sprung up to model what in the U.S. is sometimes called "the new unionism." Diverse examples abound (see, e.g., Bascia, 1998a). They include the network of California locals (both AFT and NEA affiliates) that developed "trust agreements" to support reform initiatives between 1989 and 1991 (Bascia, 1994; Lieberman & Bascia, 1991); the Learning Laboratories initiative, a nationwide network of local unions supporting reform, sponsored by the National Education Association (Bascia et al., 1997) in the later part of the 1990s; the National Coalition of Educational Activists, a grassroots organization of educators concerned about unions' ability to promote "social justice unionism" (Peterson & Charney, 1999); both the NEA and the AFT's commitment to the work of the National Board for Professional Teaching Standards; the Teacher Union Reform Network (TURN), a group of progressive union leaders focused on restructuring unions to promote reforms that lead to improved student learning; and both organizations' involvement in the Learning First Alliance, a coalition of national-level educators' groups (national member organizations of teachers, parents, teachers, curriculum specialists, school principals, administrators, school boards, state boards of education, chief state school officers, and schools of education) committed to improving student learning (see also King, this volume, chapter 10).

While they attempt to reposition themselves and to articulate more credible and convincing reasons to increase public and governmental support for teaching, it is important to recognize the particular domains where teacher unions have been working toward improving teaching quality for many decades. Unions' historical efforts in these areas represent powerful building blocks for future work rather than outmoded strategies that should be rejected in favor of new directions. The next section describes the logic behind and the nature of teacher union efforts with respect to attracting and retaining teachers and professional learning.

Initiating Strategies for Enhancing Attraction and Retention to Teaching

It is both ironic and troubling that teacher unions' traditional concerns about compensation and working conditions are perceived by many union researchers and the media as "self-interested," "mundane," and "nonprofessional," and yet these factors are so clearly fundamental to attracting and retaining individuals to teaching careers. They are persistent points of contention in local labor relations and, where salary and working conditions are set at the state level, in legislative agendas. They are also the "necessary conditions" (Alberta Teachers' Association, 1997) for teacher quality for which teacher unions are currently the only advocates.

Although influential policy documents such as Smith and O'Day's work on systemic reform (1990) and the report by the National Commission on Teaching and America's Future (1996) at least obliquely identified the importance of working conditions for teaching quality, resource support and attention to organizational arrangements and professional roles and relationships have been missing from standards-based and accountability-driven educational policy for several years.

Teachers' working conditions may be less salient to state/provincial policymakers because they cannot be as directly influenced by policy as other factors can. From policymakers' points of view, their influence on the quality of teaching and learning is not as immediate, direct, and straightforward as for other factors. They tend to cost real money, which has been in scarce supply. Resources, relationships, roles, an appropriate degree of professional autonomy, and opportunities to develop teaching skills both directly influence teaching quality and contribute to educators' sense of achievement and job satisfaction, serving to attract and retain teachers in general as well as to particular schools and districts (Johnson, 1990; McLaughlin, 1993; McLaughlin & Talbert, 2001).

The quality of teachers' working conditions has also been quite susceptible to erosion. From teachers' perspectives, working conditions are particularly sensitive to policy and administrative influence. Even while, on average, union contracts increase in size from year to year, the unpredictability of educational funding and the volatility of educational policy bring about changes in the type and degree of teachers' authority, their competence, and their professional relationships (Bascia, 1994). This issue was the straw that broke the camel's back in Washington State in recent years, prompting teacher demands that the state teachers' organization, the Washington Education Association, reduce its reform energies and redirect its attention exclusively toward increasing teacher compensation (Bascia, 2003).

Teachers are vocal when they are concerned about what they experience as inadequate or inappropriate working conditions (Bailey, 2000; Bascia, 1994, 2003). Further, teachers' concerns about the wisdom or feasibility of policy initiatives can get funneled through the narrow channel of demands for increased compensation and improved working conditions because these domains are permissible topics for negotiation (Bascia, 1994; see also Carlson, 1992; NCTAF, 1996).

Teacher unions can and do attempt to improve teachers' working conditions. The tools at their disposal—negotiating contractual items and influencing legislation through lobbying—might, for example, allow teachers some discretion on selecting teaching materials or reduce the likelihood that they would be assigned to courses and other responsibilities for which they were not prepared or competent. District-level (local) unions spend significant amounts of organizational time and effort attempting to ensure an adequate environment for teaching through the work of their legislative liaisons, collective bargaining staff, and elected union officials. In jurisdictions where teachers have no legal right to union representation (this is the case in 16 U.S. states, mostly in the South), union officials' interventions on teachers' behalf parallel, albeit less forcefully, those in settings such as New York City where the union has a strong reputation for contractual enforcement. In some union organizations, a number of designated union officials and staff spend about half of their time visiting schools. Union staff interventions may reflect more than mere concern that contractual agreements be upheld and administrative authority be scrutinized: evidence suggests many attempts to negotiate resolutions to tensions and disagreements between teachers and principals; to get to the root of conflicts by attempting to determine what organizational conditions might be challenging effective teaching and learning; and to help solve practical problems by providing information, training, and other resources.

Teacher compensation, one of the very few issues that can be directly bargained over, serves as a symbolic flashpoint both for teachers (in terms of their beliefs that the school system and the public value their work; see Bascia, 1994) and for the media and the public (in terms of evidence that teachers are "selfish"). Concerns about the ability to attract qualified teachers are the basis for teacher unions' arguments for raising teacher salaries to levels competitive with other occupations, and in the case of some states and districts, with teacher salaries in other locales. In the reform literature, compensation is often discussed in terms of the viability of a "career ladder" with accompanying differential salary, or other types of incentives for teachers' demonstrated competence. Such discussions—and lack of understanding over teachers' typically low enthusiasm for such schemes—do not address the both real and symbolic dimension of teacher compensation relative to other occupational choices they might make.

How much difference do unions' efforts in these domains make? Even though there have been no studies that attempt to capture the direct relationship between union vigilance and teacher attraction and retention, several kinds of evidence suggest their importance. First, teachers who leave teaching identify the quality of working conditions as the major factor influencing their decision (McLaughlin & Yee, 1988; Yee, 1990). Second, teachers themselves—even those who express concern about specific aspects of unions' activities—consistently report their belief in the necessity of a union presence to provide a check against what they view as "administrative excesses" (Bascia, 1994). On the other hand, given the prevailing tendencies of the educational system to discount the importance of working conditions and to view teachers' concerns about them as mere whining, unions' contract enforcement serves more as a check against too much erosion of support for teaching rather than ensuring a consistently high level of support for teaching. An educational system seriously committed to retaining good teachers must recognize the importance of working conditions to teaching quality.

Initiating and Supporting Teachers' Professional Learning

Teachers' professional learning, both prior to and during a teaching career, has long been a significant focus of teacher unions' efforts, the "other side" of what these organizations have offered for many decades (see Bascia, 1998a, and especially 2000; McClure, 1991, 1992; Rauth, 1990). This organizational priority—unions' service to their members— has been overlooked in the teacher union research, which has focused on the domains of labor relations and legislative influence, that is, unions' relationships with decision makers. On the flip side, research on teacher development, teacher learning, and teaching careers has focused almost exclusively on the more traditional providers of train- ing, such as universities and school districts, and has missed the impor- tant and unique roles unions have played with respect to professional development along several dimensions. Indeed, the "public" image of unions maintains that they are uninterested in teacher learning, tend to "trade" compensation for learning opportunities during contract nego- tiations, and encourage teachers to resist professional learning pro- vided by their employers or required by state/provincial mandate.

Like collective bargaining and governmental liaison units, profes- sional development departments, committees, and budget lines are standard elements of nearly all teacher union organizations. Profes- sional development is a constitutional requirement for many local unions in both the U.S. and Canada; central state/provincial and national offices often provide materials, speakers, ideas, and funding for affiliated local unions that seek them. One important service teacher unions traditionally have offered, then, is the direct and indi- rect provision of learning opportunities for teachers. In this way, to a greater or lesser extent, unions have either augmented or compen- sated for the availability of such learning opportunities to educators.

Such opportunities may, and often do, take the form of traditional staff development workshops. But many unions have also developed or adopted models for new forms of learning, based on teachers' own expressed understandings of what is lacking elsewhere in the edu- cational system. Educational researchers have been advocating for improvements in initial and ongoing teacher learning—a movement away from short, fragmented, Socratic delivery, which emphasizes the technical dimensions of teaching, toward the development of more opportunities for teachers to move between actual classroom practice and sophisticated skill building and complex problem solving with other practitioners (e.g., Cochran-Smith, 1991; Cochran-Smith & Lytle, 1992; Little, 1990, 1993). Teachers' organizations have been laying the groundwork for the actualization of such opportunities. A number of recently adopted innovations in teacher learning either originated in or received crucial organizational sponsorship from teacher unions.

Many of the earliest programmatic attempts at providing support for new teachers in their first teaching years—commonly known as new teacher induction and mentoring programs—were initiated by unions, starting in the late 1980s and early 1990s, out of a concern that neither principals, district personnel, nor schools of education were adequately helping educators manage the challenging transition into full-time teaching (Bascia, 1994; Kerchner & Koppich, 1993). A widespread and powerful example of these efforts is "peer review": Starting in the late 1980s in dozens of districts across the U.S., including most famously Cincinnati, Rochester, and Poway, California, new teachers have been receiving intensive in-classroom support in their first two years of teaching from released veteran teachers. Modeling and critiquing lessons, providing materials, arranging visits, and suggesting other professional learning strategies, mentors ultimately also have the authority to evaluate novice teachers and to recommend either their permanent contracts or their dismissal (Bascia; Kerchner & Koppich). Peer review not only provides the most substantive support for new teachers but also represents a switch for teacher unions, from protecting teachers' jobs under any circumstances to actively ensuring teacher quality.

Teacher unions have also pioneered and championed innovative professional learning strategies for teachers beyond their first years. Even while many teachers' organizations continue to provide traditional staff development options, such as annual workshop days, many have worked to establish the conditions for more directly teaching-related, school-based learning opportunities. Many district-level unions have negotiated the establishment of school-based professional development committees and the devolution of professional development funds and decision making to schools so that teachers can participate in selecting professional development content and processes that best match their priorities and interests, and can consider specific problems of practice in relation to new concepts and skills. An interesting innovation in New York State (concentrated in New York City) are the so-called Teacher Centers, union supported (and state funded), where trained teacher-facilitators are placed in low-performing schools to work with educators, and sometimes parents, to develop ongoing, comprehensive curriculum and pedagogical improvement projects. In both the U.S. and Canada, in order for teachers to extend their learning beyond the boundaries of their own schools and colleagues, some teachers' organizations support district- and province-wide subject- and program-based professional development networks so that teachers can focus their professional development more specifically to their teaching.

Training administrators as well as teacher leaders, parents, and other community partners is increasingly seen as crucial to ensuring collective responsibility for quality educational delivery; a growing number of unions in both countries provide school-, community-, and region-based learning opportunities for others beyond the teaching force. Many state and provincial organizations in both countries connect learning resources with schools and districts, tailor their offerings to incorporate local learning priorities and improvement goals, and even assume responsibility for developing and implementing wide-scale training. For example, in Canada, the Alberta Teachers' Association has designed and provided training for administrators and teachers with respect to using a new provincial performance appraisal system and for the educators and community members forming newly legislated school councils. In such cases, a teachers' organization can support both the purpose and the content of training—for example, less punitive and more pedagogically focused performance appraisals or more skilled, democratic councils.

One way teacher unions have contributed to educators' professional learning, then, is by serving as organizational test beds and sponsors of innovations in teacher learning that in time may gain wider currency across networks of union affiliates, become enshrined in state/provincial legislation, or end up cosponsored or adopted by district administrators. Another is to become direct or indirect providers of professional training. A third is to establish structural supports (time, money, and other resources) for teachers' ongoing learning through state/provincial lobbying efforts or district-level contract negotiations. Some teacher unions have worked extensively beyond their own organizational borders to ensure the provision of higher quality professional development

for educators. Some Canadian provincial federations have long traditions of substantive involvement in redesigning (and sometimes helping
deliver) initial teacher education programs, and a range of cooperative
experimental projects have sprung up across the U.S. between teacher
unions and colleges of education (Bascia, in press). Even more fundamentally, some unions in both countries have attempted to re-create
and improve upon eroding infrastructures that supported teacher learning in the past through the establishment of regional professional
development councils. In mundane but important ways, unions have
worked to ensure infrastructure support for professional development
by incorporating funds, time, and incentives in drafting state legislation
and collective agreements (contracts).

How much difference have these efforts made? It is not possible to
isolate the provision of professional learning opportunities from other
teaching conditions in order to compare them with gains in student
learning; but there is clear evidence that educators value these innovations (Bascia 1994, 1998b). Developed by educators, such innovations
have become more common as they have not only spread from one
union organization to another but also have been adopted by districts
and states. Without them—whether traditional or innovative—in
times of fiscal scarcity and diminished offerings, educators would have
few learning opportunities at all.

The Relative Advantages of Teachers' Organizations

The previous two sections have described the two most consistent
domains of teacher union effort. Compensation and working conditions, critical to attracting and retaining teachers and to ensuring some
level of quality of teaching practice, are the legally recognized purview
of unions and, unfortunately, domains for which teachers' associations
are the only organizational advocates. Teacher unions also have been
responsible for the development and institutionalization of innovative,
promising forms of preservice and ongoing professional learning for
teachers and others involved in the educational enterprise, helping
make these more practically relevant, intellectually engaging, and
firmly grounded in principles of adult informal learning.

Many of the initiatives and priorities described in this chapter are
common across teacher organizations, but no single union organization has either the resources or the intellectual capacity to cover all the
bases: while concerns about attracting, retaining, and training teachers
are common, specific organizations address them in particular ways,

based on the experienced needs and interests not only of union-active educators and staffs but of their teacher members, and shaped by the social, economic, and policy environments. The legal tools available to them may limit their options, and many of these reform ideas are borrowed from other union organizations within and across the two countries, but unions are most strongly influenced by their members' particular needs.

Further, union organizations are able to focus their attention on these issues to greater or lesser degrees and with varying levels of success. One reason for this variation stems from the ways in which these organizations have been marginalized vis-à-vis the formal educational system, and in particular the ways in which union concerns have so frequently appeared to challenge and resist the reform priorities of states/provinces and school districts. Union staff spend significant time and energy establishing and reestablishing their credibility with decision makers—time and energy that would otherwise be spent developing new programs. Their efforts must be more modest than those of other actors in the formal educational system because their resource capacity is far less (however, one of the ways that teacher organizations have begun to work more effectively in recent years is by pooling resources and by attracting funds from both foundations and from the government to provide educational services). A third reason, discussed more fully below, is that while teacher organizations' serious and thoughtful commitment to teaching quality appears to have been deepening and broadening in recent years, this is only a general trend, and individual organizations' success depends both on its *internal capacity* and on factors within the greater environment with which the union interacts, which might be understood as *external capacity*.

Internal capacity. Just as superintendents, ministers, and principals perform uniquely important roles in the success of states/provinces, districts, and schools in supporting quality teaching and learning, enlightened teacher union leadership is certainly one dimension of teacher union success in promoting teacher quality. But all of these organizations are obviously influenced by more than their administrative heads; other actors and factors also contribute to their effectiveness. Many studies have demonstrated that union leaders who develop reform-minded relationships with educational administrators or policymakers independently of their staffs, members, and organizations cannot sustain meaningful reform (Bascia, 1994, 2003; Bascia et al., 1997; Kerchner & Koppich, 1993; Johnson, 1988; Martin Macke,

1998). A growing number of organizations, however, have deepened and broadened their efforts through and beyond their leadership by ensuring the viability of organizational structure, relationships with members, and effective work for staff. Intellectual capacity—the ability to gather and make use of information, to generate ideas, to make sense of challenging conditions, and to see a clear direction to move—requires more than the skills of a single enlightened leader. It requires the recognition that the organization needs to continually be aware of and adapt to changing social conditions; demonstrate a willingness and ability to seek out new ideas, try new strategies, and learn from mistakes; take on multiple projects simultaneously; eschew orthodoxy in terms of relationships with both teachers and decision makers; and be simultaneously protectionist and reforming. This ongoing organizational learning can be deliberately fostered by paying attention to union structure and dynamics—by minimizing boundaries between the organization and the field, by minimizing internal organizational fragmentation and balkanization, and by seeking information and ideas voraciously and from multiple sources (see Bascia, 2000, and especially Bascia, in press, for a description of a Canadian teachers' association that exhibits these characteristics).

It is all too easy for teachers' organization staff, like other educational bureaucrats, to lose touch with educational practice, especially if staff and officials spend little time in the field or if they tend to come from a limited range of educational backgrounds. It is all too common for teachers' organizations to be driven by the needs and interests of one group of educators and ignore another (for example, elementary vs. secondary, urban vs. suburban). Careful attention to encouraging a range of special interest groups and fostering mutually respectful working relationships between elected officials and staff all help expand the range of information and ideas at the organization's disposal. By hiring educators from many backgrounds, organizations can provide a wide array of organizational services and fulfill multiple priorities. Tensions that can exist between elected officials and organized staff can be mitigated by careful organizational planning.

Another type of organizational capacity, of course, is derived from a union's resource base. Organizational size and diversification play a role in a union's ability to extend its efforts across multiple arenas of activity. Fiscal resources—dues collected from a sizeable membership base, the ability to recognize the potential value of grants from affiliate organizations and other sources of money (e.g., foundations, state departments of education, partners)—create opportunities to launch, support, or challenge the policy initiatives of others. All things being equal, larger district unions clearly have an edge over smaller locals; provincial/state-level organizations have the potential to do many things (though their distance from local classrooms and teachers' organizational loyalty can be a problem; see Bascia, 1994; Olson, 1965). The size, talents, and diversity of staff are also an important dimension of teacher unions' resource base: the more productive unions recruit individuals with practical experience in a variety of domains, provide them with a range of activities and contacts to enhance their understanding of how to work effectively within the larger educational system, and enable them to develop their skills and interests over a number of years to enhance their commitment and knowledge base. Balancing democratizing strategies that potentially bring more, and more diverse, leaders into the organization with strategies to ensure that individuals have opportunities to learn how to navigate the broader educational system over many years is an important organizational skill.

A third type of internal capacity is the union's ability to effectively articulate a link between immediate teacher work-related concerns and more future-oriented activities, to both address teachers' needs and to maintain members' support while engaging effectively with organizational players in the larger educational system. There are many examples in the research of union leaders who have been unable to communicate the logical link between present and future, of teachers feeling abandoned by their organizations and union organizations being forced to retrench (see Bascia 1994; Bascia et al., 1997). Being able to pull off this balance is strongly linked to unions' external capacity as well.

External capacity. Teacher unions obviously do not function in a vacuum; they work within the larger educational milieu. Beyond the legal conditions that shape unions' work, they also must contend with what might be called the operative discursive or conceptual framework that underlie contemporary educational policy goals. Two sets of related notions seem especially germane to how deeply and effectively unions can contribute to educational reform. The first pertains to prevailing thinking about teaching and teachers; the second focuses more specifically on assumptions about teacher unions themselves.

As noted earlier, the prevailing model of systemic reform emphasizes centralized state control and a strengthened administrative structure, standards, and policies that emphasize compliance and reduce funding for education while encouraging a significant turnover within the teaching force. This model and these conditions have emerged from but also have reinforced a conception of teaching as technical work and teachers as technicians (see Bascia & Hargreaves, 2000; Darling-Hammond, 1997). This perspective stands in sharp contrast with the prevailing assumptions embedded in the reforms of the later 1980s, which viewed teaching as intellectual work. Expectations that good teaching is a matter of obedience and compliance, and that poor teaching is the result of resistance, deny the possibility of both informed judgment by teachers and the importance of the quality of teachers' working conditions—fiscal and human resources, professional relationships, opportunities to learn, and so on. When a technical conception of teaching prevails, teachers' concerns as expressed through their unions are viewed as insubordination or irrelevance. Further, when a technical conception of teaching prevails, unions must necessarily focus on attempting to improve basic conditions.

Related to prevailing conceptions of teachers are assumptions about the actual and potential roles of their organizations. The limits of teacher unions' legal purview contribute to a view of these organizations as labor oriented rather than professionally oriented (see Carlson, 1992; Larson, 1977; Mitchell & Kerchner, 1983). Labor unions tend to lack the credibility as well as the right to influence policy or shape practice; in some jurisdictions, even where administrators and policymakers appreciate (and in some cases rely upon) the union's resource base in light of system infrastructure needs, their ability to participate as credible partners in shaping educational policy and practice is tenuous at best.

In Canada, where provinces have authority comparable to U.S. states over educational policy and where similar efforts to align system efforts with standards also prevail, teachers' organizations have recently lost significant ground with respect to the terms and purview of bargaining and their roles in helping shape provincial education policy (Bascia, 1999, 2002, in press). Some have actually managed to claim a high moral ground and to take advantage of emerging gaps in service delivery to shape the nature of school programs (developing curricula, providing professional development, and even defining the terms of school-based management frameworks). But others have responded in increasingly reactive ways, urging teachers to refuse to comply with government mandates, offering fewer supports for teaching, and engendering increased tensions with the public as well as with their members. The tensions experienced in these jurisdictions, and in those U.S. states and districts where unions must concentrate on ensuring a minimal quality of working conditions, suggest that possessing sufficient internal capacity to "take the high road" with respect to educational reform is necessary but not sufficient in policy settings where teacher unions are extremely disadvantaged relative to the power of the formal administrative hierarchy.

Conclusion: Taking Unions Seriously

This chapter has considered both the particular roles teacher unions play and the unique substantive contributions they have made with respect to improving the quality of teaching. Evidence drawn from a number of studies of union activity in both the U.S. and Canada suggests that, particularly within a larger educational policy environment that takes their contributions seriously, teacher unions provide several important functions not duplicated by other institutional actors. In advocating for the conditions teachers find especially salient with respect to their work, teachers' organizations are most directly concerned with attracting and retaining teachers. In mounting and ensuring innovative programs for teachers' professional learning, they have done as much if not more than any other entity to improve the quality of teaching practice.

Why have these efforts not been better documented? One reason is that most policy analysis has focused on the educational system's formal administrative and decision making structures, to which unions are peripheral and whose priorities often have seemed rather diverse. But unions themselves also have only recently come to recognize that they must take responsibility for making their own case, publicizing their successes and the legitimacy of their concerns—and, ultimately, for reframing the public and media discourse not only about unions themselves but about teachers and teaching more generally. Starting with the National Education Association under president Bob Chase in the late 1990s, a number of organizations in both countries have devoted sizeable resources to mounting a public relations campaign in support of public education. Unions increasingly attend to the ways they speak about themselves and to redefining themselves as proactive champions of quality education rather than reactive supporters of one occupation's narrow interests.

Given the importance of teacher attraction, retention, and professional learning to teacher quality, it is appropriate to suggest that teacher unions have played a fundamentally critical role in the state of the teacher workforce. They have been able to do this because, despite their marginal positions, they possess some unique advantages with respect to their roles, responsibilities, and resources.

Beyond the durability afforded by internal constitutional decree, labor regulation, and habits of mind, unions' sustained involvement in the areas of attraction, retention, and professional learning represent their attention to concerns of most immediate relevance and concern to teachers. These issues arise from the actual conditions of practice identified by educators themselves (Bascia, 1994). In structural terms, teacher unions represent a singularly significant source of feedback to the broader educational system about the conditions of teaching and learning in general and potentially effective solutions to problems in particular. In essence, while much policy effort in both the U.S. and Canada over the past decade or so has concentrated on aligning and harmonizing resources and expectations, teacher unions can be seen as playing important corrective functions when support for teaching is inadequate, when implementation plans are unworkable, or when the fundamental logic of reform is flawed.

Further, by virtue of their insider-outsider position with respect to the formal educational authority structure, their ongoing relationships with other educational stakeholders, and in particular what they afford their teacher members in terms of organizational sponsorship and resources, teacher unions represent important sites for experimentation and innovation (Bascia, 2000, 2003). They are important contributors to system capacity and, more specifically, they play an important corrective function vis-à-vis policy directions and administrative actions taken by others. These roles, as well as teacher unions' perennial interest in issues of teacher attraction, retention, and professional learning, are significant to efforts to ensure an adequate and quality teacher workforce.

Teachers' organizations have always existed in uneasy relationship with the formal educational authority structure. As such they have been at particular odds with attempts to align, streamline, and standardize policy efforts with respect to the teacher workforce. They are, by fundamental design, intended to challenge one-size-fits-all, remotely controlled policy efforts; their strength lies especially in their ability to be sensitive to local variation. Over at least the past couple of decades, they have contributed substantively to ensuring teacher quality at classroom, school, district, state/province, and national levels, in ways that are particularly salient during times of reduced funding and infrastructure support for education. They perform both innovative and corrective functions. The roles unions play are critical to teacher quality.

REFERENCES

Alberta Teachers' Association. (1997). *Trying to teach: Necessary conditions.* Edmonton, Alberta, Canada: Author.

Bailey, B. (2000). The impact of mandated change on teachers. In N. Bascia & A. Hargreaves (Eds.), *The sharp edge of educational change: Teaching, leading and the realities of reform* (pp. 112-128). London: Falmer Press.

Bascia, N. (1994). *Unions in teachers' professional lives: Social, intellectual and practical concerns.* New York: Teachers College Press.

Bascia, N. (1997). Invisible leadership: The roles of union-active teachers in schools. *Alberta Journal of Educational Research, 43*(2), 151-165.

Bascia, N. (1998a). Teacher unions and educational reform. In A. Hargreaves, A. Lieberman, M. Fullan, & D. Hopkins (Eds.), *International handbook of educational change* (pp. 896-915). Dordrecht, The Netherlands: Kluwer Academic.

Bascia, N. (1998b). Teacher unions and teacher professionalism: Rethinking a familiar dichotomy. In B. Biddle, T. Good, & I. Goodson (Eds.), *International handbook of teachers and teaching* (pp. 437-458). Dordrecht, The Netherlands: Kluwer Academic.

Bascia, N. (1998c). The next steps in teacher union research and reform. *Contemporary Education, 69*(4), 210-213.

Bascia, N. (1999). Collective bargaining under fire. *Orbit.* Toronto: OISE/University of Toronto.

Bascia, N. (2000). The other side of the equation: Professional development and the organizational capacity of teachers' organizations. *Education Policy, 14*(3), 385-404.

Bascia, N. (2001). Do teacher unions have demonstrated potential to promote positive forms of pedagogical, curricular and organizational change that benefit student learning? *Journal of Educational Change, 2*(2), 65-70.

Bascia, N. (2003). *Triage or tapestry? Teacher unions' work toward improving teacher quality in an era of systemic reform.* Seattle: Center for the Study of Teaching and Policy Document R-03-1. University of Washington.

Bascia, N. (in press). Learning through struggle: How the Alberta Teachers' Association maintains an even keel. In K. Church, N. Bascia, & E. Shragge (Eds.), *Informal learning: Making sense of lived experience in turbulent times.* Waterloo, Ontario, Canada: Wilfred Laurier Press.

Bascia, N., & Hargreaves, A. (2000). The sharp edge of change. In N. Bascia & A. Hargreaves (Eds.), *The sharp edge of educational change: Teaching, leading and the realities of reform* (pp. 3-27). London: Falmer Press.

Bascia, N., Stiegelbauer, S., Watson, N., Jacka, N., & Fullan, M. (1997). *Teacher associations and school reform: Building stronger connections.* External review of the NCI Learning Laboratories Initiative. Prepared for the National Education Association, Washington, DC. Toronto: Ontario Institute for Studies in Education of the University of Toronto.

Carlson, D. (1992). *Teachers and crisis: Urban school reform and teachers' work culture.* New York: Routledge Chapman & Hall.

Cochran-Smith, M. (1991). Learning to teach against the grain. *Harvard Educational Review, 61*(3), 279-310.

Cochran-Smith, M., & Lytle, S. (1992, May). Communities for teacher research: Fringe or forefront. *American Journal of Education, 3*, 298-324.

Darling-Hammond, L. (1997). *The right to learn: A blueprint for creating schools that work.* San Francisco: Jossey-Bass.

Johnson, S. (1983). Teacher unions in schools: Authority and accommodation. *Harvard Educational Review, 53*(3), 309-326.

Johnson, S. (1984). *Teacher unions in schools.* Philadelphia: Temple University Press.

Johnson, S. (1987). Can schools be reformed at the bargaining table? *Teachers College Record, 89*(2), 269-280.

Johnson, S. (1988). Pursuing professional reform in Cincinnati. *Phi Delta Kappan*, *69*(10), 746-751.

Johnson, S.M. (1990). *Teachers at work: Achieving success in our schools.* New York: Basic Books.

Kerchner, C.T., & Koppich, J.E. (1993). *A union of professionals: Labor relations and educational reform.* New York: Teachers College Press.

Kerchner, C.T., & Mitchell, D. (1986). Teaching reform and union reform. *Elementary School Journal, 86*(4), 449-470.

Kerchner, C.T., & Mitchell, D. (1988). *The changing idea of a teacher's union.* Philadelphia: Falmer Press.

King, M.B. (2004). School- and district-level leadership for teacher workforce development: Enhancing teacher learning and capacity. In this volume—M.A. Smylie & D. Miretzky (Eds.), *Developing the teacher workforce. The 103rd yearbook of the National Society for the Study of Education*, Part I (pp. 303-325). Chicago: National Society for the Study of Education

Knapp, M.S. (1997). Between systemic reforms and the mathematics and science classroom: The dynamics of innovation, implementation and professional learning. *Review of Educational Research, 67*(2), 227-266.

Larson, M.S. (1977). *The rise of professionalism: A sociological analysis.* Berkeley: University of California Press.

Lawton, S., Bedard, G., MacLellan, D., & Li, X. (1999). *Teachers' unions in Canada.* Calgary, Alberta, Canada: Detselig.

Lieberman, A., & Bascia, N. (1991). *The trust agreement: A cooperative labor compact.* Report for the Stuart Foundations. Berkeley: Policy Analysis for California Education (PACE).

Little, J.W. (1990). The persistence of privacy: Autonomy and initiative in teachers' professional relations. *Teachers College Record, 91*(4), 509-536.

Little, J.W. (1993). Teachers' professional development in a climate of educational reform. *Educational Evaluation and Policy Analysis, 15*(2), 129-151.

Martin Macke, S. (1998). Teacher unionism: Back to the future. *Contemporary Education, 69*(4), 180-181.

McClure, R. (1991). Individual growth and institutional renewal. In A. Lieberman and L. Miller (Eds.), *Staff development for education in the '90s* (pp. 221-241). New York: Teachers College Press.

McLaughlin, M.W. (1993). What matters most in teachers' workplace context? In J.W. Little & M.W. McLaughlin (Eds.), *Teachers' work: Individuals, colleagues, and contexts* (pp. 79-103). New York: Teachers College Press.

McLaughlin, M., & Talbert, J. (2001). *Professional communities and the work of high school teaching.* Chicago: University of Chicago Press.

McLaughlin, M., & Yee, S. (1988). School as a place to have a career. In A. Lieberman (Ed.), *Building a professional culture in schools* (pp. 23-44). New York: Teachers College Press.

Mitchell, D.E., & Kerchner, C.T. (1983). Labor relations and teacher policy. In L.S. Shulman & G. Sykes (Eds.), *Handbook of teaching and policy* (pp. 214-37). New York: Longman.

Murphy, M. (1990). *Blackboard unions: The AFT & the NEA, 1900-1980.* Ithaca, NY: Cornell University Press.

Murray, C., & Grant, G. (1998). Teacher peer review: Possibility or pipedream? *Contemporary Education, 69*(4), 202-204.

National Commission on Teaching and America's Future. (1996). *What matters most: Teaching for America's future.* New York: Author.

Ogawa, R. (1994). The institutional sources of educational reform: The case of school-based management. *American Educational Research Journal, 31*(3), 519-548.

Olson, M. (1965). *The logic of collective action.* Cambridge, MA: Harvard University Press.

Peterson, B., & Charney, M. (1999). *Transforming teacher unions: Fighting for better schools and social justice*. Milwaukee: Rethinking Schools, Inc.

Rauth, M. (1990). Exploring heresy in collective bargaining and school restructuring. *Phi Delta Kappan, 71*(10), 781-790.

Rosow, J., & Zager, R. (1989). *Allies in education reform*. San Francisco: Jossey-Bass.

Shields, P., & Knapp, M. (1997). The promise and limits of school-based reform: A national snapshot. *Phi Delta Kappan, 79*(4), 288-294.

Smaller, H. (1991). "A room of one's own": The early years of the Toronto Women Teachers' Association. In R. Heap and A. Prentice (Eds.), *Gender and education in Ontario: An historical reader* (pp. 103-124). Toronto: Canadian Scholars Press.

Smith, M., & O'Day, J. (1990). Systemic school reform. In S. Fuhrman & B. Malen (Eds.), *The politics of curriculum and testing* (pp. 223-268). Bristol, PA: Falmer Press.

Timar, T. (1989). The politics of school restructuring. *Phi Delta Kappan, 71*(4), 264-275.

Tyack, D., & Hansot, E. (1982). *Managers of virtue: Public school leadership in America, 1820-1980*. New York: Basic Books, Inc.

Urban, W.J. (1982). *Why teachers organized*. Detroit: Wayne State University Press.

Whitty, G., Powers, S., & Halpin, D. (1998). *Devolution and choice in education: The state, the school and the market*. Buckingham, UK: Open University Press.

Yee, S. (1990). *Careers in the classroom: When teaching is more than a job*. New York: Teachers College Press.

CHAPTER 12

Lessons for Policy Design and Implementation: Examining State and Federal Efforts to Improve Teacher Quality

MARGARET PLECKI AND HILARY LOEB

Legislative and programmatic efforts to improve teacher quality have become a major focus of state policymaking in recent years. States have employed numerous strategies in response to concerns about the preparation, quantity, and capacity of the teacher workforce. Quite often, the resulting state programs have focused on one or more of the following areas: teacher recruitment, induction, retention, certification, and compensation. These policy initiatives take various forms across states, as each state responds in the context of its specific demographic and economic circumstances.

This intensified focus on teacher quality at the state level can be viewed as a predictable consequence of the standards-based reform initiatives that began in the 1980s. To date, the reform movement has progressed through three stages (Hirsch, Koppich, & Knapp, 1999). The first focused on the establishment of more rigorous learning standards for students. The second centered on improving structural features such as raising graduation requirements, increasing teacher salaries, and promoting site-based management at individual schools (Baker & Linn, 1997). The third and current stage focuses on the classroom teacher. The higher expectations for students, the statewide assessments, and the accountability programs that are part of virtually all state reform programs have prompted significant questions about whether or not teachers have the necessary knowledge, skills, and supports to accomplish the goals of education reform (Thompson & Zeuli, 1999).

At the federal level, Title II of the No Child Left Behind Act of 2001 (NCLB) requires each state to ensure that all of its teachers in core academic subjects are "highly qualified" by the end of the 2005-06

Margaret Plecki is an Associate Professor and Hilary Loeb is a doctoral student in Educational Leadership and Policy Studies at the University of Washington, Seattle.

school year. NCLB has also placed other new pressures on states, districts, and schools by mandating the immediate creation of state standards and the implementation of annual testing for third through eighth grades by the 2005-06 school year. States, districts, and schools will be expected to make "adequate yearly progress" (defined as improvement of test scores) in order to receive federal funding. For consistently failing schools with large numbers of high-poverty students, NCLB imposes strict accountability measures, thereby further increasing the pressures on schools and teachers to produce results.

Although research documenting the significance of teacher quality has informed these state and federal policies, there is limited agreement about what it means to be a "highly qualified teacher." However, many studies have examined the relationships between aspects of teacher quality and student achievement. For example, Ferguson's (1997) Texas study found that teachers' performance on the Texas Examination of Current Administrators and Teachers, a state licensing exam administered to all teachers in 1986, had a significant positive relationship with student achievement on the Iowa Test of Basic Skills. Goldhaber and Brewer (1997) documented a relationship between teachers' undergraduate degrees in mathematics and science and the achievement of tenth-grade students and concluded that teachers' subject-specific training had a significant impact on student performance.

In a recent review of numerous empirical studies, Rice (2003) examined the relationship between student performance and five teacher attributes: experience, preparation, certification, coursework, and performance on teacher tests. Rice's analysis of the literature revealed a positive relationship between experience and teacher performance that is more notable during the early years of teaching. For teacher preparation, she found that a master's degree in mathematics or science had a positive effect on student learning in high school math and science, with mixed results for the elementary school level. Rice reported a positive relationship between teacher certification in mathematics and high school students' mathematics achievement. Teachers' coursework in content areas taught combined with coursework in pedagogy were positively associated with student outcomes, with the effect of subject matter–specific coursework being more pronounced at the high school level and the effect of pedagogical coursework being more uniform across grade levels. And finally, she reported that teacher performance on tests of verbal and literary abilities showed a more consistent positive association with student performance than did teacher performance on tests of basic skills. Rice also noted, however, that the empirical work to date does not examine the interactions among the many attributes and dimensions of teaching, leaving many important questions regarding the effect of teacher attributes on student learning unresolved.

These and other examinations of the influence of teacher quality typically focus on individual attributes of teachers and rely on a range of proxy variables (e.g., verbal ability, degrees earned, certification status, student test scores, years of experience). The result is that although these studies underscore the importance of paying attention to the teacher workforce in efforts to improve student achievement, they stop short of offering a full account of teachers' capacities and performance. As measures of teacher quality, these commonly used variables focus too much attention on what is easily counted, are only loosely connected to instructional quality, and, to a large extent, ignore how teachers apply their skills and knowledge in classrooms (Plecki, 2000). In other words, the extent to which these variables are valid and useful depends on how closely teachers' abilities, education, and training connect with the knowledge and skills that are needed and used in school and classroom contexts.

The Center for the Study of Teaching and Policy (CTP)[1] has advanced an approach to teacher workforce development that considers two aspects of teacher quality in addition to the individual attributes of teachers. According to the perspective that CTP has adopted, teacher workforce development policies need to address the quality of the teacher, the quality of teaching, and the quality of support for teachers' work simultaneously. In this approach, *quality of the teacher* refers to the individual attributes of a teacher, such as credentials, test scores, subject matter knowledge, pedagogical knowledge, and amount of experience in the profession. *Quality of teaching* refers to the quality of the individual teacher's classroom instruction and interaction with students and other features such as curriculum and instructional materials and policies regarding assessment and accountability. *Quality of support for teachers' work* refers to the quality of the variables that make up the teacher workplace such as student/teacher ratios, the assignment of students to individual classrooms, the levels and types of resources available to support instruction, the quality of school leadership, and the opportunities available for ongoing professional learning. As shown in Figure 1, these three aspects of teacher quality interact with one another, and together they are a key influence on student learning. Subsequent references to *teacher quality* in this chapter encompass all three aspects.

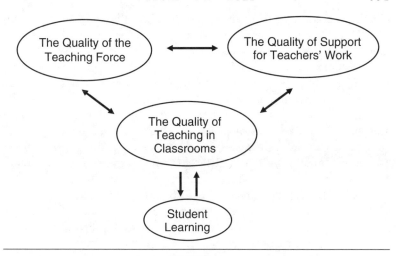

FIGURE 1

Three quality concerns confronting state policy and educational reform.
Source: Center for the Study of Teaching and Policy, University of Washington.

In some respects, the evidence to date does not support a wholesale elimination of current regulations and requirements for entry into the profession, yet the same empirical work also presents reason to question whether current policies and practices are sufficient to effect and sustain high-quality teaching for all students. We argue that the quality of individual teachers, the quality of the teaching that is present at the classroom level, and the quality of support for teachers' work inside schools and classrooms are essential components of teacher workforce development and that state and federal policies that focus on all three are more likely to result in coherent and effective programs. Although we recognize that some elements of teacher workforce development policies pose more complex and problematic design challenges than others and that developing and implementing policies aimed at improving teacher quality require attention to matters of coherence, sustainability, flexibility, accountability, and equity, we assert that state and federal policies can and should promote each of these three aspects of teacher quality.

In an analysis of state policy efforts to date, however, we have found that most have focused only on the attributes of the individual teacher and tend to concentrate on teacher recruitment and induction without sufficient attention to professional growth throughout teachers' careers. We also found that state policy strategies have suffered from both a lack of sustained focus and inadequate financial investment.

Finally, we contend that current state policy strategies do not sufficiently address the equity issues that are intertwined with the provision and support of a high-quality teacher workforce.

As compared to state policy strategies, we found the recent federal approach to improving teacher quality to be even more narrowly construed, sending a message that the policy problem can be addressed by a process of testing and inspection that focuses almost exclusively on the individual attributes of teachers. Although the federal approach may call attention to the need for improved teacher quality, the narrow framework offered by the NCLB legislation is likely to create conditions that may pressure states to alter their policy strategies accordingly. Specifically, emerging evidence about both the teacher workforce and the federal mandates suggests that a number of states will either be unable to comply with Title II or be compelled to redirect their policy efforts in the area of teacher quality. Furthermore, the federal policy assumes nationwide agreement about the attributes of highly qualified teachers, but the policy logic of state reforms addressing teacher workforce development varies.

We argue that the most promising efforts in the design of teacher workforce development policies recognize the multiple levels of a nested system—from the vantage points of individual teachers, to networks of teachers, to schools, to school systems, to broader social and policy contexts. Furthermore, because improving teacher quality is not simply a matter of training individual teachers but also of developing groups of teachers, we acknowledge that there are limitations to what may be achieved through the mandate-oriented state and federal policies. More specifically, efforts to improve teacher quality are also shaped through small-scale networks supported through building- and district-level initiatives. In short, efforts to improve teacher quality are affected by the interactions between local, state, and federal policies. Consequently, state and federal policymakers need to consider strategies that recognize and address the variable capacities of local systems to support a quality teacher workforce.

To illustrate these points, we have divided this chapter into three parts. We first introduce conceptual frameworks for understanding state policies aimed at improving teacher quality and provide examples of the teaching policy environments in four states. In the second section, we provide an analysis of Title II of NCLB by exploring the recent history of federal teacher quality efforts and reviewing the 2002 Title II legislation and related documents. In the final section, we build on our analyses of state and federal efforts by discussing the emerging critical issues in light of the pressures associated with the accountability measures posed by NCLB. We conclude the chapter with guidelines for enhancing the design of state and federal policies for improving teacher quality.

State-Level Policy Strategies to Improve Teacher Quality in an Era of Standards-Based Reform

How one views the development of policy strategies that can effectively improve teacher quality depends, to a large extent, on one's understanding of the nature of the endeavor. Part of the challenge policymakers face is ensuring that both the teacher and teaching are central to policy design. This requires some understanding of what "good teaching" is, how teachers learn to teach, and who should have voice in controlling the teaching profession (e.g., professional organizations or governmental bodies; state or local control). It also requires a recognition of the different kinds of teacher learning that need to be addressed throughout the different phases of a teacher's career (Feiman-Nemser, 2001). This extended and more complex view of teacher quality calls for differentiated but coherent responses and for an expansion of the means by which one evaluates the quality of teachers and teaching. In particular, measures in addition to traditional, input-oriented, labor-market variables such as years of experience, degrees, and clock hours spent in training (Plecki, 2000) are needed in order for policymakers to assess whether or not efforts aimed at improving teaching have been productive.

The flurry of activity at the state level calls for a careful analysis of the rapidly escalating teacher quality movement and its relation to standards-based reform. During the past decade, states not only have set more ambitious learning standards for students but also have enacted a variety of policies directed at improving the capacity of the teacher workforce to address those standards. Examples of common policy strategies employed by a number of states include upgrading teacher certification, establishing professional standards boards, intensifying recruitment and induction programs, requiring new types of teacher assessment, and approving alternative certification programs (Hirsch, Koppich, & Knapp, 1999).

From the vantage point of state policymakers, the terrain to be understood is broad, involving the politics of educational improvement, the orchestration of resources, the presence or absence of connections among bureaucratically separated programs and units, and the response of professionals at the level of practice. We maintain that the central question for policymakers is, What can and should the state be doing to improve the quality of teaching, the teaching force, and the support for teachers' work? A framework for examining how states might respond to these three components is shown in Figure 2.

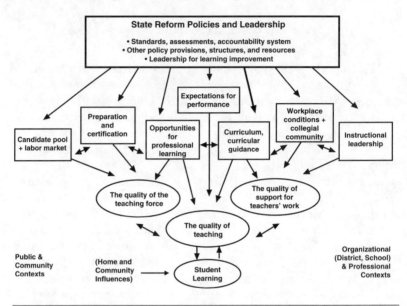

FIGURE 2

How state leadership and reform policies can affect teaching and learning.
Source: Center for the Study of Teaching and Policy, University of Washington.

Figure 2 indicates the various pathways by which states can develop and implement policies aimed at improving the teacher workforce. These policies can set in motion an array of activities—from influencing the pool of available teachers through recruitment, preparation, and certification policies to providing supports that enhance workplace conditions—that may assist in improving teacher quality. However, determining a course of action for state policy is more complicated than just selecting a set of policy strategies, developing a timeline for implementation, and setting the level of resources that will be focused on the chosen approach. A critical aspect of state policy design is coherence. Policymakers must ask: Does the approach have the effect of creating a set of mutually reinforcing conditions that together support a comprehensive strategy that addresses the full continuum of workforce development needs?

Another important challenge is to design policy strategies that recognize the value of both "top-down" and "bottom-up" perspectives on policy and that allow for adjustment based on a continuous feedback cycle. Improvement of any aspect of teacher quality requires a range of supports and an acknowledgment of the opportunities, limits, and realities at both the system and the classroom levels (Shields & Knapp, 1997). Prior research indicates that state policies are adjusted and adapted by local actors as policy is turned into practice (Elmore & McLaughlin, 1988; McLaughlin, 1976). Others have noted both the importance and the difficulty of building local capacity and flexibility through state policy mechanisms (Fisk, 1999; Spillane & Thompson, 1997; Timar, 1997). As observers of Connecticut's teacher induction program note,

We need to study programs at their level of implementation because this is where programs turn policy into practice. We need to learn what is missing, where the loose connections lie and what beginning teachers are actually able to handle. (Feiman-Nemser et al., 2000, p. 60)

It is also important to note that any state action designed to improve teacher quality takes place within a variety of public, community, organizational, and professional contexts. These contexts include public controversy about the appropriate role of testing in public education; ideological tensions about how knowledge, skills, and concepts should be represented in standards; the extent to which there is a shortage of qualified teachers; and the relative influence of professional organizations, unions, and teacher voice in shaping policy. The ability of states to develop coherent policies regarding teacher workforce development may also be influenced by policymakers' beliefs about whether supporting the ongoing work of teaching is best accomplished at the state or the local level. When states direct the majority of their efforts toward initial recruitment and certification, it reflects a belief that once teachers are certified, they are fully trained to effectively address the full range of challenges that are present inside schools and classrooms. However, ensuring that an adequate supply of highly qualified teachers enter the workforce is not synonymous with developing the profession, nor does it guarantee that teachers will be assigned to work in schools where access to highly qualified teachers is most needed.

As shown in Figure 2, we assert that states have a wide range of policy options to consider when designing strategies for improving teacher quality, and the choices that they make set the stage for the way that policies are formulated and enacted. Given the different contexts in which states are situated, it is not surprising that they vary in their specific approaches to developing the teacher workforce. Some approaches embrace broader conceptions of teacher development, from initial recruitment, preparation, and induction to providing ongoing curricular and instructional guidance, and finally, to continuous improvement of workplace conditions and enhancement of instructional leadership. States also make decisions about how fiscal and human resources will be allocated to support policy decisions and whether or not policy strategies are aimed at improving the workforce in ways that reduce existing inequities within districts, schools, and classrooms. Although the focus of this chapter is on policy *actions*, these actions take place in a context of conditions that, together with those actions, constitute an important *environment* in which teacher workforce development policies are designed, enacted, and revised.

Differences of Environment: A Look at Policy Efforts in Four States

To compare how state workforce development policies have been crafted in distinctly different policy environments, we have examined policy efforts in four states: New York, California, North Carolina, and Washington. Each was part of a longitudinal study conducted by the Center for the Study of Teaching and Policy.[2] The primary selection criteria for inclusion in the study were the active pursuit of a reform agenda and an attempt to link workforce development policies with their overall education reform efforts. The states were also selected for their differences in size, student demographics, political culture, and governance structures. They represent a variety of regions across the country. And, although each state has developed specific approaches to improving teacher quality, they vary significantly in their methods of policy formulation, which aspects of workforce development they emphasize, and how they support policies over time. In this examination, we describe the conditions that helped to shape policies regarding the improvement of teacher quality in each of the four states. We illustrate that a state's context must be considered in the development of sound policies. This is because each state context presents unique tensions and challenges that require thoughtful consideration if a coherent set of strategies is to be created. The intent of this analysis is not to determine whether these four states have succeeded or failed in their efforts but rather to explore how state approaches to workforce development might be enhanced.

New York. New York is a state of sharp contrasts, chief among them being the heterogeneity of its student population and the diverse political, cultural, and economic features across the different regions of the state. There is an asymmetrical distribution of students among the state's school districts, with five sizable urban districts (New York City, Rochester, Syracuse, Buffalo, and Yonkers) and more than 700 small districts in suburban and rural areas. Sharp disparities exist in the economic circumstances of the student population, especially in the state's urban areas. Additionally, there has been a traditional political, cultural, and economic divide that separates upstate New York from the virtual city-state of New York City.

New York has a longstanding tradition of an activist state presence in educational affairs. Perhaps more so than any other state, New York vests a great deal of authority in its Board of Regents, which governs public K-12 and postsecondary education systems. Educational lobbies are strong, and teacher associations exercise considerable influence in educational policy deliberations. A Professional Standards and Practices Board, first convened in January 1999, represents a newly created governance arrangement associated with the state's teacher quality initiatives.

Building on a period of standards development that occurred in the early 1990s, the state enacted a full set of new learning standards in 1996 and followed that with the rapid design and deployment of new assessments keyed to those standards, more detailed curricular guidance related to the standards, and a redefinition of the stakes attached to assessment performance. In short order, two years later, the state enacted a wide-ranging teacher quality initiative, as described in the 1998 report *New York's Commitment: Teaching to Higher Standards*. This initiative left few aspects of the teacher development continuum untouched. State-level activity addresses incentives for teacher recruitment and retention, promulgates high standards for teaching, reforms teacher preparation, requires professional development plans, and ties teacher recertification to additional professional development.

The process of implementing these reforms has been intentionally rapid and pushed from the top of the system. The state's policy strategy has relied on consistency of message, a massive and quick communication effort, and regulatory pressures on the state's educational institutions and localities. A prolonged budgetary process in 1999 resulted in the delay of some timelines associated with the implementation of these teacher quality policies. For example, New York's mentor teacher program has been in place since 1986 and is administered through a competitive grant process. Funding for the program fell by 50% between 1998 and 2001. New York State modestly subsidizes the fees teachers incur as applicants for certification with the National Board for Professional Teaching Standards. The state administers the Candidate Fee Subsidy Program, which uses federal funds, and the Albert Shanker Grant Program, which is primarily funded by the legislature. The Shanker awards reimburse NBPTS applicants up to $2,000 for their application fees and provides an additional $500 to LEAs to assist in paying for substitute teachers, travel, materials, and supplies for the candidate.

Consistent with its strong regulatory tradition, New York has emphasized speed, comprehensiveness, and high-stakes accountability in its policy approach. Although an impressive number of workforce development elements are included in this approach, challenges exist with respect to both building local capacities to respond to state policy requirements and fashioning state strategies that effectively address the highly urbanized settings as well as the suburban and rural contexts in the state. New York faces an additional, significant dilemma as a result of the recent court decision that found the state of New York to be responsible for addressing the inadequate education provided to students in the New York City school system. One of the inequities cited in this decision was the lack of highly qualified teachers in New York City. In fact, the majority of the state's teachers who have temporary or emergency credentials are working in New York City.

California. As the most populous and most racially and ethnically diverse state in the nation, California presents a unique set of economic, regional, political, demographic, cultural, and linguistic conditions that affect the quality of education in the state. Once considered a leader in educational innovation, California experienced a significant decline in fiscal support for schools that has been attributed to the 1978 passage of a property tax limit (Proposition 13) and the 1979 passage of a limit on state revenue growth (the Gann limit). Increased state control in education can be traced to a landmark school finance court case that mandated state responsibility for equalizing school funding (*Serrano v. Priest*). This increased control was enhanced by a former State Superintendent's pursuit of an active systemic reform initiative that began in the mid-1980s and featured the development of curriculum frameworks, a statewide assessment program, and professional development networks.

The state's reform trajectory was virtually halted in the mid-1990s due to pronounced political dissatisfaction with a new statewide assessment system that was quickly abandoned. Since that time, California has struggled to establish a coherent set of policies regarding assessment. This may be attributed to the often contentious political environment surrounding state education policies. In recent years, the state has experienced several high-profile policy debates, including those regarding affirmative action and bilingual education. Adding to the complexity is the multitude of state agencies and offices that reign over the state education system. For example, unlike New York State with its single Board of Regents, California has four separate governing boards, each having responsibility for an aspect of the state's K-12 and postsecondary education systems. Friction among the various players and the lack of structure to unify the many competing interests both contribute to a fragmented system of governance.

Among the four states, California has the most acute teacher shortage, and the problem is spread throughout the state. The number of teachers with emergency credentials doubled from 1995 to 1998, and approximately two thirds of California school districts employ teachers with emergency credentials. The state has responded to this condition through a host of policies including intensified recruitment efforts, additional alternative certification processes, expanded loan forgiveness programs, and new paraprofessional teacher training programs and university internship programs.

Since 1992, the state has invested in support for the mentoring of beginning teachers through the Beginning Teacher Support and Assistance Program (BTSA). State officials estimated that BTSA was serving more than 20,000 beginning teachers in approximately 90% of the districts in the state in 1999-2000. Given the ever-growing number of first- and second-year teachers, however, the BTSA program has proven to be of insufficient scale to meet the needs of all of California's beginning teachers.

The California Mentor Teacher Program was established in 1983 and continued through the 1998-99 school year. It was replaced with the Peer Assistance Review Program, which assists teachers who are struggling with aspects of their performance evaluations through the provision of "consulting teachers." Districts are directed to set up a teacher-administrator peer review panel to select consulting teachers, review reports, and make recommendations to the school board about participants.

To date, California has focused more of its efforts on accountability provisions than on the development of comprehensive or coherent strategies. The state implemented an Academic Performance Index that provided a basis for evaluating individual school performances on state tests relative to "comparable" schools and included provisions for performance-based rewards and sanctions. The shift toward accountability-focused policy initiatives has been accompanied by a diminished state-level focus on professional development. The state's current efforts through reading and math professional development institutes are highly prescriptive and narrowly focused, aimed at imparting the same specific teaching skills to all participants.

California's substantial 1996 initiative to reduce class size statewide significantly increased the need for qualified teachers, further exacerbating the state's teacher supply problem. The class-size reduction program was implemented quickly and broadly, affecting kindergarten through third-grade classrooms throughout the state. In 1999-2000 alone, class-size reduction for K-3 was funded at $1.5 billion. Although this significant investment in class-size reduction might be viewed as a form of support for enhancing workplace conditions, the speed with which this policy was implemented, combined with the uniform nature of the implementation across all schools, created additional equity concerns. A recent analysis of California's class-size reduction initiative revealed that the increased demand for teachers that this wholesale class-size reduction created further exacerbated the inequities that already existed in the distribution of qualified teachers in high-poverty, high-need schools as compared to more affluent schools (Imazeki, 2003). Finally, the significant downturn in California's economy in 2003 has raised concerns about whether or not the state will be able to sustain its current financial investment in teacher quality policies.

Washington. Washington State is smaller and more homogenous than California or New York. Washington residents are primarily white and middle class, though pockets of poverty and racial and ethnic diversity are rapidly growing. A cleavage between the heavily populated portions of the state in the greater Puget Sound area west of the Cascade Mountains and the primarily agricultural areas to the east of this natural land barrier also provides for a sharp intrastate contrast. The great majority of school districts are suburban or rural, leaving the urban school systems relatively isolated and poorly understood in public policy debates. Characterized by a longstanding political tradition of populism, the state has treated education as largely a local matter, and the state legislature and educational governance arrangements leave much to local discretion. However, one prominent exception to this tradition of local control can be found in the state's aggressive attempts to equalize school financing beginning in the 1970s, resulting in the state's assumption of full responsibility for funding basic education. In another departure from its decentralized tradition, Washington approved two voter initiatives in November 2000 that mandated statewide education spending provisions for specified purposes such as class-size reduction and automatic cost-of-living increases for educators.

The state initiated its standards-based reform in 1993 with legislation supported by an alliance of business interests, the state teacher's union, the governor's office, and key legislative members. The reform called for the creation of ambitious student learning standards. Assessments tied to these new standards were then developed in a slow and deliberate way, with a gradual implementation schedule and multiple opportunities for teacher and community input into the development process. The focus of reform has been relatively narrow, however, and the state has been remarkably silent about how to teach to meet the new standards. Further evidence of this gradual implementation schedule can be found in the state's prolonged deliberations about the form of its accountability system, intended to provide rewards, supports, and sanctions for schools and school districts that are tied to their performance.

Washington is slowly implementing other reforms specific to teacher policy that are conceptually linked to the performance-based student standards system. Examples of these reforms include the establishment of a two-tiered teacher certification process and the development of new program standards for teacher preparation institutions. Additionally, in 1999 Washington initiated state support for teachers pursuing NBPTS certification. The 1999 session allocated $327,000 for 15% salary increases for NBPTS-certified teachers for two years. But the limited funding allotment made it necessary for the state department to develop a competitive process to determine eligibility. Starting in 2000-2001, the bonus for teachers achieving NBPTS certification was set at a flat $3,500 per year for two years. Since 1998, teacher policy initiatives have centered around raising teacher salaries, using the traditional teacher compensation structure based on levels of education and years of experience. A Professional Standards Board, consisting primarily of teachers, was created in 2000 and aims to focus increased state policy attention on matters of teacher quality. The board's first task was to recommend a set of alternative routes to teacher certification, including a program that is focused on attracting those who are considering teaching as a mid-life career switch.

Washington has viewed teacher recruitment as largely a local matter, with no funded state programs that address the need to attract teachers to work in rural or urban areas. Some state support has been provided for mentoring new teachers through the Teacher Assistance Program (TAP), but funding for TAP has been insufficient. Approximately 20% of new teachers are not served by the program, and there is great variability in what is provided from district to district.

Compared to efforts in both New York and California, Washington's approach has been intentionally slower in pace. Strategies at the state level take local contexts into account to a much greater extent that in New York or California. However, Washington's approach is also characterized by a lack of state supports and guidance about how to align curriculum and instructional practice with learning standards and by an underdeveloped accountability system.

North Carolina. Historically a rural state, North Carolina has recently experienced rapid economic growth and diversification. The relative affluence of the resulting urban areas, including the high-tech Research Triangle, and the increasingly popular tourist economies of the mountains and coast contrast sharply with the abject poverty and significant isolation of the remaining rural pockets. The shift in the state's economy from agriculture to manufacturing and, most recently, high technology has prompted a cultural change in the state, with rising expectations for schools and pressures from business interests. Former governor Jim Hunt played a longstanding and highly visible role in the state's education reform efforts, enjoying substantial support for his initiatives from a variety of influential policy players in the state. Students in North Carolina showed marked improvements on the National Assessment of Education Progress throughout the 1990s.

As in each of the other three sample states, North Carolina's reform efforts are rooted in the development of a strong system of student standards and assessments. New curriculum standards were implemented beginning in the early 1990s. Prior to the 1990s, however, state policies had also focused on matters related to teacher quality. Starting in 1985, a Task Force on the Preparation of Teachers began examining ways to improve teacher education, and by 1990 NCATE certification was required for all teacher education programs in the state. More recently, the University-School Teacher Education Partnership (USTEP) was funded to provide more intensive clinical experiences for preservice teachers and to improve teacher education curricula. The state has also mandated tests of teachers' basic skills, subject matter knowledge, and pedagogy for more than a decade. The 1997 adoption of the state's Excellent Schools Act was accompanied by hundreds of millions of dollars in state funding for education reform, with the bulk of the money earmarked for improving both teacher education and mentoring and for increasing teacher salaries. Teacher testing and evaluation has been characterized by state-mandated basic skills, subject area, and pedagogy tests and locally developed performance-based portfolio evaluations for new teachers.

North Carolina has taken significant and highly visible steps to provide teachers with incentives and rewards for obtaining National Board certification. As a result, the state has the largest number of NBPTS-certified teachers in the nation. North Carolina also outspends most states in its support of NBPTS teachers. The state pays for the NBPTS application fees as well as for three days paid leave for application preparation, spending $2.9 million on application fees and $300,000 dollars on paid leave for preparation in 2000-2001. This is equivalent to $2.55 per pupil, up from $1.51 per pupil in 1998-99. Reaching beyond the fee subsidies, North Carolina has also distinguished itself by adjusting the state salary schedule to reward teachers for their achievement of NBPTS certification. As the population of NBPTS-certified teachers has increased, the additional salary credits have growth substantially, from $6 million in 1998-99 to $17.6 million in 2000-2001. In terms of per-pupil spending, the salary credits rose from $4.97 in 1998-99 to $14.04 in 2000-2001.

An interesting feature of North Carolina's workforce policy agenda is the provision of monetary rewards to teachers and teaching assistants based on schools' meeting or exceeding expected school performance gains. Teachers in schools that meet expected gains receive a $750 bonus, while teaching assistants receive $375; teachers and assistants in schools that exceed their expected growth by more than 10% receive $1,500 and $500 bonuses, respectively.

North Carolina's strategies have been focused on long-term goals, but short-term gains have been a more prominent component of policy action than in the other three cases in our sample. North Carolina's system for rewarding success includes attention to equity issues, by providing bonuses based on meeting or exceeding "expected growth" goals, and to accountability issues, by providing additional bonuses for meeting "exemplary growth" standards.

State Approaches to Policy Design and Implementation

The policy efforts in these four states share explicit state-level commitments to higher standards of teaching and learning. In each state, the pressure to seek solutions to the challenge of improving teacher quality statewide has typically resulted in the establishment of new standards, guidelines, requirements, or opportunities that have sometimes been accompanied by the infusion of some new fiscal resources.

Developing a broader and more detailed understanding about teacher workforce development, however, has been a challenge for all four states. North Carolina has the longest history of attempting to fashion more comprehensive approaches to workforce development that seek to support teachers throughout their careers. New York has put ambitious standards into its policy language but struggles to create approaches that meet the state's diverse needs, including the unique needs of New York City. California's conflicts with governance arrangements and teacher shortages of crisis proportions, combined with its current fiscal dilemma, present significant obstacles for the development of workforce policies that address the full continuum of teaching. Washington's efforts to influence broader conceptions of workforce development are the newest and least developed of the four states. But Washington's slow and deliberate approach to reform, combined with its relatively stable balance of teacher supply and demand, might facilitate a more comprehensive approach to workforce development in the future.

All four states have struggled with designing effective policy strategies that provide sufficient support for the ongoing professional development needs of teachers. Traditionally, each of these states has viewed professional development as largely a local matter, and this stance has contributed to state policy approaches that are more focused on the needs of beginning teachers than on those of the entire workforce. But teachers at all levels of experience are encountering new challenges in helping an increasingly racially and ethnically diverse student population meet more ambitious standards for student performance, and state approaches to date have fallen short of the investment levels needed to provide the necessary ongoing support. An analysis of national data confirms that average state and district spending on teacher professional development increased only slightly overall during the 1990s, with 17 states actually reporting a decrease from the prior decade's spending (Killeen, Monk, & Plecki, 2002). This lack of increased resources to support professional development occurred during a period (1992-98) when most states experienced an economic surge and also strengthened their focus on matters relating to improving teaching and learning.

An important component of policy design involves the extent to which fiscal resources are designated to sustain or expand existing programs and services or to promote new initiatives. In each of these four states, policy initiatives were funded by a combination of direct support to local school districts or regional agencies, competitive grant processes, and specific incentives to individual teachers. The decidedly political context in which decisions about resource allocation occur, combined with ever-changing economic conditions within states, affect how funds are directed, resulting in funding policy strategies that change with each new legislative session. This in turn results in a lack of sustained focus on programs that are aligned with state workforce development goals. State leadership for workforce development policies in these four states has been dispersed, sometimes intentionally distributed but often haphazardly assumed by various individuals or organizations involved with teacher development. An examination of the types and amounts of resources designated for new teacher quality initiatives revealed that state leaders in these four cases typically experienced more difficulty garnering new resources to support the ongoing professional development of teachers than for other policy strategies such as recruitment, teacher testing, mentoring of beginning teachers, and teacher salaries.

An examination of teacher quality efforts in these four states also revealed a lack of specific state policies aimed at addressing the equity issues that are embedded in the challenge of improving access to high-quality teachers and teaching. Although there is evidence that teacher retention rates are variable, with greater teacher turnover often occurring in high-poverty schools (Boyd, Lankford, Loeb, & Wyckoff, 2003; Ingersoll, 2001), policy attention in the four states did not focus specifically on incentives or other strategies to address the inequitable distribution of qualified teachers. North Carolina and California have made attempts to gather data about the distribution of qualified teachers across districts, but neither state has enacted specific policies that pay special attention to the equity of access all students have to qualified teachers. California recently initiated a policy that provided incentives for teachers to work in low-performing schools, but only for NBPTS-certified teachers.

Many states, including these four, focused resources on improving teacher salary levels, hoping to positively affect teacher recruitment and retention, with special attention paid to entry-level salaries. A few states, including North Carolina and California, have also provided salary bonuses for teachers and staff working in schools that meet specified targets for improved student learning. Pay linked in some way to performance is the exception rather than the rule in most states, and the issue of performance-based compensation is hotly debated at both the state and the local levels. Policy strategies regarding ways in which teacher compensation structures might be altered to focus more on knowledge production and skills development are in the very early stages of development and debate (Koppich, 2003; Odden, 2003).

The focus on improving teaching and learning affords an opportunity for states to exercise proactive leadership. Realistically speaking, however, there are limits to what can be accomplished through the vehicles of state policy action. Establishing and sustaining teacher quality is equally dependent on the capacity of school districts, regional agencies, and other local organizations and networks to productively engage in improvement efforts that are realized in the classroom (Shields & Knapp, 1997). Consequently, some state efforts focused on achieving higher levels of teaching and learning have implemented a combination of decentralization and state-level accountability standards. Under this design, the attempt is to clarify expectations while simultaneously giving schools the flexibility to meet those expectations in a manner that makes sense at the level of practice. Certainly, accountability systems can help direct the allocation of new and existing resources, but focusing on statewide accountability is not synonymous with increasing productivity because accountability alone provides only partial insight into how to best design and implement improvement efforts. Nonetheless, accountability is a major focus of recent federal policy efforts and is particularly evident in a number of features of NCLB. In the next section, we examine the federal government's role in education reform and teacher quality improvement and consider the possible effects that NCLB may have on states' efforts to impact the full range of teacher workforce development issues that must be addressed in order to sustain coherent policy approaches.

Recent Federal Efforts in Education Reform and the Improvement of Teacher Quality

Both the recent history of the federal role in educational reform and studies of federal efforts to improve teacher quality provide a context for understanding Title II of NCLB. In 1965, the Elementary and Secondary Education Act initiated a comprehensive set of programs, including the Title I program of federal aid to low-income children, to address the problems of economically disadvantaged urban and rural areas. The federal government has become increasingly involved in teacher quality since the mid-1980s. Federal reform efforts in the 1990s generally sought to build the capacity of teachers at selected sites. Title II of NCLB, however, calls for an expanded federal role in the operations of all schools throughout the United States. Research evaluating reform efforts during the 1990s yields important lessons about the challenges of this phase of systemic reform. It also helps us understand the emerging discussion of Title II and the related concerns about this federal move from building capacity to seeking compliance. To illustrate this shift toward greater federal involvement, we provide a brief overview of three significant 1990s efforts to improve teacher quality—the Eisenhower program, the National Science Foundation programs, and the Goals 2000: Educate America Act. We then discuss the reforms launched by NCLB.

Recent Measures Addressing Teacher Quality

The end of George H. W. Bush's presidency and both terms of the Clinton administration featured strong interest in public education. The first President Bush and the U.S. governors agreed on and established the first national goals for education (Jennings, 1998). Building on the work of his predecessor, President Clinton signed the Goals 2000: Educate America Act into law in 1994. Goals 2000 included a grant program to support the creation of assessment systems tied to state content standards. The 1994 reauthorization of the Elementary and Secondary Education Act (ESEA) included a revised focus for Title I. Instead of funding remediation activities, these new investments were designated to support high academic standards for all children. This new version of Title I continued to give priority to the needs of low-income students, but it also was intended to encourage systemic reform through the development of state standards and assessments and the lessening of regulations for school-level projects. These changes were made in response to public concern about U.S. students' comparatively poor achievement on the Third International Mathematics and Science Study (TIMSS). Although states expressed reluctance to implement these changes, 48 eventually accepted the funding and launched efforts to develop standards-based reform (Jennings, 2003).[3] The 1994 ESEA reauthorization also included the redesign of the Eisenhower program, which was an attempt to help students achieve high standards of learning by improving teacher quality. Although the Eisenhower, National Science Foundation, and Goals 2000 programs sought to encourage systemic instructional reforms, each fell short of expectations. Recurrent themes have emerged in both evaluations of and research on these efforts: inadequate capacity and communication at every level of the educational system. The specific ways in which each of these three federal efforts addressed the improvement of teacher quality are briefly outlined below.

Eisenhower Program. Established in 1984, the Eisenhower Professional Development Program sought to support professional development experiences for teachers, primarily in mathematics and science and to a lesser degree in other content areas. Reports on the impact of this program following the 1994 reauthorization of ESEA (Porter et al., 1999; Porter, Garet, Desimone, Yoon, & Birman, 2000) centered on its mixed effectiveness.[4] Most of the Eisenhower-assisted activities were traditional in form, utilizing workshops, courses, or conferences. Relatively few assisted activities were study groups, networks, mentoring relationships, or the like.

An analysis of survey data designed to ascertain whether participation in the Eisenhower program was a catalyst for instructional change found little reported overall change in instructional practice from 1996 to 1999 (Porter et al., 2000). Teachers participated in ongoing learning that varied in quality from one year to the next, and teachers in the same school typically had different professional development experiences. However, professional learning that introduced specific, higher-order teaching strategies increased the use of those techniques in the classroom. This effect was even stronger when the format of the professional development activity was reform-oriented (e.g., a teacher network or study group) rather than traditional (e.g., a workshop or conference).

National Science Foundation Programs. During the 1990s, the National Science Foundation (NSF) invested in the development of 13 comprehensive curriculum programs (Reys, Robinson, Sconiers, & Mark, 1999). In 1991, the agency launched the Elementary and Secondary Statewide Systemic Initiatives (ESSSI). These initiatives, which from 1991 to 1993 allocated funds to 26 states, were "created on the premise that positive reform in K-12 science and mathematics education will effectively be achieved if pursued by means of a systemic effort, coordinated nationwide on the state level rather than piecemeal" (Directorate for Education and Human Resources Division of Research, Evaluation, and Communication, 1996, p. 3).[5] National and state mathematics reforms during this period called for significant instructional change, requiring teachers to emphasize deep conceptual understandings of the subject matter rather than basic skills and operations (Spillane & Zeuli, 1999).

Both the ESSSI Evaluation (Directorate for Education and Human Resources Division of Research, Evaluation, and Communication,

1996) and Spillane and Zeuli (1999) detail the impact of the NSF programs, highlighting challenges to the implementation of reform-oriented science and math instruction. The main findings of the ESSSI Evaluation were that the states spent the largest portion of their NSF dollars on professional development and served approximately 8% of teachers in participating states. The evaluation report named five significant issues that explain the difficulties encountered in program implementation. First, although states were able to build the capacity of practicing teachers to improve mathematics and science instruction, the improvement was often insufficient to meet the objectives of the reform. Second, some state policies were not aligned with the reform goals. Third, the NSF-funded states gave only modest attention to local educational policy systems. Fourth, the states did not attend to the preparation of the "next generation" of teachers. Fifth, the mathematics, science, and education communities had limited capacity to promote reform agendas in the broader community.

Goals 2000. Like the Eisenhower and NSF programs, Goals 2000 emphasized high standards of achievement for all students. Teacher quality was addressed in its fourth goal statement: "Teachers will have access to training programs to improve their skills" (Cookson, 1995, p. 406). According to Cookson, the legislation reflected President Clinton's belief in systemic reform. According to Hannaway and Kimball (2001), the progress of the standards-based reform efforts initiated by Goals 2000 was more pronounced at the school level than at the district level. However, Hannaway and Kimball found that higher poverty districts were less likely than their affluent counterparts to establish standards, align curricula to standards, and build community partnerships.

Other scholars raised concerns about states' capacity to carry out the ambitious reforms of Goals 2000. Cohen (1995) pointed out that few educational agencies in the United States were capable of creating plans for school improvement in accordance with Goals 2000. He also noted a dilemma for this early phase of standards-based reform: "Standards set high enough to exemplify truly outstanding work could be irrelevant because they would be so far from current practice as to alienate or mystify most potential learners. But standards set close enough to current practice to be more easily understood and attained could fail to stimulate much improvement" (p. 754). Research on standards-based reform confirmed these concerns. In a nine-state study conducted by Massell, Kirst, and Hoppe (1997), teachers commonly complained of a lack of support available to carry out standards that were often broad and general in nature.

Scholarship and commentary about federal teacher quality reforms in the 1990s underscore the importance of coherence, comprehensiveness, and capacity for the improvement of teacher quality. In each of the three federal initiatives discussed above, there was a recognition of the importance of teaching but no understanding or theory of what is required to adequately support instructional improvement. The Eisenhower program evaluation suggests the value of consistency in both district- and school-level teacher-learning initiatives. Although Goals 2000 paid limited attention to teaching, Cookson (1995) and Cohen (1995) note the importance of instruction in carrying out this policy agenda. Research on the impact of the standards-based reforms initiated by Goals 2000 raises the significance of building school, district, and state capacity so that standards may be reached. The limited implementation of these three reform efforts raises the question of whether the federal outlays were sufficient given their ambitious goals. It remains to be seen how the more recent reform efforts in response to Title II of NCLB will affect state progress toward teacher quality improvement, but in the following description and analysis, we find that the federal government is taking a much more active role.

NCLB and Teacher Quality

Federal investments in teaching during the 1990s emphasized the importance of math and science instruction, but Title II of NCLB focuses more broadly on instructional improvement. Title II of the Higher Education Reauthorization Act of 1998 laid the groundwork for some of the accountability measures of Title II of NCLB. That earlier legislation implemented reporting requirements for states and teacher education programs and limited access to federal financial aid when students performed poorly on state teacher tests (Melnick & Pullin, 2000). It also called for reforms of teacher certification and licensure, including the creation of alternatives to traditional teacher preparation and certification. The federal government's position piece *A Quality Teacher in Every Classroom* (n.d.) names three objectives in improving teacher quality through NCLB: appropriations will provide assistance to states as they 1) work to enhance teacher quality, 2) elevate the teaching profession and work environment, and 3) provide new tools for teachers in specific areas of instruction. Both the legislation and the supporting documents communicate messages about teacher quality, define the vehicles for the improvement of teaching, and name eligible sites for the training and development of teachers.

The Center on Educational Policy (2003) provides an overview of the changes brought about by Title II. The center's report maintains that the Title II mandates "represent a major expansion of the federal role concerning teacher quality" (p. 76). This is the first time the federal government has created minimum qualifications for *all* teachers of core subjects. Although states will still craft teacher preparation, testing, and certification requirements, these efforts will now have to comply with federal law. In addition, programs seeking federal funding will need to document their efficacy using evidence obtained from "scientifically based research" (*A Quality Teacher in Every Classroom*, n.d., p. 7). In the following section, we first briefly describe key aspects of the NCLB legislation and its supporting documents.[6] We then present the emerging research and commentary on NCLB and its approach to teacher quality, which suggest that the emerging federal policy may narrow or restrict established state efforts to improve teacher quality.

The Highly Qualified Teacher

First disseminated in June 2002 and revised in December 2002, *Improving Teacher Quality State Grants* provides both general and specific definitions of a "highly qualified teacher." Individuals in this category either have earned full state certification as a teacher, or they have both passed the state teacher licensing examination and obtained a state teaching license. In addition, these individuals have not had certification or licensure requirements waived on an emergency, temporary, or provisional basis. Highly qualified teachers possess at least a B.A. or B.S. and have proven competence in subject area knowledge as determined by the state or in accordance with Section 9101(23) of ESEA.[7] The *Draft Guidance* presents details about the differences in these criteria among elementary, secondary, new, and experienced teachers. Although new elementary school teachers are required to pass a state test, new middle or high school teachers in this category must demonstrate "a high level of competency" (*Improving Teacher Quality State Grants*, p. 85) in their academic subject.[8] This competency may be demonstrated by passing a state academic subject test or by the successful completion of an academic major, an advanced degree, or coursework equivalent to an undergraduate major or advanced certification. The legislation provides different guidelines for charter school teachers and teachers who have earned certification through alternative routes. Individuals who teach core academic subjects in charter schools must comply with their state's charter school law regarding certification or licensure requirements and thus might not have to be licensed or certified. Charter school teachers must, however, hold a four-year degree and show competency in their subject area. In this new context, teachers who have earned certification through alternative routes must make satisfactory progress toward permanent licensure.

Vehicles and Sites for Training and Development

Title IX of NCLB includes information about the types of professional learning activities that Title II supports. These activities are designed to advance teacher understanding of instructional strategies that have been proven effective in scientifically based studies. They include learning that aims to improve student achievement or increase the skills and knowledge of teachers. Fifteen of the types of activities that Title IX describes are associated with the improvement of teaching. Among these are classroom management, instructional approaches to serving English Language Learners, effective use of technology, strategies for working with special needs children, using data and assessment to inform classroom practice, and collaboration with parents and caregivers.

Title IX also discusses the relationship of professional development to state standards and the specific types of activities and learning that are eligible for funding. The activities are described in relation to state content requirements, student academic standards, or existing curricula and programs tied to these benchmarks. The legislation privileges longer-term learning experiences that are "high quality, sustained, intensive, and classroom-focused in order to have a positive and lasting impact on classroom instruction and the teacher's performance in the classroom" (Title IX, para. 34). The legislation specifies that the eligibility of an activity for funding will be evaluated based on its impact on teacher effectiveness and student achievement. Title II includes provisions for private school teachers to participate in federally funded activities.

The Role of Scientifically Based Research

Because NCLB requires evidence from existing, scientifically based research to justify spending both in Title I schools and federally funded programs aimed at improving teaching, it is important to define "scientifically based research" and discuss its role in federal educational reform efforts. Specifically, this term refers to "research that involves the application of rigorous, systematic, and objective procedures to obtain reliable and valid knowledge relevant to education activities and programs" (Title IX, para. 37). The legislation describes six types of qualifying inquiry that draw primarily from hypothesis-driven experimental research design. It calls for transparency in methodology to allow for replication of the research or, at a minimum, the chance to build systematically on the study's findings. Scholarship fitting this definition either has been accepted by a peer-reviewed journal or has been validated by a panel of experts through an equally rigorous and objective review.[9]

The appearance of the phrase "scientifically based research" 111 times in NCLB (Feuer, Towne, & Shavelson, 2002) is evidence of its dominant role in this legislation. The U.S. Department of Education's *Strategic Plan 2002–2007* discusses this role and provides criteria that will influence Title II funding decisions. The strategic plan's fourth goal, to "transform Education into an evidence-based field" (DOE, 2002b, p. 53), names two objectives. First, the DOE seeks to elevate the quality of research that it supports or conducts. Second, the agency aims to increase the relevance of that research to better serve its customers. One performance target specifies that a minimum 75% of the new research and evaluation projects funded by the DOE between 2004 and 2007 will address causal questions and utilize randomized experimental designs. A related goal in the plan ties federal education funding to accountability for results. According to this plan, programs that do not result in student outcome improvements will be reformed or eliminated.

The Department of Education's annual reports on teacher quality for 2002 and 2003 (Paige, Stroup, & Andrade, 2002, 2003) discuss the research used to develop Title II and call for changes to state systems. The 2002 report names verbal ability and content knowledge as the only scientifically validated characteristics of highly qualified teachers. The department's negative stance on teacher preservice education programs is evidenced by the citation of an Abell Foundation report (Walsh, 2001) that claims that the research linking teacher certification and student achievement lacks scientific rigor.[10] The 2003 annual report provides more qualified claims about teacher quality, perhaps in response to scholarly critiques cited in the next section of this chapter. The authors of the 2003 report maintain that, although there is considerable evidence that teachers contribute to student achievement, there are gaps in knowledge about how individuals become effective teachers. They are, however, willing to accept the premise offered by Grover Whitehurst, director of the Institute of Educational Sciences. In his concluding remarks at the Whitehouse Conference on Preparing Tomorrow's Teachers, Whitehurst pointed out the flawed nature of an analytical focus on differences in teachers' attributes and the value of experimental research:

As we build a solid research base on this topic, one that is more specific and experimental than we have currently, we should be much better able to provide instruction for all children. . . . Individual differences in teachers will never go away, but powerful instructional systems and new, effective forms of professional development should reduce those differences to the point that every teacher should be good enough so that no child is left behind. (p. 51)

Both annual reports make recommendations about systemic changes. In the 2002 report, Paige, Stroup, and Andrade specify changes to state certification systems as a solution:

To meet the "highly qualified teachers" challenge, then, states will need to streamline their certification system to focus on the few things that really matter: verbal ability, content knowledge, and, as a safety precaution, a background check of new teachers. States need to tap into the vast pool of potential teachers who today are discouraged by the bureaucratic hoops and hurdles but tomorrow might be willing to fill their classrooms. (p. 40)

The 2003 report frames these recommendations in terms of "raising academic standards for teachers and lowering barriers that are keeping many talented people out of the teaching profession" (p. 3). It includes a section entitled "Promising Innovations to Meet the Highly Qualified Teachers Challenge" (pp. 21-31), which describes three traditional teacher preparation and six alternative certification programs.

In summary, Title II of NCLB, according to its authors, uses measures of teacher performance on state tests and certification status to determine whether a teacher is highly qualified. In the case of secondary schools, teachers may not need certification if they have demonstrated competency in their subject area by completing an academic major or additional coursework. In order to qualify for federal funding, professional learning activities must demonstrate that their strategies have been proven effective by scientifically based research. These elements imply state discretion in the implementation of teacher quality accountability measures. In this context, states define the tests, the required levels of subject matter competence, and the evaluation measures that serve as milestones for career entry and advancement. And because Title II does not include recommendations or priorities beyond the accountability requirements, states must also specify acceptable vehicles and sites for professional learning. Federal position documents that accompany the legislation offer clear definitions of teacher quality and summarize studies that claim to support these conceptions. The Department of Education's annual reports on teacher quality also recommend steps for states to raise professional standards and to decrease the obstacles to entry into teaching. In the next section, we present the emerging response to NCLB.

Responses to Title II of NCLB

Because NCLB was recently enacted, the evidence of its impact is emergent and predictive in nature. Much of the scholarly conversation about NCLB addresses its feasibility and fairness rather than its effects. To synthesize this discussion, we first present researchers' concerns about the legislation's assessment and accountability measures and about its efforts to improve teaching quality. We then consider these concerns in light of critiques of the DOE's conceptualization of the role of scientifically based research. Read together, these analyses suggest both a basis in faulty logic and an uncertain feasibility for NCLB. Unlike the four diverse state cases we presented, NCLB focuses more narrowly on the characteristics of individual teachers and on pathways into teaching. Viewed through the framework presented in Figure 2, it becomes clear that Title II includes few, if any, measures that directly address the quality of teaching and the quality of support for teachers' work. Further, these analyses reveal that Title II neglects the importance of coherence, comprehensiveness, and variable capacity in the improvement of teacher quality, themes that dominated discussions of the instructional reforms of the 1990s. As a result, some states' efforts aimed at improving teacher quality may be compromised in the near future.

Linn, Baker, and Betebenner (2002) discuss the technical problems of the assessment and accountability system mandated by NCLB. They caution that the goal of all students achieving proficiency by 2014 is unrealistic, and argue that NCLB does not recognize the volatility of school-level test results, citing problems of reliability and validity in collecting building-level data. A related concern is whether states and districts will be able to carry out the NCLB requirements by the 2005-06 deadline. Jennings (2003) notes that in the spring of 2002, only 17 states had standards and assessment systems that were considered to be in compliance with the 1994 reauthorization of ESEA. In addition, state departments of education frequently do not have staff members who possess expertise in either assessment or providing technical assistance to schools that are failing (Jennings, 2003). The Harvard Civil Rights Project's six-state analysis of the policy indicates that states are progressing at varying rates toward the 2014 goal of student proficiency (Sunderman & Kim, 2004). The authors of the project report argue that NCLB creates incentives for states to lower standards of proficiency and to deliver the largest achievement gains at the end of the timeline. Linn et al. (2002) summarize the conceptual problems with the legislation:

One can agree that schools should improve and that holding schools accountable will contribute to improvement but still conclude that the goal of having 100% of students reaching the proficient level or higher . . . is so high that it is completely out of reach. Furthermore, having a goal that is unobtainable no matter how hard teachers try can do more to demoralize than to motivate greater effort. (p. 12)

Taken together, this scholarship reveals that NCLB is built on two problematic assumptions. First, the federal policy's logic is that these ambitious student achievement goals will serve as a motivator for school staff members to alter their performance. Second, the law implies that states have well-designed, standards-based assessment and accountability systems for tracking student performance in a reliable, valid, and fair manner.

Recent research on workforce trends and federal and state funding indicates that the goals of Title II are also out of reach. Illinois, Maryland, and Pennsylvania each employ large numbers of teachers who currently do not fulfill the criteria for being highly qualified (Center on Educational Policy, 2003).[11] A large percentage of teachers in California lack certification, with the greatest concentration employed in the state's high-poverty schools (Jennings, 2003). Research reported in the DOE's annual report on teacher quality for 2003 (Paige, Stroup, & Andrade, 2003) underscores these issues. In 2001-02, 6% of the U.S. teaching force lacked complete certification, with more than 10% of teachers on waivers. In addition, high-poverty school districts had a greater likelihood of employing teachers on waivers than affluent districts, averaging 8% and 5%, respectively. The authors of the annual report cite an analysis of a Schools and Staffing Survey that found that only 54% of secondary school teachers in the United States were highly qualified in the 1999-2000 school year. Given the mandate of ensuring that there is a highly qualified teacher in every classroom by the 2005-06 school year, teacher testing may become a favored state policy tool to address this gap. Lewis (2003) points out that administering subject-area tests will be the most inexpensive way for states to comply with most of Title II's accountability provisions.

A number of states may not have the resources to make new investments in education. Although President Bush advocated a significant increase in appropriations for the first year of NCLB as part of a political concession to enact the measure, the federal budget for the second year included a much smaller increase (Center on Educational Policy, 2003). Furthermore, in a recent General Accounting Office (GAO, 2003a) analysis, officials from seven of eight states surveyed reported that they did not have the technology in place to adequately track teacher qualifications (2003b).

Mathis (2003) reviewed 10 state cost studies on bringing the states' students up to a single academic standard. First, he claims that a "standards-based NCLB education" (p. 682) for all children necessitates significant new investments in education spending, with 7 of the 10 studies predicting greater than 24% increases in base costs. In addition, although the federal government expresses confidence that it is fully funding Title I, the New Hampshire study indicated that federal appropriations will be insufficient to cover such Title II costs as additional bureaucracy, teacher and paraprofessional testing, and qualified teachers. Moreover, the National Governors Association estimates that states are dealing with a total fiscal-year deficit of $58 billion. Lastly, states with "high standards" (p. 68), such as New York, Michigan, and Vermont, will have the highest remedial needs and costs, while those with low standards will have the smallest costs.

While some scholars focus on the human and financial resources that meeting the NCLB mandates will require, others critique the ways that teaching quality is represented in Title II's position pieces and legislation. Kaplan and Owings (2003) and Darling-Hammond and Youngs (2002) take issue with the interpretations of the teacher quality research that influenced Title II of NCLB. These authors critique the DOE's 2002 annual report on teacher quality for the ways in which the document "misleadingly presented data" (Kaplan & Owings, p. 691).[12] Kaplan and Owings respond to Title II's removal of teacher preparation as a hiring requirement for secondary school teachers. Their analysis discusses the ways in which educators and policymakers understand subject matter knowledge, verbal skills, and the quality of teacher education programs, three factors explored in studies of teacher quality. The authors argue that, although these are necessary criteria for teaching quality, there is no evidence that they are sufficient. They also point out that, because college majors vary in their rigor, a prospective teacher's university transcript may not actually confirm requisite subject matter knowledge. Darling-Hammond and Youngs concur and provide detailed descriptions of the studies that informed the claims in the 2002 annual report, only one of which appeared in a peer-reviewed journal. Darling-Hammond and Youngs also claim that the report misrepresented Murname's (1983) and Hanushek's (1996) conclusions about teacher characteristics (by omitting any reference to the passages from Murname and Hanushek describing the limitations of their studies) and misinterpreted Goldhaber and Brewer (1999).

Kaplan and Owings (2003) also reason that research on credentialing is problematic. First, teacher preparation programs vary widely in quality. Second, states have the flexibility to impose their own criteria for both the performance of teacher education institutions and licensure exams. After their analysis, however, they conclude that the research "nevertheless suggests that teacher candidates from accredited, respected teacher preparation programs probably have an edge—although by no means a guarantee—in terms of potential teaching effectiveness" (p. 692). Darling-Hammond and Youngs (2002) revisited a number of studies of teacher credentialing and education and also found evidence of the positive relationship between this training and student achievement.

Initial responses to the 2003 annual report put forth similar criticisms about the federal government's potential for providing leadership in teacher quality efforts. The Education Trust (2003) expressed concerns about the accuracy and consistency of the information in the report. For example, when comparing the 2002 and 2003 reports, Education Trust observed that Utah's total number of teachers dropped by one third while Alabama's teaching force increased by 24%. This raises important questions about federal capacity to track state progress in their efforts to ensure whether students have highly qualified teachers. The Association for Supervision and Curriculum Development's (2003) critique of the annual report focuses on the federal government's approach to credentialing. They question the strategies named in the report, which advocate lowering barriers to teaching while raising professional standards:

The moves to increase accountability for teacher preparation, while also removing barriers to entering the profession, are creating a mixed policy picture. The use of tests by policymakers as a key quality gauge and the emphasis on subject-matter at the expense of teaching knowledge could have significant long-term effects on teaching and student learning. (paragraph 11)

Because states are free to choose assessments and assign cut scores, it is problematic to generalize about quality as measured by teacher exams (Hirsh, Koppich, & Knapp, 2001). Recent scholarship further warrants Lewis's (2003) concerns about dependence on teacher testing. Ludlow (2001) documented psychometric flaws in the 1999 Massachusetts Educator Certification Test that resembled the defects named in an Alabama class-action lawsuit about teacher certification. He calls for the creation of an organization that could provide oversight around technical issues associated with teacher testing. Mitchell and Barth (1999), after a content analysis of teacher tests, conclude that the exams are not able to certify whether teachers have the requisite knowledge to teach all students to high standards.

An important thread through the response to Title II is that teaching and instructional improvement are conceptually complex—indeed, more complex than the conclusions about teaching quality articulated in federal policy documents. Because we maintain that the design of workforce development policies in teaching occurs across levels of a nested system, an important question is, what aspects of our knowledge of teaching quality can be addressed within the federal definitions of scientifically based research? Among these concerns are the types of activities that are considered research and the federal government's control of research activities. Slavin (2002) and Gardner (2002) provide alternately optimistic and doubtful perspectives on these points.[13] Eisenhart and Towne (2003) name two additional issues. First, some scholars are troubled that, in the current political climate, certain ways of knowing (e.g., philosophical, historical, cultural, or practice-oriented families of inquiry) that may be relevant to effective teaching will be ignored in the efforts to pursue scientifically based research. Second, others question whether the federal perception of the "sorry state of education research" (Eisenhart & Towne, p. 31) is more a function of money and politics than of science.

The early responses to Title II of NCLB suggest that the legislation's proxies for teacher quality are necessary but grossly insufficient. Although Title II documents explain that the legislation offers flexibility to states and districts, the legislation lacks provisions that would enable the federal government to take diverse state contexts into consideration. Furthermore, this conversation provides considerable evidence of limited federal and state capacity to carry out the legislation's assessment, accountability, and teacher quality mandates.

A critical question for the next phase of research on the effects of federal policy on teacher quality is how Title II influences states' ability to foster coherence, comprehensiveness, and capacity at different levels in their efforts to improve instruction. An important lesson of the teaching reforms of the 1990s was that programs such as teacher networks and study groups show the potential to foster high-quality instruction (Porter et al., 2000). The challenge will be to discern the impact of these and other more grassroots investments on instruction and student learning from the effects of NCLB reform efforts.

In our conclusion, we reflect on the scholarship and commentary about state and federal policies addressing teacher quality. We focus on the ways this evidence speaks to four policy and design principles targeted at improving teaching.

Designing Policy Strategies Aimed at Improving Teacher Quality

As we noted early in this chapter, the quality of the teacher, the quality of teaching, and the quality of support for teachers' work are all essential aspects of what is typically referred to as "teacher quality." State teacher workforce development policies can and should address each of these aspects, and there are numerous sets of policy strategies that can be forged to do so. Our examination of state efforts to date suggests, however, that policy actions designed to improve teacher quality have been directed primarily at improving the attributes of the individual teacher, and they also tend to be concentrated on teachers' entrance into the profession. Consequently, policy strategies to date are insufficient to effectively address the full range of teachers' needs. For example, most states struggle to obtain and sustain support for the ongoing professional development of experienced teachers, even though it is this type of support for teachers' work that is essential to realizing the ambitious expectations states hold for student learning. These are critical shortcomings, given that we now know that lack of retention is a greater contributor to "teacher shortages" than inability to recruit (Ingersoll, 2001, 2003). States are also likely to face pressures to limit the range of their strategies aimed at improving teaching quality as they respond to the requirements of recent federal legislation.

To address these issues, we suggest four guiding principles that can inform the design of more comprehensive, coherent, and equitable state and federal policies for the improvement of teacher quality:

1. Policies should be informed by broader conceptions of teacher development.
2. Human and financial resource investments should be aligned with policy aims.
3. Longstanding equity concerns should be fully addressed.
4. The limitations of state and federal policy efforts should be recognized.

Clearly, these principles are ambitious and present significant challenges for policymaking. These principles do not assume that all strategies must emanate from state or federal mandates. Rather, the most successful policy strategies are likely to develop in collaboration with and in support of local efforts and initiatives aimed at common purposes because these policies will result in the capacity building necessary for comprehensive and coherent approaches. We conclude by synthesizing what we have observed about state and federal workforce development policies with respect to each of the four guiding principles.

Broader Conceptions of Teacher Development

State and federal policies addressing teacher quality can signal either a narrow or a broad understanding of how teachers develop their practice throughout their careers. There are examples of current state policy action with a broad understanding of teacher development, including North Carolina's effort to support teachers seeking certification from the National Board of Professional Teaching Standards and New York's effort to include the full continuum of teacher development in its plan for improving teacher quality.

With respect to federal policies, however, the NCLB definition of a highly qualified teacher, in its current form, suggests a narrow set of beliefs about the qualities that are necessary for excellence in teaching. Given the significant attention being paid to meeting the accountability demands of NCLB, states will be facing pressures to design teacher quality initiatives that first meet the three specific quality measures as defined in the federal policy. It is possible, especially given the fiscal stress that exists in many states, that the Title II accountability requirements may encourage a triage approach as states scramble to meet minimum requirements. In other words, NCLB may inhibit more coherent and comprehensive approaches that encompass the complexity of teaching. States can resist the pressure to adopt narrow conceptions of teaching by investing in capacity-building strategies that will result in such long-term, sustainable benefits as a more stable workforce and improved student learning. Examples of such capacity-building strategies include subject matter teacher networks, peer observations of teaching practice, more meaningful teacher evaluation systems, and a continuum of sustained support for mentor teachers as well as for those who are mentored.

Human and Financial Resource Investments

One of the most important policy mechanisms can be found in the power of the purse. Policymakers have the ability to provide new resources for particular initiatives, to reallocate existing resources away from policies that are no longer deemed viable or desirable, and to withhold resources for failure to enact established policies or meet determined outcomes. The allocation of resources can effectively focus attention on desired changes. During times of fiscal retrenchment, however, the tensions and challenges faced by states that are trying to positively affect teaching quality become intensified. The examples provided earlier in this chapter illustrate that states are currently struggling to provide adequate resources for their teaching policy initiatives. Given this period of decreases in state resources for public education, Lewis's (2003) concern about the potential dominance of teacher testing as a cost-effective measure of teachers' abilities appears warranted. States' decreased fiscal capacities combine with other concerns about the underfunding of NCLB.

Recently, Darling-Hammond and Sykes (2003) called for a greatly expanded federal role in the development of a national teacher supply policy as a way of improving teacher quality. They advocate an approach to increasing the teacher labor pool that requires additional federal resources and more coordination across states. Specifically, they offer steps to increase the supply of qualified teachers to the sites and the fields where there is greatest need; to improve teacher retention rates with a focus on hard-to-staff schools; and to create a national teacher labor market. This approach provides one example of how we might work to better align the aims of policy with the investment strategies that are most likely to support policy goals.

Equity Concerns

As Darling-Hammond and Sykes (2003) assert, "the hiring of unqualified teachers is generally a result of distributional inequities, rather than overall shortages of qualified individuals"(p. 3). Deep concerns about the equity of access to a high-quality education across the United States have prompted policymakers to think about the connections between student performance and access to high-quality teaching. States have yet to build sustainable systems that fully address inequities in the distribution of well-qualified teachers across schools and classrooms. Neither most state policies nor Title II of NCLB chart a specific course for how to provide a well-qualified teacher for every student. There are only a few examples of states offering incentives for well-qualified teachers to work in hard-to-staff or low-performing schools.

Many states are attempting to address inequities through accountability mechanisms that pay particular attention to differences in student learning by poverty level, race, and ethnicity of students. These attempts are most visible in state policies regarding the disaggregation and public reporting of student assessment data. Although accountability systems shed light on equity concerns that need to be addressed, most states have yet to fashion an educational policy agenda that connects accountability for student learning with specific teacher quality improvement strategies, particularly with respect to policies that support teachers' ongoing work and professional growth. Policy efforts aimed at eliminating distributional inequities are the least mature of all policy strategies designed to improve teaching and learning. Additional work needs to be undertaken to better understand the barriers that are limiting successful implementation of coherent policies focused on equity concerns.

Limitations of State and Federal Policy Efforts

A central theme in this chapter has been that state and federal policies can and should address the tensions and challenges that are part of improving teacher quality. We have noted that state and federal policy attention to issues of teacher quality have greatly increased in recent years. We also suggest, however, that there are limitations to policies crafted and implemented at state and federal levels. Successful design and implementation of federal and state teaching policies are dependent on and interact with local capacities at district and school levels and, even more importantly, at the teacher level. Capacity-building strategies focus on the solutions that districts, schools, and teachers need to create in order to respond to the specific contexts encountered at the local level. State and federal policies cannot realistically incorporate all the possible variables that might be affecting local practices, but they can assume that differences will exist and that flexibility is needed to respond to local conditions.

Federal and state policies must result in increased capacity that enables teachers to deliver powerful, standards-based instruction. Increasing capacity is not typically accomplished through state, federal, or district policy mandates imposed on individual schools or teachers. But there are other state and federal policy options for building local capacity that can and should be considered, including those strategies that provide supportive workplace conditions, address the inequitable distribution of teaching talent, and involve the teaching profession in shaping policy. Capacity-building strategies are by nature harder for policymakers to adopt, however, because they challenge the dominant view of the role and purpose of state policy. As Cohen and Barnes (1993) note:

Policymakers have told teachers to do many different, hugely important things in a short time. And in each case, policymakers have acted as though their assignment was to dispense answers, not to provoke thought, ask questions, or generate discussion. . . . Nor have policymakers cast policy as something that might be revised in light of what they learned from teachers' experience. (pp. 226-227)

These four guidelines highlight challenges for educational policymaking regarding teacher workforce development. Evidence from research about the complexity of improving teaching suggests the promise of recasting the definition of "highly qualified teacher" in broader terms. To this end, policy strategies not only need to consider the key supports in developing individual teachers' capabilities but also need to direct financial and human resources to the schools that are most in need. Both NCLB and the Department of Education's conceptualization of scientifically based research conflicts with this broader view because it emphasizes the use of limited proxy variables to measure teacher quality. The next wave of scholarship addressing policy efforts to improve teacher quality will need to consider state and district responses to NCLB while also assessing teacher improvement efforts that are not directly touched by the policy. Ideally, the lessons learned in this inquiry will inform policymaking and program development that approach teacher quality as a critical and complex endeavor.

NOTES

1. The Center for the Study of Teaching and Policy, a consortium of several major universities, focuses on the system-wide improvement of learning and teaching and the development of a highly capable, committed teaching force.

2. Other CTP researchers contributing to the longitudinal study include Michael S. Knapp, Barnett Berry, James Meadows, and Dylan Johnson.

3. Jennings provides a detailed discussion of the changing federal role in educational reform in his chapter in the *102nd Yearbook of the National Society for the Study of Education*, "From the White House to the Schoolhouse: Greater Demands and New Roles."

4. The titles of the reports are *Designing Effective Professional Development: Lessons from the Eisenhower Program* and *Does Professional Development Change Teaching Practice? Results from a Three-Year Study*. A third AIS report, *The Eisenhower Professional Development Program: Emerging Themes from Six Districts* (Birman, Reeve, & Sattler, 1998), documented the incipient themes about the program in exploratory cases involving six school districts.

5. During 1991-1996, the ESSSI program allocated up to $2 million annually to individual states providing substantive plans for systemic reform.

6. These documents include NCLB legislation, the NCLB Web site (http://www.ed.gov/nclb/), and such supporting documents as *A Quality Teacher in Every Classroom: Improving Teacher Quality and Enhancing the Profession* (n.d.), *Improving Teacher Quality State Grants* (U.S. Department of Education, 2002, December), *Meeting the*

Highly Qualified Teachers Challenge: The Secretary's Annual Report on Teacher Quality (Paige, Stroup, & Andrade, 2002, 2003), and the *U.S. Department of Education Strategic Plan, 2002-2007* (DOE, 2002a).

7. Section 9101(23) of ESEA provides general provisions of the legislation, providing definitions of such terms as "highly qualified teacher," "professional development," "scientifically based research," etc.

8. "Core academic subjects" as defined by NCLB are "English, reading or language arts, mathematics, science, foreign languages, civics and government, economics, arts, history, and geography" (*Improving Teacher Quality State Grants*, p. 86).

9. Eisenhart and Towne (2003) explain that definitions of scientifically based research vary in different policy documents. Definitions of scientifically based research are somewhat broader in the Education Sciences Reform Act (ESRA) of 2002, which reauthorized funding for the Office of Educational Research and Improvement (renamed the Institute of Education Sciences following passage of the Act). For example, ESRA does not have different standards for quantitative and qualitative research. It also does not require the inclusion of mandated hypothesis testing for funded research activities.

10. Darling-Hammond (2000) provides a much broader picture of the impact of teacher preservice education, reviewing studies with conflicting findings about the relationship between this training and student achievement.

11. "Illinois had estimated that about 25,000 out of 130,000 teachers in the state are teaching without full credentials or in subjects for which they are not certified" (Sack, 2002). A report of the Maryland Department of Education estimated that 10% of newly hired teachers, or more than 5,300 teachers, were hired with provisional certificates, meaning they had not yet passed the necessary state exams or coursework (Labbé, 2002). "In Philadelphia, by one report, more than half of the 600 new teachers hired this year were not fully certified" (Mezzacappa, 2002).

12. They explain that although the annual report discussed the experiences of new teachers, the NCES study it cited was actually from a survey of practicing classroom teachers, most of whom were not new to the profession.

13. Slavin welcomes the federal mandates in the hope that increased research investments will lead to improved student outcomes, but Gardner is more skeptical. Slavin claims that the greatest breakthroughs in medicine, agricultural science, and other fields have come through evidence-based scholarship, but he recognizes the value of correlational and descriptive inquiry because these strategies are critical in exploring variables that extend beyond program effects. In contrast, Gardner notes that research in schools is not conducted under the ideal conditions for randomized studies.

REFERENCES

ASCD (Association for Supervision and Curriculum Development). (2003, July). ESEA/NCLB Analysis. Retrieved November 2003 from http://www.ascd.org/cms/index.cfm?TheViewID=2038

Baker, E.L., & Linn, R.L. (1997). *Emerging educational standards of performance in the United States.* Los Angeles, CA: National Center for Research on Evaluation, Standards, and Student Testing.

Birman, B., Reeve, A., & Sattler, C. (1998). *The Eisenhower professional development program: Emerging themes from six districts.* Washington, DC: American Institutes for Research in the Behavioral Sciences.

Boyd, D., Lankford, H., Loeb, S., & Wyckoff, J. (2003). Understanding teacher labor markets: Implications for educational equity. In M.L. Plecki & D.H. Monk (Eds.), *School finance and teacher quality: Exploring the connections. The 2003 yearbook of the American Education Finance Association* (pp. 55-83). Larchmont, NJ: Eye on Education.

Center on Educational Policy. (2003, January). *From the capital to the classroom: State and federal efforts to implement the No Child Left Behind Act.* Washington, DC: Center on Educational Policy.

Cohen, D.K. (1995). What standards for national standards? *Phi Delta Kappan, 76*(10), 751-757.

Cohen, D.K., & Barnes, C.A. (1993). Pedagogy and policy. In D.K. Cohen, M.W. McLaughlin, & J. Talbert (Eds.), *Teaching for understanding: Challenges for policy and practice* (pp. 207-239). San Francisco, CA: Jossey-Bass.

Cookson, P.W., Jr. (1995). Goals 2000: Framework for the new educational federalism. *Teachers College Record, 96*(3), 404-417.

Darling-Hammond, L. (2000). Teacher quality and student achievement: A review of state policy evidence. *Educational Policy Analysis Archives, 8*(1). Retrieved December 12, 2002, from http://epaa.asu.edu/epaa/v8n1/

Darling-Hammond, L., & Sykes, G. (2003). Wanted: A national teacher supply policy for education: The right way to meet the "highly qualified" challenge. *Education Policy Analysis Archives, 11*(3). Retrieved September 16, 2003, from http://epaa.asu.edu/epaa.v11n33

Darling-Hammond, L., & Youngs, P. (2002). Defining "highly qualified teachers": What does "scientifically-based research" actually tell us? *Educational Researcher, 31*(9), 13-25.

Directorate for Education and Human Resources Division of Research, Evaluation and Communication (1996, August). *NSF evaluation highlights: A report on the National Science Foundation's efforts to assess the effectiveness of its education programs.* Washington, DC: National Science Foundation. Retrieved June 2003 from http://www.nsf.gov/pubs/1996/nsf96140/nsf96140.pdf

DOE (Department of Education). (n.d.). The facts about good teachers. Retrieved May 2003 from http://www.nclb.gov/start/facts/teachers.html

DOE (Department of Education). (n.d.) The federal role in education. Washington, DC: Author. Retrieved May 2003 from http://www.ed.gov/offices/OUS/fedrole.html

DOE (Department of Education). (n.d.). Overview of No Child Left Behind. Retrieved May 2003 from http://www.nochildleftbehind.gov/next/overview/index.html

DOE (Department of Education). (2001). No Child Left Behind Act of 2001. Title IX. Retrieved May 2003 from http://www.ed.gov/legislation/ESEA02/pg107.html

DOE (Department of Education). (2001). No Child Left Behind Act of 2001. Amended in 2002. Retrieved May 2003 from http://www.ed.gov/legislation/ESEA02/

DOE (Department of Education). (2002a, December). Improving teacher quality state grants Title II, Part A: Non-Regulatory Guidance. Retrieved April 2003 from http://www.ed.gov/offices/OESE/SIP/TitleIIguidance2002.doc

DOE (Department of Education). (2002b). U.S. Department of Education strategic plan, 2002-2007. Retrieved May 2003 from http://www.ed.gov/pubs/stratplan2002-07/stratplan2002-07.doc

Eisenhart, M., & Towne, L. (2003). Contestation and change in national policy on "scientifically based" education research. *Educational Researcher, 32*(7), 31-38.

Elmore, R.F., & McLaughlin, M.W. (1988). *Steady work: Policy, practice, and the reform of American education*. Santa Monica, CA: RAND.

Feiman-Nemser, S. (2001). From preparation to practice: Designing a continuum to strengthen and sustain teaching. *Teachers College Record, 103*(6), 1013-1055.

Feiman-Nemser, S., Carver, C., Katz, D., Schwille, S., Smith, E., & Yusko, B. (2000). Beginning teacher induction: A study of three promising programs. Final report for the National Partnership for Excellence and Accountability (NPEAT). East Lansing: Michigan State University, College of Education.

Ferguson, R.F. (1997). Evidence that schools can narrow the Black-White test score gap. *Working Paper, #H-97-04*. Cambridge, MA: Malcolm Wiener Center for Social Policy, John F. Kennedy School of Government.

Feuer, M.J., Towne, L., & Shavelson, R.J. (2002). Scientific culture and educational research. *Educational Researcher, 31*(8), 4-14.

Gardner, H. (2002, September 4). The quality and qualities of educational research. *Education Week, 22*(1), 72, 49.

General Accounting Office. (2003a, May). *Title I characteristics of tests will influence expenses; Information sharing may help state realize efficiencies*. GAO-03-389, a report to Congressional Requesters. Washington, DC: Author.

General Accounting Office (2003b, July). *No Child Left Behind Act: More information would help states determine which teachers are highly qualified*. GAO-03-631, a report to Congressional Requesters. Washington, DC: Author.

Goldhaber, D., & Brewer, D. (1997). Evaluating the effect of teacher degree level on educational performance. In W. Fowler (Ed.), *Developments in school finance, 1996* (pp. 197-210). Washington, DC: U.S. Department of Education, National Center for Education Statistics. Retrieved August 2003 from http://nces.ed.gov/pubs97/97535l.pdf

Goldhaber, D., & Brewer, D. (1999). Teacher licensing and student achievement. In M. Kanstroroom & C.E. Finn, Jr. (Eds.), *Better teachers, better schools* (pp. 83-102). Washington, DC:Thomas B. Fordham Foundation.

Hannaway, J., & Kimball, K. (2001). Big isn't always bad: School district size, poverty, and standards-based reform. In S.H. Fuhrman (Ed.), *From the capital to the classroom: Standards-based reform in the states. The one-hundredth yearbook of the National Society for the Study of Education*, Part II (pp. 99-123). Chicago, IL: National Society for the Study of Education.

Hanushek, E.A. (1996). *School resources and achievement in Maryland*. Baltimore: Maryland State Department of Education.

Hirsh, E., Koppich, J.E., & Knapp, M. (1999, December). *State action to improve teaching*. Seattle, WA: Center for the Study of Teaching and Policy.

Hirsh, E., Koppich, J.E., & Knapp, M. (2001, February). *Revisiting what states are doing to improve the quality of teaching: An update of patterns and trends*. A working paper prepared in collaboration with the National Conference of State Legislatures. Seattle, WA: Center for the Study of Teaching and Policy.

Imazeki, J. (2003). Class size reduction and teacher quality: Evidence from California. In M.L. Plecki & D.H. Monk (Eds.), *School finance and teacher quality: Exploring the connections. The 2003 yearbook of the American Education Finance Association* (pp. 159-178). Larchmont, NJ: Eye on Education.

Ingersoll, R. (2001). Teacher turnover and teacher shortages: An organizational analysis. *American Educational Research Journal, 38*(3), 499-534.

Ingersoll, R. (2003). *Is there really a teacher shortage?* Center for the Study of Teaching and Policy, University of Washington. Available at http://ctpweb.org

Jennings, J. (1998). *Why national standards and tests? Politics and the quest for better schools*. Thousand Oaks, CA: Sage.

Jennings, J. (2003). From the White House to the schoolhouse: Greater demands and new roles. In W.L. Boyd & D. Miretzky (Eds.), *American educational governance on trial: Change and challenges. The 102nd yearbook of the National Society for the Study of Education*, Part I (pp. 291-309). Chicago, IL: National Society for the Study of Education.

Kaplan, L.S., & Owings, W.A. (2003, May). The politics of teacher quality. *Phi Delta Kappan, 84*(6), 687-692.

Killeen, K., Monk, D., & Plecki, M. (2002). School district spending on professional development: Insights available from national data (1992-1998). *Journal of Education Finance, 28*(1), 25-49.

Koppich, J. (2003). Distributing the pie: Allocating resources through labor-management agreements. In M.L. Plecki & D.H. Monk (Eds.), *School finance and teacher quality: Exploring the connections. The 2003 yearbook of the American Education Finance Association* (pp. 229-246). Larchmont, NJ: Eye on Education.

Labbé, T. (2002, August 28). More new Md. teachers not fully certified. *Washington Post*, b05.

Lewis, A. (2003, February). Washington Commentary: Title II and teacher testing. *Phi Delta Kappan; 84*(6), 420-421.

Linn, R.L., Baker, E.L., & Betebenner, D.W. (2002). Accountability systems: Implications of requirements of the No Child Left Behind Act of 2001. *Educational Researcher, 31*(6), 3-16.

Ludlow, L.H. (2001). Teacher test accountability: From Alabama to Massachusetts. *Education Policy Analysis Archives, 9*(6). Retrieved August 2003 from http://epaa.asu.edu/epaa/v9n6.html

Massell, D., Kirst, M., & Hoppe, M. (1997). Persistence and change: Standards-based systemic reform in nine states. Philadelphia: University of Pennsylvania Consortium for Policy Research in Education (CPRE), RB-21. Retrieved November 2002 from http://www.cpre.org/Publications/rb21.pdf

Mathis, W.J. (2003, May). No Child Left Behind: Costs and benefits. *Phi Delta Kappan, 84*(6), 679-686.

McLaughlin, M.W. (1976). Implementation as mutual adaptation: Change in classroom organization. *Teachers College Record, 77*, 339-351.

Melnick, S.L., & Pullin, D. (2000). Can you take dictation? Prescribing teacher quality through testing. *Journal of Teacher Education, 51*(4), 262-275.

Mezzacappa, D. (2002, November 15). Pa. moves to raise teacher standard. *Philadelphia Inquirer*, 1.

Mitchell, R., & Barth, P. (1999, Spring). Not good enough: A content analysis of teacher licensing examinations. *Thinking K-16: A publication of the Education Trust, 3*(1). Retrieved August 2003 from http://www2.edtrust.org/NR/rdonlyres/5F7B8FCA-2400-47DE-9C40-AC948D93 4836 /0/k16_spring99.pdf

Murname, R.J. (1983). Understanding the sources of teaching competence: Choices, skills, and the limits of training. *Teachers College Record, 84*(3), 564-589.

Odden, A.R. (2003). An early assessment of comprehensive teacher compensation change plans. In M.L. Plecki & D.H. Monk (Eds.), *School finance and teacher quality: Exploring the connections. The 2003 yearbook of the American Education Finance Association* (pp. 209-228). Larchmont, NJ: Eye on Education.

Paige, R., Stroup, S., & Andrade, J.R. (2002). *Meeting the highly qualified teachers challenge: The Secretary's annual report on teacher quality.* Washington, DC: U.S. Department of Education Office of Postsecondary Education. Retrieved June 2003 from http://www.title2.org/ADATitleIIReport2002.pdf

Paige, R., Stroup, S., & Andrade, J.R. (2003). *Meeting the highly qualified teachers challenge: The Secretary's annual report on teacher quality.* Washington, DC: U.S. Department of Education Office of Postsecondary Education. Retrieved November 2003 from http://www.title2.org/TitleIIReport03.pdf

Plecki, M.L. (2000). Economic perspectives on investments in teacher quality: Lessons learned from research on productivity and human resource development. *Education Policy Analysis Archives, 8*(33). Retrieved November 2003 from http://epaa.asu.edu/epaa/v8n33.html

Porter, A.C., Garet, M.S., Desimone, L., Yoon, K.S., & Birman, B.F. (2000). *Does professional development change teaching practice? Results from a three-year study.* Washington, DC: American Institutes for Research in the Behavioral Sciences.

Porter, A.C., Garet, M.S., Desimone, L., Yoon, K.S., Birman, B.F., & Herman, R. (1999). *Designing effective development: Lessons from the Eisenhower program.* Washington, DC: American Institutes for Research in the Behavioral Sciences.

A quality teacher in every classroom: Improving teacher quality and enhancing the profession. (n.d.) Retrieved May 2003 from http://whitehouse.gov/infocus/education/teachers/

Reys, B., Robinson, E., Sconiers, S., & Mark, J. (1999). Mathematics curricula based on rigorous national standards: What, why, and how? *Phi Delta Kappan, 80*(6), 454-456.

Rice, J.K. (2003). *Teacher quality: Understanding the effectiveness of teacher attributes.* Washington, DC: Economic Policy Institute.

Sack, J. (2002, October 2). Illinois board adjusts teacher certification to meet federal rules. *Education Week, 22*(5), 20.

Shields, P., & Knapp, M. (1997, December). The promise and limits of school-based reform: A national snapshot. *Phi Delta Kappan, 78*(4), 288-294.

Slavin, R.E. (2002). Evidence-based education policies: Transforming educational research and practice. *Education Researcher, 31*(7), 15-21.

Spillane, J.P., & Thompson, C.L. (1997). Reconstructing conceptions of local capacity: The local education agency's capacity for ambitious instructional reform. *Educational Evaluation and Policy Analysis, 19,* 185-203.

Spillane, J.P., & Zeuli, J.S. (1999). Reform and teaching: Exploring patterns of practice in the context of national and state mathematics reforms. *Educational Evaluation and Policy Analysis, 21*(1), 1-28.

Sunderman, G., & Kim, J. (2004). *Inspiring vision, disappointing results: Four studies on implementing the No Child Left Behind Act.* Cambridge, MA: Harvard Civil Rights Project. Retrieved March 2004 from http://www.civilrightsproject.harvard.edu/research/esea/call_nclb.php?Page=2

Thompson, C.L., & Zeuli, J.S. (1999). The frame and the tapestry: Standards-based reform and professional development. In Darling-Hammond, L., & Sykes, G. (Eds.), *Teaching as the learning profession: Handbook of policy and practice* (pp. 341-375). San Francisco: Jossey-Bass.

Timar, T. (1997). The institutional role of state education departments: A historical perspective. *American Journal of Education, 105,* 231-260.

Walsh, K. (2001). *Teacher certification rconsidered: Stumbling for quality.* Baltimore, MD: Abell Foundation. Retrieved March 2004 from http://www.abell.org/pubsitems/ed_cert_1101.pdf

Part Two
COMMENTARIES

Ongoing Teacher Support:
A Critical Component of Classroom Success

ANTHONY G. VANDARAKIS

Teaching is not something one learns to do, once and for all, and then practices, problem free, for a lifetime, any more than one knows how to have friends, and follows a static set of directions called "friendship" through each encounter. Teaching depends on growth and development, and it is practiced in dynamic situations that are never twice the same.

William Ayers, *To Teach*

The next fall, I signed up as a $54-a day substitute with the Chicago Board of Education, intending only to test the waters. I had done no education coursework and had no credentials. I still wasn't sure if teaching was for me, if it was something I'd be any good at. But after just a few weeks of being bounced around as a day-to-day sub, I was, surprisingly, offered a full-time position at a South Side middle school. A teacher had quit suddenly; they were desperate. Filled with uncertainty, I took the job anyway, and in a matter of days had a classroom of my own. I've been trying to become a teacher ever since.

Gregory Michie, *holler if you hear me*

I am a teacher. My name is Anthony G. Vandarakis and I am a twenty-eight-year-old white male, a Chicago Public Schools (CPS) employee, and a graduate of the Golden Apple Teacher Education (GATE) alternative certification program at the University of Illinois at Chicago (UIC). I have been asked to reflect on my experiences throughout the various stages of my teaching career. Much of this reflection depends on the accuracy of my memory, which may be one of my finer qualities but is nonetheless flawed and to a lesser degree tempered.

Anthony G. Vandarakis completed his undergraduate work at DePaul University in Chicago, Illinois. He received his master's degree in education from the University of Illinois at Chicago and is currently teaching in the Chicago Public Schools.

My alternative path to teaching started in corporate America. I left my career as an information consultant with NetTel Technologies to become an elementary school teacher. As an undergraduate at DePaul University in Chicago, I had majored in political science and business. My motivation for leaving big business can be distilled to one simple thought: my lack of impact in corporate America pushed me to find a profession in which meaningful relationships could produce real change. Corporations are ruled and run based on their bottom line. Ends are just as important to me, but this time it's not about the number of hits on a new customer's Web site; it's about the chance to build connections between a changing world, a dynamic classroom, and a unique child.

For me, teaching provided a chance to have a real impact. But unlike a desk job that can be managed by one person, teaching has to be a collaboration between educators, administrators, students, parents, and community members. It is in the context of this complex interactive web that a teacher needs support. The crux of my commentary will look at areas under the teacher support umbrella, including preservice teacher preparation, recruitment, new teacher induction and mentoring, teacher retention, and professional development.

I obtained my "official" preservice experience through the GATE alternative teacher certification program at UIC. While I had had some substitute teaching experience in two public schools, my introduction to alternative certification began, strangely enough, on Chicago's subway. It was on the way to work that I noticed an ad soliciting professionals to change careers and enter the teaching profession. That year, 2000, the Chicago Public Schools were experiencing a severe teacher shortage; Golden Apple was one of four organizations offering "fast track certification" in response to this shortage. Several hours of research later, I had an application in hand. Fast forward five weeks, and I was delivering my college transcripts, premature ideas and philosophies on education, and letters of recommendation to the Golden Apple Foundation in person. The stars must have been aligned because I was granted an interview. The actual interview (conducted at Golden Apple's downtown office) was rather uncomfortable, stressful, and not at all what I expected. Haberman interviews may tell admissions boards quite a bit about prospective teachers, but they leave something to be desired for the person on the other side of the table. It was a high-pressure interview; I had been on several successful interviews in the business sector but had never encountered such frustrating questions. One question, which I struggled with but ultimately had to answer, was, "Do you have to love your students in order to teach them?" I honestly can't remember

392   ONGOING TEACHER SUPPORT

how I answered the question, but I do remember the frustration I felt in having to commit to a response. By this time, I knew that I wanted to teach and this interview meant more than any previous one, even though it would take a year to complete the GATE program and ultimately result in a CPS position that paid half my former salary.

The GATE teaching immersion program, which I began in the summer of 2001, was not my first experience in the classroom. Freshly discouraged with corporate America, I had decided in June 1999 to explore teaching as my vehicle for promoting meaningful change. I applied for and was granted a substitute certificate; that, along with a heartbeat, qualified me for daily assignments in Chicago's public schools. My baptism by fire came in September of that year when I had my first "permanent" substitute teaching experience. I inherited a third/fourth-grade split class that had had daily substitute teachers from their first day of school. I had only subbed for two days before I was approached by the school principal, who asked me to take on this particular classroom for the rest of the year. These students were devastated by what they had been through; they told me, "We are not wanted; we don't have a teacher."

The working conditions were difficult. Most days the teachers were not given any preparation time, we all ate lunch with our students, and the promised fifteen-minute break rarely materialized. My school was located in one of Chicago's premier neighborhoods, yet it did not attract the local children; 95% attended private or Catholic schools. Our student body, largely minority and economically disadvantaged, was bussed in from the Near West Side. At the end of the school year, 100% of my fourth graders moved on to fifth grade. The percentage of third graders moving to fourth was not as high. Much of that year I would like to forget. I was a terrible teacher; the kids forgave me, but the mirror still can't. With the exception of two fellow teachers (one a seasoned educator who saw promise in my teaching and the other a neophyte sub), my classroom door was closed to everyone. I was not formally or informally observed, critiqued, or encouraged—in fact, I was never introduced to the staff. My only interaction with the principal came prior to the first report card pickup, in November. I was told how to respond to parents who might be concerned about my lack of teaching experience.

And yet I looked forward to my teaching days and genuinely enjoyed most of my students, despite the fact that new teachers in this school were not supported. This lack of support, however, made it impossible for me to continue to teach in that environment. My experience in 1999 seemed typical of the other Full Time Provisional (FTP) instructors I worked with. There were three of us, and we all left at the end of the school year. I am the only one still teaching. While subbing provided an invaluable introduction to the classroom, the school climate left much to be desired. It discouraged *teaching*. I learned through observation how to complete the attendance book, collect lunch money, line kids up, and supervise recess, but the experience did not include real instruction, collaboration, or reflection. I stayed to the end of the year because I had made a commitment to the students. I wanted to be there, and most important, I felt I was having an impact on the students' lives. Logic still tells me that these students were better off with my consistent presence and my ability to be a role model than they would have been with yet another new teacher. Remembering this isolating and isolated experience leads me to the body of this reflection: how I was and how I am currently supported as a teacher.

Preservice Preparation

Preservice preparation is an integral but rapid process for alternatively certified educators. My preservice experience began in June 2001 with a one-week introduction to teaching at UIC led by the GATE program's co-directors, Dr. Greg Michie and Amy Rome. Without their superb leadership and dedication, the entire program could have been disjointed, impractical, a waste of time, or worse yet, an in-depth analysis of educational theory.

When I discuss my certification process with colleagues from other alternative certification programs, the ultimate variable in the overall experience is the facilitators. With limited time in a classroom and limited exposure to best practice and quality theory, reflective instructors, who in my case were doctoral candidates at UIC, are paramount to the success of the "teacher interns." For me it was important to rely on the GATE program leaders; they were, for the most part, in our classrooms, coaching us and learning with us. A more traditional approach in a typical university teacher preparation program relies on professors (good or bad) in university classrooms, at best re-creating classroom life with video clips that bring recorded children into the discussion. In the GATE program, we had living, breathing, reacting children. Equally important, Michie and Rome were realistic. They understood the shortcomings of teacher preparation in general as well as the unique challenge of alternative certification. In a system as large as Chicago's, public education varies with each neighborhood and with each school. GATE concentrated on recognizing the communities' and the students' specific needs.

I vividly remember spending the summer of my GATE internship in Chicago's Chinatown at Haines Elementary School teaching a small group of children. The GATE Summer Program at Haines was not a CPS bridge program[1] but rather serviced a mixed bag of students with wide-ranging abilities. The program was offered free to all interested students. There was quite a turnout. This experience, while beneficial in demonstrating as much about what to do in a classroom as what not to do, was not entirely realistic, involving eighteen students, two teacher interns, one "master teacher," and countless Ph.D. Golden Apple observers. In addition, the specific needs of that community (new Chinese immigrants and African American low-income families) drove the curriculum and instruction. One cannot simply transplant or duplicate that in another area of Chicago. No teacher preparation program (regardless of length) can prepare the educator for the variety of student needs in specific environments. Nonetheless, Michie and Rome (plus the GATE program itself, along with the writings and work of bell hooks, Bill Ayers, and Paulo Freire) provided the framework, and more important, the desire to see each student and her or his unique strengths in the context of her or his life. The framework seems simple enough—see the ability and the possibility in each child in order to reach her or him, while avoiding the all too common "deficit driven model of instruction" (Ayers, 2001, p. 31) and "the toxic language of labeling" (p. 29). It is a constant effort. At times every question and concern revolves around who is struggling or failing, or around the new question, à la the No Child Left Behind Act of 2001: which subgroup needs the most attention?

By late August 2001 I had completed my initial coursework and summer internship with GATE. On to certification. The process of attaining provisional certification was quite simple, provided that one had successfully completed the summer student teaching, the UIC courses, and the appropriate portfolios. Although several teacher interns did not receive the certification and were asked to leave the GATE program, most interns were granted a one-year provisional alternative certificate by the Illinois State Board of Education.

Recruitment

As a newly certified teacher intern interested in immediate employment, I attended several job fairs and visited many schools in July and August 2001. The Golden Apple Foundation orchestrated two events to bring hiring principals together with the interns. The name "Golden Apple" opened doors for us, but even with a teacher shortage, finding a position was difficult. Schools with good reputations in solid neighborhoods seldom need to fill positions. If a position becomes available at such a school, beginning teachers are rarely even interviewed. CPS provided a placement service, but like so many other programs serving a system of thirty thousand teachers, it was impersonal and generally ineffective. The district could easily create an online database that would hold current job openings, post requirements, and remove the openings when a position is filled. Knocking on doors may help build character (it is a daunting task), but if there is a true teacher shortage, why not devote more time to making both recruitment and job seeking more efficient?

Thankfully, as GATE interns we were still taking courses and therefore received the support and assistance necessary to find jobs. One of the GATE mentors, a retired principal, performed mock interviews with us and spoke directly to the issues of hiring. Michie and Rome facilitated a seminar with the COMER Institute, which partnered with a number of CPS schools, and two GATE teachers were ultimately hired because of this connection. I have not heard of this depth of support in the recruitment process from other graduates of either traditional or alternative routes.

Induction and Mentoring

Once teacher interns secure employment, the task of induction and mentoring generally shifts from the certification program to the individual schools. This is not the case with GATE at UIC, one of its real advantages over other teacher preparation programs. Michie and Rome were visible and collaborative in their efforts to support us. They responded to late night and last minute phone calls; they came in early and stayed late to meet with us; they even brought us food and took us on field trips. They modeled the ways in which invested, dedicated teachers help their students. In addition, I was assigned a mentor from Northwestern University (through Golden Apple), who visited me biweekly. The safety net for me was impenetrable, demanding yet forgiving. Even now, Kenneth M. Staral, the principal of William B. Ogden Elementary School, who is my current boss and unquestionably the driving force behind one of Chicago's most successful public schools, acts as my mentor. Under his tutelage, and aware of his boundless expectations, I have been observed, praised, and critiqued. This attention has not diminished as my tenure at Ogden continues. Staral continues to push for teacher excellence, growth, and reflection.

As I began my work at Ogden, I was expected to take part in the Mentoring and Induction of New Teachers (MINT) program, the CPS

mentoring program for all new teachers. The program made no distinction made between alternatively certified and traditionally prepared
individuals (though in all fairness, alternative certification in Illinois
was in its early stages). MINT seemed well intentioned and, at least at
Ogden, was quite visible; at some other schools it was nonexistent, or
at least that is how it seemed. GATE graduates at other CPS schools
were either not aware MINT existed or not encouraged to attend.

Teachers who attended regional MINT meetings, held monthly,
were less than complimentary because they thought the agenda was
too basic or too obvious and therefore a waste of their time; however,
most agreed that individual, school-level discussions between teachers,
new and veteran, were helpful. Currently CPS has phased out the
MINT program in lieu of a more comprehensive Golden Teachers
Mentoring Program. As a facilitator for this program I was pleased to
see distinctions made between supporting traditional and alternative
teacher preparation program graduates. These two groups bring entirely different skills, and deficiencies, to the classroom. Teaching for
an alternatively certified educator is not a first career choice or a first
job out of school. Many of the nuts and bolts "job issues" have already
been worked out.

Layers of support are critical to the success of a new teacher; one
resource is not enough. It took, for me, Greg Michie and Amy Rome
from GATE, Dr. Renee Dolezal at Golden Apple, Ken Staral at
Ogden, Bill Ayers's *To Teach*, and two master teachers, Arlene Brennan
and Eric Calderon, both of whom have been invaluable sources of
information as well as inspiration. I know that I have been lucky—
although to a degree I sought out these relationships. After listening
to others' experiences, even others from GATE, I believe that the
induction and mentoring of new teachers is hit or miss. Mentoring
cannot be reduced to a formulaic relationship between mentor and
mentee: a prescribed number of classroom visits and before-school
meetings will not necessarily result in improved instruction or new
teacher assimilation. In effect, there has to be a synthesis between the
supports offered *to* the new teacher and the aggressive seeking out of
support *by* the new teacher. All teachers, especially new ones, need to
be resourceful, rather than sitting in an empty classroom, with arms
folded, waiting for encouragement to arrive.

Retention

If one survives the induction period, additional perils await, which
workable teacher retention support can combat. I do know this: teachers

feel increasing educational and societal pressures every day. Educators are expected to do and see more. We are professionals but are not given professional resources. The medical field allows for second and third opinions; educators are required to assess, diagnose, and cure our thirty plus "patients" on the spot, during active class time. Thankfully, I was taught and am still learning real remedies—critically "seeing" each student actually decreases teacher stress and the pressure to be omnipotent. Focusing on each child's strengths instead of looking for deficiencies provides both student and educator with success, hope, and enthusiasm. That focus was the keystone of my GATE education, and it keeps me energized about teaching in spite of my mistakes. I can still remember a question from the Haberman interview: "How will you prevent burning out in a high pressure, publicly scrutinized job?" A low-level response would have been, "Take a vacation" or "Take time off." A more appropriate answer would include talking to colleagues and the school administrators, along with looking into professional development through the school district or at the university level. That was three years ago, and the last time I can remember discussing teacher retention. Focusing on students and their possibilities has afforded me this luxury: I've given little thought to the stresses that force teachers to leave the profession. Honestly, I have practiced my resignation speech only five times this year.

Professional Development

CPS has an unfortunate habit of sometimes requiring teachers to pay for their own professional development. A teacher pays thrice: first monetarily, then twice more in missed attendance and time lost in the classroom. I have paid for some high-quality professional development, and I have also sat through some very bad professional development that I received for free. Professional development can most definitely help to support teachers, provided that it is respectful, well planned, and appropriate. In order for professional development to be respectful, it must not be insulting. Professional development can never be the cure for sick teaching, but much of what is offered feels more like a lecture than an opportunity to tease out or try new ideas. The best professional development I have participated in was facilitated by teachers in a roundtable discussion, where salient issues and possible solutions were examined. Some professional development is so basic as to be almost useless, especially for seasoned teachers.

Having descriptions of specific courses prior to registration could alleviate the common problem of finding oneself in an inappropriate course. Educators needing more fundamental support should have access to it, and those who desire and need more advanced training should have such opportunities. We push differentiated instruction in the classroom; why not meet teachers at their current levels as well? This raises the issue of planning. Quality professional development needs to be planned far enough in advance so that a syllabus can be created and used for selection. Districts should find logical dates, times, and locations for professional development and not change these. Finally, for professional development to be beneficial, it needs to reflect the questions and issues facing teachers in specific schools and neighborhoods. Professional development needs to be dynamic and site specific, not generic or all encompassing. One way to achieve all three of these objectives—creating a syllabus for selection; setting a logical location, date, and time; and meeting specific school needs— could be to allow each school more autonomy. At Ogden, professional development is developed in house, required of all teachers, and paid for out of the school budget. This arrangement sends the message to teachers that professional development is taken seriously at Ogden and is designed to enhance teachers' professional growth rather than simply fill required hours.

Conclusion

Much of what I have learned about education, teaching, and children has come from those comrades who struggled and continue to struggle with me. Coursework, theory, best practice, and observation are all important components that help teachers succeed in the classroom, but they do not provide support. People do. New teachers as a rule have fewer "professional friends" to help them survive, improve, and triumph at the most crucial time in their career. And ongoing support is critical for all teachers, at all stages of their careers. From informal "teacher talk" to extensive professional development, the support offered teachers needs to be support that works.

NOTE

1. Chicago Public School Bridge Programs are designed to boost failing students' IOWA and Illinois Standards Achievement Test (ISAT) scores through a six-week summer school session.

REFERENCES

Ayers, W., & Ladson-Billings, G. (2001). *To teach*. New York: Teachers College Press.
Michie, G. (1999). *holler if you hear me: The education of a teacher and his students*. New York: Teachers College Press.

To Professionalize or Not to Professionalize? Higher Education and the Teacher Workforce Conundrum

MARY HATWOOD FUTRELL AND JANET CRAIG HEDDESHEIMER

Over the past two decades in the United States, there has been an increased emphasis on ensuring an adequate supply of teachers to serve our diverse student population. In response to this need, a movement to redefine teaching as a profession in order to attract and retain more teachers has emerged. At the same time, a countermovement has emerged, advocating that anyone who can meet minimal content and pedagogical standards should be allowed to teach. Both approaches use the phrase "highly qualified" to describe their teacher candidates. Therein lies the conundrum.

Although determining the meaning of "highly qualified" poses a challenge for P-12 schools, it poses an equal challenge for schools of education, which have the primary responsibility for preparing the teaching workforce, including teachers, counselors, and administrators. As we struggle to improve the quality of education in the United States, colleges and universities face the responsibility of ensuring that graduates from their schools of education are highly qualified members of a learned profession.

The call for more highly qualified teachers is not new, but has become louder and more strident during the current wave of education reforms. Two reports—*A Nation Prepared: Teachers for the 21st Century* (Carnegie Taskforce on Teaching as a Profession, 1986) and *What Matters Most: Teaching for America's Future* (NCTAF, 1996)—heightened the level of awareness within the profession and among the public about the need for teachers to be prepared as professional educators who effectively demonstrate mastery of the subject area or grade level they will teach.

Mary Hatwood Futrell is Professor of Educational Policy Studies and Dean of the Graduate School of Education and Human Development at the George Washington University. Janet Craig Heddesheimer is the Associate Dean for Academic Affairs for the Graduate School of Education and Human Development at the George Washington University.

400 TO PROFESSIONALIZE OR NOT TO PROFESSIONALIZE?

The need for more and better-prepared teachers also has become more apparent in the context of the critical role education plays in ensuring that U.S. workers are prepared to compete in an increasingly global marketplace (Delors, 1996; Kearns, 1988, as cited in Wheelock, 1992; U.S. Supreme Court, 1952). Additional powerful forces of change have emerged, including accountability expectations, evidence-based reforms, demographic realities, more restrictive state and federal legislation, resource constraints, and discussion about social justice. In other words, the quality of education—teaching and learning—has become a national priority for both economic and humanitarian reasons. These changes are forcing teachers and, therefore, the institutions that prepare them, to rethink who and what they are.

Redefining Teaching as a Profession

Ensuring that schools are staffed with competent, caring, compassionate teachers—prekindergarten through graduate school—means redefining teaching as a profession. This endeavor is critical to any hope of closing the achievement gap, an indicator of the quality, or lack thereof, of education in the United States. Leaders in our school districts, schools of education, and teachers' organizations, as well as individual teachers, must be its key players. We are the ones entrusted with the primary responsibility for educating Americans as citizens, individuals, and workers. We have a moral, ethical, and professional obligation to fulfill that public trust.

In particular, redefining teaching as a profession means more clearly defining 1) the specific body of knowledge to be mastered, 2) the pedagogical behaviors and skills required for competent practice, 3) the programs that offer specialized preparation, 4) the standards required for admission to these programs and for continuing practice, and 5) the set of ethical principles that should guide teachers' work. Schools of education are the primary agencies responsible for ensuring that teachers fulfill the requirements of the teaching profession, and they must examine philosophically and pedagogically what teaching means within the context of closing the achievement gap and achieving quality education nationwide. We need to define the coursework, preparation, experiences, and certification requirements a person must successfully complete to demonstrate that he or she is an accomplished teacher.

Redefining teaching as a profession also means that schools of education must work more closely with other university schools, such as arts and sciences, and with school districts to help define and enrich the quality and qualifications of teachers. In conjunction with schools of the arts and sciences, schools of education can expand and strengthen the content of subjects taught, especially in the core areas. The commitment to prepare teachers well must extend across the university, which requires a cross-representation of faculty to develop and implement teacher preparation programs. This commitment must also extend to the district level. University–school district partnerships are key to ensuring that teachers are well educated in their content areas, have experiences working with diverse student populations, and are continually enhancing their own professional growth. As part of that growth, teachers must have a stronger voice in defining and shaping the teaching profession.

In response to the call for more and better teachers, states have developed policies that attempt to articulate more clearly the skills and knowledge required to become certified to teach. Groups such as the Interstate New Teacher Assessment and Support Consortium (INTASC), the National Council for the Accreditation of Teacher Education (NCATE), and the National Board for Professional Teaching Standards (NBPTS), as well as national subject-area groups, have been even more aggressive in developing standards to define—or, more accurately, redefine—the content and pedagogical skills teachers should master.

These professional groups are also refining the requisite teacher knowledge base to specify what it means for teachers to be highly qualified. The alignment of P-12, NBPTS, and NCATE standards, along with those produced by INTASC, will provide an unprecedented level of congruence in these specifications. The work of these groups, especially NBPTS, will improve the quality and status of teaching as a profession. To date, 561 schools of education have aligned their standards with those of the NBPTS, INTASC, and NCATE, and more are in the process of doing so (NBPTS, 2003). After teaching for three years, "new" teachers who have graduated from these programs will be prepared and eligible to sit for national certification, should they choose to do so.

The Countermovement: Bypassing Teacher Certification

Concurrent with efforts to redefine teaching as a profession, a push to bypass state teacher certification requirements gathered momentum as legislatures enacted policies enabling local school districts to forgo these certification requirements entirely or to accept various "alternative certifications," thus creating a contradictory set of policies. As a result, a blizzard of alternative certification programs has emerged.

Some are programs of high quality, structured to ensure that graduates meet the same criteria as teachers graduating from more traditional teacher preparation programs. Others are making a mockery not only of what it means to be highly qualified but also of what it means to be a teacher. Within this movement, there has been a concerted, well-orchestrated effort to circumvent the certification process and what it is designed to do: keep unqualified individuals out of the classroom. Discouragingly, in too many communities, especially in rural and urban districts, hiring people who are not certified to teach has become the norm rather than the exception. Thus, "highly qualified" is in grave danger of becoming a hollow criterion for new teachers.

Many communities have cited current teacher shortages as their rationale for filling vacancies in key subject areas with uncertified personnel. However, a number of studies show that nearly six million people in the United States are certified to teach—twice the number needed to staff our classrooms—but have elected not to do so. We all have read the studies reporting that almost 50% of new teachers leave teaching within the first five years of entering the profession (NCTAF, 2003). According to these studies, many teachers leave the profession not because they dislike teaching or working with children, or even because of low salaries (although they are certainly an inhibiting factor), but because they do not receive support or encouragement to stay in the classroom and are not respected as professionals.

Professionalization to Improve Teacher Retention

If we know why teachers are leaving, what are school districts, schools of education, teachers' organizations, and communities doing to make the school environment more supportive of teachers and to provide teachers with respect for the work they do? For example, if we know new teachers need more support and mentoring before they assume full teaching responsibilities, why do we not have induction programs, similar to those in medicine and nursing, to ensure that teachers have the knowledge base, experiences, and confidence to practice their profession? In addition, what do schools of education need to do, pedagogically or structurally, to ensure that their graduates are highly qualified? What have school districts, in partnership with schools of education and teachers' organizations, done to ensure that teachers have a continuum of professional development opportunities to strengthen their understanding of state standards, the requirements of the No Child Left Behind Act of 2001, and other reforms being implemented in their schools? Finally, what are teachers' organizations and school districts doing to differentiate roles and ensure flexible schedules to support teachers as leaders within their schools, their districts, and the teaching profession?

The last point calls for a serious conversation within the profession and within communities about teachers as educational leaders and reformers and the implications such roles have in redefining teaching as a profession. For instance, teachers should be encouraged to become mentors to new teachers, staff development providers, peer reviewers, and curriculum and instructional specialists. Cultivating the teaching and leadership capacity of teachers can contribute enormously to the improvement of education in our schools.

Where Do We Start? Selecting the Best

Redefining teaching as a profession, with a focus on a continuum of preparation and support, suggests that we begin at the point of admission to the profession. Those who select future members of the profession have a responsibility to use multiple assessment strategies to determine not only each applicant's depth of knowledge in subject matter but also whether he or she has effective communication skills, respect for children and their families, and considerable cognitive flexibility and willingness to engage in self-reflection. For potential teacher candidates admitted through universities, the standard measures remain academic; they include test scores, transcripts, statements of purpose, letters of recommendation, and indicators of an understanding of the critical issues facing education. In addition to what applicants can present on paper, interviews using standard protocols and initial responses to typical classroom situations should be part of all admissions procedures. University faculty and professional staff trained in the use of these measures should be involved in the admissions process. When university–school district partnerships are in place for professional development, why not include faculty from the partner schools in the review of candidates for admission to teacher preparation programs?

In turn, when teachers are interviewed by school systems for initial hiring, it would be desirable to have direct measures of candidates' ability to handle specific classroom situations. The model used for National Board certification could be adapted effectively as part of the hiring process. This adaptation could include a portfolio documenting classroom practice during their professional preparation as well as an overview of their professional development goals for improving practice in their initial teaching assignment. Once again, responses to prompts about approaches to handling typical classroom situations, as well as approaches to teaching and learning, could also be elicited.

The advantages of these multiple measures at each step of the process of preparation for and eventual entry into a first teaching position are significant. Information about the areas called "dispositions" in NCATE and INTASC standards can guide the development and support offered to those in college and university preparation programs and to those new to the profession who are in induction programs. Such development and support could include a clinical supervision focus on the role of the teacher, the effect of the teacher's style and personality on the students, and the significance of taking initiative and managing change. Teachers in preparation, as well as those in the early stages of their careers, will gain knowledge of the effect of their actions, behaviors, and emotional reactions on those around them. More importantly, they will learn how these effects can help or hinder students' knowledge acquisition.

Although a number of universities are now including measures in their admissions processes to assess clinical skills and personal qualities, to date the focus for admission to teacher preparation programs has been largely on traditional cognitive measures. The recent move to require PRAXIS I scores as part of the admissions process is yet one more example of this focus on cognitive skills. Certainly, intellectual ability and content knowledge are essential for effective teaching. However, equally important are less measurable qualities, such as respect for and understanding of diversity, knowledge of one's emotional reactions and their impact on others, and willingness to carefully examine one's current pedagogical practice in an effort to develop increasingly powerful teaching strategies and competence.

The increased focus on standards for admission to initial preparation programs, and eventually to entry-level teaching positions, may be seen as a bold move, but it is one that deserves considerable discussion as part of the deliberation on how, or whether, to professionalize teaching. The hallmarks of a professional are a demonstrated capacity to make informed judgments that meet the profession's standards. In addition, a professional inspires a high level of trust that he or she will always act in the best interests of the individuals being served—in this case, students and their families. Using a variety of tools to form a multifaceted view of teacher candidates' potential to become a recognized and respected member of the teaching field is an important first step to professionalization.

Supporting Teaching as a Profession

Fortunately, in a growing number of school districts, policies and programs are being implemented to engage teachers in shared decision making regarding curriculum development, the hiring and assignment of personnel, and the reorganization of schools. Collaborative efforts between universities and school districts are resulting in Professional Development Schools, embedded learning communities in which students, teachers, teacher educators, and teacher interns all learn from one another. When added to the national certification process and to the growing number of induction programs that require novice teachers to be mentored for up to three years by "master" teachers, these contextualized learning experiences will lead to stronger and better-prepared professionals teaching children and, therefore, to improvements in our education system.

For example, George Washington University's Graduate School of Education and Human Development (GSEHD) has partnerships with school districts in Virginia, Maryland, and Washington, D.C. Within these partner schools, GSEHD prepares its students to be exemplary teachers and to become leaders in their schools. These teacher interns do more than work as interns; they tutor, revise curricula, mentor students, team teach, and teach independently. The research methodology sequence at GSEHD has been revised to ensure that graduates know how to use student assessment data to inform and improve their teaching. GSEHD students are also encouraged to conduct research and to publish and present their findings at conferences.

In the GSEHD Urban Initiative program at Cardozo High School in the District of Columbia, interns are able to earn a license to teach in two different areas: special education and a content area. At Cardozo, interns participate in interdependent learning groups, and self-regulated and problem-based learning. They also participate in ongoing, multiple authentic assessments. This whole process is predicated on anchoring teaching and learning in the "life contexts" of the students (UNITE & Ohio State University, 1998).

Between 5 and 10 interns are assigned to the school each year; they team teach a literacy course to ninth-grade students while also interning with the school's content and special education teachers. After spending a full year in this high-poverty urban high school, the interns involved with this program have no illusions about the demands and complexities of urban teaching. Former Urban Initiative interns have earned recognitions such as New Teacher of the Year; others are department chairs.

As new and developing teachers, they have presented at national confer-ences, testified in support of special education legislation, and had their students' work recognized in the *Washington Post*.

GSEHD graduates develop expertise in using a repertoire of peda-gogical skills to ensure that the learning in their classrooms is student focused. When they enter the profession as highly qualified, certified teachers, they understand the complexities of teaching, the educa-tional demands they will face, and the environment in which they will be working. Teacher candidates understand clearly that students need to be challenged and the curriculum enriched to ensure that learning opportunities continue beyond high school; that social justice is not simply words, but also actions; and that teachers can influence student outcomes. They enter the profession as full-time teachers who know their content areas, understand the standards students are required to achieve, and have the professional wherewithal to be effective teachers wherever they teach. They also know what it means to assume leader-ship roles within their schools and within the profession.

Changing Work Environments

Workplaces have been transformed from assembly-line, skills-ori-ented environments, where workers follow a set routine, to more infor-mation-based, collegial environments where workers are expected to use their talents and abilities, both as part of a team and independently. Individuals in today's workforce are expected to be more knowledge-able and adaptable to changing environments than previous genera-tions.

This is no less true in education, but the field has not responded as quickly or assertively as others. Although some higher education insti-tutions, including schools of education, have begun to respond to these changes, much more remains to be done. As educators, we are expected to prepare students for changing economic, political, and social envi-ronments, and we will be held accountable for their ability to apply themselves within these environments. If we are to succeed in preparing future citizens for the changes they will encounter, however, educa-tional change must occur, with educators not on the sidelines but as central players in the process of redefining teaching as a profession in the United States. Are we ready to accept the challenge of reforming schools of education and the teaching profession to be more responsive to the educational needs of our society, or will we maintain the status quo?

Schools of education should be restructured to enable them to address the educational needs of our society more effectively. Acceptance by higher education faculty, especially teacher educators, of the need to change teacher education programs in order to strengthen the teacher workforce should be viewed as constructive rather than destructive. More forthrightly stated, as go schools of education, so will go our elementary and secondary schools and, therefore, so will go America.

In many ways, institutions of higher education, particularly schools of education, hold the answer. Whether or not we continue to professionalize teaching will depend largely on the way the teacher workforce is prepared and on its ability to address the educational challenges before us. For example, whether or not we successfully implement No Child Left Behind, which calls for a highly qualified teacher in every classroom, depends on schools of education having the capacity and the fortitude to structure their programs to be more responsive to this need. It means providing schools of education with the resources to ensure that teachers understand and are prepared to implement the act's mandates and to create school environments that will encourage teachers to remain in the profession. Whether or not we succeed in our efforts to make learning more student focused depends on the willingness of school districts to work with universities to help teachers develop stronger pedagogical skills and the know-how to use them more effectively within culturally diverse classrooms. Building and sustaining a strong, effective teacher workforce requires that school districts, schools of education, and teachers' organizations work together to enhance the quality of mentoring and professional development for all teachers in order to further improve the education of students. It also means respecting and using teacher expertise and knowledge to help determine more effective ways to improve education.

Equally critical is the value that university administrators place on schools of education when determining the priorities for their institutions, a decision that sends a clear message about the importance of teachers and teaching. We need to remind university administrators and trustees that when they invest in high-quality teacher education programs, they are investing in the future of the university because the students educated in our P-12 schools will one day be the same students the university recruits as part of its student body. The willingness of policymakers and administrators to invest the necessary resources to improve the quality of teacher preparation programs will reflect the value we place on the quality of teaching and, thus, the quality of education.

Conclusion

There is no disagreement that teachers are the most critical component in student learning. The current demand for more highly
qualified teachers is a window of opportunity for higher education to
help develop teaching as a profession that addresses not only the concerns for educational quality but also those for educational equality.
We hope that, rather than reverting to the minimalist definition of
what it meant to be a teacher more than 50 years ago, when individuals did not need to earn a college degree or be professionally prepared
to teach, policymakers and educators will use this opportunity to
transform the teaching workforce into a true profession, which will
guarantee that every child in the United States is taught by a competent, caring, committed teacher who is highly qualified and certified to
teach. We can do no less for the future of our country.

REFERENCES

Carnegie Taskforce on Teaching as a Profession. (1986, May). *A nation prepared: Teachers for the 21st century*. New York, NY: Carnegie Forum on Education and the Economy.
Delors, J. (1996). Learning: The treasure within. *Report to UNESCO of the International Commission on Education for the Twenty-first Century*. Paris: United Nations Educa-tional, Scientific, and Cultural Organization (UNESCO).
Futrell, M.H. (2002). Is America ready? The transformation of teaching into a profes-sion. *Establishing a state board of teaching: A guide for state associations* (pp. 42-46). Washington, DC: National Education Association.
NBPTS (National Board for Professional Teaching Standards). (2003, November). Growth of institutions of higher education using NBPTS standards. Candidate Support & Higher Education Initiatives. Retrieved December 4, 2003 from http://www.nbpts.org/highered/highered.cfm
NCTAF (National Commission on Teaching & America's Future). (1996). *What matters most: Teaching for America's future*. New York, NY: Author.
NCTAF (National Commission on Teaching & America's Future). (January 2003). *No dream denied: A pledge to America's children*. New York, NY: Author.
UNITE & Ohio State University. (1998). *Contextual teaching and learning: Teacher educa-tion programs*. A sponsored project of the Office of Vocational and Adult Education and the National School-to-Work Office, U.S. Department of Education, Susan Jones Sears, Principal Investigator. Columbus, OH: Ohio State University; Holmes Partnership.
U.S. Supreme Court (1952, October). Brown vs. Board of Education of Topeka, KA. In *The complete oral arguments of the Supreme Court of the United States* (microform, Jacob Burns Law Library, George Washington University, Washington, DC, fiche 114). Frederick, MD: University Publications of America.
Wheelock, A. (1992). *Crossing the tracks: How "untracking" can save America's schools*. New York: New Press.

Obstacles and Opportunities: Teacher Workforce Development amid Changes in Public Funding

THOMAS W. PAYZANT

Every school district struggles to find new teachers, to hire and place them in schools, to evaluate them fairly, and to keep them through the first few years of their employment despite the ebb and flow of public funding for education. There are obstacles to developing and employing an effective pool of teachers, some that can be reduced or eliminated through effective human resources and district management and others that exist beyond the control of schools and their communities. One point is abundantly clear to everyone in education: the quality of a school is directly connected to and dependent on the instructional skills and commitment of its teachers. A second point is increasingly clear to educators: One of the essential aspects of teacher workforce development is the ability of school districts, especially the large ones in urban areas, to effectively recruit, process, hire, and support teacher applicants through the employment process and through their first years of teaching.

The experiences of the Boston Public Schools over the past three years illustrate some of the teacher workforce issues that school districts often face because of the unpredictability of state and federal budget cycles. What follows is a brief look at the effect that changes in outside forces have had on Boston's hiring and retention of teachers, along with some of the solutions Boston has developed in an attempt to create some long-term strategies for finding and keeping the best teachers for its schools.

In the fall of 2000, the Boston Public Schools and the Boston Teachers Union agreed to a new three-year teacher contract that was designed to have a significant impact on improving the hiring and employment prospects for Boston's teachers. Considerable community involvement—from businesses, parents, churches, community groups, and education advocacy groups—helped to create an agreement that refined and

Thomas W. Payzant is superintendent of the Boston Public Schools. He served as assistant secretary for the U.S. Department of Education's Office of Elementary and Secondary Education and as the superintendent of four communities, including the San Diego Unified School District, before coming to Boston. He received his doctorate in education from Harvard University.

simplified the teacher hiring process, which had been widely recognized as having a negative effect on Boston's ability to attract and hire new talent to the Boston Public Schools.

The new contract was well received by the membership of the teachers union, the community, and the local media. New contract provisions aimed at improving hiring were viewed as especially salutary, empowering principals more than ever before to have more control over hiring and staffing decisions, while speeding up the entire cycle of hiring to accommodate schools as well as applicants. A lead editorial in the *Boston Globe* praised the new agreement and expressed hope that it would greatly improve the prospects for the Boston teaching force in years to come.

An important aspect of the extensive community engagement in the hiring processes of the Boston Public Schools was a strong interest by local education stakeholders in seeing improvements in the human resources services of the Boston Public Schools. To this end, the Human Resources Department was reorganized, a new director was hired, and the administrative team supporting the director was improved to ensure better management, smoother decision making, and greater accountability.

However, a little more than three years later, in August 2003, the *Boston Globe* criticized the staffing of the Boston Public Schools, citing delays in the placement of "excessed" permanent teachers (those who had lost their positions due to school budget cuts but retained contractual rights to reassignment elsewhere within the school district) that were causing havoc throughout the city schools just as the 2003-2004 academic year was about to begin. Excessed teachers could not be placed until the state budget was resolved, and new teachers could not be hired until those under contract were reassigned.

How did Boston go from a landmark contract and a reorganized personnel department assuring hiring improvements to having a large number of excessed teachers unmatched to vacancies just before the start of a new school year? What impact do public funding issues have on teacher workforce development? Is there anything districts can do to handle staffing challenges amid the vagaries of public funding and the changing economic climate?

From 2000 to 2003 in Boston: Follow the Funding

The new Boston teacher contract in 2000 specified several changes intended to improve the hiring process for teachers. The key contract provisions were designed to compress the teacher assignment timetable and open up the hiring process to allow hiring decisions to be made sooner and to provide more opportunities to recruit outside candidates:

- The deadline for internal applicant transfers was moved up to March 1, two to three months earlier in the school year than past practice.
- For the first time, principals could "protect" their best first-year teachers (who had not yet earned seniority) from being "bumped" from their positions by more senior teachers, by making them permanent.
- Principals were able to interview candidates from outside the school district earlier than in previous years.
- "Voluntary excessing" from buildings was eliminated; teachers with an unsatisfactory evaluation (or the potential for one) could not opt to transfer out of their buildings.

Once the new contract was in place in the fall of 2000, the reorganized Human Resources Department worked aggressively to follow the earlier timetable and implement the new provisions of the contract. The results in hiring for the following school year, 2001-2002, were impressive, with all the posting and hiring deadlines met. Boston filled 1,181 open positions ahead of schedule, receiving applications for specific jobs from more than 10,000 candidates and hiring 648 new teachers, more than any previous year. The Human Resources Department managed six separate posting dates and also processed 362 retirements and resignations (five times the number from the previous year). A report on the new contract implementation, issued by the Boston Municipal Research Bureau in March 2002, hailed the "important progress" made by the Boston Public Schools in recruiting and hiring new teachers and processing staffing changes, all done well within the ambitious deadlines established by the contract and BPS.

But then the economy, in Massachusetts and across the nation, did a belly flop. Over the next two fiscal years, the Boston Public Schools, like virtually every other major school district in the United States, had to come to terms with significant revenue cuts that would force every one of its schools to reduce services and personnel. Although the 2002-2003 school year faced serious budget reductions ($30 million), the cuts for the following year, 2003-2004, were even worse ($55 million). More than 800 Boston teachers received layoff notices in the spring of 2003. After some funds were restored to the educational line items by the Massachusetts governor and legislature over the summer of 2003, schools everywhere scurried to rescind some layoff notices, stop some transfers, and hire some new teachers following retirements and resignations from a pool of applicants that had been steadily shrinking throughout the spring.

By the time the *Boston Globe* ran its article in August 2003 reporting on unfilled classrooms just days before the school year was to begin, the fiscal climate had changed drastically from what it was when the new contract had been implemented two years before. The tight budget development cycles and the misalignment between them and the decision-making points for schools to establish budgeted positions—knowing what resources will be available in order to make timely personnel decisions—were significant factors in the creation of the dilemma schools faced in September 2003.

During this time of fiscal restraint, were the provisions of the Boston teacher contract part of the problem? In fact, most were not. But delays in implementing the timelines for the hiring process, caused by uncertainty about the final budget, did cause serious problems. Most of the constraints, which involved maintaining a lengthy period for considering retirements and resignations by senior teachers, were significantly reduced by the new deadlines established in the contract but were still problematic because of budget uncertainties. The revised transfer process, generally speaking, was not an onerous impediment in Boston until 2003, when it was postponed until much later, again because of budget uncertainties.

The most controversial aspect of the Boston teacher contract in the past decade has been the existence of the so-called excess pool, or the pool of permanent teachers who, for a variety of reasons, are temporarily unassigned. The excess pool has been controversial because of the public perception that it is a large group of unwanted teachers who are kept on the district payroll because the union contract makes it difficult to fire them. In most cases, however, the excess pool is a temporary holding area where teachers who were on leave or were "excessed" from their buildings because of staff reductions await reassignment. Experienced teachers who, for one reason or another, are unable to retain their position in an assigned school still represent an asset to the school district, and the district has a contractual obligation to find them work within the system. In the best of economic times, teachers move quickly through the excess pool. When public funds are declining, the available openings sometimes do not align well with the certifications of the excessed teachers, who have the right to pick their preferred positions and are guaranteed to receive (by seniority) one of their top three choices. At such times, public pressures can have a negative effect on a school district's efforts to recruit good people in a timely fashion for hard-to-fill jobs. Traditionally, one of the attractions of the teaching profession has been its perceived stability. Talented college graduates may think twice, however, about teaching in a climate where layoffs are occurring and controversies surround teacher assignments.

In Boston, union impediments to management decisions come into play primarily when, for fiscal reasons, the central office must assign a teacher to a school against the wishes of either the teacher or the receiving principal. The best possible circumstance for transfers and teacher reassignments is always one in which both sides agree that the placement will be a good one. The district supports principals and their School Site Council personnel subcommittees in making school-based decisions on the selection of teachers in good times, but central control of teacher assignment resurfaces when teachers with rights to a position must be placed.

What can we learn from this experience? Boston had a contract in place that created earlier dates for internal and external postings, improved its central human resources functions, and engaged school-based administrators in the hiring process more than ever before—and yet still found itself racing at the 11th hour to fill vacancies in schools in 2003. If this kind of problem is to be prevented, two practices need to change: one that school districts can control, and one that will depend on the greater will of the state in which we live.

The Practice That Districts Can Control

School districts can do a much better job of supporting applicants through the hiring process. To this end, every school system needs to develop and install a state-of-the-art applicant-tracking system driven by the best available technology. Boston does not have one yet, but increasingly, large districts are using applicant-tracking systems that are sophisticated and responsive at every level of the personnel structure. These systems may require a serious initial investment. But they make it possible for central offices and schools to work together to connect with large numbers of applicants, maintain contact with them throughout the hiring process, track large numbers of résumés without excessive paperwork, pinpoint openings and qualified candidates to fit them while keeping their location and educational level preferences in mind, and maintain an active pool of potential candidates for future openings once all postings are filled. All of these tasks must be performed effectively to provide high-quality customer service and a competitive edge in the recruitment of the best candidates.

Without effective applicant tracking, the greatest disadvantages are felt at the school level, where the inundation of hundreds of résumés and the demands for organizing and conducting interviews can be burdensome, even with the most supportive central office screening services. Because most hiring decisions coincide with standardized testing and final exam periods in May and June, schools and districts will inevitably fall behind deadlines or be forced, by the time school is out and the summer is under way, to consider candidates who are less than the best available. In a time of funding reductions, a state-of-the-art applicant-tracking system may be difficult to pay for, but it is a necessity for every school district if the potential teacher workforce is to be nurtured and developed to its fullest extent.

The Practice Beyond the Reach of School Districts

Budgeting and fiscal planning at the legislative and executive levels of state government have to end the practice of 11th-hour decisions that drastically affect the educational experiences of schools and schoolchildren. We all know the saying "There ought'a be a law." In this case, there really ought'a be one. Although last-minute budget cuts invariably affect the lives of everyone in organizations that depend on public funding from states, which in turn depend on federal cycles of appropriation and expenditures, the impact is far worse for schools than for other public agencies, departments, and services. In Massachusetts, districts are required by state statute to notify teachers by June 15, before the state budget has been finalized, if they will be laid off. The same requirement exists in the contract with Boston teachers, and very likely in most teacher collective bargaining agreements; thus decisions about layoffs must be made before the finances are clear. This forces school districts into the practice of notifying all layoff candidates, even if the odds are against the layoffs eventually happening, thus adding to the instability of the profession and creating anxiety in schools on an annual basis.

No other aspect of community life is so clearly structured and constrained by the calendar. Public hospitals, fire departments, and community agencies all can conform to fiscal year spending cycles, but schools must operate on two schedules: the fiscal one and the academic one. States with year-round schedules, such as California, are for the most part the exception; for others, the academic year is not flexible.

School starts in September, and the children show up whether or not the governor has signed the supplemental budget.

As long as school districts are subject to continual changes in public-funding levels, the hiring processes for the teaching profession, probably more than any other profession in the United States, will remain somewhat unstable. This has a dramatic effect on people who might be attracted to the profession. For many years, people interested in education as a career were willing to give up earning power in return for greater control over their own working life and the satisfactions of working with young people. As federal, state, and municipal funding changes oscillate from one year to the next with increasing frequency, communities across the nation will find it harder and harder to attract and employ the best and brightest to teach the next generation. This uncertainty understandably reinforces the desire that teachers have for job security once they are hired and may very likely limit their receptivity to taking risks that might lead to school improvement. The power to change this lies with public policymakers at the state and federal levels. It can't happen soon enough for everyone in schools who must wrestle with last-minute changes in budget allocations just a few days before the buses roll up to the doors at the end of the summer.

How Real Is the National Teacher Shortage?

An all-important question for people concerned with teacher workforce development is the nature of the current teacher shortage—how real is the shortage, and in what ways are top candidates being encouraged or discouraged from entering the profession?

Among the many studies and analyses of the teacher workforce in recent years, one of the most provocative reports on the subject is *Missed Opportunities: How We Keep High-Quality Teachers Out of Urban Classrooms*, by Jessica Levin and Meredith Quinn (2003), produced for the New Teacher Project. Levin and Quinn looked closely at recruitment and hiring processes in four medium-to-large school districts and concluded, as their report title suggests, that "thanks to stepped-up recruitment efforts, high-quality teacher candidates regularly apply in large numbers to teach in hard-to-staff districts. The problem is, they do not get hired" (executive summary, p. 4).

The report cited problems that virtually every school district in the country now experiences. It showed that despite high numbers of candidates applying in each district, all four districts were "left scrambling until the 11th hour" (executive summary, p. 5) to fill their vacancies. Why? Three conditions prevailed in each of the four districts:

1. Applicants had to wait for months before receiving job offers, forcing them to withdraw and take employment either in suburban school districts that were more nimble or in other fields altogether.
2. Hiring delays forced school districts to accept weaker candidates because stronger candidates went elsewhere after growing impatient with the delays. This often meant that larger districts had to settle for higher percentages of unqualified and uncertified teachers.
3. The applicants who withdrew from the hiring pools were serious applicants. Levin and Quinn reported that "four out of five of them said they would like to be considered again for a teaching position with the urban district" (executive summary, p. 6).

Although the failures of the four districts to hire top candidates were often blamed on district human resources offices, Levin and Quinn concluded that three specific policies common to larger districts were responsible for many of the districts' hiring problems:

1. *Vacancy notification requirements*, which allow retiring or resigning teachers to provide very late notice of their intent to leave, making it impossible for schools and districts to know in a timely way how many vacancies they will need to fill
2. *Union transfer requirements*, which allow teachers to pick first from openings, with timetables and deadlines that give maximum flexibility to current teachers while creating management nightmares for school administrators and human resources professionals
3. *Chronic budget uncertainties*, which leave districts unsure of staffing levels for coming years, often extending this uncertainty into the school year and creating staffing havoc for schools

In response to these policies that work against effective human resource practices, Levin and Quinn offered a set of recommendations for school districts, including earlier deadlines for vacancy notices, transfers, resignations, and retirements; more school-level control over hiring and placements; and the development and passage of school budgets earlier in the year to ensure greater clarity on vacancies and funding levels in advance of recruitment and hiring due dates.

Although Boston was not one of the four districts Levin and Quinn studied, many of the experiences and practices they described existed in

Boston before the teacher contract of 2000. But the contract itself, which resulted from a long negotiation with very public community comment and specified significant policy changes, notably in the areas cited by *Missed Opportunities*, was still not enough to head off the havoc reported in the *Boston Globe* before the start of school in September 2003.

What About the Hard-to-Fill Teaching Positions?

It is widely recognized that there is a genuine and growing shortage of qualified teaching applicants in several critical areas—math, science, special education—and, especially, of qualified applicants of color in all teaching areas, particularly for urban school districts, where the demand is greatest (as reported in Burkholder et al., 2003, to name just one current study). Each of these shortage areas has its own challenges, and competition exists for each in other fields, especially in math and science and among applicants of color. In an era in which high standards and high-stakes testing have become part of the national educational agenda, school districts need to work closely with schools of education to find solutions to these shortages.

With a large number of universities in the Greater Boston area, many of which having schools of education with teacher preparation programs, Boston is in an excellent position to recruit top teacher candidates to its schools and collaborate with local schools of education to help prepare teachers to meet the unique demands of urban education. The Boston Public Schools, in fact, has a long-standing history of collaboration with local university communities. Begun in 1982, the Boston Compact has created a set of mutual goals for universities, businesses, and other partnership organizations and, through the Boston Higher Education Partnership, has a track record for connecting schools of higher education with the district schools and the Boston Public Schools central office.

In recent years, one of the goals of this long-standing partnership has been to address all four of the teacher shortage areas. Each university is unique, however, and the schools of education engaged in teacher development and preparation are very different: they have different educational philosophies, curricula, requirements, and expectations for practical experience and the development of demonstrable instructional skills. Although most schools of education have begun to explore ways to meet the challenges specific to large city schools, the process of sharing these methods among graduate schools is still at a fledgling stage at best.

One of the disparities in teacher preparation is that there is little agreement on what the expectations and requirements of the profession should be. Although more and more states are instituting subject-specific testing as part of their certification processes, these tests tend for the most part to assess a combination of basic literacy and subject-area knowledge. Very little in the profession assesses the ability of a person just out of graduate school to walk into a classroom and manage it effectively—with an adequate level of instructional skill, subject-area knowledge, behavioral savvy, and strategic thinking about group dynamics and children's diverse learning styles.

As noted in the proceedings from "Losing Ground: A National Summit on Diversity in the Teaching Force" (2002), the national conference sponsored by the American Association of School Personnel Administrators and other educational groups, "Currently, there is significant concern that far too many teachers graduate from preparation programs without the skills, dispositions, or appropriate experiences to teach very diverse groups of students effectively" (p. 3).

In fact, high standards, and especially the requirements of the No Child Left Behind Act of 2001, are creating more pressure than ever before on school districts to recruit, hire, and support a high-quality teaching force—one in which applicants are qualified not only because they know their subject area and have been licensed to teach but also because they have met some basic skill standards in working with the most challenging and difficult-to-teach students. In most school districts, an alarmingly high number of students receiving special education services are referred to special education not because they are disabled but because regular education teachers have not been trained to manage classroom behavior or deal with the often unique demands of children from diverse backgrounds.

Addressing the Problems

In spring 2003, in order to address the twofold issue of teacher shortages in critical areas and the difficulties of finding teachers prepared for the unique challenges of an urban district, Boston Public Schools began a new teacher preparation program of its own. The Boston Teacher Residency Program has been funded by Strategic Grant Partners for two years, with the possibility of funding for up to five years, to establish teacher residencies in the city and to prepare teachers for the challenge of teaching in a city school. The program is managed jointly by the school district and the Boston Plan for Excellence, a local nonprofit group that serves as the city's local education fund. In the first year, which began in September 2003, 16 teacher residents will complete a curriculum of coursework and placements resulting in teacher certification in their chosen areas as well as a yearlong resident internship with considerable direct experience teaching Boston children under the watchful eyes of lead classroom teachers and program support staff. Candidates will earn dual certification—in a subject area and in special education—after completing the program. The Boston Teacher Residency Program was not created to take the place of the local schools of education, but it does offer them competition, which can lead to positive change. It will provide, in addition to a cadre of well-prepared teacher candidates, a means for the school district and the Boston Plan for Excellence to work more closely than ever with local universities to influence the ways in which teachers are trained, placed, and prepared for the work of urban education. After five years, this program may provide as many as 25% of the teachers that Boston will need to staff its schools. This should have a considerable impact on colleges and universities and prompt them to take note of what Boston Public Schools wants in terms of teacher preparation.

There needs to be a much more concerted effort to set standards for the teaching profession and to engage higher education institutions involved in teacher preparation in setting criteria and standards that are broader, deeper, and more grounded in the real demands of the contemporary classroom. The Boston Higher Education Partnership has begun to tackle this challenge with its member colleges. In the absence of improved professional standards, school districts will be forced to wrestle with increased demands for performance in their schools without the benefit of increased expectations for graduates from the college programs that prepare them. Other professions—law, medicine, engineering, and architecture, to name a few—have dealt with the need for more uniformity in training and licensing standards while still allowing for unique aspects of training for each university.

We know from the recent experiences in Boston that despite relatively lower pay scales for teaching compared to the other professions named above, large numbers of people still want to teach. Last year, Boston received more than 10,000 résumés from external applicants for fewer than 300 positions posted on the district's Web site, and a vast majority of these applicants met the basic certification requirements for the positions. People want to teach. This is especially true

420   OBSTACLES AND OPPORTUNITIES

of graduates from public school systems. One of the as-yet untapped areas for recruiting future teachers may well be the ranks of our own students, especially in our large city districts.

To this end, Boston has created Teach Boston, an innovative program that works with Boston high school students who are interested in exploring the possibility of a career in teaching. Teach Boston recruits potential future teachers, provides them with work experiences and internships in schools, helps them identify and apply to colleges where they can continue their interest, and then works with the local universities involved in the program to maintain contact with the students during their college years and continue their connections with the school district. Although the numbers of students in the Teach Boston pipeline are still small relative to the numbers of teaching positions the city will need to fill over the next 10 years, the results are promising; and the students themselves are success stories with unique motivational value for the Boston schools.

In Summary

- Even with progressive union contract agreements in place, delays in public funding decisions in times of budget reductions can wreak havoc on schools despite early posting dates and large applicant pools.
- School districts need to install and use more state-of-the-art applicant-tracking systems that can help to accelerate the process of recruiting, hiring, tracking, and placement while improving connections between schools and teacher candidates.
- Fiscal decisions at the federal, state, and municipal levels that affect schools need to be made according to timelines that are more sensitive to the realities of the academic year, so that expansions and contractions of annual budgets do not happen at the last minute, which either forces schools into budgetary guesswork and scurrying for teachers to fill classrooms or, by statute, requires layoff notices before state and federal budgets have been resolved.
- Although teacher shortages are real in some subject areas and among candidates of color in particular, all school districts need to take a hard look at policies and contractual agreements that may make teacher hiring and placement decisions problematic.
- Greater coordination among schools of education and between universities and school districts can enhance the quality of teacher preparation, particularly in urban districts.

- Having school districts develop their own programs of teacher preparation and training may be an advantage, not only in helping to fill openings in areas where there are shortages but also in providing a means to cooperate more closely with university teaching schools to create more competition and to improve the long-term fit between preparation programs and the real teacher needs that districts are facing.

With more uniform requirements for the teaching profession and special emphasis on training for instructional strategies to meet high standards requirements, with close working relationships between school districts and university schools of education, and with special efforts to identify and support students in public schools as potential teachers once their college experiences are completed, it is likely that the current shortages can be addressed while the overall quality of the teacher workforce is enhanced. It will take a great deal of time and commitment, from policymakers and institutional leaders at all levels, but it can be done.

References

Burkholder et al. (2003). *Educator supply and demand in the United States: 2003 executive summary*. Columbus, OH: American Association for Employment in Education.
Levin, J., & Quinn, M. (2003). *Missed opportunities: How we keep high-quality teachers out of urban classrooms*. New Teacher Project.

Building the Teacher Workforce Bench for the Future: An Agenda for Funders

PAUL GOREN

Imagine that for the past decade you have been the head basketball coach at a university with a top-ranked program—say, Duke or Stanford or North Carolina. Your players are among the smartest and best-trained student athletes in the country, and year in and year out they compete at the highest levels. As the coach of such a team, you have learned over time the art and science of recruitment—how to attract the best and brightest students and athletes to your team and institution. In the past, retention had never really been an issue; after a senior year each player would move on, but not before. But now that professional teams are recruiting high school graduates, your own recruitment and retention strategies must change dramatically. Because you can now only depend on the best of your players to stay through their sophomore years, your recruitment process must be in constant motion so that your bench is built for future success. As head coach, you have to develop a new system that responds to the flow of outstanding players into and out of your program.

This basketball imagery in many ways fits the challenges that principals, human resource specialists, and superintendents face on an annual basis. Each year, districts must hire new teachers because of retirements, leaves of absence, and increases in student populations. Each year, districts must determine the best avenues for recruiting and retaining the best available teachers, a critical process now that federal legislation requires qualified teachers in each and every classroom. Typically these recruitment and retention strategies are independent of one another and are worked on piece by piece. But like coaches of

Paul Goren is Vice President of the Spencer Foundation, Chicago, Illinois. He is the former Director of Child and Youth Development, which included support for K-12 education, for the John D. and Catherine T. MacArthur Foundation in Chicago. He has also worked for the Minneapolis Public Schools, the San Diego City Schools, and as Director of the education policy studies program for the National Governors' Association.

422

top-ranked college teams, district leaders need to have a system, rather than piecemeal strategies, in place—one that recognizes the constant movement of educators in the short run and builds the best teams of educators at schools for the long run.

Easier said than done. If you visit the human resource operations of most districts, you will see that they are focused primarily on *triage*—handling the most immediate problem facing the school system that day. These problems can range from not having enough substitutes to meeting the No Child Left Behind mandates to finding mid-year replacements for specialists or for particular courses. As important as it is to have a full, well thought out, rational strategy for teacher recruitment and retention, it is hard to sustain this effort alone, when day-to-day emergencies must take precedence.

This is where the foundation community can work in partnership with local universities and school systems. But if these parties are to combine their expertise and resources to respond to immediate issues as well as to address long-term needs, they will need to develop and implement a system that is geared to workforce development for schools. What would this system look like? It would at the very least include 1) documentation of short- and long-term classroom needs, 2) multiple ways of meeting initial and ongoing training requirements, 3) mentoring, staff development, and problem-solving assistance, and 4) schools as centers of learning for students and adults.[1]

Documentation of Short- and Long-Term Classroom Needs

In order to determine classroom needs in the near future and to predict needs over time, a workforce development system must include a database that is site specific. How many teachers are currently employed? How many are reaching retirement age? How many teachers annually take leaves of absence? How many teachers annually leave the district permanently? What are the special needs of the district, and how many teachers fulfill these functions? How many students are predicted to be in attendance in the next year, in five years, and so on? These data are essential to knowing what recruitment efforts are necessary as well as what sort of collaborations may be required between those responsible for the supply of teachers (teacher training institutions) and those who determine their demand (districts and schools). Best-guess scenarios, without solid data, lead to triage rather than a solid strategy with a set of tactics to address current and long-term needs.

Multiple Ways of Meeting Initial and
Ongoing Training Requirements

In order to meet the pressing needs of most school districts, where demand for high quality far exceeds the supply of new teachers, potential teachers must have multiple alternatives for meeting their training requirements. Higher education institutions must think very strategically about how they might make the more traditional routes to teaching more attractive to more people. At the same time, higher education should also design training alternatives for early and mid-career retirees from other occupations. Opportunities to learn about and then practice strategies related to grade level or subject matter expertise, reading, discipline and classroom management, and the interpretation of data related to student and school performance are essential. Yet the development of these skills and competencies must be considered creatively, so that the "recruits" are actually engaged in their learning. Universities, working directly with districts, might think differently about training so that it does not end after one year. Providing an intensive initial certification experience followed by a combination of on-the-job training and reflection/analysis that is coordinated by a district, a teacher training program, the local union, and a local foundation would help to respond to short- and long-term needs. Local and national funders might underwrite the costs of such programs in order to test their feasibility.

Mentoring, Staff Development, and Problem-Solving Assistance

All professionals benefit from the relationships they have with colleagues. They gain expertise that is based on shared experiences and discover options that others have used and found successful. As we all know, professional development in schools and districts nationwide tends to follow what my friend and colleague Jane David of the Bay Area Research Group calls "spray and pray" strategies. Put an entire staff in a room, or put an entire district workforce in a convention center, have them listen to the latest guru give a PowerPoint presentation on how to improve instruction, and then quickly send them back to their isolated classrooms to try out what they have just heard. But there is much more to true professional development than attendance at such a workshop. Focused attention to real problems in a classroom or school, with actual examples of how to address them, is essential to learning how to change practice. Access to emerging data and video on classroom practices, through groups like Teachscape, is essential. It is here where the funding community can help provide access to tools and strategies for professional development that may help to address actual problems through methods proven to improve and change practice.

Schools as Centers of Learning for Students and Adults

Teaching is an isolated profession. After initial training, one is typically assigned to a classroom and told to teach. Opportunities to learn, from a teacher's perspective, come through large-scale professional development seminars, required implementations of new curricula (learn it while you do it), an occasional course (that is not necessarily related to what one teaches, but can lead to increased pay on an education-based salary schedule), and any independent work that a teacher may take on. If the profession is going to change so that the movement of teachers into and out of the profession slows down, schools and districts must be seen as centers of learning for the adults that work within them.

Again, easier said than done, especially given the pressing problems educators face, their limited resources, and the fact that there is only so much time in the day. Collaboration between districts, universities, and funders to design and model what "schools as learning organizations" truly can be is important work that might have to be initiated by the funders, but must be sustained by educators. In addition, the design and implementation of schemes where teachers can work with and learn from colleagues in the same building, colleagues across the district, and critical friends or mentors who can visit a school, through special assignments in schools or the district offices or through occasional travel to other settings, will in the long run help upgrade the profession and make it more appealing to a broader range of individuals. Again, all of this costs money, and without it there is a reluctance to try new models. Funders play an essential role here to show what is possible.

In Summary

What keeps a person in a job like teaching? Along with the obvious—pay, benefits, opportunities for advancement, reasonable hours, safe working environments—are the intangibles such as whether the working environment and colleagues are interesting, whether there are opportunities to learn new techniques and practices while interacting with colleagues, and whether there is flexibility so that one can try new methods without fear of failure. Many teachers today do not find this in the workplace called school. Those who do not will often choose to pursue other endeavors early in their careers. If they do stay, it is often because of the value they place on working with children, not because the workplace and their colleagues contribute to their job satisfaction. Recruiting and retaining teachers requires a system of workforce development that pays attention to these issues in the short run, especially during the first few years of a teacher's career, as well as in the long run for more experienced educators.

If the workforce is to be developed, if the bench is going to be built, if the team is going to be competitive at the highest levels, year in and year out, then these elements must be addressed. And because they interrelate, they must be concurrently implemented as a system. As a funder, it is essential to understand a systems approach to these issues. Funders tend to run interesting pilots, but these are not nested in the larger context of how to recruit and retain teachers for the long run. The result is a set of boutique programs that provide assistance as long as resources are available and then tend to disappear when the funding priorities change. If funders want to contribute to change and help develop the teacher workforce, they must collaborate with universities and schools to implement a teacher workforce development system and they must realize that, because they have the discretionary resources to start such a process, the ball is in their court to begin building the bench for the future.

NOTE

1. A local foundation or community trust could fund any or all of these elements and make a significant contribution to teacher workforce development. If individual elements are all that a particular funder can handle, it is incumbent upon that funder to find other partners to support the other parts of the system.

Teacher Unions: Building a Profession, Improving Our Schools

DEBORAH LYNCH

The term *professional union* (or *union of professionals*) may at first appear to be an oxymoron. How can teachers be taken seriously as professionals if they belong to unions? In fact, historically, the *only* way teachers in the United States have been taken seriously has been by belonging to a union. Furthermore, professional unions can—and do—play a major role in strengthening the teaching profession and improving our schools.

Belonging to a union is certainly important for the individual professional who may have legitimate concerns about working conditions or worker rights. But membership in a teacher union is also important in a larger, professional sense: for the negotiation of salaries and working conditions to attract and keep qualified teaching professionals in our classrooms and for the important work of improving the schools and the school systems in which union members work.

Since the education reform movement of the 1980s, there has been increasing support for the idea that teacher unions can, and must, be as effective in addressing professional educational issues as they are in addressing the more traditional, bread-and-butter issues. Good working conditions are good learning conditions. And although union leaders and system managers often find themselves in adversarial situations, they in fact have very important common goals: the attainment of a quality teaching force and the continuous improvement of schools and school systems. Both the future of public education and the future of teacher unions depend on achieving these common goals.

Teachers work in school bureaucracies, and whether these are large or small, the only real source of voice and power teachers have is through their unions. Consider the usual prerequisites of a profession: prestige, salary, professional discretion and autonomy, among other things. What little of each there is in the teaching profession exists not because educational management has freely provided it to teachers, but because teachers, through their unions (in states where collective bargaining is lawful), have negotiated for (or orchestrated strikes to obtain) higher salaries and a voice in educational decision making.

Deborah Lynch is President of the Chicago Teachers Union.

Professional Working Conditions and Recruitment and Retention

A good contract with competitive salaries and professional working conditions is vital to attracting and keeping a talented teaching force. This is a particular challenge for urban districts that lack the healthy tax base of suburban districts. In Chicago, for example, the starting teacher salary is fairly competitive with the surrounding suburban districts, but at the top of the salary scale, there is a shortfall of more than $10,000 relative to surrounding districts. This contributes to the exodus of relatively new teachers. A high teacher attrition rate (in most urban districts, 30% to 50% of new teachers leave within the first three to five years) not only represents lost investment but is also very detrimental to the success of a school system. For example, schools serving the most disadvantaged students are four times more likely to employ uncertified and inexperienced teachers as compared to schools serving advantaged students.

Teacher unions not only strive to secure a competitive salary schedule but also work to achieve improvements in other vitally important "professional" working conditions such as a voice in decision making, adequate resources, additional preparation time, and the reduction of excessive paperwork, which takes away from teaching. And although research continues to show a strong correlation between class size and student achievement, teachers still must rely on their unions to fight for smaller class sizes. All of these efforts contribute to the good professional working conditions that attract and keep the best and the brightest teachers in our classrooms.

Union Efforts to Improve the Teaching Profession

Teacher unions have also played key roles in other enhancements of the teaching profession. Mentoring and induction programs created in cooperation with unions have significantly reduced teacher turnover in many districts. Improved teacher evaluation systems, career ladders, peer review and support programs, and the creation of meaningful professional development opportunities are other union-initiated reforms, codified in union contracts and designed to strengthen the teaching profession.

The Toledo Federation of Teachers, for example, created the first union-initiated internship program in the nation, which has served all new teachers in Toledo since 1984. This program has contributed to new teachers being more effective, getting up to speed more quickly, and remaining in the profession longer. The Rochester (NY) Teachers

Association built on those ideas and has since developed the Career in Teaching program, which has greatly improved teacher retention in that district. This program has created a career path that rewards teachers who remain in the profession by providing important leadership roles (and accompanying salary increases at administrator pay levels) so that great teachers do not have to leave the classroom to get additional responsibility, salary, or recognition. These two initiatives, among others, have contributed to strengthening the teacher work force and reducing high teacher attrition rates, both of which have direct correlations with improved student achievement.

Union Efforts to Improve Schools

Unions have been playing important roles in improving schools themselves, as well as improving the profession. One of the most effective urban school reform efforts in recent years has been the Chancellor's District in New York City. This initiative, in which the United Federation of Teachers (UFT) was a full partner, transformed dozens of schools on that state's watch list. With a proven schoolwide reform model, time added to the school day, and intensive and extensive professional development, dozens of schools in the district that were in danger of closing due to low achievement scores were taken off of the state's watch list within two years.

Adapting the New York Chancellor's District model, the Chicago Teachers Union (CTU) and the Chicago Public Schools established an agreement to support Chicago public schools in danger of closing for academic reasons. Teachers vote to become a Partnership School, which involves 1) selecting a comprehensive schoolwide reform model; 2) determining the use of an additional $200,000 per school (which has gone into additional salaries to lower class size and into extending the school day); 3) having the support of union staff in implementing their reform models; and 4) getting protection from the many bureaucratic mandates that often conflict with the implementation of their reforms. Through this joint initiative, the CTU hopes to prove, as the UFT did in New York's Chancellor's District, that with the right resources and supports, schools struggling with large numbers of children at risk of academic failure can be turned around. This is the most fundamental challenge facing urban public schools today.

Union Efforts to Influence Legislation

In addition to needing unions to advocate for more professional working conditions and for vital educational issues at the district level, teaching professionals need unions to fight for them on the legislative level as well. The CTU, for example, was successful in strengthening the voice of its members in school-level decision making by lobbying for a change to the law that creates teacher committees. These committees, previously empowered to "advise" Local School Councils[1] on educational issues, are now "teacher leadership" committees, whose recommendations the Local School Councils must treat as motions for action rather than suggestions. The CTU also successfully lobbied for the passage of a bill requiring the state to decrease class sizes in the primary grades in the poorest schools in the state. There was no funding attached to the bill, however, so the goal for 2004 is to secure full funding.

At the federal level, the No Child Left Behind Act of 2001 has had a huge impact on the teaching profession. Teachers, through their unions, have worked to influence the final bill and the subsequent rules and regulations. This act includes the requirement that all U.S. school districts have a qualified, certified teacher in every classroom by 2006, an important goal for the enhancement of the profession. Yet many of the other aspects of this law, particularly the extensive testing requirements and the demands for annual progress, have negative effects for teachers. This has resulted in the exodus of teachers from urban districts that have been particularly hard hit by seemingly punitive sanctions against schools serving the most disadvantaged students, making them even harder to staff than before. Teachers need their unions to advocate for full funding for NCLB and other unfunded federal mandates, as well as effectively represent their interests and those of their students as these policies are being created.

Enhancing the Profession, Improving Our Schools

The successes of teacher unions presented here should help dispel the myths that these unions are self-interested self-interest groups, uninterested in, or even impediments to, the improvement of the profession and school reform. Teachers, through their unions, are involved in shaping and improving their profession and our schools every day. Reform efforts that do not include their voice and leadership will simply not be as effective as those that do.

NOTE

1. LSCs are the governing councils for every Chicago public school, created by Illinois law in 1989. Elementary school councils are made up of six parents, two teachers, two community members, and the principal; high schools have a student representative. By design, parents hold the balance of power.

Index

431

RECENT PUBLICATIONS OF THE SOCIETY

1. The Yearbooks

103:1 (2004) *Developing the Teacher Workforce.* Mark A. Smylie and Debra Miretzky, editors. Cloth.

103:2 (2004) *Towards Coherence Between Classroom Assessment and Accountability.* Mark Wilson, editor. Cloth.

102:1 (2003) *American Educational Governance on Trial: Change and Challenges.* William Lowe Boyd and Debra Miretzky, editors. Cloth.

102:2 (2003) *Meeting at the Hyphen: Schools-Universities-Communities-Professions in Collaboration for Student Achievement and Well Being.* Mary M. Brabeck, Mary E. Walsh, and Rachel E. Latta, editors. Cloth.

101:1 (2002) *The Educational Leadership Challenge: Redefining Leadership for the 21st Century.* Joseph Murphy, editor. Cloth.

101:2 (2002) *Educating At-Risk Students.* Sam Stringfield and Deborah Land, editors. Cloth.

100:1 (2001) *Education Across a Century: The Centennial Volume.* Lyn Corno, editor. Cloth.

100:2 (2001) *From Capitol to the Cloakroom: Standards-based Reform in the States.* Susan H. Fuhrman, editor. Cloth.

99:1 (2000) *Constructivism in Education.* D. C. Phillips, editor. Cloth.

99:2 (2000) *American Education: Yesterday, Today, and Tomorrow.* Thomas L. Good, editor. Cloth.

98:1 (1999) *The Education of Teachers*, Gary A. Griffin, editor. Paper.

98:2 (1999) *Issues in Curriculum*, Margaret J. Early and Kenneth J. Rehage, editors. Cloth.

97:1 (1998) *The Adolescent Years: Social Influences and Educational Challenges.* Kathryn Borman and Barbara Schneider, editors. Cloth.

97:2 (1998) *The Reading-Writing Connection.* Nancy Nelson and Robert C. Calfee, editors. Cloth.

96:1 (1997) *Service Learning.* Joan Schine, editor. Cloth.

96:2 (1997) *The Construction of Children's Character.* Alex Molnar, editor. Cloth.

95:1 (1996) *Performance-Based Student Assessment: Challenges and Possibilities.* Joan B. Baron and Dennie P. Wolf, editors. Cloth.

94:1 (1995) *Creating New Educational Communities.* Jeannie Oakes and Karen Hunter Quartz, editors. Cloth.

94:2 (1995) *Changing Populations/Changing Schools.* Erwin Flaxman and A. Harry Passow, editors. Cloth.

93:1 (1994) *Teacher Research and Educational Reform.* Sandra Hollingsworth and Hugh Sockett, editors. Cloth.

92:1 (1993) *Gender and Education.* Sari Knopp Biklen and Diane Pollard, editors. Cloth.

91:1 (1992) *The Changing Contexts of Teaching.* Ann Lieberman, editor. Cloth.

91:2 (1992) *The Arts, Education, and Aesthetic Knowing.* Bennett Reimer and Ralph A. Smith, editors. Cloth.

Order the above titles from the University of Chicago Press, 11030 S. Langley Ave., Chicago, IL 60628. For a list of earlier Yearbooks still available, consult the University of Chicago Press website: www.press.uchicago.edu

2. The Series on Contemporary Educational Issues

This series has been discontinued.

The following volumes in the series may be ordered from the McCutchan Publishing Corporation, 3220 Blume Drive, Suite 197, Richmond, CA 94806. Local phone: (510)758-5510, Toll free: 1-800-227-1540, Fax: (510)758-6078, e-mail: mccutchanpublish@aol

Academic Work and Educational Excellence: Raising Student Productivity (1986). Edited by Tommy M. Tomlinson and Herbert J. Walberg.
Adapting Instruction to Student Differences (1985). Edited by Margaret C. Wang and Herbert J. Walberg.
Choice in Education (1990). Edited by William Lowe Boyd and Herbert J. Walberg.
Colleges of Education: Perspectives on Their Future (1985). Edited by Charles W. Case and William A. Matthes.
Contributing to Educational Change: Perspectives on Research and Practice (1988). Edited by Philip W. Jackson.
Effective Teaching: Current Research (1991). Edited by Hersholt C. Waxman and Herbert J. Walberg.
Moral Development and Character Education (1989). Edited by Larry P. Nucci.
Motivating Students to Learn: Overcoming Barriers to High Achievement (1993). Edited by Tommy M. Tomlinson.
Radical Proposals for Educational Change (1994). Edited by Chester E. Finn, Jr. and Herbert J. Walberg.
Reaching Marginal Students: A Prime Concern for School Renewal (1987). Edited by Robert L. Sinclair and Ward Ghory.
Restructuring the Schools: Problems and Prospects (1992). Edited by John J. Lane and Edgar G. Epps.
Rethinking Policy for At-risk Students (1994). Edited by Kenneth K. Wong and Margaret C. Wang.
School Boards: Changing Local Control (1992). Edited by Patricia F. First and Herbert J. Walberg.

The two final volumes in this series were:

Improving Science Education (1995). Edited by Barry J. Fraser and Herbert J. Walberg.
Ferment in Education: A Look Abroad (1995). Edited by John J. Lane.

These two volumes may be ordered from the Book Order Department, University of Chicago Press, 11030 S. Langley Ave., Chicago, IL 60628. Phone: 1-800-621-2736; Fax: 1-800-621-8476.